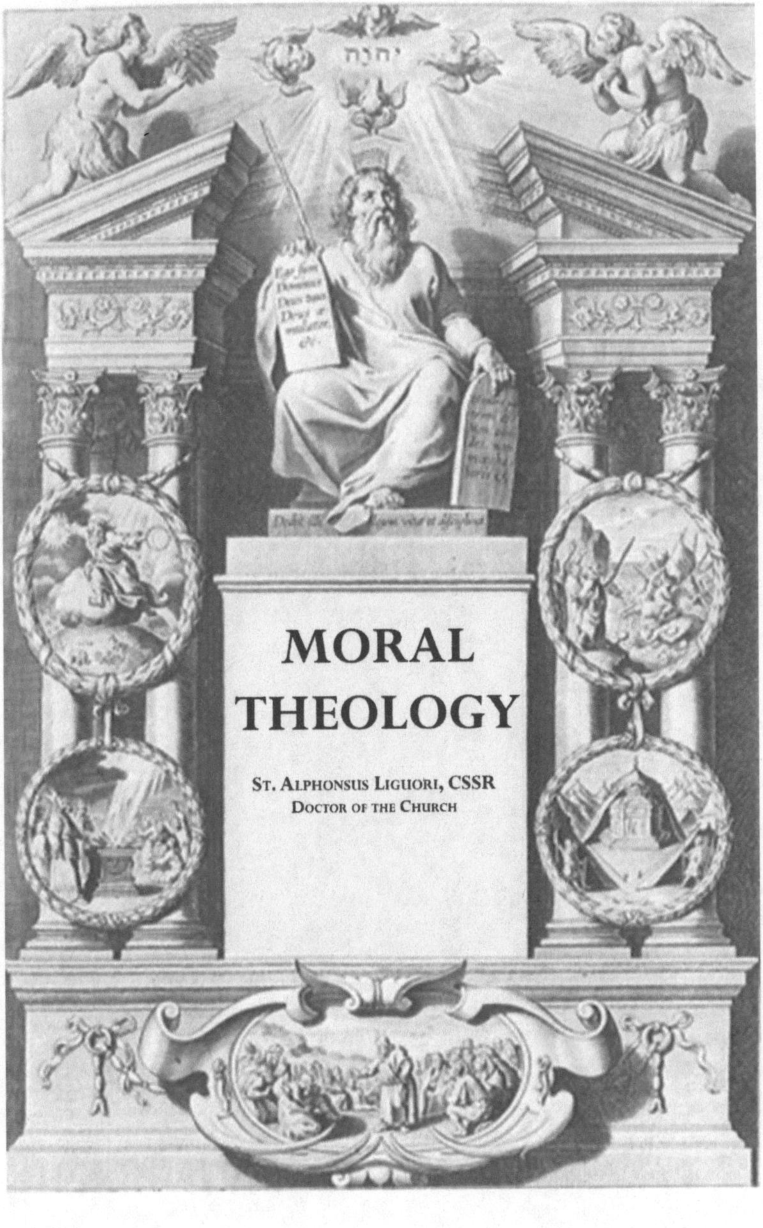

MORAL THEOLOGY

St. Alphonsus Liguori, CSSR
Doctor of the Church

MORAL THEOLOGY
VOLUME II

Book IV
On the Decalogue
1-6, 9

by
ST. ALPHONSUS LIGUORI, C.SS.R
Doctor of the Church

Translated by
Ryan Grant

First English Edition

MEDIATRIX PRESS

MMXVII
www.mediatrixpress.com

Moral Theology, vol. 2
Translated from:
Theologia Moralis Sancti Alphonsi Mariae de Liguorio
Mechlin, 1852

ISBN: 978-1-953746-21-4

© Ryan Grant, 2017
All Rights reserved. This work may not be reproduced in electronic or physical format without the express permission of the publisher except for quotations for review, journals, or educational purposes.

Cover art © Ryan Grant

Mediatrix Press
607 E. 6th Ave. Ste. 230
Post Falls, ID 83854
http://www.mediatrixpress.com

TABLE OF CONTENTS

TRANSLATOR'S PREFACE xxxix

TREATISE I
ON THE FIRST PRECEPT OF THE DECALOGUE

CHAPTER I
ON SUPERSTITION AND ITS SPECIES 2

DUBIUM I
What is superstition, and how manifold is it?

1. *What is superstition?*
2. *How manifold is superstition?*
3. *Who commits the superstition of false cult?*
4. *What is superstition of a superfluous cult?*
.... 2

DUBIUM II
On Divination. What is it and how manifold is it?

5. *What is divination?*
6. *It is one thing with express invocation of a demon, another with tacit invocation.*
7. *Whether to commit divination were always a mortal sin?*
8. *Resolution of cases. What must be thought about a divinatory staff?*
9. *Whether it were lawful to commit divination through a dream?*
10. *Whether Astrology is licit and what sort?*

v

11.   *Is it lawful to apply divination by lots?*.... 4

DUBIUM III
What and how manifold is idolatry

12 - 13 *Inclusive*......................... 14

DUBIUM IV
What, and how manifold is vain observance, and how is it deduced?

14.   *What is vain observance? And how manifold?*
15.   *Is it a grave fault?*
16.   *How can it be known?*
17.   *Resolution of cases.*
18.   *Whether it were granted and licit for virtue to be in those that are called saviors?*
19.   *Whether people are forbidden from marveling at supernatural things?*
20.   *What must be presumed in doubt?*
21.   *Whether an ensalmus is lawful?*
22.   *Whether natural fascination should be tolerated.* 15

DUBIUM V
What is a malefice, and how can it be removed?

23.   *What is a malefice, and how manifold is it?*
24.   *What remedies would it be lawful to apply against a malefice?*
25.   *Whether it would be lawful to seek from the one that carried out the malefice that he abolish it with another? And whether in doubt as to whether he knows the licit mode of breaking it?*

TABLE OF CONTENTS

26. *What about vampires? (striges)*
27. *Do malifices incur excommunication?*
28. *How a confessor ought to conduct himself with magic and malefices?* 23

CHAPTER II
ON IRRELIGIOSITY, AND ITS SPECIES. 29

DUBIUM I
What is testing God?

29. *What is testing God?*
30. *Whether paucity of the matter is granted in tempting God? And what is interpretative temptation?*
31. *Would one sin that asks God for a miracle?*
32. *Would one sin that offers himself for martyrdom? And a man sin by rejecting medicines?*
.... 29

DUBIUM II
What, and how manifold is sacrilege?

33. *What and how manifold is sacrilege?*
34. *What kind of species of sacrilege must be explained?*
35. *What are personal sacrileges?*
36. *What are local sacrileges?* 37. *Are commerce, meals, and court proceedings, etc. forbidden in Church?*
38. *Would it be a sacrilege to a man from the Church, the hall, etc.?*
39. *Is every theft in the church a sacrilege? Is it in the sacristy?*
40. *Which are real sacrileges?*

41. Would it be lawful to convert vessels and sacred garments to profane use?
42. Would it be a sacrilege to injure the goods of ecclesiastics? To detain pious trusts? To not pay tithes?
43. Would it be a sacrilege to sin mentally in a Church? To omit the sacraments in time they ought to be received?
44. Are censures against sacrileges incurred ipso facto?
45. Is it a sacrilege to steal relics?
46. Is it a sacrilege to steal on a feast day?
47. Would it be a sacrilege to violate vows?
48. See others, ibid. 33

DUBIUM III
On Simony

ARTICLE I
What is simony, and how manifold is it?

49. What is simony, and how manifold is it?
50. Could paucity of matter be granted in simony?
51. When is it simony to give temporal things for spiritual ones?
52. Would it be simony to give a benefice to someone, that he would sustain himself, either by reason of friendship or prayers?
53. Would it be simony to deduce in an agreement an antidoral obligation?
54. Would it be simony to give a spiritual thing principally on account of a temporal thing?
55. Would it be simony to receive something for the administration of the sacraments? And would it be simony principally to take it on account of temporal profit from them?

56. *What is understood by* munus a manu?
57. *Would it be simony to give a loan on account of a spiritual thing?*
58. *Would it be simony to pay a pension on account of a benefice?*
59. *Would it be simony to give something so that another would furnish something spiritual for himself when he receives it?*
60. *Would it be simony to give a benefice with some spiritual obligation? Or to resign or present with a obligation?*
61. *What about for* munus ab obsequio?
62. *Would it be simony to treat with deference on account of a benefice?* 63. *What is simony by "*munus a lingua*"?*
64. *Would it be simony to give something by a mediator so that he would obtain a benefice for you?*
65. *What if the intercessor were an intermediary?*
66. *What if you were to promise to give alms to some monastery?*
67. *What is mental simony? What is conventional and real simony?*
68. *Which is of divine law and which is of human law?*
69. *Is simony only granted in human law?*
70. *Would it be simony to sell benefices by divine law?*
71. *Would it be simony to sell a jus patronatus (right of patronage)? And is it of divine law? Would it be simony to sell the right of burial?*
72. *Can benefices be exchanged?*
73. *How can a benefice with a pension be exchanged? And by whose authority? And could bishops constitute pensions? even to n. 76.*

77. *How would it be lawful to carry out commerce in benefices? even to num. 80.*
81. *How could renunciations of benefices be made? Even to n. 84.*
85. *How manifold is "confidential" simony, and what are its penalties? Even to num. 90.*
91. *How will it be lawful to receive something for entry to a religious order?*
92. *Would it be lawful to receive something for sustenance of those entering?*
93. *Would it be lawful to receive something for catechizing, etc.?*
94. *Would it for instructing someone in sacred doctrine?*
95. *Would it for absolving, etc.?*
96. *Would it be to give a dispensation in matrimony?*
97. *Would it be lawful to give something so that the other would omit a spiritual thing?*
98. *Would it be to remedy opposition?*
99. *Could opposition be remedied by money in regard to a possession of a benefice?*
100. *What if a right to it has not yet been acquired? What if someone would corrupt electors to not elect you?*
101. *What if the other would only impede by prayers?*
102. *Could you give money to stop another candidate from opposing himself to your election?*
103. *Could you give money lest the electors would choose someone that was unworthy, or to choose someone worthy?*
104. *Could you give money that a competitor would not go to a benefice which you desire? See others with Busembaum.* 44

ARTICLE II
What is the penalty for simony?

105. What are the penalties that simony induces? Would penalties be incurred in the sale of the sacraments, or of unprovided chaplaincies?
106. To incur the penalties, should simony be carried out by both parties?
107. Would one incur penalties who obtains a benefice by a feigned promise of money?
108. Would penalties be incurred by simony that were merely so by ecclesiastical law? Would they be incurred on account of entrance into a religious order?
109. What are the penalties for a simoniacal ordination? 110. Would they be incurred on account of the conferral of first tonsure?
111. What are the penalties on account of simony in benefices?
112. Would penalties be incurred in the sale of a vicarage, or another non-moveable office? For a pension, chaplaincy, or for the sacraments and jurisdiction? Then four things are asked. Quaer. I. Are simoniacal elections to the prelatures of regulars null? Qu. II. Are penalties incurred on account of benefices simoniacally received by those who are ignorant? Qu. III. Would a simoniacal holder of a benefice ipso facto be deprived from the benefices he has obtained, and would he become unsuitable to obtain future benefices? Qu. IV. Would the simoniacal election of a Pope be null? 89

ARTICLE III
Must what was simoniacally received be restored, and to whom?

113. *Nothing spiritual received simoniacally must be restored, except for a benefice and its fruits.*
114. *The price received for a benefice, ordination, etc. must be restored.*
115. *To whom must it be restored?*
116. *To whom are the fruits of a benefice simoniacally received restored?*
117. *Who could dispense in the aforesaid penalties? Even to n. 120..* 103

TREATISE II
ON THE SECOND PRECEPT OF THE DECALOGUE

CHAPTER I
WHAT IS BLASPHEMY AND HOW MANIFOLD IS IT?

121. *What is blasphemy?*
122. *In how many ways is blasphemy committed against God?*
123. *When must heretical blasphemy be denounced?*
124. and 125. *Which jokes are or are not blasphemy?*
126. *Must it be explained [in confession] if someone directly intended to dishonor God?*
127. *To what is someone held to who does it out of habit?*
128. *What if someone were to utter: "O death of God! O wounds of Christ! being angry against a man?"*
129. Would it be blasphemy to curse created things and days?
130. *Would it be blasphemy to curse the dead? to curse the faith?*
131. *Would it be blasphemy to call down a demon on*

others or himself?
132. *Do blasphemies against God and the saints differ in species?*................ 109

EPISTOLA RESPONSIVA
AGAINST AN APOLOGETIC EPISTLE WRITTEN IN DEFENSE OF A DISSERTATION WHICH APPEARED ON THE ABUSE OF CURSING THE DEAD 123

CHAPTER II
ON SWEARING AN OATH 150

DUBIUM I
What is an oath?

133. *What is an oath?*
134. *What are true oaths?*
135. *Would it be an oath to say: "by my conscience", or "by my soul"?*
136. *Would it be an oath to say: "I swear it is so"?*
137. *Would it be an oath to say: "It is as true as the sun shines", or "it is as true as the Gospel"?*
138. *Would it be an oath to swear by creatures?* 150

DUBIUM II
How manifold is an oath?

139. *In how many ways is an oath divided? Even to n. 141.*
142. *Are all oaths of the same species?*
143. *Would it be an oath to say: "Punish me, O God, if I lie"?* 154

DUBIUM III
Is it licit to swear an oath, and when?

144. *Is it lawful? And what things are required to licitly swear an oath?*
145. *What about a requisite judgment?*
146. *What about justice? Is there a mortal defect of justice in an oath of assertion? What about in sayings like "By God I will kill you"?*
147. *What about a requisite truth?*
148. *What certitude is required to swear an oath?*
149. *Would it be lawful to seek an oath from a perjurer?*
150. *Would simple folk committing perjury be excused from mortal sin? And how must they be advised?* 156

DUBIUM IV

Would it be lawful in an oath to use an equivocation?

151. *Would it be lawful to swear an oath with a double-meaning?*
152. *Would it be lawful to swear an oath with a mental reservation?*
153. *Cases are resolved; on a confessor that affirms he does not know if what was confessed is a sin.*
154. *On a guilty man or a witness not legitimately questioned.*
155. *What if he were legitimately asked and swears ambiguously?*
156. *Would someone that is guilty of a capital crime be held to confess it?*
157. *On a penitent questioned about a sin confessed.*
158. *On a poor man needing someone else's things.*
159. *On one questioned by a judge as to whether he spoke with the guilty man, and similar things.*
160. *On a debtor that is not otherwise held.*
161. *On a creditor asserting nothing was paid to him.*
162. *On an adulteress denying the crime.*
163. *On the requisition to make a loan.*

164. On a merchant, etc.
165. On a servant asserting his master is not at home.
166. On those taken up to a doctorate.
167. On a man asserting that he received money which he did not actually receive.
168. On a man asserting what is false by adding something true in a quiet voice.
169. Would it be lawful for someone to swear equivocally when not asked?
170. See other cases with Busembaum. 171. Would it be lawful to swear an oath without a mind to really swear it? (But on this see what is profusely discussed in n. 172, dub. 5). Quaeritur: Is simulation sometimes licit?
.... 162

DUBIUM V

What is the obligation of a promissory oath and how great is it?

172. In how many ways must the truth be affirmed in a promissory oath? What kind of sin is a feigned promissory oath, and in what way does it oblige?
173. Does one sin gravely that does not fulfill a promise in a small matter?
174. Does an oath extorted from fear oblige?
175. What if it were extorted from error or treachery?
176. Would an oath oblige on a bad or vain thing?
177. What about an oath in favor of a third party?
178. Would an oath to not play exclude moderate play?
179. Would an oath made against a first oath oblige?
180. Should an oath follow the condition of a promise?
181. How does an oath to preserve the statutes of some college apply?
182. On the oath of doctors not to see someone

frequently, etc.
183. *On an oath to preserve a secret, to tell the truth and to pay a debt.*
184. *Does an oath made to a concubine to not have relations with another woman oblige?*
185. *Does a wasteful promise with an oath oblige?*
186. *Would an oath to go back to prison oblige? On the oath of parents and masters to punish sons or servants.* 177

DUBIUM VI
In what cases would a man who contracts an obligation in a promissory oath be excused from fulfilling it?

187. *Would change of circumstances excuse?*
188. *Would cessation of the final cause excuse?*. . 194

DUBIUM VII
How is the obligation of an oath abolished by invalidity, dispensation, commutation and remission?

189. *Who can invalidate oaths? And who dispenses?*
190. *Could one dispensing against vows also dispense against oaths?*
191. *On commutation and relaxation of the oath.*
192. *What if the oath is made in favor of a third?*
193. *Could it be remitted by the third itself? Appendix on adjuration and especially on adjuration of demons.* 197

APPENDIX
On Adjuration 201

CHAPTER III
ON VOWS..................................... 206
DUBIUM I
What is a vow, and how manifold is it?

194. *What is a vow?*
195. *How manifold is a vow?* 206

DUBIUM II
What deliberation and intention is required for a vow?

196. *What deliberation is requisite for a vow?*
197. *On a vow uttered from fear.*
198. *On a vow uttered from error.*
199. *Would a simple vow proposed oblige?*
200. *Would an implicit promise suffice for a vow?*
201. *What kind of purpose of the will is required for a vow? From here many things are asked: 1) Would a man be held to a vow that positively refused to promise and oblige himself? 2) Who did not have a mind to fulfill it? 3) Who negatively refused to oblige himself knowing the obligation of the vow? a) What if he did not know? b) what if someone wished to promise and positively refused to oblige himself? c) What is someone were uncertain as to whether he willed to oblige himself? or whether he knew the obligation of the vow? What if he were hesitant as to whether he had down what was proposed or vowed?*
.... 207

DUBIUM III
What matter is required for a vow?

202. *Would a vow on an impossible thing hold?*
203. *Would a vow to avoid all venial sins hold? What*

if someone would vow to avoid all mortal and venial sins collectively?
204. *Would a vow concerning a vain thing be valid?*
205. *Would it be a mortal sin to vow to do a venial sin?*
206. *Would a vow made from a bad end be valid?*
207. *Could a vow be an impediment to a greater good?*
208. *Is a vow to not seek a dispensation valid?*
209. *Is a vow to marry be valid?*
210. *Is a vow to not make a vow be valid?* 217

DUBIUM IV
What, and how great is the obligation of a vow?

211. *Would a vow on a light matter sometimes gravely obligate?*
212. *What if you had neglected a vow on a light matter through the year?*
213. *See other things with Busembaum.*
214. *Would an heir be held to the vows of the dead?*
215. *Could a father injure the legitimacy of sons by vows?*
216. *On vows that are another's de facto.*
217. *Could vows be fulfilled by another?*
218. *Would a man sin that impedes the fulfillment of a condition assigned in his own vow?*
219. *Things that must be noted in regard to the conditions in vows.*
220. *If the day promised has transpired, are you held to the vow?*
221. *Does an indeterminate vow always oblige? And what if a postponement were mortal?*
222. *What if someone would vow that he was going to enter a religious order without a certain place or a certain order?*
223. *What if someone would vow that he was not going*

to play under penalty?
224. Many notable things are adverted to in regard to oaths, and especially, whether a vow would hold if unforeseen circumstances would arise. 225

DUBIUM V
In how many ways is the obligation of a vow removed?

225. The obligation of a vow is removed: 1) By change of the matter; 2) By human authority. See resolutions.
226. Would the obligation to fulfill a vow still hold if unforeseen circumstances would arise? What about simple vows of chastity and or religion, and what of solemn ones? See book 5 n. 50.. 239

DUBIUM VI
On the invalidation of a vow.

ARTICLE I
Can the obligation of a vow be removed by direct invalidation, and how?

227. Who can invalidate vows?
228. Is it lawful to invalidate vows without cause?
229. What vows of sons could a father, grandfather, tutor, etc. invalidate?
230. Could a mother invalidate them?
231. Would the vows of subjects be valid until they are invalidated?
232. What if someone was thought to be a father, husband, etc. in error? 233. Who could invalidate

the vows of religious and nuns? What about an abbess?
234. *Could a man invalidate all the vows of his wife?*
235. *Could a wife invalidate the vows of her husband?*
236. *What if by mutual consent husband and wife were vow chastity?*
237. *Could a superior invalidate the vows made before subjection? What if there is a doubt as to whether they were pronounced before or after subjection?*
238. *Could the vows made in a time of subjection afterward be invalidated?*
239. *What if a superior ratified them?*
240. *What vows of servants could be invalidated by their master?* 243

ARTICLE II
Who can indirectly invalidate vows? 256
DUBIUM VII
What is a commutation of a vow?

243. *When can vows be commuted?*
244. *Could someone commute a vow by himself in an equal work?* 245. *Would a commutation avail less without a just cause?*
246. *See what else must be noted.*
247. *Could one having the faculty commute in a smaller amount?*
248. *Could, after a commutation has been made, the man making the vow be held to fulfill the first?*
249. *Would, in an impossible thing that was already commuted, the man making the vow be held to fulfill the first? Would someone that forgot a vow but*

*furnishes the promised work be freed from the vow*238

DUBIUM VIII
What is a dispensation, and who can dispense against vows?

250. *What cause is required to dispense?*
251. *What if the dispensation is made in good faith, but without cause? What if there is a doubt as to whether a cause is present?*
252. *What cause would suffice for dispensation?*
253. *Would imperfect deliberation or freedom suffice?*
254. *See other things that must be noted.*
255. *Could one be dispensed in a vow made in benefit of a third party? And what about a vow and an oath of perseverance, which is furnished in certain congregations?*
256. *Who is able to dispense? Does the Pope in solemn vows? Do the Bishops in simple vows? Who can delegate the faculty to dispense? Would someone having the faculty avail to dispense on their own?*
257. *Could regular prelates dispense against all the vows of religious? Of novices? Of seculars?*
258. *More notable things on reserved vows.*
259. *Would an oath of chastity or religion be reserved like a vow?*
260. *After a vow has been commuted, is the matter substituted also reserved?*
261. *Would conditional or penal vows of chastity and religion be reserved?*
262. *With pilgrims, could the Bishop of the place dispense against vows and common laws? Review book 1 n. 158..* 265

TREATISE III
ON THE THIRD AND FOURTH COMMANDMENT

CHAPTER I
WHAT IS THE THIRD PRECEPT, "MEMENTO", ETC......... 283

263. Whether this precept is natural or ceremonial?
264. Whether interior cult is commanded by this precept? And whether this precept is affirmative?
265. Whether observance of Sunday is of divine law?
266. Whether Bishops could appoint feasts?
267. From what time does the obligation of the feast begin?
268. To what does this precept oblige? On what feasts are servile works permitted in the kingdom of the Two Sicilies?
269. Is there an obligation to hear the sermon? And what sort of obligation is it for Bishops and parish priests to preach?
270. Who is held to observe feasts?
271. Whether it would be lawful to enjoin servile work on infidels during feast days? 283

DUBIUM I
What works are forbidden both by this precept and the Church?

272. What are servile works?
273. Whether to sin on a feast day would be a double sin?
274. What works are not servile?
275. Is it servile to go on a journey?

276. *Is it to drive a carriage or lead a laden beast of burden?*
277. *Would it be servile to ground flower?* 278. *Would it be servile to teach, write, sing, etc., even if these are done for profit?*
279. *Would it be servile to copy?*
280. *Would it be servile to paint?*
281. *Would it be servile to trace, stretch a canvas or to sculpt?*
282. *Is it lawful to build a printing press? to distill liquids?*
283. *Would it be permitted to hunt and fish?*
284. *What public works are forbidden on feast days?*
285. *Are sales and contracts permitted?*
286. *Are market days and commerce permitted?*
287. *Would it be permitted to excommunicate, draw up a will, and like things?* 293

DUBIUM II

What reasons excuse one from the observance of feasts that cause works to be forbidden?

288. *Who can give a dispensation to work?*
289. *What sort of laborers are excused from custom?*
290. *What about those working crops, etc. What about barbers and cobblers? And what would suffice for knowledge of custom?*
291. *How would piety excuse?*
292. *Would it be lawful to sweep a Church on a feast day, or adorn the altars, or erect a tomb, etc.?*
293. *Would it be lawful to work so as to assist the poor or pious places?*
294. *How would charity towards one's neighbor excuse?*
295. *How would necessity excuse?*

296. *Would servants be excused when their master compels them to work?*
297. *Would poor men restoring garments, etc.?*
298. *Is it lawful to cook food on a feast day, to slaughter animals, to make a meal and gather fruit?*
299. *Is it lawful to bake bread?*
300. *Is it lawful to heal, smelt iron, cook lime, or prepare blue dye? What about to shod horses?*
301. *Would it be lawful to labor on account of a great profit? And would it be lawful to miss Mass on account of it?*
302. *Would it be lawful to avoid idleness?*
303. *Would road workers, etc. be excused? And menders completing vestments for a feast day?*
304. *How will utility excuse on account of public joy?*
305. *How will paucity of matter excuse? (See also book 6 n. 346).*
306. *Would one sin gravely commanding six servants to labor for an hour?*
307. *Where is gravity of matter taken up in forensia?* 303

DUBIUM III
What works are commanded on feast days?

308. *How is the hearing of the Sermon and Mass commanded on feast days? And for parish priests to preach? Review n. 269.*
309. *Would reciting the office during Mass suffice? etc. Would serving at Mass suffice?*
310. *What omission would be grave in hearing*

Mass?
311. Is it lawful to hear two halves of the Mass in succession?
312. From what place can one hear Mass?
313. Whether internal attention is required to hear Mass?
314. Whether confessing sins during Mass satisfies the precept?
315. Would suffering spiritual experiences satisfy the precept?
316. Would sleeping satisfy the precept?
317. Would talking, turning oneself, or putting one's shoes on, or walking or gathering alms, singing etc. satisfy the precept?
318. In what Church should Mass be heard?
319. Who makes satisfaction in hearing Mass in private oratories? Would those hearing Mass on the beach or in army camps satisfy the precept? ... 318

Wherefore, the following cases are resolved:................. 319

DUBIUM IV
Whether there is an obligation for someone to hear Mass in his parish church on Sundays and greater feast days?............................. 344

DUBIUM V
What would excuse someone from hearing Mass?

324. What are excusing causes? Would one having the privilege of an oratory be bound to acquire a priest?
325. In what way would sailors, the incarcerated, the sick or the excommunicated be excused?

326. *Would those guarding houses be excused, etc.? Or those fearing lest they might be put in prison or assisting the sick?*
327. *Are wives, sons and servants fearing offense to their masters excused?*
328. *Would wayfarers be excused at some point?*
329. *What distance from the Church would excuse one from hearing Mass?*
330. *Would women be excused by reason of mourning, birth or because they do not have suitable garments? Would pregnant girls or women be excused at the time when the bans must be read?*
331. *Could a girl omit Mass knowing that there is someone filled with a filthy lust for her?*
332. *Would the loss of a great profit excuse? Would another and greater spiritual good excuse?*
333. *Would pilgrims, tarrying in some place for a short time, be held to hear Mass if it is of precept in that place?* 350

CHAPTER II
ON THE FOURTH COMMANDMENT: *HONOR THY FATHER*, ETC.
.... 362

DUBIUM I
What are children held to in regard to their parents?

333. *What are sons held to furnish to their parents in regard to love?*
334. *What in regard to reverence?*
335. *What in regard to obedience?* 361

DUBIUM II *To what matters are parents held toward their sons?*

336. *What are parents held to furnish to their sons in regard to nourishment and education?*
337. *To what is a father to give as a dowry for his daughter if she marries against his consent?*
338. *The Sanction of Naples in regard to nourishment of children.*
339. *To what else are parents held?*
340. *To what are brothers held?*
341. *Could parents at some time disinherit their sons? And what would be the just causes for it? (See also more on this in n. 948 and 949)* 368

DUBIUM III
To what are tutors, and legal guardians who stand in loco parentis *held to?* 374

DUBIUM IV
What is the obligation of masters, servants and other superiors and inferiors toward each other?

342. *What are superiors held to furnish to subjects? Are princes held to choose more worthy men for offices?*
343. *What are servants held to furnish to their masters?*
344. *Would servants that fail to stop the theft of their master's goods be held to restitution?* 376

DUBIUM V
To what are spouses held in regard to each other by the force of this precept?

351. *To what is a wife held in regard to her husband?*

352. *Whether a noble wife is held to furnish common duties?*
353. *Would an agreement for a wife not to change domicile hold? Moreover, would the wife be held to follow her husband if he were sent into exile?*
354. *When her husband is dead, is a wife held to pay debts contracted to sustain a household?* 355. *What is a wife held to restore to the sons of a first marriage?*
356. *In what way would a husband sin against his wife?* 384

DUBIUM VI
What is the obligation of parish priests toward their subjects?

357. *To what are parish priests held to in regard to residency?*
358. *To what are they held in regard to administering the sacraments, especially in a time of plague?*
359. *Are they held to celebrate Mass for the people?*
360. *Are they held to preach and instruct the people, etc.? How are parish priests held to correct their subjects? Dub. I. Whether they are held to it from charity, or from justice? Dub. II. Whether they are held to inquire into the morals of their subjects? Dub. III. Whether they are held to not desert the sheep even in danger of death?* 388

DUBIUM VII
What is the obligation of teachers and students?
.... 392

TREATISE IV
ON THE FIFTH AND SIXTH COMMANDMENT

CHAPTER I
WHAT IS FORBIDDEN BY THE FIFTH PRECEPT, *YOU SHALL NOT KILL*?
.... 394

363. What are the punishments for those who commission homicide through assassins?
364. Would the assassins themselves incur the same penalties?
365. On bull fighting..................... 394

DUBIUM I
Whether at some time it would be lawful for a man to kill, or mutilate himself?

366. Whether it would be lawful to directly kill one's self? What about indirectly?
367. Whether it would be lawful for someone to expose himself to the danger of death to avoid a harder death, etc.? Would it be lawful to burn a boat if it brings the danger of death?
368. Whether a virgin is held to suffer death rather than to be raped?
369. Whether it is lawful for a guilty man to kill himself at the command of a judge? Or to take poison so as to test out an antidote?
370. Would it be lawful for a Carthusian to abstain from meat even in extreme necessity?
371. Would it be lawful for him to reduce things that exhaust his life?
372. Is there an obligation to preserve life using extraordinary remedies or extremely difficult ones?
373. Is it ever licit for a man to mutilate himself?
374. Would it ever be lawful to castrate children?
375. Whether someone that commits suicide could

be buried in a sacred place?.................. 396

DUBIUM II

Is it lawful to kill a malefactor, and how?

376. Would it be lawful to kill an outlaw on one's own authority?

377. Would it be lawful for a prince to kill condemned men but not before they are condemned by a sentence?

378. Would it ever be lawful for clergy to condemn a guilty man to the death penalty?

379. Would a judge be held to concede a time for the condemned man to receive the sacrament of penance and the Eucharist?...................... 406

DUBIUM III

Whether and how it will be lawful to kill an unjust aggressor on one's own authority

380. Is it lawful to defend one's life by the death of the assailant? Moreover, is it forbidden to outlaws and bandits to defend themselves by arms?

381. Is it lawful for a gentleman to kill an assailant of his honor? Moreover, would it be lawful for a commoner or an ecclesiastic if he could flee without danger of life? And what if contumely were already inflicted?

382. See more resolutions of Fr. Busembaum.

383. Quaest. I: Would it be lawful to kill a thief for a thing of great value? Qu. II: What should the value be? And what, if the value were modest but the thing were taken with violence? Qu. III: What if the thief had already taken a thing and resisted the owner trying to recover it with violence?

384. Quaest. IV: Would it be lawful for clergy and

religious to kill a thief? And would they then incur irregularity?

385.   Quaest. V: Would it be lawful for anyone to defend his own possessions by arms, even through his servants?

386.   Quaest. VI: Would it be lawful to kill an assailant of one's chastity?

387.   Would it be lawful to forestall the aggressor?

388.   Would it be lawful to kill a false accuser?

389.   Whether one is held to defend the life of the innocent if he could?

390.   Even with the death of the aggressor?

391.   Whether it is lawful to kill the assailant of one's honor or the other of chastity? And what if the woman were to consent?

392.   Whether we can and are held to safeguard the goods of our neighbor even by killing the thief?
.... 409

DUBIUM IV

Is it ever lawful to kill an innocent man? 427

393.   Is it ever lawful to directly kill an innocent life?

394.   Whether at any point it would be lawful to procure an abortion? Qu. I. Whether it is lawful for a mother to take a contraceptive to directly expel an un-animated fetus? Whether it would be lawful for a woman that was raped to expel the semen of her attacker right away? Qu. II. Whether it is lawful for a mother to take medication to cure an illness, with the danger of a miscarriage of the animated fetus? Qu. III. When is the soul reckoned to be formed in children?

395.   Qu. IV. To what punishments are those procuring an abortion subjected? Qu. V. Whether

pregnant women who have an abortion incur excommunication?
396. *Qu. VI. Whether those procuring an abortion in doubt about the animation of a fetus incur irregularity?*
397. *Qu. VII. Who can relax the penalties inflicted for abortion?*
398. *When is casual homicide imputed to someone as a sin? Would an adulterer, killing the husband of the woman he committed adultery with that attacked him, incur irregularity? And would she incur it, if the adulteress preempted him?* 427

DUBIUM V
On Dueling and War

ARTICLE I
What is a duel, and is it lawful?

399. *What is a duel and is it ever lawful to provoke one?*
400. *When would it be lawful to accept a duel? And would it be lawful to begin one against a false accuser?*
401. *What are the penalties imposed for dueling?* 448

ARTICLE II
Whether war is lawful, and for how long?

402. *When is war lawful?* 403. *What should a prince do to licitly carry out a war?*
404. *When could a war be fought with only a probable opinion?*
405. *To what are princes held?*
406. *Is it lawful to call in heretics and non-*

Christians as soldiers?
407. *To what are generals held?*
408. *Could soldiers fight in a war when there is a doubt about it's justice?* 453

ARTICLE III
What is lawful in a just war? 459

CHAPTER II
ON THE SIXTH AND NINTH COMMANDMENT

THOU SHALT NOT COMMIT ADULTERY AND THOU SHALT NOT COVET THY NEIGHBOR'S WIFE, etc. 463

DUBIUM I
Whether kisses, hugs, touches, obscene words and similar things are sins outside of marriage, and how great?

413. *What is sexual enjoyment, what is sensitive enjoyment?*
414. *Why is every venereal act [outside of marriage] bad?*
415. *Whether paucity of matter is granted in a venereal matter?*
416. *Whether it is granted in sensitive enjoyment?*
417. *Whether kisses would be licit at some point?*
418. *When are kisses excused from mortal sin?*
419. *On touch and the shameful gazing at one's own body, or at the mating of animals.*
420. *On touch and the shameful gazing at another's body; and on the touch of the genitals of animals.*
421. *Is it always a shameful mortal sin to gaze on the opposite sex? Or a beautiful youth? And whether these acts of looking cover the species of the object?*
422. *Is it lawful to gaze upon non-private parts of the opposite sex?*

423. Whether it is a mortal sin to look at the chest, legs, etc. of a woman?
424. Whether it is a mortal sin to look at shameful pictures?
425. Whether it is lawful for a woman to adorn herself and put on makeup? What if she covers her breasts or uses men's garments? Review book 3, n. 52 and 54.
426. When do those mentioning foul words sin?
427. Whether those who spectate at foul comedic plays always sin gravely? Do those who cooperate with them by paying money or applause also sin gravely?
428. Do those who make the stages and dress sin?
429. Would it be lawful to dance?
430. Would a woman sin by permitted herself to be touched? Is a woman held to cry out in order to avoid unchaste touches?
431. Would a touch be lawful, etc. among the married and the betrothed?................................ 465

DUBIUM II

What are the species of natural lust?

432. Is fornication forbidden by natural law?
433. Does a woman sin not by not resisting sex on account of fear of death if she does not consent?
434. Could prostitutes be permitted?
435. In regard to concubinage it is asked: I. Whether a man can be absolved who cannot cast out a concubine without infamy?
436. II. Can a man be absolved that promises he will throw out his concubine?
437. III. Could a concubine be absolved that does not leave on account of necessity?

438. IV. Whether one who is in the proximate occasion, for the sake of exercising his craft can be absolved? What if he, after having applied remedies, always falls back in the same manner?
439. V. Whether a servant sinning with her master can be absolved?
440. VI. Whether a wife sinning with a husband can be absolved?
441. VII. Must the occasion also be removed with grave loss?
442. What are the penalties for concubinage, especially for clergy?
443. Whether "stuprum" (illicit sexual intercourse with a virgin) is a special sin?
444. To what is an abductor held?
445. What about adultery?
446. Whether heterosexual sodomy between spouses is adultery?
447. Is sex between the betrothed adultery?
448. In regard to incest it is asked: I. Whether all incest is of the same species?
449. II. Whether incest differs with in-laws?
450. III. Is it incest with spiritual kin?
451. IV. Whether it were a special sin for a confessor to have sex with a penitent? What about of a pastor with his subject?
452. V. Do near of kin commit incest having sex after a dispensation [but before the marriage]?
453. Would touches alone constitute incest?
454. How is sacrilege committed by masturbation?
455. In regard to personal sacrilege, it is asked: I. Does a priest who is also a religious commit two sacrileges at the same time if he sins against chastity?
456. II. Is it a sacrilege to have sex with another

consecrated person?

457.   *III. Does one commit a sacrilege having a vow of chastity if he induces another to masturbation? What if he takes morose delectation from the sin of the other?*

458.   *In regard to "local" sacrilege, it is asked: I. Is secret or marital sex in a Church a sacrilege?*

459.   *II. Are unchaste touches that take place in Church a sacrilege?*

460.   *What is included by the term sacred places?*

461.   *III. Are lustful words and gazes that take place in Church sacrileges?*

462.   *IV. Are sexual thoughts in Church a sacrilege?*

463.   *In regard to "real" sacrilege, when is it committed?* 484

DUBIUM III *What are the species of lust carried out against nature?*

464.   *What of unnatural sexual intercourse?*

465.   *What about masturbation (mollities)?*

466.   *What is sodomia imperfecta and sodomia perfecta?*

467.   *Whether pollution that takes place by touching a boy or a woman is a different species?*

468.   *Whether in confessing sodomy it must be explained if one was the agent or the patient?*

469.   *Whether heterosexual sodomy adds the species of incest?*

470.   *What are the penalties for those guilty of sodomy?*

471.   *What is required to incur these? Would a cleric who is patient in an act of sodomy incur these penalties?*

472.   *Are the penalties incurred before the sentence?*

473. *Does a cleric committing acts of bestiality incur these penalties?*
474. *What is the sin of bestiality?*
475. *On sin with a demon. What if the demon represented itself as a married or consecrated woman?*
.... 504

DUBIUM IV
Is it a sin to procure pollution?

476. *Is pollution forbidden by natural law?*
477. *Is the voluntary effusion of seminal fluid a mortal sin?*
478. *Is it lawful to expel corrupt semen?*
479. *Are we held to impede pollution that has already begun?*
480. *Is it lawful on account of an upright end to desire or take delight in it?*
481. *What if it were foreseen that pollution will follow from an upright act? What if it were foreseen from an illicit act?*
482. *Pollution is certainly a mortal sin when it arises from a foul cause gravely influencing toward it.*
483. *What if the action were posited on account of a just cause? Namely: I. To heal, or to hear confessions, to give an address according to morals, etc.; II. To satisfy an itch; III. To ride a horse; IV. To recline in some position; V. To eat moderately, etc. What if a surgeon or a pastor were to consent several times in pollution? And what about a simple confessor? What if someone nearly always fell back into this sin?*
484. *Is pollution a mortal sin when it arose from a cause lightly influencing it? What if the cause were in the same genus of lust? And what if the fall were*

frequent? What if the cause were in another genus? Can venial sin at least be posited for it?
485.   *On pollution following a dream. Does mutual pollution have a different malice?* 514

Translator's Preface

E are very pleased to present this second volume of St. Alphonsus Liguori's *Moral Theology*. After laying down the principles of his Moral System in book 1, St. Alphonsus then lays down the principles of law, then in book 2, as we say, he shows how to apply these principles to moral problems in questions of sins and the capital sins, the theological virtues, and here on the Ten Commandments of the Decalogue.

This book treats on the first through sixth commandments, as well as the ninth since it is connected to the sixth. The reason for this is the treatise on the seventh commandment is longer than that on the first six, taking up the scholastic commentaries from *de Justitia et Jure* not only on theft properly, but complicated subjects where in obscure and difficult questions arise, such as contracts, restitution, and above all, usury. Since this would easily have exceeded our page limits, we've decided to keep it together in its own volume.

Now, with what pertains to this work, we preface the following. St. Alphonsus will appeal to the force of some things in Canon Law from time to time; though I am not a canonist, to the best of my knowledge or after having consulted canonists, I have placed footnotes to explain any area where a major moral consideration rests upon a canon of that time which has been superceded by the current Code of Canon Law.

While we will not repeat the history of the work from volume 1, we will mention again a bit of the structure of the work. Originally, St. Alphonsus' work was a commentary on the work of Henry Busembaum, a German Jesuit. After a few editions, St. Alphonsus' notes became a full fledged commentary, and then to the point where far more of the work was St. Alphonsus' altogether. This is why some paragraphs in the work have quotation marks (")

Translator's Preface

outside of every line of the paragraph to indicate that the text is that of Busembaum's, whereas without the quotations it is purely the writing of St. Alphonsus.

Citations present a difficulty in that they are so voluminous. So we have rendered them parenthetically according to the general standards of academia. It is not our goal to produce a critical text and lead in discussion on minor points on every source, but rather to produce an accurate and readable texts for priests and moral theologians that do not have the command of Latin. For those who wish to follow up the sources, he should consult the Gaudé edition of St. Alphonsus. Nevertheless, we have taken footnotes or other discussions from Gaudé when they were important for the text.

Another thing we must note is that we followed the order of the 1852 Mechlin edition for what treatises should come in which order. Therefore, the treatise on Sin in General makes up our book II, and this causes the book on virtues to be book III in the first volume, and the work on the Ten Commandments is now book IV, whereas in Gaudé's edition of St. Alphonsus it is book III. We felt it necessary to remind the reader so that if he were to follow up with the Latin of Gaudé's edition he might find his place.

It has taken me longer to complete this work than the first volume and this is because great care has been taken to ensure the flow and accuracy of technical terms. For all that, all the care in the world would not have helped me produce the work if it was not for the generous help of others. Thus, I especially thank Fr. Chad Ripperger, PhD, for his assistance with technical terminology and assistance in a few sections. Likewise, I should like to thank Nicholas Scoville and Ashton Wilkins for their generous editing work and suggestions. I would also like to thank Paul Banducci of the Bulldog Pipe and Cigar Lounge in Coeur d'Alene, Idaho, whose establishment provided the assistance of long nights and much Virginia leaf which provided the midnight oil, as it were.

Finally, I want to thank my patient wife, Sarah, and all my

Translator's Preface

children, who have tolerated my absence to work on this and other projects which have been necessary to sustain us in the meantime.

It is my supreme hope that this text will not only be of assistance to priests and moral theologians, but also, may spark again longing for that time in theology when great names such as Bellarmine, de Lugo, John of St. Thomas, Suarez and Benedict XIV held pride of place in theology.

Ryan Grant
Post Falls, Idaho
Spring 2018

Sacerdotibus Sanctæ Ecclesiæ Catholicæ
ut opere S. Alphonsi utantur
Dirigantque animas ad Jesum per Mariam

BOOK IV

ON THE PRECEPTS OF THE DECALOGUE, AND OF THE CHURCH

TREATISE I
On the First Precept of the Decalogue

"The proper matter of this precept, insofar as it is affirmative, "is the act of the virtue of religion. Moreover, this is a moral "virtue, in which the interior and outward worship of God is "shown to be due. Its internal act is submission of the mind, "whereby we venerate the infinite excellence of God. The "outward is, in which we witness what is internal, such as "prayer, sacrifice, etc., on which see the Scholastics on 1, 2, et 3 "*parte.* Exactly as it is negative, it forbids vices opposed to "religion, which, because they are opposed to the virtue "especially among morals, they are sins. Next, those which are "committed contrary to the theological virtues are the gravest "and are mortal sins by their nature. Moreover, they are "twofold: those which are opposed by excess, such as "superstition with its species, and those by defect, such as "irreligiosity with its species."

From this, therefore, we are held by the virtue of religion to prayer, which is defined by St. Thomas (II IIæ quaest. 83, art. 1, from St. John Damascene, *Petitio decentium a Deo*). And more probably, according to the doctors, prayer is necessary for us by the necessity of means against those who think it is by the necessity of precept (Suarez, Lessius, Laym., Bonacina, Azor, etc., cited by Salamancans tract. 21, c. 9, punct. 3, §1, n. 11, St. Thomas, against Sylvius, Ledesma, Villalobos, etc.) Furthermore, when does the precept of prayer oblige? The Salamancans (*ibid.*, n. 17), with Trullenchus and Villalobos, against others, think it obliges of itself in a three-fold time, viz. in the instant of the use of reason, at the point of death, and at least once in a year. It is said *per se*, for *per accidens*, it is certain that it obliges when great temptation threatens, which cannot be conquered otherwise; or when a great calamity threatens the people or one's neighbor. (Salamancans *loc. cit.* n. 1).

CHAPTER I
ON SUPERSTITION AND ITS SPECIES

DUBIUM I
What is superstition, and how manifold is it?

1. What is superstition?
2. How manifold is superstition?
3. Who commits the superstition of false cult?
4. What is superstition of a superfluous cult?

1.—"*Resp.* 1. Superstition is a false religion, or a vicious cult "of a true or false deity. Lessius. And it fits with the common "definition from St. Thomas, in which he says it is a vice which "is opposed to religion according to an excess. He says *by an* "*excess*, not because God can be worshiped too much, or by "greater honor than is due, but it is understood according to the "circumstances, to the extent that you show worship or that "which you ought not, or to the extent that you ought not, or "to which you ought not.

2.—"*Resp.* 2. Superstition is twofold; one is of an *undue cult*, "or of one that is not suited, in which the true God, but in an "undue mode, is worshiped, by attributing to him what is *false*, "and pernicious, or *superfluous*, namely, which is against, or in "addition to, the custom and prescription of the Church. The "other is by reason of the thing worshiped, when, viz. the "worship due to God is given to a false god, or to a creature. "And this is subdivided into idolatry, divination, and vain "observance; to which magic is recalled or, rather constitutes a "fourth species. Laym., l. 4, t. 10, c. 1, from St. Thomas, qu. 92, "art. 2.

From which the following cases are resolved:

3.—"1) One commits superstition of a false cult: I. Who "offers worship to God by the ceremonies of the Old Law, *e.g.* "circumcision, immolation of a lamb, etc., because these signify "that Christ will come and has not yet come; II. A layman who "worships God as a public minister of the Church, *e.g.* by "sacrificing or absolving. Suarez teaches it is always a mortal "sin. (*de rel.* l. 2, *de superstit.* c. 2); III. One that proposes, by his "own authority, some things must be done, as if it were ordered "by the Church to the worship of God; IV. One who puts out "false relics, or claims that a miracle was done by some image, "or feigns that he himself did these things, or that he had "revelations to make a profit or to increase devotion; V. One "who, to move the people, feigns some miracle or history found "in the Sacred Scripture, etc. And this superstition, even if it is a "mortal sin by its nature, because it inflicts injury on the first "truth, and founds religion on lies, nevertheless is often excused "by ignorance of simplicity. Lessius, l. 1, c. 43; Sanchez, 2. *mor.* "c. 37; Navarre, c. 12; Laymann *loc. cit.*; Bonacina, d. 3, q. 5, p. 1, "4.

4.—"2) Superstition *of superfluous cult* is, *e.g.* a) Ceremonies "to hear Mass before the sun rises with a certain number "present in a certain order of seating, or with a priest that is "called John, or who might have the stature of Christ, etc., "because this cult is in itself inane and useless for spiritual "exercises; b) To fast on Sunday when you do not fast on other "days. (Although, from c. *Sacerdos*, caus. 26, qu. 7, it is forbidden to fast on the Lord's day to root out the heresy of the Manicheans that denied the resurrection of Christ the Lord, nevertheless, those who would fast for the sake of mortification would not sin, not even venially, as Viva says in l. 2, qu. 5, art. 1, n. 3, on the contrary they would gain merit since the Church has already dispelled this heresy. Albeit, the Salamancans in tr. 21, c. 11, num. 8 say that it is better to hold off from such a fast, and therefore the doctors teach in common that a fast promised for Sunday could be fulfilled on Saturday, and if anyone were to vow to fast for a month, he is not held to do so on the Lord's day unless he had expressly intended it).

3) "Likewise, in Mass, to make more signs of the cross "against the rubrics, to say *alleluja* or the *gloria* or the *credo* "more times against the rubrics, and otherwise to remove or "add to the ceremonies (even if it were from devotion; for this "must be corrected), because they are in addition to the practice "of the Church. Nevertheless, these and similar things, when "they are done from a good intention, are ordinarily only venial, "as Toledo, Lessius (*loc. cit.* d. 1), Navarre and Laymann teach, "because it is a light matter and an action that is not evil of "itself, and simplicity excuses many things. Still, it would be evil "of itself if you were to offer a stolen thing, or sing indecent "words in Church by word or by a notably wanton instrument, "or to sing out in a voice provoking to impurity, it is nearly a "mortal superstition, as Laymann says from the common "opinion.

DUBIUM II
On Divination. What is it and how manifold is it?

5. *What is divination?*
6. *It is one thing with express invocation of a demon, another with tacit invocation.*
7. *Whether to commit divination were always a mortal sin?*
8. *Resolution of cases. What must be thought about a divinatory staff?*
9. *Whether it were lawful to commit divination through a dream?*

Treatise I: First Commandment, Ch. I: On Superstition 5

10. *Whether Astrology is licit and what sort?*
11. *Is it lawful to apply divination by lots?*

5.—"Resp. I. Divination is, when someone tacitly or "expressly invokes the aid of a demon to know matters "touching upon or clearly what is going to happen, or "otherwise secret and naturally unknowable. Which, if they "might be the type of things which God alone can know, it "involves tacit idolatry which attributes to a demon a divine "cult; but if they are such things which the demon can "naturally know (from signs and other modes, each very secret "that he can know, even a great many thoughts of men as well "as what they are going to do, see Delrio l. 4, c. 2, q. 2, Sanchez, "2. *mor.* c. 28); just the same, it is illicit, insofar as commerce "would be held with the sworn enemy of God, which imports a "certain betrayal and apostasy from God, and perhaps even (as "Suarez would have it, against Valentia), superstition. See "Laymann, c. 3, Bonacina, p. 3, St. Thomas, "II IIæ qu. 5, art. 2.

6.—"*Resp.* 2. Divination is twofold: one, in which it is an "invocation, or an express pact with a demon, and in general is "called necromancy, such as when a demon teaches occult "matters through soothsayers, the possessed, illusions, through "persons appearing from the dead or the living, or other signs "in the air, water, fire, and mirrors. The other is in which there "is only an invocation or a tacit arrangement, whether "interpretative, such as from the geometric figures of the body, "voices, the chattering of birds and similar things, in which "demons usually mingle themselves, knowledge is understood "to which these things are disproportionate. St. Thomas, quaest. "95. Now, although there are species of each different species, "here I omit these because, according to the more common "opinion they do not differ in the kind of use, nor do they have "a special malice; and therefore in confession one does not need "to explain whether, *e.g.* divination was done with mirrors, the "air, a dead person, etc. Nevertheless, each divination must "necessarily be explained, whether an express or tacit "arrangement occurred, because these either morally differ "among themselves by species or not, still they notably change "the judgment of the confessor. (It is better because express invocation often has other sins atached to it, viz. heresy, adoration of demons, etc. Moreover, it is probable that of itself there is no obligation to explain. Salamancans tract. 21, c. 11, punct. 3, § 1, n. 29 and 30, with Victor.).

"See Laymann, *loc. cit.*, Sanchez, *loc. cit.*, Lessius, *l.c.* disp. 5, "Del. l. 4, dis. 4, c. 2; Bonacina, q. 5, p. 4.

Divination through the express invocation of a demon is called *oraculum*, if it is done by an idol. *Necromancy*, especially if through the apparent resuscitation of the dead, for generally necromancy embraces even other species of divination. *Oniromantia* if through dreams. *Praestigia* if through figures that have been confected. *Haruspicina*, if through signs in the entrails of animals. *Geomantia*, if through a figure in the ground. *Hydromantia*, through a figure in the water. *Aëromantia*, in the air. *Pyromantia*, in fire.

On the other hand, through tacit invocation there is *astrology*, if it is done by the location and movements of the stars. An *Auspice (Auspicium)* through the signs of birds. *Augury* through the signs of animals. *Omen*, if it is done by chance, *e.g.* by the meeting of a rope, etc. *Sortilegium* if it is done by lot, *e.g.* from the opening of a book by throwing a dice.

7.—"Resp. 3. Divination which is done by an express act, and "in which a demon is expressly invoked, cannot be excused "from mortal sin; but that which is done only through an "implicit act, certain doctors assert is sometimes excused from "mortal sin; namely when there is simplicity and ignorance that "is not crass, nor affected, for certain faith is not applied, but "only a certain fear or suspicion conceived over a future event. "Laymann, l. 4, tract. 10, c. 3; Sanchez, Lessius, Suarez, Cajetan, "Baldus, tract. 3, l. 4, d. 3, n. 2, etc., to the extent that then it is "truly not superstition since the intention is not so great. See "Suarez, Lessius, Sanchez, Laymann, Cajetan, Navarre, Sayr, "Valentia, and Tanner, d. 5, *de rel.* quaest. 7, disp. 1, n. 21, and "*dub.* 2, n. 25."

Thus the following cases are resolved from the aforesaid:

8.—"1) He is considered to expressly invoke or arrange and "make a pact with a demon who either invokes a demon by "words, or at least takes up some sign in fact, through which he "knows or thinks a demon cooperates.

"2) He tacitly makes an agreement who uses vain and "naturally disproportionate things to know or effect something. "It is not required that a demon would at some point make an "agreement to his involvement in the employment of such a "vain means, for because of this very thing, that someone uses "these vanities, the demon mingles himself, even if it were apart "from the intention of the one using them to invoke him, as "Suarez, Lessius and Sanchez teach.

"3) One is not excused from sin who, by using such things "that it is certain are naturally disproportionate, he protests "himself to intend no commerce with a demon, because he "really acts contrary to his protestation. For, since neither God "nor good angels mix in such things, a demon is implicitly "invoked by them, as Laymann and Bonacina teach in addition "to the cited authors.

"4) Nor is one excused, who believes such means are useful "on account of experiences, because the demon procures these "to ensnare men little by little, and to induce him to take up "similar things. See Sanchez, 2. *Mor.* c. 38. (With Viva, *loc. cit.* n. "3).

One will ask, what must be thought about the *bifurcated staff* called *divinatory* (*virga divinatoria*), which some use to discover treasures hidden in the ground, water or veins of metals, transfer the boundaries of fields and discover thieves and murderers by its prolapse? Some doctors of medicine, and even of theology, have tried to prove the use of this staff is natural and innocent; but rightly the Continuator of Tourned condemns it (*de virt. relig.* part. 3, cap. 2), with Fr. Malebranche, Fr. Lebrum, and others. The first reason is that if such a staff is moved naturally and turned around in the hand of a man, intention can confer nothing to the motion; nevertheless, the staff remains unmoved in their hands, who have protested to refuse anything superstitious, about which Fr. Lebum relates many examples; it begins to be moved in the opposite direction in the hands of those who prefaced no protestation. The second reason is a stone constituted for the boundary of a field differs nothing in matter from another stone, therefore it is impossible that the staff would naturally be moved toward the first stone, and not the second. The third reason, is that which acts physically cannot be directed by the intention of a man to do or not do, but is placed in the same circumstances, in the same mode in which he acts; but the divinitory staff is moved according to the mind of the bearer, so that if he seeks metals, not water, the staff would not be moved when he discovers water, but only if he discovers metals, and vice versa; therefore it is clear that such a motion cannot be natural.

"5) If someone were to so depend upon the stars, dreams or "similar things that would regulate nearly all his actions and "life according to them, the doctors teach he sins mortally. "Lessius, Suarez, Sanchez, *loc. cit.* (the Salamancans teach the same thing, tr. 21, c. 11, punct. 5, n. 64, with Navarre,[1] Trullenchus, and Palaus).

"6) To omit to do something once or repeatedly from the "observation of such things, to which he would not otherwise "be held under mortal sin, Cajetan and Armilla (*v. Somnium*) "think it is only venial, that to lightly fear lest they would be so "or what they portend might happen, as Suarez notes (*sup. loc.* "*cit.* the Salamancans say the same thing, *cit.* n. 64)."

9.—*Quaeritur*: Whether to divine the future through dreams is always illicit? The response is if the dreams are certainly or more probably from God, we can, nay more are held to believe them, since God promised sometimes to speak through dreams, "I will speak to him through a dream." (Numbers 12:6). So think the Salamancans, *ibid.* n. 60, with St. Thomas, St. Gregory of Nyssa, Suarez, Lessius, etc. On the other hand, it would be a grave sin to believe diabolic dreams, as in *can. Episcopo*, caus. 26, qu. 5 (*Salamancans. ibid.* n. 66, with Laym., Lessius, etc.). Still, whereas an unlearned man can be excused from mortal sin by reason of simplicity, or because he barely believed the same, as Anacletus (*tract.* 5, d. 2, n. 22) and Busembaum (below) call attention to. What if someone is in doubt as to whether the dreams are from God or a demon? The response is, if it is not certain, or the dreams are only probably from God, it is not permitted to believe them (Salamancans *ibid.,* n. 61, with Suarez, Lessius, Sanchez, Palaus, etc., and Sporer, *de 1, praec.* n. 19, from the common opinion). The reason is because God, when he causes dreams, at the same time also renders a man certain, or nearly certain, that they were sent by him. However, for a rule to discern whether dreams are from God or a demon, it must be observed whether

---

[1] Navarre, *Man.* cap. 11 n. 33, says that a man sins mortally "who, on account of the things which he dreamed, refuses to do something necessary to the salvation of his soul, or does something contrary to the safety of the same; although, if it is not of that degree, he only sins venially." Footnote b) to the Gaude edition, pg. 373.

the dream persuades to a good work or an evil one, or a presumptuous one. Likewise, whether a man feels disturbed after a dream, or less prompt to works of piety; or that he feels eager and prompt, then he can prudently reckon the dream is from God. Elbel, (*de 1. praecept.*, n. 491), and Anacl. (*loc. cit.* n. 23) so think, from the common opinion of the doctors.

"7) Commonly, and for the most part in similar matters in "which there is only a tacit agreement, one sins only venially. "Consequently, the doctors cited above, because commonly "some of these [cases] crop up which they say excuse from "mortal sin, *e.g.* because complete faith was not applied. "(Sanchez, *loc. cit.*, n. 13, Cajetan, *in summ.*, Armilla, etc. "Nevertheless, Delrio rightly notes that it is always a very "dangerous matter to direct one's self according to those "actions, even while not believing in them. See Sanchez, *loc. "cit.*

"8) The following are licit: a) *physiognomia*, which is based "on the countenance, disposition and condition of the body "and members; b) *chyromantia* which is based on the lines and "parts of the hands and considers the temper of the body, nay "more, even the inclinations of the mind, and guesses the "emotions with probability. (Salamancans trs. 21, c. 11, punct. 6, "n. 73, and 74, with Azor, Bonacina, Sanchez). c) Likewise, "divination, which guesses the dilemma from the dreams of "men, and hence, the daily affections of the mind. d) likewise, "other things, which from the voice, movement or other "actions of birds, fish, or other animals, some future natural "effects are foretold, *e.g.* serenity, rain, etc. e) Natural "astrology, which predicts corporeal and other effects such as "the winds, an eclipse, fertility, health, plague and similar "things which are conducive for medicine or agriculture; and "even when from the point of birth, or a horoscope he "probably foretells the complexion of the body and the "affections of the mind. Because these divinations are all "natural and they use proportionate means. Lessius, l. 2, c. 43, "d. 7."

10.—*Natural astrology,* which guesses the rains, storms, barrenness of the land, and similar things is another thing altogether, and it is not illicit, as Busembaum says here (with the Salamancans, *ibid.* punct. 4, § 1, n. 35), although much of the time it might be useless and uncertain. Another is *judiciaria*, which predicts future contingencies from signs in the stars, which depend upon the will of men; and this, if it is done for a particular person, is illicit, as the authors say (Salamancans *ibid.* § 2, n. 46, with Trullenchus, Sanchez, Sal, etc. against Palaus and others they cite); even if it is done not as a certain thing but conjecturally or probably, from the Constitution of Pope Sixtus V *Moderator Coeli,* in the year 1586, where even those predictions which do not dare affirm or protest anything for certain, are condemned. Moreover, they think it is licit if it were done in general, say if wars, rebellions, etc. were foretold. The Salamancans agree with this (*ibid.* n. 48) from St. Thomas, who so speaks in 1 qu. 115, art. 4 ad 3: "Many men follow their passions, with which the heavenly bodies can cooperate. Moreover, there are few wise men who resist passions of this sort, and therefore astrologers, as in a great many things, can predict what is true, and especially in common matter, but not in an individual case."

Thence it is asked, whether that astrology is licit which predicts from a horoscope, the inclinations at the point of birth, or someone's temperaments? You must make the distinction if it foretells them as a certainly, which is illicit, since all things are uncertain. So think the Salamancans, *ibid.* § 3, n. 50, with Sanchez, Trullench, Suarez, and others in common; still they think it is a light sin, as num. 52 with Laymann, Suarez, Sanchez, etc. against Filliuci and Trullenchus. But if one predicts only conjecturally or probably, it is licit. (Salamancans *ibid.* num. 53, with St. Thomas, Suarez, Palaus, Bonacina.

"9) But all the aforesaid divinations are forbidden if "something is known from them, or intended to be foretold in "regard to them, to which they are not proportioned, as in "regard to contingent and free effects, or which depend upon "God, as in regard to the state of the soul, gifts of grace, riches, "honors, fortune, marriage, state of life and similar things, the "choice of which is voluntary, depends upon the free will of "men; and likewise on occult things, as in theft, or hidden "treasure. See Lessius, *loc. cit.*, and Bonacina, d. 3, qu. 5, p. 3, n. "11, Suarez, Sanchez, *loc. cit.*, Bonacina, n. 11."

To predict free future contingencies only conjecturally from the signs of birds, etc., the Salamancans say (*ibid.* punct. 6, n. 68, in fine with Lessius, Palaus, Sanchez, Filliuci, etc.) is not illicit, because a constellation, which can move men to war, can also cause these signs in the birds.

"10) They sin who consult Egyptians for their fortune, and "indeed, if it were done with firm faith, or scandal, etc., is "mortally sinful, but from the cause of curiosity, or humor, as is "commonly done, it is only venially sinful. Filliuci and Sanchez.

"11) Superstitious divination is, that which is done through "divinitory lots, to know something that is going to happen or "something secret, as if some divine force were present in lots, "that if anyone *e.g.* by the throwing of dice and its disposition "would divine that someone is going to obtain victory, a "benefice, etc. Nearly the same thing is the case with *consultory* "*lots*, in which it is inquired what must be done in this or that "matter. I said *nearly*, because sometimes these are licit, when "the necessity and integrity of a cause demands it: a more "suitable mode does not appear for conquering doubt: provided "they are prefaced with a prayer of due reverence, and that one "does not await information except from God, as happened in 1 "Samuel 9:16 in the choice of Saul. Filliuci, Sanchez, Bonacina, *"loc. cit."*

"12) Divisory lots are without superstition and a great many "can licitly be done either for an upright game or for division of "an inheritance, or for the composition of a lawsuit provided "the litigants who have an equal right would consent, because "they comprise nothing other than a contract among them that "someone would have the right to have a thing as their own if "the lot would befall one him. So also, if many merited death "and it were not expedient to punish all, the man who must be "killed by them can be chosen by lots. I said *a great many* not "only because they are illicit for choosing ecclesiastics "(Laymann l. 3, t. 4, and Bonacina), but also because secular "duties are not divided by lot but according to the suitability of "persons, even if among a great many they are equally suitable, "and it could be done worthily by lot. See Lessius, c. 43."

Lots in the elections for secular offices are licit, but only among those worthy. (Sporer, *de 1. praec.* c. 9, n. 21, with St. Thomas, q. 97, a. 8, Sanchez and comm.) But in regard to duties or ecclesiastical benefices they are forbidden in *c. Ecclesia de sortilegiis.* Now, would such an election be null? Panormus and Villalobos (ap. Salamancans tr. 11, c. 11, punct. 7, n. 91) affirm. But Felinus, Farina, and Salamancans *ibid*, n. 86, with Suarez, Sanchez, etc. reject it. And indeed it is more true, for from *c. Ecclesia, Extra de sortil.* ecclesiastical election by lots is universally forbidden. In our case such an election of one or the other from litigants is already done by lot, even so completive. Nevertheless, the Salamancans say it is lawful if this election were to take place with the authority of the judge, because not only is the danger of a vicious entrance avoided, but also the judge, by having jurisdiction for a legitimate conferral confers the title.

Lastly, it must be noted from the Salamancans. *ibid.* n. 95, with St. Thomas, Suarez, Palaus, etc., that a divinatory lot, even if it waits upon God, is then only licit when: a) an urgent necessity of salvation is present; b) Divine things are not turned to earthly business; c) The lot is not distributed in certain ecclesiastical elections which ought to be held by the inspiration of the Holy Spirit. Hence, the Salamancans more rarely say it is licit.

"13) One can be excused from superstition who in an illicit "mode shows he means to divine the future for the sake of a "joke. The reason is, because it is not a superstitious act nor "affectation for the knowledge proper to God but only some "vanity. Suarez and Sanchez, Reginald, l. 17, n. 170." (With the "Salamancans *dict.* c. 11, punct. 3, § 2 n. 33; in fin. Provided "they believe it is false)."

DUBIUM III
What and how manifold is idolatry

12 - 13 *Inclusive.*

12.—"*Resp.* 1. It is when honor is attributed to a created "thing as just as to God. St. Thomas, II IIæ. qu. 94, a. 1. But it "happens that Lessius teaches (lib. 2, c. 43) that it is not only in "a sacrifice, but also in any sign of honor in which someone "intends to submit himself to a creature as to God, *e.g.* by "genuflection, incense, uncovering of the head before a statue "of Jupiter."

13.—"*Resp.* 2. Idolatry is two-fold: On the one hand *material*, "or simulated, as when someone without an internal affect, "from fear of death worships a cult. The other is formal and "proper idolatry, or even perfect, as when someone worships an "idol from infidelity because he thinks it is God, or imperfect, "when someone either out of hatred of God or from affect to "obtain something from a demon or another creature, that "honors it with worship rather than God. Laymann *loc. cit.*, "*from St. Augustine and St. Thomas.*

Thus, the following are resolved:

"1) Idolatry is sometimes joined with infidelity, or heresy, "when viz., a creature is worshiped in the understanding and "held for God, that is not.

"2) Even material and feigned idolatry is a grave and mortal "sin, because it is at least a pernicious lie, and against religion; "also, it is often against the outward confession of faith. "Sanchez, l. 1, c. 37, n. 21; Azor, 1. p. l. 9, c. 11.

"3) Imperfect idolatry on account of the malice of the will is "a graver sin than perfect idolatry without it. See Laym., l. 4, t. "10, c. 2; Sanchez, lib. 1.

DUBIUM IV
What, and how manifold is vain observance, and how is it deduced?

14. *What is vain observance? And how manifold?*
15. *Is it a grave fault?*
16. *How can it be known?*
17. *Resolution of cases.*
18. *Whether it were granted and licit for virtue to be in those that are called saviors?*
19. *Whether people are forbidden from marveling at supernatural things?*
20. *What must be presumed in doubt?*
21. *Whether an ensalmus is lawful?*

22. *Whether natural fascination should be tolerated.*

14.—"*Resp.* 1. It is superstition to procure certain effects by "some means that are disproportionate and not established by "God, *e.g.* sanity, knowledge, etc. St. Thomas, II IIæ qu. 69, art. "1, Bonacina and others. Moreover, it differs from divination "because this is only ordered to knowledge of occult things; but "these for an external effect. It agrees with the same thing "because each rests upon a pact with the demon, and attributes "a perfection to it that is proper to God. This is why those "things that are said to be from divination ought to be "proportionally accommodated to this.

"*Resp.* 2. It is divided 1) Just as divination, in that which "from an expressed pact with a demon, and in that which "proceeds from an implicit pact. 2) It is commonly divided into "four species; a) *ars notoria*, which to acquire knowledge "immediately and without any labor, uses the inspection of "certain figures, or some certain fasting, prayer, etc. just as "Anabaptists do. b) It is called *magic* (which is otherwise a "general name) which occupies itself in regard to various "unchangeable bodies and marvelous effects. c) *Observation of* "*events*, in which a conjecture is made about the future from "consideration of some event, *e.g.* if from that case he believes "that a fox, a dog or a cadaver, threaten certain things, and "moderates his actions by that. d) *observation of healths*, since "certain signs are applied prayers, a certain number of crosses, "sacred words, etc., as if they were necessary and efficacious to "defeat plague. The same is on the wearing of relics with vain "circumstances, *e.g.* in such a reliquary, for so many days, with "such an herb, etc. (Sanchez, c. 40, n. 11, Filliuci, t. 14, c. 6, n. "157)."

15.—"*Resp.* 3. Vain observance, just as divination, is a mortal "sin of itself. The reason is not only because it attributes divine "honor to a creature, by expecting from it what should only be "expected from God alone, but also because it depends upon a "pact with a demon. Lessius, Bonacina, Quaest. 5, part. 4 and "others. Nor can it be excused from mortal sin due to the "smallness of the matter, because simply in every material "knowledge is used or a strength proper to God. Nevertheless, it "can be done from another cause so that it would not be mortal, "as the authors cited above teach (dub. 2, resp. 3): a) by reason "of ignorance, if the pact were only implicit; b) If trust were not "employed, although he so feared it is or was going to be. See "what was said on divination, n. 8, case 7, and Lessius, dub. 8, n. "53, and 66."

16.—"Resp. 4. Vain observance can be understood: 1) from "insufficiency of the cause applied to the effect; namely, if it "were to have either natural virtue, or it was not certain that it "had a legitimately supernatural virtue; 2) From the union of "false or vain circumstances, *e.g.* if flagellation ought to take "place at a certain hour, with a certain number, in a certain "hand, with a silken whip, if unknown names are applied, or the "markings of pilgrimage, false or apocryphal words, *e.g.* Christ "had fevers, or a spasm, etc. Likewise, if force is applied in a "manner of writing, *e.g.* by a virgin of the Gospel of St. John, "while the sun rises, etc.; c) If the effects were to immediately "vanish, etc. Delrio, l. 2, quaest. 5, Sanchez, c. 40, n. 43.

From which the following are resolved:

17.—"1. It is superstitious: a) to take up some potion, or "precious stone, or whatever to use to acquire some knowledge; "b) to wear amulets, bindings, wraps, marked with false "characters against wounds or sudden death, lest they could be "wounded nor lest blood would flow, or to conciliate "invisibility, impenetrability, love, fortune, wounds and "malefices. c) To make a conjecture about an event from a "fortuitous case, *e.g* something good or bad is going to happen "to him, and therefore going out in the morning, if his foot

18   BOOK IV: ON THE PRECEPTS OF THE DECALOGUE

"should offend a stone, then he will remain at home, fearing
"something inauspicious. d) Some days have some auspicious
"things, other days inauspicious, and therefore omit business,
"*e.g.* on Friday to refuse to cut his nails; e) blessing songs of
"women and prayers and prayers to apply to strike out a
"plague; f) To cast a statue of some saint in the river so that it
"would rain; g) If Masses are not thought to benefit the dead
"unless seven are heard, with seven candles of a certain color,
"and seven acts of almsgiving; h) If a waxed safe, in which a
"sword is anointed, were cared for being absent; I) If on a
"certain feast, *e.g.* of St. John, certain prayers are employed, or
"on the feast of St. Matthew ivy leaves are placed in the water
"so that it would be understood that he ought to marry
"someone; j) If a certain and infallible force were attributed to
"certain prayers, images, or characters, or even crosses, *e.g.* to
"escape from an enemy, to expel plague, to not die without first
"having confession, of not following into misfortunes, etc.
"Nevertheless, it is a different thing to ask for these things by
"prayer, and to hope for them. Delrio l. 3, p. 2 resol. 4, sect. 7;
"Suarez, c. 15; Lessius, c. 43, dub. 10; Sanchez, n. 34, and 37;
"Filliuci n. 150."

    "2. Superstition is not: a) to observe the moon or suitable
"times for gathering herbs (*e.g.* on the day of St. John the
"Baptist), to cleanse bodies, to fell trees, etc.; b) to wear the
"words of Holy Scripture or relics for the honor of God without
"the aforesaid vanities; c) to lead a beast of burden three times
"around the Church of some certain Saint; to cut the reigns
"from the horse, if this is otherwise done, so that greater
"devotion would be exercised, and the effect ascribed to the
"merits of the saints. It would be another thing if such
"circumstances were considered infallible or plainly necessary
"or efficacious in themselves. See Navarre, in *man.* c. 11.
"Laymann adds, from Cajetan, that if unlearned men were to
"observe some rite not received by the Church but with good

"faith, and from devotion, sometimes they must be left to their "simplicity since they will be led away from that which they "received from their elders in good faith only with great "difficulty; d) Nor must certain devotions be condemned which "they call novenas, *e.g.* to celebrate Masses for nine days, or to "the example of St. Gregory, thirty, or another certain number "and with an intensity of candles and similar things, if it is done "in the memory of some mystery, *e.g.* of the nine months in "which Christ was *in utero*, or the five wounds, etc. Still, it "would be superstitious to believe these prayers would not be of "any benefit in a greater or lesser number; 5) Many also excuse "those who heal those bitten by a rabid dog, because they think "they have a grace gratuitously given for this purpose; and so "hold Navarre (*in man.* c. 11), Sanchez, Laym., Bonacina, *ll. cc.*"

18.—The question is, whether the virtue (called natural magic) were granted and would be licit in some men called *salvatores*, who are healed from plagues by the sign of the cross or sacred words, or opening of the mouth? Azor, and others cited by the Salamancans (tr. 21, c. 11, punct. 9, n. 113) affirm this, and they say a natural virtue is given. Others (*ibid.* n. 114) say no such virtue is given, neither natural nor one given by grace. Still, the Salamancans (ex. n. 115 and 116) with Delrio, Navarre, Villalobos, Trullenchus, Palaus, Hurt., and others, likewise Sanchez (dec. l. 2, c. 40, n. 47), Suarez (*de relig.* tr. 3, l. 2, c. 15, n. 25), and Lessius (l. 2, c. 43, dubio 10, n. 63) say it is probably given to some under this virtue, just as it is known the kings of France heal scrofula (as St. Thomas acknowledges, with Boniface VIII *in canoniz. S. Louis*) and the kings of Spain heal tuberculosis. This virtue, nevertheless, they say is not natural (even if it seems probable enough to some serious doctors), for otherwise all men of the same temperament would have the same virtue; but it is given gratuitously by God for the public good, according to St. Paul in 1 Cor. 12:9, "Others the grace of healing," etc.

Here, what is discovered in the *Roman Martyrology* must be noted, under 5 March on the miraculous healing from the bites of serpents for those who would touch the door of the church of St. Phocas the martyr, after his intercession has been invoked, according to the Martyrology: "At Antioch, the birth of St. Phocas the martyr, who after suffering many injuries for the name of the Redeemer, just as he triumphed over that ancient serpent, today also it was declared to the people by that miracle, because if anyone that had been bitten by the serpent, would touch the door of the martyr's basilica while believing, he would immediately be freed from the poison and be healed."

19.—Yet the same Salamancans rightly advert (*ibid.* n. 117) that men must be hindered who repeatedly handle charcoal, who warm up a furnace with vapors, or kill a man; who, while drunk heal with wine, who lose their virtue when another healer is present, who learn such a virtue from another; those that have such a virtue that were born on Good Friday, or because he is the seventh son (although in this case Viva says such a natural virtue can be given), who use certain words which they believe the virtue to be present in, when grace is conferred on a person not by words and signs. Salamancans, *ibid.*, n. 118, with Suarez, Sanchez, Delrio, Palaus, Hurt., etc.

20.—They also advert that in a doubt some effect must be presumed to have its origin rather in a natural cause than from superstition. So think Sporer (*de 1 praec.* c. 9, n. 31), with St. Augustine, Sanchez, Laymann, Elbel (n. 591), Croix, (l. 3, p. 1, n. 28) and Salamancans (*ibid.* punct. 9, n. 112), with St. Thomas, who teaches in II IIæ q. 60, art. 4 in the article: "Where the manifest indications do not appear from the malice of some man, we ought to hold it as good, by interpreting with regard to the better part, when there is a doubt." Still, the cited authors rightly advise that then a protestation should be prefaced to refuse an effect if there is any superstition. But if it is probably and certainly established that the matter has no natural force for some effect, it should be reckoned to originate more from a demon than from God, since divine permission is not held concerning that, as Sanchez teaches (*dec.* lib. 2, c. 40, n. 2), with Gerson and Spor. n. 33, with St. Thomas (II IIæ. quest. 96) art. 2.

Moreover, would the use of *symphatic* [*symphaticus*] ash be licit?

Elbel responds (n. 516), that the doctors deny it sufficiently in common, because it would seem incredible that the qualities of this ash over a distance has the force of operation; this is why Elbel reckons a use of this sort is not easily approved. Still, he says in a pressing case it can be permitted, only the wounded man should not be too far away, *e.g.* beyond 300 paces; and it is only permitted with a protestation. The reason is that it is probable for the *actionem in distans* to be granted. It seems to me it is licit enough, if such ash is not applied at a great distance; I am lead to believe this from the things the famous philosopher Purchotius says in his *Instit. phil.* t. 2, part. 1, physic., sect. 5 c. 11, where he says: "The ash of *vitriolum calcinatum* [red calks] which is called *sympathicus*, fresh in the blood from a wound injects an emission, healed in those suffering the wound from far away, and it is observed the blood stops flowing from the wound. But it cannot be begun otherwise than through substantial flow, or through acid vapors which from the calks still mixed with the blood particle, to the wound where the blood has been expressed, are imposed and just as a type of wedge opens them, from which the blood flows out and they nearly obstruct it." Moreover, to anoint at a distance a sword warm with blood from a wound, is superstitious as Croix says (n. 29) with Burghaber, and he asserts it in common. But from the same reason, as above, Sporer probably also permits it. Still, in doubt as to whether the effect has its origin in a natural cause, we already said from the most common opinion of the doctors that it is not superstitious to procure it at least when it is prefaced with a protestation.

Moreover, when some signs of the cross are applied, or so many Our Fathers, etc., in doubt as to whether there is some superstition in it, Lessius (l. 2, c. 44, n. 46) permits these, with a protestation being expressly prefaced. Sporer (n. 34) and Tamburinius (*lib. 2* c. 6, § 1, n. 12) agree, if a notable necessity were pressing. But Sporer (c. 9, n. 32) condemns, with the common consensus, as superstitious in its regular use, on certain feasts, hours, etc., to gather herbs or fruits unless the circumstances of the season would confer a virtue upon the herbs as in spring, equinox, etc. Sporer (n. 28) also condemns leading horses around through the churches of the Saints, unless the effect expected were merited by them, wherefore he says, that where a custom of this sort is present it must be abrogated; but if it could not without giving offense to the people, at least he must be taught in what state of mind it should be done.

3. It is not illicit to use the virtue of a natural thing, which is recognized through superstition, only its observance or operation must not depend upon the assistance of a demon. The reason is, because although that knowledge arose badly, still the sin passes over, and the natural virtue from it does not contract something evil. See Sanchez, 2. *mor.* c. 38; Bonacina, q. 5, p. 4; Laym., *loc. cit.* t. 10, c. 4.

21.—What about an *ensalmus*? An *ensalmus* is so called because it is commonly composed from words of the Psalms and is ordered to cure plagues. If an ensalmus is *invocative*, namely asking health from God that the effect would infallibly be believed to come from him, then it is licit. It would be otherwise if it were *constitutive*, namely if the infallible virtue were attributed to the thing itself. So think the Salamancans, tr. 21, c. 11, punct. 9 § 3, n. 124 and 125, with Navarre, Azor, Bonacina, S. Antoninus, and Suarez. Moreover, an ensalmus is certainly illicit (as St. Thomas teaches, 22. q. 96, a. 4), if one were to indirectly invoke a demon in it, or an unheard of name for some angel, or if it were mixed with something false or vain, or a certain mode of writing or composing it were applied, etc.

22.—Whether natural fascination is granted? The Salamancans affirm it (*ibid.* punct. 9, § 3 n. 104), with St. Thomas (1. p. q. 117, art. 3 ad 2), who says: "Moreover, the eyes imbue the successive air even to determined space." Hence, the Salamancans say that such a man, who experiences this pestiferous quality in himself, is held to abstain from excessive consort with men that is not necessary, or to lower his eyes. But they say in the same place, n. 135, against Azor (l. 9, c. 25) that common superstitious fascination, which is commonly believed, viz. that looking with an envious spirit causes harm, and so must be avoided just as superstitious or somewhat ugly faces, which are imposed against fascinations. But if they were applied against a natural fascination, as above, I do not know why these would be so rigorously condemned, from which it certainly appears that the aforesaid ugly faces naturally have no power to amend the malignant outlet? Sporer agrees with me (*de 1. praec.* c. 9, n. 31), who, as we related above, says in a prudent doubt as to whether a matter that was applied had natural force, which could licitly be applied, with the common opinion of the doctors from St. Augustine. To much more, because commonly certain faith is not furnished to them.

DUBIUM V
What is a malefice, and how can it be removed?

23. What is a malefice, and how manifold is it?
24. What remedies would it be lawful to apply against a malefice?

25. *Whether it would be lawful to seek from the one that carried out the malefice that he abolish it with another? And whether in doubt as to whether he knows the licit mode of breaking it?*
26. *What about vampires? (striges)*
27. *Do malifices incur excommunication?*
28. *How a confessor ought to conduct himself with magic and malefices?*

23.—"*Resp.* 1. A malefice is a force to harm others, from a "pact and cooperation with a demon. It differs from magic "because this intends to do wonders that are directed to do "harm. Toledo, (lib. 4, cap. 10); Filliuci, t. 24, cap. 8 q. 1."

"Resp. 2. Another malefice is called a *love potion* or a "*philitrum,* whose use is for carnal love or to arouse hatred, "while the demon agitates a fantasy in a man, still while doing "nothing in the will. From there it is clear, if by the malefice "those infected fall, they truly sin, because their freedom is not "taken away. Another is called sorcery (*veneficium*) in which "damage is inflicted on some other person or his goods. "Villalobos (*loc. cit.* n. 183); Azor, l. 1, l. 9, c. 26)."

24.—"Resp. 3. It is licit to use against malefices:
"1) remedies sought from medicine (seeing that a great "many herbs, such as rue, sage, etc. are naturally beneficial "against malefices because by their virtue they correct bad "humors stirred up by the aid of a demon, but it is not lawful to "use *virga lupi,* by sprinkling the ash over the body, etc. and "similar things, which cannot naturally be applied to pacify the "humors. See the Salamancans. tr. 21, c. 11, punct. 9, § 3 and "punct. 10, § 1, n. 143).

"2) Exorcisms and sacraments of the Church, pilgrimages, "invocations of the Saints, etc.;

"3) the destruction of the signs through which the demon "harms, still without another malefice; Navarre and others in "common." (It is also common with Salamancans, *ibid.* § 3, n. 157, and 158).

"4) If a warlock can destroy the malefice by a licit mode, one "is allowed to fetch him for this purpose and ask, nay more "even to induce him with money or compel him with beatings "or torments (still, not to kill him) if he refuses. (de Lugo, "Diana, part. 8, t. 7, r. 53). Therefore, even if it were certain that "he is going to do it through a new malefice, just as in the case "where it is lawful to seek from a usurer a loan at usury. The "reason is, because when I have a right to ask what can be "furnished rightly from someone, it is indifferent and if he does "something wrongly, it is imputed to the malice of the other." (So think the Salamancans, *ibid.* § 2, n. 154, with Palaus, Suarez, etc. against Cajetan) "See Sanchez, lib. 7, *de matrim.* disp. 94, n. 11; Filliuci, n. 192; Lessius, lib. 2, cap. 44, d. 6, against Delrio."

"5). It is even lawful to apply the contrary positive sin, yet it "must be upright of itself, *e.g.* if a demon were to make a pact "with a warlock, that he would cause harm as long as the one "causing the malefice would not make the sign of the cross, or "wash his body (for most of the time it is done with such a "condition, that it will endure as long as some bond remains, or "something is buried in a certain place), it will be permitted for "him to make the sign of the cross, to watch, etc. Suarez; "Lessius (lib. 2, c. 44, n. 45). Elbel also agrees (n. 534), and the "Salamancans (*ibid.* § 3, n. 161); Sanchez, Palaus, Trull., etc. "The reason is because there is no positive intention to recover "health from that means, but only to remove the sign and "dissolve the pact with the demon. Moreover, it is clear that it is "lawful to strike against the witch that touched you, for by that "strike usually the harm ceases, as Lessius holds as well as "Sanchez (lib. 7 *de matrim.* disp. 93, et 96).”

"6) If a warlock cannot remove the malefice except through "a new one, it is not lawful to induce him to do it, because that "would be to induce him to sin and to cooperate in an "intriniscally evil act. (Suarez, Sanchez, Lessius, etc.)."

"7) If there is a doubt as to whether one could remove the "malefice without a new one, it is not lawful to seek it from "them, as Laym. (lib. 4, tr. 10, cap. 4, n. 9), Sanchez and Suarez "hold, because there it is a danger to sin. Further, it can more "easily be presumed that the one who placed the signs can "destroy them without anew malefice than one who did not "place them. For that reason, if he offers his assistance, one "must first examine the mode of breaking it. See Laym., "Bonacina, disp. 3, q. 5."

25.—*Quæritur I:* Would it be lawful to seek from the one that carried out the malefice to remove the malefice with another malefice? Angelus and Aureolus (cited by Salamancans tr. 21, c. 11, punct. 10 § 2, n. 146) affirm this, just as they say it is permitted to seek the sacraments for one's own advantage from a sacrilegious priest. But the negative opinion must be held with Lessius (lib. 2, cap. 44, dub. 6 n. 35) and the Salamancans (*ibid.* n. 143) with St. Thomas and many others. The reason is, because a sacrilegious priest can minister the sacraments without committing a sacrilege. But a warlock cannot confect a malefice without cooperation with demons, which is intrinsically evil, nor is this impeded by the fact that he is prepared to it, according to what was said in book 3, n. 47.

Quareitur II: Would it be lawful to seek the remedy for a malefice from a sorcerer when one is in doubt as to whether the sorcerer does or does not know the licit manner to break it? For certain it is allowed if it would be certain that the sorcerer were not ignorant of the licit mode, even if he is going to use an illicit mode, because it would be imputed to his malice. So it is held in common with Busembaum (as above, n. 4); Salamancans *ibid.*, n. 151, and Sporer, de 1. praec. cap. 9, n. 43), with Laymann, Sanchez, and Lessius. Tamburinus says the same thing (ch. 6, §2

n. 9) as well as Sporer (n. 42), Viva (qu. 5, art. 5, n. 4), with Sanchez, Trullenchus, Filliuci, and Elbel, n. 532, with Suarez and Sayr, that it is permitted if it were probably certain that the warlock would know the licit mode. But what about in a negative doubt? Tamburinus (n. 10) thinks so, and Viva does not rebuke him (n. 3) because at sometime it is also licit to seek it because it is not rarely presumed from contingent things in common that warlocks are ignorant of the licit mode. But the common opinion contradicts this, which many authors hold. (Sanchez, *de matrim.* lib. 7, d. 95, n. 13; Lessius, lib. 2, cap. 44, n. 46; Viva, *loc. cit.* n. 3; Salamancans *ibid.* n. 152, with Palaus, Laymann, etc.) The reason is, because it must be presumed that the warlock would not know anything but illicit modes. Moreover, if in some case a just presumption were held that the warlock knew the licit mode to break the malefice, say by washing the sign, the opinion of Tamburinus seems probable enough; then the opposed common opinion would not obstruct it, for (as Tamburinus says), the contrary doctors speak about a case when the doubt cannot otherwise be laid aside. Moreover, Busembaum, Sporer (n. 43), Viva and Elbel (n. 533) with Laymann, Lessius and Delrio advert that it must more readily be presumed that the one who placed the signs would know how to break the malefice by a licit mode by taking those things away than another that did not place them.

26.—Hence it must be noted that the common opinion with the Salamancans (tr. 21, cap. 11, punct. 11, § 1 n. 172), Suarez, Lessius, Delrio, Palaus, Sanchez, etc., on vampires, which are corporally transported by demons from place to place. Nor does *cap. Episcopi*, 26, q. 5 impede this, where it is forbidden under pain of excommunication to put such trust in such incantations of little old women, for there it is forbidden to assert at the same time that they walk with Herodiadis or the goddess Diana. See Elbel, n. 527, who asserts with Delrio and others, the contrary opinion, which Luther, Melanchthon and certain Catholics held, namely that this comes about through mere illusion and the force of fantasy, and is very pernicious to the Church, because it induces men to examine witches of this sort inflicted by these penalties, which does grave damage to the Christian state.

27.—Warlocks incur excommunication from *cap. Si quis ariolos*. Moreover, some hold it is *latae sententiae*, since in the aforesaid chapter it is said: "*Anathema sit.*" (Salamancans, *ibid.* punct. 13, n. 201, with Tabiena, and Delrio). But Suarez, Sanchez, Azor, Lessius, etc. (cited by Salamancans *ibid.* n. 200) hold must be imposed; and they say that the words "*anathema sit*" in a matter of faith signify a heretic already cut off from the Church, but in other matters it only means a separation must take place.

They also incur excommunication from the Bull *Coenae*, if it is joined with heresy, or (as the Salamancans say) a vehement suspicion of it, namely when they enter into an express pact with a demon, or when they mix sacred things, or worship the devil, or take counsel from those things which he could not know. Salamancans, *ibid.* n. 203, with Suarez, Azor, etc. But this must be understood when there is an error of faith in the understanding, as Sporer says (*de 1 praec.* cap. 9, n. 35), for otherwise formal heresy is given, even if someone would outwardly expressly deny the faith, as is certain with Busembaum, as above, *de praec. fid.*, book 3, n. 19. And without formal heresy the excommunication of the bull could scarcely be incurred, as is certain with Laymann.

28.—"One might ask: What must a confessor do with those "guilty of divination, warlocks, etc.?"

"Resp. 1. They must be examined besides on various "superstitions: a) To what end they added themselves to such a "superstition, *e.g.* whether by reason of vehement passion, "sadness, revenge, avarice, or to establish for themselves a "name for sanctity, which would be the sacrilege of hypocrisy; "b) about apostasy, idolatry, and heresy, for they deny Christ "and God, would renounce the sacraments, hold a demon for

TREATISE I: FIRST COMMANDMENT, CH. I: ON SUPERSTITION

"God or a saint; they do not think they are condemned or "miserable and consequently their followers must not be "condemned; c) On blasphemies against God and the saints, "about sacrileges; for they abuse sacred things such as holy "water, the Eucharist, etc.; d) On lust and relations with a "demon; e) On damages inflicted to their neighbor. Suarez, "Sanchez, Filliuci, Bonacina, *loc. cit.*

"*Resp.* 2. They must be advised to hold themselves; a) to "abjure and absolve an express pact, if they had such with a "demon, or commerce; b) to burn their books, notes, bindings "and other instruments of the craft; c) to burn a written pact, if "they have one, but if only the demon had it, he must not "necessary be compelled to render it; because the pact is "sufficiently dissolved by penance; d) to restore all financial "loss, in the same manner as a treasurer is held (where the "goods of sorcerers are confiscated); so even heirs, if the goods "come down to them. Laym. *loc. cit.*; Suarez, t. 1, *de rel.* l. 2, c. "17; Sanchez, *loc. cit.* c. 49, Filliuci, etc.

"Resp. 3. Pastors must examine the following, types of "people, and they must be examined by confessors above all on "this precept: a) herdsmen, who are usually fond of various "observances to safeguard their flock from wolves or itches or "other losses; b) blacksmiths who use words taken either from "the psalms or the Lord's prayer to quiet horses; c) Country-"folk, who use inane and superstitious observances to heal "livestock, or have recourse to experts of such arts; d) Old "women, who apply vain and superstitious prayers over women "laboring to give birth or over animals; e) Soldiers who transfer "to themselves sacred names or prayers for certitude in war or "in a duel that they will not be wounded, and never perish by "water, fire or sudden death."

CHAPTER II
ON IRRELIGIOSITY, AND ITS SPECIES

"Irreligion, which is opposed to religion by a defect, or tends directly to the irreverence of God, and is testing God or perjury, or only tends to irreverence of sacred things, and is a sacrilege, or simony. We will speak on perjury in the Second Commandment, and here on the rest."

DUBIUM I
What is testing God?

29. What is testing God?
30. Whether paucity of the matter is granted in tempting God? And what is interpretative temptation?
31. Would one sin that asks God for a miracle?
32. Would one sin that offers himself for martyrdom? And a man sin by rejecting medicines?

29.—"Resp. Testing God is a remark or deed in which someone explores whether God is powerful, wise, merciful or has some other perfection. (St. Thomas, II IIæ. qu. 92, art. 1; Sanchez, etc.).

"It is twofold: viz. either *formal*, when someone expressly doubting on some perfection of God desires to experience it, so that if anyone would ask for a miracle whereby God would show the Catholic faith is true: or would give himself to be thrown headlong from a tower so that he might experience whether God is merciful by delivering him from injury; or it is *implicit* and *interpretative*, when someone, even if he does not expressly intend to test God, nevertheless seeks it or does it, because it seems to be related by his own nature; such as if anyone would commit himself to danger, from which one could hardly be delivered unless it were miraculously, or if he "omitted natural means hoping for an effect from God alone, *e.g.* refusing medicine for a dangerous disease, and seeking and hoping rashly for health from God. Navarre, c. 11; Lessius, n. 3. Likewise, if without necessity and for the sake of the unlearned one would preach without any preparation, hoping God would suggest concepts to him. Lessius, Laym., lib. 4, t. 10, cap. 5."

Thus, the following cases are resolved:

"1. Testing God *formally* is a mortal sin of its nature, even in each matter. The reason is that it includes doubt about the perfections of God, which overflow into grave contempt for God or great irreverence, by acting curiously with God as if in a stage-play. Lessius, l. 2, cap. 45, d. 1; Sanchez, lib. 2, cap. 3; Suarez, etc. and the common opinion.

"2. *Interpretative* testing, for which that doubt is lacking generally is only a venial sin on account of the imperfection of the act, ignorance, inconsideration, or paucity of danger. On the contrary, it is often no sin at all, when, viz. a just cause is present, *e.g.* instinct of God, necessity, or pious utility. Sayr, Toledo, Cajetan, St. Thomas, II IIæ. qu. 92."

30.—But this question is whether in *interpretative* testing of God, as above, paucity of the matter is granted? It is affirmed by Busembaum (with Cajetan, Valentia, in 2.2. d. 6, qu. 14, n. 2), Lessius, (lib. 2, cap. 45, n. 4), Sayr. (*in Clavis Regiae* lib. 6, cap. 7, n. 14), and Toledo (lib. 4, cap. 19, n. 7). These say that if anyone in a light matter and without grave danger would test God, only from curiosity of seeing some supernatural work, he would only sin venially. But more probably, other authors condemn it as a mortal sin, unless it would be excused by reason of ignorance or indeliberateness. (Sanchez, *dec.* lib. 2, c. 34, n. 5; Suarez, t. 1, *de rel.* tract. 3, lib. 1, cap. 3, n. 16; Salamancans tract. 21, cap. 12, punct. 1,

n. 2). The reason is, because it is a grave irreverence to wish that God would show his omnipotence to satisfy one's curiosity. Hence the Salamancans say that he would more probably sin gravely who in a mild illness, after rejecting medicine, would hope for health from God, although he would not seek a miracle, because (as they say) he seems, by rejecting remedies, to really desire a miracle although he wishes natural causes to be changed. Other authors rightly oppose this doctrine, though they do not recognize in this any more than a venial sin. (Sanchez, *loc. cit.* with Lessius *loc. cit.* n. 4, Bonacina, *de 1 praec.* d. 3, qu. 9, part. unic. n. 3; with Suarez, Anacletus *ibid.* qu. 1, n. 8; Elbel, d. n. 560, and Sporer *eod. tit.* cap. 10, n. 10, with Laym.). The reason is, because a grave disorder is not present, for when someone in no way seeks a miracle from his curiosity, he is justly excused from a grave sin, and sometimes I think from all fault, if he hopes for God to help him naturally to be free from such a light disease, while often in diseases of this sort nature itself often brings health.

"3. If anyone were to throw himself in a well to declare "himself for the providence of God, or walk over burning coals "to show his innocence, it is an interpretative testing of God; "such as also are these proofs which are made by burning irons, "hot or cold water, etc. (such proofs are forbidden in cap. 1 and "2, *de purg. vulgar.* just as the Salamancans in common, *ibid.* n. "5 and 6). On these see Binsfeld and Delrio, lib. 4, cap. 4, q. 4 et "5. Although God sometimes will miraculously prove such "purgations, it happens either because they were done at God's "inspiration, or because the innocent are compelled to use them "to be free. Bonacina, d. 3, q. 9, p. 1."

31.—He would sin who absolutely asks from God, or offers a miracle for the conversion of heretics, when the testimony of our faith would suffice (Salamancans, *ibid.* n. 7, with Suarez, Palaus,

Sanchez). But if at sometime there were a very firm hope of conversion, then one could ask a miracle from God under the condition that it would please him. (Salamancans). Moreover, Sporer, with the common opinion, says enough it is licit to ask a miracle from God as often as there were a grave utility for our salvation or that of others, or to fulfill the divine will. And St. Thomas clearly teaches the same thing in II IIæ. qu. 97, art. 2, where he says that a man does not put God to the test who asks a sign from him: "to demonstrate to others" and again in ad 3: "or that he might be prepared for this purpose, that something might be done that pleases God."

32.—Likewise, one would sin who puts himself forward in danger of death or mutilation to prefer martyrdom without a just cause; for in the case of necessity, if the faith or the salvation of many could not otherwise be defended, or to avoid blasphemies, in such cases martyrdom is in precept; or in the case of utility to exalt the faith or the glory of God, then it will be licit to offer oneself for martyrdom, as St. Thomas teaches (II IIæ. qu. 144, a. 3, ad 1). See Salamancans *ibid.* n. 9.

Likewise, one would sin who refuses medicines, unless it were done to mortify himself, provided there was no danger of death, as Viva teaches (qu. 6, art. 3, n. 6) with Cajetan, Navarre, and Sanchez.

It is asked whether the express tempting of God would differ in species from interpretive? Suarez and Bonacina say yes, but the Salamancans more probably deny it. (*ibid.* num. 11).

DUBIUM II
What, and how manifold is sacrilege?

33. *What and how manifold is sacrilege?*
34. *What kind of species of sacrilege must be explained?*
35. *What are personal sacrileges?*
36. *What are local sacrileges?*

37. *Are commerce, meals, and court proceedings, etc. forbidden in Church?*
38. *Would it be a sacrilege to a man from the Church, the hall, etc.?*
39. *Is every theft in the church a sacrilege? Is it in the sacristy?*
40. *Which are real sacrileges?*
41. *Would it be lawful to convert vessels and sacred garments to profane use?*
42. *Would it be a sacrilege to injure the goods of ecclesiastics? To detain pious trusts? To not pay tithes?*
43. *Would it be a sacrilege to sin mentally in a Church? To omit the sacraments in time they ought to be received?*
44. *Are censures against sacrileges incurred ipso facto?*
45. *Is it a sacrilege to steal relics?*
46. *Is it a sacrilege to steal on a feast day?*
47. *Would it be a sacrilege to violate vows?*
48. *See others, ibid.*

33.—"*Resp.* Sacrilege is a violation of a sacred thing, this is of "a consecrated divine cult, and it is a mortal sin by its nature, if "a work is specially opposed with the sanctity of the thing; but "not if it is only generally opposed, in the way that all mortal "sins are generally opposed to sanctity, *e.g.* of a church, so that "there they are committed with every venial sin. Moreover, a "sacrilege is threefold: *Personal*, in which a person; *local*, in "which a place, and *real*, in which other things are violated. St. "Thomas, II IIæ. qu. 99, art. 3 and the remaining theologians."

34.—The species of a sacrilege must be explained in confession, whether they were personal, local or real. (Viva, *de preacept. Dec.* qu. 6, a. 1, n. 1; Salamancans tr. 21, cap. 12, punct. 2, n. 17, with St. Thomas and the common opinion).

The question is, are the aforesaid species subaltern or the lowest degree?

The first opinion holds they are subaltern containing under themselves other lower species. So think Suarez, Palaus, Lessius, etc., cited by Salamancans *loc. cit.* with Busembaum (see n. 48

below) and Elbel *de sacril.* n. 565 with Filliuci. And therefore they say that striking a cleric differs in species from having sex with him.

Still, *the second opinion* holds that it is the lowest degree, as Viva (qu. 6, art. 1, n. 2), and the Salamancans with Cajetan and Trull. So that, if anyone would violate a nun by beating her, or by having sex with her, he formally commits one sacrilege. And St. Thomas thinks this in II IIæ. qu. 99, art. 3, ad 2, where he says, "It is possible that two specific sins differ in species according to the material act, but agree in species according to the one formal reasoning of sacrilege; say if someone would violate a nun by beating her or by laying with her." And this is more probable. But the Angelic doctor also teaches in the same place that the aforementioned species have different degrees signifying that they indeed constitute aggravating circumstances, but do not change the species.

Wherefore, it is resolved:

35.—"*Personal* sacrilege is the striking of a cleric, dragging "him to secular judgment, likewise lustful violation of a person "consecrated to God by a vow of chastity, on which, see below "tr. 4, ch. 2, dub. 2, n. 454."

36.—"2. A *local* sacrilege is every act in which a Church is "polluted, such as murder, the illicit and public effusion of "human blood, or of semen." (As the authors probably hold, "Viva, qu. 6, art. 1, n. 11, and Tamburinus, with Vasquez, Pont., "Diana, Con., Toledo, cited by Salamancans tr. 6, cap. 8, punct. , "n. 101, against Salamancans, *ibid.* with Suarez, Bonacina, de "Lugo, Palaus, etc. and Elbel n. 556, who more probably say "even secret effusion is a sacrilege. See what is going to be said "on the Sixth Commandment, n. 458, versic. II in regard to "place, etc.). "Likewise, the burial of an excommunicated "person, or the unbaptized; further, if certain profane acts were "done in the Church that are also opposed to its immunity, such "as business negotiations, illicit sex, and filthiness, seditions, "secular councils, stabling of horses, arson, breaking and "spoliations. Likewise, if the material of a sacred thing, or of the "Church were directly converted to profane use; if a guilty "person were taken from the Church as from a place of refuge, "still, unless he were a public thief, or a plunderer of fields at "night, or if he would commit an enormous malefice from the "trust placed in his asylum. Laymann, c. 7, Bonacina, *quaes.* 6. "But if a thing were taken *per accidens* only in the Church, *e.g.* "the purse of a rich man, the authors teach that he probably "does not commit a sacrilege (Diana, p. 1, t. 3, r. 27, ex. "Fagundez, and six others, against Suarez, Laymann, etc."

37.—Likewise, a sacred place is violated, if in it there were shouts, promenading, business, or the shouts of secular judges; but not the piety of ecclesiastics that see it. Sometimes, still, secular trials or parliaments are licit in a case of necessity, *e.g.* on account of the rain, the heat of the sun, but they must occur without noise and another local place must be lacking. Equally, it does not seem a grave sin for there to be some moderate promenading in the Church, or private consumption of food even without necessity, so long as scandal and noise were avoided. (Viva, *ibid*, n. 11, from St. Thomas with Salamancans tr. 21, c. 12, punct. 2, n. 25).

Hence, it is noticed in passing, that it is not permitted to proclaim anyone provided with a dignity (except for royalty) that the path to Church would be strewn for them; otherwise immediately services must be suspended *a divinis,* the ministers of the Church incur *ipso facto* excommunication, and the Church must be held as interdicted. This was decreed by the Sacred Congregation of Ceremonies, which says: "It was proposed in the Sacred Congregation of Ceremonies about one abuse among others, which recently crept into the city [Rome], and this same congregation, so as to altogether abolish it, decreed on the 30th day of August, 1701: 'It is not lawful for anyone, etc. (only with the exception of royal persons) to cause themselves to be conveyed to Churches strewn for them; otherwise it must immediately cease *a divinis*; because unless it were preserved, rectors and the other ministers incur excommunication *ipso facto* and the same Church must be held as interdicted'." (The annotation is thus found in a Bull of Clement XI, part. 3, decr. 1, congr. Caer.). Then it is added: "And from what was related his Holiness (*i.e.* the aforesaid Clement), approved the decree, and it was indeed promulgated, and he commanded it to be given over for execution and to be fastened to all the sacred places of the city on 3 October 1701." All this is related by Ferrara in his *Bibliotheca* (Ferrara, *Bibliotheca*, tom. 3, verbo Ecclesia, art. V, n. 28 n 29), who also relates it is forbidden by many decrees of the Sacred Congregation of Rites for the Gospel to be given to any laymen to be kissed during Mass (even to governors), just as to give them use of the baldachino, and to admit them to assist in the assembly of the clergy.

Returning to our point, however, we say:

38.—It is a sacrilege to violently extract a man from the Church, even if it has been interdicted or polluted, and from its cemetery, cloister dormitory or a walkway adjoining with the Church, likewise from the houses of religious cloistered that surround it. See the Salamancans, tr. 18, cap. 3, punct. 3, n. 81, and tract 21, c. 12, punct. 2, § 2, n. 24. Moreover, besides this use of violated immunity, to incur the species of sacrilege, by the name of a sacred place only a Church is understood, not other places when in disagreeable matters a strict interpretation must be made, as Elbel notes *de sacria*, n. 566, with Laymann, Bonacina, etc.

39.—*Quaeritur:* Whether every theft in the Church is a sacrilege?

The first opinion holds it is not a sacrilege unless the theft were of a thing accommodated to the Church or consigned to be guarded there (de Lugo, d. 16, num. 470; Tamburinus, *in Meth. Conf.* lib. 2, cap. 8; Palaus, Azor, Diana, Lessius, Coninck, Henriquez, etc. with Salamancans, Tract. 6, c. 8, punct. 4, n. 103). For other profane things are received materially *in loco sacro*, but not *de loco sacro*,² while they in no way pertain to the sacred place. Nevertheless, Cardinal de Lugo (*loc. cit.* rightly excepts theft of things which the sacristan has made for himself accommodated for decoration of the Church.

Nevertheless, the second opinion more probably affirms it, from the chapter *Quisquis caus.* 17, qu. 4, where a man is absolutely condemned as sacrilegious that steals *a non sacred thing from a sacred place*; nor is it limited to something merely deposited there fore safekeeping (Elbel, n. 587, with Filliuci, Valentia, and the Salamancans *loc. cit.*, with Palaus, Dicastillus, Vasquez, Bonacina, Laymann, etc.). Still, the Salamancans rightly call the first opinion probable.

But would it be a local sacrilege to steal from the sacristy? Sanchez says no (*de matr.* d. 15, n. 13), against others. Moreover, it is certain that theft is not a sacrilege in cloisters, nor in the oratory of a private house. But in oratories of guest housing or hermitages, although they are not blessed by the Bishop, Sanchez duly thinks these are sacrileges. See Viva, d. *loc.* n. 13.

40.—"3. *A real* sacrilege is an unworthy treatment and "administration of the sacraments, as if they were to be "ministered or received while in mortal sin. Likewise, "profanation of vessels, and of sacred instruments, *e.g.* if anyone "uses a chalice at dinner, applies the ornaments of altars or of

---

² Translator's note: In a holy place, but not from a holy place.

"priests for profane use, with the understanding about these "things, which are consecrated or at least usually blessed, for to "apply carpets at weddings or common use, candelabra, bowls, "nay more, towels and other things, which mediately "serve the sacred minister, Tamburinus teaches would not be a "sin (*Expedit. sacrif.* lib. 2, c. 2), unless it were done from some "contempt, at least implicit, as if always and indifferently you "were to use them in additional things. He affirms the same "thing about candles, branches, water, incense and things "similarly blessed, that in these small blessings the Church does "not act with such rigor, as is clear in blessed bread, wood, "charcoal, etc. (*loc. cit.* §3)."

"Likewise, violation, or unworthy treatment of sacred "images, and relics. Likewise, the abuse of Sacred Scripture, *e.g.* "to establish heresies, or indecent things."

"Likewise, robbery of the Church's goods, suppression of "pious wills, or defrauding the Church of her rights, etc. See "Filliuci, tr. 24, cap. 9; Regina, lib. 19, n. 57; Suarez."

The Council of Trent (sess. 4, in fine), calls it rash to twist the words of Sacred Scripture for scurrilous, fabulous, vain, adulatory or belittling purposes, etc. See the Salamancans, tr. 21, cap. 12, punct. 2, § 3, n. 22.

41.—*Quaeritur I:* Could vessels and sacred garments be converted to profane use? The Salamancans affirm it, (*loc. cit.*), if they lost the form and blessing. But in the same treatise, cap. 10, punct. 11, § 2, n. 145, they altogether reject it with St. Thomas, who in p. 3 qu. 83, art. 3 ad 3, and cap. 39, dist. 1, says: "The pall of the altar, the episcopal seat (*cathedra*), the candelabra and veil ... and other things which were in the sanctuary ought not be admitted into the use of the laity but must be burned." Further, other theologians distinguish the question better (Suarez, p. 3, d. 18 sect. 8; Palaus, t. 2, tr. 3, d. 1, p. 6, Bonacina, d. 3, quaest. 1, p.

4, and Roncaglia *d. 1, praec.* cap. 1, quaest. 7, with Barbosa), and say that if some thing were to be so completely changed to render it a material for common use, just as if a chalice were reduced by fire and iron to a common mass of silver, then it would be lawful to convert it to profane use. So Bonacina himself, with Palaus, Suarez, and Barbosa, but it would be otherwise if it were not first completely unformed. Hence it is not permitted to repair profane garments with a chasuble, and this adheres to that which St. Thomas said above. Consequently, others say it is not permitted to sell or pledge garments of this kind for profane use. See the Salamancans, *dict.* cap. 10, num. 147.

42.—*Quaeritur II*: Would the injury of any ecclesiastical goods be a sacrilege? Resp. No, but only of those goods which *pertain to the decoration of the Church, or are deputed to the sustenance of the ministers*, as St. Thomas says (II IIæ. qu. 99, art. 3). By "sustenance of the ministers", is understood that in which these kind of things are, as Tamburinus says (dec. lib. 2, cap. 6, §3 n. 9).

Quareitur III: Whether it would be a sacrilege to unjustly detain bequests left to the Church for its service? Lessius affirms it (lib. 1, c. 16, n. 30), but Tamburinus (*dict.* l. n. 10) with Palaus, Salamancans (tr. 21, c. 12, punct. 2 § 2 n. 35), etc. deny it, because until the aforesaid goods are possessed by the Church, they are not sacred.

Quareitur IV: Would it be a sacrilege to not pay a tithe? Lessius (lib. 2, cap. 16, n. 18), Elbel, n. 569, with Valentia, Sporer, etc. affirm, but Croix (lib. 3, p. 1, n. 52) and Tamburinus (d. lib. n. 11), with Palaus deny it. Nevertheless, they say it is a very grave sin of irreligiosity; because the paying of tithes is ordered in recognition of divine mastery.

43.—It must be noted that by purely internal acts the sanctity of the place is not violated, and therefore one does not commit a sacrilege who, while in Church, has the will to kill a man outside of it. It would be otherwise if someone proposed while outside the Church to kill a man in the Church. (Salamancans *ibid.* n. 28, with others in common).

Palaus (tr. 17, d. 2, p. 2) holds to omit the sacraments in due time is a sacrilege. But this is more probably rejected, rather it is said to be a sin against obedience due to the Church. Salamancans *ibid.* § 3, n. 38.

44.—Likewise, it must be known that censures imposed against the sacrilegious are not incurred *ipso facto* except for those who strike a cleric. And likewise, by violators of ecclesiastical immunity which is done by imposing tribute, usurping goods and by breaking into Churches and at the same time robbing sacred things, from the chapter *Conquest. 22, de sent. excomm.* See Salamancans tr. 21, c. 12, p. 2, § 2 n. 24. However, those burning Churches more probably are not excommunicated *ipso facto*, as Salamancans (*ibid.* § 3, n. 40), with Cajetan, Sylvius Navarre.

45.—One commits a grave sacrilege who steals a relic, even in a small quantity, if he knows the owner is going to be very sad on account of this. Leander Prado, Navarre, Molina, cited by Salamancans *ibid.* cap. 10, punct. 10, § 2 n. 108.

46.—*Quaeritur V:* If the occasion might be an object of sacrilege, viz. if someone were to sin on a feast day. The authors deny it, unless notable irreverence is inflicted on the divine cult, say if anyone would put on comedic plays or public games on Good Friday. De Lugo *de ben.* d. 16 n. 523, Salamancans *ibid.* c. 12, punct. 2 § n. 36, *in fin.* with Lessius, Palaus, and Tamburinus *Meth. conf.* lib. 2, c. 7, § 4 n. 40.

47.—*Quæritur VI:* Would the violation of a vow be a sacrilege? Tamburinus, with Suarez, Dicastillus (*loc. cit.* n. 12 and 13), and Palaus (tr. 17, d. 2, p. 3, § 2 n. 2). deny this. For they say it is a sin of treachery, or against the fidelity due to God, as Croix (lib. 3, p. 1, n. 55) with Tamburinus (*in dec.* loc. cit., n. 13). But St. Thomas affirms it (II IIæ. qu. 99, art. 3, ad 3) and the Salamancans follow him (*ibid.* n. 22). But one who violates a vow of chastity more probably commits a sacrilege. See Elbel., n. 584.

48.—"4. A sacrilege is also committed by a sin of omission, "*e.g.* if items used in the sacrifice of the Mass, such as the "corporal and like things, were exceedingly dirty. Bonacina *de* "*Eucharistia* (who p. 9, n. 23, with Filliuci, Suarez, Regius, etc. "says it is a mortal sin. See book 6, n. 376).

"5. In confession the species must be expressed as well as the "matter of the sacrilege. The reason of the first is, because it "often has a different malice, *e.g.* striking a priest and fornication "with the same. The reason of the second is, because it also "sometimes the matter also increases and adds to the malice, *e.g.* "if it were against the Eucharist, it adds, according to Gordon, "another sin against *latria* by the common violation of a sacred "thing. Moreover, it is not lawful for women or laymen to touch "the chalice, paten, *agnus Dei* candles, etc. that have been "anointed with chrism (although it is permitted to clerics of the "first tonsure, as Tamburinus *ibid.* n. 11 says with Suarez), short "of contempt, still it is not mortal if it is free of contempt, and if "there is a cause, it is not venial (Suarez, Tamburinus, *loc. cit.* "§1), but without a cause it is a venial sin (Suarez, Coninck and "others in common), although Tamburinus thinks from Sa, etc., "that the contrary is probable" (with Scotus and Bartholomaeus, from Angelus. But Sa, cited by Tamburinus, and del Soto, Henriquez, Sanchez, Fagundez and Tamburinus cited by Pasqualigus as Croix relates lib. 6, p. 2n. 358, thinks it is no sin. But for nuns there is a privilege, according to the Salamancans tr. 21 cap. 10, punct. 11, § 1, n. 132), "just as even the corporals "and purificators are washed by them. See book 6, n. 382. But "moreover, those things which do not immediately touch the

"Eucharist, nor are anointed with chrism, such as altar cloths,
"priestly vestments, etc. may be touched by all with nothing in
"between. Suarez, Laymann, Tamburinus, *loc. cit.*, where from
"Palaus, etc. he concedes the same on relics, just as they should
"also stand nearly the same in respect to the thecas, which
"laymen bear in processions. He teaches the same thing with
"Layman on a pyx or a ciborium, and the luna for benediction
"when they do not yet contain the Holy Eucharist. The same
"thing on corporals, palls, and purificators, when after sacred use
"they are washed (from Laymann and Bonacina), and also before
"they are washed (Laymann, Tamburinus, *loc. cit.*)."

DUBIUM III
On Simony

ARTICLE I
What is simony, and how manifold is it?

49. What is simony, and how manifold is it?
50. Could paucity of matter be granted in simony?
51. When is it simony to give temporal things for spiritual ones?
52. Would it be simony to give a benefice to someone, that he would sustain himself, either by reason of friendship or prayers?
53. Would it be simony to deduce in an agreement an antidoral obligation?
54. Would it be simony to give a spiritual thing principally on account of a temporal thing?
55. Would it be simony to receive something for the administration of the sacraments? And would it be simony principally to take it on account of temporal profit from them?
56. What is understood by *munus a manu*?
57. Would it be simony to give a loan on account of a spiritual thing?
58. Would it be simony to pay a pension on account of a benefice?

59. Would it be simony to give something so that another would furnish something spiritual for himself when he receives it?
60. Would it be simony to give a benefice with some spiritual obligation? Or to resign or present with a obligation?
61. What about for munus ab obsequio?
62. Would it be simony to treat with deference on account of a benefice?
63. What is simony by "munus a lingua"?
64. Would it be simony to give something by a mediator so that he would obtain a benefice for you?
65. What if the intercessor were an intermediary?
66. What if you were to promise to give alms to some monastery?
67. What is mental simony? What is conventional and real simony?
68. Which is of divine law and which is of human law?
69. Is simony only granted in human law?
70. Would it be simony to sell benefices by divine law?
71. Would it be simony to sell a jus patronatus (right of patronage)? And is it of divine law? Would it be simony to sell the right of burial?
72. Can benefices be exchanged?
73. How can a benefice with a pension be exchanged? And by whose authority? And could bishops constitute pensions? even to n. 76.
77. How would it be lawful to carry out commerce in benefices? even to num. 80.
81. How could renunciations of benefices be made? Even to n. 84.
85. How manifold is "confidential" simony, and what are its penalties? Even to num. 90.
91. How will it be lawful to receive something for entry to a religious order?
92. Would it be lawful to receive something for sustenance of those entering?
93. Would it be lawful to receive something for catechizing, etc.?
94. Would it for instructing someone in sacred doctrine?
95. Would it for absolving, etc.?
96. Would it be to give a dispensation in matrimony?
97. Would it be lawful to give something so that the other would omit a spiritual thing?

98. *Would it be to remedy opposition?*
99. *Could opposition be remedied by money in regard to a possession of a benefice?*
100. *What if a right to it has not yet been acquired? What if someone would corrupt electors to not elect you?*
101. *What if the other would only impede by prayers?*
102. *Could you give money to stop another candidate from opposing himself to your election?*
103. *Could you give money lest the electors would choose someone that was unworthy, or to choose someone worthy?*
104. *Could you give money that a competitor would not go to a benefice which you desire? See others with Busembaum.*

49.—"*Resp.* Simony is an eager will to buy or sell something "spiritual for a temporal price, or something connected to a "spiritual thing. (St. Thomas, II IIæ. qu. 100, art. 2; Laym., lib. 4, "tract. 10, cap. 8, etc.)."

"Dicitur 1: *The will to buy*, etc., by which words any onerous "contract is understood, whether of sale, or location or "exchange, or renunciation; because simony does not consist "without some tacit or express pact, and an obligation from a "pact. I add, that because every natural obligation, such as "gratitude or antidoral, does not suffice, *e.g.* when someone "hopes or intends something, but it does not oblige. (Sa, *v.* "*Simonia*). The reason is, because it does not make a contract. "See Bonacina, *de simonia*, d. 1, qu. 6, p. 1, and Lessius lib. 2, "cap. 35, d. 20." (But see what is going to be said here in n. 54).

"Dicitur 2: *for a temporal price*, whether that for a gift "(*munus*) or the tongue (*lingua*), that is praise, censure, "patronage or compliance, and service."

"Dicitur 3: *a spiritual thing*; by such a name a supernatural "thing is understood that is ordered to salvation, or is formally "such a thing as grace and gifts of the Holy Spirit, or causally as "the sacraments are, a sermon, prayers and sacramentals, or it "would be an effect, and use of a supernatural power, such as "consecration, absolution, dispensation, blessing, excommunication, election, presentation, confirmation, conferral of a benefice, and other acts of ecclesiastical jurisdiction."

"Dicitur 4: *connected to a spiritual thing*, to embrace those things which are not spiritual in themselves but are ordered to them, and connected to them either antecedently, such as the right of patronage with respect to a benefice; vessels and sacred vestments in respect to the sacraments, or concomitantly, such as labor in the administration of the sacraments (according to the sense that is going to be given below), or consequently, as the repayment of benefices, which are given on account of a spiritual office."

"For that reason, it is clear that the malice of simony consists in irreverence which is committed if spiritual things are valued by the character of a temporal price, and joined with contracts, and it is a mortal sin by its nature; it cannot be venial by the levity of the matter because no gift of grace, albeit small, can be sold without grave irreverence not only to the gift itself, but also to God. Nevertheless, it could be venial on account of the incompleteness of the act, or ignorance. Suarez, t. 3, *de rel.* l. 4, cap. 36; Azor, Filliuci, Layman, *loc. cit.*, Lessius, l. 2, cap. 35, dub. 1."

Moreover, Simony is fourfold, mental, conventional, real and confidential. *Mental* is, when someone gives a temporal thing with a mind to oblige him to repay with a spiritual one (or vice versa), but without any agreement. *Conventional* is when an agreement is present, but it is carried out by neither party. *Real*, however, is when an agreement has already been fulfilled. At length, *confidential* simony can take place in three ways: through agreement, regress, and through entrance. It is said *by agreement*, when you renounce a benefice to another with an agreement so that he will later resign it and confer it on another. *Through regress*, when you reserve for yourself the right to resume the benefice again in some case. *Through entrance,* if you resign a benefice conferred upon you, but there is not yet possession with an agreement to take possession of it in some case or time, see below in num. 85 and 86, where we will more profusely discuss this confidential simony and its penalties.

50.—*Quaeritur I.* Could paucity of the matter be granted in simony? In simony with regard to natural law the common opinion is negative. (Cited in Salamancans tract. 19, *de simon.* cap. 1, punct. 1 n. 8, and Croix, lib. 3, p. 1, n. 195, with Suarez, Sanchez, etc. against Molina, Reg., etc. *ibid.*). But in simony that is merely in regard to ecclesiastical law, Navarre and Zerola (to whom it seems Croix adheres, lib. 4, n. 682), teach with probability that paucity of the matter can be granted. And Croix assigns disparity, because when a temporal thing is received for the price of a spiritual thing, but the reception is forbidden to only avoid the species of simony, really it does not cause an injury to the spiritual thing, rather, it is only a sin against a precept of the Church wherein paucity of the matter can certainly be granted.

51.—*Quaeritur II:* Whether to give a temporal thing for a spiritual thing, or vice versa, is always simony?

The first opinion affirms it, with Azor, Durandus, Adrian, etc. cited by Salamancans, *ibid.* punct. 3, § 1 n. 26.

The second opinion which the Salamancans hold (*ibid.* num. 32) and which they call the common opinion with Cajetan, Sanchez, Suarez, Lessius, Laymann, Toledo, etc., denies it when it is given for free but with a mind of bringing or obliging (not rigorously from justice, but only from gratitude or benevolence) another to remunerate with a spiritual thing for a temporal one, or vice versa; so that the obligation that is principally intended of another is antidoral, or of gratitude, and repayment less principally, and they prove it from chapter *Quam pio,* caus. 1, qu. 2. And this, even if repayment were offered in the same act, from c. *Placuit,* caus. 1, q. 2, and c. *Dilectus* 2 qu. 1. Hence, they say it is permitted to give something to a Bishop, or to offer a service to him (to whom, one would not otherwise offer a service), that he might confer a benefice upon you in gratitude; provided there was no agreement, as the Salamancans say (*ibid.* punct. 4 num. 55 and 56) with del Soto, Suarez, Valentia, and the common opinion, and provided you would not offer service so that the Bishop would confer upon you a benefice, just as the price of your assistance, as the learned Fr. Elbel notes well (*de simonia*, num. 617). On the other hand, if you offer service primarily to acquire the benevolence of the Bishop, and secondarily to obtain the benefice, then you do not commit simony, even if, with all hope of a benefice removed you would not offer service, as the Salamancans say with others, and even if you express such a hope to a superior, as Valentia, Palaus, del Soto, Rodriguez, etc. add, cited by Salamancans n. 56, near the end, because it is licit, as they say, to seek from another that he would be held to furnish something from a natural obligation. Yet, Mazzota (*de dimon.* tom. 2, § 2 p. 219) and Croix (with Suarez, lib. 3, p. 1, n. 74) wisely advise that it should be avoided on account of the danger of an arrangement, or at least of scandal, especially if something were given for a time in which it is done to confer the benefice.

Moreover, Roncaglia (*de sim.* c. 1, qu. 5) and the Salamancans themselves (*ibid.* n. 57), with Sanchez, Bonacina, etc. that where another title is lacking, namely of a stipend, to remove an unjust disturbance, etc., when something is given only in consideration of obtaining a spiritual thing, or vice versa, then the intention must be presumed to be at least virtually simoniacal, viz. to exchange a temporal good with a spiritual one, unless it would be certain from the opposite, or otherwise gathered from the circumstances, namely from the paucity of the gift from piety, or from the nobility of the giver, etc. And this is certain from *c. Tua nos, de sim.* where the Pope said, speaking about one who was giving his goods to the Church and asking to be admitted to a canonry, and about the canons admitting him: "Nevertheless, if he that makes such a donation is led by that intention, that he might avail to obtain spiritual goods through temporal goods, and the clerics who admit him into their fraternity would not be prepared to admit him until they perceived suitable temporal goods, then without a doubt both they and he are judged culpable in the presence of the district judge." (See what will be said in n. 54). And one especially cannot be excused from mental simony (as Roncaglia, *loc. cit.* reg. VI *in praxi*, and Elbel *de simonia*, n. 617, rightly think) who would offer service for free to a Bishop with the mind to oblige him from gratitude, even if it is not from justice, to reward him with a benefice, according to what is going to be said in number 53.

52.—But a bishop must not be condemned for simony that confers a benefice on a cleric in recognition of gratitude on account of the services he furnished, as Elbel and Croix say (n. 619; n. 73) with Suarez. Likewise, if a bishop would confer a benefice as a favor to someone to genuinely sustain him, it is not simony; Croix, lib. 3, p. 1, n. 83, with Lessius, Laymann, etc. What's more, a conferral made to an unworthy person only by reason of consanguinity or friendship yet as a thanks, is indeed illicit, but not simoniacal. Salamancans tr. 19 *de sim.* cap. 1, punct. 2, § 2 n. 38 with Cajetan, Suarez, Palaus, etc. And St. Thomas teaches this in II IIæ qu. 100 art. 5 ad 2, saying: "If anyone would confer something spiritual on someone due to any carnal affection, it is certainly illicit ... still it is not simoniacal ... because this does not pertain to a contract ... of sale, upon which simony is based.

But would a Bishop commit simony that gives a benefice to an unworthy person due to the pleas of another? St. Thomas seems to generally uphold it (*loc. cit.* ad 3) because the Bishop seems to do this to acquire human favor; for thus the Angelic Doctor says: "It seems for this purpose (viz. human favor) principally to intend who hears the prayers poured forth for the unworthy man." And so it must be said if he would really give a benefice to obtain the favor of such a man, nay more, as the Angelic doctor duly adds, this will be simony even if the cleric were worthy of the benefice.

Furthermore, by speaking absolutely, Elbel (*de simon.* n. 612), La Croix, l. 3, p. 1, n. 84, and Laymann (l. 4, tr. 10 c. 8, n. 24) with Lessius, Suarez, Navarre, Cajetan, etc. say with probability that the Bishop is not a simoniac who also confers a benefice on an unworthy man at the request of another, but it is held in no respect to acquire human favor, because really then no sale of a spiritual thing for a temporal one took place. Furthermore, that which Croix says, namely that it is not simony if he would confer it to free from some unjust harm, I think must not be admitted, for although the harm would be unjust, nevertheless some exchange seems to take place between a spiritual thing and a temporal one.

53.—*Quæritur III:* Would it be simony to deduce in a pact an antidoral obligation? Several authors say no (Hurtad, Coelestinus, Roncaglia, etc. cited by Diana, part. 6, tr. 7, r. 42, likewise Diana himself with Vidal and John de Soria, although in p. 3, tr. 2 r 64, he does not approve this in practice). Their reasoning is because it is not thought that one commits simony when an agreement is made from the obligation of gratitude which is already in it. Wherefore, they say, if it is lawful to intend to obtain some spiritual thing from gratitude, when someone furnishes something temporal, then he will also be allowed to draw it out of an agreement. But it must be altogether affirmed with the common opinion which the authors hold (Laymann tr. 10, c. ult. § 2 num. 9; Viva in *propos.* 45, *Innocen.* XI, n. 2; Elbel, *de simon.* p. 596, and Suarez, Bonacina, FIlliuci, Covarruvias and others cited by Salamancans *de simon.* tr. 19, c. 1, punct. 4, n. 64). The reason is because from that pact a new obligation is induced.

Moreover, the Salamancans (*ibid.* n. 66, 67, and 68 with Valentia, Cajetan, Palaus, Lessius, etc.) distinguish and say that if the agreement would not add a new obligation apart from an antidoral one, say, if you would give or promise money to another man so that he would be obligated to reward you in kind, it is not simony, because no new obligation is imposed. So also, if you were to ask something spiritual for free without a rigorous obligation, in the same way that those who frequently give alms are accustomed to ask prayers from the poor; on this point really, all consent, even the authors of the second opinion. They think it would be otherwise if a new agreement would add a new obligation, and this would be when some spiritual good is asked for *in specie* for a temporal thing that was given; unless there another title would intervene, namely a stipend, apparent loss, etc. as below. But this distinction does not persuade me at all, since the arrangement always inveighs at least some new obligation of fidelity, which, when it is estimable by some price, it certainly renders the agreement simoniacal (as Viva and Roncaglia argue). Therefore, in *c. Quam pio* 1. q. 2, it is said: "Without any agreement, every agreement ceases." Because in this matter each agreement, no matter how onerous, is simoniacal, even if it does not rigorously oblige from justice. And the same must be said about an agreement of this sort in a mutual contract, as Viva proves in *prop. 42 Innoc. XI*. Besides, here we must advert with Viva, and St. Thomas (q. 13 *de malo*, art. 4) the fact that, although the borrower could demand from the lender that he satisfy his antidoral obligation (understand always without an agreement, and likewise if satisfaction is demanded but not a promise, because after permission was sought, a new obligation of fidelity is asked, as we recently said, because still it is illicit in the loan); the reason is because the borrower gives what is his own; still the one giving cannot demand something spiritual precisely on account of his conferral, because he does not furnish what is his own, but what is of Christ. This is why, although he could exercise some gratuity toward the one who confers the spiritual thing on account of his benevolent attitude, still, it cannot be exercised in gratuitous compensation for the spiritual thing itself.

54.—*Quaeritur IV:* Would it be mental simony to give a spiritual good principally on account of a temporal one, or vice versa? Del Soto, Valentia, Cajetan, Sanchez, Lessius, Laymann, etc. (cited by the Salamancans *de simonia* tr. 19, c. 1, punct. 4, n. 59) reject this, but it altogether must be affirmed, and the Salamancans rightly assert (*ibid.* n. 60), that the contrary opinion was condemned by Pope Innocent XI, in propos. 45, which said: "To give a temporal thing for a spiritual one is not simony when the temporal is not given for a price, but merely as a motive to confer or effect a spiritual thing; or even when a temporal thing would be only a gratuitous compensation for a spiritual thing, or vice versa." And proposition 46: "And it is also admissible, even if the temporal thing were the principle motive to give a spiritual thing, nay more, even if it were the end of the spiritual thing itself, so that it would be esteemed more than a spiritual thing."

This was rightly condemned, for, although there it is said on account of the motive, not the price, and it would be certain simony is not committed unless the sale of a spiritual thing would intervene; nevertheless, there the motive really is the same as the price. For when, as Viva (in dict. prop. n. 6) and the Salamancans (*ibid.* n. 58) rightly note, a merely spiritual thing is given like the sacraments, benefices, etc., principally on account of the temporal thing of some great importance (it is otherwise if it is small) which is suitable to morally overturn the will of another; then a spiritual thing is given with difficulty for free, but practically it is given with some implicit agreement to impose a new obligation on another, and so the motive is virtually converted into a price. And this is clear from the very words of proposition 46, where it is added in the end: "nay more, even if it were the end of the spiritual thing itself, so that it would be esteemed more than a spiritual thing."

55.—*Quaeritur V:* Would it be lawful to receive something for the administration of the sacraments?

Resp. 1. Because in the administration of the sacraments, and of other spiritual functions it would be simony to take money as the price of the sacred thing, or of the intrinsic labor requisite in those actions. Otherwise, if the labor were extrinsic, say, if the priest ought to celebrate with chant, or at such an hour, in such a place, and similar things. So Roncaglia (*de sim.* c. 2, q. 2, p. 208), and the Salamancans (tr. 19, c. 2, punct. 3, n. 19), with Cajetan, del Soto, Lessius, Sanchez, Palaus, Toledo, and others in common.

Resp. 2. On the other hand, it is not simony to receive money not as the price, but as the stipend for sustenance, even for the intrinsic labor impending such ministries. Each one who busies himself in what is of advantage to another, ought from justice to be sustained by it. "The laborer is worth his wage." (Luke 10:7). So the common opinion of the Doctors, as Anacletus (*de simon.* q. 3, n. 28) Cabassutius *Theor. et prax.,* l. 5, c. 5, n. 14) and Suarez, Lessius, Toledo, Sanchez, and others, cited by the Salamancans *ibid.* n. 20, and 21, with St. Thomas II IIæ q. 100, art. 3, who so teaches: "To sell something spiritual or to buy is in acts of this sort is simoniacal. But to receive or give something for the sustenance of those ministering spiritual things, according to the ordination of the Church, and the approved custom, is lawful." Moreover, this custom is found to be approved from c. 12, *de praebend.* and c. *Ex his* 22, causa 12, q. 1. And it so happens that even if the minister were wealthy from his own or ecclesiastical goods, as the doctors argue in common (Roncaglia, and Salamancans *ll. cc.* with Suarez, Lessius, Sanchez, etc), as well as St. Thomas, who, in *Quodlibet.* 7 a 10, especially notes what St. Paul says in 1 Cor. 9:7, "No man serves in the army on his own pay." Hence, it is also licit to agree to such a stipend, provided that the value or the custom is not exceeded, exactly as Roncaglia, Laymann, Palaus, Gutierrez, and the Salamancans, *ibid.* n. 22, with Suarez, Toledo, Sanchez and others say. Nor do the chapters stand in the way, *fin. de pactis,* and *c. Tua nos de simonia,* where any agreement is forbidden in spiritual matters; for the aforesaid texts either must be explained on dishonorable agreements, as Roncaglia says with the Gloss, *(c. ult. de pactis),* or as Lessius asserts (l. 2, 35, n. 99) with del Soto, in those modified by a contrary custom, exactly as he proves in the last chapter *de pactis.*

Quaeritur VI: Would it equally be simony to celebrate Masses, administer the sacraments, assist in choir, preach and similar things principally on account of a reward?

The first opinion together says that it is, with Viva (*dict.* prop. 45, n. 7), and Cardenas, with other cited by La Croix (l. 3, p. 1 n. 60) from St. Thomas. The Angelic doctor, in *Quodlib.* 8, art 11, says that one who goes to Church principally for the distributions would sin mortally on account of simony, unless he principally focused on God and secondarily on the distributions. Hence, they infer that ordinarily the ministers would commit simony since they are celebrating in mortal sin.

But the *second opinion* is more probable, which many authors hold, and it says then simony only occurs when a temporal good is received for the price of the spiritual so that one becomes equalized with the other. (Salamancans *de sim.* tr. 19, c. 1, punct. 4, n. 60; Suarez, *de relig.* tr. 3, l. 4, c. 33, n. 11; Palaus, tr. 17, d. 4, n. 3; Coreglia in d. prop. 45 with del Soto, Diana, etc. likewise Sanchez, Sylvius, Coninck, Malderus, and others cited by Croix, n. 62). Yet this does not happen not when it is received just as a stipend for the sustenance of the minister, who exercises the aforesaid offices, because the stipend is due from justice, as Elbel, n. 621, with Laymann, and Palaus. Croix confirms it (*ibid.*) rightly arguing: One who gives a stipend principally on account of Mass, which certainly is a spiritual thing, would he not be said to be a simoniac, and vice versa, would the one who says Mass principally on account of a stipend also commit simony? It is not illicit, as he notes with Navarre and Suarez, to ordinarily provide a spiritual thing, even principally to an upright temporal end.

Nor is this opposed to the aforesaid condemned proposition, "even if the temporal good were the principle motive to give the spiritual thing." For there, as we said in the preceding question, the motive is received through the same and the price of the spiritual thing. But in our case the temporal thing is received as a stipend not of the thing, but as something due for the sustenance of the person engaged for the sake of another, as it was declared above. It is also not opposed to what St. Thomas says in the citation from the *Quodlibetal questions*, n. 8, art. 11, *corp.*, for it behooves us to give attention to the fact that in our case a twofold profit can be intended, either as the end of the work, or as the end of the worker. Since the profit is intended as the end of the work, so that the spiritual work itself is intended to be sold, then certainly simony is committed, and in this way the Angelic doctor must be understood (as the Salamancans say, tr. 19, c. 1, p. 4, n. 61), while he says there: "And therefore, he that intends to sell an act of this sort commits simony ... If he receives distributions as though they were the principally intended end of his work." But it must be said otherwise when the profit is intended *as the end of the worker*, viz. by reason of the operation of a person engaged for the sake of another, because then the profit is received for a stipend of sustenance, and is not simony. Hence, the Salamancans say (*ibid.* c. 2, punct. 5, n. 32) with Sanchez, a steward licitly receives a stipend from the parish priest to furnish to his own in turn. They also say with Suarez and Layman that even if it were simony to give money to a poor man that he would apply the object or satisfaction of his prayers for you, nevertheless it is licit to give so that he would pray for you, in the mode of a stipend. But St. Thomas admits this for a different reasoning, in 4 p. d. 25, q. 3, art. 2, saying: "One who gives money to the poor so that they would pray for him, does not pay for the prayer, but gives to entice it." Moreover, those who carry out sacred ministries on account of temporal remuneration cannot easily be excused from venial sin, since it would be a certain disorder to direct spiritual things to temporal ends, as the Salamancans say (*ibid.* n. 60).

Moreover, the doctors in common with St. Thomas denominate three things which have the determination of value in simony, namely *munus a manu, munus ab obsequio; munus a lingua*, from *c. Sunt nonnulli* 114, c. 1, q. 1. Here we must view them individually.

56.—I: By *munus a manu*[3] money and any temporal thing which is estimable by price is understood. Hence it is simony to give a spiritual thing with an agreement that the other should remit what is due for it; and even that he would pay money otherwise due, because spiritual things are altogether free and are given without respect to temporal things. Salamancans *ibid.* punct. 3, § 1 n. 24, with St. Thomas, Suarez, etc. It is also a simoniacal agreement to furnish a loan for future repayment, as is certain. See Salamancans *ibid.* § 2 n. 34.

57.—*Quaeritur I:* Would it be simony to give a loan to be repaid at the same time with a benefice or another spiritual good, or vice versa? It does not seem so, equally if you will loan with an agreement that the other obliges himself to pay back the loan in the future, it would indeed be usurious; but not if with the agreement, that in the same time the other will repay you; just as in regard to a loan the authors approve (Salamancans *de contrac.* tr. 14, c. 5, § 2 punct. 8, n. 62 with Lessius, Villalobos, Diana, and as St. Thomas teaches in II IIæ qu. 78, art. 2 ad 4). The reason is because then nothing is taken by an estimable price *ultra sortem*.[4]

---

[3] Translator's note: Literally, gift from the hand, something that consists in spiritual goods. *Cf.* St. Thomas Aquinas, *Supra sententias*, lib. 4, disp. 25, 3. 3 ad 4.

[4] Translator's note: Beyond the principal.

But in our case such an agreement must be held as simoniacal because here simony is to give something temporal for a spiritual thing. (Viva, *in d. prop.* 45, n. 3; Salamancans *de simonia* tr. 19, c. 1, punct. 3, § 2 n. 36, in common with Laymann, Lessius, Bonacina, Palaus, Navarre, Filliuci, etc.

58.—*Quaeritur II:* Would it be simony within *munus a manu* if a pension were included, namely if a Bishop, giving a benefice to someone, would sin in making the agreement with the other to pay him a pension? It is answered affirmatively, since such an obligation would be estimable by price. (Salamancans *ibid.* num. 39, with Suarez, Valentia, Toledo, and the common opinion). Hence, it is certainly simony to make an agreement with someone that if he would help you to obtain a benefice you would pay him a pension. See Salamancans, *ibid.*

59.—*Quaeritur III:* Would it be simony to give something temporal under a condition, such as the other would furnish a spiritual thing in consideration of him, namely, if you promise a dowry for his daughter if she would enter into a monastery; gifts for an adolescent, if he would frequent the sacraments? It is answered negatively, because this is a simple donation, albeit under a condition, which still does not add to the obligation. (Salamancans *ibid.* § 3, n. 49, with Suarez, Lessius, Palaus. etc.) Otherwise, if a simple obligation were imposed, *e.g.* to enter a religious order, etc., as St. Thomas teaches (II IIæ q. 10, art. 2 ad 4) or if there were a condition to furnish something to the advantage of the giver, say, if their entrance into a religious order would yield a benefit to the one giving it, then it would be like an exchange of a temporal good with a spiritual one (Salamancans *ibid.* n. 41, with Laymann, Palaus, and Suarez). See what is going to be said in n. 91.

60.—*Quaeritur IV*: Would it be simony to give a benefice with an arrangement, that the other would add some obligation that is also spiritual? It is answered that if a benefice *de jure* or from its institution would place an obligation, *e.g.* to teach, sing, etc., or if some genuine obligation were imposed by a Bishop with a chapter on a vacant benefice, *e.g.* to assist the sick, etc., certainly it is not simony. (Salamancans *loc. cit.* n. 42 and 43, from the common opinion with St. Thomas from *c. Significatum de praeb.*). There is a doubt as to whether some spiritual obligation could be imposed on the one that takes up a benefice from one that resigns from it, or presented him to the benefice/ Some authors affirm it (cited by Sanchez, *Cons.* tom. 1 c. 3, dub. 15, n. 6) but it must be said, that although an exchange can be granted in other spiritual matters, *e.g.* I apply a Mass for you so that in the morning you will apply one for me, but in benefices every agreement is simoniacal, from *c. Quam pio* 1, q. 2. Sanchez, *loc. cit.* and Salamancans *ibid.* n. 44, with Suarez, Bonacina, etc.

61.—II: *Munus ab obsequio*[5] follows, whereby it is understood everything which pertains to the service, such as to serve, to teach, etc., with the end of obtaining something spiritual. Hence, it is certainly simony to confer a benefice on a servant so that he would serve you for free, or that he would be compensated for service furnished to you. And so vice versa, if a servant would serve you that in place of a salary he would obtain a benefice (Salamancans *ibid.* § 1, n. 25 and § 4 n. 50, with Laymann, Lessius, Suarez, and the common opinion). Hence, the Salamancans rightly infer with Torre, that without a doubt Bishops who only (or almost only) wish their servants to only offer service to them from the hope of a benefice are simoniacal. Nevertheless, they advert that in all the aforesaid cases penalties are not incurred, nor an obligation for restitution unless an express agreement

---

[5] Translator's note: Literally, a gift from service.

were present, from *cap. Mandatum, de simonia,* as below on penalties, n. 106.

62.—However, would a servant be a simoniac that serves a Bishop for free with the hope of a benefice, but without even any tacit agreement? Laymann, Suarez, Lessius, Sanchez, etc. (cited by Croix, n. 97) reject this. Nay more, Sanchez (*ibid.*, against Cardenas and Pith.) does not say it is simony, although principally he offers service for the benefice, but this must be admitted in no way, according to what was said in n. 51 and 52.

63.—III: *Munus a lingua*[6] follows, whereby praises, favors, intercessions, prayers and similar things are understood, which are estimable by price. See the Salamancans, tr. 19, c. 1, punct. 3, § 1, n. 25. Hence it is simony if a Bishop would give a benefice to someone so that he would praise him, show him favor, etc., or if he would say: "I will not confer a benefice on you unless such a person would ask me [on your behalf]." Salamancans *ibid.* n. 31, with Lessius, Layman, Bonacina, Suarez and the common opinion.

64.—*Quaeritur I:* Would it be simony if you would give money to a mediator so that he would obtain a benefice, or ordination for you? It must be said that if you do not give it for mediation, but for the labor taken up for that purpose, or for loss that is undergone, or for profit lost in obtaining it from someone, and the money would indeed be proportionate with those efforts, it is not simony (Lessius, l. 2, c. 35, dub. 8 n. 46; Croix n. 91; Salamancans *ibid.* § 4 n. 50, with Sanchez, Suarez, Palaus, etc.). Sanchez and Palaus say the same thing with Suarez, Mendo, etc. (cited by Croix, n. 93) if you give money to a servant of a Bishop that it would give easy access; or if you give to him for free that after becoming benevolent he would remove obstacles; but this

---

[6] *Translator's note: Literally, gift from the tongue, or oral remuneration.*

last one is very dangerous. Croix (n. 94 against Palaus) says with equal probability that it is not simony to give money to someone so that he would give you notice of vacant benefices, because these stand very remote to attaining a spiritual thing.

It is also not simony (although it is dangerous) if you give money to someone so that he would simply propose your merits to a Bishop, because it is required for simony that attainment of the spiritual thing would be the immediate end of the furnishing money; but it does not suffice if some consequent depended upon another immediate person, having no connection with him, as the authors say. (Salamancans *loc. cit.* with Suarez, Navarre, Garcia). But it must be greatly feared lest the other relinquish the office of an informant and take up the office of intercessor.

On the contrary, it must be said to be true simony (even by divine law, as Salamancans *ibid.* num. 53 hold with Suarez, Bonacina, Filliuci, del Soto, against Sanchez and Navarre), if you would give money to a mediator not freely to conciliate his friendship, whereby being moved he will help you but with an agreement that he would intercede to obtain a spiritual thing, from *Extrav.* 2, *de sim.* where it says: "Simony is committed when money is given for the conferral ... by favor or mediation." (See Salamancans tr. 19, c. 1, punct. 3 § 4 n. 52 and 53). And I think the opposite is improbable, whatever Elbel might say (n. 607 with others). For, although a temporal thing is given immediately for some merely temporal thing, exactly as the intercession is, just the same "so that you would prepare by money the way for you to obtain a spiritual thing," as St. Thomas says in a similar case (II IIæ qu. 100, art. 2 ad 5), and in our particular case, as Croix (l. 3, q. 1 n. 90), Filliuci, and Anacletus, etc. say (cited by Elbel, n. 608).

65.—*Quaeritur II:* Would it be simony to give money to a mediate intercessor, viz. that he would intercede with another who would obtain for you a benefice from the one that confers it? Sanchez (*Cons.* tom. 1, l. 2, c. 3 d. 26 n. 7), Vasquez and others think it is probably not simony (although they think the opposite is more probable): the reason is because then the money is given for a temporal thing, whereby not proximately or immediately but remotely the way is prepared for a benefice. Still Diana (p. 10, tr. 4, res. 151) and Croix (l. 3, p. 1, n. 90) say better that the contrary must be followed, and Diana doubts whether the first is probable, although he remits himself to the judgment of the wise. And he rightly doubts, according to what was just said.

66.—*Quaeritur III:* Would it be simony if you promise money to another person to pay it out in almsgiving to some monastery, or the poor, if he would obtain a benefice for you? The Salamancans reject this (*ibid.* n. 54, with Diana, Soria and Rocafull.). Understand that if the money is given altogether freely, and in almsgiving, which already constituted a just title excusing from simony, as the title of sustenance excuses, etc., as above.

67.—"*Resp.* 2. 1) Simony is threefold. The *first* is called "*mental*, when outwardly either nothing temporal is given (and "that is called *purely mental*), or when something is given (and "it is called *mental in a mixed manner*) with the intention to "oblige to spiritual repayment, without any outward "arrangement. The *second* is called *conventional*, which proceeds "to the very outward arrangement without real execution, and "it is called pure if it consists in mutual agreement; but *mixed*, if "something participates in real and conventional, as, *e.g.* if only "on the other side it is really fulfilled, and from here simony *of* "*confidence* is reduced, when someone gives a benefice to "another so that he will resign for himself or another or with an "obligation to give a certain part of the fruits. *The third* is called "*real*, which is when both sides are really fulfilled. See Lessius, "*loc. cit.* d. 6."

68.—"2) Simony is divided into that which is of divine law, "and is forbidden on account of its malice; *e.g.* to sell a "consecrated host: and that which is of human law, and is evil "only on account of the prohibition and so is forbidden by the "Church: a) *sale of benefices*, according to that which is "temporal in those matters, viz. in regard to the precise law to "enjoy the fruits; b) the outward *sale of offices* ordered only to "sacred things, *e.g.* sacristans, bursars, advocates of the Church," (obviously one who is specially constituted as an advocate by the Church. Add the office of vice lord, steward, or majordomo, from *c. Si quis* 1. q. 1 and *c. Salvator* 1. q. 3. See Salamancans *de simonia* tr. 19, c. 1, punct. 2, n. 13), "or "treasurer. c) *The offering of money* made to someone to "persuade another to give a benefice. d) An arrangement to "resign a benefice, or pay a pension if the other would obtain a "benefice. e) *The exchange* and resignation of benefices; "likewise, the reservation of a pension from a resigned benefice, "and in the case of exchange of benefices division of the fruits, "etc. if they are done without the authority of a superior, "which, if it were added, they will be licit. f) *Reception of a gift*, "even offered of one's own will, for the examination to a parish, "(ex Trid. sesss. 24, c. 18) for the conferral of orders, for tonsure, "dimissorial letters (Trent, sess. 21, c. 1). Still, an exception is "made of a tenth of a golden coin for a notary, if he does not "have a salary and custom permits. g) *Exaction of money* for "admission to a religious order, not only for the state (for that is "spiritual, and therefore by divine law unsellable) but even for "the obligation of sustenance, unless the poverty of a monastery "or a contrary custom would excuse it. See Laymann, Lib. 4 tr. "10 cap. 8 §6; Bonacina; disp. 1 *de Simonia*, q. 1 and 2; Lessius; "Azor (Part. 3, lib. 12, c. 14 quar. 2)."

69.—It is asked if simony could be granted from human law, would it be simony by divine law? Gonet rejects this (*in Clypeo, Diss de prob.* n. 141), because men, he says, cannot change the nature of things so that what is not simony would be simony.

Nevertheless, the common opinion is opposed, as the Salamancans cite it, as well as Croix (l. 3, p. 1, n. 57) with Suarez and Cardenas, who prove correctly that the Church can effect that the matter of one of its precepts would be the matter of some virtue, as here it is of religion. See Croix, *loc. cit.*

But for a greater understanding we are pressed to discuss individual cases in the following questions.

70.—*Quæstio I:* By a certain law it is simony to sell benefices. Many authors hold it is simony only by ecclesiastical law. (Navarre, *man.* c. 23, n. 108; Lessius, l. 2, c. 35 dub. 2 n. 19; with Adrian. Likewise, Garcia, Lessius, Panormus, etc. with Decius, who says it is the common opinion of canonists, cited by Salamancans tr. 19 *de sim.* c. 2, punct. 8 n. 57 and Bonacina thinks it probable.) The reason is because in benefices they say there are two laws, one to exercise the spiritual functions of the sacrament of order, or jurisdiction, and this is certainly unsellable by divine law. The other is in regard to the temporal revenues, which can be mentally separated, just as the virtue of silver and of the consecration are separated in a chalice; and therefore such right is merely unsellable by positive law.

Still, other others say more probably that it is simony by divine law (Cajetan tom. 2, *Opusc.* tr. 9, q. 1; del Soto *de justitia et jure* l. 9, qu. 7 art. 1; Sanchez, *consil.* l. 2 c. 3 dub. 24, n. 1; Palaus d. 7 p. 13 n. 3; Azor p. 3, l. 12, c. 11 q. 3; Laymann l. 4 tr. 10 c. 8 n. 44 and Salamancans *ibid.* n. 59, with Valentia, Victoria, Ledesma, Bonacina, Coninck, etc.). In this they follow St. Thomas (II IIæ q. 100 art. 5), who teaches that in a chalice one thing is temporal because it is antecedently annexed to the spiritual; the other subsequently, like in benefices, in which there is a subsequent right to revenues and it is so annexed with the law in regard ecclesiastical duties, that it can in no way be separated, since the temporal right is essentially given on account of the spiritual office, so that if the right to revenues were considered separated from the right to sacred duties, now it can no longer be called a *jus beneficiale* nor a benefice, as is gathered from *c. Si quis* 1. q. 3, and from *c. Et diligenti de simonia*. Hence, the Salamancans infer (d. n. 59) there is no dispensation in selling of a benefice even if it were obtained from the Pope. Nevertheless, the Salamancans note (*ibid.* n. 63) that the Pope can rightly separate the right to revenues from the *jus ad sacra*; and so one could concede that the revenues may be sold as merely temporal things, or as some pension imposed over a benefice by separating then the side of its fruits and by giving them to someone, which they confirm in c. 3, n. 30. Lessius teaches the same thing (l. 2, c. 35, n. 19) and Croix (l. 3, p. 1, n. 123).

Here we note in passing that it is conceded to the holders of benefices contract for the fruit of the benefice up to thirty years, but not beyond. But to contract out for tithes would be simony (See Croix, n. 124 and 125). Likewise, it would also be simony to contract out a spiritual thing, say a chalice, although compensation must be made for the temporal loss. (Croix n. 156).

71.—*Quæstio II:* Would it be simony to sell patronage? We do not speak here on the civil right of patronage, but the ecclesiastical, which is conceded by the Church to those who build Churches or give dowries. This right, in regard to the honors, and subsidies which are due to patrons, can indeed be sold, because it is not said to be spiritual in their regard to those things. Salamancans *de simonia*, c. 2, punct. 11, n. 75.

There is a doubt 1) Could a right to present someone to a benefice be sold? The response is, that if such a right were affixed to the thing, when it is sold, the right would be transferred with the thing onto the buyer, as St. Thomas teaches (II IIæ. qu. 100, art. 4 ad 3). Just as it can also be transferred in donation, or by a hereditary title. (See Salamancans *ibid.* n. 76). Outside of these cases such a right cannot be sold without simony by positive law, from *c. De jure,* and *c. Præterea extra, de Jurepatronatu.*

Hence it is simony if a patron were to sell a thing to many by reason of such a right, or to impose on the one presented, *e.g.* to sue for his expenses and to prove the law considers him a patron. But the Salamancans say otherwise (*loc. cit.* cap. 2 n. 77), when the lawsuit turns on the right of patronage, the condition is supplied that if within so many months the one presented had not pursued the presentation, the patron could present it on another, because then he remains in his freedom, nor is he obligated to prove the right of a patron for it, but for himself if he wishes to obtain the benefice. (Salamancans *ibid.* n. 77). But in this I think there is a great danger that virtually, such a presentation is sold for expenses, which ought to be made from the right of patronage.

However, would such a sale of patronage also be forbidden by divine law? Lessius, Palaus, Laymann, etc. affirm it (cited by Salamancans *ibid.* n. 78), because such a right is something spiritual, since it proceeds from the power of ecclesiastical jurisdiction. But Sanchez, del Soto, Sylvius, Navarre, Torre, Decius and others deny this, whose opinion the Salamancans say is no less probable. The reason is, such a right is rather more something temporal, since it is a temporal favor conceded by the Church, insofar as it exercises a power that is not jurisdictional, but political, eminently contained in it, to which it looks to distribute temporal favors.

Here it must be noted, that to sell the right of burial in a sacred place on account of the greater dignity of the place, is probably not simony, as Croix says (l. 3, p. 1, n. 185, with Barbosa, Burghaber and Caramuel against Suarez, etc.).

72.—*Quæstio III:* Can benefices be exchanged? It is certain that in other spiritual things, apart from benefices, exchange is licit when the things are merely spiritual, *e.g.* "I say Mass for you so that you would say so many rosaries for me, etc." But when a union is made from a spiritual and temporal thing, then a distinction must be made. If the temporal things were antecedently annexed to spiritual things, such as silver in a chalice, the reliquary for relics, these may rightly be exchanged or sold; provided that only an account of the temporal value of the thing were to be made. (St. Thomas II IIæ qu. 100 art. 4; Salamancans tr. 19 c. 3 punct. 2 § 1 n. 18; Elbel *de sim.* n. 600 with Suarez and the common opinion). But it must be said otherwise if the temporal things were subsequently annexed, such as the fruit to benefices, in which each exchange is simoniacal without the authority of a superior, now not from divine law, but from positive law, from *c. Quaesitum, de rer. permut.* Hence, Bishops can concede exchanges of benefices existing in his dioceses, as St. Thomas teaches (II IIæ q. 100, art. 1, ad 1 ex *c. Universorum, de rer. permut.*) only that the benefices may not pertain to the Pope, as in *Extravag. Dudum. Benedicti XI,* and the same can said for Abbots having the faculty of bishops (Salamancans *ibid.* § 2, from ex n. 21, with Suarez, Bonacina, etc.). Still, this does not occur if someone were only elected to a benefice, or if a suit were argued in regard to a benefice. See Salamancans *ibid.* n. 26.

However, it is licit for those wishing to exchange benefices antecedently negotiated to agree and even to oblige themselves to pay a penalty for breaking the agreement, as Lessius argues, l. 2, c. 35, n. 92, in fine. Nevertheless, it depends on the consent of the prelate, because then there is no obligation other than a conditional one. Salamancans tr. 19, c. 3, punct. 2 § 2 num. 27, with Sanchez, Palaus, Valentia, Suarez, Lessius, Laymann, etc. from *c. Inter caet. de praeb.*

Quaeritur: When afterward, an exchange does not have the effect, could they return to their own benefices by their own authority? The Salamancans deny it, with Panormus and Gomez, who advance for this opinion many decisions of the Rota; because renouncing the title he loses it as well as possession of the benefice, which is why he needs to return to it by a new conferral; still they duly say the contrary is also probable, which

St. Antoninus holds as well as Sylvius. The reason is that the renunciation is upon the condition that the prelate would consent; so if the prelate were later not to consent, it is altogether invalid.

73.—*Quæstio IV:* Could a benefice with a pension be exchanged?

We must preface that in such a case, to acquire a pension four things are required (from Lessius, l. 2, c. 34, dub. 38), namely: 1) that the one obtaining it should have the capacity, *viz.* he be legitimate, not excommunicated, and at least tonsured; 2) That a just cause would be present, *e.g.* to feed the poor, on account of the good of the Church, to compensate for uniformity; otherwise the one obtaining it will not be safe in conscience, even if the Pope will have dispensed, as Lessius argues (*ibid.* n. 204, with Toledo and the common opinion). Moreover, would the consent of the patron be required? Lessius denies it, with others, unless the benefice were resigned, in which case mention of the patronage ought to be made. 3) It is required that the pension be moderated, so that according to the use he would not exceed a third of the revenues of the benefice; 4) That legitimate authority would intervene, which is certainly [placed] in the Pope.

74.—With these having been posited, there is a doubt: 1) whether Bishops could constitute pensions in benefices? Some uphold it if a just cause were present, namely to provide for an old parish priest that is senile and unfit to bring an end to a suit over a benefice, etc., as is contained in *c. Nisi esset* 21, *de praeb.* and *c. Audivimus* 3, *de collusione*. Likewise, to compensate for uniformity in the exchange of benefices, from *c. Ad quaestiones, de rer. permutatione* (authors cited in Lessius, *d.c.* 34, n. 205; Gigas with Feline, Imola, Decius, etc.). Nevertheless, others, with Lessius, and the Salamancans (tr. 19 c. 3, p. 2, § 3, n. 31) say only the Pope can constitute pensions, because such is the style of the curia which makes the right. See n. 81, II.

But here we must note that 1) pensioners, by the bull of Pius V, are held to recite the office of the Blessed Virgin Mary, otherwise they do not earn the fruits; see Lessius, *d. c.* 34, n. 208; *cf.* St. Pius V, bulla *Ex proximo*, die 20 Sept. 1571, § 1; *in Bullarum Romanorum*, Mainardi). Nevertheless, this is understood if the pension is clerical, so that it would require first tonsure; but not if it is merely a lay pension, so that the pensioner does not demand his fruit as a cleric, but as a layman, exactly as the Salamancans hold (Salamancans *de benef. eccl.* tr. 28, *c. unic.* p. 4, n. 64, with Azor, Navarre, and Palaus). Likewise, it is understood if a pensioner were not a cleric in major orders, or a religious; for if he would recite the greater office or other prayers commanded by his religious order, but is not held to the little office (Salamancans *ibid.* with Azor, Ledesma, Palaus, Bonacina, etc.).

It must be noted: 2) that when someone resigns a benefice with a pension in favor of a third of it, he cannot exact security or a guarantee, or anticipated payment from the pensioner, unless these are admitted by the Pope at the same time. This is because laws forbid all agreements in regard to benefices that *de jure* are not present in them. This is why Lessius thinks in such a case there is not obligation to pay the pension and vacate the benefice (*ibid.* n. 95).

75.—There is a doubt 2: How could a benefice with a pension be exchanged, and by whose authority? A distinction must be made: if the pension is spiritual, an exchange can be made, but by the authority of the Pope, not a Bishop, unless that spiritual pension were erected over the title of a benefice, just like *praestimonia*,[7] because then they are true benefices and a Bishop can rightly concede exchanges of benefices, as the Salamancans say (tr. 19, c. 3, p. 2, § 3 n. 29), and as we said above in the

---

[7] Translator's note: A *praestimonium* refers to income from a foundation which, while not constituting a benefice, is intended to provide for the subsistence of a priest, the service of a chapel or the celebration of masses.

preceding question. But if the pension is merely temporal, the exchange cannot be done by Papal authority, since it would be simony against divine law, as the Salamancans teach (*ibid.* n. 29), with Suarez, Bonacina, Torre, Villalobos, etc. Nevertheless, the Pope, as supreme dispenser, by prescinding from the exchange, just as he can add more fruit to the benefice, so he can take away part of the fruits from it, and give to another, as Lessius teaches (*d. c.* 35, n. 89, and 91), where he says this is certain, with the common opinion of the Doctors. And the Salamancans agree with the cited author (n. 30) as was said in question I in n. 70.

76.—But the great question is, when unequal benefices are exchanged, would it be lawful to compensate the inequality through some pension, or money by the authority of the Pope?

The first opinion probably affirms it, which Lessius holds (*d.* c. 35, n. 101) with Cajetan, del Soto, Sylvius, Angelus, etc. The reason is, because then the bare titles of the benefices are simply commuted and separated from the provenance of the laws, which are temporal things, and through another contract the excess is compensated, as Lessius says (l. 2, c. 25, n. 102, vers. 3) and he proves it from *cap. ad quaes.* 6, *e rer. permut.* where Pope Clement VIII approved the exchange of two parochial churches, after the excess of the endowment has been compensated by money.

But the *second opinion* more probably denies it, which Anacletus holds (*de benef.* tr. 11, d. 2, q. 5, n. 50) with Laymann, Covarruvias, Vasquez, and the Salamancans (ibid. n. 34) with Navarre, Sanchez, Filliuci, Suarez, Bonacina, because simony is against divine law, provided spiritual things are bought for temporal; for that excess consequently is connected to the spiritual title of the benefice. Moreover, the Salamancans say (*ibid.* n. 35) the Pope could approve the contract, not through the mode of exchange, but by separating part of the fruits from the more profitable benefice, and giving them to the other, as we said above.

But it is certain that it is simony to compensate an excess with money, which is in a spiritual matter, say on account of a greater dignity or jurisdiction. On the other hand, it is not simony to commute the more profitable benefice with another worthier one, in the mode that no respect is held to compensate the excess of revenues with the excess of dignity. See the Salamancans, *ibid.* n. 32.

77.—*Quæstio V:* How will it be lawful to make a transaction in benefices?

In other spiritual matters it is certain that it would be lawful to do the transaction even on one's own authority (Salamancans tr. 19, c. 3 punct. 3 n. 42), just as it is lawful to exchange a spiritual thing with another as we said above in *Quæstio* III, n. 72.

But in benefices at least, the authority of the Bishop is required, even if a spiritual thing is transacted for another merely spiritual thing, from *cap. Super eo, de transact.* and *c. Statuimus, de eodem tit.,* as well as the Salamancans, *ibid.* n. 43, with Suarez, Palaus, etc. Nevertheless, we must advert that this does not forbid that they could agree to parts, by yielding their rights, or remitting themselves by their will, who are at least clerics; only no division of rights or of revenues takes place, and no obligation is imposed on those yielding, from *d. cap. Sper eo,* Salamancans *ibid.* n. 40, and 48, with Laymann, Bonacina, Filliuci, Palaus, Suarez. It is simony, however, to compose a lawsuit by the intervention of lots without the consent of a superior, since every arrangement would be illicit in benefices. Croix, l. 4, n. 1063, with Suarez, etc.

78.—Yet, there is a doubt: 1) Could a bishop licitly compose a lawsuit with some obligation, so that obtaining a benefice he would pay something to the one yielding [it]? It does not seem to be lawful for him, since a spiritual thing would be exchanged for a temporal one; but on account of some causes it can be made worthy: a) on account of the good of peace, which also leads to a spiritual good, from *c. Nisi essent, de praeb.*; b) on account of justice, lest the one yielding would remain without the support which he needs; c) on account of labor and expenses, which the one yielding would suffer, and the other is going to suffer if he would not yield (Salamancans *ibid.* n. 44, Palaus, Bonacina, etc). But truly Laymann teaches in l. 4, tr. 10, c. 8 p. 5 n. 58 with Suarez (and Abbas as well as the Salamancans *ibid.* n. 48, Palaus, Filliuci, Bonacina, etc), that it is also given with those (who are clerics) that will compose suits with such an obligation, only not with an annual pension, and only that the benefice would not be removed from the possessor; and it is certain it could be done from *cap. De caetero, de transact.*

79.—There is a doubt: 2) Could a Bishop, on account of the good of peace in such an exchange, impose upon the benefice a pension to pay to the one yielding for the duration of his life? The Salamancans, tr. 19, c. 3, punct. 3, n. 46, with Azor, Bonacina, etc. reject this. And so do a great many decisions in the Rota as Bonacina witnesses, because in the style of the curia they say transactions of this sort cannot be admitted. Still, other authors hold the contrary, which they call sufficiently probable. (Laymann, l. c. d. n. 58, with Abbas, and Palaus, Suarez, Torre, Prado, Araujo, Mandosius, cited by Salamancans d. n. 46). The reason is, because even if (as the Salamancans say in n. 45) the Pope alone can impose perpetual pensions for beneficers, as we said above, still in transactions the Doctors say in common, the rights and use have already been introduced that Bishops, on account of the good of peace, could impose pensions, but not on beneficers, but upon the same benefices for the life of the pensioners. And Laymann says this is certain from *cap. Nisi essent, de praeb.* And he also says ecclesiastical judges can do the same.

80.—There is a doubt 3: Could such a transaction be admitted by a Bishop with a pension over a benefice, if the parties would already agree upon it, but depending upon the consent of the Bishop? Laymann and Reginald deny it, but the Salamancans more probably affirm it (*ibid.* n. 47) with Bonacina and Torre.

81.—*Quæstio VI:* How can renunciations of benefices be made?

Renunciation of a benefice must be done in the hand of that prelate who can confer it; and likewise it ought to be accepted by him, from *cap. Admonet, de renuntiat.*, otherwise it is null and he does not vacate the benefice. (Salamancans *ibid.* punct. 4, n. 49, with Garcia and Covarruvias). Nevertheless, this does not occur in litigious benefices, or in elections to those which are validly renounced by their own authority, from *c. 2 De in integrum restit.* and *c. Sane, de renuntiat.*

Furthermore, a renunciation can be made in many ways.

1) *Purely and absolutely*, and in it no suspicion of simony occurs.

2) *Absolutely*, but *not purely*, if it were done without designation of person, but with the obligation of a pension, in regard to which, if the pension is temporal, as we said above in n. 75, there is now no renunciation of this sort made in the hand of the Bishop. But there is a doubt whether the renunciation would avail with the obligation of a spiritual pension? There is a twofold opinion, and each is probable as Palaus says (disp. 3, p. 17, n. 13).

The first affirms it. (Malderus, Gigas, Felinus, Imola, Navarre, Rebuffus, etc. cited by Salamancans tr. 19 *de sim.* cap. 3 punct. 4 n. 59). The reason is because it is very probable for a just cause that such a pension could be imposed by Bishops on benefices. Nevertheless, the Salamancans (dict. n. 59) with Azor, Bonacina, etc. reject this except in the case of grave necessity, because that say that such a faculty was taken away from Bishops by the Constitution of Pius V, *Intolerabilis*, n. 5. Lessius also holds the same thing (c. 35, dub. 15, n. 91).

3) Renunciation can be done *purely* but not *absolutely*, namely if it were in favor of a certain person without an obligation: and this is not forbidden by divine law if there is an upright end, but it is forbidden by ecclesiastical law unless it were done by the hand of the Pope. It is the common opinion. See the Salamancans, *ibid.* cap. 3, n. 52.

82.—But it is asked, whether such a renunciation would be simoniacal in favor of a third made in the hand of a bishop? The Salamancans correctly make the distinction that if the arrangement were to precede the Bishop, so that after the resignation has been made, a third of the benefice were conferred, it would certainly be simony; but otherwise if an arrangement were not present, because then, the Bishop remaining in his freedom, were he to confer it afterward, he would act freely. (Salamancans *ibid.* n. 53, with Sanchez, Bonacina, del Soto, Torre, etc.) Nevertheless, he would sin renouncing by such a mode against religion, and on account of it he could be deprived of the benefice by the Bishop, as the Salamancans say (*ibid.* n. 54) with Lessius, Suarez, etc.

83.—Moreover, it must be noted that it is very probable that it is not illicit, if resigning also in the same renunciation he would declare to the Bishop his desire that the benefice be conferred on a certain person, provided that there were no arrangement, as the rigorous suspending condition (just as the *Moto Proprio* of St. Pius V of the year 1568 must be understood; Salamancans *ibid.* n. 56). The reasoning is because really then the renunciation is done simply, and the Bishop is free to confer the benefice to whom he wills. Salamancans *ibid.* n. 55, with Navarre, Azor, Palaus, Sanchez, Torre and Garcia.

84.—There is a doubt whether after the resignation has been made with a condition in favor of a third in the hand of the

Bishop, this could admit resignation, after the addition has been rejected? The authors affirm because such a condition, just as it is indecent, is held that it has not been added (Sanchez, with del Soto, St. Antoninus, and Sylvius, cited by Lessius, lib. 2, cap. 3, n 86, as well as Covarruvias, Aragon, and Villalobos, cited by Salamancans *ibid.* n. 57). But others reject it, because they say a resignation for one part cannot be admitted, and rejected for another (Lessius, *dict.* lib. and Salamancans *dict.* n. 57, with Suarez, Palaus, etc.). Both are sufficiently probable, as Torre says (cited by Salamancans).

85.—*Quæstio VII*: When is the *confidential* resignation of benefices simoniacal?

It must be known that from the constitutions of Pius IV and St. Pius V (in 7 *Decretal.*, cap. 9 et 10 *de Benef. collat. juxta Trident. sess.* 24, c. 19 and *sess.* 25, cap. 7 *de Reform.*) all confidential resignations made *cum accessu, regressu, ingressu* to a benefice are forbidden, or with confidence to receive the fruits from the resigned benefice; for if the confidence were on another temporal matter, apart from the fruits of the benefice, it would indeed be simony, but not confidential, as Croix rightly notes (lib. 3, part. 1, n. 68 with Suarez, Laymann, etc.). It is said through *acessus* if you would resign a benefice to someone with a confidence, that he later will renounce it and it shall be conferred on another. By *regressus*, if you would resign a benefice, save for the right of return to it in some case. By *ingressus*, if you resign a benefice conferred on you, before you would possess it, save for the right of entering possession, *e.g.* if someone would die, etc.

If anyone resigns a benefice without another agreement, but with the hope that he would resign again from gratitude alone in your favor, or pay something from the fruits of the benefice, it is certainly not simony by divine law, nor an ancient canon, although it may be very dangerous and for the most part simony, as the Salamancans hold (*ibid.* punct. 5, n. 65).

86.—*Quæritur I:* Would such a resignation with hope but without an agreement be condemned by the new law, *dd. Constit.* of Pius IV and St. Pius V? The opinion is twofold and sufficiently probable as the Salamancans say, *ibid.* n. 66.

The first affirms it (Palaus, Suarez, Bonacina, etc.) and it is proven from the words of the bull of St. Pius V, where it is said: "If one secured anything ... even under the title of a simple donation."

Nevertheless, *the second opinion* more probably denies it. The reason is, because in those Constitutions only the decree of Trent is renewed condemning not only confidential agreements, whereby a new obligation is induced (with an express or tacit agreement, as Navarre and Rodriquez explain, cited by Salamancans tr. 19, *de simonia* c. 3, punct. 5, n. 69, *in fine*). Moreover, by the words that were advanced the Pope commanding nothing other than that simoniacal confidences should be presumed if a donation is later shown to have been made. So other theologians hold and more profusely prove. (Salamancans *ibid.* n. 67 and 68, with Suarez, Sa, Villalobos, Navarre, Lessius, Sanchez, Azor, etc.

87.—*Quæritur II:* If the one resigning declares his intention to be that another should remain obligated to resign in the future, but without the promise of the other, would it be true confidential simony? Palaus and Diana affirm it (cited by Croix, lib. 3, p. 1, n. 65), but Navarre, Azor, Lessius, Suarez and others more probably deny it, because then it lacks an agreement from both parties to the obligation. Still, it must be said otherwise, as Croix adverts (n. 66) with the common opinion, if he will resign declaring he wishes that a pension should be paid to someone from the fruits, because this is specifically expressed in the bull.

88.—*Quæritur III:* Would confidence be embraced in the aforesaid Constitutions even in exchanges of benefices? Suarez and Palaus, with Navarre deny it, (cited by Salamancans *ibid.* n. 71) since no mention is made of exchanges in those Constitutions. But the opposite must be said, with the Salamancans, Araujo and Torre. And they prove it from the bull of St. Pius V where, as they relate, it is expressly said: "And even all exchanges, presentations, conferrals ... and other dispositions are of no importance." Yet we must look more dilligently at how the aforesaid authors explain these words.

89.—Lastly two things must be noted: 1) That through this simony, even if it was only conventional, penalties are incurred, clearly a) Interdict from entering a Church; b) Papal excommunication *ipso facto*; c) nullity of the conferral and the obligation to pay the fruits; d) depravation of other benefices obtained earlier. (See Salamancans *ibid.* n. 72). Nevertheless, this last is not incurred until after the sentence of the judge, or at least a declaratory sentence. Salamancans *ibid.* n. 73, with Suarez, Laymann, Sanchez, Henriquez, Torre. See n. 112.

90.—It must be noted: 2) That if anyone resigns a benefice with a confidence, let alone with an express agreement, but on his own authority by not seeking the assent of a superior, he would indeed sin, but not incur the aforesaid penalties, because such a resignation is null of itself, even when that simoniacal agreement does not arise. (Salamancans n. 73, with Navare). But it must be said otherwise if an agreement would avail, unless simony would hinder, because then the penalties are incurred even if the resignation is null (*ibid.*). Hence, Elbel (n. 649) and Croix (l. 4, n. 958 with Filliuci, etc.) rightly infer from this, that if someone resigned a benefice in the hand of a superior, after he secretly agreed that the one resigning should give something back to himself, not only is the resignation null, but the one resigning loses the title, since among the other penalties for simony is the inability to hold the same benefice.

91.—*Quæstio VIII:* In what manner is simony committed for the entry to a religious order?

It is certain, as St. Thomas teaches (II IIæ q. 100, a. 3 ad 4) it is simony to give and receive something for entry into a monastery, from *c. Quam pio*, c. 1, q. 2. Hence 1) It is not lawful to admit someone into a monastery on account of the goods which he offers since that would be to sell the religious state, unless he simply expressed without an agreement that he wished to enter with his goods. It would equally be unlawful to offer service to a monastery as the price of admission, unless the one that serves did so to win over the benevolence of the religious to himself, that they might admit him to it. Salamancans tr. 19, c. 2, punct. 7 n. 47, with St. Antoninus, Sylvius, and Sanchez).

2) On the other hand, St. Thomas says (*loc. cit.*) it is not simony if someone would give alms to a monastery so that he would be more easily admitted from gratitude; just as it is also not simony if the religious agree to the gifts for someone to enter the monastery. Nay more, as Bonacina says, it is not simony if the monastery pays his debts to remove impediments to entrance, but still leaves him free to enter. Or even if a monastery promises to admit him after he learned a trade; because then an obligation is not imposed but a requisite condition is declared if he desires to be admitted. Salamancans *ibid.*, n. 48, with Reginald, Azor, Sylvius.

3) It is also licit, exactly as the doctors teach in common, if a poor monastery receives something for the subsistence of those entering, such as dowries for nuns, and distributions which are usually distributed to other nuns. (St. Thomas, II IIæ qu. 100, art. 3 ad 4; Cabassutius, *Theor. jur.* lib. 5, c. 5, n. 12, with Bonacina, Cajetan, Navarre, Toledo, Suarez, etc.) Nevertheless, Sanchez notes (cited by Salamancans *ibid.* n. 49), monasteries can scarcely be excused that ask a more abundant dowry on account of the ignobility of the person, or another defect, unless it would come about from this that it would be a detriment to the honor of the

monastery in goods and similar things, because this is now a temporal loss. And so it is permitted to receive more for the admittance of a poor sister, or a widow, or an old or sick person, etc. See Salamancans, *ibid.* n. 50.

92.—But the great question is, would it be lawful to receive something for the subsistence of those entering if the monastery is well supplied?

The first opinion that the doctors hold affirms it (del Soto, lib. 9, q. 6, art. 2; Palaus, d. 3, p. 9, n. 4; Bonacina, d. 1, q. 4, § 8 n. 2; Sanchez, *Conf.* c. 3, d. 23, n. 1; Elbel *de sim.* n. 604, and Salamancans *dict.* cap. 2 n. 53, with Lezana, Sylvester, Aragon, etc.) The reason is, because, as they say, this is not simony either by natural or positive law. Not from natural law, because on one side a temporal thing is not received, except what is furnished for temporal subsistence; on the other side it cannot be said that those who ask to enter have some right to the goods of the monastery since they obtain them from the monastery either by their own labor, or they were given freely to them by others. Nor is it simony by positive law, for if some laws seem to forbid it, nevertheless, no text expressly forbids something to be received by the title of subsistence. But if, as they say, such a prohibition ever existed, it is removed by a contrary custom. Nevertheless, Elbel and the Salamancans (n. 54) with Sylvius Torre, Villalobos, etc. do not deny that this could not at least excuse from the fall of avarice.

But *the second opinion* denies it, which several authors hold and follow (Cabassutius, *loc. cit.* n. 3, with St. Bonaventure, Suarez, l. 4, *de simonia*; Laymann, tr. 10, *c. ult.* § 4 n. 39; Cajetan, 2. 2.: q. 100, art. 3; Roncaglia, *de simonia* cap. 2, q. 6, and others, to whom St. Thomas clearly consents in II IIæ q. 100, art. 3 ad 4). This opinion teaches then it is only permitted to furnish something *if the monastery was of scanty means; if the wealth of the monastery would not suffice for this*, etc. But the chief reason, and the one that most persuades me, is that demanding, even if before the reception there is no law in regard to the goods of the monastery, nevertheless after one has been received, he indeed has a right to those things for his subsistence. This is why, if the monastery is wealthy, and something is furnished for subsistence of that time, he sells his right to it because after his reception he will obtain it, and although that subsistence is something temporal, it is something consequently annexed to a spiritual thing; wherefore, just as a right to return to a benefice cannot be sold, or to secure a tithe, because these come about as consequently annexed to a spiritual thing, so also one cannot partake of the right to the provisions in monastery. Hence, from *c. Quoniam, de simonia*, it was forbidden for some nuns to receive temporal things on the pretext of poverty from those entering for their subsistence. And in *Extravagantes* 1, *de simonia*, it is forbidden under excommunication for something to be received for any purpose for entry to religion, unless someone wished to give freely. And since this is simony by divine law, as we proved, common custom is asserted in vain by defenders of the first opinion (in regard to which I am very doubtful), with exception of monasteries of nuns as we will see below.

Furthermore, we must say otherwise when a monastery is poor, for when it does not have sufficient goods for the subsistence of others, then it sells nothing; then, the one that is going to be received will have no right to goods which the monastery does not have. Also, the doctors agree on this in common. Cabassutius (*loc. cit.* n. 13) adverts that to exact something from those that are going to be received strict necessity is not required, rather it suffices for that case if the monastery cannot otherwise suitably administer provisions. The Council of Trent (sess. 25, c. 3, *de Reg.*) so provides: "In temporal faculties of monasteries an account must be undertaken so that the number of nuns can *suitably* be supported."

It does not avail to say against our opinion, with the Salamancans, that just as a priest, even if rich, can licitly receive money from another to celebrate for the stipend of his subsistence, so a monastery can receive from a postulant for the same title of subsistence. The reason is because the priest, by receiving something as an alms for Mass, would licitly receive it as a stipend of his subsistence, which is due to him from justice, as we stated above, n. 55. But a monastery can exact nothing for the obligation which it assumes for the subsistence of those entering, because, (as we said) the one entering, after reception, has a right to the goods of the monastery, inasmuch as it is annexed to the reception.

Nevertheless, an exception is made: 1) If something were received from postulants for provisions during their time of novitiate, for that is expressly permitted by the Council of Trent in Sess. 25, cap. 16, *de Reg*. 2) If the one that is going to be received is sick, old, of low intelligence, or similar things, because then the monastery licitly receives something temporal from him, not only for the lack of service which another healthy or young man would furnish, but even more, for the extraordinary temporal inconvenience that the monastery is going to undergo on his account. (St. Thomas, II IIæ q. 100, ad 4, Croix, l. 3, p. 1 n. 287, with others), and this is certain among all, as the Salamancans assert (n. 51). An exception is made: 3) For monasteries of nuns, to whom Clement VIII bestowed the ability to negotiate on the dowry of those they were going to receive for their subsistence, as Navarre, Bassaeus, Lessius and Bonacina (cited by Cabassutius, n. 17), relate. The reason for this indulgence seems to be that monasteries of nuns are more easily liable to misfortunes, as is clear from experience, than monasteries of men. Yet, is the excommunication in *Extrav.* 1 *de simonia* be inflicted upon all exacting and paying for entry to monasteries today abolished in use? Navarre and Lessius seem to affirm it, but Cabassutius (n. 17) says that it is still in force for monasteries of men.[8]

Thus, the following are resolved:

93.—"It is simony to preach, catechize and offer Masses for a "price, unless one is excused by reason of labor that is not "intrinsic (for it is holy and inestimable, viz. either the sacred "action itself or one intrinsically included in it), but extrinsic , "and not annexed to a spiritual thing, as for the labor of a "journey, or to sing at Mass, or by reason of inconvenience "estimable by price. The reason is, because these actions by "their nature are ordered to something supernatural, and to "salvation, but not to something temporal, as any teaching even "of theology, which is estimable by price. Bonacina, *loc. cit.*; "Suarez, Filliuci, etc. Laymann l. 1, § 4. See what was said in "number 53."

94.—*Quæritur*: Would it be simony to receive something for the instruction of others in sacred doctrine? We make the distinction, if the instruction aims only at the spiritual good of others, it is simony; because then it is a merely spiritual matter, for which there can be no price. Hence it is simony to receive something for a sermon as the price for its intrinsic labor, just as for study or weariness, exactly as the authors teach unless it were received as a stipend for subsistence. (Lessius, lib. 2, cap. 34 n. 76 and Salamancans tr. 19, *de simonia*, c. 2, punct. 6 n. 42, with St. Thomas and the common opinion, see what is going to be said in n. 55). Otherwise if the instruction also tends to the temporal good of another, to utility, honor, delight, exactly as an instruction to interpret the Sacred Scriptures, to deduce theological conclusions, to expunge heresies, etc. as the authors

---

[8] And really, these are reviewed among the excommunications reserved *simpliciter* to the Roman Pontiff by the constitution *Apostolicae Sedis*, under 10.

say (Croix, n. 179; Lessius, *loc. cit.* n. 80, with del Soto, Cajetan, Victoria, Salamancans *ibid.* punct. 6, n. 43; Elbel, n. 620), from St. Thomas, II IIæ. q. 100, art. 3 ad 3, where he says: "One that has knowledge ... can receive the price of his doctrine as though providing a place for his works." Hence it is also licit to receive something for explaining moral theology, as is more probable with Croix (l. 3, p. 1 n. 165 and 184). Likewise, for commanding a license to teach others theology with the title of *doctor*, as is clear from the use of the Universities, or for giving moral counsel, because it is a temporal instruction, although it leads to peace of conscience. Moreover, it is otherwise if the counsel would tend to only the spiritual good of another, say, that he be moved to repentance, etc. Salamancans *ibid.* n. 45.

95.—"2. Likewise, it is simony to give or receive the price for "absolution from sins, censures, for the dispensation of a vow, "an oath, an impediment to matrimony, irregularity, etc. "Nevertheless, something can be exacted in these by the mode "of a fine to be applied to a pious cause. Laym. *loc. cit.* n. 10."

96.—Payments are taken up in the dispensations in matrimonies, etc. even by the mode of subsistence for burdens of the Pope; likewise, by the mode of commutation, just as vows are commuted in almsgiving. And it is also conceded to Bishops in such dispensations to receive something to be distributed in alms (provided nothing comes about from them or his own), through the mode of a penalty or commutation, but not by the mode of subsistence: for this is forbidden to them from *c. Jacobus, de simonia* and by the Council of Trent, (sess. 24, c. 6 and sess. 25, c. 18 *de Ref.*). The Salamancans with St. Thomas, *dict. c. 2* punct. 5 n. 26 and 27.

97.—*Quæritur:* Would it be simony to give something so that the other would omit a spiritual thing? We must distinguish and affirm, if the omission is directed from the spiritual power, such as the omission of absolution, dispensation, election, etc. from *c. Nemo presbyterorum, de simonia*, where it is forbidden to deny penance on account of a price unless such an absolution would be a sacrilege, or unjust. See Croix, n. 175. Otherwise, it is not simony if the spiritual act would depend upon freedom, such as it would be to omit prayer, to give alms, to celebrate Mass, unless the other were held to these from justice. Salamancans tr. 19, c. 2, punct. 4, from n. 27 with Ledesma, Villalobos, etc.

98.—"3. It is not simony to give something to remedy a "opposition on account of denying the sacraments in necessity. "Suarez, Lessius, Laymann; or from iniquitously impeding an "election, or possession of a benefice, to which you have the "right *in re*. I add that, if you do not yet have the right *in re*, you "could at least buy off the opposition from one that can only be "an obstacle, but not from one who can both benefit *and* block "you. The reason is, because it is not given as an equivalent "price for a spiritual thing, but that another would induced to "duly do his duty."

In this, carefully attend to the two rules handed down by St. Thomas in II IIæ q. 100, art. 2 ad 5.

The first is, that when a right is certain and in the matter already acquired, one is permitted to remove an unjust opposition, by giving something temporal (from the common opinion with Navarre, *in Man.* cap. 23, n. 102; Salamancans *ibid.* c. 3, p. 1 §1 n. 3; Elbel *de simonia* n. 616 and others). It is said, *a certain right*, for if there is a doubt then it is not lawful, because then it is acquired by a temporal thing as a certain right to a spiritual thing which was in doubt. It is said *an unjust opposition*, because if it were just then it is also not allowed. It is said likewise, *by giving something temporal*, something spiritual cannot be given to buy off the opposition, because a spiritual thing would be given for a temporal one, of the sort that the opposition is. Salamancans. *ibid.* n. 4, and 6, and the common opinion.

99.—Nevertheless, the question is, can opposition be bought off with money in regard to the possession of a benefice?

The first opinion denies it, because such a possession is a spiritual thing, or annexed to a spiritual thing, since by possession a right is acquired to exercise spiritual things. Viva, *de ben.* q. 9 art. 6; Bonacina, Garcia, Abbatius, etc. cited by Salamancans tr. 19 *de simonia* cap. 3, p. 1, § 1 n. 7.

Nevertheless, *the second opinion* is more probable, which Busembaum holds, as well as Suarez (lib. 4, c. 50, n. 31), Sanchez (*Consil.* l. 2 c. 3 dub. 30 n. 11), Palaus (t. 3 d. 3 *de simonia* p. 20 n. 3), Croix (lib. 3, p. 1, n. 140), Bonacina (c. 3, q. 4), Lessius (lib. 2, cap. 35 dub. 18 n. 109), who call it the common opinion, as well as others cited by the Salamancans. It upholds it as lawful because, although the right to a benefice is indeed spiritual, the possession is not. The Salamancans (n. 8) and Croix (*dict.* n. 140) rightly follow this, that the right is always and certainly acquired to possession; for then the opposition would not be in regard to a spiritual thing, but in regard to the fact of possession, which is temporal and St. Thomas seems to think in this way (*loc. cit.* art. 2 ad 5) teaching: "But after the right to something has already been acquired, it is lawful to remove unjust opposition with money." Nevertheless, it must be said otherwise with the Salamancans (*ibid.* in fine) if a right were recalled to a probable doubt, as we spoke of above.

Moreover, here it must be noted that in the Council of Trent (sess. 24, cap. 14), it is commanded of Bishops that they would not permit any payment or promise for admission to possession of a benefice; inasmuch as "having suspicion of a simoniacal vice or avarice," every custom to the contrary being rejected; the council only permits if it were custom, to give something to be converted to pious uses. But these are understood: 1) not in regard to all benefices, but only on canonries and what is furnished in cathedral Churches or collegiate churches, as Bonacina probably says (*de simonia* qu. 7 § 3 n. 4) as well as Barbosa in *dict*. l. Con.; 2) on those receiving something for admission to possession, but not on giving to remove an unjust opposition, as above, for the bull of St. Pius V *Durum nimis*, published in the year 1570 for the observance of the aforesaid sanctions of the council, explains and confirms it is only for those receiving it, in these words: "We command Bishops, chapters, etc. lest they would retain the fruits, and not to ask or demand other things, etc."

100.—The second rule is, that if a right were not in a thing already acquired, but to the thing, it is not lawful to remove the opposition with money, from *cap. Matthaeus, de simonia* where one is condemned who, after obtaining election, offered money lest other electors would impede confirmation, since he does not yet have the right acquired for confirmation. hence, it is simony to offer money to a Bishop who unjustly refuses me to institute what has been presented, or to choose a worthy man, because then by money I would not only remove the impediment, but would also acquire a spiritual thing. (Busembaum and Sanchez *Cons*. lib. 2, cap. 3 d. 30 num. 3; Salamancans tr. 19 *de simonia* c. 3, punct. 1 § 2 num. 9 with Laymann, Cajetan, Sylvius, etc). And they say that this would be simony by divine law, with del Soto, Suarez, etc. against Palaus, Laymann, Bonacina, and the Salamancans, n. 12.

Nevertheless, here Busembaum notes, as well as Croix (n. 144) and the Salamancans, *ibid*. n. 11 and 13, with Lessius, del Soto, Filliuci, Suarez, etc. that this rule does not apply if the opposition were from those who can only place an obstacle (Suarez *de simonia* l. 4, cap. 50, n. 23; Palaus, *de simonia* punct. 20 n. 4; Anacletus *eod. tit.* § 13 n. 310; Elbel *de sim*. n. 614). But it is otherwise if they can place an obstacle and at the same time benefit by instituting, presenting or confirming, because then, what is given to them lest they would impede them is necessarily also given to bring a benefit, namely consent by not refusing; and so then by money the path is directly laid to obtain the benefice. I think it must altogether be so held with Anacletus, n. 314, Suarez n. 18, Elbel *l.c.* and Salamancans *dict.* n. 11 and 13, with others, when money is given that an elector would not deny his vote, even if he would unjustly deny it, whatever Palaus might say, asserting that it is probable that it is not simony if money were given only to remove his minor affect. Moreover, Sanchez (*Cons.* l. 2. c. 3 d. 30 n. 5) and Lessius lib. 2 c. 35 n. 107) one does not commit simony when money is given to an elector not to benefit by furnishing a vote, but only to remedy an iniquitous opposition, whereby he would put an obstacle through force or fraud, or suborning others, as above. And this seems sufficiently probable at least in a case in which giving money would manifest that he wishes nothing other than that the other would not unjustly be an obstacle. Mazzota, cap. 3 q. 1 p. 236.

101.—*Quæritur I:* If anyone were to impede electors inclined to me not by force or fraud, but by prayers or gifts, lest they would worthily confer a benefice upon me, on account of a hatred in which they hold me, would I be able to give them money so they would stop? Domingo del Soto, cited by Lessius (dict. cap. 35, n. 109) says no. But Lessius (*loc. cit.*), Croix, (lib. 3 p. 1 n. 147) with Suarez, Laymann and likewise the Salamancans (*dict.* cap. 3 n. 13) with Sanchez, Valentia and Bonacina, rightly affirm that it is lawful because, as Lessius says, if it is licit to give money that another man would stop causing me trouble on account of justice, it is also lawful to give money so that he would stop causing me trouble out of charity, since really such opposition is a temporal thing which I remedy with another temporal thing; on the other hand my money does not pave the way to the benefice except very remotely.

102.—*Quæritur II:* Could I give money so that another man would not oppose himself to my election, although I do not know the electors are inclined to me? The Salamancans say no (*ibid.* n. 14) and they cite Sanchez and Lessius. But it must be noted that Lessius only speaks there on furnishing money to one who can be of use and as well as put up obstacles, but in regard to the other, who can only be an obstacle, and that one wills iniquitously to oppose himself to me by sinning at least against charity, it seems probable according to the same doctrine of Lessius, as above, that it would be lawful to give money so that he would give up that illicit hindrance. And Croix holds this (*l.c.* dict. n. 147) who asserts with the other doctors that always the other also without a reasonable cause would move electors by petitions and gifts that they would not favor me, but the other, it is not simony if I would give him money to stop from that iniquitous disturbance against charity.

103.—*Quæritur III:* Would it be lawful to give money to electors lest they would choose an unworthy man, or that they might choose a worthy one? It is answered, it is licit to give lest an unworthy man be chosen, if it is certain the electors were prepared or at least inclined to choose an unworthy man, because the Church holds the acquired right lest it would be given to an inept minister, as Lessius (*dict.* cap. 35, n. 112) says with the more common opinion, (Croix n. 146). Equally, the Salamancans (tr. 19 *de simonia* cap. 3, punt. 1 § 2 n. 15) with Cajetan, Laymann, del Soto, Suarez, etc. say this is lawful lest a less worthy man be chosen and even that a worthy or more worthy man might be chosen, as they say with Suarez, Lessius, Barbosa, etc. in common. It is not permitted to give money that some worthy man in particular be chosen, even if he is the worthiest in particular, except in the case of necessity, namely if among all only one is discovered worthy whom they refuse to elect. And although such an election would be null according to law, nevertheless, confirmation of it could be sought from the Pope. (Lessius, *loc. cit.*)

104.—*Quæritur IV*: Would it be simony to give money to a competitor so that he would remove himself from competition for the benefice which you are offering? Elbel (*de simonia* n. 609) and Pasqualigo (cited by Croix, lib. 3, p. 1 num. 142) say no, because, as they say, this abstinence from competition on one side cannot be said to be something spiritual, but would be bought, and on the other side, the competitor confers nothing positively in regard to the conferral of the benefice, but only bears himself negatively. But I do not assent to this opinion, and Croix says rightly with Diana and others that it must not be admitted against the common opinion. The reason is, because, as Lessius, Suarez, Palaus, Barbosa etc. (cited by Croix) teach in common with St. Thomas (II IIæ q. 100, art. 2 ad 5) it is merely permitted to remove the opposition with money when the opposition is unjust, but not when it is just, otherwise the way to the benefice would be prepared directly by money, which is altogether illicit.

Quæritur V: Would it be lawful, in a case of urgent necessity, to give money to a priest that refuses to administer the sacraments without it? St. Thomas, Alensis, etc. (cited by Lessius, lib. 2 c. 35, n. 37) reject this, because, as they say, it is never lawful to buy the sacraments, inasmuch as it is intrinsically evil. But Lessius himself (n. 38 and 39) with Adrian, Suarez, (*de simonia* lib. 4, cap. 12, n. 13), Gerson (*de simonia* rat. 6), Cajetan (q. 100 art. 2), Diana (p. 5, tract. 7, v. 16) and Sporer (*de 5 praec.* cap. 1 n. 109) with St. Bonaventure, Vasquez, Pontius and others in common rightly affirm it. The reason is because this is not to buy the sacrament, but to remedy opposition, or more correctly (as Lessius says in n. 410) to permit with a just cause the sin of another. Hence, Diana and Hurtius say this is licit only in the sacrament of baptism and penance, and a great many doctors from those cited would have it so, but also in the other

TREATISE I, THE FIRST PRECEPT, CH. II: ON IRRELIGIOSITY 89

sacraments, exactly as Lessius consents to it in lib. II, ch. 35, n. 38. And not only in the case of gravest necessity (as Suarez and Lessius say), but even in one of grave necessity, say if someone were going to fulfil the precept of Easter confession and communion, or sought viaticum or extreme unction, or were in mortal sin, or even should lack frequent use of the sacraments, and at length, lack the sacrament. But it seems this rightly adheres to those things which we said on scandal in n. 47, where we saw with St. Thomas, St. Augustine and the common opinion that it is licit for the sake of any notable good to permit the sin of another because it comes into being only from his own malice.

"4. Nor similarly is it simony to give a stipend to the "subsistence of a cleric, even if he is rich, for Masses, sermons "or even to bargain over the said stipend. The reason is, because "it is not given as the price of a spiritual duty, but for the sake "of the occupation of the other, nor for the spiritual operation, "as it is a spiritual thing, but as it is received for the sake of "another, and hence it is not almsgiving, but due from justice. "(Suarez, Laymann, lib. 4 tract. 10, c. ult. etc. against Richardus, "Sylvius, etc. (See what was said in n. 55)."

"5. It is not simony to render or buy back a merely temporal "pension, because it is not founded on a spiritual title, nor is it "related to a spiritual function. I said *temporal*, because a "spiritual thing which is given, *e.g.* to preach or assist a Bishop "on account of an ecclesiastical office, and were founded on it, "nor does it differ from a benefice except that it is not "perpetual, nor is it sold: but it is mixed, as *e.g.* what is given to "an old parish priest, or a poor cleric for subsistence, cannot "also be sold; nevertheless it can be bought back, provided the "obligation to recite the Little Office of the Blessed Virgin that "was imposed was not extinguished. But understand, even in a "place where a sale is made, the bull must be received: the "reason is because he buys back a pension, he does not buy a "spiritual thing but extinguishes a temporal burden to pay a "certain sum of money. (Lessius, cap. 35, dub. 21; Suarez, c. 26, "n. 5; Laymann, *loc cit.* n. 46)."

"6. It is not simony by divine law (even if at sometime it can "be of human law), to exchange a spiritual thing with a spiritual "thing, *e.g.* a benefice for a benefice, relics with relics, etc., or to "give a temporal thing for a temporal thing, say if you sold a "chalice or an *agnus Dei* precisely by reckoning the matter; or "to give a temporal thing for a spiritual one by the mode of a "gratuitous gift, even with the hope or intention of causing "remuneration of a spiritual gift; or vice versa, the reasoning "that gratitude does not regard a price, but a benefice; nor does "he pay a debt of justice, but an antidoral debt in which it is not "excluded that something be given for free. (See n. 51 and 54). "Nevertheless, Suarez rightly advises that one must be very "careful of gifts of this sort, on account of presumption. "Likewise, to give, to promise, or to deny any temporal thing "you like, under the condition of furnishing a spiritual work, "provided it were not done by the mode of repayment, or "exchange, *e.g.* if a parent promises a gift to their son if they "would frequent the sacraments; the reason is, because here an "onerous contract does not intervene, rather it consists either in "a liberal donation or in a donation under such a condition and "mode. Suarez, lib. 4, c. 45; Laymann, d. cap. n. 8. (See n. 59)."

ARTICLE II
What is the penalty for simony?

105. What are the penalties that simony induces? Would penalties be incurred in the sale of the sacraments, or of unprovided chaplaincies?
106. To incur the penalties, should simony be carried out by both parties?
107. Would one incur penalties who obtains a benefice by a feigned promise of money?

108. *Would penalties be incurred by simony that were merely so by ecclesiastical law? Would they be incurred on account of entrance into a religious order?*
109. *What are the penalties for a simoniacal ordination?*
110. *Would they be incurred on account of the conferral of first tonsure?*
111. *What are the penalties on account of simony in benefices?*
112. *Would penalties be incurred in the sale of a vicarage, or another non-moveable office? For a pension, chaplaincy, or for the sacraments and jurisdiction? Then four things are asked. Quaer. I. Are simoniacal elections to the prelatures of regulars null? Qu. II. Are penalties incurred on account of benefices simoniacally received by those who are ignorant? Qu. III. Would a simoniacal holder of a benefice ipso facto be deprived from the benefices he has obtained, and would he become unsuitable to obtain future benefices? Qu. IV. Would the simoniacal election of a Pope be null?*

105.—"*Resp.* 1. Only simony of confidence, and real simony "in Holy Orders, an ecclesiastical benefice and entry into "religious orders induces penalties *ipso facto*, although on "account of entry into a religious order it is rarely incurred, as "has been said, or on account of the poverty of a monastery, or "contrary to received custom." (See n. 92), Suarez, c. 56 and 57; "Lessius, dub. 23; Laymann, *loc. cit.* § 7."

In the sale of other things, namely of the sacraments, jurisdiction, pension or an unsupported chaplaincy, even if one sins, still no penalty is incurred. Lessius, l. 2, c. 53, n. 25; Salamancans tr. 19, *de simonia* c. 4, punct. 1 n. 1, with the common opinion. See n. 112.

106.—*Quaeritur I:* To incur penalties, is it required that simony be carried out by both parties? There are two opinions and both are probable.

The first opinion says no, and the Salamancans themselves hold this (*ibid.* n. 9) with del Soto, Cajetan, Palaus, etc. For they say it suffices that spiritual goods be given, since, after the thing is given a sale takes place even if the price were not paid, provided it is furnished on trust for it, from L *Inter Patrem,* lib. 2, ff. *de Contrahend. empt.*

Just the same, *the second opinion* is more common and more probable, which many authors hold. (Lessius, lib. 2, cap. 35, dub. 27; Navarre, *Man.* c. 23, n. 104; Suarez *de simonia* cap. 56, n. 33; Annacletus, n. 240; Croix, n. 112; Roncaglia, cap. 1, quaest. 2; Elbel, num. 628; likewise, Laymann, Sanchez, Covarruvias, Moya, etc. cited by Salamancans *ibid.* n. 7). Palaus and others call this opinion more probable, and it says that completion is required by both parties. Reason 1) because the sale is not altogether completed at the same time as the buying, unless the thing is given and for a price. Reason 2) (which I am more convinced of) because nowhere in law are penalties inflicted against simony that is not completed on every side, and *in penalties a gentler interpretation must be made*, as is held in *cap. 40 de reg. juris* in 6, and this is the style of the curia (which is held for a law with Elbel and the common opinion) as Navarre and others witness, namely to not judge that penalties have been incurred unless the simony was consummated on both sides. Hence, the doctors infer that one receiving a benefice with an agreement to furnish money should not be held to resign his benefice before payment, nor restore the fruits. Nevertheless, it must be noted: 1) with Lessius (*ibid.* n. 15 and Salamancans *ibid.* n. 6) that if only the part promised were paid, it is now understood to be perfect simony on both sides. It must be noted 2) that from simony completed on both sides, no matter how secret, penalties are incurred, as in *Extrav. 2 de simonia.* See Elbel, n. 620. It must be noted 3) That if the simony were confidential, penalties are incurred even by conventional mixed simony, *viz.* completed by one party, from the bull of St. Pius V, *Intolerabilis,* § 3. (See Anacletus l. 5; Decret. tit. 3, n. 284; Elbel num. 629, and see below num. 111, near the end, resp. 4.

107.—*Quæritur II:* Would one commit simony and incur penalties who obtained a benefice through a feigned promise of money that was never carried out? Pichler (lib. 5, tit. 3, n. 13 and Pontas v. *Simonia,* cas. 5) say this is enough to commit simony, because to incur the penalty it is not required that in fact a temporal thing is handed over, but it suffices that through the motive of a temporal thing a spiritual thing were obtained. Nevertheless, I think it must be said in regard to fault a man cannot be excused from the sin of simony because he at least cooperates in the simony of the one that confers it. In regard to the matter itself I reckon it more probable with Elbel n. 625 and other very serious doctors that he sins not by the sin of simony since, lacking the will to oblige himself to the promise, a true purchase (which is required for simony) does not take place. Yet, in regard to the penalties for simony, I think with Croix (l. 6, p. 2 n. 200 and 204), he does not incur them since the simony lacked completion on both sides, as we recently said in the preceding question.

108.—*Quæritur III:* Would penalties be incurred for simony that were merely established by ecclesiastical law, say, if someone buys the office of the sacristy, etc. or if he will resign a benefice with a pension on his own authority, as we noted above? Elbel, n. 627, and Navarre, del Soto, Villalobos, etc. (cited by Salamancans tr. 19 *de simonia* cap. 4 punct. 1 n. 10) affirm it, who say it is very probable, but other authors call the negative opinion no less probable. (Salamancans *ib.* n. 11, with Sanchez, Rodriguez, Diana, Aragon, etc. and Roncaglia, cap. 4, q. 1 resp. 4). The reason is because laws which impose penalties must commonly be understood as rigorous on simony, which is also against divine law, as is proved from *Extravaganti,* 2, *de simonia* which begins: "Since the authority of divine and sacred canons abhor the crime of simoniacal depravity, etc."

Moreover, it is certain that from *c. 1 Extrav. de simonia*, those giving and receiving something for entrance into a religious order incur *ipso facto* papal excommunication. But it must be noted 1) with Navarre, Sanchez, Bonacina (cited by Salamancans *ibid.* punct. 2 n. 12) that they do not incur it unless they take it for granted, as is gathered from the text. Hence those who are ignorant, even culpably, are excused. It must be noted 2) It is very probable that they do not incur them in simple entrance, but in profession. (Salamancans *ibid.* with Bonacina, Palaus, etc.) It must be noted 3) with Lessius (l. 3 c. 35 dub. 23 n. 131 and Navarre, Sylvius, Palaus (cited by Salamancans *ibid.*) this *Extravagantis*, as above, at least in regard to this excommunication is not in received use. Lastly, it must be noted that a profession done simoniacally is certainly valid, as St. Thomas teaches (q. 100, art. 3 ad 5). But if the one receiving were a whole community, or a chapter, beyond excommunication (which we say is not received in use) then it incurs suspension that is also reserved to the Pope by his office, in execution of the chapter law, and in the administration of jurisdiction. Likewise, infamy of law is incurred by both parties, and consequently irregularity. Furthermore, one that was admitted simoniacally ought to be transferred to a stricter monastery, but not before the sentence. Elbel, n. 626, *ex ead. Extr. 2.*

109.—"*Resp.* 2. On account of simoniacal conferral and "reception of orders, even of first tonsure, excommunication "and papal suspension is incurred. Lessius, disp. 24; Layman, "*loc. cit.*"

"Beyond excommunication and papal suspension, which "Bishops simoniacally ordaining and well as the mediators for it "incur *ipso facto* (from *c. Cum detes. Extrav.5 de simonia*), they "incur also interdict from entrance to the Church. And if they "will have violated the suspension, or interdict, they are "suspended from the rule of the Church and deprived from the "reception of the fruits, from the *Motu Proprio* of Sixtus V. See "Salamancans *de simonia* tr. 19, c. 4, p. 2 n. 14."

Moreover, those ordained, beyond the aforesaid excommunication and suspension *ipso facto* (from *c. 2 Extrav.* and especially from the bull of Sixtus V), they are suspended from the exercise of their orders, but only of those which ordinand received simoniacally, as Lessius teaches (c. 35, n. 135) and it is probable what the Salamancans think (*ibid.* n. 15 against Palaus and Rodriguez). And they are also suspended from the hope of ascending to higher orders. But Lessius (d. lib. num. 136), with the common opinion, and the Salamancans (d. n. 15) with del Soto, Laymann, Sanchez, note that this suspension is not incurred if the ordinate did not know that the other committed simony. Then, the Salamancans note (d. n. 15) with Palaus and Lessius (*ibid.* n. 134) that although from the bull of Sixtus V the absolution for this suspension is reserved to the Pope and the faculties conceded to religious are revoked in this regard, and also to Bishops (Trent, sess. 25, c. 6) still they say in this part (Lessius and Palaus) the bull is not received; and the Salamancans confirm the same (tr. 19 c. 4 punct. 4 n. 34 with Sa and Suarez.

110.—*Quæritur:* Would the aforesaid penalties be incurred in the simoniacal conferral of first tonsure? Busembaum and Covarruvias affirm it (cited by Lessius, c. 35 n. 133), because from the Council of Trent, sess. 21, cap. 1 *de Ref.*, it is forbidden for something to be received by a Bishop and his ministers even if hitherto it was freely offered, for the conferral of first tonsure, or for dimissorial letters or testimonials and for the seal and other things, and vice versa those doing it, are declared at the end of the aforesaid chapter of Trent to incur penalties inflicted by law. But the Salamancans (*ibid.* punct. 2 n. 14) with Palaus more probably deny it, because tonsure is not a true order according to what is going to be said in book 6, n. 734. And Lessius teaches the same thing (n. 133, although Busembaum cites him in favor of his position), saying that there is no law that establishes excommunication for these, nor did the Council mean to enjoin new penalties. He says equally, it seems harsh for Bishops to incur censure and the ministers receiving something freely offered, even if they sin. Nay more, St. Thomas permits this in II IIæ qu. 100 a. 2 ad 4 saying: "But if [something] were furnished as some type of stipend and it is approved by custom it is not simony if it lacks the intention to buy or sell ... and especially when someone pays voluntarily." Just the same, the Angelic doctor spoke of simony by divine law; but by ecclesiastical law this is forbidden by the Council of Trent (*loc. cit.*) where all customs, even immemorial ones are rejected inasmuch as they ought rather to be called an abuse. Furthermore, Croix (l. 3 part. 1 n. 167) seems to think, and not improbably, that only customs which existed before the Council were rejected as perhaps immoderate, but not those which are not to give something moderate, and which can be presumed to have been introduced for a just cause, for these can well avail according to what was said on law in book 1, n. 108.

Hence, Mazzota says (*de sacr. Ord.* cap. 1 §6) with Navarre and Lopez, a Bishop does not commit simony if he were to receive something freely offered later (but not before) order was conferred, for this is expressly permitted in *can. Sicut, caus. 1 quaest. 2*, only the Bishop cannot seek it; where it is said: "If the one, however, that was ordained, after he has received papers and the pallium wished to give something to anyone at all from the clergy out of thankfulness if it is not from an agreement nor exacted, nor sought from him, by no means do we forbid this to be accepted, because his offering brings in no stain of sin, as it does not proceed from the request of a solicitor." St. Gregory the Great agrees in *Epistle 44*. So it seems it is equally permitted for notaries according to the approved customs of places, to exact something for their subsistence, if for their work something is offered, in regard to acts confecting ordinations, no salary were assigned to them, as is deduced from the same council.

111.—"Resp. 3. On account of *real* simony in an ecclesiastical "benefice, the following are incurred: 1) Papal "excommunication; 2) the election, presentation, confirmation "or institution is made void: wherefore such a thing does not "yield its fruits. And also, although he did not know it was "provided in such a way by a third party,[9] as is held from *cap.* "*Nobis fuit, de simonia* unless he will have opposed it, or unless "money was given by a third party by fraud that you would be "rendered unsuitable; or unless he possessed the benefice in "good faith for 30 years." (As Lessius, *dict.* cap. 35, n. 149; Laymann, lib. 4, tract. 10 cap. ult.; Con l. 2 n. 20; Elbel, n. 640, with Suarez, Palaus, etc. teach in common. Nor does the rule of a chancery stand in the way, where it is absolutely required that a benefice be obtained *without simoniacal entrance*, for it is understood on one who culpably enters; Elbel, *ibid.* with Anacletus. Hence, the holder of a benefice is not held to make restitution—nor even before 30 years—the fruits consumed in good faith if the endower did not evade, as St. Thomas, II IIæ. q. 100 art. 6 ad 3; Salamancans tr. 19 *de simonia* cap. 4 punct. 2 n. 18; and Elbel n. 646, who very probably add that restitution does not need to be made for fruits taken in regard to the stole and of other parochial functions, namely funerals, sermons, administration of the sacraments, etc. The reason is because

---

[9] St. Alphonsus adds: "Exactly as it was ratified in c. 33, *de simonia*. Nevertheless, here it must be noted with Lessius, in c. 33 n. 145 and Elbel n. 652, that not withstanding your opposition, you cannot also accept the benefice if you know the money was really given by a third party for conferral of it; for the text only excuses you from the case in which 'against your prohibition', the words of the text, 'someone, while you were altogether ignorant, promised and paid.' Note that, 'while you were altogether ignorant', therefore, if you accept the benefice, knowing that it was conferred upon you by the simony of another, you cannot accept it, and if you were to do so, 'you cannot retain it'."

these fruits are not given as revenues of a benefice, but as stipends of office; so that according to the common opinion of the doctors on these, a parish priest can freely dispense, even for profane use, as de Lugo says, *de just.* d. 4, n. 13; Bonacina, d. 4. n. 13; Bonacina d. 4 p. 2 n. 19; Busembaum. See book 5, n. 185. Sanchez *Cons.* lib. 2 cap. 2 d. 45 n. 4, who calls it by far the more probable opinion, with Navarre, Panormus, Hostiensis, del Soto, Sylvester, Covarruvias, and many others, against only Innocent). "Thirdly: A man is made unsuitable to the same "benefice even with a dispensation obtained from the Bishop. "Nevertheless, he is not deprived of other benefices by law, nor "rendered unsuitable to obtain others before the sentence of the "judge. Suarez, cap. 54, n. 7." (But if someone in good faith took up a benefice, although it were obtained by the simony of a third party, the Bishop can probably dispense him for the same benefice, provided the one holding the benefice would first renounce it. St. Thomas agrees in II IIæ qu. 100, art. 6 ad 7, and Elbel, n. 642, from *c. 59 de electionibus*).

"Resp. 4. Simony of confidence that has been completed after "a benefice has been given and received (even if the recipient "turn does not fulfill the promise), induces: 1) Papal "excommunication contracted by both parties; 2) Annuls the "resignation and conferral of the benefice in the man to whom "it was attached, and he becomes unsuitable to later obtain the "same benefice; 3) He deprived of all benefices, and pensions "previously obtained, still, not before the sentence is imposed; "4) Benefices conferred in this way are reserved to the Pope "alone. Lessius cap. 35, n. 176; Suarez, cap. 43; Laymann, n. 76."

112.—Here, it must be noted above all, that by the name of benefices and offices, to which all simoniacal election is invalid by the law itself, as is discerned in *Extrav.* 2, *de simonia*, immovable vicariates, pensions, unsupported chaplaincies, or the offices of an inquisitor, legate, or of anyone having spiritual jurisdiction for a time do not come with an agreement, because these are not properly ecclesiastical offices, Although, to sell these is simoniacal by positive law, nevertheless, they do not incur penalties as the doctors say in common. (Salamancans tr. 19 cap. 4, punct. 2 n. 16, with Suarez, Palaus, Sanchez, etc. likewise Viva, *Opus de benef. q. ult.* art. 3 num. 9 with Filliuci and Reginald against Garcia). Nor is any penalty incurred in the sale of a layman's benefice, or the coadjutor of a benefice, as Croix says (lib. 3, p. 1 n. 114) nor in the sale of sacraments or spiritual jurisdiction. Lessius, lib. 2 cap. 55 n. 23, and Salamancans *ibid.* cap. 4, p. 1 n. 1 with the common opinion.

Quæritur I: Are simoniacal elections to the generalate, abbacy, provincialate, priorate, rectorate, and other spiritual offices in religious orders invalid? Bonacina (quaest. 7 p. 2) and Viva (*loc. cit.*) say no. But the truer opinion must be to affirm it, as Cabassutius teaches (*Theor. Jur.* lib. 5, cap. 8 n. 5), as well as Sanchez (*Cons.* l. 2 cap. 5 d. 104 n. 5 and 11) with Sylvester, Cajetan, Armilla and Lopez, likewise Lessius lib. 2 cap. 35 n. 137 and Elbel n. 622, who rightly adds in n. 638 that he does not see by what conscience those electors could be excused from the sin of simony who choose someone as a general with an agreement that later they would be chosen as definitors, guardians, etc. The reason for this opinion is that, although the aforesaid offices are really not benefices, nevertheless, they are expressly included under the name of offices in the same *Extravagantes* 2, where it is so said: "But through elections, provisions, etc., which it came to pass were subverted by simony, and when men are not altogether lacking in the Churches, *monasteries,* dignities, priroties, ecclesiastical offices and any benefice you like, ... a right has in nowise been acquired by anyone."

Quæritur II: Would the aforesaid penalties be incurred on account of simoniacal benefices accepted by the ignorant?

Resp. If the ignorance was altogether inculpable, certainly it must be denied, from *reg. 23 de Regul. Jur.* in 6°, where it is said:

"Someone is not to be punished without fault, unless a cause was present." Nevertheless, it must be noted with Elbel, n. 656, that not withstanding this inculpable ignorance, the provision of a benefice will always be null, since unsuitability to the same benefice is not a penalty but established in law to preclude evils. Still, A bishop will be able to dispense in that case, after the renunciation of the benefice, as was said above in n. 111. On the other hand, what if the simoniac knew that he committed simony, but was is invincibly ignorant of the penalty? In regard to censures, he certainly does not incur them, from the common opinion. See book 7 on censures, n. 43. But in regard to the other penalties, the more probable and common opinion is that he incurs them, as Elbel says (n. 657) with Azor, Laymann, etc., but n. 658 thinks the negative opinion is probable, which Pichler holds, to the extent that penalties established by law are not incurred by the ignorant, as Sanchez, Krimer, etc. say with Pichler, who says for that reason a man is excused from the impediment of the crime not knowing a woman was married, with whom he sinned.

Quæritur III: Would a simoniac holding a benefice incur *ipso facto* deprivation of benefices already obtained, and unsuitability to other benefices obtained? In regard to the penalty of deprivation, the Doctors most commonly teach with Busembaum, as above, that he is not deprived of benefices already obtained, nor their fruits before the condemnatory sentence of the judge, because there is no law designating this express penalty *ipso facto*. (Sanchez, *loc. cit.* d. 14, n. 16; Laymann, c. 8 n. 75; Bonacina, p. 2 diss. 2; Suarez c. 58, n. 6 and Salamancans tr. 19 *de simonia*, c. 4 punct. 2 n. 19, with Filliuci, Palaus, Rodriguez, etc. An exception is made: 1) simony is committed by examiners of parochial benefices elected in a Synod, who if they receive something on the occasion of examination, are deprived *ipso facto* of benefices they already rightly obtained before any sentence, as is expressly held in the Council of Trent, sess. 24, c. 18 *de Reformatione*; 2) confidential simony, from the *Motu Proprio* of St. Pius V, *Cum primum*, published in 1566, where accepting a benefice in confidence, they are deprived of all benefices, even justly obtained earlier, and they are held to lay them aside before the sentence. But to incur this penalty in these cases, it is required at least a declaratory sentence of the crime, as the authors hold (Suarez, c. 44 n. 13; Sanchez, d. 34, n. 13; Laymann, c. ult. § 8; Salamancans *ibid.* c. 3, punct. 5, n. 73 with Henriquez, etc.) The reason is, because all penalties depriving one of rights already acquired are not incurred before at least a declaratory sentence of the crime, as we said l. 1 n. 148, and according to the most probable opinion, which the authors follow. (Sanchez, *de matr.* l. 2 d. 53, n. 5; Lessius, l. 2 c. 29, d. 8 and c. 34, d. 34; Cajetan *in Sum v. Poena*; del Soto l. 1 q. 6, art. 6 and Salamancans *de leg.* c. 2 punct. 3 § 2 n. 60 with Molina, Salas, Palaus, Ledesma, Granada, against Vasquez, Bonacina, etc.). They would have it that no sentence is required if the guilty man can undergo the penalty without infamy, because it is very rigid, that the guilty suffers penalties of himself, and deprives him of the goods he possesses. But if the examiners wish to be absolved from the sin of simony, I do not know how they can be absolved except they would lay aside the benefices, since it is said by the Council of Trent: "From which (*i.e.*, from simony) they cannot be absolved until the benefices have been laid aside."

Moreover, in regard to incurring unsuitability to obtain other benefices:

The first opinion holds it is incurred before the condemnatory sentence of a judge. (Bonacina, d. 1 q. 7 p. 2, *diffic.* 2; Laymann, l. 4 tr. 10 c. 8 n. 74; Filliuci tr. 45, c. 13, q. 9 n. 26; likewise, Ugolino *de Simonia*, tab. 4 cap. 6 §6, n. 2, v. *Quoad secundam*; Henriquez lib. 13, cap. 37 n. 5; Medina *Sum.*, lib. 1 cap. 14 §20; Lopez, and Rodrigez, cited by the Salamancans in *de simonia* tr. 19 c. 4 punct. 2 n. 20). The reason is, because it is expressly held in the *Motu Proprio* of St. Pius V, *Cum primum*, as above, where it was so ratified: "Anyone that simoniacly acquired a benefice or ecclesiastical office is perpetually unsuitable to obtain it and any other benefice." But to incur penalties making one unsuitable, no knowledge is required, as was said in book 1 on law, n. 149.

But *the second opinion* is more common and probable, which many authors hold. (Sanchez, *Cons.* l. 2, c. 3 d. 104, n. 14; Navarre, *de simonia*, Consil. 92; Cabassutius, *theor. jur.* l. 5 c. 8 n. 9; Suarez, *de rel.* t. lib. 4, c. 58, n. 11; Viva *Opusc.* de benef. q. ult. art. 3 n. 2; Elbel *de simonia* n. 627, with Anacletus, Pichler, Salamancans *ibid.* n. 21; P. Navarre, l. *de rest.* c. 2 n. 43). Lessius and Palaus (cited by Salamancans *ibid.*) call it probable, and deny the aforesaid unsuitability is incurred before the condemnatory sentence of the judge.

The reason is: 1) because the bull of S.t Pius V that was related must really be understood for the external form, since he speaks about those convicted; for there he says: "Whoever has been convicted of the detestable crime of simoniacal depravity, etc." 2) Because if the bull were understood to be about the internal form, nevertheless, it was not received, as Suarez, Navarre, Sanchez, and the Salamancans show, at least, as Viva says, the bull was merely received in use in the first sense of the external forum. Nor is the opinion which we followed in book 1, n. 97 opposed, *viz.* that in doubt, as to whether a law has been received, the law rightly obliges: for here we are not continuing in doubt, but in a probable opinion, since it is very probable by the authority of the doctors, as above, that this law was not received. For, in doubt presumption favors the law, when there is a crime, in not receiving a just law, it is not presumed. For when it is probable, that the obligation of the law never began (or that the law was abolished) then the presumption in favor of the law ceases, and *libertas possidet*, as Sanchez, Laymann, and Palaus teach with the Salamancans (*de leg.* c. 2 punct. 6 §6 n. 120). Nevertheless, nobody doubts that unsuitability to the same benefice received simoniacally is incurred *ipso facto* before every sentence, since this was established on an ancient law in *Extrav.* 2, *de simonia* on whose reception there is no doubt. Moreover, Sanchez notes (*l.c.* n. 15, with Navarre and others) that after the condemnatory sentence of the judge follows, the simoniac will indeed be unsuitable in conscience to any other benefice, when through the sentence he becomes infamous and consequently is irregular.

Moreover, although I made mention on the aforesaid *Extravaganti*, 2, here I thought to annotate it, because in the end of it I found it was ratified, for there it is commanded: "for each and every individual ecclesiastic, and secular by the virtue of holy obedience, that all those who committed simony of this sort, or procured or knew there were mediators, let them not omit to reveal to the Pope as quickly as possible by themselves or through others, even if they were participants ... But if they were not, let them not avail to be absolved until they will reveal the aforesaid, and those found to be participants of this sort will be more severely punished." But the aforesaid *Extravagans* in this part was not received in use, nor is anyone obligated to it unless it were curial of the Apostolic See, as a great many serious authors say who are cited by Cabassutius, *Th. Jur.* l. 5, c. 8 n. 5, who cites Navarre, Cajetan, Suarez, etc.

Quæritur IV: Would the simoniacal election of the Roman Pontiff be invalid? Suarez (*de simonia* c. 57) and Filliuci, etc. cited by Viva (*Op. de benef.* qu. 10 art. 1 n. 8) say no, and they try to show it from *cap. Licet 6 de elect.* where Alexander III established, "that the one that is held to be the Roman Pontiff without any exception by the universal Church, who had been elected by two parts of the Cardinals, and received." The reason is, because if such an election would be made void, the Church could easily be without a head; at least for a time it would be uncertain. Nevertheless, Cabassutius (*Th. jur.* l. 5 c. 5 n. 17), Bonacina (q. 7 p. 2) and Viva (*l.c.*) more truly confirm it from the common opinion. It is clearly proved from *cap. Si Quis*, dist. 79, where Nicholas II so ratified: "If anyone by money or human favor, without the peaceful and canonical election of Cardinals and of the religious clergy following them, was enthroned on the Apostolic see, it is not considered Apostolic, but apostate." It is confirmed more clearly by the [fifth] Lateran Council held under Julius II (sess. 5) where it was said: "It is established with the approval of this sacred council, that the election of a Roman Pontiff done through simony becomes null because of this very thing; and so no faculty is granted to the one elected in spiritual or temporal things." From such words it is clear that a Pope elected through simony can not validate his election. Nor is the text cited above in *cap. Licet* opposed, nor the reason deduced that the Church would remain without a head, for as Lessius (l. 2 c. 35 n 146) and Viva rightly say, with the common opinion, from the force of *l. Barbarius*, when common error is posited with a specious title, if the simony were secret, in that case the Church would supply jurisdiction; for this reason all acts of the Pope of this sort will be truly valid, and his definitions will still have infallible authority, as it is declared in the cited chapter *Licet*. It is otherwise if the simony were public. However, the bull of Julius II as related above has not been received, as Suarez says, and Viva says it is shunned as worthless.

ARTICLE III
Must what was simoniacally received be restored, and to whom?

113. *Nothing spiritual received simoniacally must be restored, except for a benefice and its fruits.*
114. *The price received for a benefice, ordination, etc. must be restored.*
115. *To whom must it be restored?*
116. *To whom are the fruits of a benefice simoniacally received restored?*
117. *Who could dispense in the aforesaid penalties? Even to n. 120.*

113.—"*Resp. 1.* Nothing spiritual received simoniacally apart "from a benefice (under which a pension is contained, "according to Bonacina, although Lessius denies that) must be "restored. The reason is, because the rest either cannot be "restored, such as sacraments, or they must not be restored "before the sentence, because the canons did not establish "anything else. Lessius, n. 86; Suarez, Filliuci, etc. (The "Salamancans hold the same thing, c. 4, n. 23, 27, 28, with "Sanchez, del Soto, and Palaus, against Azor, Laymann, "Bonacina, d. 1 q. 7, p. 5 diss. 2).

"I said *apart from a benefice*; "because this cannot be "retained, even before the sentence of a judge; as is clear from "*cap. Si quis neque* 1, q 1, and from *4 Extravag. Cum detestabile, de simonia,*" (The same thing must be said for receiving a price for the conferral of orders and entrance into a religious order from *c. De hoc,* and *c. Veniens, de simonia.* See Salamancans c. 4, n. 29) "Bonacina adds that the fruits received must also be "restored, not only because they cannot be retained by a just "title, but even more because simoniacal acquisition of a "benefice is *ipso facto* invalid; moreover, it is expressly held in "*Extr. Cum detestabile, de simonia.* See St. Thomas, II IIæ qu. 100, "art. 6; Navarre, lib. 5, *cons. 62,* Lessius, l. 2 c. 35, dub. 31."

114.—"*Resp. 2.* The price received for a benefice, conferral of "orders, sacraments, and sacramentals, if it would notably "exceed that which could be demanded for subsistence, likewise "for admission to a religious order, must be restored by positive "law. Nevertheless, this last only after the sentence has been "imposed, if the one admitted into a monastery would remain; "because by reason of providing for many it can be retained, "provided it is converted into common use. See Bonacina, *loc.* "*cit.*; Lessius, l. 2 c. 35 d. 30." (with Palaus, Laymann, Sanchez, "cited by Salamancans *ibid.* n. 31, *in fine*, and Elbel n. 635, as is "held in *Extr.* Sanchez *de simonia*, where it is said that goods "received simoniacally for the entrance to a religious order can "be retained and applied to the common use of the monastery).

"*Resp. 3.* What was received for a benefice or another "spiritual thing, not following the conferral, must be restored to "the one from whom it was received by natural law, because "the title to retain it is lacking, since it is not furnished for "whom it was given. But if a thing were handed over, the "simony completed on every side, it is more probable that it "must be restored to the Church, not to the one giving it, "because the Church intends to punish both of them. Lessius; "Laymann, *loc.* "*cit.* § 9."

115.—*Quæritur I:* When a man has already given a spiritual thing with simony, and received the price, to whom is he held to make restitution? There are three opinions, and they are all probable:

The first holds, before the sentence the price must be restored to the one that gave it, because the recipient was incapable by positive law to acquire it, he retains ownership in view of the owner, who intends by no other reasoning to renounce his claim to it, except insofar as he would transfer it upon the seller. So Sanchez, *Cons.* l. 2 c. 3 dub. 114 n. 11; Lessius l. 2 c. 35, n. 171; with

Valentia, Soto, Bañez, Aragon, Rodriguez, etc. cited by Salamancans c. 4 n. 30.

The second opinion holds that it must be restored to the Church in which the benefice is located, from *c. De hoc* and *c. Audivimus, de simonia*. And this in punishment for irreverence inflicted upon the Church in the sale of its things. St. Thomas, II IIæ qu. 100, art. 6, ad 3 and 5; Salamancans *dict.* n. 31; St. Antoninus, Laymann, Suarez, Cajetan, etc. with Busembaum as above.

The third opinion says, from custom restitution can be made by giving it to the poor, as St. Thomas also admits (II IIæ q. 32 art. 7 and q. 62, art. 5 ad 2), with Palaus, Victoria, Covarruvias, etc. Laymann calls it probable (cited by Salamancans *dict.* n. 31) because the one receiving the price according to these, all of these opinions will be able to be sufficiently probable (as the Salamancans rightly say, n. 31), insofar as they all agree restitution must be made, whether to the one giving it, to the Church, or to the poor, and even themselves if they are needy (Salamancans *ibid.* with Sanchez). But the price for entry into a religious order must be restored to the one that gave it so that he might take it to the monastery to which he is transferred, and to supply that when he ought, as we read *c. Veniens, de simonia*. Still, if he would remain, the monastery may retain what was given, as Sanchez, Palaus, Suarez, and Laymann, cited by Salamancans *loc. cit.*

116.—*Quæritur II*: To whom the fruits of a benefice must be restored that were acquired through simony? St. Thomas teaches that restitution must be made to the Church (q. 100, art. 6 ad 4) provided those that committed simony do not receive the profit for it. But it is probable that it can also be restored to the poor, or to his successor in the benefice, or even arrange those that can receive with the Pope for the aforesaid fruits, as Salamancans *ibid.* n. 42, with Navarre, Sylvius, and Sanchez.

117.—Lastly, it must be seen who can absolve in the aforesaid penalties, or dispense? It is certain from *cap. pen. de simonia*, that only the Pope could absolve excommunication and suspension in the simoniacal order received, unless the aforesaid censures were secret, and in that case a Bishop can also absolve, from *cap. Liceat* 6, sess. 24, *de ref.* Conc. Trid. and even mendicant confessors, as Elbel says (n. 645) with Suarez, Palaus, from the common opinion. Moreover, Lessius (lib. 2 c. 35 n. 34) and Salamancans (c. 4 n. 34 in fine) say that the bull to the contrary of St. Pius V was not received in this matter.

In regard to the suspension of Orders rightly received, it is probable that a Bishop can absolve it, as Suarez holds (4 *de simonia* c. 61, n. 4) and the Salamancans (n. 34). Although they think the opposite is more probable, with Palaus and Sylvius, in a case in which a cleric was knowingly ordained from simony, and they say the same thing on suspension of the one performing the ordination.

In regard to unsuitability to obtain other benefices apart from that obtained simoniacally, a Bishop can dispense. (Sanchez, l. 2, c. 3, d. 120, art. 31 and Sylvius, Imola, Felinus. An exception is made if the simony was confidential, or if the simoniac awaits a sentence, because then he is irregular by the infamy of the law (Salamancans *d. n.* 38, in fine, and Elbel n. 631 and 645, with Lessius, Palaus, Henriquez, etc.).

118.—There is a great doubt, whether a bishop could dispense a man so that he can hold the same benefice which he received simoniacally?

We must preface in this the words of the Pope in *c. Si alicujus penult. de elect.*, "If the election of someone on account of simony, while he was ignorant and it was not yet ratified, but forfeited, if it were to come to pass that he is condemned, then the Bishop cannot in turn dispense in regard to that prelature for which he was so elected, although in regard to someone who ignorantly received a simple benefice through simony after a free resignation, the dispensation of a Bishop endures." Hence, in regard to the doubt, we answer: 1) That, if a benefice was simple (even of a canonry or a dignity, for whom there is no care of souls, as Sanchez and Navarre say with Salamancans, c. 4 n. 35) and was received ignorantly through simony (viz. when simony was commissioned by another, while the beneficer was ignorant, as the doctors understand in common, cited by Salamancans d. n. 35); then a Bishop can also dispense in that vacancy, provided the beneficiary will renounce it of his own free will, so Sanchez (l. 2, c. 3 dub. 120, n. 22); Palaus d. 3 p. ult. n. 3 and Salamancans d. n. 35, with Sylvius, Navarre and the Gloss in c. *A nobis de sim.* See what was said in 111. We answer: 2) That if, moreover, the benefice is a curature, a Bishop cannot dispense with it in that interchange, rather, he can in another vacancy with someone who was ignorant. Salamancans, *loc. cit.* n. 37; Panormus, in cap. *De simoniace, de simon.* n. 7; Palaus *loc. cit.* num. 3; Sanchez *loc. cit.* dub. 120, n. 321 and 34, etc. We answer: 3) What if someone knowingly and simoniacly received a benefice, whether a simple one, or a curature, even if he were to renounce it of his own will? A bishop cannot dispense with him to hold the same benefice, neither for that interchange or for another; just as St. Thomas teaches (q. 100 art. 6 ad 7), and Salamancans (*ibid.* n. 38) with del Soto, Palaus and Sanchez, although a Bishop could dispense to obtain other benefices, even if the simony were confidential, as we said above in n. 117.

119.—*Quæritur III:* Could even a Bishop be imparted the aforesaid dispensations in which simony was committed? Panormus denies it, and his opinion is probable. But the Salamancans (*ibid.* n. 39), with Navarre and Sanchez more probably affirm it, from *c. Si quis presbyterorum, de rebus ecclesiasticis non alienis*, and *cap. penult. de simonia,* where the faculty is conceded to Bishops without distinction.

120.—*Quæritur IV*: The Pope, when conferring a benefice on someone that he knows is unsuitable to receive it on account of simony, is he regarded to dispense? Palaus (d. 3, p. ult. n. 9), Suarez (l. 4 c. ult. n. 14), del Soto (l. 9 q. 5 art. 2) and Salamancans (c. 4 n. 40) with Torre affirm it as probable. And they say the same thing if a Pope sells a benefice to someone. (See Croix n. 232). Nevertheless, it must be noted that if a Pope confirms an election, not knowing the vice of simony, even if in a bull he would say he supplies for all defects, the confirmation is not valid, because it is understood about other defects in the election, not on simony. (Croix n. 234).

TREATISE II
ON THE SECOND PRECEPT OF THE DECALOGUE

"This precept forbids all disordered taking of the name of "God, the kind that is especially done in blaspheming, rashly "swearing an oath or taking a vow and not keeping it. It is on "such things that we take up the argument here."

CHAPTER I
WHAT IS BLASPHEMY AND HOW MANIFOLD IS IT?

121. *What is blasphemy?*
122. *In how many ways is blasphemy committed against God?*
123. *When must heretical blasphemy be denounced?*
124. and 125. *Which jokes are or are not blasphemy?*
126. *Must it be explained [in confession] if someone directly intended to dishonor God?*
127. *To what is someone held to who does it out of habit?*
128. *What if someone were to utter: "O death of God! O wounds of Christ! being angry against a man?"*
129. Would it be blasphemy to curse created things and days?
130. *Would it be blasphemy to curse the dead? to curse the faith?*
131. *Would it be blasphemy to call down a demon on others or himself?*
132. *Do blasphemies against God and the saints differ in species?*

121.—"*Resp.* Blasphemy is directly opposed to the praise of "God, it is a word of a curse or of abuse or contumely against "God, either done by attributing to him what is false, or by "denying what is true, or by attributing to creatures what ought "to be to him; or even by saying things that are true but which "aim at his dishonor or contempt, etc. St. Thomas, II IIæ q. 13; "Bonacina, *Disp.* 3, q. 8; Sanchez 3 *mor.* c. 82; Laymann, l. 4 t. 10 "c. 6, etc."

From that the following are resolved:

122.—"One blasphemes that, gnashing his teeth against God "curses him, likewise saying that he is going to act against "God's will, likewise who denies him; who swears in earnest by "false Gods, who calls God a tyrant or unjust, says that God "refuses or cannot help us and does not care for us; that a "demon is more trustworthy or can care for us more; that all "things were not rightly ordered so that certain things might "have been and ought to have been done better in creation, etc. "If anyone would believe such things are so, and utter them not "merely in anger or desperation, then it is heretical blasphemy, "*i.e.* joined with heresy; which must be added in confession "because it differs in species from imprecatory blasphemy. "Hurtad, 2.2. d. 91 sect. 12 § 54."

123.—One who hears someone advancing heretical blasphemy is held to denounce him within six days, as Viva (*de praec.* qu. 6 art. 2 n. 11) and the Salamancans (tr. 21 c. 3 punct. 10 § 2 n. 129) say, from the edict of the Inquisition; but it seems the space of six days is according to the Spanish Inquisition, for in an edict of the General Inquisition a month is assigned (See what we will say in book 5, n. 252). Furthermore, it is otherwise if the blasphemy were not heretical; for although from the decree of Julius III and Pius I, and the Lateran Council, there is an obligation to denounce (see Salamancans *loc. cit.*), nevertheless, other authors say in these blasphemies correction must come first, which, if it accomplishes its effect, then the denunciation is omitted (Sanchez, *in dec.* l. 2 c. 32 n. 47, with Medina and Lopez, as well as Salamancans *loc. cit.*, with Bonacina, Villalobos, Trullenchus and others). On the contrary, Mazotta, Tamburinus (*Dec.* l. 2 c. 6 § 4 n. 6) and Viva say that on account of disuse these decrees do not seem to oblige at this point.

124.—In addition, it must be noted that it is blasphemy to say: "God wills, refuses; Let God perish; in spite of God; I deny the sacraments." It is the same to say: "holy and all powerful demon;" but not if it were called powerful, wise, etc., according to its nature, provided one did not intend to attribute some honor to the demon.

Nor is it blasphemy when a word is changed or pronounced half way, *e.g.* "I deny holy G...; holy G ...; holy ... (Diana). This opinion is probable with Viva (*loc. cit.* n. 8), Tamburinus (n. 18) and Croix (n. 252) with Gobat and Tanner.

It is not a blasphemy to say against men: "Blood of God, Body of God." Viva, n. 9, from the common opinion with Laymann and Tamburinius (n. 25) unless the indignation were directed against God. And so it must be held with Busembaum and others (below, n. 128) whatever Croix might say (lib. 3, part. 1, n. 248), namely that these words *per se* convey contempt of God.

It is not blasphemy to say: "By the life of God" or "of the saints". It is the common opinion with Viva (*ibid.*) and Tamburinius, n. 23, with Sanchez, against Decian.

It is not blasphemy to say: "I reject God if I will not strike you." So Tamburinius says (n. 22) with Salas, and it seems probable, against Sanchez and Palaus, because then the one advancing these words has no mind to deny God, in the event that he does not strike him; but because he certainly wishes to strike, therefore he says he doesn't believe in God, if he would not strike; at length, meaning to say: "just as it is certain that I will not deny God, so I hold it certain that I will strike you."

It is not blasphemy to say: "This is true, just like God." Tamburinius, n. 16, with Azor, Bonacina, Medina (against Suarez and del Soto). And Mazzota asserts this is the common opinion with Bonacina and others, because then it is in common and created truth is not placed on par with uncreated truth, but a certain similitude mixed with hyperbole is only indicated.

It is not blasphemy to say: "It was destined by fate." (Tamburinius, *ibid.* with Sanchez), nor to assert the words of Scripture to make a joke, provided that someone does not use them for indecent things, and that it is not done so often that they savor of contempt. (Tamburinius, with Villalobos and Gobat, cited by Croix n. 251), nor to swear an oath by the noble body-parts of Christ (Tamburinius n. 23, with Sanchez). It is otherwise, if one were to swear mockingly or by the impolite parts. Therefore, it is a true blasphemy to say: "by the twat (*potta*) of Christ; by the twat of St. Paul," if it is understood by "*twat*" (*potta*) the nature of a woman, which such a word means, but such a meaning is commonly not intended, nor known; therefore by saying the aforesaid blasphemy commonly one is excused from mortal sin: so much more because the word *potta* is ambiguous, while in Italian (even of it self) it is nothing other than the interjection of anger, as is observed in the vocabulary of the Etruscan language recently published, and Mazzota thinks it is probable (*de blasph.* § 2 dub. 2).

So also, country-folk can be excused from mortal sin, who blaspheme God or the saints by adding: "Apart from God," or "If I did it." Although of itself it does not seem to be true blasphemy, because such a condition does not abolish the injury inflicted upon God or the saints by the first words, although the authors may rightly teach that for the sin of blasphemy an affect dishonoring God is not required, but merely to advance something verging on lessening the divine honor is required, whatever Gobat might say (cited by Croix) who thinks it is not a blasphemy if anyone would only advance blasphemous words falsely for a grave cause. (Sanchez, *Dec.* l. 2, c. 23 n. 3; Sporer *de 1 praec.* c. 10 n. 22; Palaus tract. 17, disp. 2 p. 3 § 1 n. 3, with Suarez and Valentia, likewise Elbel n. 180 and Croix, l. 2 p. 1 n. 250 with Tamburinius and Dicastillus) Hence, Sanchez (n. 41) and Sporer say with Tamburinus that every blasphemy, even advanced as a joke, is a mortal sin unless the joke would remove every sort of irreverence against God (which they say rarely happens) exactly as Sanchez says, if someone for the sake of a joke or derision would swear by false gods. Nevertheless, the recent author of a book, titled *Instruzzione per li confessori di terre e villaggi*, (c. 4 141) and Fr. Sarnelli the author of the book *Opera contra la bestemmia* (part. 1, p. 52) likewise Mazotta (*de blasphemia, loc. cit.*) with Diana and others say it is probable, at least on account of ignorance, that the unlearned could be excused from mortal sin, who do not otherwise intend to blaspheme the saints, such as by adding *se l'ho fatto io* (if I do it), not intending to so blaspheme. Besides that, even from saying that, it is probable such a joke is not a true blasphemy; for the true sense of each proposition is formed from its last words, and therefore it can rightly be said, that the aforesaid proposition, *Managgia Santo N. se l'ho fatto io*,[1] taken together and completely, it would not inflict a true injury on the saint, since that condition is present, "If I would have done it." Moreover, it is one thing to advance words of blasphemy outwardly, and inwardly not wishing to blaspheme, as was said above, and another to advance the aforesaid proposition, in which by it he shows, expressly advancing the condition, that he does not wish advance any injury to the saint. Yet, it must be said otherwise if he were to add such words, to not remove the malice of blasphemy, but lead by penance, even to repair a blasphemy already advanced.

125.—"2. Other signs against God are also recalled to "blasphemy, even if the words are not present; such as to spit at "heaven, to gnash teeth, etc., nay more one can also commit "blasphemy inwardly in the mind alone, just as one can also "mentally praise God."

"3. He likewise blasphemes who is contumelious against the "saints or sacred things, say as the saints are, or at least with "the virtual condition toward God, so that morally the honor of

---

[1] Translator's note: Damn St. N. if I did it.

"this is thought to be touched, because otherwise it will only be "against *dulia*, if it were spoken against them as certain men "were on earth. But it is venial if it is done as a joke, *e.g.* if they "called Sts. Crispinus and Crispiana cobblers, John and Paul "eunuchs; but it will be grave if contemptuously or from hatred "or indignation you were to say these things against the saints. "Although blasphemies against God do not admit paucity of "matter, nevertheless many admit it in those which are done "against the saints. Escobar t. 1, *extr.*"

"4. Likewise, he blasphemes who while angry, even if it is "not against God, but advances blasphemies in earnest against "others or other things, or advances the same things in earnest "which, from their meaning or manner of speech or "circumstances import diminishment of divine honor or a "reproach. Although he does not formally intend it, "nevertheless he intends it indirectly and virtually; inasmuch as "it is from talking secretly it is often venial, if it were only done "materially.

126.—"5. In confession it must be expressed if someone "(although it rarely happens) directly and formally intended to "dishonor God, or was angry and formally did it. Laymann (*loc. "cit.*)." (With the common opinion cited by the Salamancans tr. 21, c. 3 punct. 10 § 1 n. 125, with Lessius, l. 2 c. 45 n. 33 otherwise, if he would only blaspheme from anger).

"6. Likewise, he blasphemes who injuriously usurps a "member of Christ, *e.g.* "May the blood of Christ ruin you, or "the wounds, death of God, passion, sacraments, chrism, and "similar sacred things, since these were not given to destroy but "to save, and commonly men apprehend in these the greatness "of God and it contains contempt for those things. Laymann, "*ibid.*, n. 12."

127.—"7. One who has a habit of such words is held under "mortal sin to try and remove the habit in earnest. But if he

"does and still falls, he can sometimes be excused to the extent
"that the swearing was so poured forth by a natural impetus
"and not voluntarily, either in itself or in the cause, inasmuch
"as he efficaciously purposed to retract it. Laymann l. 1 t. 2 c. 3
"n. 6. See Escobar, t. 1 c. 3 n. 36. If he does not try and the
"confessor marks it, he should deny him absolution with
"discretion. Laymann, *loc. cit.*"

Here we must advert that some uttering blasphemies of this sort say they did not know the malice of blasphemy; and some doctors say that these sometimes on account of the rush of anger or a contracted habit that they can blaspheme inadvertently. But I think with the cited author of the *Instruzzione* that some advertence is always present in blasphemy, at least a confused advertence, on the malice of its enlargement; for anger, or a habit does not so ordinarily darken the intellect that the malice of blasphemy would not be noticed, even if it is not known reflexively.

"8. Meanwhile, many are excused on account of inadvertence
"in a sudden commotion, even if it seems it does not sufficiently
"excuse, because certain men say by these words they do not
"intend anything other than to give interjections signifying
"their anger: both because they can equally persuade
"themselves to other words of anger and signifying a serious
"will: and because even if they could not, just the same it does
"not seem it is lawful to take up those words which by the
"common apprehension of others dishonor God.

128.—"9. What if someone in anger against a man, not from
"indignation against God, but only man, whereby he will name
"the death of God, the seven sacraments, *e.g.* "O death of God,
"wounds, etc." without scandal and without those
"circumstances in which contempt would be imported, they are

"not blasphemies but a vain usurpation of the divine name, forbidden by this precept and a sin among serious venial sins. Cajetan and Armilla, *v. Blasphemia*; and Sanchez (See n. 124). Although on account of the danger of falling into blasphemies, and because it is rarely without scandal and just the same, in the presence of those listening they think God and his holy things are dishonored, they are rarely excused and men are rightly discouraged from similar sayings, as Laymann notes.

129.—*Quæritur:* Would it be a blasphemy to curse created things? The distinction must be made if one curses creatures with relation to God, such as to curse the rain, winds as though commanded by God, or by adding the word "of God", *e.g. Managgia il fuoco di Dio,*[2] certainly it is a blasphemy (See Tamburinus and Mazotta). The same thing must be said if one were to curse a created thing, which of itself has a special relation to God, such as our soul, the Catholic faith, heaven and similar things (see what we will soon say below). It is otherwise if the indignation were borne against created things without a relation to God. So the common opinion argues, the Continuator of Tournely (*de praec. Dec.* cap. 2 *remissive ad tract. de relig.* part 3), Viva (d. q. 6 art. 2 n. 7) with Bonacina and Lessius, from St. Thomas II IIæ q. 76, art. 2, where he teaches: "To curse irrational things insofar as they are creations of God is the sin of blasphemy, but to curse them considered as they are in themselves, is idle and vain." Hence, from Viva and others it is not grave to simply curse the hour, the day, the year, even if the word "holy" were added, unless the day bore some special holiness apart from being a day, such as the days of Easter, Epiphany, Christmas and Pentecost, as the authors say (Salamancans tr. 21, c. 3 punct. 10 § 1 n. 121; Elbel *de 2 praec.* with Sanchez, Laymann, Sporer and more expressly the author of the *Instruzzione per li conf. di terre* etc.). The reason is, because the

---

[2] *Damn the fire of God.* –Translator's note.

enlargement, where it emphasizes something special or is set forth for sanctity, always, at least indirectly, refers to God who is the author of all sanctity.

But here we ask whether it would be a blasphemy to curse the whole world, or to say in general speech, "Damn the whole world"? This case, as much as I have studied the moral authors, I have not found discussed; it is only scarcely found treated in two authors. The cited author of the *Instruzzione*, ch. 5 § *Secondo comandamento*, v. *Ma qual giudizio*, asserts in a very passing way this curse is not of itself a grave blasphemy.

But I think the opposite is altogether more true, and I am led by the argument of that common opinion which the doctors universally hand down; and they say that to swear by more excellent created things, which goodness especially emphasizes, wisdom or divine power, namely by heaven, the earth and even by the soul (as the Salamancans rightly think is more probable, *de Juramento*, tr. 17, c. 2, punct. 3 n. 28 with Suarez, Sanchez and Fagundez) and likewise thinks it is a true oath. So the authors hold in the treatise on oaths: Busembaum (n. 138), Laymann (c. 1 n. 5), Sporer (c. 1 n. 7), Palaus (d. 1 part. 1 n. 5), Salamancans (*ibid.* punct. 1 n. 12), Bonacina (q. 1 p. 1 n. 4), Felinus (*Potest* c. 2 n. 1554). And this is clearly proved from Deuteronomy 4:26 and 50:19, where Moses swore, saying: "I invoke the heaven and earth as witnesses," and from Matthew 5:34: "Do not swear at all by heaven ... and by the earth." On those words, St. Augustine says: "When you swear by heaven or by the earth, do not imagine that your oath does not bring you under obligation to the Lord." (l. 1 *de Serm. Dom.* c. 17).

Therefore, just as, I say, to swear by the aforesaid created things is a true oath, seeing that the power of God is especially resplendent in these very things, God is indirectly invoked by them as a witness, so on account of the same reasoning to curse the same created things is a true blasphemy because in these God is indirectly scorned. And indeed Felix of Panormus thinks this (*de 2 praec.* c. 1 n. 1540), where he says abuse in created things is not blasphemy unless divine goodness is especially emphasized in them, as in heaven and the earth and the soul. Nevertheless, one is rightly excused from the sin of blasphemy that curses the world, understanding that world which is opposed to God and the saints, according to that in John 15:18: "If the world hates you, know that it hated me before you." But ordinarily speaking, I think simple folk who curse the world for the most part sin gravely, until they accuse themselves of such a curse with great horror.

But Tamburinius (*Dec.* l. 2, c. 6 § 4 n. 11) thinks rightly that to curse the devil is rarely a mortal sin, because it is always customary for the author of evils to be cursed as the enemy of God; by such an arrangement, by abstracting from an act of impatience, Tamburinus says it is not even a venial sin, and Mazzota (*de 2. praec.* q. 3 c. 2 § 1) and Elbel (n. 21) agree it is probable.

Moreover, Viva notes (n. 10) as well as Tamburinus (n. 18) with Bonacina, Lezarius and Palaus, that in doubt as to whether something is or is not a blasphemy, it should not be assumed to be a blasphemy.

130.—*Quæritur:* would *the curse of the dead*, which is commonly called, "blasphemy of the dead", be a true blasphemy? The case is not discovered with the moral doctors; the only mention made of it is with the author of the aforesaid *Instruzzione per li confessori di terre*, whose little worthy book is held with great praise, and approval of the very illustrious and learned Bishop, his excellency Giulio Torni, for great erudition and outstanding repute. And in addition it is cited in the book "*Opera contra l'abuso della bestemmia*,[3] revised by his illustrious and learned lordship, Castrensis Scaja, the Bishop of Oria, at that time an outstanding professor of theology in the public academy

---

[3] Translator's note: Work against the abuse of blasphemy.

of Naples. In both books it is said, the aforesaid is by no means blasphemy, but merely a light curse. I later discovered Mazotta holds the same thing.

And so I think it must altogether be held, whatever some might say, as is shown in a certain dissertation in the form of an epistle which I published, and add here. The whole reason is in the chief point, because a curse of this sort by no means contains, either in itself from the object, nor by relation to the mind of those that utter it, some injury against the souls in purgatory, as those of the contrary opinion contend. Not from the object, because the term "of the dead" in itself does not mean anything other than *a cadaver* (for the aforesaid "of the dead" pertains properly to bodies, not to souls). To the chief point it means *men departed from life*, who can be saved and more easily damned, according to the more common opinion which would have it that a greater part of the faithful is damned; but not the souls in purgatory, unless perhaps in some circumstance of speech (and so our adversaries are answered) where express mention is made of sacred things, *e.g.* when it is said: "The Mass, the day or the congregation of the dead." Moreover, in other expressions ordinarily such a term neither in itself nor through common perception means "the souls of purgatory", as when it is said: "He is afraid of the dead; the adornment of the tomb scarcely benefits the dead", and similar things. And it does not seem that this can be called into doubt.

Those of a contrary opinion insist that those cursing the dead at least would really curse their souls, which are found separated from their bodies. But I respond that then to curse the soul of someone will be mortal when in uttering the curse the word "souls" is expressed, by denoting the excellence of the divine power which shines upon the soul, exactly as I said before in n. 129. But not when a man is cursed, if no mention of the soul is made; just as to swear by someone's soul would be a true oath, but not to swear by some man, namely by Francis or by Peter.

Whereby, just as to curse a living man is not judged a grave sin, so not a dead one. So much more, because (as I just said) the curse of the dead is more properly referred to bodies which are only dead, than to souls which are immortal. And it is certain that the kind of men cursing the dead commonly intend in no way to curse their souls; they really prescind from the consideration of souls and bodies. Nay more, in the normal manner of speech, they by no means intend to curse the dead, but to rebuke the living, to whom that curse by its nature directs the injury. Therefore, the author of the cited *Instruzzione* rightly calls the aforesaid curse more properly an *imprecation*. And this is clear from the practice of confessors who, if they interrogate penitents as to whether they intended to curse the souls of the saints, or at least the souls of the dead, respond with horror, "God forbid, may God avert it."

The general rule confirms our assertion, which Laymann assigns (lib. 4 tr. 10 c. 6 n. 12) where he so teaches: "If a penitent denies that he extended the affect of his indignation directly toward God, but only against a man with whom he was angry, then the confessor should attend to the words, 'if according to itself they express no decrease of divine honor they must not be regarded as blasphemy or mortal sin'."

For this purpose another general rule is at hand, that to condemn something for certain as a mortal sin, the malice ought to be certain. Nay more, characteristically in regard to blasphemies, Palaus, Bonacina, Lezarius, with Tamburinus (lib. 2 cap. 6 § 4 n. 19) and Viva (qu. 6 art. 2 n. 10) teach that in doubt as to whether it is or is not blasphemy, it must not be assumed to be a blasphemy. Therefore, how can the curse of the dead be condemned as a mortal sin when, of itself, as we said, it contains not injury against God or the saints; nor is it referred to the dead themselves by those that utter it, who by uttering it, do not understand what they say?

On this point I have consulted the venerable and celebrated congregations of the missionary priests of Naples to be secure in my teaching, both of regulars and seculars, and they unanimously responded that such a curse must by no means be received as a blasphemy, nor as a mortal sin. And I have inserted their responses into my aforesaid epistle.

From all of this, I think it is worthwhile that confessors and preachers would be careful when they instruct the common people on this point, thinking that it is a mortal sin, lest so many souls from ignorance would miserably sin on account of an erroneous conscience. Nor is it opposed to say that from this advertence the abuse of this curse will be more frequent, for it is answered that it is better for innumerable venial sins to be permitted than one mortal sin. And, would I that such people ignorant on account of the horror of mortal sin would no longer utter the aforesaid curse! It is an evil, but still with such a conscience of grave sin they might not desist from this vice, and on the other hand be condemned due to that ignorance. But see the response at the end of this chapter, which we recently published in regard to this curse of the dead, against a certain anonymous letter opposed to us.

Equally, we note here it is not a blasphemy in itself if anyone would curse *the faith* of someone, provided he would not express nor intend the holy faith or that of Christ, for it can also be understood about human faith. And really those cursing the faith never intend to blaspheme the holy faith. Mazotta, *loc. cit.*

But would it be a mortal sin to curse men or to call evil down on them? See what was said in book 2, n. 83.

131.—"10. To call a demon, a hail-storm, lightening, etc. "down upon others in anger, even if many confound it with "blasphemies, nevertheless is not a blasphemy, but a dire "imprecation, which more often than not (at least when it is "said against those whom the angry man loves) is done on "account of sudden commotion and inadvertence, and lacking "an earnest will, are nothing more than venial sins, because

"when they reflect with themselves, they say that they think
"otherwise by far, and sensed so that certain interjections seem
"to signify anger; even if it is hardly fitting for Christians to use
"such absurd interjections. Bonacina (*loc. cit.*) from Navarre,
"Toledo, Reginald etc., Baldellus dist. 25, n. 10, where he also
"thinks it is only a venial sin to call down a demon upon
"himself to the extent that he does not gravely wound charity."
(So it is also merely a venial sin to call down a demon upon
someone without a mind that he be taken by it. Escobar, cited
by Tamburinus, lib. 2 c. 6 § 4 n. 12). "But Molina, etc., do not
"dare excuse it from mortal sin on account of the foulness,
"horror and perversity. Moreover, it is grave if subjects curse
"their superiors, or sons their parents (even if only materially)
"in this way, especially to their face, because it is a grave sin
"against due reverence. Bald., *loc. cit.* See above, book 2 ch. 3
"dub. 6.

"11. In anger to use [the name of] a demon without an
"imprecation is not a sin of itself: nevertheless, its constant
"naming is not fitting for a Christian, and can be a grave sin by
"reason of scandal. Laymann, *loc. cit.*

"12. In confession the type of blasphemy must be expressed,
"*viz.* whether it was against God or the saints, for that these
"differ in species is probable according to Suarez, Sanchez,
"Reginald, Azor, Laymann, Diana ®. 50), de Lugo (d. 15 n. 2),
"but Trullenchus (lib. 1 n. 11 d. 2 n. 5) with Diana (p. 1 *de
"circumst.* r. 30) hold the contrary.

132.—Would a blasphemy against God differ in species from a blasphemy against the saints? Busembaum affirms it with others; but other authors deny it with probability (Bonacina tom. 2 disp. 3 q. 8 p. 4 n. 1; Sanchez, *Dec.* lib. 2 cap. 32, n. 38; Laymann, *lib.* 4 r. 10 cap. 6 n. 10; Viva d. qu. 6 art. 2 n. 6; and Salamancans tr. 21 c. 3 punct. 10 § 1 n. 124 with Cajetan, Bañez, Filliuci, etc.). Viva also thinks it is probable (dict. q. 6 art. 2 n. 6) because commonly, injuries against the saints are mediately related to God himself. Still, the Salamancans hold, with Bonacina, that on account of another reasoning it ought to be expressed in confession whether the blasphemy was against God or against the saints, because they say the aforesaid blasphemies, beyond their own malice, contain another distinct species against *latria* or *dulia*. But Viva (dict. n. 6 in fine; Tamburinius *in Meth. Conf.* lib. 2, cap. 3 § 1; Holzmann, t. 1 p. 284, n. 403; and Elbel *de 2. praec.* n. 9 with Azor, etc.) also deny this with probability, by saying that one only sins against *dulia* when the blasphemy is advanced against the saints on account of their excellence, without relation to God, so that it terminates and stops in them. But when those who blaspheme the saints more truly (by the common manner of speaking) intend to place injuries upon them, not on account of their precise and proper excellence, but insofar as they are mediately referred to God, then according to the first probable opinion of the Salamancans, they do not sin against *dulia* but merely against *latria* and on that account, are not held to explain whether they committed blasphemy against God or the saints.

EPISTOLA RESPONSIVA
AGAINST AN APOLOGETIC EPISTLE WRITTEN IN DEFENSE OF A DISSERTATION WHICH APPEARED ON THE ABUSE OF CURSING THE DEAD

Before all else I have endeavored to show that when a certain *Dissertation* appeared against what I had written on this point I promised that once I had satisfied what was opposed to me I would make no further argument on the matter. This was not only to prevent it from continuing *ad infinitum*, but so much the more that I would not repeat the same things that I had already written. But I said that I merely wished to respond (precisely as I did) to two doctrines of St. Thomas that had been raised in objection to me again. And together I showed that I had determined in my mind thereafter that I would write nothing further on this controversy (because it seemed the matter had been clearly established in public), unless I should altogether be persuaded of the truth of it by my adversary. For then, there would be no difficulty for me to desist from that opinion and I would not be ashamed to show it to all in a public statement. My mind did not recoil from doing this in some of my other opinions which, when I learned these were not in accord with reason, then I freely retracted myself.

Just the same, after I gave the last response another apologetic *Epistle* appeared in the vernacular in defense of the aforesaid dissertation, in which the author made the effort to prove that to curse the dead is in itself a mortal sin. To that epistle, not withstanding my earlier plan to not respond any further, I am compelled now to respond with another *Epistle.*—And here, I merely add this: in the following is briefly contained both the *Response* which I gave to the *Dissertation*, and the *Response* to the defense of the *Dissertation*.

To the Most Reverend Abbot D. Bartholomaeo di Marco, Basiliano.
Most Reverend Father and Venerable Lord.

Although a certain dissertation on the cursing of the dead and my own brief response were published, against the most recent publication there is another apologetic Epistle, written with many words in defense of the aforesaid dissertation. —After that Epistle arrived in my hands and I had given it an accurate reading, for a long time I considered whether to respond or not. On one side, I had taken up the purpose not to respond any further and I had decided to make good on that not to continue it forever. On the other side, it now seems expedient to respond, as my colleagues impel me to do both because I intend to retract a certain error in my earlier response, or perhaps to cut it out, although it does not bear on our argument, just as you will notice from this second response; and because in the praise for the apologetic *Epistle*, our adversary brings out other new observations whereby some ambiguities must be abolished from the midst. Thus I have taken on the need to make satisfaction with another response.

This is why I have taken care to advance this other response to you. And I ask these two things of you: First, that you read over everything that you can with the greatest scrutiny, removing, adding and correcting whatever will have seemed good to you. Second, that you might sincerely open to me your mind as to whether it seems expedient for me to have this put into print; on the one hand it would displease me to argue with a man and others of his own order whom I hold in the highest esteem and honor (especially since I know as a fact that there is no shortage of learned men in that order who adhere to my opinion). On the other hand, to remove from the hearts of the faithful this opinion, namely whether the aforesaid curse is a mortal sin when it is no such thing, for the glory of God, who holds the salvation of souls for his glory, which I regard as no small matter to discuss.

Spare me, I ask, if you see that not a few things that were noted in the earlier response and are repeated here again. I did not suppose it could be done otherwise than that everything be put before the eyes of the reader at the same time while he reads these new observations which our adversary objects to me. —In the *Dissertation* he undertakes to prove that the curse against the dead is a mortal sin and a true blasphemy for two reasons: 1) Because the bodies of the faithful departed are sacred; 2) Because the aforesaid curse cannot prescind from reference to souls. In the response given to the *Dissertation*, I said that I had already responded twice to these objections; for that reason, so as not to be always singing the same tune, I refuse to respond to all that has been objected. —Just the same, to the two authorities of St.

Thomas, which are again asserted, I cannot do anything but respond.

The first text is taken from 3 p. q. 8, art. 2, where the Holy Doctor says that Christ, because of the indwelling of the Holy Spirit, pours into the bodies of the faithful the right to be resurrected. And the author of the dissertation intends to prove this same right from another place, namely sacramental communion, that while the faithful live they are refreshed, hence from these two reasons he infers the bodies of the dead must be accounted as sacred, so much so that they must be venerated with a sacred cult emanating from the virtue of religion. But, if these reasons (I respond) would prove that the bodies of any of the dead must be held as sacred, they would also necessarily prove that the bodies of the faithful who are damned must also be accounted as sacred; for the Holy Spirit also dwelt in them, and they were united with Jesus Christ through the Eucharist. —Now, he says that these qualities were later lost through sin. As a result, I take it that as often as it is not clear to me by the authentic testimony of the Church that the soul of that body enjoys eternal glory, and as often as the Church does not elevate the honor which is due to it to the regard of a sacred cult (as we will explain below) then to me it is not lawful to hold that body as sacred. —Besides that, if the bodies of the dead are holy on account of the fact that they have received the Eucharist, and on account of the indwelling of the Holy Spirit, it must necessarily be said that even the bodies of the living faithful must be venerated as holy, so that any injury or curse inflicted against the body of the living faithful must be said to be a grave sin against religion. But this is against the express doctrine of St. Thomas, as we will soon see. —Moreover, to say that the bodies of the dead are sacred on account of the rites which the Church uses for them (namely that it gives them the benefit of sacred burial, processions and adorns them with blessings, the scent of frankincense, as well as on account of the ancient rite (as our adversary says), and formerly the custom of placing the Holy Eucharist over the breast of the deceased. I do not know why these rites should be called acts of a sacred cult when they are compared with previous ages, even in the time in which the Church enjoyed peace from the persecutions of infidels, the bodies of the faithful departed were buried in fields and roads, precisely as Thomassinus (*Vetus et nova Eccl. discipl.*, part. 3 lib. 1 cap. 66, n. 3 et 4) and Calmet (*Dissert. de funeribus et seputl. Hebraeor.*) witness. Nay more, a great many councils forbade that dead bodies be given for burial in a Church. —What if in later times the use was introduced that they be buried in a sacred place, as St. Gregory affirms, for it to happen that those nearby would more often recall the souls of the dead and help them with prayers from the sight of their tombs, or in the words of the saint: "This benefits the dead if they are buried in the Church because those near them, as often as they gather in the same holy places, will remember them and pour forth prayers for them to the Lord when they see the tombs of some of their own" (*Dialogue*, lib. 4 cap. 50). St. Augustine says the same thing (*De cura pro mortuis gerenda*, cap. 4 et 5). Furthermore, the blessings with lustral water, say Gavantus and Durandus, are applied to dead bodies, are so that they would be free from the molestation of demons. And for this same reason they are incensed, as Innocent III writes (*de Sacro altaris myster.* lib. 2 cap. 17), and on account of the same thing the most Holy Eucharist is placed on the breast of the dead, as St. Gregory also asserted (*Dialogue*, lib. 2 cap. 24), although this was condemned by Councils in the fourth, sixth and seventh century, as Fr. Vestrini relates (*Lettere teolog.*, part. 3 lett. 53). It was also forbidden that the Holy Eucharist be placed in the foundation stones of Churches, or upon demoniacs, or to remove the wounds of the sick; just as equally, to smear the forehead, eyes, etc. with consecrated blood; such a custom was held by the ancient faithful, as St. Cyril of Jerusalem (*Catech.* 23 Mystagog. 5, n. 22) and St. John Chrysostom relate. —These make it crystal clear that these pious acts (which they derived rather more from simplicity than religion), do not indicate that the bodies were sacred, for which they were applied, but only that they would attain the effects which the faithful hoped for in their use when they applied them.

But by speaking on the rites that the Church commonly used in burying dead bodies, Spondanus writes these things: "As often as you like the sign of the cross is made and adorned over them, and they are sprinkled with holy water and incensed, not only to prevent many evils but especially to ... put to flight the demons and to dissolve the tricks and spells of sorcerers; I could advance as many testimonies and examples of the Fathers as one would like." And: "Incense is applied to the bodies of the faithful departed because those who die piously are ... the good odor of Christ...; and moreover, it will be shown that the dead ... leave behind the odors of good works which still benefit them, the devoted pleas and prayers of the same which are shown ... through incense ...; and likewise, that it shows the same dead believed they, through death ... go to true immortality." —Moreover, Stephen Durandus says: "Incensation is made... to give reverence to the place as well as the divine office, etc." So also John Bethel: [The cadaver] is placed in the tomb, and there with holy water, and coals with frankincense. Certainly with holy water lest demons come to the body. ... Frankincense, however, is applied so as to remove the stench of the body and coals, to show that the ground can no longer be returned to common use." Besides, William Durandus says: "Holy Water [is placed] so that demons do not come to the body. But frankincense is placed there to remove the stench of the body or that the deceased be understood to have offered the acceptable odor of good works to its creator; or to show that the assistance of prayer benefits the dead." —From that it is clear that all the aforesaid rites which the Church applies to the dead are not a sacred cult with which it intends to honor the cadaver, but mystical ceremonies. Also note that the Church denies burial to those who were excommunicated or bound by the bond of interdict when they passed from this life even if before they breathed their last they gave certain signs of their repentance and salvation. Thus, the Church does not apply those rites to the dead because she supposes they are temples of the Holy Spirit; but because she desires the communion between the living and dead to be preserved.

The other passage of St. Thomas that is raised to me in objection is taken from the same 3 p. q. 25, art. 6, where the Angelic Doctor says that the relics of the saints must be venerated because they were a temple and organ of the Holy Spirit, who dwelled and worked in them, and also because later, through the glorious resurrection, they are going to be conformed to the body of Jesus Christ. —Our adversary infers from this that a curse against the bodies of the dead is a true blasphemy, since at some point they were also temples and organs of the Holy Spirit. But if this reasoning would avail for the dead (I say again), so much the more ought it to avail for the living, by far, more forcefully as the living are in act living temples and organs of the Holy Spirit (if they live in charity, precisely as we must piously assume). But St. Thomas (II IIæ q. 76 art. 3), with the common opinion of the theologians who follow him, all say that a curse or imprecation advanced against men does not exceed a venial sin as often as the curse is not formal but merely material, namely, without bad affect (Cajetan in 2.2. q. 76 art. 1; and *Sum.* v. *Maledictio*, § *Tertium*; del Soto *de Justitia et Jure*, l. 5 q. 12 art. 3 concl. 2; Azor part. 3 lib. 2 cap. 23 quaer. 2; Prado *Theol. mor.*, tom. 2 cap. 25 qu. 4 n. 5 and *seqq.*; Serra in 2.2. qu. 76 art. 3; Molina *de Justitia et Jure*, tr. 4 disp. 22, n. 4 and 5; de Lugo *de Justitia et Jure* disp. 14 n. 196; Laymann lib. 2 tr. 3 cap. 8 n. 8; Trullenchus *Decal.* lib. 8 cap. 8 dub. 4 n. 1). —Let us relate the whole text of the Angelic Doctor, lest I be forced to start again at the beginning: "The curses which we are speaking about at present are those whereby evil is uttered against someone [*note*] by way of command or desire. Furthermore, to wish, or provoke by way of command to the evil of another man, is of its very nature contrary to charity with which we love our neighbor by desiring his good. So, it is a mortal sin according to its genus, and so much the graver, as the person whom we curse has a greater claim on our love and respect. Hence, it is written: 'He that curses his father, or mother, dying let him die.' (Leviticus 20:9). It may happen, however, that the word uttered in cursing is a venial sin either through the slightness of the evil invoked against another in cursing him, or on account of the sentiments of the person who utters the curse; because he may say such words through some slight movement, or in jest, or suddenly, and sins of the word should be weighed chiefly with regard to the speaker's intention."

From this quote, my adversary, by inveighing against me and repeating the words of the Angelic doctor with emphasis: *It is a mortal sin according to its genus,* flares up and says "Do you understand it, or not?" —Nevertheless, it seems to me that I understood it, and so much so that nobody ought to understand the text of St. Thomas other than I do, namely that to curse a man is a mortal sin when the curse is formal, because then it is said to be such a thing, seeing that someone desired with bad intention that the evil which he uttered against him would come about, or when he induces others to utter evil against him, just as the Angelic Doctor explains himself in *article 1,* with the example of a judge who moves the ministers of justice to carry out an unjust punishment against the condemned. And the Saint says it is a mortal sin of itself because this is, as he says, "of its very nature contrary to charity with which we love our neighbor by desiring his good." For, just as charity imposed upon us that we will the good of our neighbor, so it forbids us to desire evil upon him, and to induce others to inflict evil upon him. —Yet, by speaking on a verbal curse (the only thing which we are speaking of in the present case), St. Thomas says it does not exceed a venial sin either when the evil which someone utters is light, or lacks a wicked intention (which is called a material curse), namely by uttering a curse either as a joke or without full deliberation. And then he confirms it with this reasoning: "Sins of word should be weighed chiefly with regard to the speaker's intention."

Cajetan teaches this very same thing *in 2. 2.* qu. 76 art. 1, saying: "What is properly a curse, namely to speak evil intentionally against someone is of the same sort to the extent that it is evil. And it arises from this that a curse ... is distinguished between a curse formally and materially; sometimes it is a mortal sin and sometimes a venial sin. For a curse formally is a mortal sin of its genus, as is clear; while materially, if it were optative, it is not mortal whereas if it were imperative it could be mortal. And the reason for this diversity is that without any intention cursing optatively harms nobody because it is neither from the intention nor the work. But to do so imperatively sometimes harms from the work of the minister obeying it, although not from his own intention.

Furthermore, I said: 'of its genus' because on account of the imperfection of the act, or on the side of its object that if one were to desire a small evil or command it, or on the side of the worker, that if he were to curse from anger or another passion (or as a joke, as St. Thomas adds), although it tends in affect to evil, since it does not tend to evil from the consent of reason, it lacks the perfect account of sin, and for this reason it is not mortal." So, in the progeny of St. Thomas' doctrine, Cajetan says on the one hand, that a formal curse, namely one done *intentionally,* is a mortal sin according to its genus, and that it becomes venial either on account of the imperfection of the act, namely the consent of reason, or on account of the slightness of the evil which is desired. On the other hand, he says a material curse is nothing other than venial, namely *without intention,* pronounced *optatively,* that is in the optative mode or through words expressing a desire, by taking that *optative* adverbially, to differentiate an "imperative", namely in the imperative mode. —And indeed, St. Thomas teaches the same thing although in a different mode (*loc. cit.*); there, he distinguishes a formal curse from a material. For he speaks in the first place about a formal curse, namely with the intention of willing the evil which is uttered when he says: "To wish, or provoke by way of command to the evil of another man, is of its very nature contrary to charity with which we love our neighbor by desiring his good. So, it is a mortal sin according to its genus." So, what the Holy Doctor understands to be opposed to charity and to be a mortal sin of its own genus is not simply to utter a curse; but "to wish or provoke by way of command the evil of another." Therefore, St. Thomas merely recognizes the gravity of the fault in willing the evil which is uttered or to provoke others to inflict evil. Next, he proceeds to explain a material curse, by saying it is venial if it is uttered from a light motion or as a joke, explaining the reasoning: "Because sins of word should be weighed chiefly with regard to the speaker's intention, as it was said above in Q. 72 art. 2." And in that citation, he had said earlier: "Words, to the extent that they are types of sounds, are not injurious to other persons except in as much as they mean something, and this signification depends on the speaker's inward intention. Hence, in sins of the word, it seems that we ought to consider with what intention the words are uttered." —So, it is one thing to curse *optatively*, as Cajetan says, but another to curse by a *desire*, as St. Thomas says. For he remarks that to curse *optatively* by optative words without intention. *By desiring*, however, the Holy Doctor understands to curse with a true intention of doing so; he explains himself crystal clear when he says: "But to will ..., is of itself opposed to charity, etc." And indeed this is a formal curse and so is gravely culpable and it only becomes a venial sin, as the Angelic doctor adds, either on account of the slightness of the evil which is desired, or on account of the suddenness in which the curse is advanced.

Moreover, this question between myself and my opponent is on a mere noun. Granted, St. Thomas would say generally that every curse is of its nature a mortal sin; just the same, the Angelic Doctor holds for a certainty that to curse a man unintentionally is no more than a venial sin. And I seek to prove nothing other than this. —Therefore, not only St. Thomas, but also Cajetan and all other doctors, with St. Augustine (whom the Angelic doctor cites in the same place) do not regard it a blasphemy to curse a man for the reason that a man is a temple of the Holy Spirit. For if he would have held this, he could not say a curse without a wicked intention is a venial sin; for to curse the saints or sacred things, although there is no evil intention present, is always a mortal sin. It is clearly inferred from this that according to the Angelic doctor and the common opinion of doctors, a faithful person can rightly be considered apart from the fact that he is a temple of the Holy Spirit. —And it is deduced besides (the opposite of which my adversary also agrees with), that just as it is not a mortal sin against charity and piety to curse the body of the living faithful if a wicked intention is not present; so it is not a grave sin against charity and piety to curse the bodies of the dead faithful without a wicked intention. Just the same, according to St. Thomas himself, charity, which the dead who departed in grace are going to carry out, is none other than an extension of the charity which we ought to show to the living: "The charity," says the saint, "which is the bond uniting the members of the Church, not only extends itself to the living but even to the dead who died in charity."

But my adversary says that a curse among the living and the dead is the greatest crime because the *fomes*[4] reign in the living, and hence they live in the danger of sin, from which one who has

---

[4] *Translator's note: Fomes* is short for *fomes peccati*, the tinder of sin, and is a technical term referring to concupiscence.

departed in grace is free. Wherefore (he says), it happens that a curse against the living can be venial; for although it is a sin against charity when there is no wicked intention, it cannot be grave; but a curse against the dead, since it is a sin against religion, even without a wicked intention is always a grave sin by reason of the injury which is inflicted upon religion when a sacred body is cursed. —But, that I might respond, again we seek the principle from where he asserts the bodies of the faithful departed are sacred. He himself says, according to the doctrine of St. Thomas, to curse bodies is grave because their bodies were organs of the Holy Spirit and because they received sacramental Communion. Therefore, I respond. In regard to that line of argument, that the body of a dead man, on account of communion and that it was a temple of the Holy Spirit must be held as sacred, I already said above that this reasoning would mean that both dead and living bodies must be held as sacred because even the living man is a temple of the Holy Spirit: "Your members are a temple of the Holy Spirit." (1 Cor. 6:19). But he will repeat that in the living the *fomes* are present, which render a man under the power of sin. I respond. Was the body of Adam then, before sin, sacred? Besides, the potency to sin does not effect that the species of the sanctity of the body would be changed. Likewise, neither the *fomes* nor the danger of sinning cause a living body to not be a temple of the Holy Spirit *here and now*. So much more that the *fomes* induces no guilt or stain in the soul; for the grace of the Redeemer in the baptized wipes away everything of sin, and fully repairs all its harm: "Because with the Lord there is mercy and with him plentiful redemption" (Psalm 129/130: 7); "Where sin abounds, grace abounds all the more" (Romans 5:20); "I came that they might have life, and have it more abundantly" (John 10:10). This is why the Council of Trent defined that through Baptism souls are rendered immaculate and the *fomes* causes no harm, in fact it conveys the benefit for the man who does not consent to it that he receives a greater reward:

"God hates nothing in those reborn ...; they are made innocent, immaculate, pure, guiltless and beloved to God, etc. Moreover, this holy synod affirms and believes that concupiscence, or the *fomes,* remains in the baptized, which, although it is left to struggle with, it does not avail to harm those who do not consent to it; nay more, those who genuinely striven with it will be crowned." (Sess. 5, *Decr. de pecc. origin.*, n. 5). So the reason that they are organs of the Holy Spirit does not effect that the bodies of the living faithful or the departed should be held as sacred; otherwise to curse the living, even without a wicked intention, would always be a grave sin: and the opposite is certain, as my adversary himself admits. This is why it is necessary to put to flight another argument (if perhaps our adversary should find it) that might prove the bodies of the dead are sacred.

It does not avail to say that by cursing the living, one can prescind, by not considering it a temple of the Holy Spirit, but by applying his mind to other peculiar motives, *e.g.* for injuries by which he suffered from it. And I add further: Why can this prescinding not be effected even in respect to the dead by cursing them, by reason of some trouble which he suffered from that body, but without a wicked intention? Besides the fact is (as we wrote in the first epistle), for the most part, that these curses are uttered rather more in contumely against the living than against the dead. —But, he says, this can by no means be effected because the bodies of the dead are sacred. But then we return to the question, because this is the very thing that is argued. For we say that no body of the dead is held as sacred except when the Church declares it to be holy and commands it to be venerated as sacred by elevating veneration from the human order to the supernatural and divine order; as soon we will see from the authority of St. Thomas.

But the author will again repeat that according to the same St. Thomas (3 p. qu. 25 art. 6 ad 2), the relics of the saints are worthy of veneration because the souls of bodies of this sort enjoy God in act; on that account the bodies of the dead (he says), although they cannot be venerated with the divine cult of *dulia*, still cannot be scorned since they are sacred; for it must be piously believed that their souls are saved.

I respond, must a sacred cult be shown to the bodies of the dead since they are sacred? But I mean to know what in the world is this sacred cult that must be shown to them? Our adversary affirms it ought not to be the cult of *dulia*; but I find no other that is bestowed by the Church or the holy doctors; nor can I conceive of what other cult can be bestowed upon sacred species apart from *latria, hyperdulia and dulia*. —But, he insists, surely veneration is given to altars, vestments and vessels? I respond, that the cult of *latria* is given. For these things of themselves merit no cult; but when they are employed, they are not venerated with a further sacred cult, but *relatively* or *reductively*; for this reason, the cult is reduced to the cult of *latria* by reason of the sacrifice to which they are ordered. Consequently, I say that when the bodies of the dead cannot be venerated with the cult of *latria* or any other sacred cult, they ought not be numbered among sacred things. —Father Suarez, when speaking on the veneration due to the saints and the other relics of the dead, says: "I add further, this very custom [namely, of venerating the relics of the saints as sacred things], shows by far that the Church thinks of relics of the saints in a higher mode than common people usually regard the dead bodies of men." (*Defensio fidei Catholicae*, lib. 2 cap. 10 n. 14, v. *Unde etiam*). It occurs to me that St. Gregory of Nyssa also, when speaking about the bodies of the saints and the common death of the faithful departed, says that there is no equality of honor which must be shown to the former and the latter. He adds that all shudder and flee the bodies of the other dead, but desire to approach the bodies of the saints because they are sacred, and believe they will be sanctified by touching them. We advance the words which he spoke in regard to the body of St. Theodore: "[The body of

Theodore] cannot be compared in any way to other bodies which are dissolved by common death ... For the others are to a great many abominable remains, and no man willingly passes by a tomb, nor, were he to come upon one that had been opened, would he run inside. But if he might come upon some similar place to this, where today our gathering is held, where the relics of a just and holy man are held in memory, then right away he sees with delight what magnificence these relics cause ...; he then desires himself to approach the repository, believing that blessing and sanctification comes to him from the handling [of these relics]." (*Oratio S. Theodori martyris*). —Hence we must note that it is one thing, what the Church and the faithful show to the bodies of the saints, and another altogether with which the bodies of the other dead are honored.

In regard to the veneration due to bodies, however, the souls of which enjoy God, we respond that the reasoning of St. Thomas cannot avail unless it were only for those declared as saints by the Church, which is the only thing the Angelic Doctor addresses. —St. Thomas, from that reasoning, that the souls of the saints enjoy God, proceeds to prove that their bodies must be venerated. So to perceive what the Holy Doctor thought and what is the truth of these matters, we must make a distinction between two species of cognition whereby we know and believe the soul of some man beholds God; one human, the other superhuman and divine, from the declaration of the Church. —Now, it is certain that veneration due to the bodies of the saints, on which St. Thomas speaks, cannot be applied to any but those bodies, the souls of which we know are blessed by a knowledge revealed to us by the Church, which elevates the honor which is due to them from a human order to a superhuman.

So it happens, that it does not suffice for us to hold some dead person as sacred—even from a moral certitude—and that one should or could venerate his body with a sacred cult; rather, it is required that the Church makes us authentically certain with a certitude that is itself communicated with a divine light, that the soul of that dead man now reigns with God in heaven. —Let us hear the words of St. Thomas in *Quodlib.* 9 art. 16, obj. 1. There, to the objection which prefaces that the saints cannot be venerated because moral certitude of their beatitude cannot be held, the Saint responds in this way: "It must be said that the Pope, whose [office] it is to canonize the saints, can certify in regard to the state of some man through an investigation of their life and the attestation of miracles; and especially [*note*] through the inspiration of the Holy Spirit, who probes all things, even the profound things of God." —Thus, we neither should nor can hold the bodies of the faithful departed as sacred on account of any moral certitude, let alone human and natural, nor show them a sacred cult until after their canonization. For then the Church, from supernatural knowledge, which it has from the inspiration of the Holy Spirit (as the Angelic Doctor says), transfers veneration toward that body from the human order to the superhuman and divine.

The same appears to be expressed in the decrees of Urban VIII touching on the cult of the servants of God that are still neither canonized nor beatified (see this cited by Benedict XIV, *De Canonizat. Sanctorum.*, lib. 2 cap. 11, num. 8), in which it was particularly stated, that in the written lives or deeds of such servants of God the following protestation of the author must be prefaced: "I declare that I do not wish to receive anything that I relate in this book nor for it to be received in any other sense than that which usually rests upon merely human authority; it does not rest upon that divine authority of the Roman Catholic Church or of the Holy See." —Let these words be noted: *Which rest upon human authority ... not the divine authority of the Church*, etc. Therefore, the deeds of the servants of God have no other faith and veneration than human; but when the Church declares them saints, then veneration is raised from human to divine, on account of the divine authority of the Church. Hence it is a fact that for someone to furnish a cult to some dead man which is superhuman, it is necessary that some principle and superhuman knowledge be held on the sanctity of the object, elucidation by a divine medium communicated to us by the Church. And on that account, when the saints have already been declared to be in heaven by the Church, not only do their bones become sacred, but even their garments, letters and the other things that they used and it would be a grave irreverence and sacrilege to use them for profane purposes, save for necessity. —On the other hand, in regard to the things of the dead who are still not canonized, although we might have some sort of knowledge on their heavenly beatitude, it is not forbidden to use them for profane purposes.

Nevertheless, we concede that from veneration we can have with us the relics of some dead person with the rumor of sanctity, to invoke him, to take care to paint their effigy and effect other things of that kind seeing that these cults are not carried out by reason of their being sacred, but merely as acts of religion (but not of the public authority). As John of St. Thomas says, whose authority my adversary opposes to me, and as Bellarmine (*De Canonizatione Sanctorum*, lib. 1 cap. 10 ad 7) and Benedict XIV (*De Canonizatione Sanctorum.*, lib. 2 cap. 7 n. 4 et 7) teach, it can be applied equally toward the dead and the living. Nay more, Bellarmine infers from this that it is licit to apply those acts to the dead because they can be licitly furnished to the living: "If it is lawful," he so concludes, "to honor the living whom we believe to be holy, why not the dead?" And when several seized upon this doctrine of Bellarmine, namely that he conceded that uncanonized saints could be venerated, he so vindicated it by saying that he did not concede anything other than the cult to the uncanonized is nothing other than what is usually shown to the living (*Ibid.*, lib. 2 cap. 9, n. 1). —I said "an act of religion" because a sacred cult is another thing. To kiss the hands of a servant of God, to commend oneself to his prayers, to wash his feet and the rest, these are indeed acts of religion because they emanate from religion; they are not, however, sacred cults since they are not exercised towards sacred things.

And so equally, to bury the dead in a sacred place, to incense them, to kiss their feet, to venerate their relics, these are indeed sacred ceremonies and acts of religion; but they are not a sacred cult. —Certainly, they are called sacred ceremonies and they truly are, because they regard these very things, which are sacred precisely as they are received by the Church. But they cannot be called a sacred cult because the object of the cult regards that to which they are applied. Therefore, it can never be called a sacred cult when the object is certainly not sacred. —Besides, these are certainly acts of religion. And here I confess, that in my first response (I do not know how) an error escaped me, for when I ought to have said that incensations and blessings and other ceremonies which we usually apply to the dead are not a sacred cult, I said they are not acts of religion. I indeed affirm, nor do I doubt that they *are* acts of religion; but not from this fact are they a sacred cult; and through the consequent, it is not so that on account of the aforesaid acts which are applied toward the dead that their bodies must be held as sacred, and thus, can be venerated with a sacred cult. For that reason, Alexander III absolutely forbade someone from being venerated as a saint unless the authority of the Church should be added: "Although, even if many miracles were to take place through them, you are not allowed to venerate them as a saint without the authority of the Roman Church" (Cap. *Audivimus* 1, *de reliquiis et veneratione Sanctorum*). And although formerly, some were venerated as saints by the custom of the people without a declaration of the Church, just the same, Bellarmine responds that this was allowed by the tacit approval of the Pope: "Just as other customs have the force of law from the tacit consent of the prince...; so the cult of some saint, introduced from the custom of some Churches, has force from the tacit or express approval of the Supreme Pontiff." (*De Beatiudine et Canonizatione Sanctorum*, lib. 1 cap. 8).

So, I respond: I do not doubt that the rites which the Church applies toward the dead are sacred ceremonies and acts of religion; but not a sacred cult. Precisely as the *Rituale Romanum*, when speaking on funerals, does not then call the rites which are applied in the burial of the dead a sacred cult, but only *mysteries of religion and signs of Christian piety*, so saying: "The sacred ceremonies and rites, with which ... the holy mother, the Catholic Church, customarily uses in the burial of her sons as true mysteries of religion and signs of Christian piety, as well as the wholesome suffrage of the dead faithful, ought to be preserved by the supreme zeal of the pastor." (*Rituale Romanum, de Exsequiis*, preface). —I add two other observations, from which this will become more clear. Firstly, if such a cult were sacred, the public cult would also be sacred, accordingly it would be shown by the pubic minister of the Church; and it is a certain fact that this cannot be done while the Church herself forbids a public cult to be shown to anyone at all that has not been declared as a saint or a blessed. —Besides, St. Francis de Sales says that a sacred cult is not furnished to the dead except as a declaration of the excellence of their virtue; and the knowledge of this excellence ought to be certain. Moreover, how can it be said that the rights which are exercised for the dead are a sacred cult when in regard to the dead (speaking commonly) this knowledge of the excellence of their virtue is not possessed? Nay more, it is held for a comparison that among the faithful departed there are not a few who are burned in the eternal fire and meanwhile these rites are practiced indiscriminately toward all. Consequently, it must be said that the Church does not hold such rights as a sacred cult.

I wish to forestall a certain argument that could be raised in objection: So if it is conceded that the dead may be venerated with acts of religion, it will be far from doubt that to curse them will be an act opposed to religion. —We will answer first by insistence: If this argument would avail for the dead, it would also avail for the living. For, to venerate the living servants of God with the acts described above, as we showed, is also an act of religion or a religious cult; wherefore to curse such a servant of God with this, even without a wicked intention, would equally be a grave sacrilege; but nobody says this. —Still we will give a direct response. We must make a distinction and also see from what motive such an act of religion proceeds. If it proceeds from the motive of the object itself, that it is a sacred object, then advancing a contumely against it is a sin against religion and a sacrilege. But if the act of honor proceeds from religious piety of the faithful, then it will indeed be a religious act because it proceeds from the motive of religion; but a curse against an object will not be an act against religion, because it is not an act which is referred to a sacred object.

Our adversary in the *Dissertation* regards with wonder, and with a straight face calls them imprudent, who say in confession or in a suggestion that it is not of itself a grave sin to curse the dead. —But I, and others with me am astonished at those who do not have some scruple to preach absolutely that this curse is a mortal sin and a blasphemy. For this purpose, that it would be said that some act is not a grave sin, it suffices that true probability be held that such is not. Just the same, everyone affirms it; I understand it to be the case that something which does not rest upon a weak foundation can be held and taught as safe (according to the common opinion, isolated from the question of more or less probable).

Now the two doctrines which our adversary objects from St. Augustine have no bearing—or else very little—on our argument. One: "A man would sin gravely in matters pertaining to the salvation of the soul, and in that matter alone preferring uncertainty to certainty." And: "If it is doubtful whether it is not a sin, who would doubt that it is certainly a sin?" For there, the Holy Doctor speaks about one who acted in doubt in regard to matters pertaining to the necessity of eternal salvation; in such a matter everyone is held to follow what is certain. Except the saint's discussion is on a particular Donatist who, when he was certain that Baptism was duly and rightly conferred in the Catholic [Church], was on the other hand uncertain as to whether he could rightly receive it in his sect. I will show the whole text: "Even if he should hold it to be a doubtful question as to whether or not it is impossible for that to be rightly received among the Donatists which he is assured can rightly be received in the Catholic Church, he would commit a grievous a sin in matters concerning the salvation of his soul, in the mere fact of preferring uncertainty to certainty." (*De Baptismo*, lib. 1, cap. 3 n. 4). And: "If, therefore, it is doubtful whether it is not a sin to receive baptism from the party of Donatus, who can doubt but that it is certainly a sin not to prefer receiving it where it is certain that it is not a sin?" (*ibid.*, cap. 5 n. 6). Who doubts whether that Donatist would certainly have sinned? —But St. Augustine did not say that he sins who acts from a true and solid probability, when he does not live in doubt in regard to those things which pertain to the necessity of salvation (exactly as Baptism is), and when the action is not certainly illicit. For a doubtful law does not impose a certain obligation, according to what the Angelic Doctor teaches: "No one is bound by some precept except by the medium of knowledge of that precept" (*de Veritate*, qu. 17 art. 3). And the same is proven from cap. *Cum in jure 31, de offic. et pot. judicis deleg.*: "Unless you are certain about a command, you are not compelled to carry out what is commanded." The same thing is found in can. *Sicut quaedam*, dist. 14, where St. Leo writes this: "In those maters which are either doubtful or obscure, we know that what is not found opposed to the Gospel commands nor contrary to the decrees of the most Holy Fathers must be followed." This passage holds that it can be asserted that some action is not gravely illicit. But that it be affirmed absolutely that some action is a mortal sin, probable or even more probable opinion does not suffice.⁵ For the more probable does not exclude a reasonable fear of error; for that reason, it does not effect that a law does not remain doubtful and that the opposite opinion could not be true if it is truly probable. This is why, when it is a question of the sacraments, it is not licit to follow the more probable when the opposite is probable, although less probable.

For this purpose, that some action would be gravely illicit, certitude is required just as everyone teaches with St. Raymund, who wrote: "Do not be too prone to judge things to be mortal sins where this is not certain to you from a certain Scripture." (Sum., lib. 3 tit. 34 §4, v. *Quid de venialibus*). Thus, the Saint advises that some action must not be judged a mortal sin where it is not a certain fact; and when he says: "Where this is not certain," he is always understood to condemn the assertion that something is a grave sin as often as its gravity is not a certain fact as an excess. —St. Antoninus equally says that without danger of sin it cannot be determined that some action is a grave sin unless it is found in Scripture or a determination of the Church, or evident reason: "The question which is asked concerning some act, whether it is a mortal sin or not, unless in this matter one were to have the express authority of Sacred Scripture, or a canon or determination of the Church, or evident reason, it is determined only with great danger. For, [as he adds] if something is determined to be a mortal sin that is not, a person acting against it will sin mortally because everything which is against conscience paves the way to hell" (Part. 2, tit. I, cap. 11, §28), and throws souls in danger of damnation. —Hence, Benedict XIV most wisely, in his work *de Synodo*, in a great many chapters advises bishops nothing other than that they should never condemn

---

⁵ Unless it were certain that the opposite is more probable, from book I, n. 54, 62, 83 and 88. This responsive Epistle was published in 1758, when St Alphonsus had not yet completed his Moral System. The Genuine system was first inserted in the 6ᵗʰ edition, in the year 1767. Footnote to the Gaude edition, pg. 456.

those opinions of grave sin which the doctors of both sides defend as probable.

My adversary, in other respects, has progressed to the point that he calls his opinion a theological conclusion. —I refuse to thrust myself in to decide whether his opinion has weight and upon what weight of probability it is supported. But I do not know whether it can be called a *theological conclusion*, since he has no text of Scripture on his behalf nor a definition of the Church and not even evident reason, nor the common authority of the doctors, nay more, not one of them is found who wrote according to his opinion.

He adds a text of St. Isidore of Pelusium: "The living also assault the dead and make agreements with their enemies! Why, therefore, are you above the laws of nature and the boundaries of enmities? For you seem to sharpen your tongue with embers and ashes; but in the first place you violate the sanctity which it is right that all mortals abide by. Then, it has an immortal soul, whose avenger is the watchful eye of God." —But in the book which I have, published in Rome in 1629, I found the text was in other words than the aforesaid were conceived. For there it is read: "The living customarily even assail those already dead with calumnies, they even make peace and treaties with their enemies. So why do you yourself transgress the boundaries of nature and enmities, when alive you calumniate and wound those already dead? For do you think that you only draw tight your tongue against ash and dust: but lo! You violate the very first most holy right of burial which nevertheless every man embraces, and is zealous to preserve; then he has the immortal soul, whose eye is watchful and always being awake is an avenger." —Now let others judge if this authority confers something of importance upon the opinion of my adversary, who insists all the bodies of the faithful departed must be venerated as sacred. St. Isidore calls the right of burial sacred, but not the body of the dead.

Yet besides this, my adversary agrees with himself that everything is in his favor: The Scriptures, the definitions of the Church, the common authority of the doctors and clear reasons. —The Scriptures are: "...nor will revilers possess the kingdom of God." (1 Cor. 6:10). *Revilers*, explains Calmet, are those who revile a man to his face or commit detraction when he is absent. Our adversary says the definition of the Church is the discipline that it uses in burying the faithful. He claims the authority of the doctors in common is on his side, by saying that the moralists do not dissent from this opinion because it is held for certain according to their own rules. At length, he holds evident reason to be on his side which are the very ones he published in his *Dissertation*. —Whether these persuade or not, I refuse to decide the question by my own judgment; rather, let wise men put an end to all the controversy.

Moreover, by speaking about my position, as I related in the previous pages, apart from three authors cited there who have written on this matter, I took care that this affair should be examined by many, and especially by all the Congregations of missionaries of the city of Naples, in which, especially because they are all professors of moral theology, and there (which is acknowledged by everyone) the picked clergy of Naples joined the men. Here my adversary, advancing a certain text of Socrates into the midst, intimated that not everyone there was provided with such skill to be suitable as masters to explain the questions in detail. I concede that not everyone there was a master, but when the aforesaid Congregations gave their response to me in the name of the whole body, it must be supposed the resolutions were not given by the less wise, but the wiser. —The aforesaid question, as I have already written, was discussed in Rome at the command of Pope Benedict XIV, and according to the mind of that very Pope (which in other respects I never understood to be a definition *ex cathedra*), and it was resolved that it lacked the reality of a mortal sin. But he writes that he is not held to furnish faith nor that examination was applied, nor a resolution given at Rome. I have never had the mind to force him to believe it; but I wrote it because I was moved with forceful effort not to recall it to doubt. While it was witnessed to me as a witness of its own science, and from sight (for he saw the document of the Pope with his own eyes), a certain priest, religious and most learned with scarcely any feeling in this controversy, and on that account I thought others who were indifferent to either side of the controversy could also prudently believe it and not without reason. Otherwise, in my regard, it seems so much more certain to me that I have not hesitated to publish the matter in the same moral work that I have compiled which I dedicated to the same Pope and have taken care to furnish, write and show him as a witness on my behalf.

What remains, if my adversary was lead to write with good faith, is that I also hold for certain that I have not been lead to write from some arrogance or a joy of contention (would it be the best thing that after I escaped from the snare and placed my soul in the safety of eternal salvation, only to contend to advance that which leads the soul to damnation? Why? for empty glory; I would say better that I would be held in perpetual shame for defending a false opinion!); but by a right and good end, that I might free so many from so many sins who had contracted the habit of cursing the dead, and who, not withstanding what they might believe (erroneously in my judgment) to be a grave sin, precisely as it was asserted to them, continued to utter these curses. —But my adversary would have it that I act *obstinately and driven by a false zeal*, I make this omission knowing that "he who judges me is the Lord" (1 Cor. 4:4).

***

I add to this the letter written to me in reply by Abbot D. Bartholomew di Marco, a Basilian father (to whom I sent this epistle so that he might judge it), who is indeed a man considered very experienced in doctrine, and with his order, which has adorned him with the most excellent offices, and also lived in Naples and Rome, etc. He was a teacher in sacred theology which he taught with the praise of all for a great many years, and has exercised the office of the confessional for 30 or 40 years. —I was considering whether I ought to relate here or not the following letter. But I received counsel that I should do it from two motives: 1) that it might be made known to everyone that I acted more cautiously and was not deceived by adhesion to my own feeling (which is the exact thing my adversary asserts that I am deceived by), but have always been careful to seek counsel of other learned doctors; 2) That I would make clear how other excellent men esteem my side and the opposite opinion. —The Epistle follows.

June 14, 1758
Mater Domini

Most Reverend Father, Lord and most esteemed Ruler,

It was a long time ago that I had the consolation of reading your erudite *Dissertation* about the imprecation of the dead, upholding that cursing them is not a grave fault—since that is my sentiment and that of wiser persons with whom I have often spoken with on this subject. Now, in your goodness, you have sent me the response that you had made to a man opposing you, in which I have admired your doctrine, and adding reasons upon reasons you have made it almost self-evident; I would not know on what grounds your opponent could defend that it is a grave fault since the motives adapted by him seem to me to be unimportant, in conformity with what I had read in a booklet which he sent to the printers, and which your Most Reverend Lordship solidly refuted and presently refutes. I certainly do not understand how cursing the dead could be a mortal sin.

Treatise II: The Second Precept, Ch. I, On Blasphemy

I also praise your moderation in calling this sentence 'probable' which states that blaspheming the dead is not a grave fault; you should rather have called this 'morally certain' and, consequently, that which is defended by your opponent morally false and of weak and tenuous probability.

I, therefore, am not able to change your scholarly writing; and I pray that the Lord might enlighten the mind of the one who contradicts you and of the few who keep him company in making a pompous show in finding fault in every little action.

May your Most Reverend Lordship not hold back in openly sending the above-mentioned apologetical response which will be applauded, just as all of your other works have been. I recommend myself to your prayers, making reverence to you, kissing with all respect your hands.

From the most humble, obligated and devoted servant
of Your Most Reverend Lordship,
Bartholomew di Marco, Abbot

I add these few remarks. The aforesaid most Reverend Abbot, as he writes, seems to suppose that I merely hold my opinion as probable. I did not say this; I only said that for this purpose it could be affirmed that some action lacks grave fault, and that it is sufficiently probable that it is not a grave sin. Moreover, I refuse to impose judgment as to whether my opinion is morally certain or not, since I will consign this to the judgment of the wise; but in other respects, I have held and still hold it as more than probable.

Recently our adversary published another epistle to which I hardly think it is necessary to respond; what we have already answered suffices. Furthermore, if perhaps our adversary thinks that whoever writes last remains the victor we gladly concede to him a victory of this sort.

Treatise II: The Second Precept, Ch. II, On Oaths

CHAPTER II
ON SWEARING AN OATH

DUBIUM I
What is an oath?

133. *What is an oath?*
134. *What are true oaths?*
135. *Would it be an oath to say: "by my conscience", or "by my soul"?*
136. *Would it be an oath to say: "I swear it is so"?*
137. *Would it be an oath to say: "It is as true as the sun shines", or "it is as true as the Gospel"?*
138. *Would it be an oath to swear by creatures?*

133.—"Resp. An oath is a tacit or express invocation of the "divine will, as the first and infallible Truth, in witness of some "thing. Moreover, this invocation consists in that the one "swearing, insofar as it is in him, should desire and will God to "witness to what he swears and manifest it (if and when it will "please him, either in this life or in the next), as something "known by God himself, and true. Thus the common opinion, of "the doctors, St. Thomas II IIæ qu. 89 art. 1; Bonacina d. 4 q. 1 "part. 1; Sanchez, 3 *mor.* c. 1; Laymann, l. 4 tract. 3 c. 1."

Thus the following are resolved:

134.—"1. In regard to the internal forum, he swears an oath "whoever has the inward intention, whether formal or virtual, "and invokes God as a witness either for these or those words, "and signs, or even uses neither so that if anyone would use "word by no means importing an oath, and he nevertheless "thinks these things are an oath, he truly swears an oath and "vice versa, Suarez (l. 1, c. 1), Sanchez (l. 3 c. 1), Laymann (l. 4 t. 3 c. 1). But in regard to the external forum, certain formulas of swearing an oath have a model and hence such words can licitly be used in conversation, as is clear from the following."

"2. When there is a doubt on the intention of the oath, it is usually judged according to the common reception of words which he uses."

"3. These formulas have the true model of an oath: "I give God as evidence", or, "I invoke God as a witness". Likewise, *Auf meinem Eid—bei meinem Eid*, (by my oath I swear, I add my oath) unless another were constituted with the intention of using it, because many so speak, *e.g. ich scwöre dir einen Eid—bei meinem Eid*, (I will do this or that, I add my oath), nevertheless, their mind is not to swear it in earnest, but only angrily and to more seriously affirm. Laymann, *loc. cit.* c. 2."

"4. Faith is customarily demanded of priests in place of an oath by their consecration just as even the formula of princes, *Bei unserer füerstlichen Ehre, oder Treve*, (I who am a prince, bind or call to witness fidelity and honor). Even if they are not an oath, still, in the external forum they are received in place of a sworn promise, as it is also said by illustrious or noble persons, *Bei meiner adeligen Ehre, Treve und Glaubem*, (I who am a noble, call to witness my honor and fidelity and faith). See Laymann, *loc. cit.* c. 2."

"5. These formulae: *God knows, God will witness in his time, I speak in the presence of God, God knows all things, God sees my conscience*, they are only thought to be advanced narratively, not in the form of an invocation (and so they are not oaths), unless another thing were certain, or proved from circumstances. Laymann, *loc. cit.* n. 4, Bonacina q. 1 p. 2 from Suarez, Lessius, Sanchez, etc."

Equally, to say: "As God lives, God is truth", is not an oath, if it is advanced in the fashion of enunciation. Cajetan, Ledesma, etc., cited by Salamancans *tract.* 17, c. 2 punct. 3 num. 25. But the Salamancans, with Azor, Fagundez, del Soto, and Trullenchus say such words are received in common use as advanced by way of invocation, and as true oaths.

"6. They are not oaths which are said by the mode of a "solemn promise; *e.g.* "I put forth my head, let my ears be cut "off, let it not be so", etc. See Sanchez, *loc. cit.* n. 42 (See n. 143).

"7. One does not truly swear who, so as to avoid an oath "when compelled to give one, says he swears by everything "which he can, because when there is nothing by which he "could licitly swear without necessity, it is thought through this "he intended to swear nothing.

"8. They are not oaths (which confessors and catechists "advise lest they would sin from an erroneous conscience), "truly, certainly, in truth, by the faith of a good man, by my "faith, by the faith of a good Christian, or of a priest or king." "(Salamancans tract. 17, c. 2 punct. 3 n. 23, with del Soto, "Suarez, Sanchez, Lessius, Villalobos).

135.—"Nor is it to say "by my conscience, on my conscience, "etc." as Lessius holds (c. 42, d. 1), Bonacina, (*loc. cit.*) because "they only signify one speaks from the dictate of conscience, "and the knowledge of truth; God is not adduced to witness. "Still, it would be an oath to say, "by the Catholic faith, by the "Holy Gospel", because then it is thought the Author of that "Faith and Gospel is brought to witness. See Laymann."

Therefore, to say: "By my conscience," it is not an oath, as the doctors teach (Lessius, l. 2 c. 42, dub. 2 n. 4; Elbel, *de 2. praecept.* n. 47, and Salamancans *ibid.* n. 28 with Ledesma and Villal), because no one is adduced as a witness, and the sense is: "What I say is what my conscience dictates to me." It seems the same thing must be held with the author cited above (*Instruzzione*) if you were to say: "by the conscience of my soul"; for there the conscience is principally named and intended, not the soul. It would be otherwise if you said: "By my soul", more probably this is a true oath (Salamancans *ibid.*, with Suarez, Fagundez and Sanchez, Elbel *dict.* n. 47; Renzi *de jur.* q. 17 and Busembaum n. 150), because in the soul God is singularly resplendent, who is considered then to be adduced to witness. See what was said in n. 129.

136.—Likewise, to say: "I swear it is so," is not truly an oath because then divine testimony is implored neither explicitly nor implicitly (Salamancans *loc. cit.* n. 24, with Suarez, Sanchez, Bonacina etc.), unless a question about the oath would precede, because then the questioning preceding that oath would sufficiently determine it in regard to a true oath.

137.—"9. He does not swear who says, "It is as true as the sun "shines, as I sit here, as I walk, etc." Whereby, even if the "comparison is false, it is only a lie, when no one is invoked as a "witness. Likewise, if you were to say, "What I say is Gospel, it "is after the fashion of the faith, it is *de fide*, etc." (To say this is as true as the Gospel is not regularly an oath, as Salamancans *ibid.* n. 27, with Sanchez, and Palaus. And the author of the *Instruzzione* holds the same thing, because these words denote more an assimilation than an invocation, as Busembaum adds below).

10. "Although these and similar comparisons, "It is as true as "there is a God, as there is a Christ in the venerable sacrament, "as the Gospel is true", and likewise, "as I am innocent, as the "Blessed Virgin, or St. Francis, etc.", commonly they seem to "contain an oath with a blasphemy; nevertheless, it does not "sufficiently appear because no one is invoked in testimony. "Nor does it seem to be blasphemy if it were true, and the mind "of the one declaring it were to show only a similitude, as is the "sense: This is true by its mode just as the other thing is true by "its mode. But then it would be blasphemy if the one using it

"only intended to show that it is (according to justice) a "certitude in what he said, as much as it is in a truth of faith. "Sanchez, *2. mor.* c. 31."

138.—"11. It is not an oath when someone swears by created "things in which nothing of the divine goodness is especially "manifest, because they are not thought to be adduced with "relation to God, in other words, "I swear by this beard, "garment, etc." But it is considered an oath when it is done by "more noble things of creation; since then their Creator is taken "up in these, as the one who singularly resides and is made "manifest in them, *e.g.* while an oath is sworn by heaven, the "one dwelling there is understood, when "by the earth", he "whose footstool it is, when "by the temple", he who is "worshiped there, when "by some sacrament", he who "instituted it; when "by the cross", he who was fastened on it; "when "by the Gospels", by touching or naming them, he whose "words they are. Bonacina, q. 1 p. 1 n. 4; Suarez, Sanchez, *loc. "cit.*"

DUBIUM II
How manifold is an oath?

139. *In how many ways is an oath divided? Even to n. 141.*
142. *Are all oaths of the same species?*
143. *Would it be an oath to say: "Punish me, O God, if I lie"?*

139.—"*Resp.* Several divisions are asserted in common, but "they are only accidental, and do not change the species so that "it would be necessary to distinguish them in confession. "Suarez, Lessius, Bonacina, p. 2. Therefore, it is divided:

"Firstly into *verbal, real,* and *mixed,* when viz. it is done "either by words or some action such as lifting up of fingers, "touch of the cross, a scepter, the gospels; or even by words "together with a corporal action, from whence it is called a "corporal oath. See Bonacina p. 2."

140.—"Secondly, into *invocatory*, or calling to witness, and in "*execratory*, or imprecatory. That is, in which God is invoked "simply as a witness, but this, in which he is not only called as a "witness but also as an avenger, since swearing subjects "himself, or another loved one, or something of his, or theirs to "be punished by God if what he says would is false; so that: "*God so love me, help me, may God punish me, may God cause* "*that I would never rise healthy from here; May I not see my wife* "*and children living today; May God take me by sudden death;* "*may he damn x forever; upon my soul, etc.* The scholastics deny "in such things, when it is sworn falsely, or if another species of "malice is joined against charity towards himself or his "neighbor. Suarez, Valentia, etc. deny it, because someone does "not usually call down evil on his friend in such a way; but "rather more he thinks God is not going to do it. See "Bonacina, "d. 4 q. 1 p. 2."

141.—"Thirdly, into *an asserting manner*, and *promissory*. "That is, in which past or present things are affirmed or denied; "this is in a case where something is promised in the future. "Some add *comminatory*, as *e.g. By God I will kill you.* But this "can be referred to promissory. In confession it is not necessary "to explain whether you swore by God or the Saints, because it "is a malice of the same species when the man swearing always "intends to adduce God as a witness. Suarez, Lessius, c. 24; de "Lugo, dist. 16 num. 286."

142.—*Quæritur:* Are all these sort of oaths of the same species? Palaus denies it. But the common opinion better affirms it, with Salamancans tract. 17 c. 2, punct. 2. n. 18 and 19, with del Soto, Lessius, Sanchez, *etc.*

143.—Moreover, it must be noted that the aforesaid words, "Let me be killed if this is not so," is similar, although they are true oaths if they are said by mode of execration, because they mean: "God, whom I call as a witness, shall kill me if this is not the truth", moreover, in common they do not contain anything but a certain promise or obligation under penalty, and they mean: "If this is not so, I promise my life, or that I submit myself to the penalty of death." Salamancans *ibid.* punct. 3, n. 26 with Palaus, Fagundez, Trullenchus, Viallal., Busembaum, d. 1 n. 6, Sanchez, *Dec.* l. 3 c. 2 n. 256, Elbel n. 52. But it is otherwise if God there is expressly named, by saying: "Let God destroy me if I lie", because then God is invoked as an avenger of the lie if perhaps it is advanced. Sanchez, Salamancans Elbel, with Busembaum (above n. 140). Moreover, to say: "Let me be held as a heretic if this is false," is not a true oath, just as it is not regularly by the manner of speaking to say: "May as many Angels take my soul as the number of times I have done this". Or: "Let God so favor me, etc." So think the Salamancans, *ibid.* n. 27, with Palaus and Sanchez. Nor is it an oath to say: "I swear by this cross", but not by making the sign of the cross. Salamancans, *ibid.* n. 24, with Sanchez, Fagundez, and Villalobos.

DUBIUM III
Is it licit to swear an oath, and when?

144. *Is it lawful? And what things are required to licitly swear an oath?*
145. *What about a requisite judgment?*
146. *What about justice? Is there a mortal defect of justice in an oath of assertion? What about in sayings like "By God I will kill you"?*
147. What about a requisite truth?
148. *What certitude is required to swear an oath?*
149. *Would it be lawful to seek an oath from a perjurer?*

150. *Would simple folk committing perjury be excused from mortal sin? And how must they be advised?*

144.—"*Resp.* An oath, if it is done in a due mode, is licit, and this is *de fide*. And it is also an act of religion, as everyone teaches. Moreover, it can be said to be done in due mode when these three things are observed in it: 1) It is a *judgment*, which demands that with discretion, prudence, consideration and reverence, it is done for a grave cause and not without necessity; 2) It is *justice*, which demands that what is sworn is a just matter, licit and worthy; 3) It is *truth*, as in there is no doubt that the matter is true, or at least thought to be true from a grave reason, so that, exactly as more or less from a defect of some of these, injuries are thought to redound against God, or irreverence so also one more or less commits sin.

Thus the following are resolved:

145.—"1. In regard to *judgment*, if only this is lacking then for the most part it is only a venial sin, namely if anyone would swear without necessity or from a certain levity of spirit, or from custom. See Sanchez, l. 3 c. 5 n. 22, Lessius."

"2. Nevertheless, this can be mortally or venially sinful according to the quantity of negligence, which the one swearing admits in the investigation of truth, or by abolishing custom. Sanchez n. 10."

"3. And so the status of those who do not eliminate the habit of swearing oaths without attention is mortal, whether what they usually swear is true or false."

146.—"4. In what looks to *justice*, a man sins mortally who is going to do a morally bad thing, such as he is going to kill someone, because it is a grave irreverence to oblige himself as if by divine authority to a mortal sin, so that here a twofold malice occurs: one, because he wills an evil, and the other "because for this he abuses the authority of God, who hates "every evil. Bonacina (*loc. cit.* p. 3), Lessius, (l. 2. c. 42 d. 3)."

This is certain in a promissory oath, but the question is, would the defect of justice in the assertive oath be a grave sin if someone would situate himself with an oath on some sin?

The first opinion upholds it, with Toledo (l. 4 c. 21 n. 10 and 11) and del Soto, Lessius, etc., cited by the Salamancans (tr. 17 c. 2 punct. 5 § 1 n. 46). But it must be said more probably that it is not anything more than a venial sin against religion, as Suarez (*de relig.* l. 2 c. 3 n. 6), Sanchez (*dec.* l. 3 c. 4 n. 33) and the Salamancans (*ibid.* n. 47) say, with Palaus, Tamburinus and Leander. The reason is, because in a promissory oath it is a mortal sin because the oath is then assumed to strengthen the will to carry out the evil; but in such an assertory oath it is not assumed to confirm one's own satisfaction, rather it is only pronounced to render others more certain about his sin, which is nothing more than a venial levity of spirit. Nevertheless, it must be said otherwise if someone would take up an oath to strengthen a detraction because then the oath is taken as the means to render the infamy of another more certain, as the Salamancans rightly advert with the cited authors.

Then, here it must be noted that those professing words in anger, *viz.* "By God, through Christ, I will kill you", in the common opinion does not sin gravely, because from ignorance or lack of deliberation, for the most part they are excused. In this way, the author of the cited *Instruzzione* agrees with me.

"5. Moreover, one sins venially who swears to do a thing that "is venially evil, or vain, or useless or frivolous since there, only "a light irreverence is thought to be present. Bonacina, *ibid.*, "Lessius, *loc. cit.*" (So even Tanner, Sporer, Sanchez, etc. hold. But to me the opposite opinion seems better, which Elbel holds (n. 97) with Marchant, Turrianus, etc., because it does not seem to be a light irreverence but a grave one to invoke God as a witness and surety in sin, even if it is slight).

"6. Likewise, one sins venially who swears something against "the evangelical counsels, such as he is not going to enter into "religion, not going to give alms, or lend expecting no return. "Suarez, Lessius, Sanchez, Bonacina, *loc. cit.*"

147.—"7. Now in regard to *truth*, when this is lacking in an "oath, he sins mortally because a grave irreverence is "committed against God, seeing that he is added as a witness to "falsity as if either he did not know the truth, or wanted, or "could deceive by witnessing what is false. Nor does slightness "of the matter excuse in this case, because either this is grave or "this is light, or often as a joke, equally, it is still repugnant for "God to witness what is false; and such an oath is called "perjury. St. Thomas, II IIæ q. 89, art. 7; Lessius, Sanchez, "Bonacina, *loc. cit.*" (On this matter, read *propos. 24* among those condemned by Innocent XI). "Moreover, how and when "can perjury be a venial sin *per accidens* (namely on account of "a defect of deliberation or advertence, Salmamancans tract. 17 "c. 2, punct. 5 1 n. 38 and 39), see Escobar, tom. 1 cap. 3 n. 6."

"8. Nor is one excused who swears what is true if he thinks it "is false, or who swears for certain what he is in fact doubtful "of, even if on the side of the matter it was true. del Soto, "Navarre, Bonacina, *l.c.*"

148.—Nevertheless, to swear rightly, absolute and altogether infallible certitude is not required, rather some moral certitude suffices, or a certain probability which touches upon some moral certitude. Tamburinus, l. 3 c. 2 § 1. n. 6. Nay more, Sanchez (lib. 3 cap. 4 n. 10) with Valentia and Suarez, as well as Salamancans (*iibid.* §2 n. 49) say more clearly that the probability of a truth that has been asserted or of a promise to execute the completion of a thing that has been promised suffices in an oath, whether assertory or promissory, *provided that probable reason does not stand on the opposite side.* Hence, they say one can indeed affirm with an oath that what is heard by a person is so worthy of trust, that he would make us morally certain. Still, this does not happen in judgment. Salamancans *ibid.* §1 n. 44, with Sanchez, Palaus, Bonacina, etc. See Busembaum, num. 144.

149.—"9. One who demands an oath from another knowing "that he is going to commit perjury sins equally gravely. An "exception is made if it is a just cause and necessity demands it; (but the authors say a worthy advantage suffices for a cause Palaus, tr. 14 d. 1 p. 10 n. 9 and Elbel *de jur.* n. 110), "because "then perjury follows only from the malice of the one "committing perjury, the other is morally censed for its cause, "when he might use his right. Still, outside the judgment it "rarely has place in private persons. St. Thomas, q. 29; Suarez l. "3 c. 13 and 14; Sanchez, lib. 3 c. 8."

"10. One does not commit perjury that swore something that "is really false because he thought it was true with good faith "and with reason.

150.—"11. It seems that very simple men may to be excused "from the mortal sin of perjury by reason of inconsideration, "since they take up certain formulas for oaths, such as: "By my "soul, may God punish me." Even if they knew it is called an "oath, they still do not apprehend that to swear something "grave is to invoke God as a witness, but only apprehend some "confused reasoning of an evil that is not of great importance. "See Bonacina, *loc. cit.* Laymann, c. 14."

Nay more, we must note that in general, simple people do not apprehend the gravity of perjury. When confessing themselves concerning oaths, they do not or scarcely distinguish true oaths from false ones; and I understand this from long practice in missions.

This is why for those who have the habit of perjuring themselves in this way, I rather more think confessors ought to refrain from instructing men such as these about the grave sin which really is found in perjury so that when they go out from the confessional the material sins in them due to their bad habit do not become formal sins. From the general rule, as Busembaum teaches *de sacr. peon.* with de Lugo, Sanchez, and Laymann, etc. (See book 6, n. 610). Still, those that are accustomed to this must be strongly advised, that in turn they should stop swearing falsely. Moreover, it is not always expedient to warn an unlearned penitent of this sort about the gravity of perjury, if the admonition would not be foreseen to bring profit easily.

DUBIUM IV
Would it be lawful in an oath to use an equivocation?

151. *Would it be lawful to swear an oath with a double-meaning?*
152. *Would it be lawful to swear an oath with a mental reservation?*
153. *Cases are resolved; on a confessor that affirms he does not know if what was confessed is a sin.*
154. *On a guilty man or a witness not legitimately questioned.*
155. *What if he were legitimately asked and swears ambiguously?*
156. *Would someone that is guilty of a capital crime be held to confess it?*
157. *On a penitent questioned about a sin confessed.*
158. *On a poor man needing someone else's things.*
159. *On one questioned by a judge as to whether he spoke with the guilty man, and similar things.*
160. *On a debtor that is not otherwise held.*
161. *On a creditor asserting nothing was paid to him.*
162. *On an adulteress denying the crime.*
163. *On the requisition to make a loan.*
164. *On a merchant, etc.*
165. *On a servant asserting his master is not at home.*
166. *On those taken up to a doctorate.*

167. *On a man asserting that he received money which he did not actually receive.*
168. *On a man asserting what is false by adding something true in a quiet voice.*
169. *Would it be lawful for someone to swear equivocally when not asked?*
170. *See other cases with Busembaum.*
171. *Would it be lawful to swear an oath without a mind to really swear it? (But on this see what is profusely discussed in n. 172, dub. 5). Quaeritur: Is simulation sometimes licit?*

151.—"Resp. To swear with an equivocation, when there is a "just cause and the equivocation itself is lawful is not evil, "because where there is a right to conceal the truth, and it is "concealed without a lie, no irreverence it made in swearing. "But if it were done without a just cause, it will not be perjury "when one swears what is true at least according to some sense "of words or a mental reservation, nevertheless it will be from "its nature a mortal sin against religion, since it is a grave "irreverence to take up an oath so as to deceive another in a "grave matter. So the common opinion of the Doctors, Sanchez "(lib. 3 cap. 6); Bonacina (p. 12); Laymann (cap. 13)."

For greater clarity on the aforesaid points, as well as what must be said on this very difficult matter, we must make a great many distinctions. In the first place, we must make the distinction: an *ambiguity*, or an equivocation, is one thing, but *a mental reservation* is another.

An ambiguity can exist in three ways: 1) when a word has a twofold sense, exactly as *"volo"* means to wish, and to fly; 2) When a phrase has a twofold principal sense, *e.g.* "This is Peter's book" can mean that Peter is the owner of this book or that he is its author; 3) When words have a twofold sense, one more common, the other less so, or one literal and another spiritual, such as those words which Christ said about John the Baptist:

"He is Elijah". And the Baptist said, "I am not Elijah." In such a sense spiritual men say delicate foods harm them, that is, harm their mortification, and when they say they are afflicted with sufferings to be healthy, that means in regard to the strength of the spirit. (Cardenas *diss.* 19 n. 47). So also, a man who was asked about something which is expedient to conceal, can answer, "I say no," *i.e.* I say the word "no". Cardenas (n. 52) is hesitant about this, but save for better council, it unjustly seems when the word "I say" truly has a twofold sense, for it means to advance and assert. Yet, in our sense "I say" is the same as "I advance" [*profero*].

Now that we have posited these points, it is certain and common among all writers that for a just cause it is licit to use an equivocation in the modes we have explained, and to strengthen them with an oath (Lessius (l. 2 cap. 42 n. 47; Cardenas diss. 19 n. 35; Salamancans tr. 17, *de juram.* cap. 2 punct. 8 § 3 n. 115, from St. Jerome, *Utilem* 21, caus. 22 q. 2, who says: "One must take up a useful simulation at the right time." St. Thomas, explaining the matter in II IIæ q. 111 art. 1 ad 2, says: "St. Jerome employs the term "simulation" in a broad sense for any sort of pretense." The reason is, because then we do not deceive our neighbor but from a just cause we permit that he deceives himself. On the other hand, we are not held to speak according to the mind of others if there is a just cause. Moreover, a just cause can be any worthy end to preserve goods useful to the spirit or the body. Salamancans *ibid.* § 1 n. 109 with Valentia, Sanchez, Bonacina and Leander.

Is it a mortal sin to swear with ambiguity or a reservation that is not purely mental (as we discuss below) without a just cause? Viva affirms (*prop. 27 damn. ab Innoc. XI*), likewise, Toledo, Angelus, Armilla, Navarre, etc. with Sanchez (*Dec.* lib. 3 c. 6 n. 22). And Busembaum holds the same thing with Laymann, Sanchez, and the common opinion, as he asserts it. But he incorrectly cites Sanchez and calls his opinion common, for

Treatise II: The Second Precept, Ch. II, On Oaths

Sanchez follows the opposite (*loc. cit.*). And de Lugo holds the same thing (d. 4 sect. 5 n. 64) as well as Cajetan (2. qu. 89 a. 6 ad 4, dub. 2), Salamancans (*loc. cit.* n. 108) with del Soto, Valentia, Prado, Hurtadus, Candidus, Leander etc. Lessius (lib. 2 cap. 42 dub. 9 n. 48) also thinks it is probable along with Palaus, tr. 14 d. 1 p. 7 n. 3), and Busembaum in n. 170, 3. The reasoning of this more probable opinion is that in an oath of this sort truth and justice are present while only judgment or discretion is lacking, whose deficiency is nothing more than a venial sin. Nor does what Viva says hinder us, namely that swearing in such a way in practice invokes God to witness to what is false, for he really would invoke him to testify what is true according to his reckoning, although he permits it for a just cause, that the other, from his lack of care, or inadvertence, be deceived. Nevertheless, an exception must be made that this not be done in a judgment or in contracts. (Salamancans *loc. cit.* and others in common). But from the aforesaid opinion it is inferred (apart from in judgments and contracts), that an absolutely grave cause is not required to swear in such a way, rather, any reasonable cause would suffice, say to free oneself from importune and unjust questioning of another, as the doctors teach (Salamancans *ibid.* n. 109, with Viva, Sanchez, Bonacina, Palaus, etc., Roncaglia *de jur.* c. 4 q. 2 r. 3; Elbel n. 129). Still, we must note here: 1) With Roncaglia (*loc. cit.*), greater cause is required to equivocate with an oath, than without one; 2) With the Salamancans (n. 109), the more the occasion to err that the words offer, the greater the cause should be weighed, which is why they say that when the words offer nearly no cause of error, such as words that are equivocal in themselves which equally hold a twofold sense, then the lightest cause excuses.

152.—*A mental reservation* is on the one hand *purely mental*, which can be perceived by others in no mode, while the other is *not purely mental*, which can be made known from the circumstances present.

A *purely mental* reservation is never licit, and neither is an oath upon it, which is clear from three propositions condemned by Innocent XI. The first of those which were condemned (n. 26), said: "If anyone either alone or in the presence of others, would swear with another end that he did not do something which he really did do by understanding inwardly something else which he did not do, or another road from that which he was on, or any other true addition you like, whether it was when questioned or done of his own will or for the sake of recreation, or whatever, then it is really not a lie nor perjury."

The second (n. 27) of those that were condemned, said: "There is a just cause for using these ambiguities as often as it is necessary or useful for health of the body, honor, or to keep domestic affairs safe; or for any act of virtue so that the concealment of truth were thought then expedient and devoted."

The third of those condemned, n. 28, said: "One who, by the medium of commendation or duty, was promoted to a magistracy or a public office, will be able with a mental reservation to furnish an oath which is usually exacted at command of the king, not held in respect to the intention of the one exacting it, because he is not held to affirm a secret crime."

On the contrary it is licit, for a just cause, to use a restriction that is not purely mental, even with an oath if it cannot be perceived from the circumstances. It is proved from John 7:8 where Christ said: "I do not go up for this feast day." And still Scripture says that he later when up; "I do not go up" is *manifestly*, as the disciples were asking, but *I go up secretly*. Equally from Matthew 24:36, where the Lord said: "On that day no man knows ... not even the Son," by understanding *to manifest*, as the disciples were asking, exactly as St. Augustine explains (*in* Psalmis, VI, n. 1). St. Thomas thinks in the same way (3 p. q 10 art. 2 ad 2), saying: "He is said not to know the day, because he does not cause [them] to know." In other words, he said I do not know to manifest it to others. And St. John

Chrysostom, St. Hillary, St. Ambrose, St. Athanasius, St. Basil, St. Hilary, etc. all think the same thing, as Suarez shows (in 3 p. q. 10 a. 2). The following authors hold this opinion in common: Gonet (*Man.* c. 5 tr. 8 c. 2 § 3); Laymann (tr. 3 l. 4 c. 13 n. 7 *v. Interim*) Paludanus (in 4 d. 9 q. 3 a. 3 concl. 1); Adrian (in 4 *de sacr. confess.* d. 6 § *Ad Argum*); Major (in 4 d 15 q. 18 q. 1); del Soto (*de secreto, membr.* 3); Wigandt (tr. 10 exam. 4 n. 61 resp. 3, Cardenas in 2 *crisi*, diss. 19 n. 81, who in prop. Innoc. XI diss. 19 n. 48 with Suarez and de Lugo says the same thing must be held if he would respond to the mind of the one asking); La Croix (l. 3 p. 1 n. 287); Holz. (t. 1 *de juram.* p. 273 n. 490); Elbel (*eod. tit.* t. 2 p. 52 n. 44); Sporer (tr. 3 c. 1 n. 115); Viva (in prop. 27 Innoc. XI n. 4); and Salamancans tr. 17 c. 2 punct. 8 § 3 n. 117), where they say this opinion is the common opinion of nearly all the doctors.

The Continuator of Tournely (*de relig.* part. 2 c. 3 art. 5, in fine) with Vanroy and Boudart, while noting that even the stricter theologians deny these broadly mental restrictions (which is not the same as a purely mental reservation) are illicit, following St. Augustine who, in his book *contra mendacium*, c. 10, says: "Although everyone who lies wants to conceal what is true, but not everyone who wants to conceal that which is true, lies." Even the most rigid Contensonius (t. 4 diss. 2 c. 1, in resp. *ad Instabis*); while explaining that of John 7 on the ascent of Christ to the feast day, he says Christ applied somewhat obscure words in which a prudent man could easily understand the sense of the words in interpretation. St. Thomas favors this (as Wigandt rightly says) in II IIæ q. 69 art. 2, where: "It is one thing to be silent about the truth, but another to propose falsity." Likewise, in q. 110 art. 5 ad 4, he says: "It is not licit to tell a lie for this purpose, that someone would free another from any danger; nevertheless, it is lawful to cover the truth prudently under some dissimulation, as Augustine says in his book *Contra mendacium.*" Furthermore, the reasoning of this opinion is that if it were not lawful to use a purely mental reservation, then the mode to licitly cover a secret would not exist, if anyone could not open it without loss or harm; which indeed would be equally as pernicious in human commerce as a lie. Thus the condemnation made by the Pope of a mental reservation is correctly understood and strictly taken up on a purely mental reservation; for only a true mental reservation ought to be said to be that which is only made in the mind, and so remains secret and in no mode avails to be understood from human circumstances.

153.—Hence it is inferred: I. A confessor can affirm even with an oath that he does not know the sin he heard in confession, by understanding in addition *as a man*, but not *as a minister of Christ*, as St. Thomas teaches in II IIæ q. 70 art 1 ad 1. Cardinal de Lugo, disp. 22 (who, nevertheless, explains in n. 75 that it could be understood in another mode, *to not know by knowledge which would be useful to make a response*), likewise Sporer *de praec.* n. 119, and Elbel *de jur.* n. 149, with others very much in common. The reasoning is because the one asking does not have a right except to know communicable knowledge, but the confessor does not have such knowledge. And this is so even if another man would ask whether he heard it as a minister of Christ because the confessor must always be thought to respond as a man since he cannot speak as a minister of Christ (de Lugo, n. 66; Viva *in prop. 27 Innoc.* n. 3 and 13; Roncaglia *de 2 praec.* c. 4; Reg. *prax.* n. 2 and Elbel *de jur.* n. 130 with others).

Hence Cardenas and Felix Potestà say that as often as someone is held to conceal the infamy of another man, he may licitly say "I don't know," viz. "I do not have useful knowledge to make a response" or "I do not know anything that can be manifested," as Cardenas says with de Lugo (d. *loc.* n. 43 and 44) and others (Cardenas, *diss.* 19 n. 39 in fine, and 67; Felix Potestà *de jur.* n. 1734). And if anyone would rashly seek from a confessor whether he heard such a sin in confession, the latter can rightly respond:

"I did not hear it," that is, "as a man, or to make it known". (Cadenas with de Lugo, n. 66).

154.—II. A guilty man or a witness, when not legitimately asked by a judge, can swear they do not know the crime when they really know it, by understanding in addition to not know the crime *about which one can legitimately inquire*, or to not know *to divulge* (Cajetan *Opusc.* tom. 1 tr. 31 r. 5; Sporer *de 2. praec.* c. 1 n. 120 and 121; Azor tom. 1 l. 11 c. 4; Roncaglia *de 2. praec.* c. 4 q. 2 r. 3; Sanchez *Dec.* l. 3 c. 6 n. 23 and 26, with Navarre, Toledo, Valentia, etc., from the same thing that St. Thomas says in II IIæ q. 69). The same is held if the witness were not held to divulge as a result of another heading, namely if it is certain for him the crime lacked sin, as the Salamancans say in tr. 17, c. 2 punct. 8 § 6 n. 139, and Elbel in n. 145, or if he knows the crime but under a secret, since no infamy would go before him, as Cardenas says (*ibid.* n. 51).

Still, a guilty man or a witness who is legitimately asked by a judge, cannot use any equivocation because he is held to obey the just precept of a superior and that is the common opinion (Salamancans *ibid.* n. 146, with del Soto, Lessius, Sanchez, etc. with Busembaum). And the same must be said about an oath in burdensome contracts, because otherwise injury would be inflicted upon another. (Salamancans *ibid.*) Except in a trial, if the crime were altogether secret, for then on the contrary a witness is held to say the guilty man did not commit it (Tamburinus, c. 4 § 2 n. 4, with Caredenas, and Potestà as above). And the guilty man can do the same thing if there is not incomplete proof, etc. (Tamburinus § 3 n. 2, with the common opinion), because then the judge does not legitimately ask.

155.—*Quæritur I:* If such a guilty man actually entering into a contract deceived by swearing equivocally, could he be absolved on condition that he would manifest the truth? Some deny this as improbable, but Sanchez (*Dec.* l. 2 c. 7 n. 8) and the Salamancans (*ibid.* n. 147) with Philiarchus, affirm it as more probable, because by such an oath (which cannot be called perjury) he did not sin against commutative justice, but against legal justice and due obedience to the judge, whose precept to detect the truth is transient, and endures only while the judge asks him. And Sanchez says the same thing (*ibid.*) about a lying witness. And therefore both can be absolved provided that they reveal the truth. But both are held to make satisfaction to the other man, if they can by another way. Still, if they cannot, the Salamancans say they are held to again reveal the truth in court. But I would excuse them if they were altogether powerless to make satisfaction in the present and future.

156.—*Quæritur II*: Can a guilty man deny the crime when he is legitimately asked, even with an oath, if grave harm would threaten him from the confession? Elbel (n. 44) denies this, with St. Thomas (*ibid.* art. 1 ad 2) and indeed it is more probable because the guilty man is held to undergo that harm for the common good. But it is probable enough what other authors say, that the guilty man can deny the crime even with an oath (at least without grave sin) if the penalty of death, prison or perpetual exile would threaten him, or the loss of all his goods, ships and similar things, by understanding in addition "he did not commit it insofar as he is held to affirm it," provided there is a hope of avoiding the penalty. The reason is that human law can oblige men *sub gravi* with such a burden. And Elbel adds that this opinion (although it is less probable) sill would have to be understood by the guilty men and their confessors so that they would be freed from the grave sin in which they will easily fall should they bound to confess the crime. See what is going to be said in book 5, n. 274.

157.—III. The penitent, being asked by the confessor about a sin already confessed, that he did not commit it by understanding in addition, "that which he has not confessed." (Cardenas *diss*. 19, n. 48, Salamancans tr. 17 c. 2 punct. 8 § 3 n. 118, Sanchez, lib. 3 cap. 6 n. 14; Sporer *de 2. praec.* cap. 1 n. 105). But this must be understood, unless the confessor would justly ask to learn the state of the penitent, from number 58 of the propositions condemned by Innocent XI.

158.—IV. A needy man can respond to a judge about goods hidden for his subsistence that he has nothing (Salamancans *ibid.* § n. 140). Equally, an heir who, without discovery, hides goods; if he is not held to make satisfaction to creditors from them he may respond to a judge that he has hidden nothing, understanding in addition "from the goods which he would be held to make satisfaction". (Salamancans *loc. cit.* and Roncaglia, c. 4, *reg.* 2 *in praxi.*)

159.—V. Someone that takes out a loan, but later satisfies it, can deny he has taken up a loan, understanding in addition: "such that he ought to repay." (Salamancans *cit*. n. 140, and Sporer *de 2. praec.* c. 1 n. 122, with Suarez, Navarre, Azor, Laymann, Covarruvias and others).

So equally, if anyone were coerced to matrimony, they can assert to the judge even with an oath *that they did not contract it*, that is to say freely, as is just. (Toledo, lib. 4 c. 21; Laymann, c. 14 n. 8; Navarre, in c. *Humanae aures*, caus. 22 q. 5; Sporer *loc. cit.*). Sporer says the same thing about someone who entered into an invalid betrothal. Equally, a man who promised matrimony, but then would not be held to it, can deny the promise, viz. *that he was held by it*, as the Salamancans say (*ibid.*).

Someone who is not held to a tax can respond that he brings nothing with him, *viz.* from which he owes a duty. (Cardenas n. 77, Salamancans *ibid.*; Sporer *loc. cit.* n. 121 with Ledesma). One who comes from a place falsely thought to be infected can deny he came from it, *viz.* a pestilential one, because this is the mind of the guards. (Salamancans *ibid.* n. 141; Lessius, c. 42 n. 47, Sanchez *Dec.* l. 3 cap. 6 n. 35; Sporer *loc. cit.* n. 140, with Toledo, Navarre, Suarez, Henriquez, Rodriguez, etc.). Nay more, Toledo and Lessius admit this as well as many others cited by Sporer, even if he quickly passed through an infected place, provided it were certain he did not contract the plague, because it could be understood he did not come so that danger would not be feared from him; but I do not altogether acquiesce to this. The Salamancans (n. 141) admit this, with Busembaum, because if someone were forcefully obliged by a thief to promise money with an oath, he could understand in addition: "I will give, if I owe you without an oath"; because they say that promise from circumstances can admit such an ambiguity. Equally a wife, for whom it is certain the marriage is null, can promise with an oath to a judge, or a confessor who would not otherwise wish to absolve her, that she will cohabitate with her husband, even if she did not so intend, understanding from that licit cohabitation. (Salamancans *loc. cit.*).

160.—VI. A man asked by a judge whether he spoke with a guilty man can deny it, understanding he did not speak so as to cooperate with him. A canon lawyer, obligated to a secret, can swear he manifested nothing, if he manifested nothing of those things which he is held to conceal *sub gravi*. The Salamancans agree (*ibid.* n. 142) who assert all these things obvious to all authors. Equally Lessius, c. 52 n. 48, with Alexander, Bartoli. etc. One who is going to be chosen for an office, being asked whether he had some impediment can deny it if it is really not such a thing that would impede him in the exercise of office.

Equally, if anyone were summoned and asked whether the food is good, which really is insipid, he can respond it is good, viz. *for mortification* (Cardenas, *diss.* 19 n. 74). So also Cardenas (n. 76) and la Croix (lib. 3 p. 1 n. 302) say ceremonies can licitly be advanced, "I kiss my hand," etc. "I offer myself as a servant," etc. because from common use they are received as material words advanced only for honor. It is also licit to conceal the truth with cause, *e.g.* if someone asked you for money, you can respond: "Would that I had it!" or "I would be glad to have some", etc. (Cardenas, *diss.* 19 n. 53).

161.—*Quæritur I:* Could a creditor assert from a document with an oath that nothing was paid to him, if really a part has been paid but he has a loan from another person, which he could not prove? It is answered that he can, provided he did not swear the quantity due to him by that document, lest it be inferred he suffered loss from other previous creditors. Salamancans tr. 17, cap. 2 punct. 8 § 6 n. 143, with Sanchez, Palaus, Leander, etc.

162.—*Quæritur II:* Could an adulteress deny the adultery with a man, understanding, that will reveal him? She can equivocally assert she did not break a marriage which truly persists. And if she had sacramentally confessed the adultery, she can respond: "I am innocent of this crime," because by confession it has been taken away. So thinks Cardenas, *diss.* 19 n. 54, who still adverts that she could not affirm it with an oath, because to assert something probability of the fact suffices, but to swear an oath certitude is required. But the response is made that moral certitude would suffice to swear an oath, as we said above in *dubium* 3, n. 148, with the Salamancans (tr. 17 c. 2 punct. 5 § 1 n. 42), Lessius, Sanchez, Suarez, Palaus and the common opinion. Such moral certitude of the remission of the sin can indeed be held, when someone morally disposed receives the sacrament of penance.

But in regard to the question, the Salamancans (*ibid.* punct. 8 § 6 n. 144) with del Soto say a woman cannot deny the adultery because it would be a pure mental reservation. Still, Cardenas (n. 60) admits that in danger of death it is permitted to use a metaphor which is common in scripture where adultery is taken for idolatry, as in Ezechiel 23:37: "Because they committed adultery ... and fornicated with idols." Nay more, if the crime is truly secret, according to the probable opinion of the authors, a woman can deny it with an oath and say: "I did not commit it"; in the same mode in which a guilty man can say to a judge that does not officially question him, "I did not commit the crime," by understanding he did not commit to the extent he is held to manifest it. (Busembaum, below, and Lessius, Trullenchus, *ibid.* and Sanchez, lib. 3 *dec.* c. 2 n. 42, with del Soto, Sayr and Aragon, as Tamburinus holds *ex comm.* c. 4 § 3 n. 1 and 2, as well as Viva q. 7, art 4 n. 2).

163.—*Quæritur II:* Could someone requested to make a loan swear that he did not have any money when he really has some, by understanding that he has no money *to furnish a loan*? The Salamancans (*loc. cit.* n. 145, with del Soto, Henriquez) deny this. The reason is because that reservation cannot be perceived from the circumstances. But this must be understood, if the truth can in no way be perceived; for if it could be thrown out there from some circumstance, namely of poverty or neediness of the lender, one could rightly understand "I have nothing superfluous that I could lend". So think Roncaglia (*de 2 praec.* c. 4 reg. 2 *in praxi*), Viva (q. 7 a. 4 n. 2) with Sanchez, Bonacina, Sylvius, etc. Cardenas (diss. 19 n. 48) with Suarez and de Lugo, who so teaches: "One that has one loaf necessary for himself truly responds that he has nothing for one that asks for bread to be loaned to him, because he has nothing which he could loan and it is the only thing the other man asks." (*de poenit.* disp. 23, sess. 4 n. 74). Cardenas says the same thing (n. 73) on money that is sought, if it is necessary to its owner.

164.—*Quæritur IV:* Could merchants swear their merchandise is more expensive for them, by understanding with other merchandise? Some affirm this, but the Salamancans (dict. n. 145) rightly deny it. Still, Croix, with Gobat says that it is probable he can when they do not consider the mere price of the thing, but compute it in expenses for taxes, for the storehouse, etc. (Croix l. 3 p. 1 n. 301).

165.—*Quæritur V:* Could a servant, at his master's command, deny that the latter is at home? Cardenas (*diss.* 19 n. 75) admits that he can fasten a stone to his foot and answer "he is not here," because it is not a mental reservation; but I do not assent to this, if the other man could notice it by no means. I would rather more concede that he could say "he is not here," viz. not here at the door, or at the window, or (as the Continuator of Tournely says, *de relig.* part. 2 cap. 3 art. 5, in fine): "he is not here," insofar as he can be seen. Cardenas says likewise, that he can respond, "he has left the house," by understanding in the past; for we are not held, as he says above with Lessius, to respond to the mind of the one asking the question if a just cause is present. It would be otherwise if he were asked, did the Lord go out this morning, as Croix says (lib. 3 p. 1 n. 284). In this way, even Cardenas (n. 72), speaking about a nobleman who is in bed, says that the servant can respond that he is outside, viz. he is not to be seen, as it is usually understood from the common manner of speech.

166.—*Quæritur VI:* Could those that are going to take up a doctoral degree swear the requisite condition with an equivocation that is not true, *viz.* to have freed himself up for that science for so many years, etc., if they were equally suitable as other doctors? See Tamburinus, *Dec.* lib. 3, cap. 2, who affirms it and says then there is a just cause for swearing in this way, lest worthy candidates be rejected. But whatever about this, it seems to me more probable that those who are going to get their doctorates at Naples do not commit perjury who, by the usual custom, write in their own hand on taking up their registrations: "*Dico con giuramento essere il primo anno institutista,* etc.,[6] when

---

[6] Translator's note: "I swear to be registered for the first year, etc."

it is really not so. The reason is because that verb "*giuro*" or "*dico con giuramento*," as we said above (dub. 1 n. 136) with the Salamancans (tr. 17 c. 2 punct. 3 n. 24), Bonacina, Sanchez, Suarez, is not of itself an oath, unless questioning would precede about an oath; but this questioning at Naples is either altogether not done or is not done from a true oath, but only on that written material which seems from the common use not to take up a true oath.

167.—*Quæritur VII:* Could someone licitly assert, in the presence of a notary, that he received money which he truly did not receive? Tamburinus (*ibid.* n. 20 and 23) affirms he can by changing the sense, viz. by swearing he has or receives money for a portion, because he is morally certain another man is going to pay him in a short time. And it seems probable from the common use of speech.

168.—*Quæritur VIII:* Is it lawful to swear something false by adding a true circumstance in a low voice? Hurtad and Prado (with others cited by Salamancans *ibid.* punct. 8 § 5 n. 136 against Torre), affirm it, who say that it suffices to make the speech true, that it would outwardly harmonize with the concept of the mind either to be explained by trifles or a quiet voice, and it is *per accidens* that the other would not hear it. But the Salamancans admit it better (*ibid.* n. 138) if the pronouncement could be perceived by the other in some mode, although his senses did not perceive it; it is otherwise if it were altogether hidden from the other man.

169.—"1. He sins gravely who uses an equivocation when "questioned, but swears by his own will, because then he is held "to use terms according to their common meaning, as Cardinal "Toledo says (lib. 4 c. 21) to the extent that they do not have the "reasoning of an equivocation."

Nevertheless, the Salamancans more probably say the contrary with the common opinion, namely that when a just cause of necessity or utility is present, one can use ambiguities in swearing, even if he would offer to swear of his own will.

170.—"2. Likewise one sins gravely that uses an equivocation "when an oath is justly exacted from him, such as by a judge or "a superior in a grave matter. Bonacina p. 12."

"3. Moreover, if such an oath were made on a light matter, "for a joke and short of disobedience and notable loss to "another it will only be venial, as Sanchez probably teaches (l. 3 "c. 5 against others), because he lacks only discretion or "judgment. See Bonacina, *loc. cit.*"

"4. It is lawful to swear equivocally if an oath were unjustly "exacted, *e.g.* if someone were to demand an oath who has no "right to, say a judge with no competence, or that does not "preserve the order of law. Likewise, if it were exacted by force, "injury, fear, *e.g.* if a man were to demand an oath from a wife "about a secret adultery; if thieves demanded from you a "ransom with an oath. (Sayr l. 4 c. 3 and lib. 1 c. 17; Lessius, "Trullenchus lib. 2 cap. 1 d . 15).

171.—"5. Someone that only swore outwardly without a mind "to swear is not obliged, except perhaps by reason of scandal, "since he did not swear but play-acted. Still, in the external "forum he can be compelled to keep it. (Sanchez, 7 *Mor.* cap. 10, "num. 11; Trull, lib. 2, c. 1 d. 10). But on this see what is going to "be said in the following n. 172."

Lastly, it is asked whether simulation is sometimes licit? It is answered: *formal* simulation, namely when someone intends by an external act to signify something which he has in mind, this is never licit because it is a true lie of fact, as St. Thomas teaches (II IIæ q. 111, art. 1). But *material* simulation, viz. when someone does something not so intending to deceive another man but some other end, this is licit with a just cause, and others could always conjecture from the circumstances that it is done for another end, exactly as it was said about a reservation that is not purely mental in n. 152. So in Joshua 8 he licitly fled, not intending to show fear but so the enemy would be led far away from the city. So even Christ the Lord did in Luke 24:28 at Emmaus, "And he pretended to go further," not intending that the disciples would believe this, but meaning to show that he really was going to go further unless they would invite him. (Croix l. 2 p. 1 n. 298).

DUBIUM V
What is the obligation of a promissory oath and how great is it?

172. *In how many ways must the truth be affirmed in a promissory oath? What kind of sin is a feigned promissory oath, and in what way does it oblige?*
173. *Does one sin gravely that does not fulfill a promise in a small matter?*
174. *Does an oath extorted from fear oblige?*
175. *What if it were extorted from error or treachery?*
176. *Would an oath oblige on a bad or vain thing?*
177. *What about an oath in favor of a third party?*
178. *Would an oath to not play exclude moderate play?*
179. *Would an oath made against a first oath oblige?*
180. *Should an oath follow the condition of a promise?*
181. *How does an oath to preserve the statutes of some college apply?*
182. *On the oath of doctors not to see someone frequently, etc.*
183. *On an oath to preserve a secret, to tell the truth and to pay a debt.*
184. *Does an oath made to a concubine to not have relations with another woman oblige?*
185. *Does a wasteful promise with an oath oblige?*
186. *Would an oath to go back to prison oblige? On the oath of parents and masters to punish sons or servants.*

Treatise II: The Second Precept, Ch. II, On Oaths

172.—"Resp. 1. In a promissory oath two truths are affirmed: "one primarily on the present, namely that the one swearing "should have the mind to fulfill what he promises; the other "secondarily on the future that he is going to fulfill it in the "time which he promises; whether he makes the promise to "God, and it is a vow with an oath, or to man and a human "promise is sworn. From there, the obligation to fulfill it arises, "if he reasonably could. So the common opinion of the doctors; "Laymann, lib. 4 tom. 3 cap. 6, and Bonacina, p. 7."

Thus the following are resolved:

"1. From a defect of the first truth the one swearing truly and "mortally commits perjury, if he either did not have a mind to "fulfill it, whether the matter was small, great, licit or illicit; or "if he hesitated as to whether he was going to do what he swore "or not; or if he thinks it is morally impossible for him to fulfill "what he promises because in regard to this present truth, a "promissory oath does not differ from an assertory one; "wherefore the paucity of the matter does not excuse." (Indeed one who promises something with an oath, thinking it is impossible sins. So here Busembaum. But it must be added with the Salamancans, tr. 17 c. 2 punct. 5 § 2 n. 49 with Azor, Suarez, Fagundez, Leander, etc. that it is otherwise if he had probable reason to fulfill it).

Quaeritur: What sort of sin would a feigned promissory oath be, and to what does it oblige? I distinguish: Someone can falsely promise with an oath in three ways: I. Without a mind to swear; II. Without a mind to oblige himself; III. Without a mind to fulfill it. I. If anyone would swear *without a mind to swear*, he sins, from the 25th proposition condemned by Innocent XI, which says: "It is licit to swear an oath without a mind to swear whether the matter is light or grave with cause." The reason is, because then he mocks divine testimony. Moreover, would he sin gravely? *Resp.* He would if he swore an oath without a mind to fulfill the promise; if truly with a mind to fulfill it, he would only sin venially, as the common opinion of the doctors says (Sanchez, *Dec.* lib. 3 c. 6 n. 10; Roncaglia *de juram.* c. 4 q. 1 r. 3; Tamburinus *de juram.* lib. 3 c. 3 § 2 n. 4; Elbel *de jur.* n. 120; Mazzotta *eod. tit.* c. 3 q. 3). But they rightly make the exception if the oath were made in contracts, or in the presence of a judge, because then, although it is not perjury, still it is a grave deception against justice.

II. But if they swear *without a mind to oblige themselves*, but with a mind to fulfill it, the doctors hold he sins mortally, both because so swearing he falsely signifies he has the intention of obliging himself that he truly does not have, and because, as Croix sensed as more probable, it seems a grave irreverence to adduce God as a witness and refuse to be bound by his testimony. (Cajetan 2. 2. qu. 89 art. 6; Croix, lib. 3 p. 1 num. 521, likewise St. Antoninus, Navarre, Scotus, Tamburinus and others more commonly cited by Sanchez, *loc. cit.* num. 5). But some of the same authors hold very probably he does not sin except venially. (Sanchez, n. 7; Tamburinus n. 6; Elbel n. 21; Renzi *de juram.* and Ant. *à Spir. S.*, to whom Roncaglia adheres). The reason is because swearing in such a way, when he has no mind to fulfill it, although he does not intend to obligate himself, on that side he does not swear what is false because he asserts rightly the truth on the present, on the other side, since he would not have the will to be obliged in any way by the force of the oath, from its intrinsic reasoning it is to induce an obligation of religion, he really does not swear, as the authors say from the common opinion, and therefore this oath is the same and if it is done without a mind to swear, that is no more than venial when the truth is asserted, as was said above (Salamancans tract. 17 cap. 1 punct. 1 § 3 n. 19 and n. 23; Elbel *loc. cit.*; Sporer in *2. praec.* cap. 1 n. 134, etc.).

Furthermore, would someone swearing an oath with a mind to swear, but without a mind to be obliged, be held to keep the oath?

The first opinion says no, not only because an oath of this sort would be invalid, as above, but even more because God does not accept promissory oaths except according to the intention of those that swear them, from *c. Humanae aures*, qu. 5, where it is said: "Divine judgments hear such as these [our words] and profess their inmost value." (Palaus, tract. 24 d. 1 p. 8, n. 7; Salamancans *ibid.* n. 23; Roncaglia r. 4; Tamburinus n. 7; Mazzotta *loc. cit.*; Elbel n. 125 and Sanchez *Dec.* lib. 3 cap. 10 n. 8, with St. Bonaventure, St. Antoninus, Scotus, Sylvius, Navarre, Armilla, Gabriel, Angelus, and others in common, as Azor asserts). And St. Thomas clearly favors this in 3. dist. 39 qu. 1 art. 3, where he says: "Moreover, if one swears without treachery *simpliciter*, then in the forum of conscience he is not obliged except according to his intention." And he confirms the same thing in II IIæ. qu. 89 art. 7 ad 4, "But if the man who swears the oath does not apply treachery, he is obligated according to the intention of the oath." Yet, he swears without treachery (as Elbel says n. 118 *cum Ill.*) who swears to someone having no right from justice to the thing promised.

Nevertheless, *the second opinion* affirms that he is held to preserve the oath. (Lessius, lib. 2 cap. 42 n. 37, though he calls the opposite opinion very probable; Cajetan 2. 2. q. 89 art. 7; Suarez, cap. 7; del Soto lib. 8 q. 1 art. 7; likewise, Valentia, Sayr, Filliuci, Aragon, cited by Bonacina tom. 2 d. 4 qu. 1 pag. 7 num. 3 and Renzi *de juram.* pag. 125 qu. 5). The reason is because, one who swears with a mind to swear, now utters a true oath, and so is held to effect it, to preserve the reverence for the divine name so that the truth, which he swore, would go out; nor can one separate the obligation to fulfill what was promised from the oath, when the obligation arises from the oath itself, whose nature is that it should have the effect which is sworn lest God would be called as a witness to falsity. And in this the difference between a vow, or a contract and an oath appears, for in them the obligation depends on the intention of the one vowing or contracting, but in an oath from the force of the oath itself. Both opinions are probable, but the first is more probable; for the reasoning of the second opinion supposes as certain that such an oath without a mind to oblige oneself to what he uttered, is a true oath. Nevertheless, it is more probable and common what the Salamancans assert (tr. 17 cap. 1 punct. 1 § 3 n. 19) with others, as above, and even Viva (in prop. 25 Innoc. XI n. 13 against Lessius, n. 37), that an oath of this sort is not a true oath both because it lacks the necessary condition for the nature of a promissory oath, whose character is the mind to oblige oneself, and because the oath follows the nature of the promise which he confirms, as is certain with Busembaum n. 280, with Lessius, Bonacina, etc. But the promise made without such a mind is indeed not a promise but a simple proposition; therefore, when the promise vanishes, so also the oath vanishes, and it is held as a deed without a mind to swear, which certainly, as we saw, is null. But if no oath exists, then no obligation to fulfill it exists.

III. At length, if someone swears *without a mind to fulfill it*, but with a mind to swear and oblige himself, he certainly sins mortally because then there is a defect of truth in the present. Moreover, would he be obliged to fulfill what was promised? We answer affirmatively, because then the essence and obligation of the oath is in force (Tamburinius, n. 7; Mazzotta l. c. and Sanchez, lib. 3 cap. 10 n. 5 with St. Bonaventure, Leonardo and Suarez, who call the opposite improbable). And this must be said even if he had no mind to oblige himself from the force of the promise, because he is obliged from another source—the force of the oath, as Sanchez holds (n. 6), as well as Tamburinus (*ibid.*), and Mazzotta (*loc. cit.*) who also rightly adverts that he who has a true mind to swear and thinks nothing on the obligation of the oath is truly obliged because the obligation follows from the very nature of the oath, and one who wills an act consequently wills its properties. He says the same thing of a man who is ignorant of the obligation of the oath; but the Salamancans more probably contradict this (*ibid.* n. 23) while speaking on a vow, where they say from the common opinion, that if someone were ignorant that a vow carries with it an obligation, and utters the vow with his error, by refusing the obligation, he is not obliged to the vow because no man contracts an obligation unless he willingly imposes it on himself. (See what is going to be said on vows, n. 201, *Quaer.* I. And see what was just said above, where we saw with St. Thomas that an oath does not oblige beyond the intention of the one vowing it). Moreover, if someone is unjustly compelled, say by a thief, to promise something with an oath, he can licitly intend to not wish to fulfill the promise if he obtained relaxation of the oath. So probably Croix (lib. 1 p. 3 num. 278) with Suarez, Sanchez and Diana.

173.—"2. By a defect of the second truth he truly commits "perjury who promises something, and later does not fulfill it if "he could reasonably fulfill it. Here there is only a doubt as to "whether a man who promises a scanty thing with an oath, say "to give someone one apple, or a coin for alms, or to castigate a "child, or among things going to be sold to refuse to sell for a "lesser price, or to refuse to occupy the first place or precede in "the entrance of a gate, etc., would he, I ask, be held to keep "these under grave sin? It seems speculatively that he truly so "adduced God as a witness to the fact that he was going to do it, "therefore, if he does not without cause, insofar as in itself he "makes God a false witness. Just the same, others hold the "contrary with probability, as Sanchez. See Laymann, sup. c. 4."

There is a great question as to whether paucity of matter is granted in a transgression of a promissory oath, so that the one promising to give some modest thing, if he had a true mind to furnish it when he swears, but later does not furnish it, would he sin lightly?

The first opinion very probably denies it. (Cajetan 2.2. qu. 89 art. 7 dub. 1; Toledo lib. 4 cap. 22; Lessius l. 2 c. 42 dub. 5 n. 23; Bonacina t. 2 disp. 4 quaest. 1 p. 14 num. 2; likewise, Valentia, Reginaldus, Medina, Candidus etc. cited by the Salamancans tract. 17 cap. 2 punct. 5 § 2 n. 52). The reason is, because then an oath is violated in a way that paucity of matter is scarcely granted by the violation. And it seems St. Thomas Aquinas agrees with this in II IIæ qu. 89 art. 7 ad 3, where he says that if someone were compelled unwillingly to promise something under an oath, even if later he could later demand what he pays back in a trial, still in the meantime he is held to pay what was promised, "Because he ought more sustain the temporal loss than violate an oath."

But the *second opinion* is no less probable, on the contrary, it may be even more probable, and it affirms it. (Suarez *de relig.* lib. 3 *de juram.* c. 16, n. 9; del Soto *de justit.* lib. 8 q. 1 art. 7 dub. 1; Azor, lib. 5 cap. 27 qu. 2; Castro. tr. 15 disp. 1 p. 6 n. 8; S. Antoninus part. 2 tit. 10 cap. 4 § 1; Navarre, *Man.* c. 12 n. 10; Sylvius *v. Juram.* 4 q. 1; Laymann lib. 4 tr. 3 cap. 14 n. 6 and Salamancans *ibid.* n. 53 with Aragon, Sanchez, John of St. Thomas, Rodriquez, Trullenchus etc.). The reason is, because in a promissory oath God is not properly adduced as a witness (for otherwise he would commit perjury even if then the promise were not fulfilled for a just cause), but only as offering authority to the obligation. This arises from the promise made in God's presence, exactly if someone would promise something in the presence of a prince, intending from his authority to strengthen his promise. Hence, they say that when the man making the promise later does not fulfill it, now he does not sin by perjury, because perjury must not only be carried out, but even more, God must be invoked as a witness to a lie. But it is not a lie where the man swearing had the will to fulfill what he promised, but does not fulfill it; so it is not a lie, but infidelity, and a good deal more grave by reason of the irreverence which is inflicted upon God, seeing that it was promised in his presence. Still, when a matter promised is not grave, infidelity of this sort does not pertain to grave fault.

So also the Salamancans say (cit. c. 2 punct. 7 § 2 n. 88) with St. Antoninus, Navarre, Castropalaus and others related above, that if someone swears to keep a secret and later does not keep it, he does not sin gravely unless he manifests it with grave injury to his neighbor or the community.

"3. It is certain that if you only did not keep some of what
"you swore, it is not grave; *e.g.* if you swore that you would not
"drink wine, you do not sin mortally by drinking a little.
"Sanchez, t. 1 c. 12 n. 21, because then paucity of the matter
"excuses. And in this way they are excused who swear to
"preserve the statutes of some chapter, college, university, etc.
"if later they would violate some small part of the statutes. And
"the same thing is said of legal clerks that swear an oath, and
"other ministers of justice, as well as of a man who would take
"away only a little from the sum which he swears that he will
"give to another man. Navarre, Suarez, Sanchez. See Laymann,
"Bonacina, p. 14."

174.—"4. You are probably obligated by a promissory oath,
"even if it was extorted from you by an injury or fear, that if
"forgetting to use an equivocation, you swore to pirates to give
"a ransom, or usury to a usurer. (Becanus 2. 2. qu. 82, etc.)
"Nevertheless, Azor denies this (p. 1 lib. 1 cap. 11 qu. 13) in the
"matter of matrimony because matrimony compelled by
"yielding to a resolute man is null; hence even an oath extorted
"from the one contracting it seems relaxed by the law itself, as
"he says in *v. Perjurium*, Suarez, cap. 9, Sanchez, and Bonacina
"p. 9."

An important question is whether an oath extorted by fear would oblige in conscience? It is said *in conscience,* because in the external forum, where it is presumed that there is no mind to swear, such an oath certainly does not oblige, from *c. Verum, de juramento.*

However, in regard to the internal forum, *the first opinion* denies it obliges, held by Azor, St. Antoninus, Sylvius, Lopez, Angelus, Panormus, and others cited by Sanchez (*de matrimonia,* lib. 4 d. 20 n. 3) who calls it probable, and from *Authent. Sacramenta,* c. *Si adversus venditionem,* where it is said that such oaths are held to be of no importance. Hence they say that a promise so sworn by suffering fear is either void, or rescindable.

Nevertheless, *the second opinion* is by far more probable, which St. Thomas holds (II IIæ qu. 89 art. 7 ad) as well as the Salamancans *de contrac.* cap. 1 punct. 2 n. 16 with Bonacina, del Soto, Lessius, Sanchez, Suarez; and likewise Elbel n. 57 (who calls it most common) and Viva (*de juramento,* q. 7 art. 4 n. 7, who call it common), and it says such an oath obliges. The reason is because we are held to effect what we swear for it to be true, lest we make God a witness to what is false. Therefore, from *cap. Cum contingat, de jurejur.* in 28 and others, as below, the rule is whatever is sworn must be kept, which can be fulfilled without sin. Moreover, it is responded the *Authentica* cited is not received or was expressly revoked by c. 8 and 15 of *de jurejur.* Furthermore, it must be noted that one suffering fear in the time in which fulfillment is held from force of the oath, can seek its relaxation from the Bishop or anyone who can commute oaths, as the Salamancans hold (*l.c.* n. 65) with de Lugo, Villal. and Ledesma. And if he has already paid what was promised, he can seek it back in court or secretly compensate himself, as Viva holds (*loc. cit.*). See *On Contracts in* book 4 n. 717 vers. *Quaeritur II.*

175.—"5. Likewise, you are obliged, even if the oath were "extorted in error or treachery, or the error turns only on "accidental circumstances that are not of great importance, for "if it turns upon the substance, as *e.g.* if you swear to give a ring "to another, thinking it is iron, when it is really gold, or in "regard to circumstances of great importance, in which you "would not have sworn had you known, you are not obliged. "See Sanchez, lib. 3 cap. 11, n. 11; Suarez, etc."

The Salamancans think this doctrine concerning accidental qualities is probable. *de Contract.* cap. 1 punct. 3 n. 21. But they think the opposite is more probable. See n. 187 *v. Sed dubium* and *de voto* here in book 4, n. 198, vers. *It is certain*, and n. 225.

176.—"6. It does not induce any obligation if you swear an "evil, vain or useless thing, or (as Cajetan holds) an indifferent "thing, which is not made worthy either by the end or the "circumstances, because the oath cannot be a bond of iniquity "or vain things, or of idle things, to which God does not wish us "to be obliged. Bonacina and others in common. There, note "what Laymann says in cap. 6, that an oath does not become "valid, even if such an illicit and vain thing would later, after a "change of circumstances, become worthy, seeing that "according to Reginaldus (18, *de reg. juris* in 6), what is not "present in the beginning is not strengthened by the progress of "time." (With the Salamancans. *ibid.* punct. 7 § 1 n. 58. Here also, add with Elbel, n. 60, Palaus and Tamburinus, that, if an oath were on keeping something forbidden by law, it is not valid even if the law only forbade it under penalty; it is otherwise if it were on something permitted by law).

177.—An oath in favor of a third can always be fulfilled without sin, and must be fulfilled even if it is against evangelical councils. (Salamancans tr. 17 *de juramento* c. 2 punct. 6, n. 69 with

Palaus, Lessius, Sanchez, Suarez, etc.) And even if the promise became void by law in hatred of a wicked creditor, such as a promise to pay usury, as from *c. Debitores, de jurejurando*. And Sanchez asserts that this is certain (*Dec.* l. 3 c. 11, n. 5) that even if a promise made to a prostitute, although such an oath would be illicit (Molina, Suarez, Cajetan, Sanchez with Salamancans *ibid.* in the middle). Note: if the prostitute had already supplied her work; it is otherwise if not. (Spor. c. 1 n. 55; Laymann c. 6 n. 2; Elbel n. 88).

Still, it must be said differently if the promise were made void by law, because it would be against the common good; the reason is because then the fulfillment would be illicit. Therefore, an oath extorted by fear does not oblige over profession, matrimony, betrothal, renunciation of ecclesiastical forum, if one is a cleric; likewise over donation by a cleric, or made by a soldier to a concubine. (Salamancans *de contr.* c. 1 punct. 7 § 2 n. 67 from c. *Diligenti de foro compet.* with Busembaum n. 174).

Quaeritur: when a contract is made void by law in favor only of the men that promise, would the oath then strengthen the contract so that the one to whom it was promised would acquire the right to justice from it? Azor, Sanchez and others affirm it. But Elbel (n. 61) and Sporer (c. 1 n. 53) with Tamburinus, Potestà, Pichler, etc. deny it with probability. The reason is because in no way does an oath have the force to strengthen a contract of this sort, not of itself, because it only obliges by virtue of religion; not from positive law; for although from c. 28 *de jurejurando*, etc. such contracts ought to be kept on account of the oath, still, in no place is it held that they must be preserved from justice; and therefore this obligation does not pass to heirs of the one that swore the oath, and the very one that swears it is disobliged after the oath has been relaxed. See Elbel, n. 64.

"7. You are not obliged to fulfill if you swore something "against evangelical councils, such as not to enter religion, and "not to give alms, etc. (Molina, Sanchez, Laymann, l. 4 t. 3 c. 6). "And even if you were to sin by swearing such things, "nevertheless you do not sin by not fulfilling it. Cajetan *v.* "*Perjurium.*" (So the Salamancans think in tr. 17 *de juramento* c. 2 punct. 5 § 2 n. 58, unless the oath were done in favor of a third, with Lessius, Sanchez, Suarez, Palaus, etc., as just above, and Busembaum below).

"8. You are held to fulfill, nor could you commute it into "some better work, *e.g.* a work of religion, if you swore "something to the advantage of, or for the sake of some man, or "of others, provided it is worthy and can be fulfilled without "sin. Thus, *e.g.* an alumnus who swore himself to the service of "a prince, or to this or that Church, etc., cannot enter religion "without relaxation. Still, an exception is made if you swore to "Titia that you would marry her; in that case you can, after she "has been left behind, enter religion because the oath chooses "the nature of the acts to which it is assigned and moreover, "this tacit condition enters into a promise of matrimony, *unless I "would enter religion.* See Laymann, c. 6; Bonacina d. 4 q. 1 p. 3."

178.—*Quæritur I:* Would an oath to not play oblige one to abstain even from licit play and of a modest quantity? *Resp.* If the oath were made not to play in general, everyone agrees this does not oblige one to abstain from worthy and moderate play. (See Salamancans *ibid.* punct. 7 § 4 n. 95). The doubt is if the oath was expressly and specially made to abstain even from licit and moderate play, would it oblige? Dicastillius, Navarre, Rodriquez and Bassaeus (cited by Salamancans *ibid.* n. 94) deny it, because such play pertains to the virtue of eutrapelia. But it must be answered in the affirmative with the Salamancans (*ibid.,* n. 96), Tamburinus, Palaus, Bonacina, Sanchez and the common opinion; because it is an act of greater virtue to abstain even from some virtuous act for greater perfection. Hence, if someone swearing an oath for a greater good expressly intended to abstain from play, say, to free himself for God, to mortify himself, etc., he is held to fulfill it; but it is otherwise if he would have sworn the oath without such an end (Salamancans *ibid.* n. 95 and 100, in fin.) But in this play, paucity of matter can rightly be granted which must be measured according to the end intended by the oath. (See Salamancans *ibid.* n. 98). Such a person swearing the oath can even give money to another to play and observe him, and even help him, because this is not properly play. (Sanchez, l. 3 *dec.* c. 18, n. 5; Bonacina t. 2 d. 4 q. 1 p. 16 n. 5; Palaus tr. 16 d. 2 p. 7 n. 5 and Salamancans *ibid.* n. 99 with Candidus, Trullenchus, Fagundez, etc.

179.—*Quæritur II:* Would an oath made against a prior oath oblige? A distinction must be made if the oath is opposed to the other *in the act of swearing it*, say if you swore an oath to never swear an oath again and later you did so, *e.g.* that you were going to observe fasting, you are held to fast; because according to the oath it is then licit from the matter, although you sin by swearing it. On the other hand, the second oath is null if it is opposed to the prior *in the matter that was sworn*; because then it would be illicit from the matter: hence, if you swore to marry Caja (even if you promised simply, as Sanchez teaches *de matrimonio*, l. 1 d. 50 n. 2) and later swore to Titia, this second does not oblige even if later Caja remitted the promise, from the rule: "What is not present at the beginning is not strengthened by the progress of time." (*de reg. Jruis* in 6). So Croix supposes (l. 3 p. 1 n. 232), with Sanchez, Palaus, Tamburinus and Salamancans tr. 17 c. 2, punct. 7 § 5 n. 102 and 103), with Suarez, etc. Nevertheless, Croix (*ibid.*) with Sanchez, Tamburinus and the common opinion, because, if the contract sworn were later fulfilled then it is valid, although illicit because by the oath the act is not invalidated, which could otherwise be validly done.

Moreover, would a vow avail against another vow? See below on vows, n. 210, v. *It must be noted.*

180.—"Resp. 2. A promissory oath has the same condition, and must be explained in the same mode as a promise or resolution annexed to it. The reasoning is because an accessory follows the principle; and therefore, when a promise does not oblige, neither does the oath based on it. (Lessius l. 2 c. 42 d. 2; Bonacina d. 4 q. 1 p. 6; Trull. l. 2 c. 1 d. 17).

Thus the following are resolved:

"1. Titius, who promised with an oath to marry Bertha, a rich, healthy maiden of good repute, etc., is not held to remain in the oath after Bertha falls into poverty, infirmity, fornication or ill-repute, because the promise itself does not oblige in that case." (And this is held in c. 25 *de Jurejurando*).

"2. One who swears an oath for the sake of urbanity that he is not going to sit, drink, or enter a house, etc. in front of another does not sin against the oath if he were compelled by another to sit first, drink or enter; both because that promise or purpose has a tacit condition joined to it, unless you will compel me, whereby it is removed, it would not oblige and consequently neither does the oath; and because it is relaxed by another yielding to his right. (Bonacina *loc. cit.*, Sanchez, Lessius, Trull.)

"3. One who swore that he was going to keep decrees and rules or statues of some congregation, university or chapter, are only held to preserve those things which are in vigor and to the extent they are in use or preserved by a greater part of the chapter; nevertheless, unless another thing were certain from the mind of the one swearing the oath, or he would will to oblige himself to those things independently from the statutes. The reason is clear, because the promise itself does not otherwise oblige. Trull, *l. c.* Azor, Lessius, Diana, p. 2 tr. 6 r. 39." (See what is going to be said in n. 181).

In every promissory oath, however, by a fashioning of law, the following conditions are understood in addition: I. *If I can,* because no man is thought to have obliged himself to a thing that is impossible physically or morally, viz. with a great difficulty that was not foreseen (Sporer c. 1 n. 77; Laymann, c. 9 num. 4; Elbel n. 70); II. *Save for the law of superiors, from* c. 19 *de jurejurando;* III. *If he, to whom the promise is made, will accept or not remit:* for this is the nature of the promise which follows the oath. (Elbel, *ibid.*); IV. *If the matter were not notably changed.* See n. 187; V. *If even another party will have kept the trust:* Understand if the promise was mutual, c. 75, *de R.J.* in 6.

181.—*Quæritur,* How does an oath to preserve the statutes of some college, congregation, etc. oblige? Attend to the four rules commonly handed down by the Doctors on this point: I. That such an oath is understood about published statutes, not that are going to be destroyed. (Salamancans tr. 17, c. 2 punct. 7 § 1 n. 77); II. Such an oath is understood to oblige *sub grave* or *sub levi,* or only to punishment, or only under counsel, just as a statute obliges. (Elbel, n. 91; Salamancans *ibid.* n. 78, with Palaus, Sanchez, Bonacina, etc.); III. That such an oath does not oblige to statutes, which do not impose an obligation on account of an impossibility, or on account of lack of conformity or because they are so received in use, even if an oath were furnished on some particular statute (Salamancans *ibid.* n. 79 with Suarez, Bonacina, Sanchez, Prado, etc.); IV. Such an oath also does not oblige if some of the statutes are not observed by a greater part of the community (Salamancans *ibid.* n. 80, with Sa, Sanchez, Azor, etc.). Hence, the Salamancans infer with Sanchez, Palaus, Trullenchus, etc., that the officials who swear to preserve the value of what has been prescribed, do not sin by receiving something other if the value or stipend were not sufficient.

182.—We ask further, in what way does an oath oblige which doctors in colleges furnish by the precept of St. Pius V in his *motu proprio* for the year 1566 *Supra gregem*, to not visit the sick more than a third of the day unless they are made certain about the confession of the sick man by the rescript of a confessor? The Salamancans say (*ibid.* § 3 n. 91) with Sanchez, Cajetan, Prado, Trullenchus, Leander, etc. such an oath does not oblige if it has not been received in use exactly as they witness it is not received in Spain (nor is it received in Naples). Hence they say there, then the doctor is only held when he foresees in a sick person a probable danger of death and if at the same time he believes probably he is in mortal sin, or it is necessary that he disposes of his things to pay his debts, remove suits, etc. (Salamancans *ibid.* n. 92 and P. Elbel *de jur.* n. 91). Moreover, in the diocese of Naples it was done in the last synod that reserved cases with an excommunication, for before it was without an excommunication; for there, n. 4, it is so said: "Doctors who visiting the sick in bed, after three days from the visitation that do not see to it that the aforesaid sick would confess their sins to a suitable confessor, or otherwise do not desert them according to the limits of the constitution of St. Pius V and Innocent XI. But, as I said, a constitution of this sort has not been received in use at Naples, as a many wise man asserted to me, when the sickness is light: but when it is dangerous, the constitution and reservation is in force. Hence, Mazzotta, (*de sacram penit.*) speaking on the aforesaid reserved case, says the constitution of St. Pius is modified by custom, so that it is only understood on dangerous sicknesses. Nevertheless, a doctor would be excused if he would advise a sick man through another, or if he would certainly think the admonition was not going to be beneficial. It is said *certainly*, he is held in doubt to advise him (Elbel, *dict.i n. 89, cit.;* Sanchez, Bonacina, Tamburinius, etc.). Mazzotta says the same thing, and he adds that the testimony of domestic servants suffices, or of the sick man himself that he has recently gone to confession, if they are worthy of trust. But in this I say domestic servants are regularly and easily held suspect. See what is going to be said on this point in book 6 tr. 4 *on the Sacrament of Penance*, n. 664 and in the *Practice of Confessors*, n. 53.

183.—"4. One that swore an oath to keep a secret does not sin "against the oath by divulging it when it cannot be concealed "without grave loss to him or another, because the promise of "the secret itself does not seem to oblige except under this "condition, *if it would not cause harm.* (Sylvius, Bonacina, "Sanchez, Trullenchus *loc. cit.*)" (In regard to revealing the secret, see what is going to be said in book 4, n. 971).

Moreover, oaths to keep a secret which are furnished in congregations on elections or other things, gravely or lightly oblige according to the harm which they can inflict. So Elbel n. 90 thinks, with Henno, because the obligation of the oath follows the obligation of the secret. Other authors say the same thing (Spor. r. 3 c. 1 n. 42; Croix l. 3 p. 1 n. 329 etc.) on an oath to keep the secret in regard to the art of confecting some medicine. Nay more, not withstanding the oath, you are held from charity to reveal it, if otherwise someone would undergo grave danger of death since the oath must not be a bond of iniquity (Croix, with St. Thomas, Suarez, etc.).

"5. A man who swears an oath to a judge that he is going to "say what he knows, is not held to reveal secret things. The "reason is clear. Lessius, Bonacina, Trull, *loc. cit.*

"6. A man who swore an oath that he was going to pay what "was owed within a month, is not held to do so by force of the "oath if the time of payment were prorogued by the creditor; "because he yields to his right, the obligation of the promise "would cease, and consequently the oath. Azor, Bonacina, "Trullenchus, *loc. cit.* n. 18."

184—*Quæritur I:* If a man who promises a concubine with an oath that he is never going to have sex with another woman, would he be held to it? Diana rejects this, with Fagundez, because the end of such a promise was depraved, namely to preserve friendship and because such an oath would offer the occasion of remaining in sin. But the Salamancans ®. 17 c. 2 punct. 6 n. 70) with Sanchez and Prado more probably affirm it, because from the general rule one ought to fulfill an oath always and when he can without sin; but the occasion comes *per accidens.*

185.—*Quæritur II:* Would a prodigal promise with an oath oblige? Some affirm it (cited by Salamancans *ibid.* n. 71). But the Salamancans (*dict.* loc.) with del Soto, Suarez, Trullenchus, etc. more probably deny it, because such a promise is at least lightly evil, and therefore the oath, since it may not be a bond of iniquity, does not oblige, from the *regulis Juris,* n. 6: "An oath furnished against good morals is not obligatory. (*Cf.* Salamancans, *ibid.* n. 68). See what is going to be said *On Matrimony,* book 6, n. 851.

186.—*Quaeritur III:* Would someone that promises to go back to jail with an oath, be held to do it with probable fear of death or of very grave and unjust harm?

The first opinion denies it, because it would be a bad action to freely offer himself to death. Navarre, *Man.* c. 12 n. 18; Vasquez, Navarre, Pontius, Covarruvias, Tamburinus, Reginald, cited by Salamancans *ibid.* n. 74.

The second opinion much more probably affirms it, because, after the promise has been posited, it would be a work of virtue to return. Toledo, l. 4 c. 22 n. 2; Suarez, l. 2 c. 10 n. 14 and 15; Lessius l. 2 c. 42 n. 28 and Salamancans *ibid.* n. 75 (although they call the first probable) with Bonacina, Sanchez, Lessius, Suarez, Laymann, Toledo, etc.

Parents or masters, swearing to punish children or servants, rarely sin if they do not fulfill the oath, or because the delinquents have already emended, or promised to emend themselves; or because the oath was on a useless thing, or rather more from disordered revenge. Laymann, n. 9 c. 14; Anacletus, d. 2 n. 22 and Elbel, n. 87, with Gobat, and it is sufficiently common. And Elbel adds, many such oaths are made without the intention to swear them, but only to terrify. See what is going to be said in n. 187 ad IV.

DUBIUM VI
In what cases would a man who contracts an obligation in a promissory oath be excused from fulfilling it?

187. Would change of circumstances excuse?
188. Would cessation of the final cause excuse?

187.—"*Resp.* Such cases, apart from those which are gathered "from the higher ones, these are reviewed by Toledo and "Cajetan: I. If what was good in the time of the oath, were later "illicit on account of the circumstances, or vain or impeding a "greater good, or better if it were omitted than fulfilled "(Sanchez, c. 15); II. If you will change the oath into some work "that is clearly better and more pleasing to God, for anyone can "do that *per se* as Toledo holds (c. 23). Still, there is always the "exception that if you swore something advantageous to a man, "since God does not wish him to be defrauded; III. If the state of "the thing will be notably changed, as if, *e.g.* you were to swear "to punish someone with a just punishment, but he, begging, "would seek forgiveness and do penance, you could pardon him "without perjury because the oath obliged, while the same state "was preserved, in which he was not sorry (Laymann, c. 9); IV. "If the matter sworn became useless to the intent, especially if it "is more destructive, such as if from correction of the "impenitent son it were noted he is going to be more destroyed "than emended, or if the family would be disturbed, that "quarrels with his wife would follow and in this way he brings "to bear to not correct him. Reginald l. 18 c. 56; Bonacina l. c. "14." (Hence, if the punishment that the father threatens, is hardly conducive to correction, he is not held to fulfill the matter sworn at least not *sub gravi*. Salamancans *ibid.* § 3 n. 63 with del Soto and Sanchez. Moreover, he is excused from fulfilling the oath who swore menacingly from anger, or not in earnest, as children usually do. Salamancans *ibid.* n. 62 and 62 with Bonacina and Cajetan. See what was said in n. 186, at the end). "V. If those conditions which so impose, which in any "promissory oath you like are tacitly understood in addition to "the nature as the Doctors teach. Moreover, such are, as "Laymann, says (sup. c. 9): 1. If I can; 2. Save the right of a "superior; 3. Unless the matter were notably changed" (What if unforeseen circumstances would arise? See what was said in n. 180); "4. Unless the obligation were abolished. From which "doubt follows."

Someone is not held to fulfill an oath when a notable change comes up, *e.g.* danger of death, infamy or of other grave loss which is not considered in such a case to have willed to obligate himself when by the change then the matter is different from what was promised; but in doubt as to whether the change is notable, he is held (Palaus tr. 15 d. 1 p. 20 n. 4; Sanchez, *dec.* l. 4 c. 2 n. 34 and Salamancans *de juramento* c. 3 punct. 2 n. 20 with Trull., Leander, etc. See *de voto* n. 225).

But there is a doubt as to whether that change would be sufficient of itself, even if it were not notable, still which if they were foreseen, he would not have made the oath?

The first opinion affirms from St. Thomas (in 4 dist. 48 q. 1 art. 3 ad 1) who so teaches in this way. Something frees from the obligation of a vow (or an oath), if, were it known from the beginning, it would have impeded these things from being done. The reason is, because the intention to oblige himself then is either lacking or understood in this way (Navarre, *Man.* c. 18 n. 7; Sylvester v. *Votum*, 2. q. 17 in fin; Molina, to. 2 *de just.* d. 272 coll. 2 and 7, likewise St. Antoninus, Henriquez, etc. cited by Salamancans d. c. 3 n. 21).

The second opinion holds that it does not suffice because the obligation must not be taken up by a man from a promise which will not be made in the future, but from that which has already been made. (Suarez, l. 4 c. 9 n. 8; Sanchez *Dec.* l. 4 c. 2 n. 22; Palaus tr. 15 d. 1 p. 20 n. 3 and Salamancans *ibid.* n. 22, with del Soto, Cajetan, Val, etc.). Still, they duly say the probability of the first opinion cannot be denied. On the contrary, the Salamancans themselves (*ibid.* c. 1 punct. 6 § 3 n. 152) think it is a notable change when something, were it known from the beginning, then the man swearing would not promise, but at any rate, adhere to the first opinion. See *de voto* n. 226.

188.—Add that the obligation of an oath or vow would cease if its final cause would cease, *e.g.* you promised to a poor man to give alms, but later he becomes rich; you promised that you were not going to enter such a house due to danger of death, but it would cease: you promised a pilgrimage on account of the health of the father, but he died and similar things (Sanchez l. 42, Suarez l. 2 *de voto* c. 18 n. 3, Bonacina d. 4 q. 2 p. 3 § 2 n. 10; Palaus tr. 15 d. 9 p. 20 n. 1; and Salamancans *eod. tr.* c. 3 punct. 2 n. 16 with Prado, Trullenchus, Tamburinus, etc). But it is otherwise if the impulsive cause would cease. (*ibid.* n. 17).

DUBIUM VII
How is the obligation of an oath abolished by invalidity, dispensation, commutation and remission?

Treatise II: The Second Precept, Ch. II, On Oaths

189. *Who can invalidate oaths? And who dispenses?*
190. *Could one dispensing against vows also dispense against oaths?*
191. *On commutation and relaxation of the oath.*
192. *What if the oath is made in favor of a third?*
193. *Could it be remitted by the third itself? Appendix on adjuration and especially on adjuration of demons.*

189.—"*Resp.* On this from the conditions already posited, and "the power of superiors against their own and their vows, these "are commonly handed down by Laymann (c. 11) and others:

"1. When it comes to invalidating, every superior, husband or "master can invalidate and annul an oath who also can "invalidate their vows. (Sanchez v. 69, n. 7; Suarez, Azor, "Filliuci, l. 25 c. 9 p. 17 dub. 6). See the following chapter "following from n. 227.

"2. And the same can invalidate promissory oaths made in "favor of a man as often as the promise itself or contract "weakens what was conceded to them."

"In regard to dispensation, each has the ordinary or "delegated power; or the privilege of dispensing in vows, can "dispense against the same even if it were sworn with an oath."

190.—*Quæritur*: Could a man that has the delegated faculty to dispense against vows, also dispense against oaths?

The first opinion is probable and denies it, because the bond of the vow, and of the oath is different; and therefore from the style of the curia the faculty in regard to oaths is specially conceded. So Lessius, l. 2 c. 42 n. 60 and Sanchez, Bonacina, Azor, and Ledesma cited by Salamancans *de juram.* c. 3 punct. 1 n. 3.

But *the second opinion* no less probably affirms it, because oaths furnished to God alone, although they are different bonds from vows, still, in order for dispensation, as vows are reputed, in the argument *l. Ut tantum, ff. de servo corrupto*, where it says: "One disposed in one of two equal things, is reckoned disposed in the other." Moreover, that special concession in regard to oaths following the style of the curia is done for greater caution (Salamancans *d.* n. 3 with Cajetan, Pontius, Suarez, Palaus, Trullenchus, Diana, Prado, Arag., etc.). But this not withstanding, the first negative opinion must altogether be held, for the obligation of the oath has already been contracted, so is certain and should be followed. It does not avail for it to be taken away by a dispensation that is only probably valid. Moreover, it seems it must be said otherwise in regard to oaths made to a man when they are harmful to the common good; nay more, oaths of this sort are null of themselves. See what was said in n. 177.

191.—"4. In regard to commutation, the reason is the same as "on dispensation.
"5. What attains to remission, or relaxation, an oath made in "favor of a man cannot be relaxed except by the one to whom it "was made, or to whom he and the promised matter are subject.
"6. He can even remit, even if such a favor was sworn to him "on account of God, *e.g.* if someone on account of God swore to "marry a poor girl, she can relax that oath, as is held by Navarre "and others, against del Soto and Sylvius, because although the "oath was made principally on account of God, nevertheless, "because the execution is in favor of man, it also depends upon "the will of man."
"7. Could the civil power also relax oaths of their subjects in "temporal things, when there is a just cause to overturn them, "*e.g.* because they were extorted from fear or another injury? "Some deny it, but others say with Laymann that it is probable "what Sanchez teaches (l. 3 c. 12) with Suarez, that he cannot "relax it directly just as the ecclesiastical power does when it "dispenses, but only indirectly, *e.g.* by reason of the matter or "by supplying in its turn, to whom it was sworn, and who

"ought to remit it. For more considering an oath in the external "forum, see Laymann, *supra* c. 11; Bonacina, *loc. cit.*"

192.—For greater clarity it must be said: I. That if a promise that had not yet been made in which is favor of a man were strengthened by an oath there is no obligation to fulfill it and it can be revoked, because then the oath is accessory, and follows the nature of the promise; but it is otherwise if the promise was principally made to God. This is certain. See Salamancans *de juramento* c. 2 punct. 5 § 2 n. 56, with Suarez, Lessius, and more profusely *de contractibus* c. 4 punct. 4 § 1 n. 70.

It must be said: II. That if such a promise were received by a third party, to whom it was made, then it cannot be relaxed, not even with the consent of the Pope. And it is common with Laymann, *de jur.* c. 11 n. 25, with St. Thomas, II IIæ q. 89 art. 9 ad 3; Tamburinus l. 3 c. 7 § 3 n. 3; Salamancans c. 2 n. 68; Croix, l. 3 p. 1 n. 358. And this, even if the oath is principally made in honor of God, as Croix says (*ibid.* with Sanchez, Suarez, Lessius, de Lugo, Diana, Moya, etc.), always and by reception the right is acquired for the third. But this oath, principally uttered to God, turns on a great question on which you can see what will be said in c. 3 *de voto* n. 255.

Nevertheless, the second declaration is limited and only imposed on three cases:

Limitation I: If the one swearing were a subject and the oath were in regard to those things which are subject to the power of a superior, as St. Thomas teaches. Therefore, the Pope can invalidate all oaths in regard to benefices, ecclesiastical offices, etc. Parents can also invalidate oaths of their prepubescent children, but not after they have attained puberty in regard to their own things; tutors of students; religious superiors, men in regard to the goods of their wives' dowry, masters those of servants. See everything cited by Salamancans, *de juramento* c. 3 punct. 1 from n. 4 and 5 with Busembaum n. 2.

Limitation II: If an oath could not be preserved without common loss, according to whether the oath would be to not denounce and not accuse, etc., or in a contract made void by law, *e.g.* to pay a penalty, if anyone would recoil from betrothals, which is forbidden from *cap.* Gemma, *de desponsat. impuberum.* (Even paying for play that is forbidden, as the Salamancans say. See what is going to be said on play in treatise 5, *de contr. dub.* 13). Such oaths more truly do not need relaxation when they are null of themselves, according to what was said in n. 177. Nevertheless, be they valid, they can be relaxed by the Church. Salamancans *ibid.* n. 6, with Sanchez, Palaus, and Guttierez. Moreover, by the name of Church come not only the Pope but also Bishops, chapters in vacant sees and others having episcopal jurisdiction (Salamancans *ibid.* n. 7 et 8), and even confessors having a delegated faculty to dispense against vows, who can also relax such oaths as Busembaum n. 3 and Salamancans *ibid.* n. 9 with Rodr. and Ledesma.

Limitation III: If an oath were extorted by fraud or fear, for then it can also be relaxed by the same, as above, in punishment of those extorting it, as is certain among all authors; even if the oath were extorted by another third party, unaware of the principal oath. (Salamancans *ibid.* n. 7 with Suarez, Sanchez, Palaus, Molina, Arag.). On the contrary, this coincides, even if the promise was in doubt, say, on paying some true debt, not to mention were it unjustly extorted; and even if an oath were twisted out *from a light fear*, at least for the internal forum, as the Salamancans hold (*ibid.* n. 8), with Sanchez, Suarez, and Palaus, from *c. Sollicite* and *c. Accepta de restit. spol.*, where the only oath that cannot altogether be relaxed is a voluntary oath.

193.—Moreover, it is certain that an oath in favor of a third party can be freely remitted by him without any relaxation of the Church, as all teach with St. Thomas (II IIæ q. 89 art. 9 ad 2). But the question is, would an oath made in favor of a third party cease from his remission, even if the promise were principally made to God? St. Thomas denies it, unless a condition were supplied, *viz.* if it will so seem to the one to whom the promise is made; and the Salamancans hold the same thing (*ibid.* n. 10) speaking generally, with del Soto, Sylvius, Sanchez, Bonacina, Palaus, etc. On the other hand, Busembaum (in this article, n. 6) with Navarre, and Croix, l. 3 p. 1 n. 358, with Gobat and Tamburinus, hold with probability that the obligation ceases. The reason is, because even if the promise were made to God, nevertheless it was always made dependent upon the will of the man to whom it was sworn, namely, if he would not remit the execution. And the Salamancans (*ibid.* n. 14) with Sanchez, Palaus, Trullenchus Prado, Fagundez, Leander, etc. also follow this, against Scotus, Sylvius, etc., that it is always lawful for an oath to be made principally in honor of God, still, the whole promise yields in favor of a side, say, if someone from the aspect of piety would swear that he was going to give a chalice to this Church, alms to this pauper, to enter into this religious order. But could an oath or a vow *of perseverance*, which is usually uttered in some congregations, be relaxed or dispensed by bishops without the consent of the congregation? See what is going to be said in n. 255, below.

APPENDIX
On Adjuration

I. Adjuration is an invocation of God, or of sacred things, or even of the Saints, to induce someone to do a certain thing, or to omit one. (St. Thomas II IIæ, q. 90 art. 1). One is *solemn*, which is done by ministers and by the modes which the Church has constituted; the other is *private*, without solemn rites of this sort. Likewise, another is *deprecative*, exactly as was that of the chief priest: "I adjure you by the living God, to tell us if you are Christ, etc." (Matt. 26:63). Another is *imperative*, which is only suited for superiors towards subjects, and exorcists towards demons.

II. For the adjuration to be licit, three things are required, just as in swearing an oath: 1) *Truth*, *i.e.* that the one swearing truly intends to obtain what he seeks, and the cause on account of which he seeks it, is true; moreover, lacking the truth will rarely be more than venial, namely if a man pretending to be poor asks for alms from God, as Sanchez says (*Dec.* l. 2 c. 42 n. 5) and Sporer (*de 2 praec.* c. 1 n. 163) and Elbel (*conf.* 6 n. 153); 2) *Justice*, from the lack of which one would certainly commit a grave sin in asking a thing that gravely evil, from the common opinion of the Doctors. What if, he seeks a matter that is only lightly evil? The doctors say it is venial. (Salamancans tr. 22 *de 2. praec. Decal.* c. unic. n. 4; Sporer n. 165 with Suarez, Bonacina, Sanchez, Tab.) But Elbel (n. 97) says better that it is mortal, because it seems the irreverence is grave enough to induce another to a bad thing with the help of divine authority. See what was said in n. 146; 3) *Judgment*, *i.e.* the discretion that is due, the lack of which is certainly nothing other than venial.

III. Only intellectual creatures can be directly adjured, that is men and demons. Moreover, irrational things can be indirectly adjured, such as salt, clouds, locusts, etc., by adjuring either God that he would help us with their uses; or demons, that they would cease to cause harm through these things, exactly as St. Thomas teaches in II IIæ q. 90, art. 3 in common with others.

IV. Privately it is lawful for anyone to adjure; but solemnly only for the ministers of the Church constituted for this, and with the express license of the Bishop. (Commonly Salamancans *ibid.* n. 5 with others, from Luke 10:19: "Behold, I have given you power to tread over serpents and scorpions, and over every power of the enemy." And from Mark 16:17: "In my name they will cast out demons."

V. Moreover, especially in regard to the *adjuration of demons*, two things must especially be noted here: 1) That with them the adjuration is imperative, but not deprecative; 2) that they are only done to remove damage and vexation of the obsessed, but not for vanity and curiosity; hence the Doctors say in common with the Salamancans (*ibid.* punct. 6 § 1 num. 55), that one cannot be excused from grave sin who gives many useless sermons while the demon is obsessing.

Quæritur I: would it be a mortal sin to ask a demon one thing or another out of curiosity? Palaus says yes, because then the exorcist seems rather more to deprecatively ask something, than imperatively. But it is more probably only venial, if the adjuration is really done in the imperative mode. (Sanchez, *Dec.* l. 2 c 42 n. 25; likewise, Cajetan, Suarez, Navarre, del Soto, commonly with the Salamancans *ibid.* n. 55 and 56).

Quæritur II: On what things may exorcists interrogate a demon? It is indeed lawful to ask about anything which leads to its expulsion (Salamancans *ibid.* n. 51, with St. Thomas and the common opinion). Hence, they can ask their number and names, who dwell in the obsessed, and how long they have been there, as it is held in the *Rituale Romanum.* Likewise, the cause of their entrance, the sign for their exit, as the authors more commonly permit against del Soto (Sanchez, n. 28; Salamancans *ibid.* n. 54; with Palaus, Delrio, Trullench., etc.). But would it be lawful to imperatively seek a manifestation of truth from the demon? Elbel (*Conf.* 6 n. 156) rejects this, because (as he says), the ministers do not seem to have any other power except to only question about those matters which will direct them to expel it. But more probably and commonly it is affirmed it is lawful if it were conducive to divine glory. Sanchez, (n. 24) and Cajetan, del Soto, Coninck, Tabiena, etc. with the Salamancans (*ibid.* n. 59), and also St. Thomas expressly teaches it in II IIæ q. 95, art. 4 ad 1, where he says: "It is one thing to seek after something from a demon occurring freely, because at sometime it will be lawful due to the advantage of others, especially when he can be compelled by divine power to tell the truth. And it is another thing to invoke the demon to acquire knowledge of secret things from it;" which certainly is evil.

What if a demon would assign for the cause of his entry that the obsessed was invalidly baptized, would he need to be re-baptized *sub conditione*? On one side it seems this must be denied because no trust must be placed in the demon. On the other hand, it seems it must be affirmed, because the demon is held by the force of exorcism to make plain the truth. The Salamancans reasonably opine on this difficulty (*ibid.* § 2 n. 69) that he must not be re-baptized, unless there were a valid conjecture from another source that he had not received baptism, namely if the man who baptized him had been a warlock or a heretic, or a woman that was not well trained, or a bitter enemy of the parents who said he wanted revenge, and similar things.

But the exorcist, to truly free the obsessed, should carefully see to it that he observes the following: 1) That he should first explore whether they are really obsessed by a demon; 2) to fortify themselves with faith, confidence and charity, in addition to prayer and fasting as well as great humility, otherwise he will be of little benefit. Still, the Salamancans (tr. 22 punct. 2 n. 7) say his exorcism has force, even if it were done by a man that is in sin; 3) That he induce the obsessed to confession, confidence and prayer; 4) To use the exorcisms approved in the Roman Church, or at least in his diocese. He should also use the invocation of the names of Jesus and Mary, and likewise the sign of the cross and relics of the Saints, or Holy Water, an Agnus Dei, etc.; 5) Let him be careful lest he would joke with the demon, but rather more should relate a few things and not permit him to say more, but command him to silence; 6) Let him also be careful to know the *Rituale*, lest on account of a saying of the demon he have recourse to warlocks to dissolve a malefice. Nevertheless, he ought to command the demon to say whether he is in that place on account of a malefice, and that he should give or reveal the signs of the malefice; 7) He should regularly do exorcism in a Church, with the doors open, unless there was a worthy cause (as it says in the *Rituale*) that it be done in a house; 8) to exclude women, children and idle men, whose simple faith can be an obstacle to expulsion [of the demon]; 9) Let him repeat many times the threat and words with which he shall observe the demon in pain, always by increasing the penalty. At length let him know there are no infallible signs of exit, but probable signs, such as if for a long time the obsessed were free from aggravations; likewise, the confession of the demon, a large quantity of vomit of putrid things, or exceedingly foul-smelling breath. Likewise, great shouts, which are heard there, likewise if the obsessed would remain on the ground dejected and as if dead, and similar things. More probably, however, it is not lawful to concede to a demon that he might invade another body whether of man or beast, that he might go out from the possession, just as he promises, as Elbel thinks (n. 167) with Bonacina, Tamburinus, and others against Palaus, etc.

Moreover, the Doctors commonly say that exorcisms have infallible force to expel demons *ex opere operato* as it were. So Sporer (*de 2. praecept.* n. 167), Sanchez, (c. 42 n. 16), Palaus (p. 4 n. 19) Elbel (n. 160) and Salamancans (*ibid.* p. 3 n. 17 and 22) with Cajetan, del Soto, Trullenchus, etc. Nor is it opposed that a great many exorcisms do not have effect, for as the Salamancans say, these always obtain some effect, if not completely, at least imperfectly, by weakening the strength of the demon. See other things with Delrio, who treats more profusely on this matter (lib. 6 cap. 2, sec. 3, in 4° remed.).

CHAPTER III
ON VOWS

DUBIUM I
What is a vow, and how manifold is it?

194. *What is a vow?*
195. *How manifold is a vow?*

194.—"*Resp. 1.* It is a promise made to God, deliberately, on a "possible and better good. St. Thomas II IIæ q. 88. See Sanchez, "and Laymann, l. 4 t. 4. For that reason it is clear that a vow is "an act of *latria* due to God alone. This is why, when we vow "certain things to the Saints, the sense is that these are vowed "to God at the same time in honor of the saints,[7] just as we "build Churches and altars to God in honor of the same. "Furthermore, from individual parts of the given definition, "many cases are resolved, which, so as to avoid confusion, and "to pay attention to history, I propose them in separate *dubia*.

195.—"*Resp. 2.* A vow is divided: 1) Into *absolute* and "*conditional*. That is, what is done without any condition, such "as, I vow to give alms; but this which is done with a condition "so that, unless this has been posited, the obligation is not "pressing: such as I vow to give alms if I am restored to health, "or (what is called penal) I vow to make a discipline if I will do "this; 2) Into *solemn and simple*. That is something that is so "received by the Church and these are two: a vow of chastity, "which is connected to major orders, and a vow of religious "profession. Moreover, a simple vow is everything else which

---

[7] From the common reception of the Church, Salamancans *de voto*, tr. 17, c. 1. punct. 1 § 4 n. 29.

"does not have such solemnity. There it must be known that a
"solemn vow renders a person by law unsuitable to contract or
"act against the vow, such as to matrimony or to have
"ownership of goods. (See below, book 5 ch. 1 in *the Treatise on
"the state of religion*). Moreover, such a simple vow, *e.g.* of
"chastity (I make an exception for the vow made in the Society
"of Jesus after novitiate), or to enter a religious order, even if it
"would render a contract, *e.g.* of matrimony, illicit, still it would
"not be invalid. See below in book 6 *On Matrimony*; 3) Into *real
"and personal*. The former is, when money or another outward
"matter promised by an estimable price, such as a chalice,
"almsgiving; but the latter, when some action of man or
"cessation from the action, such as a vow to fast, go on
"pilgrimage, to abstain from play. Some add to these mixed
"from each, as if you were to vow a pilgrimage with the
"offering of some thing. See Lessius, l. 2 cap 40."

DUBIUM II
What deliberation and intention is required for a vow?

196. *What deliberation is requisite for a vow?*
197. *On a vow uttered from fear.*
198. *On a vow uttered from error.*
199. *Would a simple vow proposed oblige?*
200. *Would an implicit promise suffice for a vow?*
201. *What kind of purpose of the will is required for a vow? From here many things are asked: 1) Would a man be held to a vow that positively refused to promise and oblige himself? 2) Who did not have a mind to fulfill it? 3) Who negatively refused to oblige himself knowing the obligation of the vow? a) What if he did not know? b) what if someone wished to promise and positively refused to oblige himself? c) What is someone were uncertain as to whether he willed to oblige himself? or whether he knew the obligation of the vow? What if he were hesitant as to whether he had down what was proposed or vowed?*

196.—"*Resp.* When the obligation of a vow is very serious, the "intention, deliberation, and perfect freedom is required, "whereby someone freely and directly willed to promise in "itself, with a mind to oblige himself. So the doctors in common. "Lessius, Bonacina d. 4 q. 2 p. 1."

Thus the following are resolved:

"1. Age and the use of reason suffice to vow those things "which, is enough for mortal sin if one willed to act against "them perfectly and directly in a human act. Nevertheless, this "excepts a solemn vow of religion, which is invalid before a "certain age."

"2. A vow made with partial knowledge or deliberation does "not impose an obligation, *e.g.* from a sudden movement of the "mind, or a habit, the tongue preceding the mind, or from the "heat of anger, taking away the use of reason. Azor, Sanchez, "Trullenchus, l. 2 c. 2 d. 1, where he notes it is not a sufficient "indication that perfect reason or deliberation is absent, if the "one vowing changed his mind soon after making the vow; just "the same, a movement of anger rarely and hardly ever impedes "the use of reason." (Hence it must be seen whether other connected circumstances are present. See Salamancans tr. 17 c. 1 punct. 1 § 1 n. 11. Moreover, he sins at least venially who utters vows of great weight from a light consideration. Salamancans *ibid.* n. 13, although there, one would be obligated, *ibid.* n. 14).

"3. What if a man who knows he made a vow becomes "uncertain as to whether he did so with sufficient deliberation "and the use of reason, on account of a defect of age? If he did "indeed make a vow before his seventh year, it does not oblige "unless it is certain that it came from the sufficient use of "reason, because the law does not presume it in such a matter,

TREATISE II: THE SECOND PRECEPT, CH. III, ON VOWS 213

"then the possession favors freedom. But if he made the vow
"after his seventh year, it obliges since possession favors the
"vow when the use of reason is presumed unless the opposite is
"certain. At length, if one were uncertain as to whether before
"or after his seventh year he had made the vow, Sanchez and
"Palaus would have it that he is held by the vow, while Diana
"rejects it." (But Sanchez is more probable).

But in every doubt, as to whether there was full deliberation, the vow is valid (Salamancans c. 1 n. 147, with Suarez, Sanchez, Palaus, etc.). Likewise, in doubt as to whether the one that made the vow was coerced by fear, or whether the fear was grave. (Salamancans *ibid.* with Bonacina and Trull.). It is otherwise in a doubt as to whether the matter was worthy or possible, because then one could not follow the vow. (Salamancans *ibid.* with Palaus, Sanchez, and Suarez).

"4. Vows made while drunk, even if foreseen before, and so
"in a case, are not valid since they were not willed in
"themselves and directly; furthermore, good does not spring up
"except from the integral cause, although to sin it is enough for
"it to be indirectly voluntary in the cause. Laymann, l. 4 t. 4 c. 1
"n. 4."

197.—"5. Vows made in fear, but not instilled to this purpose
"that a vow would be extorted, are valid because they are
"voluntary and deliberate *simpliciter*."

(Just as also vows made from intrinsic fear, or justly fear justly instilled are valid. Salamancans tr. 17, c. 1 punct. 6 § 5 n. 161, from *c. 1 et 2 de adult.*).

"Moreover, vows made in fear instilled unjustly to twist out
"the vow itself, are invalid by *the common opinion*, not because
"they are voluntary, but because either the law invalidates
"them, or God does not accept them lest he would give force to
"an unjust coercion, and either the fear would be grave or light,

"provided someone formally made the vow only from such a "fear. Suarez, *de voto* lib. 1 c. 8; Filliuci t. 26 c. 1."

But the question is, whether a vow uttered from grave fear, instilled unjustly, is invalid, at least by ecclesiastical law?

The first opinion denies it. (Suarez, *de relig.* lib. 6 c. 14 n. 6, and *de voto* c. 8 n. 5; Sylvius, v. *Metus* 8 fin. and *v. Votum* 2 q. 12; Pontius, lib. 7, c. 19 n. 9; Palaus, t. 3 tact. 15 d. 1 p. 5 n. 13 and probably Palaus, Bas., Sylvius, and Bonacina and Trull rightly call it probable, cited by Salamancans *ibid.* c. 1 n. 163). Nevertheless, with the exception of a solemn vow uttered in religious profession, which is certainly null, from *c. Perlatum, de iis quae vi*, etc.

The second opinion affirms it with probability, as Busembaum and Sanchez (lib. 4 c. 3 n. 11), Lessius (l. 2 cap. 40 dub. 3 n. 18), Azor (p. 1 lib. 11 cap. 16 qu. 6), Navarre (cap. 12 n. 52) and Salamancans (*ibid.* n. 164) with Trullenchus, Bonacina, Valentia, del Soto, etc., from *c. Ad audientiam de iis quae vi*, where it is said: "A vow ought to lack the intensity of force which comes from fear."; from *cap. Cum locum de spons.*, where it says: "Since consent has no place where there is fear or coercion." Nevertheless, it is excepted if the fear were justly inflicted, from *cap. 1 et 2 de adult.* See Salamancans *ibid.* n. 161. But would a vow from a light fear unjustly pronounced, be invalid? Here Busembaum affirms it, with Suarez and Filliuci. Likewise, Navarre and many others cited by Sanchez (*Dec.* lib. 4 c. 3 n. 24). The reason is (as they say) because, the fear invalidates the vow to the extent that it takes away full consent of the will: therefore a mild fear will also invalidate it, when it takes away the same freedom and is the reason why the vow is made. And Sanchez calls this opinion probable. But the opposite opinion is more probable, which Sanchez holds (n. 24) with del Soto, Valentia, Sa, Azor, etc. and the Salamancans (*ibid.* n. 161), who call it the common opinion and prove it from *c. Perlatum, de iis quae vi*, etc. The reason is because the cause of the thing is not reckoned so grave, as a vow is, that light fear which can be easily rejected, as we will equally say on contracts, n. 718.

198.—"In regard to vows pronounced from error, if the error "were in regard to the substance of the promised matter, or in "regard to the substantial condition, or in regard to the end or "the formal reasoning and motive to vow, the vow is null. (with "Salamancans tr. 17 cap. 1 punct. 6 § 4 n. 155). For example, 1) "In regard to *substance*, if anyone would vow someone his "chalice, which he thinks is silver, when it is gold, or that he is "going to enter a certain monastery, thinking it is a Benedictine, "when it is really Carthusian; 2) In regard to the *substantial* "*condition*: if someone, *e.g.* would vow that he was going to "enter a monastery where he thinks religious discipline and the "essentials of religion are exactly preserved, and still it is not so; "or if he vowed to make a pilgrimage *ad limina apostolorum*, "thinking it is a distance of a hundred miles, when it is actually "three hundred; 3) In regard to the *final cause*; if anyone, *e.g.* "vowed something in thanksgiving for a parent being restored "to health, and they really were not sick, or died (with "Salamancans *ibid.* n. 158 and c. 3 punct. 2 n. 15 and 16). And "the reason for the nullity of such vows is because here there is "a defect of free consent, which is not conveyed on an "unknown, and nothing is as contrary to consent as error. "Filliuci t. 25 c. 1."

It is certain that error in regard to substance invalidates a vow, even if it were concomitant, *i.e.* not giving cause to the vow, say, if still, after the error were known, you were to vow. (Sanchez, *de matr.* lib. 7 d. 18 n. 6 and *Dec.* l. 3 c. 11 n. 43). And even if such an error were as crass as you like (Sanchez *ibid. de matr.* n. 7). And it is also certain that an error in regard to substantial circumstances invalidates a vow, *i.e.* what pertains to the substance of a thing promised, according to the examples that Busembaum places here. But it is otherwise if the error, although it would give cause to the vow, would be in regard to conditions which do not affect the substance of the thing, say, if someone would vow to give alms to a pauper thought to be good and a friend, he is held to give even if later he would learn he is wicked and an enemy, even if, had he known these things, he would not have made the vow in the first place. Thus, Salamancans *de voto* c. 1 punct. 6 § 4 n. 156. Otherwise, as they say, how many contracts, how many marriages, how many professions, how many ordinations would need to be broken, if additions would open up the way to annul these on account of accidental circumstances apart from substance, not foreseen? The Salamancans cite for their position del Soto, Lessius, with Sanchez. But not rightly because Sanchez (*loc. cit. Dec.* lib. 4 c. 2 n. 11) adheres to Busembaum, who above (n. 175) says it is probable (with Suarez) that an error even in regard to accidental circumstances invalidate an oath (and the same for a vow) if these are of great importance, and if after they are known, the oath would not have been made. And this in regard to contract the Salamancans think is probable (*de contract.* c. 1 punct. 3 n. 21). And therefore in regard to vows it also seems probable. See what is going to be said in n. 226.

"7. Vows which are made after novitiate in every approved "order, after the fashion of carnal matrimony, are not "invalidated on account of any error, except only substantial in "regard to substance."

"8. If an error in regard to a substantial condition were on a "matter of little importance, it does not render the vow invalid: "as if the journey of pilgrimage, which someone vows to make, "were a little longer than is thought, because a little thing is "reckoned for nothing. Likewise, if the error were only in "regard to an impulsive cause, the vow is valid, (Salamancans *de* "*voto* tr. 17 cap. 1 punct. 6 § 4 num. 158), because that is only a "secondary cause, after such is separated, the act is sufficiently "voluntary according to the substance. Nor does such an error "in the remaining contracts vitiate the act; *e.g.* someone vows a "pilgrimage to Rome with zeal to worship God, and at the same "time also has a secondary impulsive cause to see his brother, "whom he thinks is at Rome, even if he understood that he was "not there, then the obligation of the vow does not cease. And it "is clear from these, how it must be understood, which is "usually said to be vows not to oblige beyond the intention of "the one making the vow. Sanchez, lib. 4 c. 2 n. 45. Lessius, c. 40 "dub. 2 n. 11."

199.—"A mere intention does not suffice for a vow, even if it "is very firm, because one who only intended something is not "held to furnish it under sin; but one who promised is obliged "under sin, and unless he would furnish it, acts against trust "given to God. Bonacina, p. 1, Laymann, *loc. cit.*"

Would someone neglecting a good intention sin at least venially? Lessius, Palaus, etc. (cited by Salamancans *de vot.* cap. 1 punct. 1 § 2 n. 17) affirm it, on account of the inconstancy without a cause then intervening. Still, Busembaum, Sanchez (*Dec.* lib. 3 cap. 2 n. 21) with del Soto, Aragon, Azor, and Salamancans (*ibid.* n. 18) with Dicastillus, Palaus, Suarez, Toledo, etc. reject it, because (they say) a defect of constancy of itself is not a fault, unless there is a precept. Both opinions are probable.

200.—"10. An implicit promise sometimes suffices for a vow, "as is clear in the reception of sacred orders, where, although *I* "*vow* or *promise chastity* is not said, nevertheless, this vow is "made implicitly by the very fact that you receive them, "knowing the Church has annexed that vow to these orders."

"But there is a doubt whether if someone were plainly "ignorant of the fact, would he still be reckoned to have vowed "from implicit intention? Some say yes, some more probably "deny it, and say such is held to chastity, not by vow but by a "precept of the Church. Sanchez *de matrimonio*, l. c. d. 87, n. 23; "Bonacina c. 2 p. 1 and the common opinion." (But Laymann thinks more probably he is held by the precept of the Church to pronounce the vow. Still, see what is going to be said on this in book 6 on Holy Orders, from n. 806).

201.—"11. If anyone had an intention to promise, but "nevertheless not to oblige himself, the vow is null, according to "Navarre, Sylvius, Sanchez (n. 27), Lessius (l. 2 c. 40 dub. 1 n. 6), "Bonacina and others against Cajetan, because such a person "does not wish to vow when he adds the condition against the "substance of the act. This is why de Lugo (d. 24 *de just.* sect. 1) "and others contend such a man cannot be said to promise "something. Certainly it seems to be an argument on the term. "But if he had a mind to make a vow and put himself under "obligation, but not to fulfill it, then he would also gravely sin "and the vow would be valid. Sanchez, Filliuci, Bonacina (p. 1 n. "14), Laymann, etc."

Here it behooves us to distinguish many things: 1) If someone vowed with a positive mind to not promise, nor to oblige himself, certainly the vow is null, as the Salamancans hold (tr. 17 c. 1 punct. 1 § 3 n. 19) with St. Thomas and the common opinion; 2) If wishing he had a mind to promise and oblige himself, but with the intention to not fulfill it, it must be said he is held to the vow from the common opinion, as the authors teach (Lessius l. 2 c. 40 dub. 1 n. 7; Sanchez, *Dec.* l. 4 c. 1 n. 23; Salamancans *ibid.* n. 21 with Suarez, Cajetan, Azor, Bonacina, etc. against Valentia). The reason is, because the obligation of the vow does not depend upon the intention to fulfill it, but upon the will which is present to put himself under the obligation; 3) If a man, while making a vow, has the mind to promise and fulfill it but without a positive mind to put himself under an obligation, then if he sufficiently knows the obligation of the vow, but does not give his attention

TREATISE II: THE SECOND PRECEPT, CH. III, ON VOWS 219

to it when he makes the vow, and is in the negative by not willing, or by not excluding its obligation, indeed he is held to the vow because one who wills an antecedent act, wills (at least implicitly) its consequent obligation. (In common Sanchez, *de matrimonio* lib. 1 d. 9 n. 11; Palaus t. 3 tr. 15 d. 1 part. 3 n. 2; Tamburinus, l. 3 c. 12 § 1 n. 6; Salamancans *loc. cit.* n. 23 and others here and there).

Quæritur I: Would a man be held to a vow who does not know the obligation of a vow and is in the negative, that is not explicitly or implicitly meaning to undertake it? Palaus (l. c. n. 2) and Suarez (*de voto* cap. 3 n. 9) affirm it, because he must be thought to have wished to promise according to the mode and intention which others rightly making a vow have. But Sanchez (*de matrim.* l. 1 d. 9 n. 2) with Ledesma, Aragon and Manuel more truly deny it, likewise Croix (l. 3 p. 1 n. 365), and Tamburinus (l.c. n. 8) and Salamancans (*cit.* n. 23) who assert this is truly the doctrine of all. The reason is, because no man contracts an obligation unless he wills to impose it on himself; but here the man in no way means to undertake it, either formally in itself nor virtually in a promise, since he would err in substance by judging such an obligation is not annexed to the vow. Nevertheless, it must be said otherwise, as Sanchez and Tamburinus advert, if someone wished to make a vow in the ordinary mode, in which others make vows, because then he implicitly wills to contract an obligation.

Quæritur II: Would one be held to a vow that wishes to promise and knows the obligation of the vow, but does not wish to obligate himself to the vow?

The first opinion, which some authors hold, says he is obligated because after his will have been posited to pronounce a true vow, the obligation cannot be separated, which arises from the vow. (del Soto *de justitia et jure*, l. 7 q. 1 art. 2) and Prado, Aragon, Gutierrez, etc. cited by Salamancans, tr. 17 c. 1 punct. l. § 3 n. 24).

But *the second opinion* is more common and probable, and it denies it. The reason is, not only because a man that wants to add a condition contrary to the substance of the contract renders the contract invalid, but even more, because the law (exactly as a vow is a particular law) does not obligate except according to the mind of the legislator (Sanchez, *Dec.* l. 4 c. 1 n. 27; Lessius l. 2 c. 40 dub. 1 n. 6; Palaus tom. 3 tract. 15 d. 1 p. 3 n. 2 and Salamancans *ibid.* n. 25 with Suarez, Azor, Bonacina, Valentia, Trull). Hence, the Salamancans infer that if someone promises betrothal, or receives sacred orders, or pronounces a religious profession with a mind to not obligate himself, he is not held to betrothal, nor to the vow. But see what is going to be said on this on Orders, in book 6, dub. 2 n. 809. Furthermore, would it be a sin for a man to make a vow without a mind to obligate himself in this way? Some authors say that ordinarily it is no more than a venial sin, on account of a certain disorder. (Sanchez, *loc. cit.* n. 38; Palaus, *loc. cit.* n. 5; Salamancans *ibid.* n. 27 with Suarez, Bonacina, Trullenchus, Reginald, and Villalobos). I said *ordinarily*, because in a religious profession, and reception of sacred orders there is no doubt it would be a mortal sin, because it would be a deception in a very grave matter. See what was said on oaths in n. 172.

Quæritur III: Would a man be held to a vow if he doubts whether he willed to obligate himself by making the vow? Tamburinus thinks it is probable that it does not obligate him; but the opposite must be said with Croix (l. 3 p. 1 n. 384), Gobat, Diana and others with the common opinion, because until the invalidity of the act is established, the presumption is in favor of its validity, as Menochius, etc. teach in the common opinion.

The same thing must be said as Croix (n. 386) rightly says against Gobat, if someone were uncertain as to whether he knew or took notice of the obligation of the vow because commonly from contingent circumstances everyone is thought to know that every vow begets an obligation to fulfill it. What if someone were uncertain as to whether he made the vow, or purposed something, but recalls that he believed it, would he gravely sin if he did not fulfill what he promised? Croix (n. 366) thinks that he is not obligated, because at least the vow is doubtful since many common folk still making a bare proposition think erroneously that they are held to it under sin. But I do not agree with this, and I think this man must truly be thought to have made a vow and to have contracted the obligation of the vow, for since he already apprehended that he sins by not fulfilling what was promised, it is rightly argued that he really knew it and imposed it on himself.

DUBIUM III
What matter is required for a vow?

202. Would a vow on an impossible thing hold?
203. Would a vow to avoid all venial sins hold? What if someone would vow to avoid all mortal and venial sins collectively?
204. Would a vow concerning a vain thing be valid?
205. Would it be a mortal sin to vow to do a venial sin?
206. Would a vow made from a bad end be valid?
207. Could a vow be an impediment to a greater good?
208. Is a vow to not seek a dispensation valid?
209. Is a vow to marry be valid?
210. Is a vow to not make a vow be valid?

202.—"*Resp.* A vow should be possible (since an impossible "thing can neither be efficaciously intended nor would there be "an obligation to it); and not only good but even better than the "opposite, or its omission; obviously the intrinsic end of the "vow is to give honor to God through it, but it cannot be done "unless something pleasing were offered to him, but it cannot "be pleasing that someone would be obliged to relinquish that "which is better. Sanchez, l. 9 c. 7; Laymann, Navarre, etc."

What if someone were to vow a possible thing together with an impossible? We answer he is held to the possible part, if it is divisible, say if a spouse would vow chastity, they are held to not seek the marital debt. So also the vow is valid if its principal part is possible, even if the accessory part were impossible. It is otherwise, if vice versa. See Salamancans tr. 17 cap. 1 punct. 2 § 5 num. 75.

What if the vow were disjunctive? See the following number.

Thus the following are resolved:

203.—"A vow to never sin venially is invalid, since it is "morally and ordinarily impossible. Nevertheless, some wish, so "vowing to be held by this vow to avoid mortal and more "serious venial sins. See the Scholastics on this matter, Navarre, "c. 12 n. 63, Suarez, l. 2 c. 3; Sanchez *de matrim.* l. 9 d. 35."

The Salamancans (*ibid.* n. 80, with Sanchez, Palaus, Trullenchus, Prado) assert that a vow on avoiding all venial sins, even if it were from full deliberation is altogether invalid, precisely as it is on a matter that is morally impossible. (Council of Trent, Sess. 6, from can. 23 *de justif.*). In regard to the vow of St. Teresa [of Avila], one would understand to do anything more perfectly, the response is that she made it by a special inspiration of the Holy Spirit. See Salamancans *ibid.*, n. 84 and 85. But Croix (lib. 3 p. 1 n. 401, with Suarez) says more truly that the vow is valid to avoid deliberate venial sins, since this really is not impossible and those persons loving perfection will sufficiently avoid them. But a vow to abstain from venial sins in some determined matter is commonly valid, especially in persons of great virtue; in others of more modest virtue the matter will be impossible; nay more in some matters, say of unworthy and idle thoughts, etc., since they are inevitable in regard to all, the vow is null. Salamancans *ibid.* n. 81, with Cajetan, Sanchez, Suarez, etc.

A vow on avoiding mortal and venial sins collectively is equally null. And even a vow to avoid venial or mortal sins divisively, because that disjunctive vow is null, part of which is suitable, part of which is inept, and vowing to neither he willed determinately to oblige himself, say, if you would vow that you were either going to pray or play, the whole vow is null. (Salamancans *ibid.* n. 83 and punct. 6, n. 141, with Sanchez, Trullenchus, Villalobos, and Leander, and also Palaus (p. 8 § 1 n. 3) and Croix (*loc. cit.* n. 402). Nevertheless, they rightly advert that if someone were to obligate himself to such a vow, inasmuch as he can, he is indeed held to at least flee mortal sin. And I think he is also held to avoid deliberate venial sins, according to what we said above.

204.—"A vow on a vain useless, or indifferent matter is "invalid, except from the circumstances or it is done from a "good end,[8] because a stupid promise displeases God, and hence "he does not accept it; and one sins venially vowing such "things, as *e.g.* if anyone getting off a horse, would vow to "never again mount one. Navarre, c. 12; Sanchez 4 *mor.* c. 7" (with Salamancans *ibid.* n. 55).

205.—"3. It is invalid to vow evil things, and one who will "vow a mortal sin, sins mortally, but who vows a venial sin, he "only sins venially (Sa, Sylvius, etc. *v. Juramentum*), even if he "wills to sin morally (Cajetan, *v. Votum*, and Lessius, lib. 2 cap. 4 "d. 5) which seems more probable."

It also seems more probable to me that to vow an evil, even a venial sin, of itself is a grave fault; since of itself it is a blasphemy to will that an evil would fall to the honor of God; but in common on account of ignorance this is not more than venial, as the

---

[8] Provided the circumstances are not only from relation to the one vowing, but of itself is conducive to a good end. Salamancans tr. 17, c. 1 punct. 2 § 3 n. 57.

Salamancans rightly note (*ibid.* § 4 n. 71). We said the same thing on oaths in n. 146.

206.—"4. A vow is invalid to which an end is joined or other "circumstances that are evil, holding itself on the side of the "thing vowed, as *e.g.* someone will vow to give alms to obtain "vainglory, or to obtain from it an unjust victory, a happy "success for theft, adultery, etc., or in thanksgiving for success "in some sin; because almsgiving for such an end is a "blasphemous action, as if God would give progress to sins; and "therefore it cannot be the matter of a vow. Cajetan, Navarre, "cap. 12; Sanchez, c. 6; Laymann, lib. 4 t. 4 cap. 2 n. 6; Filliuci, t. "26, cap. 5.

"5. Nevertheless, a vow is valid even if a bad end is joined to "it, or another evil circumstance, that only exists on the side of "the man making the vow: say if someone from vainglory or "from anger toward an importune poor person would maintain "giving alms to him, because then the matter is good which he "vows, although he would vow it wickedly and with sin. *Ibid.*"

Therefore, note here the difference between a wicked end on the side *of the thing vowed*, and on the side *of the man vowing*.

1) The end on the side *of the thing vowed* is, when the matter promised is directed to a wicked end, namely if you were to vow fasting, so that you would receive applause for it; and then the vow is null, as the authors commonly teach. (Busembaum, Laymann, lib. 4 tract 4 cap. 2 n. 7; Salamancans *ibid.* n. 67). And the Salamancans say, with others, that the same thing must be held, even if a wicked end is vowed that is not the primary but only the secondary motive, or it is impulsive, but without which the vow would not be made. The same must be said if the end were indifferent, or merely temporal. Wherefore, if someone would vow fasting to spare costs, almsgiving lest he be thought greedy, the vow is null. But a vow uttered to obtain temporal

things from God or to make thanksgiving to him is valid, because it is good to hope for these things from God, or to make thanksgiving for them. So Laymann, *ibid.* n. 10 and Salamancans *ibid.* n. 70, with Sanchez, Palaus, Trullenchus, Bonacina, etc. Nevertheless, Laymann (n. 7) and the Salamancans (*ibid.* n. 69, with Cajetan Sanchez, Bonacina and the common opinion) note that if an evil work is placed as the end of the vow, but as a simple condition, namely if someone would vow fasting if he would kill an enemy, if he would commit theft; then the vow is valid, because after the fulfilled condition has been placed, it is worthy in itself to fulfill the vow.

So, we speak this way when a wicked end is on the side of the thing vowed.

2) Nevertheless, it would be otherwise when a wicked end is on the side *of the man vowing, viz.* when the matter is not vowed, but the act of vowing itself is directed to a wicked end, say, if someone would externally vow fasting, so that from the act of making the vow he will be praised by others, then the vow is valid, as Busembaum (n. 5) rightly says with the common opinion. Hence, Laymann says (*ibid.*) that, one who vows from a disordered appetite to eat fish so as to enter the Carthusian order, is held to the vow. But this seems hardly to be proved to me if the eating of fish, not indeed the spiritual good of religion, were the end of the vow, for then the matter of the vow itself, which is the taking up of the state of religion, is directed to a vain end, which weakens the vow, as was said above with the common opinion.

"6. Likewise, a vow made from a desire toward a good thing "is valid, as it is good, even if it is joined with a bad cause, as if "anyone would vow almsgiving, if he would come out of a duel "safe; if he would not be caught in the act of theft; if a son "would be born to him from adultery, which he carries out, etc., "for even though to will a duel, theft, and adultery is evil, "nevertheless, when these have been posited, to not be harmed, "to not suffer disrepute, to beget a son, are not evil, but gifts of "God; and a vow is not made not over the former evils, but over "the latter goods, considered (as I suppose) insofar as they are "good in themselves. Navarre, Laymann, *loc. cit.*"

207.—"Likewise, it is invalid and a venial sin to vow a good "which is an impediment to a greater good, especially vows "against the evangelical counsels, such as *e.g.* to remain in the "world, to marry, to go into the army, to carry out trade. "Navarre, n. 29; Suarez, Filliuci cp. 1 q. 7 n. 8; Sanchez, etc."(The Salamancans say the same thing, tr. 17, c. 1 punct. 1 § 2 n. 37, with St. Thomas, II IIæ qu. 89, art. 7 ad 2).

"8. Still, if something good, *per se* and absolutely less good, "the greater good would be done *per accidens*, when he avails to "vow such things: *e.g.* if someone would see the taking of orders "as ruinous to him. See Bonacina, p. 1."

208.—So also the Salamancans (*loc. cit.*) But the question turns to: would a vow to not seek dispensation, commutation, or invalidation of a vow be valid, even with a just cause (for without a just cause, it is certain it would avail)?

The first opinion rejects it, with del Soto, Trullenchus, Tamburinus, Sanchez, etc.

But *the second opinion* affirms it with St. Antoninus, Bonacina, Suarez, Filliuci, etc., cited by Salamancans *ibid.* n. 49, and 50. And this seems more probable; by adverting to the fact that in a case in which it is more useful on account of a spiritual good to seek a dispensation, the vow does not oblige, although it was valid. Nevertheless, the vow can always be relaxed by a superior, whose power is always untouched. (Salamancans *ibid.* n. 51, with Sanchez, Palaus, Suarez). Moreover, it must be noted that the one vowing to not seek a dispensation can seek a commutation and vice versa. See Salamancans *ibid.* n. 52.

209.—"9. Ordinarily, a man invalidly vows matrimony "because ordinarily, celibacy is better. I said *ordinarily*, because "it is validly vowed: a) If anyone were obliged to this, or "because without injury or grave infamy to the betrothed, or of "the children conceived by her he cannot recede from "betrothals; b) If it were thought to be very useful to the "common good, because *e.g.* from it peace was hoped for "between princes, conversion of heretics, tranquility of the "kingdom; c) If anyone on account of fragility, and inveterate "custom to sin were so prone to falling that prudent men would "judge after consulting with him that he should marry, "although in that last case, Laymann and others disagree. See "Bonacina, *loc. cit.*, Filliuci, num. 6; Navarre, Suarez, *loc. cit.*, "Laymann n. 12."

A vow to marry, speaking *per se*, is null, even if it were to marry a pauper, a whore, or to put a stop to someone else's sins, because celibacy is always more pleasing to God. This is the common opinion, among the Salamancans, *ibid.* n. 38 and 39, with Sanchez, Leander, Palaus, Torre, Prado, etc. Otherwise, if the vow were pronounced to repair scandal or the honor of a young woman from obligation, or for the common good, as Busembaum adds, or from what is supposed, that vowing he willed to marry, he is held to the vow. (Salamancans *cit.* n. 38, in fine).

But the great question is, whether one who vows to marry on account of the experience of his weakness, is held to the vow?

The first opinion says no, because such a vow would of itself be an impediment to a greater good, namely entering a religious order, or of preserving celibacy. Then, because such a vow would be useless, since, such a vow not withstanding, the man vowing could freely enter religion; especially seeing that matrimony is a lower remedy for concupiscence. Lessius, lib. 2 c. 40, dub. 7 n. 44 and Palaus, del Soto, Prado, and others with Salamancans *ibid.* n. 40.

But *the second opinion* by far is more probable, which many authors hold. (Busembaum, Sanchez, *Dec.* lib. 4 cap. 8 n. 53; Viva *de Spons.* qu. 1 art. 3 from n. 3; Salamancans *de voto* c. 1 punct. 1 § 2 n. 41 and 42, with Bellarmine, Navarre, Cajetan, Bonacina, Trull., etc.). It says that the vow is valid, supposing that such a man refuses to use other remedies; because in such a case matrimony is the greater good, since matrimony is conceded by God to pacify the concupiscence for those who refuse to take up better remedies. For on these sorts the Apostle says: "It is better to marry than to burn." Especially because the man frequently relapsing [into sin] would be held by natural law to marry once it is posited that he refuses to use other remedies.

Someone will ask: so, a subdeacon who vows chastity could not marry, if he could not contain himself when to marry would be a better good for him? But the response is, that this is expedient on account of the common good to vow more to remain in health than it would be to take account of his frailty. See the Salamancans *ibid.* n. 45. Moreover, the Salamancans say he is held to matrimony who refuses or *cannot* apply other remedies. But Laymann says better (l. 4 tract. 4 c. 2 n. 12) citing St. Jerome and Ambrose, as well as Sporer (*de voto* n. 61 and 62) that he is held to matrimony who *refuses* to apply other remedies, but not who *cannot,* for no one that wills to use opportune remedies can be said to not be able to apply them; moreover, who is forbidden to use at least prayer? It is far from doubt that he could overcome all concupiscence from what we read in Luke 11:10, "Everyone that asks, receives".

210.—*Quaeritur:* if someone was exceedingly prone to make a vow, and would vow to not make any more vows except with the license of a confessor, but later made another vow, *e.g.* fasting, would the vow be valid? I respond with Laymann (lib. 4 tract. 4 c. 2 n. 5) and I say: 1) That the first vow is indeed valid, since it is on a better good; 2) That he sinned by making the second vow; 3)

I say that, the first vow not withstanding, he is held to the second because since it had a good object, it is valid enough. I make the exception, unless he would have established that he refused to avail of future oaths, unless the counsel of a confessor were added, for then there will be no second vow provided he did not expressly or virtually retract it, viz. if being mindful of the first vow he pronounced the second.

Lastly, it must be noted that a man that makes many very different vows should keep the worthier of them, otherwise the first is preferred to the second (Laymann, with Trullenchus, and Busembaum n. 225 v. 2 against Sanchez, who says then it is in the will of the man vowing to keep what he prefers). Moreover, on an oath against another oath, see what was said above in n. 179.

DUBIUM IV
What, and how great is the obligation of a vow?

211. *Would a vow on a light matter sometimes gravely obligate?*
212. *What if you had neglected a vow on a light matter through the year?*
213. *See other things with Busembaum.*
214. *Would an heir be held to the vows of the dead?*
215. *Could a father injure the legitimacy of sons by vows?*
216. *On vows that are another's de facto.*
217. *Could vows be fulfilled by another?*
218. *Would a man sin that impedes the fulfillment of a condition assigned in his own vow?*
219. *Things that must be noted in regard to the conditions in vows.*
220. *If the day promised has transpired, are you held to the vow?*
221. *Does an indeterminate vow always oblige? And what if a postponement were mortal?*
222. *What if someone would vow that he was going to enter a religious order without a certain place or a certain order?*
223. *What if someone would vow that he was not going to play under penalty?*

224. *Many notable things are adverted to in regard to oaths, and especially, whether a vow would hold if unforeseen circumstances would arise.*

211.—"*Resp.* To the extent that both the quantity of the "matter permits, and the intention of the man making the vow, "whereby he means to obligate himself to either much or a "little, or absolutely, or with a certain condition, restriction of "time, of quality, he plans in such a way that even if the "obligation of the vow were of natural law, still, its force would "depend upon the will and the deed of the man as a foreseen "condition, so that it only obliges so much. Thus the common "opinion. See Laymann, c. 3; Bonacina, p. 5."

Thus, the following are resolved:

"1. In a light matter no man is obligated under mortal sin "because the matter does not permit it" (Not even if one would "wish to oblige himself under grave sin; Salamancans tr. 17, c. 1 "punct. 4 2 n. 106), "Navarre, n. 40; Sanchez, lib. 4 c. 12; "Laymann, *loc. cit. E.g.* you vowed to daily recite the *Salve* "*Regina*: by omitting it once in a while, you would not sin "mortally because it is a light matter. Sanchez, lib. 4 c. 12; "Laymann *loc. cit.*, Azor lib. 21 cap. 15."

Quaeritur: Would a transgression of a vow be a mortal sin when its whole matter is small? Cajetan, Toledo and Cardenas affirm it (cited by *Salamancans ibid.* n. 112) in the same mode in which in a promissory oath, if something is lightly promised, a man would sin gravely (as they say) if he did not fulfill it. But the opposite must be held with Busembaum and Lessius (lib. 2 c. 40 dub. 9 n. 56), del Soto, Suarez, Trullenchus, Bonacina, Palaus, etc. (Salamancans *ibid.* n. 113) because a vow is a particular law and the law does not oblige except according to the gravity of the matter. Nay more, the same must be said on a promissory oath. (Salamancans *ibid.* n. 115, and 2 punct. 5 2 n. 53, with others, as we said above in n. 173).

Hence it is inferred, that a vow to avoid sin does not oblige except according to its gravity; say if you were to vow to avoid lying, you would only sin lightly by lying, but in two ways, against veracity and against the vow (Salamancans c. 1 cit. n. 115, with Sanchez, Trull., Navarre etc.). Still, unless avoidance of that sin on account of causes is of such great importance, just as lying is very unbecoming for a person constituted in a dignity, or even if by that sin one were very much impeded from the progress in virtue. Salamancans *ibid.*

212.—"On the contrary, even if you were to omit it for a "whole year, it is only a venial sin, to the extent that these small "matters do not coalesce into one, as the authors probably "teach. (Diana, t. 5 *misc.* n. 24; from del Soto, Aragon, and "Tanner, 2. 2. d. 3 dub. 3 against Valentia, etc.)."

Just as the Salamancans say (*ibid.* with Villalobos, etc.). But they advert this must rightly be understood when a promise of these light matters was made in honor of a day, just as it is thought in all personal vows, unless it would be certain from the opposite, as the authors commonly say (Salamancans *loc. cit.* and Croix lib. 3 p. 1 n. 450, with del Soto, Suarez, Laymann, Diana, Palaus, etc.). For on the other hand, if a promise of a light matter were made by the mode of one thing, so that a day were not assigned as the terminus, but the obligation were not delayed beyond it, then the matters coalesces and may arrive at a mortal sin. This is why, if someone would vow that he was going to give a little in almsgiving daily, he would sin gravely if he omitted it daily by a vow made through the mode of one thing (Salamancans *d.* num. 115, with Sanchez, Suarez, Trullenchus, Leander, etc.). Hence they note, that in regard to real vows, unless another thing were established, a day is regularly not appointed to finish, rather to stir up the obligation and therefore the matters coalesce, as the authors teach in common. (Salamancans tr. 17 c. 1 punct. 5 num. 131; with Suarez, Bonacina, Palaus, Vasquez and Croix, *loc. cit.* with others, as above. See what is going to be said in n. 220.)

213.—"In a grave matter, even if someone could oblige "himself only lightly, still in the common opinion, it is thought "that he wills to oblige himself gravely, unless it is certain from "another source. Wherefore, one violating such a vow sins "gravely from its nature. See *ibid.* §1 n. 93 and § 2 n. 105."

"3. One who after he has bound himself with a grave vow, "then is seriously sorry that he did it, he does not sin gravely, "provided he would retain the mind to fulfill it. See Sa, *v.* "*Votum.*

"4. One who violates a vow on a matter that is already "commanded, *e.g.* one who, after making a vow of chastity "would fornicate, should add in confession that he had a vow or "that he had received Orders, if the confessor does not know, "because the malice of the sin is twofold; Suarez, cap. 6; Lessius, "d. 7; Sanchez, c. 5; Filliuci, cap. 2, q. 7." (From the common opinion, for a vow rightly avails on a matter otherwise commanded Salamancans *ibid.* punct. 2 § 1 n. 32 with St. Thomas against Gerson, St. Antoninus, etc.)

"5. No man is obliged by someone else's vow from the force "of that vow. Wherefore, if some canons seem to indicate that a "son whom his father has vowed should enter religion were "held to profess it, they must be understood to mean if the son "would at some time ratify the vow of the father. Suarez, cap. 9, "Sanchez, Laymann, c. 5 n. 6; Salamancans *ibid.* punct. 4 § 3 n. "118.

"6. When an heir is held to pay real vows of the dead, he is "not held by the force of the vow, but from justice: just as he is "held to pay his other debts, and things bequeathed to him, etc. *Ibid* n. 123."

214.—Certainly, an heir is held to pay real vows of the dead just as other debts, from *l. 2 Secunda, ff. de pollic.* and from *c. Licet de voto.* From which he can be compelled to pay by excommunication. Hence, he ought to satisfy such debts before the bequeathment, but later what is due to justice.

215.—*Quaeritur:* Could a father in death injure the right of his sons?

The first opinion affirms it, with Navarre, Sylvius, Diana, Lopez, Vega, etc., cited by Salamancans *ibid.* n. 126. As also (as they say) a father can burden the right with gifts to remunerators.

But the opposite must be held with *the second opinion.* For a father can, in his life, diminish with moderate vows in some way the right of sons, or of those ascending to that right, but not in death, where according to the law he ought to dispose his goods, and the right, when it is of the law, cannot be burdened with voluntary debt, from Ecclesiastes 34:21: "You immolate from wickedness, the offering is stained." So Salamancans *ibid.* n. 127, with Sanchez, Laymann, Bonacina, Palaus, Trull., etc.

216.—"7. In the same manner, if the community would vow "something, concerning which they later did not agree, they are "not held to keep it by the force of the vow, but now and then "by reason of the pact, statute or of long custom. See Laymann, "*hic* c. 3.

"8. When someone vows the deed of another, the sense is "that he is going to see to it that in that mode in which it can "licitly be done, *e.g.* by asking, persuading, or even by "commanding if he is a superior; or even sometimes by "negotiating and by supplying the costs. So a parent, who vows "their son for a religious order, is held to nothing other than "that they should try to persuade the son, so he who vows to "take care of Masses or a pilgrimage for another when he pays "the stipend and the costs for him, is not held to substitute "another with new costs, if the prior did not furnish for which "he obligated himself. (Sanchez, Laymann, n. 7).

217.—"9. Personal vows are not fulfilled except by the man "making the vow; wherefore, someone who vows to make a "pilgrimage, say to Rome, does not satisfy it if he would employ "another, but he is not held to it if he could not. Salamancans "tr. 17 c. 1 punct. 4 § 3 n. 121."

"10. Real vows must be paid from one's own means, "wherefore, someone who cannot from his own means is not "held to beg from another. What if he could from his own and "still another, whether asked or of his own will, wants to pay "for him? It would be valid because what the other man gives "becomes his, however, the action of another person cannot be "done for another. *Ibid.* n. 122."

Nay more, he rightly satisfies the vow or the oath to give alms, who that furnished by another for that end, unbeknownst to him, he would later ratify when he learns of it, because then the vow is already fulfilled with the consent of the one that makes it. (Salamancans *cit.* n. 122, with Sanchez, Bonacina, Trull., etc.) And it seems probable enough since by such a mode he would rightly satisfy the promise made to the other man, so also he satisfies the promise made to God.

218.—"11. Conditional vows do not oblige when the "condition ceases, even if the one vowing was the cause that "the condition were not placed; provided that he did not impede "it from deceit, force or malice, *e.g.* you vow a pilgrimage if "Peter approves it, then you submit to persuade him not to "approve it; consequently, when he does not approve it, you are "not held. On the contrary, even if you impeded it maliciously "by fraud or deceit, still it is probable that you are not held to "the vow, as Laymann holds (cap. 6 from Suarez and others).[9] "Meanwhile, Laymann rightly advises that we must be attentive "to the intention of the one vowing, *e.g.* if a son vows that he is "going to enter religion unless his father would contradict him, "it seems his intention was unless he contradicted it of his own "will, left to his devices, etc."

But if you were to impede it deceitfully you would sin. You vowed, say, to enter religion if the father approves: if you would impede consent of your father by petitions and reasons, you do not sin; otherwise, if you were to impede it with force or fraud. Likewise, you vowed chastity if God would free you from mortal sin for a year, if you fall from frailty, you do not sin in respect to the vow. It is otherwise if you eagerly sin so that you would be free from the vow. And so, on the rest. (Salamancans *ibid.* n. 171, with Laymann, Palaus, Sanchez, etc.)

219.—In regard to the conditions of vows, it must be noted: 1) That all indecent or impossible conditions render vows null. (Salamancans *ibid.* n. 165). It must be noted: 2) That it would not suffice for the obligation of a vow that the condition were equivalently fulfilled, rather it ought to be specifically fulfilled. *E.g.* you vowed to enter into a religious order if your sister would marry, it does not suffice if she would die. Salamancans *ibid.* n. 169.

"12. A man who vows a certain and determined thing, *e.g.* "this chalice, if the thing would perish, he is not held to another "since it is usually not intended: but if he sold it, it seems more "probable that he is held to give him the money that he

---

[9] And this is more probable, from Salamancans *ibid.* punct. 6 § 6. n. 173, with Palaus, Filliuci, etc. against Azor, Bonacina, etc., because now the condition is not fulfilled, although by the fault of the one vowing.

"received, because the man who vowed the thing is thought to "promise its every advantage."

220.—"13. A man who vows to do something in a certain "time, say to fast on this or that day, after it has passed, either "with or without his fault, he is held to nothing, and if he had "foreseen the impediment was coming up in that time, he was "not held do it earlier since this is not usually the intention of "the one making the vow. Suarez, lib. 1; see Bonacina, p 5."

But the same rule comes to mind here which we spoke of above (n. 212), from the common opinion with Salamancans tr. 17, c. 1 p. 5 n. 130. For you are held to nothing after the day has transpired, if the day was appointed to end the obligation as it happens in personal vows, unless it is certain from the opposite, as Croix (lib. 3 p. 1 n. 450) with del Soto, Palaus, Laymann, Diana, etc. say in common. Salamancans (*ibid.* punct. 4 § 2) with Trullenchus, Suarez, Sanchez, etc. It is otherwise if you appointed the day only to bring its fulfillment, just as on the other hand it must regularly be judged in real vows, precisely if that day had no more special reasoning than others, as Salamancans *ibid.* punct. 5 n. 131 with Suarez, Palaus, Bonacina, etc. and Croix l. c. with others, as above.

Furthermore, whether in a doubt as to whether the day was appointed to end or to stir up the execution of the vow, are you held to the vow for the days transacted? Diana says no (p. 3 tract. 4 r. 26) because, as he says, vows do not oblige in doubt, when they must be interpreted strictly, from the rule commonly handed down by the doctors, with Cajetan and Laymann, etc. But generally speaking, Sporer (*de 2. praec.* n. 109) and Salamancans *ibid.* n. 132, with St. Thomas, Sanchez, Palaus, Trullenchus, Azor, and Bonacina affirm. The Salamancans give the reason that when a vow is certain and there is only uncertainty about the excusing circumstance, possession stands for the vow. But this reasoning does not clearly prove the matter, for it could be answered that here there is a doubt on the circumstance, which affects the substance of the vow, and therefore it would render the vow itself doubtful, according to what was said in n. 198. Hence, it seems more correct to me to distinguish and say that in personal vows you are not held, when in doubt, to satisfy for the days transacted; but it is otherwise in real vows. The reason is because on the one side the rule is firm, that possession favors that which the presumption favors, as the doctors commonly teach with Busembaum (l. 1 n. 26), Croix (l. 1 n. 509), Sanchez (*Dec.* lib. 1 cap. 10 n. 13), with del Soto, Molina, Aragon, and Menochius. On the other side, the most common opinion is that unless it were established from the opposite, as was fore-noted above on real vows, the appointed day is only presumed to stir up the obligation, as the Salamancans (*ibid.* 1 n. 131 with Suarez, Sanchez, Vasquez, Palaus, Bonacina, Prado and Croix, l. 3 p. 1 n. 450 with Laymann, del Soto, and Diana). Nevertheless, unless the vow had a special connection to the day, say if you were to have vowed to give alms in a jubilee week, or on Saturdays through the year, for example, in that year you received grace (Sporer n. 106 and Salamancans tr. 17, c. 1 p. 5 n. 129 with others). It is otherwise if the day had no connection to the vow, namely, if you vowed that you were going to give alms on the Saturdays of a year, having no special relation for that year, as Sporer rightly says (n. 106 in fine). On the other hand, in *personal* vows, the appointed day to end the obligation is presumed, as the Salamancans (*ibid.* p. 4 § 2 n. 115) and Croix (*loc. cit.*) say, with others noted above. Hence, in real vows, because the presumption is in favor of the vow, possession also favors it and so it must also be fulfilled for the transacted days. But it must be said otherwise in personal vows in which the presumption is on the opposite side, and so the Salamancans must be understood, when they assert as certain, that in personal vows the appointed day should be presumed to extinguish the obligation.

238   BOOK IV: ON THE PRECEPTS OF THE DECALOGUE

221.—"14. A man who vows something without a certain "time, *e.g.* a pilgrimage, is only held to fulfill [it] as soon as he "suitably can. Everyone is morally thought to understand their "promise so that when the suitable time comes, they should not "delay for very long, although a lesser cause would suffice to "delay it than to omit it. (Filliuci cap. 4 q. 10; Suarez lib. 4 cap. "12 n. 6, 7 and 13; Laymann, lib. 4 tr. 4 cap. 3; Bonacina disp. 4, "qu. 2 punct. 5 §1 n. 1, etc.)."

An indeterminate vow in regard to time, *e.g.* to recite a daily rosary, to fast on Saturdays, perpetually obligates a man unless something else were gathered from the circumstances. (Salamancans tr. 17, c. 1 punct. 6 § 1 n. 140, in common). Nevertheless, if there were a doubt as to whether a vow were for a year, or a month, you are only held to the lesser time. Salamancans *ibid.* n. 146 with Sanchez, Trullenchus, Suarez, Bonacina, etc. from c. 18 *de Censibus.*

Quaeritur: Would a man that makes a vow for an indeterminate time sin mortally if he would put off fulfilling it? It is certain that if a vow were for perpetual service to God, say to enter a religious order, to run a guest house, and similar things, one would sin mortally who delayed it for a long time if the opportunity were present to fulfill it, and a reasonable cause would not excuse him. Moreover, Armilla, Rodriguez, and Ledesma (cited by Salamancans *de statu relig.* tr. 15, c. punct 3 n. 32) say that to delay a vow of religion for two or three years is not a mortal sin; but this opinion rightly seems lax to others, such as Sporer (*de 2. praecept.* n. 117), the Salamancans and Croix with Palaus, who, speaking generally, say it is a mortal sin to delay for six months, and the Salamancans adhere to this (*dict.* n. 32), with Trullenchus and Garcia, thinking it is a mortal sin to delay beyond six months. Sporer also agrees if the man that makes the vow should go beyond 40 years of age; still Tamburinus thinks a youth of 15 or 16 years is excused from mortal sin who delays for three or four years because (as they say) this time seems a small matter in respect to lifelong service, but I can hardly acquiesce to this unless there were a just cause for the delay. Just causes for delaying are, if the one making the vow hoped by the delay to soften the blow to his parents or, if a grave spiritual or corporal necessity of corporal sisters or brothers would stand in the way. (Croix l. 3 p. 1 n. 443, with Palaus and Gobat, Bonacina *de voto* disp. 4 q. 2 p. 5 n. 3, with Aragon, and Tabienus, Sanchez *dict.* l. 4 c. 11 n. 5 and 6 and Salamancans *d.c.* 2 n. 30 with Suarez, Mach. Pell. Trullenchus and Garcia). Still, Sporer and the Salamancans rightly advert in these cases that great care must be taken lest a delay would be excessive or there was a danger of never fulfilling the vow. Such a danger is frequently present in vows of religion, for the execution of which the demons rouse innumerable quarrels and impediments.

Moreover, if a vow were in temporal assistance, viz. so many fastings, pilgrimages, etc., the authors think each delay does not arrive at a mortal sin. (Sporer, *2 praec.* n. 116 with Tamburinus). And Sanchez favors this (*dict.* l. 4 c. 14 n. 21) referencing St. Antoninus who says it is a mortal delay, "when the delay is made for a long time and from the delay itself there is the danger of forgetting it or powerlessness to fulfill it." But it must more truly be said that he sins mortally who without a just cause notably delays fulfilling the vow, say, beyond two or three years; and the authors rightly think that if you vowed to confess every month, you could delay for two or three days beyond the month with cause. (Croix l. 3 p. 1 n. 446; Salamancans *de statu rel.* loc. cit. n. 32, with Palaus, Trullenchus, Garcia and Diana).

222.—"15. A man who vows something without a certain "place, *e.g.* he is going to enter the Benedictine order, satisfies "by entering any monastery of that order in which the "substantial parts of the rule are preserved. Nor is one held to "travel to a province for admission, but it is enough to enter "some places that are not too distant. And he satisfies the vow "if, after he entered, he is remitted or he goes out before "profession (at least with a just cause, *e.g.* grave and long "lasting sadness, anxiety, or by nature itself, or born for another "life; Escobar, from Sanchez, t. 1 l. 4 c. 16 n. 10). See Trullenchus "l. 2 c. 2 d. 20 n. 7 and 8." (And see l. 5 from n. 72).

"16. Someone who vows something without a certain quality, "*e.g.* that he is going to enter a religious order in general, can "enter any, even a laxer house, provided essentials are "preserved and it is approved. Similarly, if anyone would vow "wheat, etc. he is not held to give the best that he has, but it is "enough (speaking precisely on the obligation) that he give "what is not plainly defective." (The Salamancans say the same thing, *de voto* tr. 17 c. 1 punct. 6 § 1 n. 140, with Laymann, Suarez, Bonacina, etc. Someone that makes a vow that he is going to give a chalice, build a Church, ought to fulfill the vows according to the common use).

"17. Someone that vows that he is going to give something, "without a certain quantity, *e.g.* almsgiving, money, grain, etc., "satisfies by giving as much as he wills, provided he would not "give so little that it would seem that he rather makes a "mockery of his vow than fulfills it. The reason for all these is "found in the intention of the man making the vow, whereby "no man is thought to oblige himself except to that which he "can suitably give and is commonly thought to be decent. "Suarez, Sanchez, l. 4 c. 13."

"18. In doubt on the mind of the one making the vow, the "interpretation is made according to the propriety of the words "which he uses, or rather more the common and customary "reception. Filliuci t. 26, c. 2, Laymann c. 3." (Salamancans *ibid.* from n. 134).

223.—"19. Someone that vows if he will play with paper, he is "going to give ten imperials, is held according to Sanchez to "give ten as many times as he plays, because the penalty is "accessory to the act. Still, it seems Laymann denies this (l. 4 "tract. 4 c. 5 n. 4). See Trull., Diana, p. 5 t. 9 r. 60."

The Salamancans rightly make a distinction (*ibid.* § 7 n. 177): If a vow was simple on paying a penalty if he were to play, then it suffices to pay the penalty the first time (with Sanchez, Bonacina, Sa, Diana). And Laymann calls it probable enough, as well as Palaus. It is otherwise if the vow were twofold, namely on not playing and on paying the penalty; then as often as he transgressed the vow, he must pay the penalty; unless this is very serious, such as a pilgrimage, bestowing a large sum in almsgiving, which is not usually found. (Salamancans *ibid.* with Laymann Palaus, Trullenchus, Sanchez, Diana, etc.)

Here it must be noticed that in such a twofold penal vow, if the first is relaxed, the second is also relaxed, precisely as it is accessory to the first (Salamancans *loc. cit.* n. 176 with Palaus, Laymann Sanchez, etc.) Then it must be noted that one who is invincibly ignorant, or forgets the principal vow, or the vow on the penalty, is not held to it (See Salamancans *ibid.* n. 175, and 177).

224.—Lastly, here many things must be equally noted: 1) That vows must always be interpreted with benignity (Salamancans *ibid.* § 3 n. 148, with Laymann, Cajetan, and the common opinion); 2) That fractions of vows are of the same species. For this reason, if someone, having a vow of chastity would fornicate, he can confess a fraction of the vow separately (Salamancans tr. 17 c. 1 punct. § 1 n. 101). But what if someone would vow fasting from a special motive of temperance? Valentia, Sanchez, Bonacina, etc. (cited by Salamancans *ibid.* n. 102) probably hold that he commits two sins by breaking the fast. So equally a spouse vowing chastity from the motive of love for chastity, if they were to seek the debt, they say they commit two sins. But it must more probably be held with the Salamancans (*ibid.* n. 103) and Cajetan, Trullenchus, Suarez and Prado, that such people only commit one mortal sin against the vow, because from the vow they only impose upon themselves the obligation of fidelity toward God, not another. 3) That if someone would vow disjunctively a good thing, or a bad thing, or a vain or impossible thing, the vow is null. (Salamancans *ibid.* punct. 6 § 1 n. 141). But if each part is suitable matter, that which is chosen must be furnished, even if after the choice the other part would perish, or be rendered impossible. On the other hand, if one part would perish or be rendered impossible before the choice, you are not held to the second, unless the matter would perish by your fault, or you made delay in giving it, or determining it. (Salamancans *dict.* n. 141 and 142, with Sanchez, Palaus, Molina, etc.)

Quæritur: Could someone vowing one part already chosen commute it with another?

Palaus and Sanchez, with others (cited by Salamancans *de voto* c. 3 punct. 12 n. 107) deny it with probability. For that reason, if the part were chosen, whose matter were reserved, such as chastity, etc., a papal dispensation is required. Nevertheless, Leander and Tamburinus (with many others) affirm it, and the Salamancans call it no less probable. The reason is, because not withstanding the choice, the vow still remains disjunctive, and the one making the vow does not deprive himself of freedom to choose the other part by carrying out a determination.

Someone vowing that he is going to hear Mass for a month is probably not held to hear two on feast days. Just as it is also probable if it was imposed on him by a confessor for penance. (Salamancans tr. 17 c. 1 punct. 6 § 1 n. 136, with Palaus, Tamburinus, Suarez, Trull., etc. Sporer, *de 2 praec.* c. 2 n. 96 and Croix *de poenit.* n. 281).

Someone vowing that he will recite the rosary makes satisfaction by reciting a third of it because this is commonly understood by the word "rosary" (Salamancans *ibid.* n. 136, with Palaus, Tamburinus, Prado, etc.). And he satisfies by reciting it in turns, because such a vow obligates after the fashion of the Divine Office (Salamancans *ibid.* in fine with Trullenchus, Tamburinus, Diana, Leander, etc.). And he also satisfies it by dividing the decades (*loc. cit.* in fin. with Sanchez, Trullenchus, Bonacina, etc.)

Someone who vows to fast can eat food with milk products (Salamancans *ibid.* n. 137 with Sanchez, and Palaus). If he vowed fasting for a month, he is not held on Sunday; or if he vows on the vigil of some Saint, which would fall on a Sunday, he can anticipate the fast on Saturday (Salamancans *ibid.* with Bonacina, Trullenchus, Diana, etc.) If someone vowing to fast eats meat, he is not held to the fast; in regard to a distinction of the precept of fasting by the Church, which imposes by a twofold precept both fasting and abstinence from meat, according to the Salamancans, with Sanchez, Azor, Sylvius, etc., and exactly as the reigning Pope, Benedict XIV has declared (see l. 5 n. 992). Would someone vowing fasting on each Saturday be held to the vow if the Saturday would fall on Christmas? Molina, Azor, Fagundez, Diana, Rodriguez, Villalobos (cited by Salamancans *ibid.* n. 138) probably deny it, and Bonacina (*de voto* tom. 2 disp. 4 q. 2 p. 6 n. 9) and Tamburinus (*de voto* § n. 13) call it probable, unless he expressly intended still on that day to oblige himself, because then without doubt he is held. The Salamancans affirm it as more probable, with Suarez, Sanchez and Vasquez. See what is going to be said in n. 226.

If someone forgot the vow, or a penance enjoined upon him, etc., and he furnishes the work that is due, then he truly satisfies it by the general will, as each is censed to have satisfied the earlier obligations (Sporer tract. 1 *de consc.* n. 50; Sanchez, *dec.* l. 1 c. 14 n. 15; Lessius, l. 2 c. 37, num. 11; Laymann l. 4 tract. 2 c. 11 n. 9). If anyone, however, is certain about a vow, but has probable reason that he satisfied it, the authors say the one willing is held to nothing. But we have already said of this opinion in the treatise on conscience that it must not be adhered to, because the obligation of a certain vow is by no means fulfilled by probable satisfaction.

DUBIUM V
In how many ways is the obligation of a vow removed?

225. *The obligation of a vow is removed: 1) By change of the matter; 2) By human authority. See resolutions.*
226. *Would the obligation to fulfill a vow still hold if unforeseen circumstances would arise? What about simple vows of chastity and or religion, and what of solemn ones? See book 5 n. 50.*

225.—"Resp. It can be removed in two ways. 1) for nullity "with intervention of authority, and that either by change of "the matter, say if the matter before was worthy and became "indecent, indifferent, or impeditive to a greater good, by "reason of a new circumstance, or of prohibition, or it becomes "absolutely or morally impossible or by cessation of the "condition upon which it depends; 2) with the intervention of "human authority: and that is threefold, by invalidation, "commutation or dispensation, upon which we will treat in the "following *dubia*. It is common, with Sanchez, l. 4 c. 24; Lessius, "l. 2 c. 24; Suarez, Filliuci t. 26 c. 8."

Thus, the following are resolved:

"1. Even if the matter became impossible, useless, etc. by "your fault, nevertheless, after it has become such, the "obligation ceases and it suffices to do penance for the fault.

"2. If the obligation of two incompatible vows coincides, the "one that is more urgent, and pleasing to God must be fulfilled "and the obligation of the other would cease. But if it were "neutral, or you did not know, both are better, it must be "fulfilled which you first vowed, and let the other one fall; if

"you do not know this, the choice is free. See Trullenchus l. 2 c.
"2 d. 9."

"3. If the matter of a vow were to become impossible, in
"regard only to a part, then if such a matter can not be suitably
"divided, or it is not customary, you are held to nothing, e.g.
"you vowed to build a Church, if you cannot build the whole,
"you are held to build a part."

"4. But if it can be suitably divided, and it is customary, the
"obligation remains to that part which can be fulfilled, so that:
"a) Someone who can not fast for a whole week but can on
"some days is held to the latter; b) Someone that contracted
"matrimony and consummated it after a vow of chastity, is held
"to not seek the debt, insofar as the vow is still possible (for he
"ought to render the debt). See Bonacina, p. 7 § 1.

"5. What if a vow could be divided but into one principal
"part, while the other is only an accessory, not intended as a
"separate thing *per se*, but dependent upon the first like an
"appendix to it and the mode; then if the principal would
"become impossible, the obligation of the accessory falls to ruin,
"but not vice versa. Say you vowed a pilgrimage to Rome in a
"hair shirt, and there to offer a certain something; if the
"pilgrimage became impossible, you are not held to wear a hair
"shirt nor to make the offering. See Sanchez, l. 4 c. 10;
"Bonacina, d. 4 c. 2 p. 4 § 4; Trullenchus l. 2 c. 1 d. 10."

226.—*Quæritur:* would there be an obligation to fulfill a vow if such notable circumstances would arise that, if he had foreseen them, the man would not have pronounced the vow? It is the common opinion with the Salamancans, in tract. *de juramento*, c. 3 punct. 2 n. 19 and 20, with Sanchez, Palaus, Trullenchus, etc. (see what was said in n. 187), that in every promise, exactly as it is also a vow, notable change of the matter of itself removes the obligation. The reason is because by change the matter becomes different from that which was promised. But what if a new circumstance that was not foreseen were added, say, if someone that had vowed to fast on all Fridays would be held to fast on Christmas day, when he would have excluded such a day if it were foreseen? The Salamancans (*de 3 praec. Decal.* c. 2 punct. 5 § 2. n. 104), with Navarre, Vasquez, Sylvius, and others uphold this position with Sanchez, in *Dec.* l. 4 c. 11 n. 61 (but we must note that Sanchez speaks in this place on a precise case of fasting, because he thinks the circumstance of a feast does not cause a notable change: but in regard to our question he holds the opposite opinion, as below). The reason is, as they say, to remove the man who makes the vow from it's obligation that which he promised, if he remembered it, must not be applied, but rather that which he promised in act. And they prove it from *c. Explicari, de obs. jejun.* where Honorius III said: "Men are bound neither by vow nor by regular observance on Friday if it would happen that the feast of Christmas should fall on that day, for on account of the excellence of the feast they can eat according to the general custom of the Church."

But Molina *de just.* disp. 272; Azor 1 p. 1. 11 c. 20 q. 3, and Fagundez, Diana and others cited by Salamancans *loc. cit.* de 3. praec. n. 103, deny he is held to the vow, by speaking on the aforesaid case of fasting (on which we also spoke of in n. 224), as well as by speaking generally on every new notable circumstance that arises, St. Antoninus, Navare, Sylvius, Henriquez, etc. (cited by Salamancans in tract. as above *de jurmamento* c. 3 punct. 2 n. 21). And St. Thomas expressly holds this opinion in his commentary on the sentences, 4. dist. 38, q. 1 art. 3 ad 1, where he so teaches: "Something that would have impeded the vow from being made if it were known in the beginning frees one from the obligation of a vow or an oath." The reason is, because then the intention to obligate himself is either deficient or interpreted in this way. And the Salamancans say for this opinion that probability cannot be denied; on the contrary, the Salamancans themselves (tr. cit. c. 1 punct. 6 § 3 n. 152) think that it is a notable change which, if it were known from the beginning, the one making the vow would not have obligated himself to it. This second opinion seems no less probable to me, nay more, perhaps more probable than the first. The general reason is because when unforeseen circumstances arise whereby the vow is rendered onerous, the matter of the vow becomes different from what was promised. And so the response is made to the opposite reasoning, because the one vowing would be held to more than he promised. Moreover, the response to the definition of Honorius III, as above, which there the Pope did not explain, when the circumstance of Christmas was actually not foreseen, because the text can be explained (as Azor understands it) on those who expressly vowed to keep the fast even on Christmas day, in which case he is certainly held to the vow, as we said above in n. 224.

DUBIUM VI
On the invalidation of a vow.

ARTICLE I
Can the obligation of a vow be removed by direct invalidation, and how?

227. Who can invalidate vows?
228. Is it lawful to invalidate vows without cause?
229. What vows of sons could a father, grandfather, tutor, etc. invalidate?
230. Could a mother invalidate them?
231. Would the vows of subjects be valid until they are invalidated?
232. What if someone was thought to be a father, husband, etc. in error?
233. Who could invalidate the vows of religious and nuns? What about an abbess?
234. Could a man invalidate all the vows of his wife?
235. Could a wife invalidate the vows of her husband?

236. *What if by mutual consent husband and wife were vow chastity?*
237. *Could a superior invalidate the vows made before subjection? What if there is a doubt as to whether they were pronounced before or after subjection?*
238. *Could the vows made in a time of subjection afterward be invalidated?*
239. *What if a superior ratified them?*
240. *What vows of servants could be invalidated by their master?*

227.—"*Resp.* Since ownership of something should not be "violated, and every master can use his freedom, hence, if "someone's will were subject to the dominative power of "another, he can invalidate all the vows of his subject, whatever "kind they are, at his pleasure, validly make them void without "any cause, directly, *i.e.* he can will and pronounce that those "vows are null so that in no case would the obligation later to "revive them (even if they sin, if they invalidate without cause, "as Lessius teaches, l. 2 c. 40 n. 75; Navarre, Suarez, Filliuci). "Thus, this right comes into being from positive law, wherein "dominative power is given to someone over the will of "another. The doctors commonly hold it in this way. See "Sanchez, l. 4 c. 24 n. 30 and 31." (But it also comes into being from natural law, as the Salamancans hold, *de voto* tr. 17 c. 3 punct. 3 n. 27, with St. Thomas II IIæ q. 185, art. 5).

228.—*Quaeritur:* Is it lawful to invalidate vows without cause? It is certain in favor of the value of the invalidation that no cause is required, and it is common that it is not a mortal sin, as the Salamancans teach (*ibid.* n. 29 and Lessius l. 2 c. 40 n. 69) to whom it seems certain, with Paludanus (in 4, dist. 38, qu. 4 art. 2, concl. 2 num. 20); Sylvester (v. *Votum IV*, q. 2 vers. *Sextum*); and Angel (v. *Votum II*, num. 10). There is a doubt as to whether it is a venial sin.

The first opinion affirms with Busembaum, Lessius, etc., because it is discordant for a superior to use this power without cause. But of itself, by speaking more truly, there is no sin because the vows of subjects are made under the condition of consent of superiors, for which reason, obedience suffices for the cause (Salamancans *ibid.* n. 30 with S. Antoninus, Cajetan, Sylvius, Azor, Tamburinus, etc.). I said by speaking *of itself*, because it can be excused from another source from venial sin with difficulty, because he makes the act idle, or because he irrationally impedes the advancement of another, as Lessius says (*loc. cit.* n. 70). But each reasonable cause suffices to excuse from venial sin, as Elbel (n. 254) and other say. And Sporer (*de 2. praec.* n. 34) with del Soto, Valentia, and Medina, etc., more commonly say that the superior does not sin gravely when he permissively gave license and later revoked it; on the contrary he thinks it probable that it is not even a venial sin unless he would have promised that he was not going to revoke it. Moreover, the invalidation of all vows is valid in general, even made over future things, and even if suddenly refused. Salamancans (*ibid.* n. 34 and 35), with Palaus (tr. 15 disp. 2 punct. 4 n. 6), etc.

Thus the following are resolved:

229.—"Any father, and in his absence a paternal grandfather, "tutor,[10] and moreover, even the mother, not only if she is the "tutor, but even in the absence of the first or second, certain "ones, if there are no others, even a teacher or master, as Suarez "and Lessius say (d. 10 n. 78 against Sanchez) can directly "invalidate vows of prepubescent children as is gathered from c. "*Mulier, caus. 32,* q. 2 etc., 1 and 2 c. 20 q. 1, etc., *Si quis de reg.* "Prepubescence, however, according to the laws, is defined in "males as completed in their fourteenth year, for women in

---

[10] Translator's note: A tutor, in the 18th century, is not to be understood as it is today; rather a tutor had guardianship of a child, normally of the gentry, to ensure he was educated in Latin, French (depending on the country), and the basic liberal arts; a tutor had full authority in regards to the child's discipline.

"their twelfth year, reckoned from the day of birth. (Sanchez, *loc. cit.*; Laymann tom. 4 c. 7 n. 10; Bonacina, tr. 4 disp. 4 q. 2 p. 6 § 2)."

The particular points must be explained more clearly.

A father, or paternal grandfather if he is absent, can invalidate every vow of prepubescent children, whether personal or real, even of chastity and religion, and even if the son had the capacity for deceit, and even if the vow were over the *peculium castrense*,[11] as it were (Salamancans *de voto* c. 3 p. 5 n. 45 from St. Thomas, II IIæ q. 88, art. 9, with Cajetan and Sanchez, Suarez, Trullenchus, Laymann, Lessius, Palaus etc., from c. 1 c. 20 q. 1 and 2). And the reason is, as Sanchez says (l. 4 c. 18 n. 5) because in such an age they do not have perfect deliberation for such an obligation; this is the reason why nature provides for such a defect, by offering parents the faculty to invalidate such vows. But in doubt as to whether a vow was made before or after puberty, still a father can invalidate it because his power prevails. Sanchez, Diana, Michel, with Elbel, n. 251, who rightly says that in doubt a son after puberty should ratify the vow. Moreover, parents cannot invalidate the personal vows of their post-pubescent sons, namely of chastity, frequenting the sacraments, etc.; unless they were prejudicial to domestic governance, such as vows of long abstinence, pilgrimage, and fasting, which are incompatible with the mode of life of the family, etc. (Salamancans *ibid.* n. 46 with St. Thomas, Lessius, Palaus, Sylvius, Tamburinus, Palaus, etc.) Moreover, they can rightly invalidate (but indirectly, as Busembaum says with Laymann n. 242), real vows of post-pubescent children of minority age, because they lack the administration of goods (Salamancans *ibid.* n. 47, with St. Thomas, Sanchez, Trullenchus, etc.). An exception is made if the

---

[11] Translator's note: A *peculium castrense* goes back in definitions to Roman Law. Under the legal systems St. Alphonsus is referencing, it would essentially mean the child's allowance deriving either from the paternal or maternal side.

vow were over the *peculium castrense*, or something like it; or if the son went out of from the father's power (Salamancans *ibid.* n. 48). Likewise, a vow to go to Rome for absolution of excommunication, from *c. Relatum de sent. excomm.* But the faculty which the father has towards his legitimate sons, is the same which he has toward his illegitimate sons (Sanchez, l. 4 c. 35 n. 82, with Palaus and Tamburinus, and it is common with the Salamancans *dict.* c. 3 n. 53). Here it must be noted that what was said about the father is also said about a tutor in respect to the pupil, and on a guardian in respect to a minor. And if there are many tutors, or guardians, each has the same power. Salamancans *ibid.* n. 49 with Suarez, Sanchez, Bonacina, Trullenchus.

230.—*The question is:* Could a mother invalidate the vows of her sons? If a mother were designated as a tutor or a guardian, certainly she can because tutors, and the others (as above) are able to. But what if she were not so designated, and the son lacked a father or a paternal grandparent? Sanchez, Suarez, Palaus, etc. (cited by Salamancans *loc. cit.* n. 50) think then the son is *sui juris*; but they say the opposite opinion is probable, viz. that in that case it is incumbent upon the mother to be the guardian, as the Salamancans more probably hold with Tamburinus, Prado, and Leander because it is reasonable that a mother, or a grandmother would provide for the minor; and therefore she can invalidate their vows as *curatrix*.

But it is more uncertain whether a mother, when the father is present, or a tutor, could invalidate the vows of her sons? There is a twofold probable opinion.

The first denies it, and says that only in absence of the father and a tutor could the mother invalidate the vows of prepubescent children, and failing the mother, the grandfather can do the same and a grandmother for the part of the mother (Suarez, Sanchez,

Tamburinus, Laymann, Palaus, Trullenchus, Bonacina, etc. cited by Salamancans *ibid.* num. 51).

But *the second opinion* is no less probable, as the Salamancans rightly say (*ibid.* n. 52, which Prado, Philiarchus and Roncaglia, *de voto* c. 5 q. 3 r. 3 hold). It asserts that the mother, even if the father or tutor are present, can invalidate all the vows of prepubescent children, even of chastity and religion; and also the personal vows of post-pubescent children which are prejudicial to the governance of the home, but not real ones, the administration of which pertains to the father or a guardian. The reason is, because such power is naturally also in the mother (although not civilly), whom her sons are held to obey even if with subordination to the father; so that the father can invalidate the vows of sons over the mother's opposition, but not so the mother when the father opposes it, and it is proved from St. Thomas (*Op.* 17, c. 13 art. 10) who indiscriminately furnishes the faculty to parents to invalidate the vows of sons.

231.—*Quaeritur:* Would the vows of sons and of other subordinates, such as religious, wives, etc., as below, be valid in those things which are not prejudicial to the commands or jurisdiction of a superior until they are invalidated?

The first opinion says no, and hence it says they do not need relaxation if they are pronounced with the consent of a superior. Because such vows lack the use of the will, whose mastery is in the power of superiors. So Valentia, Angelus, Marchant, Richardus, Rosella and others; and Leander, Torres, and Peyrinus (cited by Salamancans *de vot.* tr. 17 c. 1 punct. 7 n. 182) call it probable. And they say St. Thomas favors them in II IIæ q. 88, art. 8 ad 3, who says: "No vow of a religious is firm unless it is from the consent of a prelate." And he says the same thing on the vow of a wife, etc.

Nevertheless, *the second opinion* is more probable, which the Salamancans say must altogether be held (*ibid.* n. 183, with

Cajetan, Navarre, Tamburinus, Palaus, Trull., Filliuci, Azor, Sanchez, Suarez, and many others). It affirms that such vows are valid whether they are real or personal, unless they will be invalidated; because subjects really do not lack the will, but they ought to subject it to the will of superiors if they would contradict it. And so St. Thomas must be understood in that citation to teach nothing other than such a vow is not *firm*; because as he says in the response, ad 1 et 4: "In their vow the due condition is understood, if it would please their superiors, or if they would not resist." This is why it suffices that they do not resist that the condition of the vow be fulfilled and the vow is firm.

232.—*Quæritur:* If by common error someone with a title were thought to be a prelate, a husband, a father, etc., would the invalidation of vows which they make be valid, just as they are valid acts of jurisdiction according to *l. Barbarius, ff. de offic. præt.*? Sanchez, Bonacina, Trullenchus, Palaus and others (cited by Salamancans *tr. cit.* c. 3 punct. 8 n. 71) deny it, because the act of ownership differs from the act of jurisdiction. Still, the Salamancans (Salamancans *ibid.* with Prado) think the contrary is probable, because in these matters the same reasoning proceeds.

233.—"2. The vows of religious, (but not of novices), even "pronounced under their predecessors, can be directly "invalidated, not only by the Pope, but also by abbots, "guardians, priors and rectors, and probably also abbesses as "Suarez holds, l. 6 *de voto*, c. 7 n. 19; Reginald l. 81 n. 242; "Filliuci, Bonacina, *loc. cit.* n. 79. Still, an exception is made for a "vow to transfer to a stricter religious order. See Binsfeld "*Enchir. theol. pastor.,* part. 3 de 10 præceptis, cap. 9, I. f.; "Lessius, n. 73; Sanchez l. 4 c. 33 n. 13; Bonacina, l. 4." (Not even the Pope can invalidate this vow. Salamancans *ibid.* num. 38). (All vows, even internal ones, as the Salamancans say in punct.

4 n. 37, with del Soto, Sanchez, Laymann and Roncaglia q. 2. In regard to novices, even if their personal vows are suspended. See Salamancans *ibid.* n. 42. In regard to the Pope, indeed he can directly invalidate all vows of religious, as well as the Bishop of consecrated religious subject to him, Salamancans *ibid.* n. 33. Moreover, even secondary prelates, in addition to those above, can do this when the primary prelates are absent).

234.—"3. A husband can do the same thing, according to "Sanchez (l. 9 *de matr.* d. 39) in respect to the vows of his wife; "although others more probably limit that power to the vows "which are prejudicial to the right of a husband. (Laymann *hic.* "c. 7; Filliuci, tract. 26, c. 8 qu. 8; Lessius, d. 19, n. 93 and d. 15."

Nevertheless, at least externally, it seems the contrary opinion is more probable, namely, that a man can directly invalidate all vows of his wife even if they are not prejudicial to the use of matrimony or the education of children or the domestic governance (as the doctors merely concede to the contrary opinion, cited by Salamancans *de vot.* tr. 17 c. 3 punct. 6 n. 57). And it is especially proved from Numbers 20:7 and 9, where it is said: "If she has a husband and he vows something ... (if the husband) hearing would oppose it on the spot, and he made her promises invalid ... the Lord will be merciful to him." But the translators of the Septuagint interpreted not only on a vow of abstinence, but every vow; and St. Ambrose (cited by Salamancans *ibid.* n. 58) so says: "It evidently appears that a husband is so the head of his wife that no vows to offer God abstinence or religious life are lawful to her without his permission." Equally, St. Thomas (II IIæ qu. 88 art. 8 ad 3) teaches that the vow of a wife is thus null without the consent of her husband, just as the vow of a religious without the consent of a prelate: "No vow of a religious is firm unless it is from the consent of a prelate, nor the vow of a girl living in the home, unless it were from the consent of her father; nor of a wife unless it were from the consent of her husband." And the reason is, because it is very expedient to the peace of the family to foster mutual love seeing that the wife has a will totally dependent upon her husband, and so the impetus of women is weakened." (Sanchez, *de matr.* l. 9 d. 39 n. 4 with del Soto, Sa, and Salamancans *cit.* n. 58 with Sanchez, Prado, Tamburinus, Diana, Rodriguez, Fagundez, Villalobos, Ledesma, Leander, Aragon, etc. against Sporer *de voto* c. 3 n. 27 with Navarre, Sylvius, Azor, etc.) But they call the contrary opinion probable (Salamancans *ibid.*) Hence a man can even invalidate his wife's vow of chastity and religion to be carried out after his death (Salamancans *ibid.* n. 59, with Soto, Aragon, Leander, Fagundez, etc. Likewise Sanchez, *l.c.* n. 16, and disp. 40 n. 17 with Palaus, Ledesma and Vega, against Navarre, Cajetan, etc.).

235.—On the other hand, it must be noted: 1) That a wife cannot invalidate the vows of her husband unless they were prejudicial, such as a vow to make a long pilgrimage, great abstinence, to cloth himself in the habit of a hermit, and similar things (Salamancans with Busembaum, n. 242, v.2). Likewise, even a vow to seek what is due, as the authors say, because it would be a very grave shame for the wife to be compelled always to seek it (Sporer *l. c.* n. 28, with Laymann, Trullenchus, Henriquez, Fagundez, etc., against Lessius, Sanchez, Basilius, etc. cited by Salamancans *ibid.* n. 56). Such vows, the doctors teach in common must be invalidated: but it seems rather more to be invalid inasmuch as it is on an unworthy matter, as the Salamancans suppose (*ibid.* n. 55).

236.—It must be noted: 2) that if spouses would vow chastity or religion by mutual consent, they cannot invalidate each other's vows, because virtually both yield to the other's right. It is the common opinion; so the Salamancans (*ibid.* n. 59) with Sanchez,

Suarez, etc. and Busembaum, (n. 242 v. 7), who rightly adds it is otherwise if they would both vow independently of the other. But see what is going to be said in n. 239. These spouses, if after such a vow, made by mutual consent, would revoke the agreement, and have carnal relations, although they would not sin against chastity, still they would sin against the vow unless it were excused for a grave cause. (Salamancans *loc. cit.* in fin. with Suarez, Palaus, Bonacina, Sanchez, etc.

"4. Someone who once invalidates a vow, if later he changes "his mind, the vow is not revalidated as Sa says, *v. Irritatio voti*.

237.—"5. None of the aforesaid can directly invalidate a vow "made before subjection, *e.g.* before marriage. Still, they can "invalidate them when they are made within the time of "subjection on a matter that must be fulfilled after the time of "subjection, *e.g.* in puberty, or after the death of a husband. "Bonacina, *loc. cit.*" (With Salamancans *ibid.* n. 74, Valentia "Diana, Tamburinus, etc. as Sanchez *de matr.* l. 9 d. 39 n. 16 "with del Soto, etc. See what was said in n. 234).

A man cannot directly invalidate vows made by a wife before marriage, but can rightly suspend their execution insofar as they are prejudicial to his power (Salamancans *ibid.* n. 75, with Sanchez, Valentia, Palaus, Suarez, etc.). But the vows of religious are certainly extinguished by profession, as is held from *c. Scripturas, de voto*. See Elbel n. 253, and Salamancans

"6. A vow on which there is a doubt as to whether you "pronounced it in a time of liberty or subjection, a superior "cannot invalidate, as Salas teaches (1.2. q. 21) and Caramuel "(*Theol. fundamental.*, tom. 3, l. 3 c. 1 d. 1). But Suarez, Sanchez, "Bonacina, etc. with Bardi (l. 6 c. 1 § 28) hold the contrary."

Quaeritur: Therefore, could a husband or a prelate directly invalidate the vows of a wife or religious, respectively, on which there is an uncertainty whether the vows were pronounced before or after subjection? Sanchez (*Dec.* l. 4 c. 32 n. 7), from Suarez (with others, cited by Busembaum above). The reason is because, as they say, possession of the present will of the subordinate is certain, when it is certain she is a wife or this man is a religious; but an exception in regard to those vows is doubtful; this is why, until the exception is proved, viz. that the vows were made before subjection, the possession of the superior will prevail as certain. Just as a spouse that is uncertain about the validity of the marriage is held to render the debt to the other spouse when they seek it on account of their certain possession, as is held from *c. Dominus, de sec. nuptiis*. So Sanchez. But with respect to that doctor, I think the opposite. I do not doubt (as we said in n. 229) that a father can invalidate the vows of the son when there is a doubt, when the son arrives to puberty, or not, because in that case possession favors the power of the father, as we said in n. 229. But otherwise, in reverse order I say here it must be held that when the vows are certain and the possession of the husband, or the prelate is doubtful, to the extent that it is uncertain whether the vows were or were not pronounced in the time in which the subjection would have begun. Yet, the equality of the spouse seeking the debt differs, for there he has certain possession over the whole body of the uncertain spouse, and from possession he has a certain right to use it. Nevertheless, it is otherwise in our case, in which a man, or a prelate, does not have total possession over the will of his wife or a religious. Indeed, he has possession over the present will of the subject, but does not have it over the past will. And therefore the aforesaid cannot directly invalidate vows on which there is uncertainty as to whether they are from the matter subjected to them. Still, they can indirectly, according to the following article in n. 241.

238.—"7. Vows made in the time of subjection can still be "invalidated after it, *e.g.* when a son is an adult, which is true "even if he ratified it in puberty, thinking from error it is firm; "nevertheless, it is otherwise if he knew it was weak and "independently ratified it from the first. Lessius, l. 2 c. 40 dub. "10." (and Elbel n. 252 with Spor., Tamb.)

And this is more probable, namely, that vows made in the time of subjection can also be invalidated by the father even after that time, as the Salamancans hold against other opinion (*de voto* tr. 17 c. 3 punct. 8 n. 73) with Sanchez, Suarez, Trullenchus, Cajetan, Bonacina, Palaus, etc., provided the son does not confirm the vow in puberty; and provided he knows then the vow was not weak, as Busembaum adds with probability, together with Lessius.

Still, a father cannot invalidate real vows of sons that have grown up, after they are emancipated. (Salamancans *dict.* n. 73). Nor a prelate the vows of religious if the latter is no longer subject to him, nor a man the vows of his wife after a formal divorce is made. See Salamancans *ibid.* n. 72.

239.—"8. The aforesaid can revoke as well as directly "invalidate vows, even if they once ratified them, because they "do not deprive themselves of mastery or their power. See "Suarez, *de voto* l. 6 c.6, nevertheless, if it were done without "cause, it will be a mortal sin according to certain authors, "although Suarez and Layman more probably deny it."

That superiors can validly invalidate the vows of subject, even if they ratified them, seems certain, because the, even if they willed, cannot take away dominative power from themselves which they have over subjects. So in common Sanchez (*Dec.* l. 4 c. 27 n. 9), Elbel (*de voto* . 259) and the Salamancans (*ibid.* num. 66) with Cajetan, Suarez, Palaus, Sayr, Trullenchus, Prado, etc. And this avails not only for a father in respect to his son, and a prelate in respect to a religious, but even for a man in respect to his wife and Sanchez holds it is very probable (*de matr.* l. 9 d. 40 n. 17) with del Soto, Ledesma, Aragon and Vega, likewise Tamburinus, *in Dec.* l. 3 . c. 16 § 3 n. 48, and Salamancans *l.c. ex n. 65* with others cited (against Elbel, n. 259, and Sporer *de 2. praec.* c. 3 n. 32, etc.). The reason is because a man has true direct power to invalidate the vows of a wife, even of chastity, and religion, as was said in 234.

On the other hand, it is certain that all the aforesaid superiors, if they invalidate the vows of subordinates without a just cause, even after they positively approved them, both they and their subordinates seeking relaxation would sin (I said *if they positively approved*, for it would be otherwise if they permitted their subordinates to make the vow, and pursued the matter promised by the vow, as the Salamancans say, *ibid.* n. 69, with Sanchez and Palaus). But there is an uncertainty as to whether they would sin gravely or lightly by invalidating them. There are two probable opinions.

The first asserts that they would sin gravely, from Numbers 30:16 where on a man knowing about the vow of his wife, and later invalidating it, it is said: "He will bear his iniquity." The reason is, because after he has placed his consent, he is held to not impede the vow. Salamancans *ibid.* n. 68, with Cajetan, Sanchez, Laymann and Ledesma, etc.

But *the second opinion* is perhaps more probable, and asserts that they would sin lightly, if scandal and contempt were avoided, because the superior uses his right and by invalidating the vow it is not the cause of that violation, since the subordinate does not then violate the vow. The authors hold this with Busembaum; Suarez (l. 6 c. 4), Bonacina (p. 7 § 2 n. 29), del Soto (*de justitia et jure* l. 7 q. 3 art. 1), Tamburinus (*loc. cit.* n. 37), and Trull., Pellizario, Diana, Peyrinus, cited by Salamancans *ibid.* n. 67. Sporer holds the same (*l.c.* n. 54) with Valentia, Medina, and the more common opinion. But even so, the same Sporer (n. 32) and Lessius (lib. 2 c. 40, n. 95) as well as Elbel (n. 258) make an exception from these for a man who by his positive consent approved the vow of his wife, especially if it were a vow of chastity, because then (as they say) he has yielded to her right; wherefore he could not properly invalidate it, and if he would invalidate it would be a grave sin. But these authors speak according to the opinion which they hold, *viz.* that a man can only have indirect power over the vows of his wife. For they say in this that a prelate in respect to a subject differs from a husband in respect to his wife because the prelate, since he has direct power to invalidate, cannot renounce his right; still, the husband can only use what indirect power considers. But we say with St. Thomas according to the aforesaid opinion in n. 234, that the same dominative power which a prelate has over a religious, a husband has over his wife; for that reason, just as a prelate cannot deprive himself, so neither a husband in respect to his wife. Hence, it seems probable enough to opine according to what Tamburinus said above (*l. c.* n. 53), that a man, invalidating a vow of chastity of his wife without cause, even after he positively approved it, does not sin more than venially.

Moreover, what if spouses would vow chastity by mutual consent? Certainly, a husband in that case remains bound by his vow, which cannot be invalidated by his wife. So also Sanchez (*dict.* d. 40 n. 20) says a husband cannot invalidate a vow of his wife and the Salamancans (tr. 17 c. 3 punct. 6 n. 39) follow him (as well as others in common). Bu I do not find a certain reason whereby I could condemn Palacius and others (cited by Sanchez, *loc. cit.* n. 19) who contradict it, for if a man (insofar as Sanchez concedes, as we saw) can validly invalidate a vow of his wife that was pronounced with his approval, why could he not, Palacius argues, if by mutual consent he also vowed chastity? Just the same, since this opinion is against the common opinion, and Tamburinus, wrapped in this difficulty left the *dubium* undecided, so I also remit it to be discerned by the wise.

"9. A prelate can invalidate the vow of a subordinate either "confirmed by an equal predecessor, or a lower superior, but "not by a higher. See Bonacina on these, *loc. cit.* § 3, Laymann, "cap. 7." (And he does this validly and licitly, Salamancans with Sanchez, Palaus, Suarez, Tamburinus, etc.).

240.—If we speak about slaves, a master can invalidate all their real oaths, unless they have something of their own, and personal oaths which are prejudicial to their master, namely of religion, long pilgrimage, etc. But not of chastity or moderate prayer, or fasting, etc. (Salamancans *ibid.* punct. 8 n. 62 and 63, with others.

Moreover, the vows of servants cannot be invalidated by a master, but only suspended for the time of service, insofar as they are prejudicial to due service. Salamancans, *ibid.* n. 75, with Sanchez, Suarez, Bonacina.

ARTICLE II
Who can indirectly invalidate vows?

241.—"*Resp.* If not the will of the man vowing to someone, "but the matter of the vow is subjected, so that he would hold "right over it, he can invalidate such a vow by indirect "invalidation, *i.e.* to suspend his obligation inasmuch as it is "prejudicial to his right; and that is from natural law, which "teaches that no man can promise another man something "prejudicial to a third party. St. Thomas 4 d. 38, Suarez, Lessius, "etc. *loc. cit.*

Thus the following are resolved:

242.—"1. So, apart from those named above, a father can "invalidate in respect to postpubescent sons, so long as they "remain in the paternal house and are not emancipated;

"likewise, a tutor of the same in those matters which impede their power even to the 25th year of age. Laymann, cap. 7." (See n. 229)."

"2. Likewise, a wife can invalidate, in respect to her husband, *e.g.* if he will have vowed a longer pilgrimage so as to live in another place, to sleep apart, which detracts against the common life and use of ownership which she has over the body of her husband. Lessius, n. 83; Filliuci n. 273." (See sup. n. 235).

"3. Likewise, a master and mistress in respect to servants, that if they were to vow a fast whereby they become useless for service to their master, such a vow is not of chastity or of brief prayer. Lessius, n. 86."

"Likewise, not only the Pope in respect to all the faithful, but even Bishops and princes can invalidate in respect to subjects, when the matter is prejudicial to them. Lastly, superiors in respect to novices in those matters which impede the exercises of the novitiate. Lessius d. 13 n. 8."

"5. Vows cannot be invalidated indirectly on a matter otherwise commanded, *e.g.* to not steal, because they are prejudicial to no one. Likewise, nor must vows then be fulfilled when the matter of the vow will no longer be subjected; *e.g.* to fulfill the vows of a servant when he is free, and of a spouse after the other is dead. (But more probably this is denied on a husband in regard to the vows of his wife, as above, n. 234).

"6. Someone can also indirectly invalidate vows made long before, as the matter would be subject to himself, *e.g.* made by a spouse long before marriage." (Salamancans tr. 17 cap. 3 punct. 8 n. 75, as above n. 237).

"7. Someone can also indirectly invalidate vows that were conceded and confirmed by a predecessor, as is clear from an article above. Nevertheless, an exception is made, unless he would yield his right, and the subordinate would accept this concession, *e.g.* in a vow of chastity, made mutually from the "consent of a husband and wife. Still, it would be otherwise if "either the wife alone or both independently from the other "would make the vow. (See above, n. 239).

DUBIUM VII
What is a commutation of a vow?

243. *When can vows be commuted?*
244. *Could someone commute a vow by himself in an equal work?*
245. *Would a commutation avail less without a just cause?*
246. *See what else must be noted.*
247. *Could one having the faculty commute in a smaller amount?*
248. *Could, after a commutation has been made, the man making the vow be held to fulfill the first?*
249. *Would, in an impossible thing that was already commuted, the man making the vow be held to fulfill the first? Would someone that forgot a vow but furnishes the promised work be freed from the vow?*

243.—"*Resp.* A commutation is a substitution of another "worthy work in place of what was promised by the vow, but "under the same obligation. In regard to which, that it would be "done licitly, these rules are handed down:

"*First*: for a commutation of a vow ecclesiastical authority is "required: 1) When a commutation is made that is a little less "good, that if it were notably less it is called a dispensation; 2) "When there is a doubt, on the equality of the good (with "Salamancans *de vot.* tr. 17, c. 3 punct. 14 n. 130); 3) When it is "done in an equal good, although some might then think one's "own authority suffices. Nevertheless, this suffices for a "commutation in a better thing, because in a better thing the "lesser is contained." (And it is the common opinion with the Salamancans, *ibid.* n. 132, still with the exception of reserved vows). "Moreover, I call a thing *better*, which is such in the "order to the spiritual advantage of the one making the vow "and more pleasing to God." (With the Salamancans ibid. punct. 15 n. 142. A commutation is safer in frequenting of the sacraments; Sanch., Tamburinus, Bardi, Bassius, cited by Salamancans loc. cit.)

244.—*Quæritur:* Could a vow be commuted on one's own authority into an equal work? A twofold opinion is present.

The first more probably denies it, from St. Thomas in 4 dist. 38 q. 1 art. 4, who advances the reasoning: "Because the commutation is indeed a contract which cannot be carried out without the consent of the one who stands in the place of God on earth, viz. a prelate." Next, because by that supposed permission, supposing the promise, it is thought more pleasing to God that the one making the vow be faithful by furnishing to him the thing he promised than another equal thing. So Sanchez, *in Dec.* where although previously (lib. 3 c. 19 n. 9 in fine; and lib 4 c. 5 n. 28) he censed the contrary, he revokes himself in book 4 cap. 49 n. 12 and 21 with Cajetan, Covarruvias, Del Soto, Azor, and Suarez, Palaus, Leander, Laymann, Filliuci, Reginald, etc. with Salamancans *ibid.* punct. 14 n. 134. Since that opinion has been posited, other say such a commutation is only a light sin, such as Sanchez, Ledesma, Diana, Mendochius and others (cited by Salamancans *ibid.* n. 135) because, as they say, it would be infidelity in a modest matter. This is why, if the aforesaid matter were commuted, it suffices that the man making the vow should supply something. And they assert the same thing must be said if the matter furnished were less than what was promised. Still, others think it is a grave sin, such as the Salamancans, with Palaus, Suarez, Azor, Prado, etc., because on such a commutation, exactly as it is invalid, the reasoning held is null. On this, see the following n. 245.

Nevertheless, *the second opinion,* which the Salamancans call probable enough (*ibid.* n. 133) affirms that it is lawful for anyone to commute his vow with a work that is clearly equal. (Elbel n. 304, Henriquez, Medina, Major. cited by the Salamancans, likewise Tamburinus *Dec.* lib. 3 c. 16 § 5 n. 14 with Sa, Rodriguez, Bonacina, Fagundez, Diana, Villalobos, Suarez, Aragon, cited by Sanchez and Trullenchus calls it probable). The reason is, because God is presumed to accept a work that is equal in regard to equal substance, on account of divine benignity, at least as an offering is more happily offered to him. Now after supposing that presumption, the reasoning of the promise, as above, would cease. Moreover, the doctrine and reasoning advanced by St. Thomas must be understood on a lesser work, for otherwise, a commutation for a clearly better thing would not even avail, which the common opinion does not hold any doubt that it in fact avails, even if the matter were unequal. (Salamancans *ibid.* n. 132, with Sanchez, Azor, Valentia, Suarez, Laymann, and others against a few, and it is proved from *c. cap. Super his, de voto.* Moreover, the doctors of the first opinion also agree that if the matter were certainly equal, and probably, or doubtfully better, then the commutation is rightly done on his own authority. So the Salamancans, tr. 17, cap. 3 punct. 14 n. 134, in fine, with Sanchez, Suarez, Palaus, etc. because then the matter is always morally better, as Salamancans *ibid.* punct. 16 n. 144, in fine. But these not withstanding I would not recede from the first opinion, for the reasons advanced by St. Thomas are very persuasive. At least that reasoning is conclusive for an equal work.

"*The second* rule. Cause is required for the commutation of a "vow for an equal thing, even if less than for a dispensation, "because a dispensation clearly frees one from the obligation of "a vow, but a commutation substitutes another. This is why, if "it is done for a better thing, no cause is required; if in an equal "thing with the authority of a superior, a greater consideration "suffices." (as the Salamancans, *ibid.*, n. 145 and 146 with Laymann, Cajetan etc. or less danger of transgression, as Elbel, num. 306, with Sanchez, Palaus and Croix). "But if there is a "doubt as to whether it would be equal notable annoyance in "fulfilling it suffices. See Lessius, lib. 2 ch. 40.

245.—*Quaeritur*: If a commutation is made in a lesser thing without a just cause, would it not only be illicit but also invalid?

The first opinion says it is valid, provided a defect is supplied for, because if it were not a greater obligation toward men than supplying so much more toward God, with whom he deals more mildly (with Sanchez, l. 4 cap. 52 n. 8, and Diana, *Candid.* etc., cited by Salamancans *ibid.* n. 147 and Tamburinus *de voto* § 5 n. 9). And this is akin to the second opinion related above in n. 244.

But *the second opinion* says it is invalid just as St. Thomas teaches that a dispensation without a just cause is invalid. (II IIæ qu. 88 art. 12). The reason is, because a prelate cannot exceed the faculty which he has been delegated to him by God, viz. to commute only with a just cause (Salamancans *ibid.* n. 148 with Mur., Palaus, Trullenchus, etc.). Both are probable, but in doubt as to whether the cause for a commutation were sufficient or not, St. Thomas teaches (*ibid.* ad 2) the one vowing can acquiesce to the judgment of the one commuting.

Thus the following are resolved:

246.—"1. Although prayer is absolutely better than fasting, it "is still not lawful to commute the former for the latter on one's "own authority, since here fasting can be more pleasing to God, "inasmuch as it is more useful to the spiritual good of this man. "Lessius, d. 16, Sanchez cap. 56."

Lohner asserts in his *Instructione de Confessione* (part 1 cap. 3 § 1 qu. 8 reg. 5), that one confession or communion would avail for a rosary for the whole week. But I do not acquiesce to this, generally speaking.

"2. All personal vows can be commuted on one's own "authority in a vow of religion; nay more, by the law itself all "real vows are so changed in profession." (*So St. Thomas, cited by Salamancans tr. 17,* cap. 3 punct. 14 n. 129).

"3. One that has a vow of religion, cannot commute it on his "own authority in reception of the Episcopacy; both because "this does not cause the man to be more perfect than religion, "although it supposes him to be more perfect; both because it is "not certain that it is more pleasing to God here and now, and "because Innocent III so responds (ap. Bonacina *in secundum* "*praeceptum* d. 4 q. 2 p. 7). Likewise, other doctors teach this. "(Lessius lib. 2 cap. 4 d. 16 art. 103; Azor, Sanchez, Laym. l. 4 t. 5 "cap. 6 n. 15; Palaus d. 3 t. 16 n. 2; Fagundez., p. 6 t. 6 r. 62)."

"4. One that has the faculty to dispense," (even delegated, as more truly Laymann, Lessius, Palaus, Suarez say, with Salamancans ibid. punct. 9 n. 81 against Navarre, Sanchez, *etc.*), "has also the faculty to commute; but not vice versa, because a "commutation is part of a dispensation. So one who commutes "it for a greater thing, can also for a lesser. Moreover, one that "has the faculty to commute such a thing, cannot change it "except for an equal thing, because it must be valued morally, "and not scrupulously, as Laymann advises (cap. 8). In such an "estimation, Cajetan says that the concomitant things must not "be neglected, *e.g.* in a vow of a pilgrim the accounting must be "made not only of the labor, but even of the expenses, which he "will accrue. Suarez, Lessius. See Bonacina, p. 7 § 3." (*And c.* "*Magna, de voto*).

247.—*Quæritur:* Having only the faculty to commute, could someone commute for a slightly lesser work?

The first opinion (which the Salamancans rightly call probable enough, *ibid.* punct. 15 n. 138) affirms it provided there is no notable excess. The reason is, because if the power to commute were not such, it would be liable to a great many anxieties, consequently it would be useless, since it would be very difficult to discover an equality in a thing substituted. Next, if it is probable that a commutation can be made on one's own authority in an equal thing, it should also be probable that it ought to be the one having the faculty to commute that can commute in something less, otherwise such a power would do nothing. So Sa, Bonacina, Trullenchus, Diana, Leander, Medina. And Lessius calls it probable (cited by Salamancans *dict.* n. 138).

But *the second opinion* holds the commutation must be made in an equal thing, still by a moral equality, not a mathematical one, so that a small thing is believed to be different, and no excess would manifestly appear. So Salamancans *ibid.* n. 139, with Cajetan, Palaus, Suarez, etc. with Busembaum (here) and Laymann. And so this opinion is really conciliated with the first.

It must be noted, that a personal work may rightly be commuted into a real one and on the other hand, also perpetually into a temporal one. Salamancans *ibid.* n. 140, with Lessius, Suarez, Laymann, Palaus, etc. Moreover, Elbel (n. 308 with Gobat and Tamburinus), rightly advises the confessor that he should try to substitute such works by a vow, which seem to the penitent more useful and no more difficult.

248.—"5. If a man, whose vow is commuted, prefers then to "fulfill the first one, he can do it, not only because it is better, or "equal, but even more, because it is done in his favor with the "tacit condition that it would please him. Lessius, n. 97; "Sanchez, Filliuci, n. 289."

If a vow is commuted in a lesser or equal thing, there is no doubt that the first work can still be chosen. It is the common opinion with the Salamancans (*de voto* tr. 17, cap. 3 punct. 18 n.

167) with Sanchez, Palaus, Suarez, etc. There is a doubt if the commutation were made in something known to be and received as better: then Suarez, Filliuci, Reginald, etc. (cited by Salamancans *ibid.* n. 168) reject that the one making the vow can go back to the first vow. But more probably, Lessius (lib. 2 cap. 40 dub. 16 n. 111), Sanchez (lib. 4 cap. 55 n. 26, cap. 55 n. 26), Elbel (n. 318) and Salamancans (*ibid.* n. 169) with Laymann, Bonacina, Palaus, Tamburinus, Diana, Trullenchus, etc. with Suarez n. 27 hold with the common opinion that it can if such a commutation were done deliberately, and in greater worship of God. But the Salamancans say more truly (*ibid.* n. 170) with Palaus, Prado, and Villalobos, that still such a commutation does not oblige at least *sub gravi* unless a new vow were made; because each proposition does not place an obligation, according to what was said in book 1, n. 28.

249.—"6. If the matter of a vow is legitimately commuted by a "superior, or a work becomes impossible or indifferent, he is not "held to return to the first because the obligation has been "extinguished. See Laymann, Bonacina, *ll.cc.*"

When a commutation is made on a vow, even if the matter substituted became impossible by the fault of the man making the vow, or if he did not fulfill it, he is not held to the first; *e.g.* fasting on such a day is substituted for almsgiving, if then you could not fast, or refused, you sinned, but you are not held to almsgiving, because by commutation the first obligation is extinguished (Sanchez, lib. 4 cap. 56, n. 15, and Salamancans tr. 17, cap. 3 punct. 18 n. 165, with Laymann, Palaus, Trullenchus, Suarez, and Elbel, n. 317, and Sporer c. 5 n. 136, with the common opinion). Still, this does not occur if the commutation were made on one's own authority, for then if the second work is not fulfilled the first must be fulfilled, since then the first obligation is not extinguished, rather it is satisfied by a superabundant fulfillment, or at least an equivalent one, as above; and this is certain. (Salamancans *ibid.* n. 166, with Tamburinus, Leander, etc).

Lastly, for completion of this doubt:

Quæritur I: Would someone having the faculty to commute vows for others, also have the faculty for himself?

It is answered in the affirmative, just as the doctors teach in common on the faculty to dispense. (Sanchez, *de matr.* lib. 8 d. 3 n. 8 and 9 and l. 4, *Dec.* c. 18, n. 42 and 45; Bonacina, disp. 2 q. 4 n. 7 § 4 n. 31). So Salamancans (*ibid.* punct. 14 n. 128, with Tamburinus, Suarez, Trull., Azor, Diana, Prado, Leander, Rodriguez, etc. and it is proved from St. Thomas, II IIæ. q. 185, art. 8, where he teaches a prelate can dispense himself.

Quæritur II: Would one who forgot a vow but furnishes the work promised by the vow, be freed in the second? See what was said in n. 224, near the end, and what is going to be said *on Restitution* in n. 700, *quæritur: II.*

DUBIUM VIII
What is a dispensation, and who can dispense against vows?

250. *What cause is required to dispense?*
251. *What if the dispensation is made in good faith, but without cause? What if there is a doubt as to whether a cause is present?*
252. *What cause would suffice for dispensation?*
253. *Would imperfect deliberation or freedom suffice?*
254. *See other things that must be noted.*
255. *Could one be dispensed in a vow made in benefit of a third party? And what about a vow and an oath of perseverance, which is furnished in certain congregations?*
256. *Who is able to dispense? Does the Pope in solemn vows? Do the Bishops in simple vows? Who can delegate the faculty to dispense? Would someone having the faculty avail to dispense on their own?*
257. *Could regular prelates dispense against all the vows of religious? Of novices? Of seculars?*
258. More notable things on reserved vows.

259. *Would an oath of chastity or religion be reserved like a vow?*
260. *After a vow has been commuted, is the matter substituted also reserved?*
261. *Would conditional or penal vows of chastity and religion be reserved?*
262. *With pilgrims, could the Bishop of the place dispense against vows and common laws?* Review book 1 n. 158.

250.—"*Resp. 1.* A dispensation is an absolute pardon of the "obligation of a vow, made in the name of God. For it to be "valid, a just cause is required, such as: 1) the good of the "Church or the common good of the commonweal," (and even of a household; or the greater progress of the one making the vow. *Salamancans de voto* tr. 17 cap. 3 punct 13 n. 125; with St. Thomas, Suarez, Sanchez. And also in a doubt about this: Palaus and Suarez, *ibidem*); "2) A notable difficulty in the "observance of a vow; 3) The imperfection of an act or levity "and readiness, from which a vow proceeds. Suarez, l.c. c. 17, "Filliuci n. 260, Sanchez, l. 4 c. 45. See Bonacina, p. 7 n. 24, "Laymann, c. 8 n. 5." (Hence Innocent III warns in *c. Magnae, de voto*, three things must be applied in the dispensation of vows: 1. That it would be lawful according to justice; 2. That it is lawful according to worthiness; 3. What would be expedient according to utility; from which Elbel says (n. 277) with Sporer c. 3 n. 43, then it must be dispensed against a vow when it would lead to ruin or become a snare for the soul on account of perplexity, or when a greater spiritual utility is hoped for.)

251.—*Quæritur:* Would a dispensation if it were believed in good faith that a just cause were present when really it was not?

The first opinion affirms that the dispensation is valid. This is because such a thing is considered to be the divine will, so that they would not be anxious in their conscience and the determinations of their pastors would remain firm just as it seems necessary for the right rule of souls (the authors hold with

Busembaum, lib. 1 n. 180, Sanchez, *Dec.* lib 4 cap. 41 n. 10; Lessius, l. 2 c. 40 n. 119; Salamancans *ibid.* n. 119 with Tamburinus and Leander, and in the same tract. 11 *de legibus* cap. 5 punct. 6 § 2 n. 71, where they also cite Laymann, but not rightly as we will see below).

But *the second opinion*, which Palaus holds (*de voto* tract. 15 d. 2 p. 9 n. 4) with Basilius and Salas, contradicts it, and we follow this if later it were found certain that a cause, or at least an insufficient cause were not present. The first opinion, although it is defended by such authors, nevertheless is opposed to a certain principle, that an inferior invalidly dispenses against the law of a superior without sufficient cause. Moreover, I think it must be said otherwise if there were a doubt as to whether cause or a sufficient cause were present: both because in a doubt then it favors the validity of the dispensation and because in that case the reasoning of the first opinion persuades, that it would be a matter too liable to scruples if men after obtaining the dispensation were held to inquire of its validity; and since this frequently would happen, then God is rightly presumed to hold that dispensation as valid to spare consciences as well as for good government. Furthermore, where nullity of cause is certainly detected, Palaus rightly says that God is hardly presumed to wish to favor a manifest error (whatever Diana might say, p. 1 tract. 10 r. 33). And so really, Laymann speaks (tract. 4 *de leg.* cap. 22 n. 12) where he says the man that acquiesces to the dispensation can rightly be dispensed, *unless the truth does not appear to the contrary*, citing del Soto, Navarre, Suarez, etc. And Palaus agrees with us, and says in that case where there is a doubt, legitimate dispensation is presumed (Salamancans tr. *de legibus* cap. 5 punct. 6 § 3 from n. 75) the dispensation is valid, even if it were sought in bad faith from the one dispensing, if there really were a just cause, as we said in book 1 *on Laws*, n. 181.

252.—Moreover, a danger of transgression on account of a particular indisposition of the man making the vow, or on account of the common frailty of men, suffices for the cause to dispense. A great difficulty in execution also suffices, not only if it were unforeseen, as Sanchez, Palaus, Suarez, etc. say, but also if it might have been unforeseen, as the Salamancans think (*de voto* tr. 17 c. 3 punct. 13 n. 124) with Leander and Tamburinus. Then, because the danger of transgression is also present, and because a much more difficult matter is apprehended while the execution approaches than while it is deliberated. And even if such a difficulty has its beginning from the frailty of the one making the vow, as Suarez, Palaus, Laymann, Trullenchus, with Salamancans *ibid.* It also suffices if the one making the vow is troubled by great scruples. Salamancans *ibid.* with Sanchez, Trullenchus, Fagundez, and Tamburinus.

253.—Besides, even if the danger of transgression is absent, as well as great difficulty in execution, it suffices for the cause that the vow was immaturely pronounced, viz. with too much readiness, or from imperfect deliberation, or without perfect freedom (Sanchez, lib. 4 cap. 45 n. 28 and Cajetan, Palaus, Suarez, etc., with Salamancans *ibid.* n. 121). On account of this reasoning, in vows of prepubescent children without any cause one can absolutely be dispensed without any commutation (Sanchez, *ibid.* n. 30 and Tamburinus, Palaus, Cajetan, Suarez, etc. with the Salamancans, *ibid.* num. 123). The same must be said if a vow were pronounced on account of a light fear instilled from an outward thing (Sanchez, n. 32 and Palaus, with Salamancans). The same when imperfect deliberation or freedom proceeds in a vow from sadness or anger, whether from inward fear of shipwreck, death or of another evil because then they usually make vows immaturely. Consequently, the vow can be dispensed against them without commutation. But if it were certain that mature deliberation was present, then some commutation is mixed with the dispensation. Just it should also be done if the impulsive cause of the vow were to cease. (Salamancans *eodem* n. 123 with Palaus, Sanchez and Tamburinus).

254.—"1. When the cause is insufficient for the whole "dispensation, it can be partly dispensed against the vow and "partly commuted. Bonacina, *loc. cit.*"

"2. A prelate, seeing and not opposing it (when he easily "could), seems to dispense, as Sa says."

"3. Even delegated power to dispense against vows extends "also to vows and pious oaths, sworn to God alone. See Suarez, "l. 6 *de voto*, Sanchez lib. 8 *de matrimonio* dub. 4." (As we said above in n. 190. Moreover, would oaths of religion, chastity, etc. be reserved, as vows? Each is probable, as we will say below in n. 259, *Quaeritur 1.*)

"4. Before the reception of a vow by a certain person, or "Church, it is reckoned he has not acquired the right, and "therefore can without injury be dispensed against it, or have it "commuted."

255.—But here the question must be profusely discussed: Could a vow overflowing with advantages for a man be dispensed or commuted without his consent?

Resp. 1: If the vow has not yet been accepted by a third party, it is the common opinion that it can be commuted (Elbel, num. 309, Sanchez *Dec.* l. 4 cap. 41 n. 7 with Cajetan, Sa, Navarre, Sylvius, Azor, Suarez, etc.) Even if the promise was not directed to God alone, but specifically to a person, say, if vowing someone will have said: "I promise with my vow to give to such a pauper, etc.," but the promise was not received either by the poor man, nor by any in his name, as the authors add (Sanchez, *ibid.* n. 10 and 11, with Suarez, Sylvius, Armilla etc.). And even if the promise were made in honor of the saint of that Church, reception is required by its rector for the commutation to no longer be able to be done. (Sanchez, n. 12, with Cajetan, etc.)

Resp. 2: That if the promise were made to God alone of giving something to indeterminate paupers, then it can always be commuted, even if the promise were manifested to someone from the poor and received by them. (Sanchez, *ibid.* n. 14 with Suarez, de Lugo, *de justitia et jure* d. 29, n. 93; Tamburinus, lib. 2 cap. 7 § 6 n. 3, with Palaus).

Resp. 3: That if on the other hand the promise were made for the advantage of the man alone, and were accepted, by no means can it be revoked without his consent, as we said above in n. 192.

There is a great doubt: Can a vow uttered principally in honor of God, but secondarily, or less principally, also in favor of a determined third party, say such a Church or pauper, can it be commuted after it has been received by them without their consent? Elbel rejects this (num. 309) along with Lessius (lib. 2 c. 40 dub. 11 n. 90), Sanchez (*ibid.* n. 18), Salamancans (*de voto* tr. 17 cap. 3 punct. 17 n. 156), with Suarez, Moya, etc. The reason is, because then the right is acquired by the Church receiving it, or the pauper, of whose reason is held in together in the vow, *e.g.* on account of special affection or its necessity. Nevertheless, other authors say it is probable enough that such a vow can rightly be commuted on the authority of a prelate, or one's own authority, even after it is received (Sporer *de 2. praec.* cap. 3 n. 113 with Henr., Viva *de Jubilaeo* q. 12 art. 1 n. 3 and Fagundez, Trullenchus, Leander, cited by Salamancans *ibid.* n. 155). And Cajetan (cited by Sanchez, *ibid.* n. 17) who, speaking on *cap. Licet de regular.*, where it is laid out that one professed in religion, even if his prelate has accepted it, can pass into a better one; Cajetan gives the reasoning that there, on account of God and not on account of the prelate, he gave himself to religion, and consequently, can commute his vow on his own authority even after it has been received for a better one. Navarre also agrees, who says: "When someone pronounces a vow to give a certain quantity to someone, even after it has been received, the Pope could commute it because the promise is not principally made for the sake of men, but in worship of God." And what Navarre says about the Pope, the same must be said (as Sanchez says) about other prelates, on account of the reasoning advanced. Therefore, the reason for this opinion, as Fagundez says (cited by Tamburinus, lib. 3 cap. 17 § 2 n. 15), is that these vows are principally directed to God as the purpose *of it*, and the pauper is only the purpose *to whom*, less principal or accessory, which ought to follow the principal end. Even if the promise were specially made to this pauper, still it is made on account of God; as a result God is the whole cause of the promise and it is *per accidens*, that the poor man received it, who, if he still would have acquired some right, nevertheless he acquired it dependent upon it being acceptable to God for whom the promise should be kept.

It must be noted equally: 1) That such a simple promise, made to a man, as well as received, even if it would oblige, still would not oblige *sub gravi*, according to the very probable opinion of the Salamancans (*de contr.* cap. 4 punct. 4 § 2 n. 82, with Cajetan, Bañez etc.) as we will say more profusely on Contracts, n. 720. It must be noted: 2) That the same thing which was said on a vow must be said on an oath made principally in honor of God, as Tamburinus thinks with probability (l. 2 cap. 8 § n. 3 and c. 17 § 2 n. 15 with Fagundez), which can be relaxed by a Bishop without consent of the party. But it must be noted: 3) that this is understood only on a gratuitous promise, but it would have to be said otherwise if the party receiving it would oblige itself to some burden to the advantage of the one that makes the promise, for then, although an obligatory and onerous contract would intercede for both parties, the promise, and consequently an oath, cannot be remitted by the one that promises it unless the other party would consent, according to the law of contracts. And so it comes about that in an oath *of perseverance*, which is furnished in the fifth congregation of the missionary Fathers of St. Vincent de

Paul, and not the least in our congregation of the Most Holy Redeemer, where oblates, although they principally promise an oath in consideration of God to persevere in the congregation, nevertheless, because in the same time the congregation by receiving them obliges itself to give them subsistence and instruction, and also to not dismiss them without a just and grave cause (on which, even superiors are not held to render an account for those dismissed). Thus, when this contract intercedes, obligatory on latter and former side, the oath cannot be remitted by any other than by the congregation itself or the Supreme Pontiff, as the supreme Lord of ecclesiastical goods. It is clear from the monitum of our Most Holy Lord Benedict XIV, or the bull *Convocatis*, published on 25 November 1749, § 32, for the Jubilee year of 1750, where it is said: "Lastly, in regard to vows let them (confessors) abstain from commutation of them (vows), in which it is a question of prejudice to a third party. Hence, let them not betake themselves to that, which pertains to vows, no matter how simple, or of perseverance, or others usually pronounced in some congregation or community, and in obligatory vows received by a third party." So our aforementioned Pope, with Fr. Theodore of the Holy Spirit, *in Tract. de jubil.* recently published at Rome in the same year, 1750, in chapter 11 § 2 n. 10, proposing the question as to whether a vow or an oath of persevering taken in congregations by priests, or female oblates, could be commuted by the force of a jubilee, responds negatively, providing this reason: "Not because it is reserved but because it was taken in the mode of an onerous contract obliging both parties. For the Supreme Pontiff never confers the faculty to commute a vow where the right of others is injured, from *cap. Cum sit, de rescriptis*. Nor is it opposed, that this vow to persevere is principally made for the worship of God and secondarily in obedience to congregations, because this does not admit that a contract that is obligatory on every side would follow between the one that makes the vow or swears an oath, and the congregation, and hence that the right sought by the congregation would be wounded if the vow were commuted without requiring its consent. It follows from the same reasoning, the vow cannot be commuted by alumni of colleges that was pronounced for missions to infidels, etc. treated from prejudice of a third party, etc." And the same Supreme Pontiff, Benedict XIV, in the bull *Inter praeteritos* (published 3 December 1749), n. 66, so says: "But what attains to the commutation of vows in which it is a question of prejudice to a third party, which indeed is forbidden to penitentiaries, Suarez suitably writes of in t. 2 *de relig.* lib. 6 c. 5 n. 7 in regard to vows of perseverance, which are made by certain men when they enter some congregation, each assume the nature of the contract and the reciprocal obligation among themselves and the congregation, which receives them, in which the penitentiaries cannot dispense."

256.—"*Resp.* 2. The power to dispense is fitting for all prelates "who have jurisdiction in the external forum, or privilege "(Lessius, lib. 2 cap. 40 n. 12, Sanchez, cap. 37 and the common "opinion). For this reason, the following can dispense: 1) the "Pope in respect to all the faithful against every vow; 2) The "bishop in respect to the vows of his subjects; but not a parish "priest, because he only has jurisdiction over the internal "forum, as Suarez says, *loc. cit.* c. 12; 3) Regular prelates in "respect to their religious and novices, and that in regard to "vows which they made either in the world or even in the "novitiate (Lessius, n. 80 and 107; Sanchez, lib. 9 *de matr.* d. 29), "but not prelates nor abbesses." (*Nor penitentiaries, nor vicars of* "*the Bishop, unless the faculty is specially delegated to them.* "*Salamancans tr. 17 c. 3 punct. 10 n. 84*). "Suarez, Lessius, *ll.cc.* 4) "From the privilege of the Pope, confessors of mendicant orders "according to the concession and moderation of their superiors, "as Lessius notes, d. 13 n. 108."

Quaeritur: Could the Pope dispense against solemn vows? In regard to clergy in sacred orders, he probably can against a vow of chastity, since it is probable enough that this vow is only connected to holy orders by ecclesiastical law. See book 6, n. 808. (St. Thomas, II IIæ qu. 88 art. 11; Salamancans *de ordin.* tr. 8 cap. 6 dub. 1 n. 11 with others, against Gonet, etc.)

A greater doubt is whether the Pope could dispense against the vows of Religious? del Soto, Sylvius, Aragon, Turrianus, etc. (cited by Salamancans *de statu relig.* c. 1 punct. 3 n. 41) deny it, because these vows are essentially connected to the religious state by divine law.

But more probably and commonly, others affirm it (St. Thomas in 4 d. 38 qu. 1 art. 4 ad 3, and Salamancans *ibid.* n. 42 with St. Antoninus, Palaus, Suarez, Lessius, Sanchez, Pontius, Cajetan, Lezana, Pellizzarius). Although, it seems St. Thomas reverses himself in II IIæ q. 88 art. 11. But Cajetan (*ibid.*) and the Salamancans (*dict.* n. 41) with Azor and Basilius are not inept when they explain that the Angelic Doctor understood the Pope, only in that sense, cannot dispense a man in such a way that he could be married and a monk at the same time.

Moreover, in the first citation, he expressly taught that the Pope can rightly dispense, but with a very pressing cause, evidently on account of the common good of the Church, or of some kingdom or province. The reason is, because it is rightly thought this is conceded to the Pope, to whom God conceded rule of the whole Church.

Then, it is certain that the Pope can dispense against simple vows, and Bishops against those that are not reserved. For an account of why they can do it, see what is going to be said *on Matrimony*, book 6, n. 986. It is also certain that all prelates who have the faculty to dispense against vows by ordinary right can also delegate it to others, according to the Salamancans (*de voto* cap. 3 punct. 10 n. 83).

Furthermore, although, one who has the faculty to dispense, whether ordinary or delegated, cannot invalidate his own vows because no man can take a vow under condition of his consent, as is certain with Sanchez, Palaus and Croix, l. 3 p. 1 n. 485. Nevertheless, they can duly dispense against these by himself, since it is an act of voluntary jurisdiction (Lessius, l. 2 c. 40 n. 116; Croix *loc. cit.* and l. 1 n. 799 with Laymann, Suarez, Sanchez, Bonacina, Filliuci, etc., Elb. n. 278 with those who assert it is the common opinion against Henno and some others.)

257.—But prelates themselves cannot dispense against the vows of religious, even if they took them with their license; and even if a vow were to pass over to a stricter religious order, if he knew it were more useful to remain in his own order (See Salamancans *ibid.* c. 3 punct. 11 n. 90 and 91). Just as a Bishop can also dispense with his subjects in a vow to enter into a stricter religious order, while leaving the vow of religion untouched in regard to its substance; since with no right is such a reserved dispensation is discovered (Lessius, lib. 2 c. 40 dub. 13 n. 107 and del Soto, Sanchez, Aragon, Ledesma, etc. with Salamancans *cit.* n. 91). But the faculty to dispense can be delegated by the aforesaid prelates even in a simple clerical tonsure. See Salamancans *ibid.* punct. 10 n. 85. Still, in substantial vows, or those connected to them, just as in a vow to not eat meat, to renounce dignities, etc. which are usually taken in some religious orders, it cannot be dispensed except by the Pope. It is common with the Salamancans, *ibid.* punct. 11, n. 92. Besides, in vows of novices, if they are reserved, it can be dispensed both by prelates of the order and even by their own bishops, as Sanchez, Palaus, Bonacina, and Pellizarius teach (with Salamancans *ibid.* n. 89).

Nay more, from the common opinion of the doctors (Lessius, lib. 2 c. 40 dub. 18 n. 134, and Navarre, Sanchez, Palaus, Tamburinus and as many as you like with Salamancans *ibid.* n. 94) all regular confessors can dispense against vows of any of the faithful inside and outside of confession (for it is not required that someone who has a faculty must dispense in confession): and this from different pontifical privileges, which the Salamancans (*dict.* n. 94) and Elbel (n. 280) advance.

Legates *a latere* have the same faculty as well as nuncios in provinces consigned to them; likewise, a chapter, during a *Sede vacante*, and episcopal abbots having jurisdiction. See Salamancans, *ibid.* n. 86.

"*Resp.* 3. All the aforesaid inferiors to the Pope can dispense "against all vows, except for five reserved to the Pope alone, viz. "a vow of perpetual chastity, approved religion, pilgrimage *ad "limina apostolorum*, to Santiago de Compostela, beyond the "sea or in the Holy Land (See Bonacina, Lessius, Laymann)."

258.—Many things must be noted in regard to reserved vows. It must be noted: 1) That the faculty to dispense against these is not understood to be conceded by the Pope unless a special concession were present, or at least a general one by a clause, because such a faculty is expressly conceded from *Extrav. Et si Dominici*, 5, *de pooenit. et remiss.*, where the Pope commands such vows not to be relaxed, "except by a special license and our certain knowledge." And also, in *c. Si Episcopus, eod. tit.* it is said: "These do not come in a general concession, which did not have some appearance that they were truly conceded *in specie*." This is the common opinion. See Salamancans *de voto* tr. 17 cap. 3 punct. 12 n. 116. But if a reserved faculty to dispense is extended to all, then no vow es excepted. Suarez, Palaus, etc. with Salamancans *ibid*.

It must be noted: 2) That bishops and those having similar jurisdiction can rightly dispense against reserved vows in an urgent necessity, say, if there were no easy access to the Pope, and a delay would cause danger of grave harm whether spiritual, such as a violation of the vow, scandal, quarrels or of another sin;

or the danger of temporal loss to oneself or another, namely grave infamy of a woman and similar things (Lessius, lib. 2 cap. 40 dub. 18 n. 126 and 127; Sanchez lib. 4 cap. 4 n. 44 and Laymann, Barbosa, Suarez, Palaus, Sylvius, Tamburinus, and others with Salamancans *ibid.* punct. 11, n. 96). Yet in that case, could even mendicant confessors dispense against these vows? The more common opinion denies it (Tamburinus, Croix, Sanchez, Sporer, etc.). But Elbel (n. 279) with Anacletus, Henriquez, Bassaeus, etc. think it probable that they could because bishops dispense by ordinary right, as Lessius teaches (*ibid.* with Navarre, Sylvester and del Soto). See what is going to be said in book 6, *on Matrimony* n. 1128.

Moreover, notice here that the aforesaid matters proceed when a dispensation is made against a reserved vow, say of chastity, for the purposes of contracting matrimony; for then it is required that the danger were in delay, and it is clear that there is no easy recourse to the Pope. For, if matrimony is already contracted, even without such a danger the bishops can dispense against a vow of chastity for a due petition, just as the mendicant confessors. (See *on Matrimony*, book 6, n. 987).

Moreover, it must be noticed that the aforesaid faculty, which is probably conceded to the Bishops, and others, to whom the power to dispense against reserved vows is communicated by them, with urgent necessity, as above, is not conceded to confessors in a jubilee having the faculty from the Pope to dispense against simple vows, for, what is conceded to Bishops on account of the power of their ordinary power is not conceded to confessors in a jubilee. So rightly, F. Theodore of the Holy Spirit said in *de jub.* cap. 11 § 2 n. 21. We must also advert that the mentioned dispensation must not be conceded except insofar as necessity obliges. Wherefore, if it would suffice that a vow is suspended, it cannot be dispensed; likewise, if it were dispensed with from a binding vow of chastity to marry with some woman to repair her honor, he cannot marry another. Sanchez, n. 40 and

Salamancans tr. 17 c. punct. 12 n. 101, with Laymann, Suarez, Palaus, Tamburinus, etc.

It must be noted: 3) That the aforesaid vows are not reserved: a) If they are taken under a light obligation (Sanchez, *Dec.* lib. 4 cap. 40 n. 47; Salamancans *ibid.* n. 103 with Palaus, Trull., etc.); b) If they were taken from fear, even light, at the insistence of another, because then they were not made with full liberty (Salamancans *ibid.* with Tamburinus, Bassaeus, and Leaner, etc.); c) If the vow were not perfect on the side of the matter, and therefore a vow not to marry, or not to fornicate is not reserved, nor to seek a debt, nor to preserve virginity if only its conservation is intended; otherwise, if abstinence from every sexual act, and not a vow of chastity for some period; and not to take a vow to take a vow of chastity or religion, or to receive Holy Orders, because a vow of chastity was not made, but is going to be made (Laymann, Suarez, Palaus, Prado, etc., with Salamancans *ibid.* n. 104). Nor a vow to preserve conjugal chastity (Salamancans *ibid.* n. 104, with Sanchez, Trull., etc.); d) Likewise, an unapproved vow of religion is not reserved, nor a vow for pilgrimage to Rome, etc. if it is not taken only for the sake of devotion, but precisely for those places, *e.g.* someone vows to go to Rome to visit an image at St. Mary Major, etc. the vow is not reserved (Sanchez, *ibid.* n. 77 and Palaus, Fagundez, etc. with Salamancans *ibid.* n. 105); e) Even if the vows are reserved, still their circumstances are not reserved, say to make a pilgrimage as a beggar, to enter a stricter religious order, for the Bishop can dispense so that he might enter a laxer order, likewise, if it were a vow to enter immediately, the Bishop can dispense it with cause, so that the entrance will be delayed (Sanchez, n. 74, and Palaus, Tamburinus, Bassaeus, etc. with Salamancans *ibid.* n. 106); f) Nor is a disjunctive vow reserved, say of religion or fasting, at least if he did not choose a reserved part (Sanchez, n. 46; Lessius, l. 2 c. 40, dub. 18 n. 124, and Palaus, Laymann, etc. with Salamancans n. 107). There is a doubt, would it be reserved if the reserved part were already chosen? Sanchez, Palaus etc. affirm it. But the Salamancans also probably deny it, with Leander, Tamburinus and many others, according to what was said in n. 224, *Quaeritur*.

Nevertheless, could a Bishop dispense against a vow of chastity taken by a spouse after contracting matrimony? See what is going to be said *on Matrimony*, book 6 n. 987, where it is probable with Sanchez and others, that he can whether the vow was taken before or after matrimony. And mendicant confessors can do the same, as it is said in n. 987 of that book. But many questions remain here to be resolved.

259.—*Quæritur I:* Is an oath of chastity or religion reserved just as a vow? There are three opinions.

The first opinion affirms it, with Lessius, Filliuci, Laymann, and Azor (cited by Viva, *de jub.* qu. 12 n. 12), because in equal things it is thought to be administered as one, even from another, from *c. Postquam de elect.* in 6. But this reasoning does not seem firm enough, when the Doctors teach in common that the bond of a vow, which obliges from fidelity and reverence toward God, is greater than the bond of an oath which only obliges from reverence, as St. Thomas teaches (II IIæ qu. 80 art. 8) and therefore, such oaths are not usually reserved to the Popes, as Viva (*loc. cit.*) and Diana (p. 4 tract. 4 resp. 69) say with others.

The second opinion, with Sanchez (*de matrim.* lib. 8 d. 13 n. 4, and del Soto, Cajetan, Azor, Valentia and Salamancans n. 108 with others), distinguishes if the oath includes a vow or an obligatory promise to God, it says that it is reserved; it is otherwise if it does not include that. But this opinion also does not seem to speak fittingly; for when two bonds are supposed to be present in such an oath, viz. of the oath and the vow, then it must be said the vow is reserved but not the oath.

Therefore, *the third opinion*, with Viva and Diana (*loc. cit.*) with Trullenchus, Tabienus, Ledesma, Pellizarius, etc. which Sporer calls probable (*de 2. praec.* cap. 3 n. 97 with Tamburinus) speaks more fittingly, and holds that such an oath is hardly reserved. And if perhaps in the oath itself a vow were included, indeed the vow will be reserved but not the oath. And I think this is what Sanchez understood.

But there is a great doubt: When must a vow be judged as included or not in such an oath? Sanchez (*ibid.* num. 4), Diana and Viva think for the most part that a vow is also included in such an oath; especially, Sanchez says, when a thing is offered regarding divine honor. Nevertheless, he admits he can give such an oath without a vow when someone is induced to swear by some human motive, say, on account of loss of office, or if he would swear to enter religion from anger toward neighbors. But by speaking more properly, I think it must be said that if such a person swearing intended to oblige himself to religion by a twofold bond, namely of a vow or obligatory promise *sub gravi*, and more by the bond of swearing, then, although if he were dispensed from the oath, nevertheless, he would remain bound by the vow. But if he intended only to gravely obligate himself with he bond of an oath so as to take an oath of religion but not to strengthen his promise by another bond, rather, to strengthen his bare proposition or promise which is not obligatory of itself, then he is held *sub gravi* only by the bond of the oath, then he is altogether freed from the obligation through relaxation of the oath. Because then he obliged himself to God, not receiving his promise as a creditor, but as a witness exacting the truth of his testimony in the matter promised, or proposed; as in this Sanchez rightly speaks (*dict.* n. 4, with Lopez and Valentia.

But in a doubt as to whether such a vow or obligatory promise was present, there is already a common rule, that a vow doubtfully taken, does not oblige.

260.—*Quaeritur II:* After a reserved vow has been commuted, is the matter substituted also reserved? Azor and others affirm it, because then the same bond of the vow is transferred to it. But other authors commonly and more probably deny this (Lessius, lib. 2 cap. 40 dub. 18 n. 124; Sanchez, *Dec.* lib. 4 cap. 40 n. 46 and Suarez, Laymann, Palaus, Tamburinus, Busembaum, etc. with Salamancans tr. 17 *de voto* cap. 3 punct. 12 n. 109). The reason is, because although the matter substituted should have the same bond of the vow, since it is not reserved, it hardly carries the reservation with itself, which had only been added to the first matter.

Quæritur III: Would a conditional vow of chastity, etc., be reserved? We must preface: a) That if the condition were on the past or present, certainly the vow remains reserved, because then really it is not said to be conditional, but absolute, since the condition does not suspend the obligation (See Salamancans *de matrim.* tr. 9 cap. 8 n. 1). The same thing must be said if the condition were on a future necessary thing, which is held as not suitable; or even on a future contingency, which is common, *e.g.* "If I live, if I can, etc." Likewise, if the condition supplied with a mind to suspend not the obligation but the execution of the vow, *e.g.* "I vow that I will enter a religious order when I will have reached 20 years old; If I will have completed a course of studies...." (Salamancans *de voto* c. 3 punct. 12 n. 110). It must be prefaced: b) It is certain that if a condition were not yet fulfilled, he can be dispensed by anyone having the ordinary faculty because the reservation is understood on the consummated obligation. And it is common with the Salamancans, *ibid.* n. 11.

261.—There is a great doubt whether a conditional vow would be reserved for the future when the condition has already been fulfilled? There is a threefold probable opinion.

The first affirms it, whether the vow were conditional or penal; because after the condition has been shown to be true, the vow is completed and becomes absolute, as if it were taken then (del

Soto, Azor, Pontius, Covarruvias., etc. with Salamancans tr. 17 cap. 3 punct. 12 num. 113).

The second opinion says that a conditional vow is indeed reserved, but not a penal one, since a penal vow is not made from emotions toward religion or chastity, on the contrary it is rather more from horror toward those things promised as a penalty (Lessius, lib. 2 c. 40 dub. 18 n. 132 and Laymann, Suarez, Bonacina, etc. with Salamancans *ibid.*).

But *the third opinion* is much more probable, which many authors hold (Sanchez, *Dec.* l. 4 c. 40 n. 94; Croix, l. 3 p. 1 n. 545 and 546; Salamancans *ibid.* n. 114 and 115 with Toledo, Trullenchus, Prado, Ledesma, Diana and many others, as well as Elbel, n. 286, who calls it most probable, with Palaus, Filliuci, Sporer and Marchant). It teaches, that all vows, whether conditional or penal, are not reserved; the reason is, because a vow, to be reserved (just as everyone seems to admit, even the authors of the second opinion), ought to proceed from a perfect and sole affect to the matter promised; so a reservation must be understood. But a penal vow is no such thing, as is certain; nor a conditional vow, where a condition is advanced to the thing promised, and therefore the principal affect is more to the condition. Therefore, although, once the condition has been fulfilled, the obligation is rendered absolute, nevertheless, when the vow proceeds from an imperfect affect, it is not reserved. Still, it must be said otherwise, as a recent author rightly says (Fr. Theodore *in tract. de jubil.* cap. XI § 2 num. 9), if someone would vow religion with the condition, *e.g.* "if my mother would agree"; the particle "if" does not rarely equal the particle "when".

262.—But could a dispensation be made against vows and oaths with pilgrims, where they are found, by the Bishop of the place? It is more probably denied by other authors in common (Sanchez, *de matrim.* l. 3 d. 25, n. 12 and 13; Salamancans *de leg.* c. 3 punct. 5 § 1 n 55 and others against Pontius, Palaus, and Joseph de

Januario), unless they remained there for at least a year for the greater part of that year (see what we said more profusely on this question in book one *on Laws*, n. 158, and also what is going to be said in n. 332 near the end, where it is probable enough with Suarez, Pontius, Salas, Palaus, Sanchez, Slam. etc. that pilgrims become true subjects of the superior of that place where they are, even if they tarry there for only a short time.

TREATISE III
ON THE THIRD AND FOURTH COMMANDMENT

CHAPTER I
WHAT IS THE THIRD PRECEPT, "MEMENTO", ETC.

263. *Whether this precept is natural or ceremonial?*
264. *Whether interior cult is commanded by this precept? And whether this precept is affirmative?*
265. *Whether observance of Sunday is of divine law?*
266. *Whether Bishops could appoint feasts?*
267. *From what time does the obligation of the feast begin?*
268. *To what does this precept oblige? On what feasts are servile works permitted in the kingdom of the Two Sicilies?*
269. *Is there an obligation to hear the sermon? And what sort of obligation is it for Bishops and parish priests to preach?*
270. *Who is held to observe feasts?*
271. *Whether it would be lawful to enjoin servile work on infidels during feast days?*

263.—"This precept, insofar as it means some time is to be "sanctified, or of fulfilling the divine cult, is natural and still "obliges. Insofar as the time it designates is on the Sabbath day "(Saturday), it is ceremonial, and abrogated in the New "Testament, and for this the Lord's day is designated by the "Church. The mode of keeping the feast holy was prescribed so "that certain works would be done on those days others not; the "latter are forbidden, but the former are commanded. Bonacina, "Laymann, from St. Thomas, II IIæ q. 122."

Quæritur I: Was the precept on making the Sabbath day holy a *natural* or *ceremonial* precept? It is answered together with Busembaum that the precept, inasmuch as it determined a certain time of the year must be freed up for God, it was natural and obliges all, and therefore is reckoned among the precepts of the Decalogue; but inasmuch as it determined the day of the Sabbath from evening to evening (as in Leviticus 23), it was ceremonial and only obliged the Hebrews. This is the common opinion with the Roman Catechism (3. p in *praec. Dec.* n. 4 and 6) and St. Thomas, who thus teaches: "The precept on the sanctification of the Sabbath ... is partly moral and partly ceremonial. It is certainly moral insofar as it is for the purpose that man prepare some time of his life to be free for divine things ... But insofar as in this precept a special time is determined as a sign of the creation of the world, in this way it is a ceremonial precept. ... For this reason ... it is placed among the precepts of the Decalogue, insofar as it is moral, but not insofar as it is ceremonial." (II IIæ q. 122, art. 4 ad 1). See Salamancans tract. 23, *de 3 praec.* c. 1 where they make a more profuse dissertation on this point, from number 1 even to number 7.

264.—*Quaeritur II:* Does this precept also command an interior worship of God? Scotus affirms this, along with Angel, and Tabienus, cited by the Salamancans (*dict.* c. 1 punct. 2 n. 8), and they say this is because the faithful are held from this precept to elicit acts of charity and contrition; consequently the sanctification of the soul is obtained, which is commanded by this precept. On the other hand, the more common opinion of the authors denies it (St. Antoninus, p. 2 tit. 9 c. 7 §2 q. 4 a. 4 concl. 2 dub. 1; Sanchez, *dec.* l. 2 c. 35 n. 8; Salamancans *ibid.* ex n. 9 with Covarruvias, Filliuci, Bonacina, Sayr, etc., from St. Thomas, I IIæ q. 122, art. 4, where he teaches that we are not compelled to the interior cult, rather we are moved by the Holy Spirit: "And ... therefore in the third precept of the Decalogue the outward worship of God is commanded." The Roman Catechism teaches the same thing, where it says: "By this precept of the law, that outward worship which is due to God from us is prescribed." (*Catech. Rom.* de. 3 *praec.* p. 3 n. 1). Moreover, sanctification of the soul is indeed the end of the precept, but the end of the precept does not fall under the precept; according to the common axiom of theologians; St. Thomas teaches the same thing (I IIæ q. 100 art. 9, in the body of the article) and he says it more expressly in *ad 2*: "For, that which is given in the precept is not the same as the end."

Quaeritur III: Is this precept affirmative or negative? We answer that it is affirmative, seeing that it does not oblige always and everywhere. Suarez, Sanchez, Palaus, Leander, Fagundez (with Salamancans *ibid.*, n. 15) uphold that it is negative against Cajetan, Filliuci etc., since it commands nothing positive upon the Jews; but this should be denied. See the Roman Catechism, n. 11.

265—*Quaeritur* IV: Is observance of Sunday of the natural law, divine law or merely ecclesiastical law?

The first opinion asserts that it is of divine law because Sunday takes the place of the sabbath, which was instituted by divine law for the worship of God. So think Abbas, Angelus and Panormus, cited by the Salamancans (*ibid.* punct. 4 n. 37) and Croix adheres to this (l. 3 p. 1 n. 691) with Marchant and Sporer, who says that one excused from Mass on a feast is held to worship God on Sunday at least by an internal act.

But by far, the *second opinion* is more probable and common, that it is an ecclesiastical law, from what we read in the Roman Catechism (3 part. n. 19): "Yet it pleased the Church of God that the worship of the Sabbath would be transferred to Sunday." St. Thomas teaches the same thing (II IIæ qu. 122, art. 4 ad 4): "The observance of Sunday succeeded the observance of the Sabbath, not by the force of law but from the institution of the Church." And therefore, the observance of Sunday can be changed by the Church and dispensed by it, although it could not dispense against this in such a way that there would be no festive day especially appointed for the divine cult, precisely as Pope Alexander III dispensed against this so that on Sundays men could fish for herring, as is held in c. *Licet de feriis,* where he says:

"Although both the page of the Old as well as the New Testament specially set aside the seventh day for human rest, and both it and other days were set aside for the majesty of the most high, just the same the Church decreed that the birth of the holy martyrs must be observed. We concede that it is lawful on Sundays as well as feast days (apart from greater solemnities of the year), if herring were fished from necessity." Many authors also hold this opinion (del Soto, *de justitia et jure*, l. 2 qu. 4 art. 4 ad 2; St. Antoninus, p. 2 tit. 9 c. 7; Navarre in *Manuale*, c. 13 n. 1; Azor, tom. 2 l. 1. c. 2 q. 2; Suarez, *de relig.* l. 2 c. 4 n. 8; Sanchez in *Cons.* l. 5 cap. 2 dub. 1 ex n. 2; Elbel n. 340 and the Salamancans, *ibid.* n. 38, in common with t. Thomas, *loc. cit.* n. 263, Filliuci, Cajetan, Bonacina and with them Cardenas, tr. 52, p. 2 n. 15 and Bellarmine *de cultu Sanctorum*, lib. 3, cap. 11). But a great opposition arises, namely: The precept of the sabbath was certainly natural and moral, therefore it was numbered among the precepts of the Decalogue; therefore, Sunday, which was substituted for the Sabbath, is also of natural law, that is to say, divine. We respond that although it is of divine and natural law that some determined time is designated to worship God, nevertheless the determination of this worship, and of the days in which it must be furnished was from the arrangement left to the Church by Christ. Then the Pope could discern that the observance of Sunday should endure only for some hours, and that some servile works would be lawful, as the Salamancans say (*dict.* n. 38). And as a result, this precept, inasmuch as it is an exhibition of worship, is indeed divine but insofar as it is a determination of the cult and time, it is ecclesiastical (See the Salamancans, *dict.* num. 38 and 39, and at the end of the introduction of tract 23 *de tertio praecept. Decal.*).

266.—*Quaeritur* V: Could Bishops appoint feasts for their dioceses? It is certain that they can, from c. *Conquestus, de feriis*. But there is a doubt because of the Bull of Urban VIII where he advises Bishops in the Lord that they should abstain from establishing feasts. But it is more probable that these words are rather more advisory than in the form of a precept. See Salamancans, tr. 23, c. 1 punct. 6 §1 n. 105 and 6.

An even greater doubt comes to mind, whether the consent of the clergy and the people are required? It must be affirmed with Azor, Covarruvias, Bonacina, Trullenchus, etc., and the Salamancans, *ibid.* n. 108 and 109 commenting on the aforesaid chapter *Conquestus, de feriis*. Still, it must be noted that it suffices if the clergy and people do not contradict it. Thereupon it must be noted that although the Bishop could not appoint perpetual feasts over their opposition, still he could on one or another day in turn. Nay more, other authors say that only the consent of the clergy suffices from custom (Suarez, Bonacina, Trullenchus, Palaus, Barbosa, etc., cited by Salamancans *ibid.* n. 110); but the Salamancans oppose this (n. 111) according to ancient law. Still, they note that after heed has been given to the new law, from the bull *Universa* of Urban VIII, published in 1642, that Bishops can institute perpetual feasts without the consent of the people and clergy (Salamancans *ibid.* n. 112 and 113, with Bordono). But Croix opposes this, saying the people are not held to keep a feast day appointed by the Bishop without their consent as well as that of the clergy, with Barbosa, Gavantus, Gobat (n. 619), etc. And indeed, more probably, for on the one side it is certain from the aforesaid chapter *Conquestus*, that a Bishop cannot appoint feasts without the consent of the clergy and people; on the other hand, in the aforementioned bull (according to its words related by the Salamancans) nothing else is said except that bishops should abstain from easily instituting feasts. Consequently, it is not rightly, or at least not sufficiently deduced that this faculty is absolutely conceded to bishops.

Moreover, whether bishops could appoint feasts in honor of saints that are merely beatified? Suarez, Trullenchus, Fagundez etc. (cited by Salamancans tr. 23, c. 1 p. 6 §1 n. 114) affirm this.

But the Salamancans (*ibid.* n. 114) more truly deny it with Sanchez, Barbosa, Villalobos, Diana, etc. Secular princes can also appoint feast days, at least in regard to abstinence from servile works, as Sa, Sylvius, etc. say. But the common opinion denies this, with Azor, Sanchez, Filliuci and a great many others with the Salamancans, *ibid.* § 2 n. 117.

267.—*Quaeritur VI:* From what time does the obligation of a feast begin?

Angelus and Panormus, etc., hold that it begins from evening to evening. But it more probably begins from the middle of the night to the next; such is the current use of the Roman Church. Nevertheless, it is true that feasts can be established even to noon, or night. (Navarre, Suarez, etc. with the Salamancans, *ibid.* punct. 7 n. 124, and Elbel *de 3 praec.* n. 331). Yet it must be noted that if a feast were transferred to another due to an impeded day in regard to the office, the obligation of hearing Mass and abstaining from servile works would not be transferred with it. This is the common opinion; see the Salamancans *ibid.*, n. 126, which they argue because it is the common practice of the Church.

268.—*Quaeritur VII:* Would this precept oblige *sub gravi* and to what does it obliges?

We answer the first affirmatively, since proposition 52 condemned by Pope Innocent III says: "The precept of preserving a feast does not oblige under mortal sin, provided scandal is removed, if there is no contempt present." To the second we respond that it obliges one to hear Mass from c. *Vice illius, de treuga,* and c. *Si quis, de consecr.* dist. 1. Furthermore, to abstain from servile works, as we read it in Leviticus 23:7 and *c. 1 Licet de fer.* And this is not only on Sundays, but also on other feasts.

Here, we must opportunely notice, that from the *Brief* published on 22 December 1748 by our Pope, Benedict XIV for the Kingdom of the Two Sicilies, servile works are permitted except for, "feast days with the exception of Sundays of the Easter season, as well as Pentecost, and all other Sundays of the year, nor may servile works be done on the days of the Circumcision, Epiphany, Ascension, Corpus Christi and Christmas, on the days of Purification, the Annunciation, Assumption, or the Birth and Immaculate Conception of the Blessed Virgin Mary, nor on the feasts of Sts. Peter and Paul, All Saints day and the particular patrons of Churches of dioceses." For other feasts, it is only commanded to hear Mass.

269.—Whether there is also an obligation to hear the sermon?

It seems to be so commanded in *c. Sacerdote, de consecr.* dist. 1. But we answer in the negative with Busembaum (below, 308 as well as n. 323) as well as the Salamancans (tr. 23, c. 1 punct. 8 n. 134). Moreover, the Gloss explains the cited text as speaking only of those that scorn the sermon. Suarez also notes in *de religione* (l. 2 c. 16 n. 8) that nothing else is commanded but that Bishops and parish priests give a sermon on Sundays and on more solemn days either themselves or through other suitable ministers as well as to preach at least three days of the weak in Advent and Lent, if it will be fitting. From such words no other obligation is placed except upon Bishops and parish priests to preach. Here we must notice in passing that in the Council of Trent (sess. 5, c. 2, *de reformatione*), both Bishops and parish priests are given the obligation of preaching to their people on Sundays and solemn feasts in these words: "All Bishops ... and ... prelates are held to preach directly (if they are not legitimately impeded, or through suitable men if they are impeded), ... However, if anyone will pay no heed to fulfill this, let him be subject to rigorous punishment. Archpriests, curates and anyone that has care of souls shall feed the flock consigned to him either in his own person or through another suitable man at least on Sundays and solemn feasts by teaching those things which are necessary for all to know for salvation, and by announcing to them with brevity and ease of speech what vices they must avoid and the virtues that they must follow."

The same command to the Bishops is renewed in the same Council, sess. 24, c. 4. Hence, I do not doubt, along with the Salamancans (*ibid.* n. 136 and 137) as well as Barbosa, that the aforesaid precept obliges both Bishops and pastors gravely and absolutely. Nor is what Suarez thinks opposed (cited by Bonacina d. 5 q. *unic.* p. 2 in fine), namely that this command does not oblige so rigorously that parish priests who omit to preach at times, or more often, would sin mortally. Suarez thinks it is so from the customary interpretation of the law, which is from the Council itself, where in the aforesaid ch. 4, sess. 24, when the discussion is on this obligation of Bishops, it is said "if they shall think it will be necessary;" and Bonacina (*l. c.*) as well as Palaus (tr. 9 d. 9 p. 4 n. 5) adhere to this interpretation. Just the same, the Salamancans answer rightly since that condition is related in regard only to Advent and Lent, as is clear from the real context of the Council, but not in regard to other times of the year. Nevertheless, the doctors in common admit smallness of the matter in such a precept; Roncaglia would have it that smallness of matter is only for a twelfth of the sermons of the year (*de 4 prace.* c. 5, q. 6); but this seems too rigid. Furthermore, the Salamancans (*loc. cit.* n. 138) reasonably assert that parish priests frequently omitting preaching are not excused from grave fault. Hence, Bonacina and Palaus do not appear to hold improbably (*ll. cc.*) that parish priests do not sin gravely who omit to preach only once in a while; but it is otherwise, as they say, if they omit for one whole continuous month, or for three months separated throughout the year. So much more because in the Council of Trent (*sess.* 5 c. 2) it is said that if these parish priests are "warned by the Bishop and will have failed in their duty for three months then let them be compelled by censures and other measures to fulfill their office." From that, it seems the smallness of the matter has a greater latitude. Lastly, the Salamancans note (*d.* n. 138) that parish priests can duly omit sermons to supply them more opportunely later. But Bishops are held to give sermons more rarely than parish priests.

270.—*Quaeritur VIII:* Who is held to observe feasts?

We answer that all the faithful of sound mind, that is about the end of their 7th year. So also from the common opinion (Croix l. 3 p. 1 n. 615) and the Salamancans (tr. 23, c. 1 p. 9 § 1 n. 144) against other authors whose opinions are everywhere rejected. Hence, children that have attained the use of reason for certain before their seventh year are held, as other authors more probably hold and who call this opinion more probable (Suarez, 3 p. t. 3 d. 88 *sect.* 4 in fine, Navarre, *in Man.* c. 21 n. 7; Azor t. 1 l. 7 c. 2 qu. 1 and Salamancans *ibid.* n. 145, with Fagundez and Diana, p. 10 tr. 12 r. 37). However, they are not held, even if it is after their seventh year, if they still lack the use of reason. The reasoning is because the law obliges everyone who attains to the years of discretion. Yet, other authors do not unduly think the opposed opinion is probable, namely that children before their seventh year, even if they have acquired the use of reason, are not held to positive laws because these do not oblige except according to common contingencies, as is held in l. *Nam ad ea ff. de leg.* where it says: "For the law should be more suited to these matters which come about frequently and easily than those that happen in exceptional cases." (Elbel, *de leg.* n. 369; Diana *loc. cit.* with Trullenchus, Rocafull, and Pasqualigo, and Croix, l. 1 n. 676, with Burghaber, Illsung. and John Sanchez, Zaccaria, l. 3 p. 1 n. 615). St. Thomas also uses this reasoning in II IIæ q. 147 art. 4 ad 2, to excuse young men before the age of 21 from fasting, even if someone does not need food frequently, "Because the legislator attends to that which happens commonly and in many cases." Likewise, Santius, Diana, and Burghaber (cited by Croix, l. 6 p. 2 n. 2026) on the precept of yearly confession; but it must be held with Palaus in *de sacr. peon.* p. 20, § 2, n. 2, where he says that it is the common opinion with Sylvius, Suarez, Concina, Navarre, Laymann, Vasquez, Bonacina, etc., is that children who have a mortal sin on their conscience are obligated to go to confession, while it is commanded by c. *Omnis utriusque sexus, de poen. et rem.* that all the faithful are held to annual confession after they have attained to the years of discretion. The Gloss explains that *the years of discretion* are "those with the capacity for cunning [*dolus*]." But after their seventh year, in doubt as to whether children have obtained suitable reason they are certainly held to all laws, because then without a doubt the presumption from common contingencies favors the obligation, as Elbel and Sanchez hold, as well as Bonacina, Diana, etc. (quoted by Salamancans, n. 145). But someone that was blind, deaf and mute at the same time would not be held to be present at Mass because he could not furnish moral assistance; it is otherwise, if he were only blind, or only deaf (Croix, l. 3 p. 1 n. 616). Are pilgrims held to the observance of feasts? See what was said in book 1, n. 156 and what is going to be said in this book, n. 332.

271.—Would it be lawful on feasts days to enjoin servile works on infidels?

Fernandez, cited by Tamburinus (c. 3 § 1 n. 17) rejects this. But Diana, Merolla, Laymann (l. 1 t. 4 c. 9 n. 3), Croix (l. 1 n. 579) affirm it, along with Viva, Tamburinius, and Elbel (n. 410 who thinks it is merely non improbable). Laymann permits servile works to always be enjoined on the insane, for both are outside the law, while the Apostle instructed us "that the Church does not judge concerning those who are on the outside." 1 Cor. 5:12.

DUBIUM I
What works are forbidden both by this precept and the Church?

272. What are servile works?
273. Whether to sin on a feast day would be a double sin?
274. What works are not servile?
275. Is it servile to go on a journey?
276. Is it to drive a carriage or lead a laden beast of burden?
277. Would it be servile to ground flower?
278. Would it be servile to teach, write, sing, etc., even if these are done for profit?
279. Would it be servile to copy?
280. Would it be servile to paint?
281. Would it be servile to trace, stretch a canvas or to sculpt?
282. Is it lawful to build a printing press? to distill liquids?
283. Would it be permitted to hunt and fish?
284. What public works are forbidden on feast days?
285. Are sales and contracts permitted?
286. Are market days and commerce permitted?
287. Would it be permitted to excommunicate, draw up a will, and like things?

272.—"*Resp.* 1: On a feast day all servile works are forbidden, "*i.e.* those which are conducted in regard to an external matter, "and even mechanical and unworthy, *e.g.* to sow, to make "something; or they require only the labor of the body and are "usually done by workers and servants. So the common opinion "of the doctors. See Laymann (l. 4 tr. 7 c. 2), Suarez, Filliuci, etc. "from St. Thomas, *loc. cit.*"

We must preface three kinds of works are given by the authors in common. Some are works of the body, which are exercised by the body and ordered immediately to the advantage of the body, such as to dig, to sow, etc. And these are called *servile* because they are usually done by servants. Hence, a servile work is defined by Illsung, cited by Croix (l. 3 p. 1 n. 574): "An action which is done immediately more advantageous to the body than to the powers of the soul." Others are works of the *soul*, which especially proceed from the soul and look to cultivate the mind, such as to read, to teach, sing, play instruments, etc. And these are called *liberal*, because they are exercised by freemen. Lastly, others are called *media* or *communia*, which are exercised in common by both freemen and servants, such as to go on a journey, hunt, etc. (Laymann tr. 7 c. 1 n. 1; Bonacina dub. 5 q. un. p. 2 n. 6; Anaclet., *Viva*, etc.).

273.—*Quaeritur:* would those who sin on a feast day sin against this precept? St. Bonaventure, St. Antoninus, Medina etc. (cited by the Salamancans, *de 3 praec.* c. 1 punct. 11 § 1, n. 216 and 217) affirm this, because, (as they say), the sin is opposed to divine worship which is commanded on a feast day; but the more probable and more common is the contrary opinion, held by many authors (Navarre, *in Sum.* c. 6 n. 9; Suarez, *de rel.* l. 2 c. 18 n. 3; de Lugo, *de poenit.* d. 16 sect. 12 n. 116 and the Salamancans, *ibid.* from n. 218 with Cajetan, del Soto, Sylvius, Sanchez, Bonacina, Palaus, Medesma, Trullenchus). St. Thomas also teaches this in 3, d. 39, qu. 5 art. 5 r. 2 ad 2, where he cites the Gloss which says in c. 13 of Luke that the law does not forbid a man on the sabbath "to take care of man, rather to do servile works, *i.e.* to be weighed down by sins," and he so answers: "Servile works are mystically understood as sins, but are literally said to be deputed to be exercised by the servants we have." It is not opposed that the holy doctor says in II IIæ q. 122 art. 4 ad 2: "He acts more against this precept that sins on a feast day than he who does some licit corporal work." For this understands the end of the precept, but not the obligation of the precept; but the end of the precept does not fall under the precept, as was said in n. 264 by the same St. Thomas.

TREATISE III: THE THIRD AND FOURTH PRECEPTS CH. I   301

274.—"1. It does not pertain to the accounting of servile work "whether it was done for profit or for recreation; or whether it "was from this or that intention, pious, vain or indecent. "(Cajetan, Suarez, Laymann, *loc. cit.* etc., against Sylvius and "many Canonists)."

"2. It is also of no importance whether it was done with "exhaustion and labor or not; whether it was for a short or long "time, etc., because nothing changes the nature of the work.

"3. It is not servile, and therefore not forbidden, to play on a "feast, to hold a dance, to play musical instruments, to make a "journey on foot, horse or carriage, or boat. Wherefore what is "necessary for these are licit (Navarre, c. 13; Toledo, Laymann, "Suarez *de festis*, c. 27."

275.—Would it be licit to make a journey on foot, horse or carriage on a feast day? Abulensis, Cajetan, Sylvius, etc. say no. But it must be affirmed with the common opinion following Busembaum, Viva (*de 3 praec.* q. 9 n. 8), Elbel (n. 404) and the Salamancans (tr. 23 c. 1 punct. 11 §3 n. 239). And the opposite opinion must now be left behind as antiquated, which Roncaglia duly notes (c. 3 q. 4).

Would it be lawful to be carried on a litter by men? Croix says no (l. 3 p. 1 n. 577) but it is affirmed by Tamburinus (Tr. 9 *de 3° Praec.*, qu. 1 cap. 3 qu. 4 resp. 3), with Palaus (tr. 9 punct. 5 n. 12). But in this I say the custom of places must be attended to, which now flourishes in the city of Naples, and excuses from fault as Mazotta duly notes (*de 3 pracept.* cap. 1 § 1).

276.—"4. It is not servile to lead a beast of burden without the "burden when it is to make a journey, as Filliuci says (c. 9 n. "170). But, to ride a pack animal, carriage, or boat laden with "wares is servile (Suarez *loc. cit.*, Filliuci *loc. cit.*). But if before a "feast, a man began such journeys, their continuation is "permitted, either on account of public utility or a loss which "would otherwise follow."

There is a grave question, would it be lawful to drive a carriage or lead a beast of burden laden on a feast day? There are three opinions.

The *first opinion* holds this is in itself a servile work, regardless of labor (Busembaum, Bonacina (disp. 5. q. un. p. 2 n. 25) with Reg. and S. Antoninus, Navarre, Cajetan, and Sylvius (cited by Salamancans *loc. cit.* n. 242).

The *second opinion* holds this although not *sub gravi*, nor *per se*, but by reason of the labor if it were serious in imposing or lifting burdens; it is otherwise if the labor were modest. (Croix, l. 3 p. 1 n. 578; Tamburinius; Dec., l. 4 c. 3 § 1 n. 12, with Diana, Sanchez, Cons., l. 5 c. 2 dub. 7 n. 10, Palaus, cited by Salamancans, *ibid.*, Elbel, de 3 *praecept.* n. 404).

The *third opinion* is the more probable, at least today, which Viva (q. 9 art. 1 n. 9), Roncaglia (c. 3 q. 4), and the Salamancans (*ibid.* n. 243) hold with others. It holds that it is altogether licit, not only to continue a journey already begun, but to begin one. The reason is, because in such a labor mule-drivers do not employ a notable time, and, if perhaps it were a notable time, it is excused either on account of avoiding grave loss, or then because a universal custom is present which Mazzota duly asserts is; and the same about boats.

277.—Would it be lawful to mill [flour] on feast days? Sanchez "(*Cons.* lib. 5 cap. 2 d. 13) concedes so if the mill is operated by "water or wind; but not, however, if it is operated by animals, "especially if much labor and employment is required. From "such a doctrine Tamburinius (n. 14), and Croix (n. 578) infer "with probability, that when the cooperation and application of "men is modest, it would not be illicit, at least not gravely, to "mill even with animals."

Would it be lawful then for a blacksmith to shod horses making a journey? See Dubium II, n. 300 below.

278.—"Likewise, it is not servile whether gratuitously or for a "price, to teach, study, write, transcribe, and according to "certain men (Medina, Lopez and Armilla, whose opinion "Laymann thinks probable, against Filliuci, Azor and many "others), to paint even with colors[12] (for a great many concede "simple drawn lines); still, to prepare the colors and not paint "but touch them, for example, to preserve them or the canvass, "to whitewash walls is ignoble."

Here, many things must be distinguished.

Quaeritur I: Are teaching, writing, playing, singing, etc. *servile*, if they are done for profit? Abulensis, Azor, Tabienus etc. (cited by Salamancans tr. 23, c. 1 punct. 12 n. 255 and 256) affirm, because, although such actions are liberal, still they become servile from the profit. But the opposite must be held from St. Thomas (II IIæ q. 122 art. 4 ad 3) with del Soto, Navarre, Suarez and the Salamancans (*ibid.* n. 257). The reason is, because the intention of the worker cannot change the nature of the work.

279.—*Quaeritur II:* Is transcription a servile work? Cajetan, Navarre, Sanchez, Sylvius etc. (cited by Salamancans, *ibid.* n. 261) affirm that it is because they say transcription is not a work of the mind, since many transcribe even what they do not understand. On the other hand, it is very commonly denied, and the authors hold more probably that to transcribe, just as to write, is ordered to instruct the mind (Elbel, n. 399; Roncaglia, c. 3 q. 4 resp. 1; Salamancans *ibid.* n. 262, with Suarez, Sa, Trullenchus, Bonacina and Viva, q. 9 art. 1 n. 3 with Palaus and

---

[12] Translator's note: "With colors" refers to the fact that in St. Alphonsus' time, colors had to be prepared from pigments and their preparation was very labor intensive. Today, one merely removes a cap from a tube.

the common teaching). So, Elbel (n. 400) and Viva (*ibid.*) note from Tamburinius that it is lawful even to transcribe music notes, accounts, and even to brand (Laymann, with Diana, Busembaum, n. 282, Mazzota and Elbel, n. 401, with Sporer, Tamburinius, Sayr. and many others against Palaus).

280.—*Quaeritur III:* Is painting a servile work? *The first opinion* denies it with Lopez, Medina, Angelus, Sylvius, Sayr, Armilla, Rosella, Barbosa (cited by Salamancans, *ibid.* punct. 11 §3 n. 250), and with Busembaum and Laym. The reason is because, as they say, such a work is not properly servile, but rather more liberal, as it is very similar to writing. Azor, Reg., Filliuci, etc. (cited by Bonacina, disp. 5, q. un. p. 2, n. 25) admit that at least it is not servile if it is done for the sake of recreation. Sporer (n. 45) calls this opinion most probable.

Nevertheless, *the second opinion* is more common and holds that to paint is a servile work because it cannot be called a liberal action, since it does not intend to instruct the mind, as writing has for its end, but only to imitate the images of things. Then, because to paint is similar to sculpture and embroidery, which are servile works in the common opinion (Salamancans *ibid.* n. 231, with Cajetan, Suarez, Palaus, Sanchez and others).

Still, these things not withstanding, Laymann (tract. 7 c. 2 n. 3), Viva (q. 9 a. 1 n. 4), Elbel (n. 395), Holzmann (n. 541), Roncaglia (*ibid.* q. 4) Anacl. (tr. 10, q. 2) Tamburinius (l. 4 c. 3 § 1 n. 8) with Sa, Pellizarius, and Palaus, all admit that the first opinion is probable provided it was done without a lot of set up, namely by mixing colors and setting up tables, etc. The reason is to paint, although it requires material operation, does not seem to properly be a servile action, but rather must be called liberal. Just as a writing expresses internal concepts, so a picture expresses images of things, as Castropolaeus, Tamburinius, Viva, etc. say, or as Laymann says, to paint seems to be a liberal action insofar as its end is recreation for the mind. It cannot be denied that the aforesaid opinion is probable enough, as Mazotta rightly says; for even if it is not certain that painting is a liberal work, it is also not certain that it is servile, and at any rate, it must be established to be for certain if it is to be forbidden. It seems more probable that the action is at least in the mean and common to servants and freemen, while we often observe that noble men do not blush to learn the act of painting as well as to do it. St. Thomas says (II IIæ q. 122 art. 4 ad 3), "Insofar as works are common to servants and freemen, they are not called servile." At least, as Roncaglia says (*in reg. prax.*), those who follow this opinion as probable must not be dismissed without absolution.

281.—Moreover, the authors commonly admit that it is not a servile work to draw, trace images or to make patterns with a needle, as women customarily do, for this (as Tamburinius says) is related more to the exercise of talent than to mere work (Sporer, tr. 3 in *Dec.* c. 4; Felix Potestà, n. 2033, Mazotta and others cited by Tamburinius and Viva). Other authors also excuse girls doing embroidery so that they might learn (Azor, Filliuci, Sylvius and Ang. cited by Bonacina, *ibid.* n. 25, with Palaus, Sa, Marchant, cited by Busembaum here in n. 283).

Nevertheless, the art of sculpture, at least in the estimation of men, is numbered among the mechanical arts. See Tamburinius with Palaus, *ibid.* n. 10.

282.—"6. Those placing letters in a printing press also seem to "be excused when they do so without much thought after Mass, "as Laymann holds. Still, to print is considered servile labor "(Escobar, E., 5 c. 4, Suarez, Laymann, etc.).

"7. Filliuci (n. 169) also excuses distillation, which is done "without weariness to the body and rather more from "experience and expertise than from duty and craft." (Croix admits this in n. 57 if the application is small. But on account of this reasoning, would it be lawful to clean wheat with the hands? Tamburinius, §1, *in fine*, calls this into doubt. Moreover, Fr. Michel, cited by Elbel, n. 408, permits light labors to avoid idleness, such as to pick roses, to peel apples, etc. But in these I think it must rather be said that a greater space of time is required for grave matter.)

283.—"8. Some men do not think hunting is servile (Granado "2. 2. c. 3 t. 12, d. 4 sect. 7 n. 65, others hold the contrary and "excuse it for custom or to avoid idleness or worse vices), or "fowling, waging war, boxing, fishing (at least in rivers for the "sake of recreation) and like things; still fishing ought to be "moderated. See Laymann and Filliuci (tr. 27 c. 9 q. 12), "Bonacina (d. 5 q. 1 p. 2 n. 25), and Escobar who teaches it is "laborious and formally not permitted. Likewise, certain men "excuse girls doing embroidery to avoid idleness (Armilla, Azor, "Palaus, Sa, Marchant. See Diana, p. 5 t. 6 r. 15 and p. 4 tr. 4 r. "92)."

Quæritur: Are hunting, fowling and fishing forbidden works on feast days? There is a twofold opinion.

The first affirms it, because they say they are servile works, especially if they are done for employment, such as Sylvius, Angelus, Corella, etc. (cited by the Salamancans, tr. 23, c. 1 punct. 11 § 3 n. 234).

But the *second opinion* is more probable and common, which denies they are forbidden, even if they are done for the sake of profit. This is either because they are not servile works (as Laymann, c. 2 n. 4; Elbel, n. 402; Sanchez, *in Cons.* l. 5 c. 2 d. 14 et 15; Navarre, Medina, Granado, Rodriguez, and Lopez hold), or because they are at least excused by custom (Holzmann, n. 542; Viva, art. 1 n. 15 with Palaus, Sanchez, Trullenchus, Filliuci, Leander, etc.). This is provided they are done without great labor; otherwise it would seem that the Pope dispensed the fishing of herring in vain, in c. 3 *de feriis*.

284.—"Resp. 2. Besides these, certain works that are not servile are forbidden which are called *forensia* (public), such as fairs, agreements, court trials where death and punishment is involved, all *strepitus judicialis*, that is, actions which pertain to the decision of cases, both civil and criminal, secular and ecclesiastical. So the common opinion of the authors, from c. 2 *de feriis*."

Thus the following are resolved:

"On a feast day it is not lawful to cite, call witnesses, that is, to exact a judicial oath, impose or execute a sentence, which, if it is imposed, is null and void. See Laymann, l. 4, t. 7 c. 2 n. 7."

It is forbidden to furnish a judicial oath on feast days for temporal matters, as St. Thomas observes (II IIæ q. 89, art. 10). But it is licit to furnish an oath to inquisitors and even oaths in which a contract of a promise is confirmed on a feast day (Viva art. 2 n. 15). Also forbidden are the formation of processes, the citation of a party and the postponement or execution of a sentence, unless necessity or piety would otherwise require it, from the last chapter of *de feriis*.

285.—"2. It is not licit to buy and sell unnecessary things, to conduct business publicly or privately, to enter into contracts for sale, rents, exchanges, etc. (unless they were excused by custom or other just causes) because they are embraced by the term *mercatus* (fairs), which are forbidden by c. 1 *de feriis*, as Bonacina teaches from Suarez, c. 13, Filliuci t. 27, c. 10, q. 2 n. 180." (See more below).

286.—Universal market days are now permitted by custom, and in some places even particular markets on any week, as Viva says (q. 9 art. 2 n. 2), with Palaus and the Salamancans (tr. 23, c. 1 punct. 13 § 1 n. 269 ad 270), and Sanchez, Cajetan, del Soto, etc., Croix n. 606, who with Palaus and Tamburinius says that from custom now it seems altogether licit for there to be a fair. But sales of wares are certainly forbidden by canonical law, as Sanchez says (d. 25, n. 3 etc.) cited by the Salamancans (*ibid.* n. 272). But where there is a contrary custom, they are excused (Sanchez *loc. cit.* num. 4, and Viva *loc. cit.* num. 2). For custom (Mazzota says, §2), for the most, part abrogates the law in this. Hence, the Salamancans (*ibid.* n. 273) note that the sale of food and drink is permitted on feast days, even if it tends to gluttony (with Cajetan, Sanchez, Navarre, and Busembaum, according to a decree of the Sacred Congregation of Rites cited by the Salamancans, *ibid.* n. 279). Likewise, to sell shoes, candles and similar things, the price of which has already been determined. Likewise, to sell a house, horse, wares, even presents, even though much time is consumed in this; both because the use of the God-fearing is advanced and because the Church only forbade sale in public offices by reason of scandal (Salamancans *ibid.* ex n. 275 and 276, with Sanchez, Navarre, etc., and Croix, n. 606, with Palaus, Tamburinius, and Illsung).

Moreover, by the word "fairs" are renting and negotiations, and similar things forbidden? Busembaum affirms it, with Tab., Sylvius, etc. But the more common opinion denies it (Sanchez *ibid.* c. 1 n. 277, with Trullenchus, Palaus, Azor and Leander). This is because such is the custom of the wise, whereby it seems it was repealed by the decrees of St. Pius V *Cum Primum*, of 1566, and of the Sacred Congregation of Rites (cited by Salamancans *ibid.* n. 279). Hence, all contracts are licit if they are made without instruments, and the authority of the judge, as Sanchez, Illsung and others with Croix n. 606. Therefore, Mazotta condemns a sale of great importance when it is done on a solemnity as a mortal sin; but Viva asserts from the common opinion (with Palaus q. 9 art. 2 n. 4) that it is permitted to make wills, celebrate contracts and similar acts which do not require *strepitum judicialiem*; and really, they everywhere use instruments in making contracts among us on feast days. Still, notaries in some places customarily ask for a general license from their ordinary for this purpose, which is commonly conceded.

287.—"3. On a feast day it is lawful to excommunicate, "dispense, inform a private judgment, consult a defense "attorney, make councils, hold elections, etc., because these do "not require *streptium judicialem*. See Bonacina, *l.c.*" (It is common teaching, as Viva cites in q. 9 art. 2 n. 4). It is licit even to confer benefices and even to exercise jurisdiction without *strepitus judicialis* likewise to free a servant and also make an appeal. Viva *ibid*.)

DUBIUM II
What reasons excuse one from the observance of feasts that cause works to be forbidden?

288. Who can give a dispensation to work?
289. What sort of laborers are excused from custom?
290. What about those working crops, etc. What about barbers and cobblers? And what would suffice for knowledge of custom?
291. How would piety excuse?
292. Would it be lawful to sweep a Church on a feast day, or adorn the altars, or erect a tomb, etc.?
293. Would it be lawful to work so as to assist the poor or pious places?
294. How would charity towards one's neighbor excuse?
295. How would necessity excuse?
296. Would servants be excused when their master compels them to work?
297. Would poor men restoring garments, etc.?
298. Is it lawful to cook food on a feast day, to slaughter animals, to make a meal and gather fruit?

299. *Is it lawful to bake bread?*
300. *Is it lawful to heal, smelt iron, cook lime, or prepare blue dye? What about to shod horses?*
301. *Would it be lawful to labor on account of a great profit? And would it be lawful to miss Mass on account of it?*
302. *Would it be lawful to avoid idleness?*
303. *Would road workers, etc. be excused? And menders completing vestments for a feast day?*
304. *How will utility excuse on account of public joy?*
305. *How will paucity of matter excuse? (See also book 6 n. 346).*
306. *Would one sin gravely commanding six servants to labor for an hour?*
307. *Where is gravity of matter taken up in* forensia*?*

"Such are especially seven: First the *dispensation* of a bishop, or one having quasi-episcopal power, namely the superiors of religious orders. Furthermore, even pastors, when easy access to a Bishop is not granted to them. Suarez, c. 33, Laymann, c. 4 n. 2, Bonacina, p. 1 n. 20."

288.—In the *first place*, the Pope can dispense against the precept of abstaining from servile work as the supreme legislator and pastor; he does this on all festivals and for the whole Church. *Secondly*, a Bishop in his diocese; and even the chapter when the see is vacant; still regular prelates toward their religious subjects as well as their household. It also must be noted that Bishops can dispense even against common feast days. Nevertheless, it must also be noted that if they were to dispense against these without a just cause, they sin gravely and the dispensation is invalid; it is otherwise, if they dispensed against synodal feasts or particular feasts of the place. *Thirdly*, the pastor can dispense when, as a subject, he cannot approach the Bishop but only the Church, and for some particular case. So Sanchez *Cons.* lib. 5 c. 2 d. 20, n. 2, Cajetan, del Soto, Navarre, Suarez, Palaus, Azor, Trullenchus, with the Salamancans, tr. 23, c. 2 punct. 14 § 4 n. 352, and Viva art. 2 n. 13, who notes that the vicar general can also dispense, but only by a special mandate; for those things are not communicated that have the sense of grace, as Tamburinius says (l. 4 §2 n. 3) with Merolla, Barbosa, and Sanchez. Even with the bishop present, a pastor can dispense from custom against minute and frequent necessity; still only in those matters in which it was introduced by custom for them to dispense against, such as against fasting and against the abstinence for servile works on feast days. (Viva, *loc. cit.*; Tamburinius, as above, n. 37, and c. 5 § 7 n. 56, with Thomas and John Sanchez, Sporer, *de legibus* c. 1 n. 349) with Suarez, Mazotta, *de leg.* tr. 1 d. 4 q. 1 cap. 2 and Salamancans *de leg.* c. 5 punct. 4 §2 n. 40). Moreover, Elbel thinks (*de 3 praec.* n. 414) with Suarez, Sylvius, Filliuci etc., that with urgent necessity even a presumed dispensation would suffice if the dispenser could not be approached. But we must note here that one having ordinary power can delegate it to another, but not if he had delegated power. Croix, n. 584, with Tamburinius, etc.

289.—"Second *custom*; those fairs are licit that are "customarily held on feast days everywhere, as well as "preparations of unnecessary delicacies as dainties, cakes and "similar types of pastries, likewise buying and selling of things "of scarce importance. Bonacina, *l.c.*, Laymann, *l.c.*"

290.—Hence, from custom, the Salamancans (tr. 23 c. 1 punct. 14 §3 n. 341), and Sanchez (cited by Viva, art. 2 n. 12) excuse those who work on the threshing floor or separate wheat, and gather the branches into barns. Fernandez, however, (cited by Diana, with Tamburinius n. 13, excuse barbers from custom (and Viva says the same thing can be said for cobblers shoeing feet with new shoes). But Viva notes that the doctors more commonly doubt the approval of such a custom, upon which Sanchez (d. 27 n. 1) and the Salamancans (*ibid.* n. 336 and 337) equally have doubts, with Cajetan and Cardinal Toledo. Still, the continuator of Tournely (de 3 *decal.* praec. art. 1, *colliges* 4), Mazotta (tom. 1 c. 2) Croix (lib. 3 p. 1 n. 591), Elbel (n. 417), Tamburinius (§2 n. 13, and Viva (*l. c.*) that they can be excused either for paucity of the matter, namely if one or another were to cut, or from the necessity of country life, for which it is merely conceded on feast days that they should cut. And the Salamancans concede it with Trullenchus and Pasqualigo (n. 341) not only when the country folk live elsewhere, as Sanchez admits, but even in the same place where the barber lives from a custom already introduced. Viva, Mazotta and Tamburinius (with Fernandez *ibid.*) and Croix (with Diana and Illsung n. 591) excuse them by reason of the loss of notable profit, if otherwise it would be relinquished by so many with a grave loss of profit; with Sporer (n. 55) who universally permits it with Fernandez, Diana, etc., from the custom tolerated nearly everywhere.

We must also note in regard to that custom, what Viva says (art. 2 n. 8), clearly, that to excuse probable custom suffices. It suffices, as the Salamancans say (*de leg.* c. 6 punct. 3 § 2 n. 18, with Salas, Granado, etc.) according to the saying of one outstanding and also modern doctor who advances custom. But Mazotta adverts (*de 3 praec.* c. 2) that in a doubt about custom, *preceptum possidet*, wherein a dispensation must be sought; it is otherwise if it is probable that the custom exists.

291.—"Third, *piety* toward God, whereby works are licit that "proximately (not remotely) consider the worship of God, such "as to ring the bells, process with images or crosses in "supplication. However, to adorn the Church and sweep "Churches, and similar things which do not embrace divine "worship itself, if they are delayed to the feast without reason "then they are considered a venial sin. Filliuci, n. 218, Bonacina "*loc. cit.*."

292.—*Quaeritur I:* would it be licit to sweep the Church on a feast day, bake the hosts, adorn the altars or decorate the Church, to raise floors necessary for a festival or a tomb, or similar things? There are three opinions.

The first opinion with Corrado, and others cited by Diana, says this is illicit *sub gravi*, unless a reasonable cause would excuse it, because these are truly servile; but this is against the common opinion.

The second opinion with Viva (art. 2 n. 10), Suarez, Toledo, Croix, n. 586 and Tamburinius (§2 n. 3) says that it is not servile; but if it is expedient that they be done on the preceding day, it would be venial to transfer to the feast day.

The third opinion holds with sufficient probability that to do these on a feast day are not even *sub levi*, both because it is the common custom, and because this work *per se* runs proximate to divine worship. So think Elbel, n. 420; Salamancans, tr. 23, c. 1, punct. 11 § 4, n. 251, with Diana, Pasqualigo, Leander, etc. But Viva and Tamburinius note that to knowingly prepare a platform on a feast day to see a procession would of itself be a grave sin; but if they were not made the day before, they are licitly made on a feast day and Mazotta holds the same thing (*loc. cit.*).

293.—*Quaeritur II:* Would it be lawful to work on a feast day due to piety alone, without actual necessity, namely to make clothing for the poor, to till the fields of the Church, to carry stones and wood to his building, to whitewash the walls of the Church? Angelus (v. *Feriae*, n. 9, 28 and 32), Tamburinius (*v. Feriae*, n. 18 and 37), the Gloss (*in c. Conquestus de feriis, v. Pietas*), Sa (*v. Fest.*), Villalobos (c. 22, n. 80), Filliuci (tr. 27, n. 156), and likewise, Perez, Sylvius, Palacius, etc. cited by Sanchez (*cons.* lib. 5, cap. 2 dub. 23) affirm this. Still, Sylvius places the limitation provided it were not on Sundays and more solemn feasts, nor to the last exhaustion. They are moved from that which is in c. *Conquestus, de feriis,* judicial matters are excused, "if necessity demands, or piety persuades," therefore they say in like manner that servile works are excused. This reasoning does not seem to be spurned since by the same ecclesiastical law, as above, n. 265, judicial and servile matters are forbidden; but in equal part, where the same reasoning occurs, the same disposition of law follows, as we said from the common opinion in book 1, *On Laws*, n. 106. But others deny this is allowed, except that necessity would urge by act, or at least, unless a license of the Bishop would intervene, since such works are servile in themselves, and only remotely coincide with divine worship. But judicial matters, as above, are not servile of themselves and consequently, are permitted on account of piety. But the precept to worship God and abstain from servile works is of a higher order than works of piety. This second opinion seems to me certainly more probable, not only is it licit to labor when a poor man is gravely needy in act, or (precisely as Roncaglia and the Salamancans add, with the authors cited below) he is so needy that unless one would work on this feast day, he could not provide for his necessity and he were otherwise poor so that he would not be able to pay his workers their wage (Sanchez, *l.c.* n. 3; Palaus, tr. 9 d. *unic.* p. 10 n. 2; Bonacina, p. 3 n. 6 and the Salamancans, *loc. cit.* n. 260 with Suarez, Cajetan, Navarre, etc.). Escobar holds the same thing (*de 3 praec.*) saying it is lawful to build a Church, till its fields, etc., if it were so poor that it would not be able to provide for itself from another source. Tamburinius (*l.c.* with Fagundez) adverts that for this purpose common necessity does not suffice, rather, it is required that a poor man of this sort be known in particular, or there were a grave and certain necessity in some corporate body. By speaking about pious places, the Salamancans so say: "Moreover, because nearly all Churches and monasteries labor in need in these times, so for these, or for hospitals, confraternities, and similar things, man can licitly labor by building temples, harvesting wheat, tilling the fields, etc." (*ibid.* punct. 11 § 4 n. 253). Suarez, del Soto, Palaus, Bonacina, Trullenchus, Cajetan,

Sanchez, etc. So equally Mazotta permits labor to make necessary ornaments for a needy Church.

294.—"Fourth, *charity* towards one's neighbor; whereby "judicial acts for poor orphans, widows and miserable persons "are licit and valid, lest they be weighed down with expenses. "So also can civil cases be roused for country folk in small "towns and if they cannot be present on other days. In like "manner it is lawful to assist the poor and infirm, as well as the "needy. So also to buy and sell from country-folk who are "impeded on other days." Laymann, cap. 2 n. 7; see Diana, t. 1 r. "34.

295—"Fifth, one's own *necessity*, or another's of body or "soul: if it is certain it cannot be omitted without grave "inconvenience or detriment." (St. Thomas generally excuse those who labor to avoid loss of goods in II IIæ q. 122 art. 4). "In "such a matter the following are excused: 1) judgments, which "require speed, e.g. if a thief would run away unless he were "caught here and now; 2) Servants and maidservants compelled "to work by their masters and daring not to refuse: still, it if "would frequently happen, they ought to desert them" (Suarez, Laymann, *loc. cit.*).

296.—Servants, compelled by their master to labor on a feast day, unless it were in contempt of the feast, are excused enough on account of fear of the master's grave indignation, or of grave inconvenience, *e.g.* if they fear lest they might be dismissed and might not be able to find another right away and easily. So think Croix, with Illsung n. 593, Roncaglia, c. 3 q. 5, Elbel, de 3 praec. n. 37, Viva art. 2 n. 9, Salamancans tr. 23, c. 1 punct. 14, § 3 n. 339, with Palaus, Suarez, Azor, Bonacina, Navarre, Sanchez. What if there was no such fear present, then Sanchez (n. 18) and the Salamancans (*ibid.* n. 340) and Roncaglia say more truly against Busembaum that they are held to desert their masters unless they apprenticed or obligated to serve up to a certain time, if they would truly suffer grave loss. The same thing that is said about servants is said about sons or wives that are compelled to labor by their husbands; if they cannot refuse without fear of grave harm or indignation, as Viva and the Salamancans say (*ibid.* with the cited authors and Mazotta).

297.—"3. The same and similar are excused for mending their "garments when it cannot be done on other days."
"4. Poor men, who cannot feed themselves or their "household, working privately without scandal, especially "when many feast days coincide. Bonacina, n. 13." (with "Sanchez, lib. 5 c. 2, dub. 18 n. 15, and the Salamancans, *ibid.* "§ 2. n. 324 with Azor, Suarez, Palaus, etc.)"

298.—"5. Cooks and kitchen servants are excused."
It is certain that it is lawful to cook food, as the doctors teach in common with St. Thomas, II IIæ q. 122 art. 4 ad 4 et 5. (And because it pertains to prepare food, it is also licit to slaughter animals and skin them if it could not suitably be done the day before, as usually happens in great cities; but not in small towns unless it was in the summer time or unless many feasts coincided. Sanchez, *ibid.*, dub. 18 n. 6, with the Salamancans c. 1, n. 326, with Palaus).

It is also licit for bakers to make pastry, at least by custom, as Sanchez (n. 3) and the Salamancans say (*ibid.* n. 327), with del Soto and Trullenchus. But Tamburinius rightly denies it (§2 n. 11) unless they were only preparing it for their own food on the same day, or if it were fitting for public abundance, as he says.

Whether it would be lawful to bake bread for delectation, say to decorate them with frosting, etc. Sanchez and Roncaglia deny it, and the Salamancans adhere to them (*ibid.* n. 331) unless they were (as the Salamancans say) *ad modum victus diuturni*; or unless some special improvised reason for inviting friends were to occur, or unless (Roncaglia adds), such food could not conveniently be made on the preceding day. But Palaus (cited by Tamburinius, n. 9) says these foods, even if they are superfluous and made for delectation, are excused from custom, and Tamburinius rightly thinks it is probable (n. 10) with Fagundez. And Viva agrees (art. 2 num. 6 vers. 2) with Azor and Mazotta (c. 2).

Mazotta and Viva (*ibid.* n. 6) as well as Fagundez, Palaus (cited by Tamburinius, dict. l. et n. 22) permit the gathering of fruit on a feast day, even if it is not necessary for the use of the day so that it might be preserved whole. And this is more easily permitted if there was a danger that they might be taken by others or ruined by the rain, for which reason it is received in use in many places to gather olives, chestnuts and other forest fruits on a feast day. It is also certain that it is lawful to furnish works that are necessary for daily use, such as to make beds, clean the house or clothes, wash kitchen utensils and like things. Elbel, n. 394, with Sporer n. 42, Henno, and the common opinion.

"6. Bakers and butchers and those in similar occupations are "also excused when they live in populous towns and when a "number of feasts coincide." (The Continuator of Tournely, *de 3* "*praec.* art. 1, *Colliges* 4, with Pontas and Juenin, rightly excuse "bakes and men selling their wares if they otherwise could not "sustain themselves and their household, or if they do not labor "they would suffer a grave inconvenience in other things)."

299.—Is it lawful to prepare and bake bread? In regard to bakers, Viva says they are more commonly not excused by the doctors if they could have baked it the day before, and Sanchez says the same thing (d. 18 num. 3) and Bonacina (punct. 3 n. 9) but they excuse them if many feasts coincide or a multitude of buyers or the advantage of the people. Still, the authors excuse them and with probability, even if they sift flour to prepare bread, or grind the wheat (Mazotta, *loc. cit.* and Salamancans tr. 23 c. 1 punct. 14 § 2 n. 328, with Sa, Azor, Pasqualigo, Leander, etc.). The reason is both because there is always some excusing cause present, which Sanchez and Bonacina soon assigned, and because daily bread is more suited for consumption; and otherwise, the least scarcity is enough to stir up the people; then because the custom is present at Rome and I believe it can be said everywhere with Sporer, n. 55.

So also in regard to bakers. But in regard to others, is there is a custom present permitting them to prepare bread? Tamburinius is rightly uncertain (n. 9) unless many feast days were to coincide, or unless the bread that was baked were not suitable enough, or then, unless it were necessary for the use of the day, as I said about pastry makers, because then it is reduced to the preparation for one's own consumption. So also Tamburinius, n. 9 and 11, with Sanchez, Bonacina and Fagundez. On butchers, however, selling meat, see what was said in n. 298.

300.—"7. Surgeons, apothecaries.
"8. Castors of iron and lead, bakers of bricks, limestone, etc.
"and whoever is engaged in work that once it has been started
"it cannot be interrupted without loss."

It is licit to prepare limestone, lead and soap because the heating of such things requires many days; and this can be started at some time on a feast day to avoid grave loss, as Sanchez teaches (n. 21) with del Soto, Palaus, Turllenchus, Navarre, etc. with the Salamancans (*ibid.* §3 n. 341).

It is equally licit to show horses that are making a journey, or those that are making their journey at the crack of dawn, or going out in a field to work when otherwise grave loss would be suffered. This is the common opinion of the authors (Salamancans *ibid.* n. 346, with Sanchez, *loc. cit.* n. 14, del Soto, Trullenchus, Navarre, etc. and Mazotta *dict.* c. 2). This is why their plowshares and tools can equally be mended when it cannot be done otherwise on the following day. So also for those who repair roads and bridges, as Mazotta says (*ibid.*).

"9. Millers are excused (see above, dub. 1 n. 277) as well as "ship captains depending upon the winds.
"10. Fisherman of herring and tuna, etc., who can only do it "at a certain time of the year."

301.—*Quaeritur I:* Would an occasion for seeking great profit excuse one from servile works exercised on a feast day? There are two probable opinions.

The first affirms it, and there are many authors that uphold it (Cajetan, *Summ. v. Festor. violatio*, Angel, *v. Feria* n. 34, Armilla *v. Festum*, n. 20, Holzm. tom. 1 n. 546, *v. Quarta*; Sanchez, *Cons.* lib. 5 c. 2, dub. 19, with Palaus, Rosell., an Alcoz. p. Zachar. l. 3 p. 1 num. 588; Renzi *e III praec.* cap. 3 q. 13; Sporer *e 3 praec.* c. 4 n. 51; Mazotta, c. 2; Elbel n. 402; Bonacina, p. 3 n. 15; Viva art. 2 n. 9 in fin.; Tamburinius, c. 3 § 2 n. 80, with Diana, Filliuci, Sayr and others cited by the Salamancans, *ibid.* n. 342). The reason is, because the loss of great profit (that is to say an extraordinary one, not merely a daily wage) is the same as to suffer a great loss; thus, in *c. Licet de feriis*, Alexander III is related to have dispensed so that men could fish for herring on Sundays and other feast days with the exception of more solemn days (but not under mortal sin, as Sanchez notes, n. 4). And Busembaum, Gobat, Cajetan, Navarre (cited by Sanchez) rightly extend this to fishing for tuna.

The second opinion denies it, and this is held by Roncaglia (c. 3 q. 5 r. 11) and the Salamancans *ibid.* n. 343, with Suarez, Reginald., Palaus, Abulensis, etc., and it denies that it is excuses them because, as they say, to lose a profit is not the same thing as to suffer a loss. But the first opinion seems more probable, since in common those who support themselves by their labor have rare occasions to acquire such a great profit, and they think they have suffered a great loss when they lose profit; for they amount to the same thing, to lose something and to be forbidden to acquire, which means it cannot be acquired any further. For as Sporer (*dict.* n. 51) says in *C. unic. de sent.* letting go of a great profit is compared to a great loss. At least in such a circumstance it seems it must be said that the precept of the feast, insofar as it is human, does not oblige when there is such a loss, as Tamburinius says. Still, Roncaglia, who disagrees, does not refuse to excuse those who hope for a great profit, if it is so great that a man suffering many necessities could provide for himself and his own from it, with Suarez, Reginald, from Filliuci.

Tamburinius (l. 4 cap. 2 § 2 n. 7) and Mazotta (*de 3 praec.* cap. 3 §2 against the Salamancans, tr. 23 c. 1 punct. 14 § 3 n. 345) say with probability that the same reasoning also excuses from hearing Mass due to the loss of a notable profit (see below, *dubium* 5, n. 532). But the Salamancans rightly rebuke what Tamburinius still reckons probable (cap. 1 § 3 n. 9, and Viva agrees with him, q. 4 a. 3 n. 12) that one can begin a journey on Saturday to hunt in a far off forest, although he could not hear Mass there on Sunday; for commonly (as Tamburinius says) those on a journey are excused as well as purveyors of wares, who go out on a journey the day before the feast. Those who will go out to hunt on Thursday are commonly excused (with Viva, *ibid.*, Sanchez, Marchant and Palaus).

302.—*Quaeritur II:* Would the reasoning of leisurely hunting excuse?

The first with Suarez, Comitolus (*Respons.*, lib. 4 qu. 58 num. 6, v. f, and others cited by Croix, in n. 586), altogether denies it, because a pious end of leisurely hunting cannot cause it to not be a servile work; but this reasoning is not persuasive because the cause, when it is just, although it would not change the nature of the work, nevertheless excuses it.

Hence, the *second opinion*, which Sa and Sylvius hold (and that Laymann follows in l. 4 tr. 7 c. 4 n. 2 as well as Mazotta with Pellizarius, and Burghaber, cited by Croix), excuses those who, unless they will work during an occasion of leisure, live in a probable danger of sinning. For if, as they say, danger of temporal loss excuses, how much more ought spiritual danger excuse? Tamburinius (cap. 3 § 9 n. 18), Viva (art. 2 n. 10), Sanchez (dist. 15 n. 13) Croix (d. n. 586), Zaccaria (l. 3 p. 1 n. 586), admit this opinion only in the case in which temptation presses on, which otherwise cannot be conquered except by laboring. And so also Laymann truly speaks, who consequently says with Viva and Sporer (n. 54) that such a necessity to labor rarely happens and this is the *third opinion*, which I gladly subscribe to myself.

303.—"11. Men that restore fountains, bridges, public roads "and similar things which do not suffer delay, are excused.
"12. Patchers in necessary works, such as ropes, marriages, "etc., if it cannot otherwise be done that they make satisfaction "[of their jobs]."

For patchers who cannot sow garments on non-feast days, it is lawful for them to complete them on feast days when necessity urges, *e.g.* funerals and weddings and similar things, say (as the Salamancans assert), if a guest lacked decent dress, since decency of state excuses them (Salamancans *loc. cit.* n. 337, with Laymann, c. 2 n. 2, Trullenchus, Diana, Pasqualigo.). Viva (a. 2, n. 7), Mazotta (c. 2), Sporer (n. 50), and Croix (n. 562, with Laymann and Diana) also excuse them, if others are waiting to use the promised clothes; but it must be understood (as Croix rightly says) if patchers would otherwise suffer a grave inconvenience. The Salamancans say the same thing (*ibid.*) about cobblers with Viva (n. 12) and Mazotta who excuse those making new shoes when it has been introduced from custom.

"13. Likewise, farmers, to avoid loss, working in rural areas, "so that if they must gather their crop or straw on account of "rain. Bonacina, n. 13, Filliuci n. 211." (Croix n. 558).

"14. Next, merchants are also excused, who sell certain "things when they have closed their shops, seeing that they "could presuppose that these are necessary things to buyers and "they could not suitably buy them at another time." (See above, n. 286). "On the aforesaid, see Suarez, Filliuci, Laymann, "Bonacina, *ll. cc.*"

304.—"Sixth, *utility* that is necessary not simply but for "common joy or splendor; for it is lawful to work on the arrival "or birth of a prince so that theaters, fires, garments, etc. would "be completed. Although, Suarez wisely advises that to furnish "the labor in this case one ought to seek the permission of their "pastors. See Bonacina."

It is certain that it is licit on account of a public cause as well as a genuine necessity or public joy, say, due to a victory, the arrival or birth of a prince, etc., to make garments, theaters and similar things. The authors extend this so that it can be done also on account of putting on a play (Sanchez, dub. 18 n. 27, Toledo, and Trullenchus, Pasqualigo, cited by the Salamancans tr. 23 c. 1 punct. 14 § 3 n. 347), who from the foregoing extend it also to the stirring up of bulls, provided that such things could not be suitably done on a non-feast day. The reason is, because such signs of joy are morally necessary to the state, and therefore are permitted from custom. Probable necessity suffices for all these things, as Viva notes, or probable custom. So Mazzota equally permits theaters to be set up, the garments of servants, etc. for the sake of weddings if they cannot be completed on the day before (d. c. 2).

305.—"The seventh likewise excuses, at least from grave sin, "the *paucity* of the work, or time. This is why it does not seem "grave to work for one hour, as Suarez holds (l. 2 *de fest.* c. 32), "especially as Laymann notes, if the labor were not too servile "and not tiring to the body. Nay more, it seems harsh to "condemn it as a mortal sin, if anyone were to expend two or "three hours. See Filliuci, tr. 27, c. 1 q. 1 n. 105."

Quaeritur I: Is there grave matter in this? Some canonists (cited by Suarez), as the Salamancans say (*loc. cit.* § 1 n. 312) posit for grave matter a third of the day; but this opinion is commonly rejected. On the other hand, others very rigorously, as Azor, Bonacina, and Reginald (cited by Croix, n. 594) place one hour and Suarez and Palaus especially impugn them, as Busembaum notes with Laymann, if the labor were not too tiring. Others posit for grave matter two hours, such as Roncaglia (c. 3 q. 5 r. 5) with Sanchez, Trullenchus and the Salamancans (*ibid.* n. 313), with Palaus, Elbel (n. 395), Holzmann n. 545. And Sporer, as well as Mazotta (with March.) call this the common opinion. Henno thinks the same thing), cited by the Continuator of Tourney (*de 3 Dec.* praec. art. 1, concl. 1, in fine, *quaeres*), if the labor were very servile, such as to cut stones, dig holes, etc. In other matters he requires three hours. In other labors, however, he requires three hours. But others, speaking generally, require for grave matter (and not improbably), at least two, and somewhat more than two hours, as Viva asserts with the common opinion, as well as Diana, Granado, Henriquez, Bassaeus, Leander, Valentia, Illsung, cited by the Salamancans (*ibid.*, n. 312 in fin) and Croix, d. l. with Tamburinius cap. 3 § 2 n. 1, who says this is the opinion received in our time. Others, such as Marchant, and Gobat (cited by Croix) require three hours,[13] which Viva and Mazotta also admit, if some sort of necessity or other cause would occur, only by itself not sufficing to excuse. Busembaum equally, with Filliuci, says it is harsh to condemn the labor of two or three hours as a mortal sin.

---

[13] Translator's note: St. Alphonus says in *Homo Apostolicus*, tr. 6 n. 25, that his opinion is too lax.

Croix consents (lib. 3 p. 1 n. 594) and concludes that now the opinion is more common and probable that it is not a mortal sin unless one would labor more than two hours, say two and a half.

306.—*Quaeritur II:* Would one sin gravely who commanded six servants to labor for an hour? Coninck (*Clypeus,* tom. 3 art. 5) affirms, and Arsdekin (tom. 2, part. 2, tr. 5 cap. 3 § 1, qu. 4) does not deny it, whose opinion Croix says is more probable (c. 581) in the case in which the master commands that they labor successively, if it was at the same time, all agree with Sanchez, Bonacina, Trullenchus, etc., (*ibid.* n. 580) that it is not a mortal sin. Moreover, there is an opinion that is more probable and by far more common, that in each case it is not a mortal sin (Viva, art. 2 n. 11, with Bonacina, Sanchez *dec.* l. 1, c. 4 n. 12, Roncaglia, c. 3 q. 5, *in fine*; and the Salamancans, *ibid.* n. 317 with Trullenchus, Pasqualigo). The reason is, because the works of servants do not unite into one. Moreover, the master cannot sin more than these servants who only sin venially in this, since each one only fails lightly in his obligation to God. Otherwise, it would be certain, if the master were to command one servant to labor many times on a feast day that it even [arises] to grave matter.

307.—"But in public courts, and in judicial matters, the "quantity of matter is not from the quantity of time, but the "quality of the work taken up, as Escobar adverts (*E.* 5. c. 3 n. "14, from Palaus, lib. 1 tract. 9 d. 2 p. 3 n. 4). So it is a grave sin "to assert the sale of a thing of great importance, with great "solemnity, even if it were done in a short time. Understand "that (according to the aforesaid), unless custom or necessity "were to excuse it." (See what was said in n. 286, at the end).

DUBIUM III
What works are commanded on feast days?

308. *How is the hearing of the Sermon and Mass commanded on feast days? And for parish priests to preach?* Review n. 269.

TREATISE III: THE THIRD AND FOURTH PRECEPTS CH. I   325

309. *Would reciting the office during Mass suffice? etc. Would serving at Mass suffice?*
310. *What omission would be grave in hearing Mass?*
311. *Is it lawful to hear two halves of the Mass in succession?*
312. *From what place can one hear Mass?*
313. *Whether internal attention is required to hear Mass?*
314. *Whether confessing sins during Mass satisfies the precept?*
315. *Would suffering spiritual experiences satisfy the precept?*
316. *Would sleeping satisfy the precept?*
317. *Would talking, turning oneself, or putting one's shoes on, or walking or gathering alms, singing etc. satisfy the precept?*
318. *In what Church should Mass be heard?*
319. *Who makes satisfaction in hearing Mass in private oratories? Would those hearing Mass on the beach or in army camps satisfy the precept?*

308.—"*Resp.* It is commanded: 1) Hearing the sermon, but "not under pain of mortal sin, except insofar as anyone is held "to learn what is necessary for salvation. See the Council of "Trent, sess. 24, cap. 4 *de reform.*, Filliuci, c. 8, Bonacina, t. 1 d. 5, "qu. 1, p. 2, n. 27; Suarez, etc. I said, *except insofar as,* etc., "because more unlearned men, being ignorant especially of the "mysteries of faith, especially those which they are held to "know under pain of mortal sin, as was said above (book 3, tr. 1 "c. 1), are held by the law of charity under grave sin to be "present for the sermon (if they cannot conveniently learn them "otherwise), or better yet, catechism. Bonacina (d. 2 *in praec.* 2. "n. 28), adding in that case the sermon of the Mass is to be "preferred. Trullenchus l. 1 c. 1 d. 4 n. 12, Fagundez, etc." (But "when Bishops are held to preach, see what was said in 269).

"2) It is commanded by a special precept, obliging under "mortal sin, to hear Mass, this is to be present at it by moral and "human assistance, or presence. This is the common opinion "from *cap. Omnes fideles,* and from *c. Missas, de consecrat.* dist. 1 "against Angelus and Rosella, who said to neglect it once or "again is venial." (Besides, that is a condemned proposition, n.

"52, of Innocent XI). "This precept obliges all baptized that have "the use of reason on all feasts; but not infants and the insane, "or catechumens. The reason for the first part is, because it is "universal. The reason for the second is that they cannot have "human assistance. The reason of the third is because they are "not subjects of the Church. Cardinal de Lugo, d. 22, sect. 1 and "2, from Navarre, Sanchez, and Coninck."

Wherefore, the following cases are resolved:

"1. There is no obligation to hear a sermon in one's own "parish: both because many doctors acknowledge that nothing "is commanded on this matter, seeing that the Council of Trent "in session 24, c. 4, *de ref.* says "one is held where it can be "conveniently done"; and because, if there was some obligation "it is set aside by the privilege of regulars and the general "contrary custom. Suarez (*de rel.* l. 2, cap. 16, Azor, Navarre, "Cenedo, Zerola, p. 1 *verb. Praed.*, Trullenchus, l. 2 c. 1 d. 4. See "Barbosa, in *Trid. sess. 24, c. 4*). Nay more, the Dominicans and "Franciscans, and those who share in their privileges, preaching "in their Churches in every season of the year, can concede to "those listening to them an indulgence of 18 years and 220 days "in the name of the Pope. Diana, p. 4 t. 4 r. 22, from Rodriquez, "etc." (See what was said above in n. 269, and what is going to be said by Busembaum in n. 323).

"2. There is no obligation to hear Mass on Maundy "Thursday, Good Friday and Holy Saturday in Great Week, nor "on the days of Rogation. Azor, Henriquez, Suarez, d. 88 sect. 5."

"3. On Christmas you are only held to hear one Mass. "Navarre, Suarez, Filliuci.

309.—"4. One satisfies the precept who recites during Mass "the Canonical hours (when he is under obligation), or a "penance enjoined in confession, as Cajetan, Sylvius, Angelus, "and Armilla teach against Suarez, Sa, Rodriguez, Filliuci, etc. "The reason is, because those two precepts can be satisfied at once." (Sporer, c. 4 n. 16, Elbel, n. 359, the Salamancans, tr. 5 *de* "*Sacrif. Missae*, c. 6, punct. 2 n. 20 teach the same with Palaus, "Bonacina, Sanchez, and the most common opinion). "See what "was said above in book 1, n. 164. Likewise, on one who "confesses during Mass, Reginald (l. 19 n. 14) affirms it, "provided that he had the intention to hear Mas. But Suarez (d. "88, sect. 6), Azor (c. 7 q. 6), Gordon (lib. 6, qu. 7 n. 13), Cardinal "de Lugo (*l. c.*) deny it, if they could delay the confession, and "the necessity of precept of confession were not present. "Bonacina says the same thing (*disp.* 4, last article, p. 1). On the "other hand, he excuses the practice to the contrary of some, "either on account of the necessity to communicate, or the "intention to hear another Mass, or even on account of good "faith." (See below, n. 314).

"5. They also satisfy the precept who serve Mass if they "leave but are going to offer necessary things, *e.g.* the wine, the "host, incense, etc., because seeing that these are ordered to the "office, they are not thought to be absent, provided they do not "leave the Church, or at least not for a long time. See Bonacina." "(So also *de Lugo*, disp. 22, sect. 1, n. 24, and the Salamancans, "*ibid.*, n. 21, with Sa, Navarre, Sylvius, Dicastillus, etc. And so it "must be held with Elbel, num. 556, Palaus, and Bonacina, if it is "for a short time, or they are not gone from the Church against "Dicastillus, Leander, and Diana, cited by Salamancans *dict.* n. "21).

310.—"6. One sins that does not hear the whole Mass; and "indeed venially if they omit a small part, mortally if they omit "a notable part, *e.g.* the middle or third part. Still, Laymann, and "others think it harsh to condemn someone for mortal sin who "is present from the offertory even to the end. And add, that "commonly one is excused from mortal sin who hears from the "beginning of the Epistle, or, according to others, from the

"Gospel even to the end; or from the beginning even to "communion.[14] See Bonacina, l. 1 d. 4 q. ult., Cardinal de Lugo, "d. 22, sect. 1 n. 3."

Quaeritur I: Would the omission in hearing Mass be a grave sin? There are different opinions.

The first says it is grave to omit from the beginning even to the epistle exclusive; so think Toledo, Bonacina, Navarre, and Torrianus cited by Croix, l. 3 p. 1 n. 665.

The second, says it is grave if it is omitted inclusively even to the epistle, so Viva holds (q. 9 art. 3 n. 2) as well as Croix and the Salamancans (*de Miss. Sacrif.* c. 6 punct. 1 n. 2) with del Soto, Suarez, Tabienus, Azor, Fagundez, Concina, Henriquez, Dicastillus, etc., with the more common opinion, as the Salamancans assert.

The third opinion says it is not grave if it is omitted from the beginning even to the Gospel inclusive, provided that it is heard even to the last Gospel. So think Dicastillus, Palaus, de Lugo, Tambienus Sa, cited by Salamancans *ibid.* and Croix. And Holzman thinks this is probable (*de 3 praec.* n. 525), as well as Elbel (n. 258), the Salamancans, *loc. cit.*, Suarez, Bonacina, Laymann, Henriquez, Rodriguez, etc. Even if the *Credo* were omitted, as de Lugo, Henriquez, and Burghdahl cited by Croix (*loc. cit.*) because the *Credo* is not a regular part. Hence they say one cannot sin gravely who comes before the Offertory, from which, as Isidore witnesses, formerly began the Mass. The second opinion seems more probable to me, but who would deny this last (as the Salamancans rightly say) to be probable *in re,* which depends on the estimation of men, since it is supported by so many and so great authors?

---

[14] Translator's note: In this context the communion of the priest is meant, not of the faithful. The communion of the faithful did not take place during Mass apart from Maundy Thursday and Corpus Christi until the reign of St. Pius X where it was moved into Mass after the priest's communion as a rule.

Moreover, were someone to omit everything after communion, he would not sin gravely and this is the common opinion with Croix, n. 666. Nor would it be if someone were to omit everything before the epistle together with everything after communion, as Suarez, Illsung, Fagundez, cited by Croix. What if one were also to omit the epistle? Bauny and Llamas also excuse it, but Palaus, Suarez and Concina, as well as the more common opinion cited by Croix oppose them. Moreover, to omit the offertory whether before or after the consecration is not grave, as Pasqualigo says with Croix, n. 667.

In regard to the Canon, however, it is certain that the least omission is grave. This is because of the omission of the consecration, together with communion (Salamancans tr. et punct. cit. n. 3; Croix d. n. 667). Likewise, if there were an omission from the consecration even to the *Pater noster* exclusive. (Salamancans, *ibid.*, Croix, l. 3 p. 1 n. 667; Leander and others cited by Croix). But there is an uncertainty as to whether to omit only the communion, or the consecration would be grave? Authors from the more common opinion uphold this (Reginald, Bonacina, Concina, Aversa etc., with Croix, *ibid.* Roncaglia, c. 2 q. 1, Palaus, *de Euch.* p. 16 n. 6, Holzman c. 1 n. 52, Salamancans *ibid.* n. 4). Nay more, Pasqualigo says it is grave even if one consecration were omitted, because the sacrifice more probably consists in the consecration. Still, others, such as de Lugo (*de Euch.* d. 22, n. 4), Tamburinius (l. 6 c. 2 § 1 n. 3), Diana (p. 5 t. 13 r. 61), Escobar (d. 17, *num.* 126) excuse it from grave sin, even if the whole consecration were omitted; seeing that it is not certain enough whether the essence of the sacrifice were truly in communion or the consecration; and Elbel (n. 358) with Suarez, Hurtad, Fagundez, Burghaber, etc. thinks it probable (and Sporer, Viva, Laymann and Mazotta very much adhere to this). *The first opinion* seems more probable because (as the Salamancans and Holzman say), although it is not certain whether the essence of the sacrifice consists in the consecration, or communion, nevertheless it is certain that both pertain to the substantial integrity of the Mass. But since, on the other hand, it is not certain whether the Church commands the faithful under grave sin to be present at both parts, consequently, the second opinion does not seem improbable. Yet on Good Friday there is no obligation to hear Mass, if the feast of the Annunciation falls on it, as Mazotta says (*de 3 praec.* c. 3 §1) with the common opinion, against Vasquez.

Quaeritur II: Whether one who comes before the consecration that could not also hear another Mass, is held to hear at least that part? Sancius denies it, but it must altogether be upheld with Sanchez (*dec.* l. 1 c. 19 n. 6), the Salamancans (*de Sacrif. miss.* c. 1 punct. 1 n. 13) with de Lugo, Suarez and the common opinion, because these remain in which the sacrifice consists. But if he were to come after the consecration, then Henriquez and others (cited by Salamancans) say he is not held to hear the rest, according to what is going to be said in book 6 *On the Sacrifice of the Mass*, n. 305, where we will say that it is exceedingly probable that the essence of the sacrifice consists only in the consecration of each species. But the Continuator of Tourney (*de 3 Decal. praec.* art. 2 sect. 1 *Colliges* 3), says that the obligation of Mass is considered in respect to the nature of the Office, which should be recited in part if the whole cannot. But this is not persuasive, because prayer is commanded in the Office, which is why a man that cannot satisfy the whole prayer is held to the part which he can; but where the essence of the Mass fails, the obligation altogether ceases since the precept is on hearing Mass, but not on hearing that part which is not Mass. Moreover, this affirmative opinion is very probable and held in practice (as Fr. Zaccaria says, l. 3 p. 1 n. 668), for another reason, namely, a notable part of the sacred ceremony commanded by the Church can be heard.

Quaeritur III: Whether omitting a minor part of the Mass, one is held to supply if he can? Filliuci denies it, because if he omits with cause, then he did not sin; if without cause, then he already

TREATISE III: THE THIRD AND FOURTH PRECEPTS CH. I   331

committed a venial sin. But the Salamancans (*ibid.* n. 15, with Leander) more probably say the opposite, because, when one can, he is held to hear the whole Mass.

311.—"7. He does not sin, at least not mortally, who hears "from two priests two half Masses (Navarre, c. 21, Sa, del Soto, "Henriquez, Diana, tr. 1 tr. 3 r. 18, Bonacina, d. 4 q. ult. punct. "11 n. 13, Hurtad, against Suarez, Concina, Fagundez). The "reason is, because he hears a whole Mass. This is why it is "probable" (*in his time, but today it is improbable on account of proposition 53 condemned by Innocent XI*), "even if they are heard "together, as Bonacina (*l.c.*) Hurtad and Diana argue, against "Reginald, Concina, Cardinal de Lugo, etc., whose opinion "seems more probable."

Quaeritur: So, would a man hearing two halves of the Mass in succession from two different priests satisfy the precept? We must preface the discussion with Proposition 53 condemned by Pope Innocent XI, which said: "He satisfies the precept of the Church to hear Mass who hears two parts, or even four at the same time celebrated by different priests." But the doubt is, can they be heard in succession?

The first opinion, which several authors hold, affirms that he satisfies the precept, even if he were to hear two half parts of the Mass in reverse order, and even with the passage of some time, namely of an hour, as Mazotta thinks (Navarre, c. 22 n. 2, Sa, *v. Missae auditio*, n. 2, Laymann, c. 3 in fine, Cabassutius, t. 1 l. 2 c. 32, n. 5, P. Zaccaria l. 3 p. 1 n. 611, Marchant, tr. 4 tit. 2 qu. 1 d. 2, likewise del Soto, Bonacina, Palaus, etc., cited by the Salamancans in *de Sacr. miss.*, c. 6 n. 7, Cardenas cited by Croix in l. 3 p. 1 n. 611, and the Salamancans and Croix, *ll.cc.* think it is probable, likewise Viva, *de 3 praec.* quaest. 9 art. 3 n. 1, with Diana, Pasqualigo and Tamburinius, *de 3 praec.* cap. 2 num. 10, Mazotta c. 3 § 1). The reason for this opinion is both because hearing is then well completed to one whole Mass, if not physically then at least morally, and because seeing that Christ is the principal celebrant offering Mass, now those two parts are united into one; then, because these two halves, although they do not suffice for the unity of the sacrifice, still suffice for the unity obedience commanded by the Church, since assistance is furnished to those parts comprising the sacrifice. —We say this opinion is not probable enough.

Moreover, if someone were to hear Mass from one priest even to the consecration exclusive, and from the other from the consecration to the end, we think it probable. But if he were to hear from one even to the consecration inclusive, and from the other even to the end, we think the *second opinion* is more probable, which is that it does not satisfy, as other authors hold (Suarez, *de festis*, sect. 2, Continuator of Tournely, *de 3 Decal.* praec. art. 2 sect. 1 coll. 5; Sporer *de 3 praecep.* c. 4 n. 23; Tamburinius, d. n. 10, de Lugo disp. 22 n. 8, with Azor and Coninck). The reason is most especially, because the Church prescribes one to hear and assist at Mass which is one whole sacrifice; but just as that Mass is not called one sacrifice, which is celebrated by one priest even to the consecration, and by another even to the end, so also one should not be said to assist at one sacrifice, because he hears two halves of the Mass from different priests.

It is also not opposed to say 1) as Viva says, that if the Mass were said by one priest, and he died, if it were completed by another it is called one sacrifice, for we respond then that truly one sacrifice is completed, but the matter is otherwise in regard to our case, where two half parts hardly unite to make one. It is not opposed: 2) To say with Croix, that since Christ is the principal one offering it, one sacrifice is confected from those two parts; we answer that although Christ is the one offering in those two Masses as one celebrant, still, because then Christ is offered twice, therefore one sacrifice is not confected, but truly there are two different sacrifices which someone assisting at half of each, and a man cannot be said to have assisted at one sacrifice, but two imperfect sacrifices. Moreover, all agree and say that someone that without a just cause would hear two Masses in this way, could in no way be excused at least from venial sin, as the Salamancans, Viva and others say in common.

312.—"8. A man does not satisfy the precept who sleeps "during Mass, paints or teaches" (see below, n. 316), "nor "someone who is behind a wall or another thing, in such a place "from where nothing can be seen, heard or be known, which "were it to happen then one is not reckoned to have been "morally present.

"Nevertheless, the following satisfy the precept: the deaf, "blind and anyone that is present in such a way that he could "gather from external signs what the celebrant is doing when "the nature of the place is considered (although he might be "behind a door or pillar or in a window or far from the Church, "even if *per accidens* he heard nothing, saw nothing, or "understood nothing), and he is part of the multitude by his "moral union, which is called "*praesens*", and is in sight of the "altar. Bonacina, *l.c.*"

De Lugo, Reginald, Dicastillus, Leander, Gordon (cited by the Salamancans, *de Sacr.* missae, c. 6 punct. 2 n. 23), teach the same thing which Busembaum asserts. For it suffices to hear Mass in choir behind the altar, or though a window through which one can see into the Church, even if he cannot catch sight of the priest, provided that assisting through others he could know what is done. So thinks Croix, n. 541, and Mazotta, *l.c.* who adds that one can rightly hear Mass behind the altar, even behind a wall or pillar, provided that in his assistance he were united to the other people hearing Mass. And still, from a place outside the Church, if he has been joined to the multitude extending even to the altar; as Croix (n. 642) and Elbel (n. 334) also admit with the common opinion. Moreover, Mazotta says he does not satisfy who is in a great basilica in some chapel, and Mass were offered at a very distant altar, but this does not seem probable if he could rightly look upon the celebrant and did what everyone who is present in the Church does, although he were far away from the altar, he would sufficiently furnish moral assistance, as Sporer rightly says (*de 3 praec.* c. 4 n. 8).

Now, could a man hear Mass from his house if it were across the road and he could look upon the altar? Sporer (n. 9 and 211), de Lugo, Dicastillus, Gobat, etc. with Croix, n. 643) affirm this. Mazotta (*l.c.*) and Elbel (n. 355, with Escobar and many others) admit that it is not improbable if the distance were small, because he now assists enough morally. And the Continuator of Tourely (*loc. cit.*, concl. 2, num. 3) does not dissent. Moreover, Cardinal de Lugo and Escobar do not oppose a distance of 30 paces. But Tamburinius and Gobat (cited by Croix) do not admit it.

313.—"9. A man hearing Mass ought to be attentive, at least "virtually even in a confused state, so that he might know in "some way what is done. Hence, if anyone is attentive here, but "converses later, that nevertheless he could always know what "is happening, although he would sin from irreverence, still, it "must not be condemned as a mortal sin. Moreover, Concina (3. "p. q. 83, with Sylvius, Rosella and Med.) teaches that one "satisfies the precept who is voluntarily distracted through the "whole Mass, provided he were actually present at it and "assisted with external reverence. Laymann teaches that this is "probable (against Suarez, Bonacina and others). See Concina, "*l.c.* and Cardinal de Lugo, n. 26 and 27. For much more on this "whole matter, see above in book 1, n. 163 and 165."

In regard to due attention at Mass:

Quaeritur I: Is internal attention also required to satisfy the precept of Mass? There are two opinions on the matter.

The first denies it, because the Church does not command interior acts; thus, it suffices to assist from an external moral attention, so that we can witness what happens (De Lugo, *de Euchar.* d. 22 s. 2 n. 71, and Concina, Dicastillus Pellizarius, Henriquez, Sylvius, Medina, Hurtad and many others cited by the Salamancans *de Sacr. Miss.* c. 6 punct. 4 n. 38, and Laymann, Lessius, Mazotta, c. 3 § 1, Zachar. l. 3 p. 1 n. 658, with the common opinion as he asserts as well as Sporer n. 18, who calls it probable.

Nevertheless, *the second opinion* is more common and probable, which St. Thomas holds in 4 d. 15 q. 4 art. 2 qu. 4; Elbel, n. 335, Sporer n. 14, Laymann, Bonacina, Diana and others with the Salamancans (*loc. cit.* 6, n. 39) uphold that internal attention is required because the Church, although it does not directly command internal acts, still it can do so indirectly. Furthermore, according to this opinion virtual attention, namely for someone to have the intention to be attentive from the beginning and not change it suffices to make satisfaction, as in the Office (as the Salamancans say, *ibid.* n. 41, with Cajetan, del Soto, Suarez, Navarre, *l.c.*, n. 10). If later he were distracted, even advertently, but he did not notice that he is distracted from the Mass or from the Office, he also makes satisfaction, because he, although voluntarily distracting himself, still, is not voluntarily distracted from Mass. So the Salamancans (*ibid.* n. 42, with Cajetan, del Soto, Suarez, Navarre, and Sanchez, with a great many others. Moreover, sufficient attention at Mass is twofold: 1) To the words and actions of the celebrant, with a mind to worship God; 2) To the mysteries, or to God, namely to contemplate his attributes, love, etc., provided that one is attentive to the more principal parts of the Mass, and especially the consecration and [priest's] communion. But after the fact, as Elbel wisely adverts (with

Tamburinius and Sporer, n. 16) that no man should be anxious on account of a scruple for not having furnished this attention, because it suffices to have had a general intention to worship God.

Moreover, the first opinion, which Croix calls more probable after considering the reasoning (l. 4 n. 1341), as well as common (l. 3 p. 1 n. 658) cannot be denied to be probable enough according to what will be said on the *Canonical Hours*, in book 5 n. 177. And from the foregoing, in regard to hearing Mass, it suffices to offer moral assistance, as the cited authors say (with Renzi, *de 3 praec.* c. 3, q. 5), so that prayer is not expressly required. At least (I say), favoring the authority of so many authorities that uphold this opinion, the law of the Church (taken up by the contrary authors) seems doubtful enough, which also obliges those hearing Mass to both internal attention and prayer, since many serious authorities, such as Lessius, Suarez, Medina, etc. teach that it is not necessary to pray in order to hear Mass, but only to intend to worship God. Hence Croix (l. 6 p. 2 n. 1740) places the contrary among the rigid opinions, dangerous in practice due to the danger of the scruples that those opinions are liable to cause. Nevertheless, it is understood unless the distraction were of the kind that a man could in no way attend to Mass, as he notes in l. 3 p. 1 num. 659.

314.—*Quaeritur II:* Would someone satisfy the precept, who goes to confession during Mass? *Resp.* He would not, following the common opinion (Cont. Tournely, *de 3 Dec. praec.* art. 2 sect. 1 concl. 2, with Tabienus, and Pontas, the Salamancans, *de Sacr. Missae* c. 6 punct. 4 n. 46; Tamburinius, *de 1 praec.* c. 5 n. 23; Escobar, c. 9 n. 183, Bonacina, *de Eucharistia*, q. ult. p. 11 n. 26, who changed his mind from the contrary opinion, Holzman *de 3 praec.* c. 1 n. 527, and he calls the opposite improbable). Likewise, among others, de Lugo (*de Eucharistia*, d. 22 n. 22) teaches that this, our opinion, must altogether be held. Furthermore, they make different arguments. Bonacina and Bassaeus reject it because the man would not pray, but this is opposed to what Suarez, Lessius, Medina and Gobat teach, as we already said, namely that it would suffice to hear Mass by worshiping God, for such worship it is not absolutely necessary. Tamburinius, Dicastillus, Pasqualigo, etc. say it better, because external attention is not furnished, while one makes confession then he is present as a guilty man, and not as one offering sacrifice with the priest.

Now, the *second opinion* affirms that the man would satisfy the precept if, while confessing his sins, he would at the same time attend to Mass in some way (Palaus, tr. 22 punct. 16 n. 4, with Reginald, and Molfesio, Gobat, tr. 5 n. 258, Lessius, although he requires that at least a good part of Mass be heard before confession; Cons. *mor. v. Missa*, cas. 2, likewise Hurtius, *de resid.* p. 1 r. 8 n. 26 and Croix calls it probable, l. 3 p. 1 n. 655, Zaccaria l. 3 p. 1 n. 655 and Elbel, *de 3 praec.* n. 345 with Pichler and Pellizarius). The reason is, because such a man would indeed assist morally while, by the pious action of confession he would sufficiently worship God directly. Likewise, (Gobat and Elbel say), confession made to a priest is as if it were made to Christ; who will deny that confessing one's sins to Christ does not satisfy Mass? And Elbel (n. 342), Zaccaria n. 656 (which he asserts is the common opinion) and Palaus as well as Gobat (cited by Croix, n. 656) say the same thing about the priest hearing confessions. This *second opinion* does not seem altogether destitute of probability, and I myself once thought it was probable; but because later I observed that it was rejected by a number of serious authorities, I no longer dare to say it is probable. Furthermore, Croix absolutely holds it (*l.c.* with Lessius) and consults in a case in which the servants are obligated to Mass, who could not confess otherwise, for then (as he says) it is at least presumed that the Church would consent. See what is going to be said in n. 332. But the common opinion is that a man who makes an examination of his conscience during Mass satisfies the precept, just as one who reads a spiritual book unless he was reading sacred history with a mind to learn style (Suarez, Croix, n. 654, etc.). Just as the celebrant can also hear someone else's Mass, as Croix (n. 657), Zaccaria (n. 657) and Sporer (n. 16), because while he celebrates he is now praying.

315.—*Quaeritur III:* Would one satisfy the precept who, while he hears Mass, undergoes an ecstasy? Some authors deny it (de Lugo, Turrianus, Leander, cited by the Salamancans and de Lugo *de Eucharistia*, d. 22 n. 19, likewise Torre, c. 1 n. 205). This is because, while alienated from the use of his senses he might not assist with a human and moral presence. But the Salamancans (ex. n. 206), with Suarez, Trullenchus, Ledesma and others because then his attention is on God, which is more perfect than that given by others, as the authorities commonly teach with St. Thomas Aquinas (II IIæ q. 83 n. 13). Both are probable. But the second is more probable, with the Continuator of Tournely, *de 3 Decal. praecepto*, art. 2 sect. 1 concl. 2, because in an ecstasy one does not lose free will as St. Thomas says (I IIæ q. 113 art. 3 ad 2).

316.—*Quaeritur IV:* Would one that is asleep during Mass or the recitation of the Divine Office satisfy the precept? It is answered with Sanchez (*Cons.* lib. 7 c. 2 d. 33), Navarre and the Salamancans (tr. 5 c. 6 punct. 4 n. 48), that he would satisfy, or at least not sin gravely if after due intention to hear Mass, or recite the hours with that attention, whereby he at least knows that he is not omitting to hear or say any word, although when he is disturbed from sleep he does not attend to the meaning.

317.—*Quaeritur V:* Does a man satisfy the precept that hears Mass while holding conversations? Here Busembaum upholds it, if the discussion would not impede him from paying attention to what is going on, at least in a confused state. But other authors more truly contradict this (Salamancans *ibid.* n. 50, with Suarez, Dicastillus, and Filliuci, and Laymann, Bonacina, Trullenchus adhere to them with del Soto, Medina and others cited by Croix, n. 653, in fine). They say he does not satisfy the precept if the discussion continued through a notable part of the Mass, and on a serious matter; otherwise if it were for a small part, or discontinuously on a light matter which would not impede all attention; and Elbel (n. 343) also thinks this. But I do not altogether acquiesce to this last one since discussion, even on a light matter, can impede external attention.

Furthermore, someone that puts on clothes during Mass, or his shoes, probably satisfies the precept, as Dicastillus, Leander, Navarre, Cajetan, and Bonacina say, with the Salamancans (*ibid.* n. 52). Still, in regard to someone that walks around while hearing Mass, Bonacina is uncertain if he sins gravely or not; but Dicastillus and Gobat (with others cited by Croix n. 652) say he satisfies. Moreover, someone who consumes a great part of the Mass in gathering alms, is excused by many authors if it is in a small Church, but it is otherwise if it is in a great Church; so Henriquez thinks with others cited by the Salamancans (*ibid.* n. 52). But Lessius (as Croix cites, n. 652) excuses them without distinction if they attend to Mass at the same time; and truly such a distinction does not seem possible at the same time. Musicians, organists and others also satisfy if, while they sing or strike instruments, they attend to Mass at the same time, provided it is related to the same worship of God (Croix, d. n. 652, and Sporer, n. 16).

318.—"10. The precept to hear Mass is fulfilled in any place, "whether in a parish church or a cathedral, or in a church of "regulars, private oratories or even if it is heard outside of a "Church. The reason is, because the Church merely commands "the hearing of Mass but not the place; therefore, the precept is "fulfilled in any place." (Salamancans *de Sacrif. missae,* c. 6

punct. 1 n. 1, with de Lugo, Dicastillus, etc. in common. But in regard to private oratories, see what follows in n. 319). "Toledo, "l. 9 c. 7; Azor, c. 6, Rodrigez, Navarre, Filliuci, Nuñez, Suarez, "Concina, Bonacina, d. 4 q. ult. c. 32 n. 4 and many others). "Such a doctrine, although it seems certain enough, just the "same, because after all the authors cited above it was called "into doubt by an otherwise learned author, an examination of "this peculiar doubt must be made lest a scruple or an "erroneous conscience arise from it (because the book is easy to "find)."

Here it is worthwhile to recall to judgment the privilege of a private oratory, and before relating everything to annotate the words of the Papal Brief by which an indult of this sort is usually conceded.

Clement XIII: To you N. N. of the diocese of Naples, who (as you assert) are from noble birth, we grant one Mass for each day in the private oratory existing in your house in the city of N and the diocese of N., which has been decently constructed for this purpose with a wall, that may and must be decorated, free from all domestic use, that has been previously visited by the Ordinary and approved and by his license, so long as he wishes it to endure. This is provided that in the same house the license to celebrate which still endures was not already conceded to another, for any secular priest approved by the same ordinary or a regular with permission from his superiors, if it is not in prejudice to any parochial rights with the exception of the feasts of Easter, Pentecost, and Christmas as well as the more solemn feasts of the year to be celebrated in your presence as well as that of your children and household, and also of your noble guests you can and may licitly and freely avail yourself. Not withstanding, etc. ... Moreover, we will that household servants that are not necessarily in your service by act during the aforesaid time, being present at a Mass of this sort are hardly reckoned free from the precept to hear Mass in the Church on feast days.

Now we must briefly put to examination each clause of the indult that might run into difficulties.[15]

Clause I: "To you N. N. of the diocese of Naples.

Here, the question arises: Would the one obtaining the privilege, by transferring his domicile into another diocese, be able to use it here? The most common opinion upholds this. Barbosa, *de jure ecclesiast.* l. 2 c. 8 n. 16; Salas *de leg.* d. 20, sect. 15, n. 123; Pasqualigo *de Sacrificio Missae*, q. 629; Pellizzararius *Man.* t. 2 tr. 8 c. 2 sect. 2 n. 152; Tamburinius, *Meth. celebr. miss.* l. 1 c. 6 § 4 n. 2; La Croix, l. 6 p. 2 n. 269, with Sylvius, Bonacina and Diana, p. 4 tr. 4 r. 208, with many others. Their reasoning is, because this privilege is personal since it is not conceded to the place but to the person on account of his nobility, whereby, just as when the cause of the privilege ceases, the privilege ceases, so while it perseveres, namely the nobility of the person, the privilege would persevere. They also argue that it is not opposed that it says, "To you, N. N. of the diocese of Naples," for it is not affixed comprehensively, but demonstratively, namely, "To you who are now in the diocese of Naples", and this is so the privilege could not be usurped by someone in another diocese that perhaps had the same name. Nevertheless, the aforesaid authors advert that an inspection of the place is required as well as approval from the Ordinary of the other diocese. But these not withstanding, I think with Fr. Fortunatus of Bruges (*de oratorio domest.* p. 62) and Fr. Gatticus (n. 20 *eod. tit.* c. 22) as well as Morella (cited by Diana, *loc. cit.*) that after domicile has been transferred to another diocese, the privilege would cease. The

---

[15] Translator's note: Because English grammar requires a reordering of the Brief from its legal Latin, the English translation of Clement XIII's Brief is ordered differently. The explanation of the clauses below follows the ordering of the Latin.

reason is, because modern examples of an indult of this sort, the name of the city and the diocese is not only applied to the person, namely "To you of diocese N.," but also to the oratory itself, since it is said there: "In a private oratory of your customary habitation, existing in the city of N.," and sometimes even the name of the diocese is added; therefore, just as the privilege is limited in regard to the person, so also in regard to the place. And therefore, I think the authors cited in favor of the first opinion, once held that in common because formerly the name of the diocese was not affixed, only that of the person, and not even the place; for that is what we see in the example related by Tamburinius (*loc. cit.* n. 1), "To you of the diocese of N., that in a private oratory that you customarily inhabit, decently constructed for this purpose, etc." But today, because the name of the city or even of the diocese is affixed and even the place, there is no uncertainty that is affixed not demonstratively but comprehensively. Besides that, even if there were a doubt, a privilege of this sort must be interpreted strictly. I know Tamburinius (*loc. cit.* §4 n. 31) by citing Pellizzarius in favor of himself is opposed to me, saying that such an indult for an oratory ought to be interpreted broadly, since it is a privilege of a prince, from which no prejudice is induced. But the opposite appears more true to me, and Fr. Fortunatus of Bruges (*l.c.* c. 3, *animadv.* I, p. 91) asserts it is common among everyone. The reason is because the authors commonly teach otherwise (Sanchez, *de matr.* l. 8 d. 1 n. 1 and 5; Bonacina, *de privil.* d. 1 q. 3 p. 7 § 1 n. 5; Suarez, *de legibus*, l. 8 c. 27, n. 28; Salamancans *de privil.* tract. 18 c. 1 punct. 6 n. 79 with Palaus, Laymann, Bassaeus, Tamburinius, and others). They say that although privileges, insofar as they are favorable, must be interpreted broadly, nay more very broadly, nevertheless, those privileges which set aside the common law (as this one does) ought to be regularly interpreted strictly, because a privilege against the common law contains and imports a dispensation which is always odious.

Thus, it is confirmed from *reg.* 15 *juris* in 6, where it is said: "Those matters which detract from common law must by no means carried be to a consequence." I said "regularly", because some cases constitute exceptions, which we will review in the *Appendix* on privileges, placed at the end of the work, see there n. 7.

Moreover, Pignatellus and Pasqualigo say that a nobleman can, even if he would remain in the country for a short time, use the privilege of the oratory there since this privilege would be personal. But this also must be denied with Roncaglia, *de Sacrif. missae*, c. 5 q. 3, *vers. Quarto*, according to the words of the indult related above, where it is said: "In a private oratory of a house you normally inhabit." Moreover, a country house where a nobleman abides for a short time cannot be said to be a place that he "normally inhabits."

Clause II: "Who (as you assert) are of noble birth."

We must notice in the first place, with Tamburinius (*Meth. cel. missae*, l. 1 c. 6 §4 n. 5) that when this condition of nobility has not been verified, this privilege altogether collapses; because from the common doctrine handed down by Sanchez (*de matr.* l. 8 d. 21 n. 8) since the condition is not verified, which, if it did not exist, the privilege is not conceded, the privilege ceases for the very reason that the condition then is required as the final and principal cause of the concession. Moreover, Pignatellus (*Cons.* 68 n. 100) and Pasqualigo, *de Sacrif. Missae*, qu. 622) as well as Clericatus (cited by Fr. Fortunatus of Bruges in the cited work *de orat. dom.*) say that any nobility suffices for it, whether it is of birth or privilege, or dignity or state, or by another mode. But the aforesaid Fr. Fortunatus of Bruges denies this, saying the Pope is principally moved on account of nobility to impart this privilege on someone, and therefore it is not presumed that he means one participates in it if he is not really of the nobility. On the rest, Tamburinius says one is reckoned noble who has not exercised manual labor for so many generations.

Hence, I think these passages must always be distinguished, since someone that perhaps is reckoned to be of the nobility in some city will not be so regarded in another.

Clause III: "That in a private oratory of a house that you customarily inhabit, existing in the city of N., decently constructed for this purpose with a wall, decorated and free from all domestic use."

Note: 1) The words, "constructed with a wall". Here, La Croix (l. 6 part. 2 n. 266) and Tamburinius (*loc. cit.* n. 8) say that it is not necessary that it be enclosed with four walls and a door for them to divide the oratory from other places, but they can put four tapestries or blankets adapted in place of walls which open or close for the suitability of those hearing Mass.

But Fr. Fortunatus of Bruges does not think that wide armoires within the cavity of the wall would suffice, which are closed with a wooden door after the sacrifice has been carried out. No one has any doubt that an oratory of this sort is more decent within four, or at least three walls constructed in a separate room; but I know the aforesaid armoires are in use at Naples, and I know they are approved by the Archbishop. And really, oratories of this sort formed in this way do not seem, according to the tenor of the indult (as Fr. Bruges supposes) do not seem to be forbidden. This is because the lateral doors are sufficient to act in place of walls; still, provided that the wooden altar is so bound to the wall that it is not movable, according to the decree of the Sacred Congregation of Rites published on 3 December 1661, in which it was said: "having an indult to choose an oratory in their own home, if someone would wish to build a wooden altar there, he does not need the apostolic faculty provided the wooden altar with the altar stone is united to the wall and cannot be moved, and a portable altar does not display an image."

Note 2) the word "decorated". Everyone agrees that the place of the oratory ought to be so constructed that it is considered different from other rooms designated for profane use; it should appear sacred from its decor. Nay more, Pasqualigo (qu. 618 n. 3) says that in these oratories a more splendid decor is required than in Churches in which, when the place is permanently dedicated to divine worship, *per se* the place calls for veneration; but when it ceases in private oratories, the splendor with which it is decorated ought to supply veneration.

Note 3) The words, "free from all domestic use." Pasqualigo says (*de Sacr. Miss.* q. 618) as well as Tamburinius (*l.c.* n. 9 from Sa, *verb. Ecclesia*, n. 3) that when necessity arises, just as it is also permitted in a consecrated Church to eat, sleep and similar things, so much more are these things to be permitted in an oratory which is only reckoned for the use of the Mass for a time. La Croix (lib. 6 p. 2 n. 266) adds that actions of this sort, although they might be done without necessity, do not exceed a venial sin, for the authorities (cited by Bonacina and Suarez, *de relig.* lib. 3, cap. 5) teach that these, even if they were in a consecrated Church, are not mortal sins unless they were done constantly and by a mode of habit, by using a Church or oratory as any sort of profane place. Nevertheless, in that case, Pasqualigo (*l.c.* q. 618 n. 8) thinks, with others, the place is made inept and therefore the privilege ceases. At least, Tamburinius says (following Castropolaeus) then the place would need a new approval of the Bishop.

Now, would it be licit to place beds upon the roof of the oratory or Church, or to exercise other profane things? Several authors reject this, saying that to refrain from doing these things will be from the fittingness, but not from precept (Roncaglia, *de Sacrif. miss.* c. 5 qu. 3 *v. Primo*, in fine with Pignatellus and Croix (n. 266) with Quarti and Tamburinius, n. 9 vers. *Illud*, from Sanchez l. 1 n. 26 and the Gloss in *cap. unic. de consecratione Eccles.* in 6). If someone sleeps on the roof of a Church, he sleeps outside the Church. On the other hand, St. Charles Borromeo forbade a place in which someone might sleep or live or do anything profane whatsoever to be set up above a Church, chapel or oratory where Mass is offered. (*Concil. 4 Mediol.*) But Fr. Gatticus (c. 23 n. 6) supposes that if it could not be provided otherwise on account of the scant space of a privileged house, something must be permitted in this affair.

Clause IV: "that has been previously visited by the Ordinary and approved and by his license, so long as he wishes it to endure."

The oratory certainly should be visited and approved by the Ordinary that it is suitable and in a decent place, but only once and for free. Moreover, after the oratory has been approved, then the Ordinary cannot impede Mass from being celebrated in it, precisely as Barbosa relates was decided in the Council of Trent (sess. 22 *Decr. de Observ.* etc. n. 19). The term "Ordinary" embraces both the vicar general of the Bishop and the Cathedral chapter if the see is vacant (Sanchez *de matr.* lib. 3 disp. 29 n. 3 and 5). But a Bishop can also consign this faculty of visitation to another, since this faculty is perpetually connected to the episcopal office (Sanchez, *ibid.* d. 31 n. 1 and others).

Those words, "and by his [the Ordinary's] license, so long as he wills it to endure", Tamburinius asserts (n. 15) are not placed in all indults, but where they are, if the Ordinary were to revoke the license, then Mass can no longer be celebrated in the oratory, but he can be compelled to concede it if he denies it unjustly (Tamburinius, *l.c.* n. 14 and 15). Nevertheless, the same author adverts (n. 16, as well as Sanchez, *Consil.* lib. 7 c. 1 dub. 55 num. 7) that the word "*arbitrio*" differs from "at his pleasure" (*libera voluntas*), which is why he says the Ordinary cannot revoke a license of this sort without a just cause. Still, if a just cause exists, then he can rightly suspend the celebration, not only by the force of the aforesaid clause, but also by the force of the cited Decree of Trent, where the power of establishing or forbidding those things which they see in regard to the celebration of Masses was universally given to Bishops as well as apostolic delegates.

Clause V: "One Mass on each day ... provided in the same house the license to celebrate which still endures was not already conceded to another."

Note, "one Mass" *that is only a single one*, as Pope Benedict XIV declared in his bull *Magno* (whatever others might say; see what will be said on this point in book 6, n. 359, "We must note III"). But by the words, "Provided it is in the same house, etc." even if one of two noblemen had the proper oratory in his separate dwelling (an apartment in the vernacular) of the same house, by no means could the other nobleman obtain the privilege.

Clause VI: "for any secular priest approved by the same ordinary or a regular with permission from his superiors."

Tamburinius cites a certain author (n. 33) that thought this clause means priests require special permission to celebrate Mass in a private oratory, but Tamburinius rightly denies it, because everywhere priests usually offer Mass in the aforesaid oratories with only a universal approval to celebrate.

Clause VII: "if it is not in prejudice to any parochial rights."

This clause imports that those celebrating cannot announce marriages, periods of fasting and similar things that are the provenance of parish priests. It also imports that they cannot minister the sacrament of the Eucharist (whatever Tamburinius says) just as Benedict XIV expressly forbade it in a certain Encyclical to the Bishops of Poland (see what we will say in book 6, n. 359). Moreover, the *Roman Ritual* prescribes that no one may administer the sacrament of Penance in a house except for a reasonable cause.

Clause VIII: "with the exception of the feasts of Easter, Pentecost, and Christmas as well as the more solemn feasts of the year."

Tamburinius adverts (n. 7, from Gavantus, p. 1 tit. 10 § *Sciendum*) that by the name "Easter" and "Pentecost" only the first day is understood in which it is really a solemnity. For which days are understood by "the more solemn feasts" see book 6, n. 359, "From which it is deduced 1)" where we discuss a decree of the Sacred Congregation of Rites explaining the matter.

Clause IX: "be celebrated in your presence as well as that of your children and household, and also of your noble guests."

By the word "yours" (*tua*) the presence of the nobleman is altogether required. Formerly, Roncaglia (*de Sacr. Missae*, c. 5 q. 3 vers. *Quinto*, with Barbosa) thought it was a probable opinion that Mass could be celebrated with the household assisting even if the lord were absent, saying the particle as well (*ac*) *in tua praesentia, et natorum, ac familiae*, is understood for "or" (*vel*); otherwise (he says) the presence of the lord would not suffice if the household were absent. But today, in the beginning of his decree *"Cum duo nobiles"*, Pope Benedict XIV has ratified that Mass cannot be celebrated in a private oratory unless some person is present in act from the number of those to whom the indult was principally conceded and directed (see the constitutions of Benedict XIV are extensively related at the end of this work, *De Romanorum Pontificum Decretis*, part. 2 c. 2 decret. 5).

By the word "children", Pignatellus (tom. 6 *Cons.* 58, n. 105) and Pasqualigo (*de Sacrif. Missae*, q. 654 n. 1) say that even illegitimate sons may come, provided they were certainly born of the father and there is no question of it. Fr. Gatticus (*de orat. dom.* c. 25, n. 25) and Fortunatus of Bruges (*eod. tit.*) with Barbosa, hold only legitimate sons may come, but not bastards of an unknown father or natural children until these have been legitimized by a subsequent matrimony, or by the authority of the prince; and also I adhere more to this opinion, since a privilege of this sort must be interpreted strictly, exactly as we proved in our explanation of the first clause.

By the word "household" (*familia*) indeed both cousins and in-laws may come. But could all relatives of any degree of relation come? Pignatellus (*Cons.* 94 n. 102) and Pasqualigo (q.

654) affirm it. Just the same, Gatticus (*l.c.* n. 76) thinks the privilege is not extended beyond the fourth degree of relations, because (as he says) the present discipline after an impediment to matrimony from carnal relation that is restricted to the fourth degree, does not look further to lower degrees. Besides, Tamburinius says (with Pellizzarius) relatives enjoy the privilege, even if they live on their own expenses and in their separate parts, provided they dwell in the same house. But the more common and truer opinion denies this (Pignatellus, *l.c.* n. 95; Pasqualigo, q. 649; Roncaglia, *de Sacrificio Missae*, cap. 5, q. 3, *v. Sexto*; Croix, lib. 3 p. 1 num. 627 and Fr. Fortunatus of Bruges). This is because it is required by the indult that relations not only abide in the same house but are also of the same household.

By the word: "guests", Fr. Fortunatus of Bruges (with Pellizarius and Gatticus) says a guest (provided he were of the nobility, according to the indult), can also be admitted for one day; and even one invited to lunch by the nobleman possessing the privilege for the purpose that he participates in the privilege. Still, the servants of the guest cannot enjoy the privilege because he is not from the household of the one possessing the privilege.

Clause XI: "Moreover we will that household servants that are not necessarily in your service by act during the aforesaid time, being present at a Mass of this sort are hardly reckoned free from the precept to hear Mass in the Church on feast days."

As a result, for household servants to enjoy the privilege of the oratory it is required: 1) That they live at the expense of their master and depend upon his service, from *cap. Sicut nobis, de verb. sign.* in 6; 2) That by act they are necessarily in their lord's service; 3) It is required that by act they are necessary, not only sometimes for a day, but in the time in which the Mass is celebrated; so rightly Fr. Fortunatus says with Gatticus, and it is clear from the words of the indult. Moreover, Pignatellus (*Cons.* 98 n. 107) thinks that household servants useful in their service are considered necessary; and Gatticus admits this (cap. 25 n. 19) at least in the case in which the servants are necessary for the lord's suitable decor. But Fr. Fortunatus concedes neither from the principle repeated many times above, that this privilege must be interpreted strictly and according to a rigorous propriety of words. He only admits, with Gatticus, one servant who is considered morally necessary to assist his master in those things which can happen during the time of the Mass. Moreover, servants of relatives do not enjoy this privilege, unless they are taken up by the one possessing the privilege to assist and they are necessary to the relatives in the aforesaid mode, who are under the care of the nobleman possessing the privilege.

319.—There is a doubt: 1) Whether servants, living at the expense of the master, but dwelling outside his house would enjoy the privilege? Many authors deny it (Bonacina, Barbosa, Lezana and Gobat, cited by Croix, book 6 part. 2 num. 272). But others affirm it (Fr. Pazzotta, Pellizzar, *Man.* tract. 8 c. 2 sect. 2 q. 22, Gatticus, cited by Fortunatus of Bruges, and Palaus, Diana Quarti and others that Croix cites). Their opinion does not appear to be condemned, if the servants immediately assist their master and are really necessary at the time of Mass (as we already said).

There is a doubt: 2) Whether anyone not apart of the household hearing Mass in a private oratory, would satisfy the precept? Busembaum affirms it, with Azor and others. But other authors rightly reject this opinion from the words of the indult where it is said: "Moreover, we will that household servants who are not necessarily in your service by act during the aforesaid time, being present at a Mass of this sort are hardly reckoned free from the precept to hear Mass in the Church" (Tamburinius, *meth. celebr. miss.* lib. 1 c. 4 § 4 n. 34; Sporer *de 3 praec.* c. 4 n. 14; Mazotta *de Sacrif. miss.* c. 3 and others). It is not opposed to say that those not apart of the household now hear Mass; they say concerning that place there is no precept; for those words, "We will, etc." are affixed from the style of the curia for the time in which Mass was once heard in the parish Church. But

Tamburinius rightly responds that the Pope, by saying "we will, etc." imposes, clearly enough, a precept even on the place by commanding that those who are not of the household are held to hear Mass not necessarily in a parish Church, but in a public Church, to the exclusion of a private oratory.

There is a doubt: 3) whether a nobleman is sometimes held to use the privilege of the oratory if he could not go to a Church? It seems it must be denied, because, if he were held to use his privilege, the privilege would be rendered onerous. But they duly affirm that he is held if he can suitably find a priest, but not from the force of the privilege, but of the precept to hear Mass which obliges all to hear Mass who have the ability to fulfill it without grave inconvenience. Hence it is that the one having the privilege is held, if he can suitably do so, to provide a priest not only for himself but even for others in his household if any of them cannot go to a Church (as Fortunatus of Bruges rightly says with Nuñez, Pasqualigo and Gatticus).

Moreover, it is probable that he satisfies who hears Mass on the shore or in an encampment (Croix n. 629, with Bonacina and the cited authorities). Here we must note that an oratory in the houses of Bishops, religious or of privileged missions, or erected somewhere else and blessed by the Bishop, when the door is on the road (say like the houses of laity), now they are not private oratories, but true Churches; by what means do those hearing Mass in them truly satisfy the precept and do they on any feast? See Croix, n. 626 and our treatise on the Eucharist, book 6 from n. 357.

DUBIUM IV
Whether there is an obligation for someone to hear Mass in his parish church on Sundays and greater feast days?

320.—"*Resp.* Even if it were fitting, still it is not an "obligation. This is the common opinion of the authors (whom "you can see above in a case of the last dubium), and Cardinal "de Lugo says it is certain (disp. 23 sect. 1 n. 2); even if "Marchant in his *Candelabro mystico*, t. 4, cap. 7 and in "*resolutionibus moralibus, in forma manualis editis*, c. 8 calls it "into doubt and tries to provoke a scruple.

"The reason is: 1) Because no precept on the matter exists; "2) Because in the chapter *Ut Dominus*, the pastor is "commanded before Mass to throw out those who mean to hear "Mass in contempt of their own pastor, and so, without formal "contempt it is lawful; 3) Because c. *Si quis, de consecr.* dist. 1, "those who have an oratory in their home are commanded to "hear Mass in their parishes or in cities on major feast days; 4) "Because all of the faithful, and also their learned pastors and "confessors (who do not ask penitents about this matter), do not "observe this custom as Marchant manifestly teaches; 5) "Because the Council of Trent (sess. 22 c. 7) only says that "people should be advised (but not held) that they might be "present frequently in their parishes, at least on Sundays and "greater feasts. See Fagundez, de Lugo, Barbosa, Zened., "Trullenchus, lib. 3 c. 1 dub. 6.

321.—"Nor is what Marchant objects opposed to us: 1) "Because ancient laws discern the contrary, for the very reason "that Sixtus IV, *De Treuga et pace*, commands the Mendicants "not to preach that [the faithful] are not held to hear Mass in a "parish on Sundays and feasts. In the first place, by that decree "of Sixtus nothing follows, since a man is not said to be held, "rather, he only forbids them to publicly *preach, that they are* "*not be held.* Since it was the most just thing for the people to "hear Mass in the parish Church, and fitting to persuade it "would hardly be fitting to dissuade (especially in public). For "thence, scandals and contempt of their own parish priest could "follow; and this is what Sixtus wanted to prevent. Then, even if it is the case that they have some ancient laws, it has been repealed in later times through various privileges, and universal custom received (Cajetan, de Lugo, and the other cited authorities)."

"Nor is it opposed: 2) that he asserts that many canonists follow this opinion; be that as it may that at one time someone so thought, still at this time, after so many and such ample privileges, after such clear and long-lasting custom, after the declarations of most eminent cardinals, and even contrary decrees of Popes (as you will see in the following response), whether some teach it, I do not know."

"Nor 3) the citation of Trent cited recently in the response, which he objects to, as is clear from the very words and declaration of the most eminent Cardinals, and the common explanation of authorities."

322.— "*Resp. 2.* The Bishop cannot compel one to hear Mass in his parish Church by censures, fines and other penalties. This is against Marchant (*loc. cit.*), where he says, "Regulars commonly respond to the effect that they might magnify the fringes of their privileges, and they increase their phylacteries," and against the prestige "of parochial obedience."

"Moreover, the reason is, because, as Navarre says, the Bishop cannot abolish (nor restrict) common law and the general custom of the world. On the contrary, the authors cited above teach in this way (St. Antoninus, p. 2 tit. 9 c. 10 § 1 n. 4; Sylvius, v. *Missa*; Toledo; Laymann l. 4 t. 7 cap. 3 etc.) as well as the common teaching of all theologians and modern canonists. Azor (t. 1 l. 7 c. 8 q. 6), and Cardinal de Lugo (disp. 22 lib. 1) assert in favor of this opinion the declaration of the Cardinals at Trent which expressly holds: "The Ordinary cannot compel the faithful with fines and penalties to hear

"Mass or a sermon in their own parish, even in the case of "negligence and contumacy." And if anyone refused to trust "these two because they are regulars, he can read the same "declaration cited by Barbosa in *Trid.* sess. 22, c. 8 *de Sacrif.* "*missae* and sess. 24, *de reform.* c. 4 n. 12. Likewise, in his "treatise *de Officio et potestate Parochi*, where Barbosa himself "follows the same opinion and cites more than twenty famous "authors, partly theologians and partly canonists, both regulars "and secular clergy (See the same author's *Remissiones in* "*Tridentinum*, published at Antwerp in 1644, and Zerola *in praxi* "*episcopali*, p. 2 v. *Parochia* and p. 1 v. *Missa*, §6).

"Pope Clement VIII confirmed the same very precisely on 22 "December 1592 in his decree in regard to this very controversy "which was roused by Duaci, who broke it with these words: "We ratify with our present decree, that it is lawful for secular "clergy and all the faithful of Christ to hear Masses on Sundays "and other great feasts in the Churches of both the Friars "Preachers [Dominicans] and of other Mendicants, and even in "the colleges of the Society of Jesus according to their privileges "and ancient customs, provided that they do not do so in "contempt of their parish churches. One can also confess his "sins to the aforesaid Friars Preachers and priests of the "aforesaid society as well as to others provided with an indult "from the Apostolic See not only during Lent and Easter, but at "any time of the year; nevertheless, they must be approved as "suitable by the Ordinary."

"Moreover, if one would like to know better the aforesaid "privileges and other similar ones, let him inspect the "compendium of privileges of the Society of Jesus (that I might "pass over others), where after the words of Leo X we have the "words of Paul III in *Extrav.* given in November 1549, which "begins *Licet debitum*, wherein he says: "It is conceded to all the "faithful of Christ of whatever condition that are present for the "preaching of the word of God in the Churches of the same "society that they may avail themselves to hear Masses and "receive the sacraments in the same place freely and licitly, and "they are not held to go to their parish Churches." Moreover, "lest someone would marvel at such ample privileges conceded "to Regulars by various Popes, it would behoove him to inspect "their bulls, in which he will find very serious motives. Or, if he "does not feel like inspecting them, let him at least consider that "God himself showed to Innocent III (when he saw the Church "of the Lateran falling to ruin) that it was held up by St. "Dominic and St. Francis. Let him consider the fact that just as "in various regions of the world once, and in Germany itself, "the doctrine of Christ was carried over by the work of "regulars, so without their assistance it would not have been "preserved, or at least would have flourished less. And then, lest "anyone would be angry with the Regulars because they hold "these privileges, it must be known that they can neither "renounce them nor yield them without the consent of the "Apostolic See (See lib. 2 *Decret.* tit. 43, *de arb.* c. 5). Nay more, "even if they did this, it would be invalid and they would sin "because it would inflict an injury to their order and the whole "Church.

323.—"Now I briefly respond to the arguments of "Marchant."

"1. He asserts the authority of a certain Capuchin father, "who wrote *Parochianum obedientem*, and I showed many "serious authorities in opposition to this a little earlier.

"2. He says the practice of certain Bishops is the contrary "and it is founded and an ancient law as well as a new one from "Trent (*loc. cit.* sess. 22 and sess. 24) where he says each and "everyone is held to be present in their parish Church to hear "the word of God and to be instructed in the rudiments of faith; "moreover, these things are taught in many rural places in "Mass, therefore they can even be compelled to go to Mass.

"*Resp. 1.* That practice (if it exists anywhere) is only of a few and contrary to the common practice of Bishops in all kingdoms, provinces and moreover of the Supreme Pontiff."

"2. That practice is not founded on an ancient law, since (if it exists) it would be set aside and custom would abrogate it; nor is it founded upon a new law because, while Trent was speaking on sermons and catechism, it made no mention of Mass and that conclusion would not avail in penal works; not only because Trent expressly added (what Marchant omits in his citation, although it would bear the most on the matter), "If it could be done suitably", but even more, because the Universal Church shows there is not even an obligation in regard to sermons received by custom for the very reason that perhaps regularly "it could not be done conveniently," as Cardinal de Lugo notes (*loc. cit.*). Nor are the faithful commonly taught Catechism during Mass unless perhaps it were in the country where Regulars rarely contend with parish priests on the present matter."

"Lastly, I do not know whether or not the Bishops of whom he is speaking are perhaps from the number of those whom Pius V was speaking of in his bull *Etsi Mendicantium* because, seeing that the Bishops rightly ought to cultivate and help the mendicant orders, adding that should they afflict them with inconvenience and disturbances not only would they neglect the Council of Trent, but they would twist the words of the Council into a deprave sense."

"3. He cites the decree of the Synod of Leodiensis (Liège), and Namurcensis (Namur), adding: "But who would dare to condemn this and the Fathers of this synod, among whom many learned theologians were present?"

"*Resp.* These decrees (and if perhaps there are some similar ones) must be understood, lest they hear Mass outside the parish in contempt of their own pastor; or, if they have some other sense, they were not received or were abrogated by use.

"Thus argue the cited authors in common. It can be seen with "Cardinal de Lugo (*loc. cit.*), Barbosa and Zerola (*ll. cc.*) and by "a reading of the very worthy pamphlet of Francis Pontanus, a "preacher with royal title: "The responses to the queries of a "certain prelate, etc." first written in French at Nantes, in the "year 1625, but later it was rendered into Latin and published in "Vienna, Austria, published by Michael Rictius in 1634. I "provide other arguments whereby he tries to persuade that "one should frequent the parish Church (still without "obligation). Whereas the pamphlet scarcely meant to condemn "a conscience, inasmuch as it is especially upright and decent, "rather, it only intends to impede an erroneous conscience, "clearly lest they would frequent the Churches of Regulars with "the persuasion of a parochial obligation or apprehension of "sin."

Pope Benedict XIV, in his work *De Syn.* book 11, c. 14 n. 7, shows (against Juenin and Van Espen) that today there is no obligation to hear Mass in a parish Church.

DUBIUM V
What would excuse someone from hearing Mass?

324. What are excusing causes? Would one having the privilege of an oratory be bound to acquire a priest?
325. In what way would sailors, the incarcerated, the sick or the excommunicated be excused?
326. Would those guarding houses be excused, etc.? Or those fearing lest they might be put in prison or assisting the sick?
327. Are wives, sons and servants fearing offense to their masters excused?
328. Would wayfarers be excused at some point?
329. What distance from the Church would excuse one from hearing Mass?

358   BOOK IV: ON THE PRECEPTS OF THE DECALOGUE

330. *Would women be excused by reason of mourning, birth or because they do not have suitable garments? Would pregnant girls or women be excused at the time when the bans must be read?*
331. *Could a girl omit Mass knowing that there is someone filled with a filthy lust for her?*
332. *Would the loss of a great profit excuse? Would another and greater spiritual good excuse?*
333. *Would pilgrims, tarrying in some place for a short time, be held to hear Mass if it is of precept in that place?*

324.—"*Resp.* There are two causes: One of which, if it is "present, you are not held to see to it that [Mass] is celebrated "privately with a privilege, nor (even if it were advisable) to say "prayers in the meantime in place of Mass, as Navarre (c. 13), "and Suarez, Filliuci, t. 5 c. 5 q. 11 assert.

"The first cause is *impossibility*, whether simple or moral, or "a difficulty from one's own notable inconvenience, or "inconvenience to a neighbor, of body, or goods or even of "honor, because this is the mind of the Church, the nature of "the commanding discretion, and the benevolence of our "mother. Bonacina, d. 4 q. ult. p. ult., Navarre, Filliuci, t. 5 c. 7 q. "11, Suarez d. 85.

"The Second cause is some rational motive, in which "someone thinks he is excused in good faith. See Suarez, in 3. p. "sect. 6, c. 5; Laymann, and Bonacina, *l.c.*"

Thus, one is excused from hearing Mass for any moderately grave cause; namely, which involves some notable inconvenience or loss to the goods of the soul, or of their own body, or of their neighbor. The doctors teach this in common. Busembaum, DD. cited by Croix, l. 3 p. 1 n. 675; Salamancans *de Sacrif. missae*, c. 6 punct. 5 n. 63; Mazotta, *de 3 praec.* c. 3 § 2; and Zachar. l. 3 part. 1 n. 575, with Suarez, Azor, Palaus, Filliuci, Tanner, etc.

Thus, the following are resolved:

325.—"1. They are excused, who are at sea, or in prison. "Likewise, those who are sick or convalescing, whereby it "would be harmful to venture out of doors. Likewise, those who "are excommunicated, or under an interdict that has been "imposed on the place."

The sick are excused when they prudently fear no small harm or a notable delay in their recovery. So the doctors hold in common that it also excuses one who, laboring with a strong illness, would fear a notable headache by going out, or exhaustion of his strength, indigestion, etc. Cajetan, del Soto, Navarre, and others with the Salamancans, *de Sacrif. missae*, c. 6, punct. 5 n. 58, and Elbel, *de 3 praec.* n. 366, with whom Gobat and Sanchez agree. But what if he were uncertain as to whether the inconvenience would be light or sufficiently grave? He must favor the counsel of a doctor or a superior, or a pastor or another prudent man; and the sick man can also acquiesce to his own judgment if he prudently judges it is so. But what if still, after he has sought counsel, he is in doubt? Suarez says that then he must seek a dispensation, but Palaus, Gobat, Bonacina (cited by Croix, n. 679) and the Salamancans (*ibid.* n. 59) say absolutely he is not held to hear Mass. The reason is, while the danger of harm is present then, the precept of the Church does not hold possession [*non possidet*] against the sickness; and de Lugo thinks the same thing. Gobat says, then it must be judged that in such a case mother Church does not put one under obligation. See Croix, *ibid.* It is exceedingly probable with Mazotta, *l.c.*

A man that has been excommunicated or is under interdict does not sin by omitting Mass, and so equally one that is in jail. Even if they do nothing to obtain absolution or in the latter case freedom, because they are not obliged to remove remote impediments. This is the common teaching a against a few, cited by the Salamancans (*ibid.* n. 53) with Navarre, Suarez, Azor, Bonacina, Sa, Palaus, etc. Provided (as Sporer, tr. 3 c. 4 n. 26 and Elbel, n. 365 rightly advert) they do not disregard their liberation from their own will so that they would not be held to hear Mass. Nay more, others more probably say that in that case, they would not be excused if it would be easy to obtain absolution or their freedom and they refuse to do so because every man is held to remove light impediments to satisfy a grave precept (Bonacina and Trullenchus, and the continuator of Tourney, *l. c.*).

326.—"2. Likewise, they are excused who guard a camp, "city, flock, house, or have care of infants or a child (who "cannot be contained quiet in Church and without "disturbance to others), or that ought to bring consolation to "the sick or cook for them and to take care of similar matters "which cannot be omitted. Bonacina, Con. n. 86 and 314."

As a result, those guarding houses or flocks are excused by the common teaching (Laymann, l. 4 tract. 5 c. 4 n. 3; Palaus t. 22; the continuator of Tourney, *ibid.* concl. 4 num. 2 in fine; Bonacina, d. 4 q. ult. n. 3; and the Salamancans *ibid.* n. 68). But if there are many guards and one Mass is said, they should hear Mass alternately. So think the Salamancans, n. 68, with Suarez, Navarre, Coninck, Laymann, Covarruvias, etc. And so equally, if a husband or wife must remain home to guard it, the husband cannot compel her to always remain at home since she is a companion, not a servant; but a lord can also remain at home sometimes so that his maid servant can hear Mass, for her advantage would excuse the lord (Croix lib. 3 part. 1 n. 686; with Stephan of St. Paul, tr. 5 disp. 4 dub. 16 n. 102, and Gobat tr. 5 n. 494).

In an equal manner mothers that do not have someone at home to entrust the care of children without danger, and on the other hand cannot bring them into the Church without a notable disturbance to others, are excused (Bonacina, *l.c.* n. 2, and Salamancans *loc. cit.* n. 73 and Suarez, Trullenchus, and Elbel, n. 389, with Laymann, etc. in common). They are probably also excused who fear being put in prison, if they go to Church (Croix, n. 689, with Henriquez, Dicastillus, and Gobat, as well as Zachariah, l. 3 p. 1 n. 689).

They are also excused who cannot go to Mass because they will leave a sick man without assistance for food or medicine; or that the sick man, left behind by him, would suffer grave disturbance (Palaus, Dicastillus, Filliuci, Suarez, del Soto, etc., with the Salamancans, *de Sacrif. missae*, c. 6 punct. 5 n. 76). And this, even if an assistant were present but the sick man reckoned their assistance were necessary for him and otherwise would suffer grave sadness. (Pasqualigo, cited by Croix, n. 680, and Mazotta, *loc. cit.*).

327.—"Likewise, one is excused for whom there is the "danger of grave offense to a husband, parents or masters "(Henriquez, Suarez, Filliuci, n. 226). Nevertheless, if it always "happens, the servant must find another means of "employment."

Servants are excused when their service is commonly necessary and they cannot omit it without grave inconvenience to their masters; still they ought to apply average diligence so that they would not miss Mass (Suarez, d. 88 sect. 6 n. 5; Palaus, *loc. cit.* n. 5; Cont. Tourn. *de 3 Dec. praecepto* art. 2, sect. 1 concl. 4, *l.c.*; and the Salamancans, *ibid.* n. 74, with Concina and Dicastillus). Nay more, Croix notes (n. 685) with Palaus, that servants are still held to hear Mass, who have average annoyance or lack of sleep, but not, however, when there is a notable loss of sleep. But if their service is not so necessary, there is little doubt that their masters sin if they impede their servants from hearing Mass. Furthermore, these servants are then held to hear Mass, though it is against the command of their master, unless they fear grave indignation or if they could not easily find another master right away (Croix, l. 3 p. 1 n. 685, with Palaus, tr. 22 p. ult. n. 6), whatever Sporer (*de 3 praec.* c. 4 n. 34) and the Salamancans (*ibid.* n. 75) might say, knowing servants are normally excused for so many times. Mazotta notes (d. 5 § 2) that masters hardly sin if they command their servants during the time of Mass to do those things that cannot be delayed according to the common mode of life (it must be understood, without grave inconvenience to the masters). And then, even servants are rightly excused if during all of the Mass times they are occupied with their actual and necessary duty, as Sporer says (*ibid.* d. n. 34, with the Salamancans, n. 74, etc. as above).

So equally, a wife is excused if she fears the indignation of an angry or jealous husband from her arrival at Church; the case is otherwise if it is mild anger (Palaus, Suarez, Bonacina, Azor, with Salamancans tr. 5 c. 6 punct. 5 n. 68, Mazotta, *loc. cit.* and Elbel num. 369). Just the same, this must rarely be admitted. For a just cause, Croix notes in n. 688, with Tamburinius and Fagundez, that a father can detain his son locked up at home as a punishment, even if the latter would not hear Mass. Elbel says the same thing (n. 380). He is also rightly excused by the Continuator of Tournely (*loc. cit.*) who would omit Mass to stop the quarrels of others, or stop the theft of another's goods.

328.—"4. Likewise, if anyone would otherwise lose a "suitable time to make a journey, *e.g.* a guide if they do not "know the road, or fear dangers. But otherwise he is held to "hear Mass before the journey or while he is on it. Suarez, "sect. 6; Rodriquez, Bonacina *l.c.*"

Wayfarers are also excused if they would otherwise spend the expenses of the journey which a companion had made for them, as Suarez, Dicastillus, Gobat (cited by Croix, n. 582) say, as well as the Salamancans, *ibid.* n. 69, with Bonacina, and Elbel n. 383. Or, if he ought to undergo greater expenses if he would lose the occasion on account of hearing Mass, as Elbel adds. Or, if he were not secure on the journey without a companion. Or if that society would assist him well enough and take away the exhaustion of a long journey, which certainly seems to be a grave inconvenience, or at least joined with the danger of a grave inconvenience, as Tamburinius, Suarez, Dicastillus, Gobat, Henriquez, cited by Croix (*ibid.*).

329.—"5. One is excused if there is a great difficulty of "going to Church on account of distance, *e.g.* of one or more "German miles, or even of a lesser space, particularly if the "road is very troublesome, or it is raining. In that case, the "account of persons must be held, as well as of the place, time "and custom. Bonacina, Suarez, Filliuci, *loc. cit.* Marchant, "*Resol. past.* t. 4 c. 6 n. 7."

For distance to excuse, some assign three of our miles, others two, others one. But this must be judged from the circumstances of person, time, etc., as Busembaum, Viva, and the Salamancans teach from the common opinion. Still, ordinarily the distance of a mile does not excuse, as Croix rightly says (n. 687). But Dicastillus does not oblige noble or young women to a mile and a half; but he obligates the middle of that group, as well as country folk to a longer space. On the other hand, the Salamancans, with Suarez, Palaus, Trullenchus, Filliuci, etc. (to whom Zaccaria adheres, l. 3 p. 1 n. 687) and Croix, with Diana, Gobat and Fagundez), say that regularly the distance of a *leucae* or three miles, *i.e.* of one good hour, or of 5 quadrantium made on foot, and less if it would be difficult due to snow, rain or another cause. And Mazotta holds the same, saying absolutely that distance of three miles excuses everyone.

330.—"6. If from the custom of the country women do not "usually go out during a time of mourning, or even after birth. "Sylvius, Cajetan, and Filliuci, n. 227."

Consequently, widows are excused by reason of mourning, as Sporer (n. 35) and Elbel (n. 384) teach, and even their daughters and sisters, as Mazotta adds, with Suarez. Yet, as Filliuci, Villalobos and others say, such a custom must not extend beyond one month from the death of her husband. St. Charles Borromeo only permitted one month (conc. 1 Mediolanensi). Although, if there were another custom present in some place, they must not be condemned for a grave sin as Palaus, Dicastillus and Filliuci teach (with the rest of the authors cited by the Salamancans, *dict.* c. 6 n. 82). Still, those women that go out of their house to do other things must not be excused, as the Salamancans note, with Palaus. In some places virgins are excused from mass by the custom of the place lest they would go out in public (Salamancans *ibid.* n. 81, with Filliuci, Palaus, and Suarez, who still rightly advert with Azor and the other authors that such a custom must be moderated as much as it can).[16]

"7. If anyone did not have clothes suitable to their state. "Navarre, Henriquez, Sa, Azor, Bonacina, *l.c.*

"8. If some woman that was pregnant from a secret "fornication feared it would be discovered, she is excused if it "would benefit her. Laymann, l. 4 t. 5."

Women that do not have decent clothes according to their state are excused (with Busembaum and Elbel, n. 367), whether a servant, or a wife, without which they would swell with shame as Mazotta says (*l.c.*). But the authors rightly advert that they are not excused from hearing Mass very early in the morning if they can, or in a remote Church where the people do not gather (Salamancans tr. 5 *de Sacr. miss.* c. 6 punct. 5 n. 64; Ledesma,

---

[16] Translator's note: In *Homo Apostolicus*, tr. 6 n. 42, St. Alphonsus is much harsher on this: "By no reasoning can this custom (which is better called an abuse) be reputed as licit, whereby young girls should stay away from Mass lest they go out in public."

TREATISE III: THE THIRD AND FOURTH PRECEPTS CH. I 365

Suarez, Filliuci, Dicastillus, Palaus, etc.). The same thing is said about a girl that is pregnant out of wedlock if it could be done in a secret place and hear Mass without it being known. This is the common opinion (Busembaum, Elbel, n. 367, the Continuator of Tournely, *de 3 Decal. praec.* art. 2, sect. 1 concl. 4 n. 2, *Qui sacro*, and Palaus, Laymann, Reginald, etc. with Salamancans, *ibid.* in fine).

So also, the girls who go out from the Church when proclamations of their matrimony are read can also be excused if they would suffer a notable shame on that account, although they would omit Mass. So Elbel (n. 374), and Sporer thinks the same about noble woman (c. 4 n. 35). Moreover, I think this can rarely be admitted and only with difficulty; but if a girl really suffered shame from only this so that she would undergo a great inconvenience, in that case I would not condemn it. But Croix (n. 690), absolutely excuses such girls where a custom of this sort is present. Equally, custom excuses women that have just given birth and confine themselves at home after the birth for some time (*e.g.* from the common use for six weeks as Sporer and Elbel witness), even after they have recovered (Sporer num. 35; Elbel n. 384; Salamancans c. 6 n. 79 with Palaus, from cap. *Unic., de Purificat post partum*). But women are not excused on account of menstruation. (Salamancans, *ibid.*, n. 80).

331.—"9. If a woman knew that a man desperately lusted "after her and an occasion of sin would follow were she to go "out. Sa, Filliuci, n. 227."

It is an important question, whether a young lady that knows someone lusts foully after her could miss Mass? There are three opinions.

The *first* says that she can omit Mass and is held to do so two or three times (Laymann, *de char.* c. 13, n. 10; Sporer *de 6 praecept.*

c. 1 n. 29 and 37; Villalobos, Lopez, cited by the Salamancans *ibid.* n. 77).

The *second* opinion with Palaus and Henriquez says she is held to hear Mass, not withstanding the ruin of the other man, which comes about from his own will.

The *third* opinion teaches that she indeed can omit Mass to avoid the injury to her neighbor, but she is not held to do so because she uses her right, and he suffers injury by his own fault (Mazotta c. 2 §2, who asserts it is the common opinion with Suarez, Sa, Filliuci, Bonacina, Sanchez, etc., all of whom are cited by the Salamancans, n. 77). All of these opinions are probable, but the first is more probable. The reason is because the natural precept to avoid scandal must be preferred to the positive precept to hear Mass. On the other hand, because charity does not oblige with grave inconvenience, the young lady is not held to abstain from Mass more than once or twice. See what was said on charity in book 3, n. 51 and 53.

332.—*Quaeritur:* would the loss of a notable profit excuse one from hearing Mass? The Salamancans reject this (tr. 23 *de 3 praec.* c. 1 punct. 14 § 3 n. 345). But other authors affirm it with probability, on account of the same reasoning. From what we said above (n. 301), one is excused who labors on a feast day to avoid the loss of an extraordinary profit according to general reckoning, because an ecclesiastical precept does not oblige with grave inconvenience (the learned Fr. Holzmann, *de 3 praec.* c. 1 n. 258; Viva, art. 3 n. 7; Mazotta, *loc. cit.*; Elbel n. 368, with Anacletus, Diana, Tamburinius, c. 2, with Azor, Basseus, cited by Croix, n. 681). Gobat holds the same thing, who excuses a poor man even on account of the profit of one ducat, and another of two and for a small fortune. And the Salamancans unjustly reject the aforesaid second opinion, since in tr. 5 *de Sacrificio Missae,* c. 6 punct. 3 n. 69, with Suarez, Palaus, Bonacina, etc., they did not refuse to excuse a wayfarer who omits Mass lest he might lose some expenses which he hopes for from a companion. But would one be excused who went out to hunt on Saturday, where he cannot hear Mass? See what was said in 301, near the end. But Dicastillus and Gobat (cited by Croix, n. 684) excuse coach drivers who cannot hear Mass lest they would give up their fees with a notable loss. Mazotta says the same thing (*ibid.* § 2) about shopkeepers and duty officials, who fear a notable loss; and he says the same thing of sailors and merchants who cannot hear Mass without grave inconvenience. However, we do not admit what some authors add (that Croix cites), namely, that even if someone could omit a fee without a great loss, still he could be excused from the custom of others that have something to convey. Equally, Suarez and Gobat excuse millers if they would suffer a moderately grave loss because of Mass. It is very probable that those men are excused who, on account of hearing Mass, should omit business that would bring grave loss (Suarez, Dicastillus, Cajetan, etc. with Salamancans, tr. 5 c. 6 punct. 5 n. 70).

Following the more common opinion with Pasqualigo (cited by Croix n. 683), one is not excused who omits Mass on account of another spiritual good, even if it is greater. Still, Illsung admits with probability that one would be excused who omits Mass to confess his sins if otherwise he would remain in the state of mortal sin for some time; and Croix (with Lessius, n. 665) holds the same thing. Likewise, they are excused from Mass who otherwise could not stop blasphemies, quarrels, theft etc. (Elbel n. 391).

Moreover, are pilgrims held to hear a Mass which must be heard from the peculiar precept of the place where they are, even if they tarry there for only one day? Several authors uphold this. The reason is, because pilgrims truly become subjects of the superior of the place where they are, even if they tarry there for a short time (Suarez, *de rel.* l. 1 c. 14, n. 9; Pontius *de matr.* l. 8 c. 4 n. 7; Joseph de Januario and Salas, cited by Palaus *de leg.* d. 1 p. 24 n.

12, who rightly calls it probable with Sanchez, *Dec.* l. 1 c. 12 n. 37 and the Salamancans, *de legibus* c. 3 punct. 5 § 1 n. 56).

Still, Sanchez more probably denies it (*l.c.* n. 38) with Toledo, Azor, Sayr, and Bonacina (d. 1 q. 1 p. 6 n. 6 and 43, Sylvius, *v. Jejunium*, q. 2 n. 7; Elbel *de 3 praec.* n. 383, and so do St. Antoninus, Granado, Vega, etc., cited by Salamancans *ibid.* n. 58. The reason is, because the superior of the place does not have jurisdiction over pilgrims unless they would remain there or at least have a mind to remain there for the greater part of a year, according to what was said in book 1 *On Law*, n. 156.

Here it is of importance to note the indulgence of Pope Benedict XIV in his Brief *Cum sicut, etc.* given on 22 December 1748 in regard to the Kingdoms of Naples and Sicily, dispensing from servile works on feast days, except for Easter and Pentecost, and all other Sundays of the year, likewise on the Circumcision, Epiphany, Ascension, Corpus Christi, Christmas, the Purification, Annunciation, Assumption, Nativity and Immaculate Conception of the Blessed Virgin Mary, likewise on the feast of Sts. Peter and Paul and of All Saints, as well as the principal patronal feast of any city or county region of that diocese. But in other feasts he ordered that only the faithful are held to hear Mass.

CHAPTER II
ON THE FOURTH COMMANDMENT: *HONOR THY FATHER*, ETC.

DUBIUM I
What are children held to in regard to their parents?

333.   *What are sons held to furnish to their parents in regard to love?*
334.   *What in regard to reverence?*
335.   *What in regard to obedience?*

333.—"*Resp.* Everyone is held by the force of this precept to "furnish *love, reverence and obedience* both to parents and "superiors in those matters in which they are subject to them "and for whatever time they subject to them. To the extent that, "if there were a notable defect of these in a grave matter, he "would sin gravely. This happens more easily in respect to "parents than others. Thus the common opinion. See Filliuci, t. "28, p. 2 c. 1, Reginald, lib. 20 cap. 1, etc."

Wherefore, the following are resolved:

"1. A son gravely sins against *love:* a) If he shows signs of "hatred to his parents and treats them bitterly; b) If they always "look upon them with an attitude and speak so bitterly as if "they hate them; c) If they do not assist them in a grave "spiritual or corporal necessity." (Hence, sons also sin gravely "neglecting to offer prayers and sacrifices for their parents. "Salamancans. tr. 24, c. *unic.* punct. 1 § 1 n. 4). "d) If he will not "fulfill their wills and bonds, provided he is the heir; e) If a "grave evil, *e.g.* he desires their death (Navarre, Reginald, l. 20 "n. 8; Filliuci, t. 28, c. 1 q. 3 and 7)."

Therefore, sons sin gravely if they will not see to it that their parents, constituted at the point of death, receive the sacrament of penance and the other rites. Bonacina, *de IV praec.* p. 4 n. 5; Filliuci n. 3; Salamancans *cit.* n. 4 in fin. with Azor, Navarre, Trullenchus. Likewise, if they would prevent their parents from making a will (Bonacina, *ibid.*, Tamburinus, n. 5). Still, that is understood if they impede it with wicked designs; otherwise, if they did it with permissible means, then they will be free from all fault.

334.—"2. A son sins exceedingly against *reverence*: a) If he "strikes his parents even lightly, according to Reginald; b) If "he raises his hand deliberately to strike" (So all hold in "common, as Sporer rightly adverts, *de 4 praec.* c. 5 n. 32, "because in these matters the son sins doubly, against justice "and against piety); "c) If he would gravely sadden his "parents. Reginald l. 20, n. 24; Filliuci, c. 17, n. 17."

(Even if the words would not be gravely contumelious, as Busembaum more probably says later on, and Bonacina, *de 4 praec.* p. 3 n. 4, against Elbel, *eod. titl* n. 357, saying it is not mortal if, resentment of parents does not arise from word or deed, since this is lightly injurious, but from a sinister state of mind, or from their indisposition; for if then reverence is not gravely wounded, at least love for his parents is gravely violated, by bringing them grave sadness without a just cause and deliberately).

"d) If he would provoke to anger from a deliberate intention "with contumelious words, or with such whereby he would "know that he offends them gravely."

(Hence, Roncaglia, in *de 4 praec.* c. 1 r. 1 rightly says in practice he is not excused from a mortal sin who calls his mother "crazy", a "drunkard", a "bitch", a "witch", or a "thief", and similar things. But one who would merely say she is "old", "stupid" or "ignorant", and similar things, I think cannot be absolutely condemned for a mortal sin unless the parent were gravely offended by these words. Moreover, the son would sin gravely who frequently shows his parents a bad attitude, or addressed them with bitter words to show he hates them. Busembaum, as above, and Bonacina, num. 3 with Sylvester, Graffius, Elbel, n. 550, Roncaglia, r. 2).

"e) If he hurls curses and abuse at them." (With the "Continuator of Tournely, *de 4 Dec. praec.* cap. 1 art. 1 sect. 2 "concl. 2 n. 2. Understand in their presence as we will see in the "subsequent annotation. Likewise, if he would mock his parents "deliberately with a gesture or derision, as Sporer says in n. 31 "as well as others. It is said *deliberately*, for in these matters and "similar ones, as above, sons are often excused from a mortal sin "on account of the indeliberate nature of the act, as Bonacina "and Elbel note).

"f) If he would despise his parents because they are poor, or "refuses to acknowledge them. Nevertheless, if he would "dissimulate outwardly that he did not know them and refused "to have them under his roof for a just cause so long as he "provided them what is necessary, Bonacina excuses him from "grave sin, precisely to the extent that they are not reasonably "unwilling." (Hence probably Salamancans, *de 4 praec.* punct. 1 §1 n. 5; Azor, Navarre, Toledo and Trullenchus excuse the son in that case from a mortal sin: 1) if he would suffer a serious loss; 2) if the parents were known for an infamous crime; 3) if he would only dissimulate outwardly without internal contempt because then, as Bonacina says, the parents themselves are not considered gravely or reasonably reluctant).

"g) If in the external forum a son would also accuse his parents of a true crime; outside the crime of heresy, treason or of an oath against the prince, since there would be no other mode of correction. See Bonacina, *l.c.*"

Sporer (d.c. 5 n. 30 and 31) says absolutely that a son cursing his parents or mocking them is not excused from a mortal sin, whether he does it in their presence or in their absence. I do not know how this author, although he is just in his other opinions, and maybe sometimes is more mild than he should be, could assert this absolutely. For, as he himself affirms (*de 8 praec.* c. 6 n. 135) and all authorities teach, reverence or honor is not wounded except by a contumely inflicted in the presence of the offended, or in their absence, but with the purpose that someone else should know. Besides, it happens that many more serious doctors say that by secret fornication in a Church a sacrilege is not committed, nor a Church polluted because, as Coninck hands down (cited by Salamancans *loc. cit.*) the reverence due to the Church consists in the opinion of men, such as reputation, therefore, just as men do not become infamous unless their crimes are made known, so the reverence of a sacred place is not violated unless the crime is publicly made known (Coninck, *de Ritu ven. Sacr.* art. 3 dub. 1 num. 230; Pontius *de matr.* l. 10 c. 10 n. 15, and he asserts it is the common opinion, Toledo, l. 5 c. 8 n. 11; Navarre, c. 27 n. 256 in fin.; likewise, Azor, Vasquez, Sa, etc. cited by the Salamancans *de matr.* c. 15, punct. 5 n. 64; see below on the 6th commandment, n. 458). Whatever the case may be about this opinion, which is probable enough (although the opposite seems more probable to me, because the irreverence in that case is inflicted against God, who assists in the Church and a special way and regards all secret things), what is important to me here, is the reason adduced, namely that reverence is not wounded except by a manifestation of contumely. Therefore, how will a son gravely sin when he curses a parent secretly, or mocks him in his absence, when then there is present neither contumely nor irreverence? And I think this must be said, even if he did this in the presence of others. Nevertheless, I do not deny in this a certain contempt is exercised that is opposed to the reverence due to parents, and a special malice against preserving piety, but such that does not pertain to a mortal sin except in the case in which a son would curse them with a malevolent will or with great contempt, namely if he would curse them in the presence of others with the purpose thereupon they would fall upon his parents or at least by way of presumption that they will fall upon them.

Moreover, Viva, Elbel, Tamburinius, Mazotta and Bonacina (with others) say a son cursing his parents gravely sins whether they are living or dead; but the aforesaid authors (to some extent too inconsiderately) do not explain whether the curse is made with a mind to do so or without a malevolent mind. But even so, it must altogether be understood that he does not sin gravely if he curses without such a mind. And really, Navarre and Filliuci, whom Bonacina cites in favor of this doctrine, so understand it; for Navarre (*Man.* c. 14 n. 12 v. *Sexto*), says the son sins, "who intentionally curses his parent whether living or dead; but if he only cursed them vocally, he commits no more than a venial offense." And Filliuci confirms that in almost the same words.

335.—"3. A son sins gravely against *obedience*: a) If in a "grave matter he were disobedient in regard to those things "which pertain to the governance of the house, good morals, or "the salvation of the soul (Filliuci, n. 20); b) If he takes an "unbecoming [*indigna*] wife against the will of his parent. "Unbecoming [*indigna*] however is said to be a woman with "whom he cannot contract marriage without dishonor "according to the use of his region,[17] still, he cannot be "disinherited (see n. 949); c) If he refuses to marry according to

---

[17] See what will be said in book 6 on Matrimony, n. 851.

"the will of the parent without a just cause, especially if from "that hatreds would be put to rest or the necessity of his "parents would be lifted. On the other hand, it will be a just "cause *e.g.* if the family were inferior, if she was sick, deformed, "foolish or uncivil; d) If he weds without consulting his parents, "as Sanchez holds. Nevertheless, after he has consulted them, he "can prudently contract marriage against their will with a "worthy woman,[18] since the choice of state is his right. Lessius, "lib. 2 c. 40 n. 43; Sanchez, l. 4 c. 14; Filliuci, q. 10 n. 20. Would, "children sin by stealing from their parents, and how? See "below, n. 543.[19] Likewise, whether they can lose possession of "their goods? See below, n. 918."

Therefore, a son is held to obey his parents in those matters which were just discussed and he sins gravely by a special sin that must be explained in confession if the matter were grave, and the parent commanded it in earnest by an express precept. It is otherwise if the parent only warned them, as the authors say (Sporer, *de 4 praec.* c. 5 n. 14; Roncaglia, c. 1 q. 3 and Holzmann, n. 555). Cardinal de Lugo, *de poenit.* d. 16 n. 226 and Bonacina *eod. tit.* part. 6 n. 3, with Navarre and Rodriquez, add that then the son commits this special sin when the parent commands something intending to oblige him with obedience due. Nay more, the authors say then the son sins gravely when he ordinarily transgresses the precept; it is otherwise if once in a while from negligence (Sporer n. 16, Elbel *de 4 praec.* n. 555, with Marchant).

Besides, here we must advert that sons are not held to obey in those things which pertain to the choice of state. Hence, parents sin gravely when they compel their sons against their will, even indirectly, to choose a state of life, whether religious, clerical or conjugal, or on the other hand, if they unjustly force them back,

---

[18] See book 6 on Matrimony, n. 849.
[19] Translator's note: Nos. 543 and 918 will be in the 3rd Volume, on the 7th Commandment.

even without force or fraud from the religious, clerical or conjugal state without a just cause, because it is especially incumbent upon parents to consider the spiritual good of their sons (Molina, t. 5 d. 51 n. 2; Elbel n. 538 and Sporer n. 21 with the common opinion). This is why, if the son thinks he is called by God to the religious or clerical state and knows his parents will unjustly impede him, he may deliberately conceal the matter and carry out the divine will (Elbel, *l.c.*, Bonacina, *l.c.* n. 2 with Sayr, Molfesius, Filliuci and others). I said *unjustly*, for it would need to be said otherwise if the parents would oppose it for a just cause, say, if they would remain in necessity, or if otherwise a most noble family would be extinguished (Elbel n. 539). Still, in the second case I do not think the son would be held to desert his vocation (see the rest that will be said more profusely on this matter in book 5, n. 66).

"4. Children are held to feed needy parents; so much so that "in a grave necessity where they could not be helped otherwise, "a son would be held to remain in the world (unless it were "certain to him, or else very probable that it would threaten a "danger to his salvation), and if he were to enter religion, he "would be held to go out from it and help his parents, provided "their necessity preceded his profession. Filliuci, q. 5 n. 9, "Bonacina, q. 1 p. 6." (See book 5 n. 67).

"5. But if a necessity should come up after profession, if it is "extreme he is held to go out, first seeking permission and then "even if pardon is not obtained. If however it is only grave, in "which they could live to some extent, he is certainly not held, "still he can go out if his superior would permit it. In such a "case he is held, insofar as it does not stand in the way of his "purpose, to delay the habit and observe the substantial things "of religion, but, after assistance has been provided to his "parents, to return. Lessius, l. 2 c. 41, dub. 3." (See below on the "state of religion, l. 5 n. 67)."

DUBIUM II
To what matters are parents held toward their sons?

336. What are parents held to furnish to their sons in regard to nourishment and education?
337. To what is a father to give as a dowry for his daughter if she marries against his consent?
338. The Sanction of Naples in regard to nourishment of children.
339. To what else are parents held?
340. To what are brothers held?
341. Could parents at some time disinherit their sons? And what would be the just causes for it? (See also more on this in n. 948 and 949)

336.—"Parents, by which term those rising up to take their "place are also understood, *e.g.* grandparents, great-"grandparents, etc., are held by a grave obligation of natural "law to see to the preservation and education of children. "Bonacina, disp. 5 q. 1; Azor, p. 2 l. 2 q. 17; Filliuci tr. 28 c. 2.

Thus, the following cases are resolved:

"1. Parents gravely sin, who without a just cause abandon a "child in a hospital or in public places. See Bonacina and "Filliuci, t. 21 p. 2 c. 2 and below treatise 5, c. 1." (But a just cause is, if the child is illegitimate, as Layman, Diana, Henriquez, the Salamancans, *de IV praecept.* punct. 2 n. 36 all say with probability. See *on restitution,* n. 656).

"2. A mother is held (though under venial sin) to nurse with "her own milk, unless she has a just excuse." (*E.g.* if she were

TREATISE III: THE THIRD AND FOURTH PRECEPTS CH. II 377

weak, or noble due to custom. Salamancans, *ibid.* n. 35, with Navarre, Azor, Trullenchus, etc.).

"But then she is held under mortal sin to seek a good nurse "(Bonacina, d. 6 q. 1 p. 6; Laymann). Likewise, she is held, "according to rights, to feed and nurse her child until the end of "the third year." (But if the mother cannot give milk, the father is held to the expenses of lactation. Croix, l. 3 p. 1 n. 697, and the Salamancans, *loc. cit.* n. 34, with the common opinion).

"After education, even to emancipation, looks to the father. "Except, unless he were poor and the mother rich. Filliuci, "Laymann, l. 5 tr. 10 c. 3 n. 4; Reginald, l. 20 n. 32."

"3. The father is held to see to the nourishment of his "offspring, not only legitimate, but even illegitimate (where we "see civil law is corrected by canonical law, according to *c. Cum* "*haberet*), this is, food, drink, clothing and genuine skills, "according to their state. Nevertheless, it is otherwise if he "could provide for himself from another place and would not "need it. Lastly, he is held to provide a dowry for his daughter."

In respect to sons, the authors say that the father is held to furnish nourishment not only to the son, but even to his wife, even if he married her without a dowry and against the will of her father (Sanchez, *de matr.* l. 4 d. 26 n. 21; Bossius, *de effectu matr.* p. 2 c. 4 num. 95, with the Gloss in *c. Admonere* 33 q. 2 and *Surdus as well as Megala*). Besides, Azor (p. 2 l. 2 c. 4 q. 12) as well as Merenda (*Controv.* l. 4 c. 34 n. 6) with Baldus (Authent. *Quod locum, c. de collation.*, n. 7 et 8), and Jason (Authent. *Si captivi, c. de episcopis et clericis*, n. 12) hold that the father ought to feed his son even if the son viciously consumed the portion already given to him.

"And clerics certainly also can furnish, from ecclesiastical "fruits, these things for their illegitimate offspring. Filliuci, *loc.* "*cit.* t. 28 c. 2 n. 28; Laymann, l. 5 t. 10 p. 3 c. 5. See below, tr. 5 c.

"4 d. 5 q. 1. Hence, they sin: a) If the do not apply diligence, at "least moderate, to acquire the goods with which their sons are "to be fed and have an inheritance according to their state; b) If "by squandering goods they render themselves powerless to "genuinely educate and give dowries to their children according "to their state (Bonacina, d. 6 § 2, from Azor, Filliuci, etc.); c) If "without a legitimate cause they refuse a dowry to their "daughter (or disinherit a son), *e.g.* because she wants to enter "or has entered religion, or because she married against their "will even if it was out of her state (Bonacina, *l.c.* from Azor, "Reginald, etc.), or because a son receives holy orders; just as a "father is held to provide a dowry to his daughters for marriage "or entrance into religion, so also to sons when they receive "holy orders. And this gift is not revocable, nay more, what has "been so given, cannot include in the reckoning against the law, "or a division with brothers, as Barbosa teaches (c. 17). Still, "Molina holds the contrary, with Diana (p. 8 t. 6 r. 91 and 92)." (And the Salamancans, tract. 24, *de IV praec.* punct. 4 § 2 n. 78. But see what is going to be said about contracts, n. 956, where we will see about other goods that will be contracted in conference by sons).

337.—There is a question, whether the father is held to give a dowry for his daughter when she marries against his will? We distinguish and affirm if the daughter were married for more than 25 years, even if out of her state, as the authors hold (Sanchez, *de matrimonio*, l. 4 d. 26, n. 11; the Salamancans, *ibid.* punct 2 n. 40, with Bonacina, Trullenchus, etc.). But there is a greater doubt: what if she was married for less than 25 years? Some affirm it absolutely, but others, only if she married unworthily, others say the father is held only to provide her sustenance, but only if she needs it, and this, even if she married unworthily. Sanchez, n. 18 and 19; the Salamancans, *ibid.* n. 20, with Molina, Trullenchus, Covarruvias. And this is more probable. Hence, Sanchez (n. 20) infers, with Trullenchus and Bonacina (cited by the Salamancans, *loc. cit.* n. 42) that if the son also entered into marriage against his father's will, the father provides for him and his wife when they are needy. See what is going to be said in n. 949.

338.—Here we must note in passing the most recent Council at Naples, with the four halls joined, in a sanction to which his royal Majesty assented on 15 December 1742. There, it was ratified that it is not lawful for parents to expel their children and sons, or some of them, unduly from their own house and then to furnish sustenance to them outside the home without a just cause approved by law or by a judge. And on the other hand, the right is not imparted to sons, children or any of them have to depart from obedience to their father of their own will and to demand sustenance outside the paternal home; rather, the will to not live with a parent so as to benefit the other sons by furnishing sustenance from outside the home, since the will of the sons would be the cause of virtue, not of vice. This must be observed inviolably hereafter as perpetual law, not withstanding any other interpretation of matters to be judged being taken to authority.

339.—"4. A parent is held to assist his child after they have "relinquished religion, in the same cases in which children "would the parent. See the previous dubium, cases 4 and 5, n. "335.

"5. Parents are held by a grave obligation to instruct their "children personally or through others in matters necessary to "salvation. Hence, they gravely sin: a) If they do not see to it "that their children are imbued with good morals, learn "Christian doctrine or the rudiments of faith, avoid the "company of bad children, observe the commands of God and "the Church, frequent the Sacraments and avoid sins (Azor, "Filliuci, Bonacina *l.c.*); b) If they do not turn them away from "occasions of sin or permit them to spend time in suspect places "or houses (Trullenchus, t. 1 d. 3 n. 4); c) If their children "become corrupted by their counsel or bad example; d) If they "do not scold and punish dissolute children, but moderately. "Nevertheless, they do not sin even by beating them "immoderately, *e.g.* that they are notably injured. (del Soto, "Sylvius, Bonacina, *loc. cit.* and d. 3 *de contr.* q. ult. p. 3)."

"6. Parents are held also to leave to the child freedom in "regard to choice of state. Wherefore, they sin in compelling "their children to marry against their will or to choose religion, "or by removing them from it.[20] And even the Council of Trent, "sess. 25 *de Reg.* c. 18 excommunicates anyone compelling their "daughters to enter a convent."

340.—"Even though a brother is held to assist his brother or "sister in an extreme necessity (or at least in an apparent "extreme necessity), both by the law of charity and piety, still, it "is not the same obligation which exists between parents and "children, since there is no dependency (See Lessius, l. 2 c. 31 n. "34). This is why, if he is professed in religion, he is not held to "go out to succor them. Trullenchus, l. 2 c. 2 d. 24 n. 8, from "Suarez, etc." (See book 5, n. 67).

Still, we must note here that everyone is held in both forums, if he could, to furnish sustenance and dowries for his brothers or sisters not only in an extreme necessity, but even in a grave necessity (Salamancans, tr. 24 *de IV praec.* punct. 4 § 1 num. 69, with Azor, Trullenchus, Fagundez, Barbosa, Menochius, etc.). The authorities extend this doctrine to brothers born from the same father, even if they are from a different mother; for these are lawfully considered to be joined on every side from the law *Cum plures* §. *Cum tutor. ff. De administratione tutorum.* But if brothers, just as if sisters, are only related on the side of the

---

[20] See above, n. 335 and what will be said in book 5, n. 850.

mother, then the obligation is to provide sustenance, but not dowries to their sisters.

341.—"One might ask whether a son at some point could be "deprived of his inheritance by his father?
"*Resp.* He can for a just cause, otherwise he cannot. The "same should be expressed in his will. *Auth. Sed si post, c. de* "*inoff. test.* A just cause, however, would be considered: a) "Ingratitude (unless he returned to the grace of the father and "did penance before the will has been drawn up) such as if he "caused a grave injury to his father, or plotted against his life, "or raised his hand against him, or will have mixed himself in "malefices (Bonacina, d. 3 quaest. 7 p. 4, from Covarruvias, "Sanchez, Azor, Molina, etc.); b) If he carnally knew the "stepmother or wife of the father; if he refused to help a frantic "parent or refused to offer bail for one found to be detained in "prison, or if he would impede his father from giving evidence, "if he would bring the goods of his parents to ruin with grave "expense to them; c) If a daughter younger than 25 years chose "a lustful life, etc. Note, in regard to those things which impact "these causes, when the son has from another source what is "necessary to live, since he cannot be deprived of the necessary "sustenance for life as it is due by the law of nature, it also "cannot be taken away by civil law. Bonacina, disp. 6 qu. 1 p. 6 "§3, from Sanchez, Molina, Azor, Reginald, Filliuci, "Trullenchus, lib. 1 cap. 1 d. 3 n. 16 and t. 2 lib. 7 and cap. 17." (It is otherwise in regard to things necessary to state. Salamancans, *ibid.* punct. 2 n. 43 with the common opinion. In regard to disinheritance of sons, see on contracts, n. 948 and 949).

DUBIUM III
To what are tutors, and legal guardians who stand in loco parentis *held to?*

"A Tutor (it is the same for a legal guardian) is held to "manage the care of the pupil, and his due goods, and to "faithfully administer them. The reason is because he is "constituted for this purpose and the pupil assigned to him in "place of the father. This is why if he fails or is notably "negligent in this matter he sins gravely and is obliged to "compensation for the loss which the pupil receives from him "(and at least from the fraud and sin conveyed). Nay more, if he "exercises the office of tutor for a price (nevertheless, which if "it was not constituted from the beginning, it is reckoned he "took the job for free), he is also held to venial sin. Bonacina, *de* "*contract.* d. 3 qu. 19 p. 4."

Wherefore the following are resolved:

"1. A tutor is held to safeguard the person of his pupil, as "long as it is necessary, and imbue him with good morals and "educate him rightly in his own person or through others. "Bonacina, *l.c.*"

"2. He is held to faithfully administer the goods of the pupil "and therefore (receiving the office of tutor) to draw up an "inventory, otherwise to make good the losses that follow from "its defect; nor is it lawful for him to concede to the pupil too "much money for nugatory uses."

"3. The tutor (and also a legal guardian) is held to preserve "all rights, goods and actions of the pupil (or a minor) and to "sell goods lest they go to waste and convert the money into the "purchase of stable goods, or in an estimate, etc., exactly as it "will be more useful (*Ibid.* ex Rebello, *de oblig. justit.*, p. 2 lib. 17 "q. 1).

"4. If the tutor or guardian converts the money of the pupil "into his own use, he is held to make restitution of the whole "*lucrum cessans*, or make good an emergent loss that the pupil or a minor receives thereafter. *Bonacina, Rebell.* q. 17."

"5. Likewise, he is held to make restitution of the fruits (after expenses have been deducted), which he could have gained for the goods of his pupil but did not by his own fault. *Sylvius, v. Tutor,* § 4; Reb. *loc. cit.*"

"6. He is held to examine the names of debtors and pay the debts of the pupil; still, as much as it can be done, so that he might look out for the good of the pupil (Sylvius, Rebello *ll.cc.*, Tabienus, *ibid.*)"

"7. The tutor or guardian cannot make donations or gratuitous abatements from the goods of the pupil, because he was not constituted to ruin him, but to safeguard him (*ibid*). An exception is made for a donation of remuneration, then he can, *e.g.* adding a stipend due for free service from a free donation (Molina, de Lugo, d. 23, sect. 10, Sanchez, Trullenchus, lib. 7 cap. 18, d. 8. See Diana, p. 8 t. 6 r. 17)."

"8. Lastly, he is held (by the purpose of his office), to render accounts because this is the common burden of those who administer another's goods (see Bonacina, *de contr.* d. 3 qu. 19 p. 4 and later in this book, n. 917 *et seq.*)"

DUBIUM IV
What is the obligation of masters, servants and other superiors and inferiors toward each other?

342. What are superiors held to furnish to subjects? Are princes held to choose more worthy men for offices?
343. What are servants held to furnish to their masters?
344. Would servants that fail to stop the theft of their master's goods be held to restitution?

342.—"*Resp.* 1) Masters and superiors are held to have care of their servants and of their other subjects. This is clear from

"1 Timothy 5:8, 'But if any man does not have care of his own and particularly, of those of his own household, he has denied the faith and is worse than an infidel.' And the reason is, because they are their head and stand in the place of parents, so they are held to the same things as parents in the same way. In the first place, they are held to see to it, as much as they can, that they keep the precepts of God and the Church. Bonacina, dub. 16, q. 1 part. 8."

Quaeritur: Albeit it is in passing, the question arises as to whether secular princes are held to choose more worthy men to secular offices? The following authors affirm this: The Salamancans, *de IV praec.* punct. 6 § 2 n. 103, with del Soto, Bañez, Lessius, Trullenchus, etc. But Cajetan, Vasquez, de Lugo etc. deny it, provided that offices are not distributed to the unworthy, because, as these authors say, these offices do not pertain to distributive justice, nor are they common goods, but rather more of the king, who satisfies if he rules the state for the common good, but not in the worthiest manner possible. Both opinions are probable, but the first opinion is more probable, because otherwise the state would suffer a serious injury. For that motive de Lugo concludes (although in n. 19 he held the opposite), that at length, princes are normally held to choose those who are more worthy for any specific job (d. 34, n. 21). But could kings sell secular offices? Many authors deny this, such as Adrian, Angelus, Turrianus and Medina, cited by the Salamancans *l.c.* n. 94 from 1 *Haec lex ff. ad leg. Jul. de ambit.* where it is expressly forbidden. But Navarre, Cajetan, del Soto, Sanchez, Azor, etc. with St. Thomas (Opusc. 21, cited by the Salamancans *ibid.* ex. n. 95) say they can, provided the sale were altogether necessary for the advantage of the commonwealth, and provided it were sold for a modest price, and to worthy men, and inasmuch as it can be done, to the worthier. Moreover, all agree with St. Thomas that this sale is not expedient; understand on greater offices of magistrates, to whom it is given to administer justice; but not on lesser ones, in which it is only fitting to carry out the duty. See the Salamancans, *l.c.*

"1. Masters sin gravely: 1) If they would impede their "servants from hearing Mass on feast days without a just cause; "or that impose servile works upon them on feast days; or if "they command those things which cannot be done without "venial sin. Navarre, cap. 14, etc. 2. If they permit an occasion of "sin when they could impede it, or if they do not correct those "who are gravely delinquent, or do not advise those who are "unaware of what is necessary for salvation, and do not rebuke "them. Bonacina, *l.c.*" (The common opinion with the "Salamancans, *de IV praec.* punct. 7 § 4 n. 140).

"2. Likewise, they sin gravely: a) If they afflict them with "grave injuries, calling them devils, dogs, etc. Bonacina, *l.c.* and "Trullenchus, l. 4 c. 1 d. 5, although Diana (p. 7 t. 7 tr. 47) "excuses such contumely from sin when it arises from anger, "and is usually advanced from a lack of deliberation." (And really, these are not commonly considered grave injuries).

"b) If they do not furnish them with suitable sustenance, a "just wage (provided they faithfully serve them), do not pay "them or delay the payment without a reasonable cause. *Ibid.* c) "If before their term of service is at an end they rashly expel "them from the house; in which case (unless they did it from "grave cause) they are held to pay their whole wage. Lessius, "Azor, c. 14, q. 1; Filliuci, n. 117, Reginaldus, Molina, etc. "Escobar, t. 3 e. 9 . q. 3." (as the Salamancans say in tr. 24, punct. 7 § 4 n. 151, with the common opinion. Nor would a servant, unjustly expelled, be held to go back to complete the time of his service; say, if the suitable time were already completed say, if the suitable time were already transacted, and he did not fulfill it by his own fault, then the master would be held to pay the promised salary. But there is a doubt, if the servant suffered no loss from the expulsion, would the whole salary be due to him? In this we can opine with probability, according to what will be said in n. 345, that the master is held in a penalty of injustice in conscience to pay him more than half his salary, nay more to give the whole wage as Lessius notes in l. 2 c. 24 num. 8, from l. *Qui operas*, 38 and l. 16 ff. *Locati;* but we say this, not until after the sentence, according to the rule of all penalties).

"d) If he, who corrupts children and other domestic servants "with words or example or poor morals and is not corrected by "a rebuke, would not dismiss him from the house. Navarre, c. "14, Azor, Trullenchus, d. 61 n. 2."

"3. A master is not held to give a salary to a sick servant "(while he is sick) except *in extremis*, or in grave necessity (for "then he ought to from charity), nay more, he can demand back "the expenses taken up in his care. Molina, l. 1 t. 28 c. 4 n. 8; "Escobar, t. 3 e. 9." (Salamancans *ibid.* n. 149 with Molina, Azor, "Lessius, commonly n. 7. See what will be said in this book, n. "864)."

343.—"Resp. 2. Servants and other subjects are held to "furnish to their masters and superiors in some manner the "same love, reverence and obedience which they show their "parents. the reason is clear from the aforesaid, because they "are for them as if in *loco parentis*. St. Thomas, II IIæ. q. 103; "Reginald, l. 20 n 26."

Wherefore, the following are resolved:
"1. Servants sin gravely: a) If they will not work or faithfully "carry out their service, and they are held to make "compensation for the loss (Molina, Lessius, l. 1 c. 24)."

"b) If they inflict grave loss or permit it to be inflicted when "they could have impeded it (Navarre, c. 14, n. 22; Filliuci tr. 28 "c. 3 q. 10; Reginaldus, *l.c.* And indeed, if that loss were inflicted "whether by a relative or a stranger in matters over which care "was consigned to them, they cannot be excused from "restitution. Molina, Lessius, l. 2 c. 23 p. 30 n. 65, Filliuci tr. 36 c. "9 q. 9 n. 114."

"c) If they depart from their master before the tenure of "their service has elapsed without a very serious reason; but "they are not held to remain beyond this, even if they could not "offer their service for some time due to being impeded by "illness. Molina, *l.c.* Reginaldus, n. 517, Escobar, e. 7 n. 50."

"d) If they do not obey their master in matters of great "importance."

344.—*Quaeritur I:* Would servants that do not impede thefts of their master's effects be held to make restitution? Some uphold this in all respects, such as Renzi (*de IV praec.* cap. 1 quaest. 21 and *de VII praec.* sect. 3 quaest. 25, with Pontius and Diana, against Rebello, Molina and Bonacina). Because, as they say, by reason of his service the Lord seems to have consigned his effects to the custody of every servant. But others, such as Lessius (l. 2 c. 13 n. 75), de Lugo, (*de justitia,* d. 19), Holzmann (*de rest.* n. 437), the Salamancans (*de 4 praec. cit.* n. 138), with Molina, Azor, etc., more commonly and probably distinguish the matter, saying that if the loss comes about from a household member, and the servants were not particularly consigned the care of those things (as altogether must be held with Busembaum and the common opinion), then the servants are not held to make restitution. Then, the servants only sin against charity but not justice, because they are not obliged from justice to safeguard their master's things from household members. Nevertheless, it is otherwise if the theft were committed by a stranger, as the Salamancans say (*l.c.*) with the common opinion, as well as Tamburinius (*dec.* lib. 8 tr. 4 c. 3 §6), who adds in that case each servant is held to make restitution *in solidum*,[21] for each of them, when they can, are held to impede the theft and if they cannot

---

[21] Translator's note: Of the whole.

impede it alone, they at least ought to call for their fellow servants to impede the theft.

345.—*Quaeritur II*: Whether a servant, offering his labor for a year, if he departed before a year by his own fault, could seek his pay for the time that he was in service? The more common opinion affirms it, against Molina (unless grave loss would come about to his master from it); because the service rendered merits its wage, although not the whole of that which was agreed; for that reason, the master is held to pay at least a little less than half of the stipend (Azor, p. 2 l. 2 c. 3 q. 6; Filliuci, tr. 28, p. 2 c. 3 n. 68; Sylvius, *v. Fam.*, q. 6 and Trullenchus, Diana, Fagundez with the Salamancans *de IV praec.* punct. 7 §3 n. 132.

346.—*Quaeritur III*: Whether a servant, offering his labor for a year, if he were sick for months, is held to supply the lost labor? No, from the common opinion with the Salamancans, *ibid.* n. 133, as well as Azor, Bonacina, etc., because the promise is bound to a determined period of time. But he cannot seek the salary for the time in which he was sick, as was said above with Busembaum, n. 342, at the end.

347.—*Quaeritur IV*: Whether a servant, after three years has elapsed after he departed from his master, can seek his salary and secretly compensate himself? Some authors uphold it because, although the servant loses the right to seek the stipend in the external forum, following the prescription of three years (as Covarruvias, Medina and Lamas say against Molina), according to Spanish law, or bull 33 of St. Pius V wherein, after two years after service was furnished the servant is deprived of the right to seek the salary, or according to the sanction of the Council of Naples with all the halls joined, (related below in n. 516), wherein after two months have elapsed after the servant departs from his lord, the right of seeking his wage in a judgment is denied him

TREATISE III: THE THIRD AND FOURTH PRECEPTS CH. II 389

(Sanchez, *de matrimonio* l. 7 d. 37 n. 17 and the Salamancans, *ibid.* n. 134, with Molina, Fagundez, Villalobos and others). Nevertheless, the servant always retains the right in the forum of conscience and the master, if he is certain that he did not pay, always seems to be held to the payment; so much the more because in the aforesaid decision (published for the Kingdom of Naples) it is said the action must be denied to the servant, not from the support of the claim but from the force of expected payment. But this must be understood, if it were morally certain to the servant that the master did not legitimately pay him; for if the master otherwise ordained a payment for three years with a title, and in good faith, in that case neither would the master be held to pay, nor could the servant compensate himself, even if he were certain that the payment was not made because then the master acquired the right of not paying by reason of the claim, according to what is going to be said below *On the Seventh Commandment*, n. 517.

348.—*Quaeritur V:* Whether a servant, serving with no wage established, could seek a just stipend (at least the lowest) or filch it secretly? Distinguish, if a master of this sort usually borrows the work of servants, then affirmative. It is otherwise if not, seeing that it happens with boys whom nobles or Bishops are asked to admit into their household; for then it suffices if the masters give them meals, clothing and lodging, seeing that such is the custom (Salamancans tr. 24 punct. 7 § 3, n. 135, with Molina, Azor, Trullenchus, Villalobos, Fagundez, etc). Moreover, no salary is due for servants who learn their trades from their masters while they serve them (Salamancans *ibid.* n. 136, with Azor, Molina, Rebello, Fagundez). Unless it were otherwise in use in regard to some trade, from the nobility of the trade seeing that the master demands something from the student, like the art of constructing a clock. From the ignobility of a trade a student should often receive something from the teacher, such as is the art of one who pounds with a hammer, etc. Therefore, it must be seen according to prudence of the will, what is heeded from use in any art.

349.—"2. Servants do not sin if they use secret compensation "when sustenance or a just wage are refused them by their "master (Molina, *l.c.*, FIlliuci, tr. 36 c. 6, q. 3), provided that "there is no other mode to seek it, they did not receive more "than is due, and scandal or another inconvenience is not "feared. See Bonacina, *de rest.* d. 2 q. ult. p. 2 n. 16." (Still, in this "matter take note of the 37th proposition condemned by Pope "Innocent XI. See *On the Seventh Commandment*, n. 522).

"3. Similarly, for services rendered to which they are not "held (if they were not freely and liberally furnished, but done "with a mind to remuneration), it is lawful for him to take "compensation from the goods of his master which he "otherwise could not attain (Navarre, c. 17 n. 108; Lessius, *l.c.*). "For more on these see below, tr. 5 c. 1 d. 4 and c. 3 d. 10, as well "as Bonacina d. 6 q. 1 p. 8." (Unless they increased their work of "their own will. Salamancans, *ibid.* n. 136, with Molina, del Soto, "Diana, etc.)"

But could servants compensate themselves the salary for the greater work furnished? See n. 522.

350.—Here it must be noted in passing the question unto the practical utility, whether slaves taken in a just war can licitly flee to their homes? Molina, Sylvius, Panormus and others cited by the Salamancans (*ibid.* § 1. n. 115) deny it, because such servants are considered to be perpetually condemned to servitude, since the master justly possesses them. Still, Lessius (l. 2. c. 5 n. 24), del Soto, de Lugo, Palaus, Filliuci, Vasquez, and a great many authors, with the Salamancans (*ibid.* n. 116) more commonly and probably hold the contrary. The reason is, because such a law of nations to make men taken in a just war slaves, has been accepted in such a way that freedom to flee is left to them. And it is clear from *Instit.* l. 2 tit. 1 *de rer. divis.*, where in n. 17 it is said of them: "Nevertheless, if they evade our power and return to their own, they recover their former state.

DUBIUM V
To what are spouses held in regard to each other by the force of this precept?

    351. *To what is a wife held in regard to her husband?*
    352. *Whether a noble wife is held to furnish common duties?*
    353. *Would an agreement for a wife not to change domicile hold? Moreover, would the wife be held to follow her husband if he were sent into exile?*
    354. *When her husband is dead, is a wife held to pay debts contracted to sustain a household?*
    355. *What is a wife held to restore to the sons of a first marriage?*
    356. *In what way would a husband sin against his wife?*

351.—"*Resp.* A wife is held to obey her husband in those "matters which pertain to the governance of the house and "good morals; nevertheless, he is to treat his wife not as a "servant but as a companion. The reason is because the "husband is the head, and the wife the limb. Navarre, c. 14, n. "20; Trullenchus, Filliuci, t. 28 c. 9 q. 6 n. 144, and the common "opinion.

Thus the following are resolved:

"1. Spouses sin: a) If they do not contract matrimony with "the intention that is due; b) If they omit the reading of the "bans without a dispensation; c) If they contract the sacrament "of matrimony in a state of mortal sin; d) If they use matrimony "against nature, or in an undue mode, or with danger of "miscarriage; e) If they refuse the marriage debt without a just "cause; f) If they have unchaste contact with the danger of "pollution."

"2. A wife sins gravely: a) If she were to provoke her "husband to great anger or blasphemy with quarrels, or other "words (Filliuci, *l.c.* n. 145 and Bonacina); b) If she were to "expend something notable against the will of her husband and "the custom of women of a similar state, except from her own "goods outside her dowry, if she has such; c) If , despising her "husband, she claims mastery over him; d) If she refuses to "follow her husband when he changes domicile, provided it can "be done without danger to life and safety, and there are no "contrary arrangements, and her husband does not become a "vagrant after marriage (Navarre, Toledo, Bonacina, p. 7. See "below, . 5 c. 1 dub. 4); e) If without sufficient information she "judges badly in regard to the continence of her husband; f) If "without a just cause she refuses the marriage debt (see below, "book 6); g) If she thrusts herself into the management of the "house without a just cause, such as, if her husband wastes the "goods of the household (Sylvius, Trullenchus, c. 1 d. 4 n. 18)."

Or, if he were careless or less suited to manage the household. Elbel, t. 2 *conf.* 21, with Filliuci, Gobat, and Henno).

352.—*Quaeritur I:* Is a noble wife held to furnish common duties when her husband commands, such as to prepare food, sweep the house, etc.? Angelus (*v. Uxor*, num. 2), Tiraquellus (*de Nobilitate*, cap. 20 n. 95) etc., uphold this. But other authors more probably deny it, because the wife is a companion, and therefore not held to furnish the work of the household which is unbecoming of her state (Sanchez, *de matrimonio*, l. 6 d. 6 n. 14, Salamancans, *de IV praec.* punct. 3 §2 n. 59, with Sylvius, Gar., Fagundez, etc.). And if she does furnish it, she can compensate herself, as they say.

353.—In the case of the wife's refusal, an agreement to not change domicile more probably avails (Sanchez, *de matrimonio*, l. 1 d. 40 n. 2, with Lopez, Palaus, etc., against others). But this must be understood, unless a new and grave cause would arise (Sanchez, n. 23, Salamancans *ibid.* n. 61, with Navarre, Sylvius, Fagundez, etc.).

Quaeritur II: Would a woman be held to follow her husband if he were sent into exile? Henriquez and Baldus (cited by Salamancans *ibid.* n. 62) reject this because the innocent wife is not held to undergo the penalty of her husband. But the Salamancans (*ibid.*) as well as Sanchez (lib. 1 d. 41 n. 11) more probably uphold this with others because the wife is held not to suffer the punishment, but the misfortune of her husband. The Salamancans (*loc. cit.*) and Palaus say the same thing if the husband were excommunicated somewhere. On the other hand, the Salamancans with the same doctors say that if a woman being compelled by necessity were to change domicile, the husband ought to accompany her.

354.—*Quaeritur III:* After the death of her husband, would a wife be held to pay debts he contracted to provide for the family from the goods of her dowry?

The first opinion answers in the affirmative if the husband was poor when he contracted the debts; it is otherwise if he was wealthy, because the poor man was not held to provide for his wife; therefore, she is held to pay what was converted into cash for her utility. So think Fagundez, Bartolus, Lupus, and others with Sanchez, l. 9 d. 4 n. 28.

But the *second opinion* more probably denies this whether the man was poor or rich. The reason is because the action of repaying loans made that were contracted to their creditors is personal, that is, only against the husband; and although the obligation to provide for his wife was suspended by reason of poverty, still it was not extinguished. This is why if he provided from a loan, he is responsible for his own debt. (Sanchez, n. 29,

Salamancans *ibid.* n. 64, with Molina, Trullenchus and Bonacina, who still places the limitation if the husband contracted the debts in the name of his wife either with her knowledge or if the husband was publicly witnessed to have not wished to, favoring his poverty, to freely provide for her. And what was said here on support of the wife, is also said on support for the sons (Salamancans *loc. cit.*).

355.—*Quaeritur IV:* Whether a woman going into her second marriage should reserve something she received from her first husband for the sons of the first marriage that was retained as a usufruct? It is upheld by the law *Ex testamento*, and *In donatione* c. *de secundis nupt.*, if she receives from a profitable title; still, otherwise if it were onerous or if she received it from an outside source. And the same is said in respect to a husband concerning something given by his first wife. Sanchez, lib. 6 d. 41; Salamancans tr. 23 punct. 3 § 2 n. 66, with others.

356.—"3. A husband sins gravely: a) If he afflicts his wife "with contumelious or defamatory words." (And such a sin would be of a twofold malice, as the Salamancans say *ibid.* § 1 n. 46). "b) If he impeded her in regard to the precepts of God or "the Church without a just cause. Sayr, l. 7 c. 7, Navarre, c. 14. "But if he were also to impede her without cause in regard to "those goods which are only of counsel, *e.g.* confession, "communion, etc., the common opinion is that he only sins "venially unless it were certain that she would secure great "advantage from them (Sayr., Filliuci, Bonacina, q. 1 p. 7; "Trullenchus); c) If he should strike her gravely; whereas he "can moderately castigate her with words or even, due to a "grave cause, mild beatings, held by reason of condition and "state." (Elbel consents to this, *Conf.* 21 n. 58 with Gobat.) "d) If "he refuses support, unless the wife departs the common life of "her husband by her own fault." (Or unless she commits adultery, according to Sanchez, *de Matrimonio* l. 10 d. 8 n. 25, Palaus, *de spons.* d. 3 p. 6 § 5 and Croix l. 3 p. 1 n. 714. But the husband cannot retain the dowry of an adulterous wife if she departs from the house of her own authority before the sentence; although he could oppose the exception for adultery and seek the dowry from a repentant wife that it be applied to him exactly as Croix says with greater probability, with Abbat, and Palaus, against Sanchez). "e) If he neglects the governance "of the house and domestic business; f) If he does not cohabitate "with his wife or is away for a long time without a just cause; g) "If when he could he did not procure sustenance. See Filliuci n. "140 and 141; Navarre, c. 14, n. 19; Toledo lib. 5 c. 2, Sanchez, l. "10 *de matr.* disp. 18 n. 18; Bonacina p. 7."

DUBIUM VI
What is the obligation of parish priests toward their subjects?

357. *To what are parish priests held to in regard to residency?*
358. *To what are they held in regard to administering the sacraments, especially in a time of plague?*
359. *Are they held to celebrate Mass for the people?*
360. *Are they held to preach and instruct the people, etc.? How are parish priests held to correct their subjects? Dub. I. Whether they are held to it from charity, or from justice? Dub. II. Whether they are held to inquire into the morals of their subjects? Dub. III. Whether they are held to not desert the sheep even in danger of death?*

357.—"*Resp.* The curate, or pastor, is held by divine law: 1) "To reside in his own parish. (Council of Trent, sess. 23, c. 1, *de* "*Reformatione*; Barbosa, *de off. paroch.* c. 8 n. 1). Otherwise, in "conscience he does not generate his fruit, and he is held to "make restitution for a fixed absence to the upkeep of the "Church or a pious cause. Nevertheless, he can, for a just cause "and with the permission of the Bishop, be absent for a brief period. See Navarre, c. 5; Azor, t. 2 l. 2 c. 4; Possevino, Barbosa, Trullenchus, l. 4 c. 1 d. 8." (In regard to residence, see what is going to be said on benefices in book 5, n. 121 and 123).

358.—"He is held to administer the sacraments." (Not only in extreme necessity, but even in a grave one, according to the Salamancans, tract. 21, *de Charit.* c. 6 punct. 3 § 1 n. 33, with St. Thomas and the common opinion. And there Bonacina adds that the parish priest is held also to inquire after the seriously needy.)

359.—"3. To pray for the people and celebrate that the people might hear Mass; he is also held to apply it for them at least on feast days and on a few other days as Cardinal Toledo teaches (l. 3 c. 5). But Suarez (*De Sacramentis*, qu. 83, n. 199), and Coninck (in 3 p. q. 83 art. 1), reject this, since no law stipulates this. See Bonacina, *qu. ult.*, Barbosa, *loc. cit.*"

Note here what our most Holy Pope, Benedict XIV, established in his Encyclical Letter *Cum Semper*, published in the year 1744, that any pastor, whether having suitable proceeds or not, is held to apply Mass for the people on all Sundays and feast days. And although it was conceded to some pastor if he could not otherwise live to apply the Mass for alms offered on feast days, nevertheless, it was ratified that they should supply Masses for the people on other ferial days. And in regard to vicars, or managers of ecclesiastical vacancies, the faculty was given to Bishops to assign a fitting portion of the fruits for them, so that they could equally celebrate for the people on feast days. See Book 6, n. 326.

360.—"4. To teach the people by preaching, argument, etc. personally or through others. Toledo, l. 5 c. 5 c. 5; Possevino, Barbosa, Trullenchus, *ll.cc.*" (See what was said on the third "commandment, n. 269. Equally, superiors of religious are also "held to shepherd their subjects by preaching, just as pastors. "Elbel, *Conf.* 21, n. 583, with Henno)."

"5. He is held on every Sunday as well as solemn feasts, to "explain Christian doctrine to the people either in himself or "through another, as is certain from the Council of Trent, sess. "24, c. 4 *de ref.* and it under a grave obligation even of divine "law, because of the supreme necessity on account of which "they can be compelled by Bishops and other prelates under the "penalty of excommunication (and all others that they might "listen to it, learn and know) as Trullenchus (l. 1 c. 1 d. 4 n. 7 et "8), Bald. (t. 2 l. 1 d. 48), Sanchez, Palaus, Barbosa and others "teach. (He can rightly be understood to satisfy this obligation to explain Christian doctrine through another. Trullenchus, and Ledesma, cited by Salamancans tr. 21, c. 2, punct. 5 n. 55).

"6. He is held to visit the sick and have care of the poor, to "rebuke sins, etc. Possevinus, Reginaldus, tom. 2 l. 20 c. 5 sect. "3; Barbosa, c. 7; see above."

Pastors (and so much more Bishops) are held *sub gravi* to correct the sheep persisting in mortal sin and the proximate occasion of sin, even with a crisis of life and not only in extreme, but even their grave necessity, as if the hope of correction were always present. So runs the common opinion (Bonacina, d. 3 q. 4 p. 4 n. 5, with Valentia, Maldero, and Reginald; likewise Viva, de praec. q. 21 art. 6 n. 12; Mazotta tom. 1 p. 458, Salamancans tr. 21 c. 6 punct. 3 § 1 n. 33, with Suarez, Coninck, and Trullenchus; see also what was said in book 2, n. 40). Besides, pastors are held to remove scandals with any inconvenience, whereby if one of their subjects were incorrigible, and by his bad example the occasion of ruin were present to others, the pastor is held to impede such a loss, at least by apprising the Bishop not only once, but as long as the scandal continues and hope gleams that it could be impeded.

But there is a doubt: I. Whether pastors are held to it from charity or justice? Suarez and Tapia cited by the Salamancans (*eodem* tr. c. 7 punct. 4 § 2. n. 58) think they are held only from charity. But he is more probably held by justice, as others think. The reason is because for this purpose, at any rate, that a stipend is given to pastors by the community to procure the salvation of each and ever member of it; hence, correct vices (Roncaglia, *de char.* quaest. IV, q. 1; Holzmann, *eod. tit.* n. 192; Palaus tr. 6 d. 3 p. 7 n. 8; with Cajetan and Coninck. Salamancans *l.c.* with Sanchez, Valentia, Diana and Trullenchus).

There is a doubt: II. Whether pastors are held to look after the morals of their subjects? It is answered affirmatively from the common opinion, as St. Thomas teaches (II IIæ q. 33 art. 3 ad 1) as well as the Salamancans with Laymann, Cajetan, del Soto, Ledesma, Villalobos, etc. The reason which St. Thomas hands down is that those who have a special obligation to press on for the salvation of some certain person, just as pastors have towards each of their sheep, are held not only to correct the wayward, but also to see to it that they satisfy their obligation. But it must be said otherwise about others, who have a general obligation toward their neighbor; for these it suffices to merely correct them after they have fallen, to alert their neighbor to the danger of falling.

There is a doubt: III. Whether Bishops and pastors are held to not desert their sheep even in danger of death? We respond with St. Thomas: "When the salvation of his subjects demands the personal presence of the pastor, the pastor should not withdraw his personal presence from his flock, neither for the sake of some temporal advantage, nor even on account of some impending danger to his person, since the good shepherd is bound to lay down his life for his sheep" (II IIæ q. 185 art. 5). So it is also held in John 10:11, and these words contain not only a counsel but also a precept as the Salamancans duly prove (tr. 21 c. 2 punct. 6 n. 76 from *c. Sciscitaris* 7 q. 1 where this is clearly expressed). St.

Thomas also adds: "On the other hand, if the salvation of his subjects can be sufficiently provided for by another person in the absence of the pastor, it is lawful for the pastor to withdraw his bodily presence from his flock, either for the sake of some advantage to the Church, or on account of some danger to his person." (*ibid*). There are certain causes excusing pastors from residence (see book 5, n. 125).

Moreover, it must be noted: 1. That a Bishop, when he receives the rule of his episcopate, ought to exact an account from the principal vicar about everything done during the period in which his see was vacant (Council of Trent, sess. 24, c. 16 *de Ref.*); 2. A bishop is held by the same session of the Council of Trent (c. 3) to visit his diocese at the same time, and he can receive nothing during that visitation apart from provisions. There it is said: "Bishops shall not neglect to visit their respective dioceses, either personally or, if they are lawfully hindered, through their vicar-general or visitor; if by reason of its extent they are unable to make a visitation of the whole annually, they shall either themselves or through their visitors visit at least the greater part of it, so that the whole may be completed in two years. ... Let them strive to complete the visitation as speedily as possible, yet with due attention. Meanwhile they shall exercise care that they do not become troublesome or a burden to anyone by useless expenses, and neither shall they nor any one of theirs, either by way of compensation for the visitation or from wills made for pious purposes, except what is by right due to them from pious bequests, or under any other name, receive anything, be it money or gift of whatever kind or in whatever way offered, any custom, even though immemorial, notwithstanding; with the exception, however, of food which shall be furnished them and theirs frugally and in moderation during the time necessary for the visitation only and not beyond that. It shall, however, be left to the option of those who are visited to pay, if they prefer, what in accordance with a fixed assessment they have been accustomed to pay in money heretofore, or to furnish the food; inviolate also shall remain the right of old agreements entered into with monasteries or other pious places, or with churches not parochial.... But if anyone, God forbid, should presume to receive something more, ... in addition to the restitution of double the amount to be made in one month, he shall also incur penalties.

DUBIUM VII
What is the obligation of teachers and students?

361.—"*Resp.* Among teachers (the same with tutors) and "students there is, in a certain measure, the same obligation "which exists among parents and children.

Thus the following are resolved:

"1. Students sin: a) If they do not show honor and reverence "to teachers and tutors; b) If they do not obey in matters "pertaining to study and good morals; c) If they were to exhibit "abusive or contumelious words to them; d) If they studied "negligently, or leave during time for school and study for play "or be at leisure; e) Bring the money of their parents to ruin or "spend it uselessly; f) If they study with a bad end; g) If they do "not keep the laws of the school or the statutes of the academy "(if indeed these oblige to sin); h) Were they to learn known "superstitions or forbidden things, or read forbidden books; I) "They were not to pay the stipend due to their teacher when "they could (see Navarre, c. 23 and 25; Filliuci, tr.28, part. 2 c. 10 "q. 1)."

362.—"2. Teachers and tutors sin: a) If they were to ignore "the sins of their disciples and not correct them when they can; "b) if they did not eagerly promote the progress of their

"students in letters; c) If they would not teach them good
"morals; d) If they purposely teach false things as true, or
"superstitious things and others harmful to salvation; e) If they
"are not zealous that they might satisfy their duty; f) If they
"demand a higher stipend than is just, or than the laws of the
"school or custom permit; g) If they refuse the dress of the
"doctorate to a worthy candidate or confer them upon the
"unworthy, which Navarre says is a mortal sin, especially in
"theology, canon law, civil law and medicine; for in philosophy
"perhaps it would be a venial sin, as Cajetan thinks (*verb.
"Doctor*); h) If they were a bad example to students; I) If they
"admitted to schools those imbued with bad morals and who
"are pernicious to others, or do not dismiss such from their
"schools. See Trullenchus, l. 4 c. 1 d. 11."

TREATISE IV
ON THE FIFTH AND SIXTH COMMANDMENT

CHAPTER I
WHAT IS FORBIDDEN BY THE FIFTH PRECEPT, *YOU SHALL NOT KILL*?

363. *What are the punishments for those who commission homicide through assassins?*
364. Would the assassins themselves incur the same penalties?
365. *On bull fighting.*

363.—"The murder of a man is forbidden, as well as "mutilation, beating and other similar unjust affliction; "wherefore the question arises, when would it be unjust?"

Here we must note in passing what is contained in *cap. Pro humani, de homicidio,* in 6, which declares that those commanding a Christian to be murdered by assassins, or receiving, defending or hiding assassins, incurs *ipso facto* excommunication and deposition from every dignity, office and benefice. Moreover, by *d. Cap. Pro humani,* such are held as bandits; so that they lose all their goods and the right is conceded to anyone you like to kill them. Nevertheless, this must be understood after a declaratory sentence, however only probable arguments suffice to make this clear. So it is held at the end of this declaration, where it is said: "And after probable arguments have been established that someone committed so execrable a crime, in nowise is any further sentence required against him." Understand, no further decisive sentence is required. *Cf.* Molina tr. 3 disp. 25, num. 4; Bañez 2. 2. q. 64 art. 3 dub. 2 ad 4; Gomez *Variar. resolut.,* tom. 3 cap. 3 n. 10; Farina *Prax. et theor. crimin.,* q.

123, n. 15 et *seqq*, and others cited by the Salamancans, *de V praec.* c. 1 punct. 8 n. 190.

But here we must advert: 1) That they incur *ipso facto* excommunication after the declaratory sentence, as we noted above, and they are deprived of dignities and benefices, which they lose by the law itself, as Azor and Gonzalez say (cited by Salamancans *ibid.* n. 191); 2) That by the mere command [to commit the murder] the aforesaid penalties are incurred, since in the aforesaid chapter it is said: "Although death perhaps would not follow from this command." And so think Molina, Covarruvias, etc. cited by Salm, *d.* n. 191.

364.—Still there is an uncertainty as to whether assassins would incur the aforesaid penalties since the text only imposes them upon the men who command the murder.

The first opinion upholds this, because the assassins more nearly engage in homicide; for that reason, the law includes them by the identity of this motive. So much more, because in that citation the Pope expressly does not include them seeing that there he spoke about infidel assassins on whom he could not impose penalties. So argue the Salamancans (*ibid.* n. 188) with Farina, Barbosa, Gomez, and others. Moreover, the Salamancans note (*ibid.* n. 193) with Aliciatus, Gabriel, Farina, etc., that men who perpetrate a homicide from an agreement are considered assassins, seeing that the one commanding the act pays them something temporal.

Nevertheless, *the second opinion*, with Cajetan, Navarre, Suarez, Azor, Fagundez, Sylvius, etc. (cited by Salamancans *ibid.* num. 187) more probably deny it, both because the penalties were not extended and because the text speaks about those who killed Christians by means of infidel assassins; wherefore the motive of the law appears formally different.

365.—Here it must be noted that St. Pius V forbade princes under excommunication *ipso facto* lest they would permit the fighting of bulls or of wild beasts in the market place; and individual Christians lest they would join in; likewise, clergy, lest they would assist at such spectacles. Still, Pope Clement VIII later took away these punishments not only for the kingdom of Spain, but from all except religious. See the Salamancans, *de V. praec.* c. 1 punct. 9 § 2 n. 200, *et seq.*

DUBIUM I
Whether at some time it would be lawful for a man to kill, or mutilate himself?

366. Whether it would be lawful to directly kill one's self? What about indirectly?
367. Whether it would be lawful for someone to expose himself to the danger of death to avoid a harder death, etc.? Would it be lawful to burn a boat if it brings the danger of death?
368. Whether a virgin is held to suffer death rather than to be raped?
369. Whether it is lawful for a guilty man to kill himself at the command of a judge? Or to take poison so as to test out an antidote?
370. Would it be lawful for a Carthusian to abstain from meat even in extreme necessity?
371. Would it be lawful for him to reduce things that exhaust his life?
372. Is there an obligation to preserve life using extraordinary remedies or extremely difficult ones?
373. Is it ever licit for a man to mutilate himself?
374. Would it ever be lawful to castrate children?
375. Whether someone that commits suicide could be buried in a sacred place?

366.—"*Resp.* Without divine authority it is not lawful for a "man to directly kill himself, even intentionally. The reason is, "because it is against charity for himself and would be an "injury to himself and God, who is the only absolute and direct "master of human life." (Would someone killing himself sin even against justice? The Salamancans uphold this in *de V praec.* c. 1 punct. 5 § 1 n. 111, with Lessius and Bañez but de Lugo, Navarre, Fagnello etc. reject it).

"1) I said "without divine authority," on account of Samson "and certain martyrs who killed themselves, either from divine "inspiration, or inculpable ignorance. I said 2) *directly* because "at some time it is permissible to kill one's self *indirectly, i.e.* to "do something or omit something whereby, contrary to one's "intention, death would certainly follow; because the precept to "preserve life, inasmuch as it is affirmative, does not always "oblige, but can be omitted on account of a good end, necessity "or great utility. St. Thomas, II IIæ, q. 64 art. 5 ad 4. See Filliuci, "tr. 29, c. 4 q. 5 and Becan 2.2. t. 3 .c 7 q. 8."

Thus the following cases are resolved:

"1. A soldier can, nay more is held, to remain at his station, "even if it were morally certain he is going to be killed. Cardinal "de Lugo, d. 10 q. 1." (On account of the common good, or on account of a special obligation which a soldier, governor, bishop, parish priest, etc. has from an agreement or duty, they can licitly prefer death and are held to do so. Elbel, n. 10 Salamancans tract. 13, *de rest.* c. 2 punct. 2. § 3 n. 33).

"Likewise, he can overthrow an enemy citadel, or destroy "enemies, or burn it to the ground, even if he were to know "that he would burn himself; *e.g.* to sink a boat, or burn it, lest "an enemy should take power over it with grave loss to the "state, as Lessius teaches, l. 2 c. 9 n. 32; Fagundez, t. 1 l. 5 c. 11." (And the Salamancans, *ibid.* n. 37 with Bonacina, Trullenchus, etc.) "Similarly, it is lawful to throw himself in front of a bullet, "or a blow, to save the life of a prince, to undergo death in place "of a friend unjustly condemned (Lessius, l. 2 c. 9 dub. 6 n. 30); "or to give a friend a plank in shipwreck (though drowning "would result), from Toledo, Lessius, *loc. cit.* Lopez, p. 1 c. 95."

(Even if the plank were already taken, against Sotus, Rodriquez, etc., Sylvius teaches cited by the Continuator of Tourenly, *de praec. dec.* cap. 1 art. 3 sect. 4 punct. 1 in med. Gravior, and the Salamancans, *ibid.* n. 34 with others, whom you will find cited in n. 971, v. *Hoc* from St. Thomas, who in 3. d. 29, art. 5 ad 3, says that to hand oneself over to death on account of a friend, would be a most perfect act of virtue, whereby the virtuous seek after this act more than their own life. Moreover, Sylvius rightly notes that he cannot throw himself into the sea to yield his plank, because no man can positively kill himself. Hence, one cannot throw himself into a river to baptize a child, as the Continuator of Tourenly says, *loc. cit.*)

"Likewise, to serve those infested with plague, or to flee a "burning building by jumping from the top, with certain danger "of death (Lessius, and Filliuci, *l.c.* Laymann, *ibid.* n. 35). Still, "where taking a citadel and the burning of a ship indeed held "no hope of escape, it is conceded that it can be done only "fearfully and for the gravest reasons, e.g. for the sake of the "public good. See where de Lugo teaches the same thing, n. 51, "52 and Malderus, tr. 3 c. 1 dub. 19, Diana, p. 5 tr. 4 r. 26, "Fagundez, p. 5 c. 11 n. 6 and *seq.*

"2. Although it is also not lawful for a virgin to directly kill "herself to preserve her chastity, it would be to expose herself "to the certain danger of death, even for her corporal integrity "alone, although she may reasonably presume she is not going "to consent because her integrity is of great value. See "Laymann, c. 1 n. 3."

367.—*Quaeritur I:* Would it be lawful for one to kill himself to avoid a harder death? *Resp.* It is never lawful to directly kill one's self; even if men revere some who did this, it must be said they did it from a divine instinct. So the common opinion of the doctors, whatever St. Jerome may say in c. 1 Joann, related in c. *XI caus. 23 quest. 5*, where it is read: "In persecutions it is not lawful to perish by one's own hand except for that where chastity is in danger." But the phrase "except for that" can be explained and *not even with the exception of a case in which chastity is in danger*, as Laymann explains.[1] Although, for one to kill himself indirectly, say if anyone threw himself out a window to escape burning, especially if some hope were present to evade death (Busembaum, de Lugo, d. 10 n. 50, with Lessius, the Cont. Tournely, *de 5 Dec. praec.* art. 1 concl. 2. *Secundus*, and Sporer, *de V praec.* c. 3 n. 24 and Elbel, n. 13, permit this even to guilty men detained in prison to evade a certain sentence of death, or even perpetual jail, as in n. 16).

Quaeritur II: Would it be lawful to burn a ship with a clear danger of death lest it would come into the hands of your nation's enemies? Renzi denies this (*de V. praec.* c. 2 q. 3) with Diana from St. Thomas, II IIæ q. 64 art. 5. But de Lugo (n. 52) answers in the affirmative with Lessius that it is lawful if there were some moderate hope of avoiding death, or, even if death were certain, provided it were expedient to avoid public loss. Moreover, Mazzotta says (*de rest. ob homic.* c. 1 with Busembaum n. 2) that a virgin can throw herself into certain danger of life to preserve her chastity from an invader, but not certain death. That does not seem improbable since on account of the good of virtue the Doctors do not hesitate to assert in common that it would be lawful for one to expose their life to danger, *e.g.* to give up a plank after a shipwreck to a friend, as Busembaum noted above in 366 with Lessius, Toledo and the Salamancans, etc. So much more, because in the aforesaid case of rape the danger of consent is always present.

---

[1] "Nisi cum excusando dicere velis cum Glossa, *ibid.* Joanne Majore in 4 dist. 15 q. 19, Pet. Nav. lib. 2 c. 3 n. 32, voculam *absque eo* non sumi exclusive, sed inclusive, ut sensus fit, etiam ubi castitas periclitatur: quo modo sumitur Cant. 4:3, *Sicut fragmen mali punici gena tua, absque eo, quod intrinsecus latet.*" Paul Laymann, *Theologia Moralis*, lib. 3 tr. 3 part. 3 cap. 1 num. 3.

368.—But here a third question urges even more: Would a virgin be held rather to permit herself to be killed than violated, say, if the invader threatened her with death if she refused to have carnal relations with him? There is a two-fold opinion.

The first, says that although she could, a woman is not held to suffer death but can appear permissive while the copulation passes, provided she positively resists it in her will and the danger of consent is absent; because, as the authorities say, that permission is then not moral cooperation, but only material, and therefore on account of the danger of death she is sufficiently excused Navarre (Sum. c. 16 n. 1), del Soto (*de just.* l. 5 qu. 1 art. 5) as well as Cardinal Toledo, Lopez and others cited by the Salamancans (*de V. praecept.* c. 1 punct. 5 § 2 n. 127).

The second opinion teaches this is altogether illicit because in that case a woman could impede copulation, if she permits it induced by fear, then her cooperation is truly moral and voluntary; for in that woman the permission for copulation is regarded as an action (Salamancans hold (*loc. cit.* n. 128) with de Lugo, Azor, Bonacina, Filliuci, Palaus, etc.). Still, this reason does not convince because that permission of the woman cannot really be called an action, provided it were in no way positive; therefore, the first opinion (speaking speculatively) does not seem to lack probability. Still it must not be denied that the second opinion is persuasive in practice at least on account of the danger of consent, which can easily be present in that permission.

369.—"3. It is not lawful for the guilty man to flee, nay more, "he can voluntarily stop the punishment although he could not "positively destroy himself, even if that were permitted to him "by a judge. See Lessius, c. 9 d. 6, Cardinal de Lugo, d. 10 *de just.* "sect. 1 n. 38, against Vasquez, 1.2. d. 173 c. 3."

Quaeritur: Whether a guilty man could kill himself at the command of the judge? Vasquez, Bonacina, Victoria, Aragon, and

Corduba (cited by the Salamancans, *de V. praec.* c. 1 punct. 5 § 1 n. 118) all affirm it. They say, if the guilty man can open his mouth so that poison may be poured in, he can also draw it out to swallow it with his own hands, and in like manner, pierce himself with a sword. The reason is then the judge constitutes the guilty man as his own executioner, which appears may probably be done with Elbel, *de homic.* n. 9, who cites Haunold, Illsung, etc. But the Salamancans (*ibid.* n. 117) with St. Thomas, Busembaum, Suarez, del Soto, Laymann and the more common opinion deny this because suicide, as an intrinsically evil act, cannot be commanded by a judge nor carried out by the guilty man. Still, the common opinion concedes that a guilty man may climb a ladder [to the gallows] or stretch out his neck for the sword, etc., since these actions only remotely have death as their aim.

But it must be noted with the Salamancans (*ibid.* n. 120), Navarre, Lopez, Salon, etc. that someone would indeed sin gravely who drinks poison or suffers himself to be bitten by a snake to test out an antidote. That is unless it were certain for them by the experiment or the judgment of experts that they did not expose themselves to a probable danger of death, which Henno approves. And the same thing must be said about rope dancers or those playing with a rope in high places with the probable danger of death (Salamancans *ibid.* with Henno and Sylvius).

370.—"4. Although, a Carthusian in extreme sickness could "save his life by eating meat, and it would probably be licit for "him (further, if one were to offer food made from meat the "Carthusian while he was unaware, he probably would not sin; "Sanchez, Diana, part. 8 t. 7 r. 70), still, he would also licitly and "in a praiseworthy manner forego it with certain danger of "death, as Diana teaches in par. 5 d. 4 r. 32 against Vasquez, and "Granadus from Victoria, Lorca, etc., because he reasonably "neglects his life for the common good of the Order." (Even in probable danger of death, as Azor, Medina, Victoria, hold against Vasquez, Granadus and the Salamancans, *de leg.* c. 2 punct. 7 n. 137 and 138; who still call the first opinion probable enough. The Salamancans thought it is certain that he could eat the meat, *loc. cit.* n. 136). "Cardinal de Lugo (d. 10 n. 33 against "Azor and Escobar, t. 6 c. 7) teaches that he is held to eat the "meat if necessity demands it, where he could not preserve his "life otherwise. Sanchez distinguishes this in part. 2 *Cons.* l. 5 c. "1 d. 35 with six others, if the necessity to eat were *ab* "*intrinseco*, *e.g.* from plague, where in the judgment of the "doctors he could not get well unless he were to eat meat, then "he says it is more probable that the Carthusian is not held to "eat meats (even if he could do it licitly) because he will die "naturally from the plague, of which he is not the cause; but if "it were *ab extrinseco*, *e.g.* if on account of the want of other "foods he would die of hunger, he is held to eat them because "that death, since it is violent, would be imputed to him." (And the Salamancans rightly judge this to be most certain, in *de rest.* c. 2 punct. 2 § 2 n. 27, and *de leg. l.c.* n. 135).

371.—"5. If someone noticed that abstaining from meat and "moderately fasting on vigils notably diminished his health and "continued just the same, he would sin gravely, as Laymann "notes (l. 3 *de just.* t. 3 p. 3 c. 1 n. 5), even if many would excuse "it on account of good faith and the zeal to please God. See "Bonacina, d. 2 q. ult. sect. 1 p. 7 n. 9; Filliuci, *loc. cit.*, Cardinal "de Lugo, *de just.* d. 10 sect. 1 n. 32, 33 and 36, etc. There, he "rightly notes that it is one thing to manage life in such a way "that it is short, or in a way that causes death for himself, and "another to permit or undergo danger of it, or to not apply the "means to avert it. Earlier he says it is illicit, *e.g.* by indiscreet "penances, and mortifying himself by foregoing meat to notably "shorten his life; but later he often says it is licit." (So also de Lugo *de just.* d. 10 sect. 1 n. 32; the Continuator of Tournely, *de*

5 *praec.* art. 1 quaer. 3 r. 2 and the Salamancans, *de vest.* c. 2 punct. 2 § 2 n. 30, with Granado, Villalobos, Sayr, etc. If the mortifications were done at the counsel of a prudent prelate, or confessor, so life were also shortened by 12 years, as others say. And really, if it were licit for craftsmen and blacksmiths, as the Abbot of Rancé, the founder of the Reformed Trappists says, to shorten their life by laboring daily in the midst of fire, a deep swamp whereby he could easily be killed, or where human life is lacking; if it will be permitted for scholars to weaken their health to gain knowledge; if it is lawful for soldiers to expose their lives to so many toils and dangers of death, why will it not be lawful for a religious man to embrace corporal austerities to bring his rebellious flesh into subjection?)

"So a Carthusian is not held to eat meat, nor to use some "precious and expensive medicine to avoid death; nor is a "secular priest, leaving behind his domicile, to seek healthier air "outside of his country." (Cardinal de Lugo Bonacina, Trullenchus, with the Salamancans, *ibid.* num. 26, since it suffices to use ordinary medicines).

372.—"6. Sick men are excused who, a little before death for "the sake of humility, or a good example, ask to be placed on "the ground because they do not intend to shorten their life. "See Vasquez, *l.c.* Laymann adds (lib. 3 t. 3 p. 3 c. 1 n. 5) that no "one is held to preserve his life by extraordinary means and "excessively hard ones, *e.g.* amputation of a leg, etc, unless it "were necessary for the common good." (So the common opinion with de Lugo, del Soto, Bañez, Bonacina, the Salamancans, *ibid.* punct. 3 n. 50. The Continuator of Tourney teaches the same thing, *l.c.* concl. 2, *quartus casus* in fin. with Sylvius. Nevertheless, he adds that a father, a tutor, or another superior can command the limb of a subject to be amputated if the subject will only suffer modest pains, against Henno). "See "Lessius, *loc. cit.*, Sanchez, *in opusc.* tom. 1 l. 5 c. 1 d. 34, where "he says that a weak man in danger of death, if there were hope of health, cannot refuse medicine. Still, it does not seem a sick virgin (speaking *per se*) is held to undergo the hand of a doctor or a surgeon when it is a very serious matter for her and it terrifies her more than death itself. Escobar, e. 7 c. 8, from Turrianus, *sum.* p. 1 c. 263, d. 5." (So the Salamancans, *de rest.* c. 2 punct. 2 § 2 n. 28, with Lessius, Sanchez, Diana, etc. Still, a virgin could permit that she be touched, nay more is held to permit it if she is under the care of another woman, as Diana rightly says).

373.—"*Resp.* 2. It is not lawful to mutilate oneself unless it were necessary for the preservation of the whole body, because nobody is absolutely the master of his members. Lessius, lib. 2 cap. 9 disputation 14."

Thus, the following are resolved:

"1. It is not lawful for a man to castrate himself to preserve his chastity and defeat temptations, because this is not necessary to that end. St. Thomas, II IIæ q. 65 art. 1; Lessius, Molina, Filliuci, t. 20 c. 4 q. 3, etc.

"2. Parents sin who castrate their sons, even with their consent so that they would be profitable as singers. See Laymann, l. 3 tr. 3 c. 1."

374.—*Quaeritur:* Is it lawful to castrate boys to preserve their voice?

The first opinion more probably denies it with Busembaum, Sporer (*de V. praec.* c. 3 n. 35) and the Salamancans, *ibid.* punct. 3 n. 45 and *de V. praec.* c. 1 punct. 5. §1 n. 121, in fin. as well as de Lugo, Bonacina, Diana, Villalobos, etc. They say, if it is not lawful for the good of the soul, how much less for temporal profit? Therefore, they say that preservation of the voice is not a good of such importance that it would be lawful to do what nature forbids.

Still, *the second opinion*, which other authors hold, upholds it as lawful provided there was no moral danger to life, and it were not done to children against their will (Tamburinius, l. 6 c. 2 § 3 n. 4; Trullenchus, Salon., Pasqualigo cited by the Salamancans, *de rest.* dict. n. 45 and Mazotta, *de rest.* q. 3 c. 1 § 1 and Elbel n. 29 think it is probable. Elbel thinks it has crept in on account of tolerated practice). Their reasoning is not only because eunuchs are advantageous to the common good by singing the divine praises more sweetly in Churches, but also because the preservation of the voice is of no small importance and said to be a good for them, and since by that condition they will change notably for the better, and through their whole life acquire a rich and notable income, such a good seems to be a just cause that could licitly make good such a harm to the body; so much more because day by day this is deduced in use as well as tolerated by the Church, as Elbel says.

375.—"One might ask, whether a man that has committed "suicide should be buried in a sacred place.

"Resp. The canons of the Church forbid this. Nevertheless, "they are not to be understood on those who do this from rage, "madness or suffering extreme sadness or disturbed by fancy, or "someone who truly suffered from this before death. And if it "were certain that any man killed himself and it were uncertain "whether this were done from a deliberate intention, in practice "he is deprived of sacred burial since it is presumed according "to the external work that this was done voluntarily, unless the "contrary could be gathered from the circumstances. But if it "were uncertain whether for example, a man had drowned "himself or were drowned by another, a crime so atrocious and "against nature is not presumed without clear evidence. "(Molina, t. 3 d. 20). See Laymann, *l.c.* n. 8. See also Escobar, e. 7

"q. 8, where he says that the man who dies from a wound "received in a duel, if he left the place while still living, must "not be deprived of ecclesiastical burial."

DUBIUM II
Is it lawful to kill a malefactor, and how?

376. Would it be lawful to kill an outlaw on one's own authority?
377. Would it be lawful for a prince to kill condemned men but not before they are condemned by a sentence?
378. Would it ever be lawful for clergy to condemn a guilty man to the death penalty?
379. Would a judge be held to concede a time for the condemned man to receive the sacrament of penance and the Eucharist?

376.—"*Resp.* Outside a case of necessary defense, on which "we will speak below, it is lawful for no one except the public "authority while preserving the order of law, as is clear from "Exodus 22 and Romans 13.

Thus the following are resolved:

"1. It is not lawful for a husband to kill his wife or a father "to kill a daughter caught in adultery because they do not have "the public authority for this; and civil laws permitting this are "corrected in canon law as unjust." (Moreover, the contrary "opinion was condemned by Alexander VII, prop. 19).

"It is otherwise with outlaws, whose killing pertains to the "public authority and so it is not done unjustly since it is "necessary for the defense of the common good." (Provided the "killing were not done outside the territory of the outlaw, "except with the license of the other ruler. Salamancans, *de V* "*praec.* c. 1 punct. 2 n. 19. See n. 380). "Still they sin who do not "do this from the zeal for justice but out of hatred or for the "sake of private vengeance. See Laymann, *l.c.*"

377.—"2. Princes or magistrates (properly speaking) sin, who "command outlaws to be killed when they have not been cited "for their crime, were not heard in court or were not "condemned, even if it were certain from private knowledge "that they were causing harm; because by the law of nature a "public act ought to be done from public knowledge and "authority. See Cajetan, *v. Homicidium,* Filliuci, tr. 29, c. 2 q. 6 n. "27, Bonacina *l.c.* p. 1. n. 7. Also, see below in book 5, c. 3 d. 1." (An exception is made 1. If the crime were notorious; 2. if there were danger of sedition or if there would be dishonor to the king were he to proceed judicially. Salamancans, *ibid.* n. 18).

378.—Here we must note: 1) For clergy, even having lay power, it is illicit to condemn outlaws to death, from *cap. Continentia, de cler. percussore.* Still, in this case the Pope can dispense, as the Salamancans teach (*ibid.* n. 13 and 14, with St. Thomas, etc.) And the Bishops themselves, or similar, having temporal dominion of some place, can licitly commit their power to laity in capital cases. Salamancans, *ibid.*, n. 16, with St. Thomas, Bonacina, Trullenchus, etc. See what is going to be said in book 7, n. 467.

379.—We must note: 2) That a judge is held *sub gravi* to concede sufficient time for the guilty man to go to confession, even if he fears the danger of escape. Salamancans, *ibid.*, n. 21 with Navarre, Sylvius, Trullenchus, etc. He is also held to concede time for him to take communion (unless grave harm were feared); since the guilty man would then be at the point of death in which the precept of communion obliges by divine law as the authorities teach. (The Salamancans (*ibid.*) with Suarez, Navarre, de Lugo, etc). They also adduce in this case a Motu Proprio of St. Pius V.

Then, even a guilty man that is not fasting can communicate because then he is truly on the point of death. Salamancans, *l.c.* n. 21, with Navarre, Bonacina, Suarez, de Lugo, etc. And he can communicate in a praiseworthy manner on the same day that he is to die, provided the communion were an hour before the execution, as Sa and Fagundez say (cited by the Salamancans, *ibid.* n. 22).

We must note: 3) That if the guilty man refuses to confess his sins after an exhortation, he can be licitly killed by the executioner, because then his damnation is attributed to his own fault. Salamancans, *ibid.* n. 23, with Trullenchus, Bonacina, Salon, and others.

DUBIUM III
Whether and how it will be lawful to kill an unjust aggressor on one's own authority

380. Is it lawful to defend one's life by the death of the assailant? Moreover, is it forbidden to outlaws and bandits to defend themselves by arms?
381. Is it lawful for a gentleman to kill an assailant of his honor? Moreover, would it be lawful for a commoner or an ecclesiastic if he could flee without danger of life? And what if contumely were already inflicted?
382. See more resolutions of Fr. Busembaum.
383. Quaest. I: Would it be lawful to kill a thief for a thing of great value? Qu. II: What should the value be? And what, if the value were modest but the thing were taken with violence? Qu. III: What if the thief had already taken a thing and resisted the owner trying to recover it with violence?

384. *Quaest. IV: Would it be lawful for clergy and religious to kill a thief? And would they then incur irregularity?*
385. *Quaest. V: Would it be lawful for anyone to defend his own possessions by arms, even through his servants?*
386. *Quaest. VI: Would it be lawful to kill an assailant of one's chastity?*
387. *Would it be lawful to forestall the aggressor?*
388. *Would it be lawful to kill a false accuser?*
389. *Whether one is held to defend the life of the innocent if he could?*
390. *Even with the death of the aggressor?*
391. *Whether it is lawful to kill the assailant of one's honor or the other of chastity? And what if the woman were to consent?*
392. *Whether we can and are held to safeguard the goods of our neighbor even by killing the thief?*

380.—"The law of nature permits that you may repel force "with force and that you may forestall and kill an assailant who "unjustly tries to take your life from you or those things that "are necessary for you to lead a worthy life, such as temporal "goods, honors, chastity, or the integrity of your members. "Nevertheless, that it is done with a mind to defend yourself "and with *moderamen tutelae inculpatae*, namely not by causing "greater damage or using greater force than is necessary to "prevent harm. So the common opinion, St. Thomas, II IIæ, qu. "74, art. 7; Molina, etc. Lessius, dub. 8 n. 44."

Note here, the author of a recent book titled: *Esposizione della Dottrina christiana*, errs by saying that St. Thomas with St. Augustine deny it is licit to kill an assailant in defense of one's own life; for the Angelic Doctor teaches expressly the opposite, saying: "Nor is it necessary to salvation that a man omit an act of moderate defense to avoid the slaying of another." He only adds in the response *ad primum* where he explains the doctrine of St. Augustine and says: "That in the act of killing he cannot intend the death of another but only their own defense."

And with St. Thomas the Roman Catechism admits this (*de 5. praec.* n. 8) where it is said: "It is lawful to kill another for the sake of one's own safety," adding that a homicide of this sort is not forbidden by divine law. And the authors agree (de Lugo, *de just.* d. 10 n. 138; Lessius, l.2 c. 9 d. 8 with St. Antoninus, Azor, Bonacina, del Soto, etc., and commonly against Gerson, Richard of St. Victor, Hugon., etc. cited by the Salamancans, *de 5. praec.* c. 1 punct. 4 § 2 n. 51). St. Thomas proves it (*loc. cit.*, cited by Busembaum) from Exodus 22:2, where it is said: "If a thief be found breaking open a house or undermining it, and be wounded so as to die: he that slew him shall not be guilty of blood." Thus, the Angelic Doctor adds: "Yet it is much more licit to defend one's own life than one's own house." St. Bonaventure teaches the same thing (Serm. 6 *de 10 praec.*), as well as St. Antoninus (p. 2. t. 7 c. 8 § 1) and the Continuator of Tournely (*de 5 paec. Dec.* art. 3 sect. 2 punct. 1) with Estius, Sylvius, Pontas, Nöel Alexander and innumerable others, with Salon, who calls the opposite opinion temerarious, since it is opposed to the common opinion of the doctors, a great number of texts and especially against *c. 3* and *c. Significasti* 8 *de homic.* and *c. Si vero 3 de sent. excom.* where it is said: "Since all laws and all rights permit one to repel force with force."

But someone will say: "A man that kills an unjust assailant to save his life exceeds moderation by preferring his own temporal life to the next eternal life." We can answer with the Continuator of Tournely (*l.c.* ad 2, *Fateor*), Lessius (lib. 2 c. 9 n. 51), del Soto (q. 1 a. 8) Petrocorensis (l. 4 c. 3 q. 3) and others in the common opinion, both that we are held to prefer the next higher order to our inferior good when, for example, our life were absolutely necessary for the spiritual salvation of another, say, if an infant would otherwise die without baptism. But it is otherwise if the assailant throws himself into the danger of damnation by his own malice; for then, since everyone has the right to defend his life, he licitly repels force with force even if it causes the damnation of the assailant. And the same reasoning avails if a grave wound were feared from the assailant, or that he would inflict deformity, as the Salamancans say (tr. 10 c. 8 punct. 4 n. 45 and 45) and Roncaglia (*de 5 praec.* c. 3 q. 1). And the same reason proceeds for the defense of honor, and of a fortune, as we will say below. Hence, even clergy or religious can kill an assailant of their life and then not incur excommunication or irregularity as the Salamancans say (*loc. cit.* n. 45 in fine) with others, from the cited canon *Significasti* and *Clem. Si furiosus, de homicida.* (See what is going to be said *on Censures,* book 7 n. 382). But could it happen that an adulterous cleric would not incur irregularity who, to defend himself from the husband, were to kill him? See below n. 398, where the distinction is made, if the invasion were foreseen as proximate or remote. Moreover, I said "can kill;" for nobody is held to kill an aggressor, but can licitly and laudably permit their own killing lest the other man be deprived of temporal and eternal life, as the common opinion holds (Lessius, *loc. cit.* n. 55, with St. Antoninus, Sylvius and the Salamancans, *ibid.* n. 47, with del Soto, Bañez, etc. against Abulensis and Fagundez, who are not to be heard). The Salamancans make the exception: 1) When the life of the man assailed would be exceedingly useful to the common good. Lessius (n. 56) with St. Antoninus, the Salamancans and others make the exception: 2) When he a man is in mortal sin, because then he is held to defend himself by every means.

Thus the following are resolved:

"1. It is not lawful for an outlaw to kill ministers of justice "that come to take him to jail or punishment, because it is not "permitted to the outlaw, as Laymann notes from the common "teaching (lib. 3 t. 3 p. 2) because they are not unjust "aggressors."

Decius and Carterius (cited by Tamburinius, l. 6 c. 1 n. 8) and a great many authors cited by Clarus and Nellus, as Azor relates (p. 3 c. 1 q. 11) hold that it is licit for outlaws to defend themselves because human law cannot take away a right which everyone has to defend their life; Azor thinks this opinion is probable (*loc. cit.*) and Tamburinius seems to agree (*loc. cit.*) But the opposite must altogether be held with Roncaglia (*de 5 praec.* c. 3 q. 3), Croix (l. 3 p. 1 n. 816), the Salamancans (tr. 25 c. 1 punct. 2 n. 19), Elbel (*de homic.* n. 35) with Sa and the common opinion. The reason is because human law can rightly grant to anyone the right to kill a criminal, and vice versa, to take away from the criminal the right to defend himself; otherwise outlaws could also defend themselves against the executioner, which nobody admits. Moreover, it is certain that it is lawful for anyone to kill outlaws; but not other criminals, even if they were highwaymen and even if condemned to death, unless they meant to take a great quantity from you, according to what will be said in n. 383 (Croix, lib. 3 part. 1 n. 796, and Elbel, n. 55 and 56). Hence, accomplices, or soldiers who kill a guilty man whose capture they have been entrusted with if they resist or flee will sin, unless this were commanded by the public authority: but that can only be done if the criminal to be apprehended were guilty of a sufficiently notorious capital crime and could not be taken in any other way; and it is feared he will commit worse evils in another place if he escapes. So think Croix, n. 797, Elbel, n. 54 and Diana, part. 8 tr. 7 r. 44 with Farina and Clarus.

381.—"2. Even if on account of some contumely, *e.g.* if it "were said to a gentleman: "you lie," it would not be lawful to "kill him for the reason that he could and usually is repelled in "another manner (Lessius, Azor, Hurtius, etc., Diana part. 5 t. 1 "4. r. 12 and 13); still it is permitted if the assailant were to "attempt to strike a blow or a club upon the gentleman which "he could not in any way avoid, as Diana teaches (*l.c.* r. 4),

"Lessius, Hurtad, and others." (But in practice it is very rarely permitted for the aforesaid opinion to be used, for Sylvius, in 2.2. quest. 64 art. 7 qu. 9, rightly says: "Even if honor were a good of a greater excellence than riches, we think there is either no case, or very rarely a case, in which it would be lawful for one to kill for the sake of honor alone.")

"3. If one can ward off unjust violence with a club, or a "wound alone, or cutting off of an arm or in another manner, "then it is not permitted to kill. For this reason, if someone were "the type of person from whom it would not be a dishonor to "flee, he should preferably flee if he is able and save himself." (Unless there were a danger of being attacked in flight; and so it must be held with de Lugo, d. 10 n. 166 and the Salamancans tr. 25, c. 1 punct. 4 § 2 n. 60, with Tapia, etc., against some men, *ibid.* n. 59, who say improbably that flight would also be ignominious for a commoner. This is why clergy and religious are held to flee if they could without danger to their lives, because it is not shameful for them to flee, but rather honorific, as de Lugo says (*l.c.*). But even in regard to seculars and nobles, Sylvius wisely acknowledges this in 2.2. qu. 64 art. 7 q. 9, saying: "Even if honor were a good of greater excellence than riches, we think there is either no case, or very rarely a case, in which it would be lawful for one to kill for the sake of honor alone.")

"Nevertheless, it is otherwise if it would be a disgrace to "flee, *e.g.* for a nobleman or a military official; again, unless in "the actual moment it would not be a disgrace on account of "the superiority of the assailant or due to other qualities, say if "he is drunk or mad, for it is not lawful to kill such a person "when he can flee. Malderus, Diana, part. 5 tract. 4 r. 9. See "Laymann, lib. "3 tom. 3 part. 3 c. 3.

382.—"4. It is not lawful to kill a thief on account of a trifling "thing. Hence the opinion saying a thief can be killed to save a "single golden coin was proscribed by Pope Innocent XI "(Proposition 31). It is lawful, however, if someone would steal "a very notable dignity or goods of great importance, still, "unless they could be protected or recouped in another manner, "*e.g.* by a court. This is why when the laws indicate that a "nocturnal thief is killed with impunity, but not during the day, "they presuppose that in most cases at night they could not "otherwise be warded off as they can be during the day. "Otherwise, if a nocturnal thief can be taken, he should not be "killed, and if a thief that strikes during the daytime cannot be "taken, and what he steals cannot be taken back from him "except by killing him, it is lawful; nevertheless, these things "must not be of small importance and at least of one golden "coin, according to Molina, t. 4 t. 3 d. 16, n. 7. See Laymann, c. 3. "Or rather more, according to others cited by Diana, p. 3 t. 4 "r. 18, of two coins; although in this Diana seems too lax. Nay "more, Bonacina (*de restitutione*) does not think it is a thing of "great importance, even if it were three or four coins. Still, if "such a thief would take such a thing while its owner, or a "guard see it and resist, or threaten him with force, *e.g.* they "began to demand it back from the assailant with a sword, "Bonacina and Diana permit the killing (*l.c.*).[2]

"5. It is more probable that this is also lawful for clergy and "religious on account of temporal goods. But the customary "rights are advanced against the contrary, say, when "*moderamen inculpatae defensionis* is not preserved. Laymann, "*l.c.*, Tanner, t. 3 d. 4 q. 8 d. 4, Escobar, e. 7 c. 8, where he also "teaches from Tanner (*ibid.*, n. 68) that it is lawful for a virgin "to kill a man assailing her chastity if she cannot otherwise "avoid being violated." (See below n. 386).

"6. Nevertheless, when a hostile assailant is in danger of "salvation, someone can spare him from charity and prefer to "suffer the injury, but he is not held, for the very reason that

---

[2] See what is going to be said below in n. 383, *Quaeritur II*, towards the end.

"the assailant places himself in danger from his own malice. "Laymann, *ibid.*

"7. It is not lawful to kill if the injury was already contracted "or the assailant has already fled; because it would not be to "defend oneself but to avenge, as the authors teach. (Toledo, "Rodriguez, etc.). But Henriquez, Navarre (c. 15, n. 5), and "Fernandez (p. 1 c. 9 § 1) say if being wounded would cause a "great loss of honor, so long as he pursued the man fleeing right "away, he could follow after and strike him, inasmuch as it "would be enough for the defense of his honor."

Here the opposite must altogether be held with de Lugo, d. 10 ex. n. 189 *et seq.*, Viva *in prop. 17 Alex. VII*, n. 9 with del Soto, Molina, Vasquez and others in common, cited by Cardinal de Lugo. The reason is, because then he does not recover his honor *per se*, rather, by the harm to the other man's honor among wicked men, which is intrinsically evil. And I cannot understand why the contrary opinion ought not to be said to have been proscribed by the 30th proposition condemned by Pope Innocent XI that we related above in n. 381, which was condemned because it permitted striking the one who flees if he cannot avoid another disgrace.

"Nevertheless, Cardinal de Lugo, Molina, Lessius, etc. with "Diana, p. 8 tr. 7 misct. r. 47 say it is lawful to pursue a fleeing "thief with your horse and dispatch him with a weapon or an "arrow because the invasion still endures [see below, *Quaeritur* "I]. But even if it were not lawful, after one has returned to "safety, if still he cannot recover the thing stolen by a judge, he "can enter the place where it is being held and claim it, and if "the other man would impede him with force, he may repel him "with force. Tamburinius, Lessius, Malderius, Hurtad, Diana "(part. 5 resol. 37 and part. 8 resol. 47)." (See below, *Quaeritur* III).

383.—Let us be attentive here to four condemned propositions: 1) Prop. 31 condemned by Innocent XI, which says: "I can regularly kill a thief for the preservation of a single gold coin"; 2) Condemned Proposition 32: "It is not only licit to defend with defensive killing over those things we posses in act, but we also have a *jus inchoatum*[3] to those things and for what we hope we may possess"; 3) Condemned proposition 33: "It is permitted for an heir as well as a legate to defend himself against one who unjustly prevents either an inheritance being assumed, or legacies being paid, just as it is permitted a man who has a right to a chair or a benefice against one who unjustly impedes his possession of them"; 4) Proposition 18 condemned by Pope Alexander VII: "It is permitted to kill a false accuser, false witnesses, and even a judge, from whom an unjust sentence threatens with certainty, if the innocent man can avoid harm in no other way." Now with these being posited, let us proceed.

Quaeritur I: Is it lawful to kill a thief over a thing of great importance?

The *first opinion* denies it, which Gerson holds (tract. *de Euch.* as well as Abulensis, Abb. Covarruvias, Sylvius, and Tamburinius, cited by the Salamancans *de 5 praec.* c. 1 punct. 4 § 4 n. 80). The reason is, as they say, that we ought to prefer the life of our neighbor to temporal things. And they prove it from *c. Suscepimus, de homicida*, where the Pope condemned two religious because one of them killed two thieves trying to steal their vestments, "since," as the words of the text go, "it was more expedient to sustain the loss of goods than to be bitterly enraged against others for the preservation of lowly and transitory things."

Nevertheless, the *second opinion* affirms it and is very probable and common. St. Antoninus holds this in 3. p. t. 4 c. 3 §

---

[3] Translator's note: Essentially "a right only just begun", or a partial right.

15, and in the same place, c. 3 *in princ. ex Jac., Aret. et Petro* he hands down: "For, if I can kill a thief where I do not know and cannot make provision against the theft of my goods through a judge (as *l. Furem. ff. ad l. Cornel*), it is much more lawful to kill where the person cannot otherwise be safe." St. Antoninus taught the same thing, *l.c.* § 2, saying: "Likewise, a defense *cum moderamine* is licit, not only for one's own person but even for his goods; and not only for his own but even for goods lent to him or deposited with him, and even for the goods of his friends and neighbors, namely by assisting them." Sylvius holds the same thing commenting on 2.2. q. 64 art. 7 q. 8, saying that it is licit to kill an assailant of goods if "they were of great importance and could not otherwise be defended or recovered, than by the death of the one stealing them." Domingo del Soto likewise writes in *de Justitia et Jure*, l. 5 q. 1 art. 3: "While someone assaults anyone you like to murder him or steal his goods, the latter may kill him by repelling force with force." Angelus (*v. Defensio*, n. 4), Sylvester (*v. Excommunicatio*, in 6 n. 8), Amrilla (*v. Defensio*, num. 2) hold the same thing. D. Raymundus once taught the same thing (lib. 2 *de raptu* § 18) where he so spoke: "I cannot repel from possession unless I would kill them, and so such a defense will be licit." del Soto teaches the same thing (l. 5 q. 1 art. 8), along with Lessius (lib. 2 cap. 9 d. 11), de Lugo (d. 10 n. 175), Cajetan (2.2. q. 64 art. 7) Croix (l. 3 p. 1 n. 808), Elbel (*de hom.* n. 64), Roncaglia (*de 5 praec.* c. 3 q. 5) and the Salamancans *ibid.* n. 81, with Bonacina, Suarez, Prado, etc. St. Thomas (II IIæ q. 64 art. 7 v. *Sed Contra*) clearly adheres to this, and it is shown 1) from that of Exodus 22:2, precisely as we related above in n. 380. From such a text, St. Thomas (*l.c.*) infers that it is much more lawful to defend one's life, saying: "Rather, it is much more licit for someone to defend his own life than his own house," therefore he supposes for certain, the text permits the assailant of his goods to be slain. Nor do the words in the same passage of Exodus stand in the way of this, namely: "But if he will have done this when the sun rises, he will have committed homicide, and he will be killed." For Cornelius à Lapide responds to this (*in cit. loc.*), that it is not said there that because after the light the danger of death is absent, but because at high noon a thief can be better recognized and so it is easier to recover one's goods by means of a court; moreover, because after the sun rises he can repel the thief better by calling for the aid of his neighbors.

2) It is proven from the chapter *Dilecto de sent. exc.* in 6, where it is said: "It is indeed lawful for a dean to defend himself, if the aforesaid bailiff should presume to despoil him of his worldly goods. ..." Then it is added: "And because sufficient temporal defense was not present for him against excessive power, etc." From which, the Pope supposes that he could defend himself with secular arms if they were supplied with sufficient strength.

3) It is proven from the reasoning that Cardinal de Lugo and the Salamancans hand down (which seems better to me) that the precept of charity does not obligate one to prefer the goods of a neighbor of a higher order, except when (as we said above) one's neighbor is in extreme necessity; but not when he exposes himself to the danger of death of his own will. And so the reasoning of our opponents is altogether crushed since otherwise it would not even be licit to kill a man that unjustly tries to kill you, which all laws admit. Now, in regard to the text in *c. Suscepimus*, the Salamancans respond with the opposite, as above (*de V. praecept.* c. 1 punct. 4 § 4 n. 84), and rightly, that those religious were condemned because the thing was not of such an importance, nor could the killing be excused by the fear of death imposed upon them by the thieves who were already bound there because they were trying to free themselves from their bonds, since in the meantime they might equally try to escape and so free themselves from danger. Hence we say with Lessius (*dict. dub.* 11) and del Soto (*l.c.*) and the Salamancans (*ibid.* n. 88) with Bonacina, Prado, Trullenchus, Dicastillus, Sayr, and others in

TREATISE IV: THE FIFTH & SIXTH PRECEPTS CH. I   427

common, that it is lawful to kill a thief with a weapon out of a sword's reach if he removes a thing and, being forewarned about his danger refuses to lay aside the thing, as Bonacina explains well in p. 10 n. 2.

Quaeritur II: How much should the value of the thing be for it to be lawful to kill a thief? It is certain that two things are required to kill a thief. 1) Firstly, that the thing cannot be recovered in another way; 2) Secondly, that the thing is of great importance, of a value above a gold coin, as it is held from the aforesaid condemned proposition 31. Except in some rare case, in which the theft of such a thing would afflict vast harm, say (as Viva says in his commentary on *prop. 17 condemned by Alexander VII*, n. 10), if an instrument of his trade were taken away of similar value which, once it were removed, he could not support his life and that of his household. Hence, by speaking generally, Viva and Elbel say that thing is a great price which, once it is taken away, the sustenance for some man would fail for himself and his household (Viva, *l.c.*, Elbel, *de hom.* n. 65). And Nöel Alexander (*Theol. de V. praec.* art. 2 prop. 6), the Salamancans (*ibid.* n. 87) as well as Vasquez and Molina, cited by de Lugo (d. 10 n. 178), say that loss suffices which inflicts notable harm on the owner, according to the quality of the person. For, as Roncaglia duly says (*de 5 praec.* cap. 3 qu. 5) the theft of ten gold pieces, which could be a grave harm to someone, would be light to another man who was wealthier. Moreover, Cardenas (*in. 2 Crisi* d. 21 n. 88) supposes, in respect to any sum of 400 silver pieces (with us that is 40 ducats) is great. And the Salamancans regularly (and correctly) follow the opinion of del Soto and Aragon (with whom Sayr, Bonacina, and Trullenchus agree, and Viva rightly rejects the opposite) that it is not lawful to kill someone for a theft of four or five gold coins. Still, Cardinal de Lugo (n. 178) and the Salamancans (*ibid.* n. 86) point out the fact that in the time of Domingo del Soto five gold coins, or ducats were valued more than ten are now because with the progress of time the abundance of money increased as well as the price of things.

Would it be lawful to kill a thief taking a thing of modest value when the owner or the guard offers resistance? Molina (t. 4 tr. 3) and Bonacina (p. 10 n. 1) affirm it and others seem to adhere to this (de Lugo, d. 10 n. 178; Sporer, tract. 5, c. 2 n. 157 and Viva *l.c.* n. 40, as well as Roncaglia *l.c.*, although the last two say if it were a nobleman resisting). This is because then his honor is also taken away with that thing. Tamburinius does not condemn this opinion (lib. 4 c. 1 § 2 n. 3). But the contrary opinion is much more satisfactory to me, which the Salamancans (*ibid.* n. 85) and Diana (p. 5 tr. 4 r. 18) hold, not admitting it. The reason is, because although such a removal takes place with a special injury to it's owner by reason of violence, just the same, since not every injury causes dishonor, here it seems to me that honor is neither properly nor gravely wounded by that removal, according to the estimation of men. For, who is thought to be gravely dishonored because a thief violently stole something from him?

Quaeritur III: Is it lawful to kill a thief if he put a thing that he stole and that still exists in safety and you wanted to recover it? St. Antoninus, del Soto, Bonacina, Sayr, and others (cited by Salamancans, tr. 25, c. 1 punct. 4 § 4 n. 92, although they think this opinion is probable) deny it. The reason is because in that case the thief is not an assailant, but only an unjust keeper of the thing and therefore, it is not lawful to kill him, rather only to accuse him before a judge. Otherwise great disturbance would follow for the common good. But the affirmative opinion seems more probable to me, in a case where there is no hope of recovering the thing in another way. The reason is because then the thief, although he is not an assailant of the person, nevertheless is the assailant of the thing, since he would fight you to keep back your thing. So Lessius (lib. 2 c. 9 dub. 11 n. 75); de Lugo (d. 10 sect. 9 n. 181) and Vasquez, Tanner, Malderus, Diana, cited by the Salamancans (*ibid.* n. 91) with Busembaum, as above, n. 382.

384.—*Quaeritur IV*: Would it also be lawful for clergy and religious to kill unjust assailants of their goods of great importance? Busembaum, de Lugo (d. 10 n. 175), Elbel (n. 83) and the Salamancans (*ibid.* n. 81) with Lessius, Becan and others more commonly affirm it and with greater probability. The reason is because the right of defense is of natural law, and therefore, suited to both. Would they, however, incur irregularity in this case? See *de irregularitate,* where the negative opinion is proved.

385.—*Quaeritur V*: Whether it would be lawful for someone to defend his household by arms, even through servants? Sporer (n. 169) and Elbel (n. 66) with Navarre, de Lugo, Layman, etc., because that which someone can do per se can also be done by another. Hence, Elbel (*ibid.*) infers that it is lawful for both by reason of charity to repel the other by force, unjustly entering to despoil the house of his neighbor; and the Salamancans agree it is probable (*ibid.*, §5, n. 104 with others; just as it is also said for the defense of honor and chastity. See what is going to be said in n. 392.

386.—*Quaeritur VI*: Whether it is lawful to kill an assailant of one's chastity? If this is lawful to defend honor, and offices, it must be said all the more that it is lawful for the defense of chastity when there is no other remedy at hand. St. Antoninus so thinks in p. 2 t. 5 c. 6 *in fi.* where he says: "And if it is lawful not only to defend one's self and goods, why also not to prevent the loss of chastity?" And therefore, he says that a girl does not sin if, repelling force with force, she were to kill the assailant. The Archbishop says in another place: "Because a woman uses her natural right, in as much as it is lawful to repel force with force, she is held to provide for her safety more than for a stranger, for she exposes herself to the danger of consenting to the act of sin, by permitting herself to be oppressed on account of the difficulty of desire" (p. 2 tit. 7 c. 8, and p. 3 tit. 4 c. 3 § 2). Other authors teach the same thing (Fr. Cuniliati, *de V. praec.* c. 2 § 3; de Lugo, tom. 1 disp. 10 sect. 10 n. 195; Molina, d. 17 n. 10 and 11; Lessius, lib. 2 c. 9 dub. 12; Anacl. *de 5 praec.* q. 2 n. 19; Elbel *de homic.* n. 61; Sporer *tract.* 5 in 5 *praec.* c. 2 n. 265; Salamancans *de 5 praec.* c. 1 punct. 4 § 3 n. 72; with Bonacina, Trullenchus, Filliuci, and others in common). And here, Cardinal de Lugo (n. 196) and Roncaglia (*de Quinto Praecepto*, c. 3 reg. 5 *in praxi*) duly notice that it will not only be lawful for the girl while she is violently struck by the act of the other man, but even immediately after, to strike him with blows, fists, a club and even threatening strikes. The reason is, because unless she shows her displeasure and constancy in such a manner, he will not easily depart.

Moreover, a woman should never be permitted or counseled to kill out of vengeance, since, should the other man at least come to his senses, he would not attempt it another time.

387.—"8. It is also lawful to kill a man when it is known as a "certain fact that he lays plans to kill you, *e.g.* if a wife would "know for certain that her husband is going to kill her that "night, if she could not flee it is lawful for her to attack first. "Navarre, Lessius, n. 45, Filliuci, n. 39."

Nevertheless, the question is, whether it is lawful to preempt the assailant:

The first opinion rejects this, with Sylvius, Navarre, Trullenchus, etc. (cited by the Salamancans, *ibid.* §2 n. 54) because to preempt an enemy that is only prepared to attack him, would not be a true defense.

The second opinion affirms it with de Lugo, Bañez, Vasquez, Molina, etc. (*ibid.* n. 55) because, they say to kill an invader for one's own defense it is not necessary that the other man begins attack you, rather, it suffices if he were prepared to attack.

Just the same, Tamburinius (*in Dec.* lib. 5 c. 1 § 2 n. 15) and Roncaglia (c. 3 q. 2) and the Salamancans (*ibid.* n. 56, 57 and 58) with del Soto, Azor, Covarruvias, Diana and others) unite these two opinions and make the distinction: If anyone knew from some action that an enemy was determined to invade, say, if he were morally certain someone already prepared arms for this purpose, or had given the command to a servant; then, if he could not otherwise flee then he can licitly anticipate him. Otherwise, as Roncaglia says, "It would be ridiculous to compel him to wait for the attack when he would justly fear he could not repel it more." But it must be said otherwise if he did not know for certain, but only had a suspicion, or were to have doubtful fear about the invasion; for it is altogether wicked to deprive your neighbor's life on account of a doubt. Nevertheless, these not withstanding, I think, according to the second opinion, even supposing this distinction, it could hardly follow in practice on account of the danger of error which can be present in a matter of this sort.

388.—"9. Hence, others also say (such as Sanchez, *2 mor.* c. "29) and others, it is lawful to kill a man who, in the presence of "a judge presents false accusations or testimony and it will "happen that you know for certain that you are going to be "killed or mutilated or even (what others more morosely "contend) you will lose temporal goods, honor, etc., because this "is not an invasion but just defense, after it has been posited "that the injury of another is certain, and there is no other "mode of escape. Nevertheless, Lessius, Filliuci and Laymann do "not dare to defend this, on account of the danger of great "abuses. See Escobar, ex. 7 c. 8; Hurtius, de Lugo, dub. 10, sect. "7, Diana, p. 8 t. 7 r. 52."

The aforesaid opinion of Sanchez was expressly condemned in Proposition 18 proscribed by Alexander VII: "It is lawful to kill a false accuser, false witnesses and even a judge, from whom an unjust judgment threatens if the innocent man can avoid the harm in no other way."

389.—"10. Whenever someone according to the aforesaid has "the right to kill another, another man can carry out this task "for him when charity persuades it. Filliuci, Tanner, t. 3 d. 3 q. "4, Molina, d. 18. When, however, and when is he held to this? "See Lessius, l. 2 c. 9 d. 13, Diana, p. 5 t. 4 res. 6, 14, 20."

390.—It must be said, therefore: I. It is lawful to defend the life of a neighbor with the killing of the unjust invader. So think the Continuator of Tournely (*de 5 Dec. praec.* art. 3 sect. 2 u. 3) with the common opinion of the Doctors and St. Thomas (II IIæ, q. 60 art. 6 ad 2) where he says: "Or it can be said that Moses killed the Egyptian by defending the one who suffered injury, blamelessly with moderate protection." Wherefore, St. Ambrose says that someone who does not repel an injury from a friend when he can, he is in the same vice as he who does it (*de Offic.* lib. 1 c. 36) and he induces the example of Moses. And this happens even if your neighbor, while innocent, means to permit himself to be killed, since he is not the master of his own life and therefore cannot deprive others of the right of defense (Lessius, l. 2 c. 9 num. 87; de Lugo, Bonacina, Dicastillus and others in common with the Salamancans, tr. 25, *de homic.* c. 1, punct. 4 § 5 n. 94).

But someone will say: If the one invaded yields his right, how can you defend his right with the death of the attacker? *I respond*: That neighbor who was invaded has (that I might so say) two rights in a certain measure in regard to his life; one to life and the other to defend it; he certainly cannot yield the right to his life since he does not have mastery of it, for which reason he could not induce another to kill him; although he might permit himself to be killed, the killer will always sin against justice. But he can rightly yield the right to safeguard his own life by permitting another man to kill the assailant, according to what was said in number 380. Moreover, when you kill an attacker of the innocent, you do not defend a right which he has to defend himself, which he already yielded, but you defend the right which he has to life that he cannot yield. Nor would killing in that case incur irregularity (Salamancans *Tr. 25.* n. 95, with Suarez, Bonacina, Sporer, *de 5 praec.* cap. 2 n. 169, and the very common opinion; see book 7 n. 388).

Quaeritur: Here we must ask whether there is an obligation to defend the life of the innocent from the invader? *Resp.:* Because magistrates and princes are indeed held to do this from justice, and when it is argued about the common good, they are also held with danger of life inasmuch as they remove public thieves from the midst, etc. And equally soldiers are specially held to be conducted to defend the city; but they are not held to defend the life of a private man with such danger (Salamancans *ibid.* n. 98, with Lessius). Though it is in passing, notice that Bishops and parish priests, constituted in orders for spiritual things, are held to help their sheep still when they are in danger of life, as the Salamancans note (*ibid.*). Hence, parish priests are also held with danger of life to minister the sacrament of baptism or penance to their sheep, but not the Eucharist, not even in a time of plague, as Dicastilius and others cited by the Salamancans hold (tr. 4 *de Euch.* cap. 9 punct. 3 n. 30), which they think probable. See what was said in book 3, n. 27, and below in book 6 *On the Eucharist,* n. 233.

But there is a greater doubt: If you could not defend an innocent man that positively refuses to be killed without the death of the invader, are you held to kill the invader without danger to your life?

The Salamancans affirm it (tr. 25 *de V. praec. Decal.* c. 1 punct. 5 n. 100) with Navarre, Molina, Bonacina, Sa, etc., because, they say, everyone is held to defend the life of the innocent by the precept of divine charity when he can suitably do it.

Nevertheless, Lessius (l. 2 c. 98 n. 92) and de Lugo (dis. 10 sect. 11 n. 208), to whom the Continuator of Tourney adheres (*loc. cit.* r. 2) deny it with a more probable argument. The reasons are: 1) That the precept of charity does not oblige in that case since it is better to avoid the eternal death of the assailant than the temporal death of the innocent; 2) Because in the slaying of another man he can never avoid great detriment on account of fear of enmities, public justice, etc. At least, will someone not say the fear of polluting his hands with human blood inflicts a great detriment to which the precept of charity is not thought to obligate him? Except in the case where the person invaded were necessary to the public good. Sporer even makes the exception (with the common opinion, as he asserts *loc. cit.* n. 170) that if the one invaded were a parent, son, wife or brother, then piety would obligate their defense. The Continuator of Tourney also rightly makes the exception (*de praec. char.* sect. 4 punct. 1, *Colliges 2*, with Verricelli, *De apostol. missionib.*, tit. 2 qu. 60 n. 6), if the one that is going to be killed is drunk and in a state of mortal sin, because he is truly in extreme necessity of soul.

391.—It must be said: II. It is equally lawful to kill an invader of chastity or honor of your neighbor if the invasion in fact happened, namely by striking, etc. Otherwise, if it is only by words (as was said above in 381). De Lugo, *disp. 10* sect. 11, n. 203, Lessius, c. 9 d. 13 and the Salamancans, *ibid.* n. 96 with Bonacina, Filliuci, Dicastillius, Trullenchus, etc., against Sporer, n. 169, who denies it, though with less probability, unless the person affected with contumelies were married, or a prince, or a nobleman).

Moreover, when a woman consents, or at least, if she does not positively resist, it is not lawful to kill an invader of her chastity, because then it would not be a case of repelling force with force (Salamancans *ibid.* n. 97). But if she were your kinswoman and near in relation, Lessius and Sporer (n. 173) along with others cited by the Salamancans, say that you can kill her attacker, even when the woman consents to sex if you cannot otherwise avoid your infamy. Moreover, this must be understood before the fact, for in the very fact or after, certainly it is not lawful to kill, as is clear from the 19th proposition condemned by Pope Alexander VII, which said: "A husband does not sin killing a wife taken in adultery on his own authority." Lessius (l. 2 c. 9 art. 88) and the Salamancans (*dict.* n. 97) note the fact that it will not be lawful for a man to kill his wife if she impudently willed to commit adultery, because the man can repair the injury by other means, by striking her with a stick or by driving away the adulterer with threats. Notice here, however, that which is held in *c. Si vero* 3 *de sententia excommunicationis*; where it is defined that any man striking a cleric acting disgracefully with a mother, daughter, sister and wife, is immune from excommunication, but not from fault.

It must be said: III. We are held by charity to defend the goods of our neighbor when we suitably can, or with a light injury to ourselves, but not with a grave injury. Bonacina, Trullenchus, Dicastillus, etc., in common with the Salamancans, *ibid.* n. 102. But if we expend something for the defense of the goods of another, we can also secretly compensate him (authorities cited by the Salamancans, *loc. cit.*).

Quaeritur: But we ask whether someone, on account of defending his neighbor's goods when they are of great importance, could also kill the thief if it is necessary? The Doctors who deny it on account of the defense of one's own goods, deny it all the more in regard to someone else's goods, such as Gerson, Sylvius, etc., cited by the Salamancans (§ 4 n. 79 and 80, and §5 n. 103). Because, they say, charity obliges more the defense of one's life than another's goods. But St. Antoninus and others hold the contrary. The reason is, because we ought to prefer the life of our neighbor to the goods of another when he is in involuntary necessity; but not when he puts himself in necessity of his own will, as we have repeated often enough in the present *dubium*. Moreover, there is a question as to whether it is lawful to expel the fetus to defend the life of the mother? See what is going to be said in the following dubium, n. 394, *Quaeritur I* and *II*.

DUBIUM IV
Is it ever lawful to kill an innocent man?

393. Is it ever lawful to directly kill an innocent life?
394. Whether at any point it would be lawful to procure an abortion? Qu. I. Whether it is lawful for a mother to take a contraceptive to directly expel an un-animated fetus? Whether it would be lawful for a woman that was raped to expel the semen of her attacker right away? Qu. II. Whether it is lawful for a mother to take medication to cure an illness, with the danger of a miscarriage of the animated fetus? Qu. III. When is the soul reckoned to be formed in children?
395. Qu. IV. To what punishments are those procuring an abortion subjected? Qu. V. Whether pregnant women who have an abortion incur excommunication?
396. Qu. VI. Whether those procuring an abortion in doubt about the animation of a fetus incur irregularity?
397. Qu. VII. Who can relax the penalties inflicted for abortion?
398. When is casual homicide imputed to someone as a sin? Would an adulterer, killing the husband of the woman he committed adultery with that attacked him, incur irregularity? And would she incur it, if the adulteress preempted him?

393.—"Resp. It is never lawful with direct intention and "knowingly (unless God, the master of all life would concede it); "but indirectly and *per accidens* it is sometimes lawful, namely "by using his right and by laboring in a lawful and necessary "matter, as well as of such importance that it would be "equivalent to life. So think St. Thomas and all the doctors in "common."

Wherefore, the following are resolved:

"If a tyrant threatened to burn a city unless an innocent "man were killed, it is not lawful to do it directly. Nor would it "avail that just as it is permitted to cut off a limb for the "salvation of the body, so also even the citizen for the common "good; because a man is an equal moral part of the state and it "is not the reason why he exists and lives in the way that a "member of the body does from the body. Molina, t. 4 c. 3 d. 10; "Lessius, Filliuci, etc." (St. Thomas, II IIæ, q. 64 art. 6; Salamancans *de rest.* c. 2 punct. 4 § 1 n. 52).

"2. Nevertheless, the state can, in that case, compel such a "man that he should go to the tyrant, and, if he refuses hand "him over since from charity and legal justice it is held to "abandon his life for the sake of the republic. Wherefore, if he "were to refuse, harm can be done. And this will not be to "cooperate in his death, but only to permit it, since handing him "over is indifferent and death would only follow indirectly, and "apart from the intention of the state. Molina, *l.c.*, Lessius, l. 2 c. "9 d. 7 n. 38; Filliuci, tr. 29 n. 11, Laymann, etc." (Del Soto, "Aragon, Turrianus, etc. with the Salamancans, *ibid.* n. 57, who "say the state cannot hand him over against his will, because it "would cooperate in his death because it is intrinsically evil. But "the first opinion seems more probable with de Lugo, d. 10 n. 13 "and Busembaum, Molina, Lessius, Filliuci, and Laymann, as "above, because it seems that it cannot be denied in that case "the innocent man would be held to hand himself over, as del "Soto concedes the same; therefore, if he is held to hand himself "over, the state can rightly hand him over, if he culpably "refused; for then he is no longer innocent, as the Continuator "of Tournely agrees (*de 5 Dec. praec.* art. 2 sect. 1 quaer. 5, with "Sylvius, Bañez, and Salon)."

"De Lugo places the limitation (d. 10, *de just.*) if the innocent "were a subject or a pilgrim held to die for a foreign state."

"3. If you could not flee death while the enemy pursues, "except by a narrow way in which anyone sitting there will be "crushed, just the same it is lawful (still, provided if it is an "infant it is baptized, as Cardinal de Lugo warns, as well as "Escobar, e. 7 c. 8) to flee with that danger and with that death "apart from your intention. Lessius, n. 58, Filliuci, n. 36." (Salamancans *de rest.* c. 1 punct. 4 § 2 n. 64 in med. with Prado, Villalobos, Tapia, Sanchez, Dicastillus, etc.)

"4. Similarly, to storm a city and gain victory, if it were "necessary, it is lawful to direct siege equipment against that "place where there are many innocent people because it follows "their deaths are apart from the intention. Lessius, *l.c.*

"5. It is not lawful to kill hostages, even if those who sent "them do not keep good faith; because they are innocent. "Bonacina, t. 2 d. 2 q. *ult.* sect. 3 p. 7; Diana p. 5 l. 4 4. 35, against "Azor, etc."

394.—"You might ask, when will it be lawful to procure an "abortion?

"*Resp.* Whoever maliciously procures an abortion in "themselves or another sins gravely, whether the fetus were "animated, because it is true homicide, or not, because it aims at "the murder of a man, and is against the nature of generation. "Lessius, l. 10 n. 61.

"Nevertheless, if it is altogether necessary to preserve the "life of a mother, the following rules are held:

"1. If the fetus is probably going to bring death to the "mother, and is not yet animated with a rational soul (males are "commonly said to be animated on the fortieth day, but females "on the eightieth, though the matter is very uncertain), certain "men permit it even by direct expulsion, such as Sanchez, l. 9 *de* "*matr.* d. 20 n. 9 and 10; Henriquez, etc. against Lessius, l. 2 c. 9 "d. 16 and others, whose opinion is persuasive in practice; to "what point you may directly expel it when it is lawful "indirectly and would suffice?

"2. But if the fetus were animated and the mother were "judged to be about to die with the child unless she would take "medicine, it is lawful for her to take it and according to what "certain men hold, by directly intending only her health, even if "indirectly and consequently the fetus were destroyed; because "in equal necessity the mother can look to herself more than the "child."

"3. But if with the death of the mother, the hope of life and "baptism of the child would seem favorable, the mother is held, "according to many, under mortal sin to abstain from every "remedy that is destructive to the child, because she is held to "abandon bodily life for the extreme spiritual necessity of the "infant. Still, Louis Lopez teaches the contrary, which Sa (*v.* "*Charitas*) says is probable. See Lessius, *l.c.*, Sanchez, Filliuci, t. "29, c. 6 q. 1, Bonacina t. 8 art. 3."

Quaeritur I: Is it lawful for a mother that falling into extreme illness to take a contraceptive to directly expel an unanimated fetus? It is certain that to expel a fetus, although it is not yet animated, is *per se* a mortal sin, and the one expelling is held to be guilty of homicide, as it is said in *c. Si aliquis, de homicidio*; because, although she would not take away the life of a man, nevertheless she proximately impedes the life of a man. It is certain with all that it is licit to offer a remedy to a pregnant woman so as to directly cure her even with the danger of miscarriage if the sickness is mortal; otherwise, if it were not such as the Continuator of Tourney rightly adverts (*de 5 praec. Dec.* art. 3 sect. 1 r. 2).

There is a doubt as to whether then it would be lawful to give a woman a contraceptive to directly expel the fetus?

The first opinion affirms it, and very serious authors affirm it (Sanchez, *de matr.* l. 9 d. 20 n. 9; Laymann, l. 3 tr. 3 p. 3 c. 4 n. 4, with Sylvius, Navarre, etc. Likewise, Petrocorensis, t. 2 l. 4 c. 3 q. 1, Viva in prop. 34 Innoc. XI, n. 11, Mazzotta t. 2 p. 470, Habert t. 7 p. 749 and others). The reason is both because that fetus is part of the womb and the mother is not held to save it with such a crisis to her life, and because a mother can, in that case, expel it as an attacker of her life; and although the fetus is not a voluntary attacker, nevertheless, the mother is not held to overlook her present life to save the future life of her child; especially, because were the mother to perish, the fetus will scarcely be animated. St. Antoninus favors this opinion (p. 3 tit. 7 c. 2 § 2) where he says: "But if the offspring is not yet animated, then [a doctor] may and must give such a medicine because, although it would imped the animation of such a fetus, nevertheless, it would not be the cause of death of some man; and this good follows, because it would free the mother from death." But Sanchez rightly makes the exception (n. 7, and here asserts it as common among all authors, against a few) if there is a doubt present whether the fetus were animated or not, for that very reason then it would be intrinsically evil to positively expose the innocent to danger of death.

The second, more common opinion teaches that, although it is certainly lawful for a mother to take medicine for the purposes of directly curing a plague even if it would indirectly cause the expulsion of the fetus, it is still not lawful to directly expel the fetus. (Lessius, l. 2 c. 9 n. 61; de Lugo *de justitia* d. 10 n. 131; Pont. *de matr.* l. 10, c. 3 n. 2; Filliuci t. 2 tr. 29 c. 9 n. 140; Cabassutius l. 5 c. 20 n. 8; Cont. Tournely *loc. cit.* r. 1 and 3; Sporer *de matr.* c. 4 n. 704; Cardenaz *in prop. 34 Innoc. XI* n. 28; Bonacina *de rest.* d. 2 p. 7 n. 3; Salamancans *de rest.* c. 2 punct. 4 § 2, n. 62; Croix l. 3 p. 1 n. 825; Holzmann *de 5 praec.* c. 1 n. 579; Elbel *de matri.* n. 464; and a great many others). The reason is, because if it is never licit to expel semen, even if death were feared from an abundance how much less lawful is it to expel the fetus, which is nearer to human life? It does not avail to say the unanimated fetus is part of the mother, since that is answered by the fact that the fetus does not pertain to the integrity of the maternal body, but is from its beginning a distinct individual human. An exception is made here, as Sporer (*l.c.* n. 706) and Holzmann (*l.c.*) rightly advert, that if the fetus were corrupted then it could be expelled because then it is no longer a fetus but a putrid mass which no longer has the capacity for animation.

Both opinions are probable, but I regard the second as safer and in our case it must altogether be embraced since the first can be of no service in practice, and it seems that the doctors that burn so much time on the question do so in vain. As Fr. Busembaum rightly notes here, what purpose is there to take a potion to directly expel the fetus since it could also suffice for it to be expelled indirectly? The first opinion could only be deduced into practice in two cases. The first would be if the mother otherwise experienced in giving birth were to undergo the danger of death; but on account of this it is not lawful to expel the fetus as Sanchez (*l.c.* n. 10), Petrocorensis (d.q. 1), and Azor (c. 4 q. 2) teach against some. The reason is, because in that case the fetus is not a present aggressor, since the danger would be very distant and the mother could die from another cause in the meantime. And it is confirmed from another common doctrine which St. Thomas, Navarre, Cajetan and others cited by Sanchez (n. 2 *ex c. Aliquando 22*, q. 2) hand down, namely that it is never licit for a mother to take a potion to impede conception on account of some danger. Now, the second case could be when a mother, unless she would expel the fetus, would undergo the danger of death from her kin, or dishonor. But this is certainly illicit from what we read in proposition 34 condemned by Innocent XI, which says: "It is lawful to procure an abortion before animation of the fetus to prevent a girl caught pregnant from being killed or defamed." The reason is, because it would be one thing if the fetus were an aggressor *per se* and *ab intrinseco*, but it is another when it is *per accidens* and *ab extrinseco*. For anyone can kill an aggressor so that they are not killed by him, nevertheless one cannot kill another lest he be killed by an enemy.

Moreover, Sanchez (*de matrimonio* l. 2 d. 22 n. 17) and Viva (on the aforesaid *prop. 34*, n. 17) say that a woman, if she were raped by a man, could expel the seed she had received as an assailant of her honor to avoid infamy; equally it is lawful for a noble man to kill an aggressor when willing to strike him in act with a club (as we said above, n. 381), although this would not be lawful after the blow had been struck. But I cannot acquiesce to this opinion: for if a woman could then expel the semen as an aggressor of her honor, she could also afterward, which the authors themselves do not concede. Nor would it avail to say, with Sanchez, that it is licit for a woman to immediately expel the semen in that case, because then the semen is still not in the peaceful possession of the uterus (*in pacifica possessione uteri*); for, as Pontian rightly teaches (*de matr.* l. 10 c. 13 n. 1) as soon as the man pours out the seed, the womb of the woman receives it and it is closed. And this cannot be denied by Sanchez himself (lib. 9 d. 16 n. 3) with the Salamancans (*de matr.* c. 15 punct. 6 n. 75), Sporer (*de matr.* c. 2 n. 493) and for others in common (see *de matrimonio* book 6 n. 971), who say a wife would not sin mortally who renders the debt on top; indeed, this is so because (as we just said) the womb of the mother is closed immediately and receives the semen. Otherwise it would be dissipated and blocked, and for that reason it would be far from doubt that it is a mortal sin. Moreover, the Salamancans correctly argue (*cit.* n. 75) that a wife would not sin if, for a just cause, she would stand up immediately after the reception of the semen unless she were to do this with a bad mind to disperse it, as Sanchez also says (l. 9 d. 20 n. 3). Moreover, we duly admit what Sanchez says in l. 2 d. 22 n. 17, namely, that a woman, if she were raped, could licitly turn herself and interrupt the *coitus* even if the semen of the man would be poured out; this is because it would come about *per accidens* and on account of the malice of the man. This is why Croix rightly concludes, in l. 3 p. 1 n. 824 (with Cardenez) that it is indeed licit for a woman that was being raped to repel the semen unless it would be inserted; but not to eject what has already been inserted. See what is going to be said on *de Matrimonio*, book 6 n. 954, v. Dub. 1.

Quaeritur II: Would it be lawful for a woman to take a potion to directly expel a plague if she feared that the abortion of an animated fetus would indirectly result? It is answered: If the remedy directly aimed at the killing of the fetus, such as cutting the womb, striking the stomach, etc., this indeed is never lawful. Moreover, if it aims at directly saving the life of the mother, such as a purgation of the body, bleeding, baths, etc., these are certainly licit when it is morally judged for certain that the mother is going to die with the child otherwise. So think Habert (t. 7 p. 748) and the Continuator of Tournely (*de 5 Dec. praec.* art. 3 sect. 1 r. 4) with the common opinion. But the question is, would it be lawful for a mother to take a medication when there is a doubt whether after the mother dies the child could survive and be baptized. Holzmann affirms it, (*de 5 praec.* c. 1 n. 79), the Salamancans (*de rest.* c. 2 punct. 4 § 2 n. 66) with Prado; because (as they say) the obligation to prefer death to procure eternal life of one's neighbor constituted in extreme necessity is then alone present, when it is certain the loss of temporal life is absolutely necessary to the spiritual life of the other (as the cited Doctors say as well as others cited by the Salamancans speaking generally); moreover, not when the spiritual salvation of the neighbor is uncertain, exactly as in our case there can be many doubts. And Sanchez (*de matr.* lib. 9 d. 20 n. 17) as well as Roncaglia (*de 5 praec.* c. 2 q. 3) seem to favor this opinion, saying then it is only illicit to take a remedy when there is danger to the life of the child, when it is certain or at least very probable that the child will be brought forth alive. But I do not see how I could agree with this opinion, since when the death of the child is certain if the mother takes the medicine, and otherwise the death of the mother is certain she does not take the medicine, the mother is certainly held by the order of charity to abstain from the medicine and prefer the spiritual life of her child to her own bodily life; for thus, she is held by the same charity to abstain when there is a doubt about the salvation of the mother and the child, as Tournely says (*l.c.* concl. 2 and r. 5, with Habert.), unless the danger of miscarriage were equal whether she were to take the medicine or not; because then without a greater danger for the fetus the life of the mother is justly chosen. And even if the death of the mother would be morally certain, if she did not take the remedy, nor even then would I dare to permit her the medicine if some reasonable hope would appear favorable, because after the death of the mother the child would survive and could be baptized; because it is licit for no one to safeguard their own temporal life to positively expose their neighbor constituted in necessity with danger of eternal death. Otherwise, I think it must be said with Elbel, Petrocor (t. 2 d. 4 tr. 2 c. 3 q. 2) and the Continuator of Tournely (*l.c.* r. 3) with Sylvius, Hab., Comit. and the common opinion, if there were no reasonable hope in regard to the life of the child after the death of the mother, so that it could be brought to the grace of baptism; because then charity does not seem to oblige the mother placed in extreme necessity, so that she should neglect her life by abstaining from remedies on account of the scanty and very remote hope of the life of the child. Furthermore, the Salamancans (*ibid.* n. 65) reasonably say that doctors, in this case, insofar as medicines are furnished to mothers, should not scrupulously press them to the extent that something might be very probable which the same Salamancans, as well as others say is a very rare case and morally impossible to the point that it would be a miracle that after the mother dies the child would survive and could receive baptism (Salamacans, *l.c.* n. 65; Sanchez, d. num. 17; de Lugo d. 10 num. 135; Roncaglia, dict. q. 3). And a great many experts in medicine have confirmed this for me, whom I have consulted, because while a mother is laboring with a fatal disease the humors are corrupted and they infect the nourishment of the fetus.

Now, is a mother held to suffer a cesarean section so that children be baptized? See what will be said in book 6, n. 106.

Quaeritur III: When is the soul of the child considered to be formed? We must first state proposition 35 of those condemned by Pope Innocent XI, which said: "It seems probable that every fetus, so long as it is *in utero*, lacks a rational soul and then first begins to have the same when it is born; and consequently homicide is not committed in any abortion." Conversely, some wrongly said that the fetus in the first instant in which it is conceived is animated because the fetus is certainly not animated before it was formed, as is gathered from Sacred Scripture, Exodus 21:22, where it says according to the Septuagint: "He who strikes a pregnant woman and causes a miscarriage, if the fetus was formed, he will render life for life, if it was not yet formed, he shall be fined."[4] Therefore, it is certain that the fetus is not immediately animated. Hence, Lessius (lib. 2 cap. 9 n. 65) supposes from Hippocrates that a male child comes to the point of animation on the 30th day, or the 35th, or the 40th or 45th from conception, while a woman on the 35th, or 40th, or 45th or 50th after conception. And many authors affirm the same thing (de Lugo, d. 10 n. 133 and Bonacina, as well as Filliuci, cited by the Salamancans, *de restituione*, c. 2 p. 4 §2 n. 59). Just the same, Busembaum (as above, n. 394), Elbel, *de matr.* n. 470, and the Salamancans with St. Thomas, Azor, Sylvester and the common opinion, as P. Holzman affirms, say the male is formed and animated in a space of 40 days, while a woman 80. And Anacletus and others, cited by Elbel (n. 470), witnesses this opinion follows

---

[4] Translator's note: Whatever the case with the Septuagint, the Vulgate reads: *Si rixati fuerint viri, et percusserit quis mulierem prægnantem, et abortivum quidem fecerit, sed ipsa vixerit: subjacebit damno quantum maritus mulieris expetierit, et arbitri judicaverint.* Moreover, the Vulgate is actually more accurate with respect to the Hebrew which says the same thing. See the next footnote for more information on this topic.

in the external forum in regard to penalties inflicted for homicide. Nay more, St. Thomas (3 dist. 3 q. 5 art. 2) says: "The conception of a male is not completed until a period of 40 days after conception, as the Philosopher says in 9. *de animalibus*, but women to the 90th day. Still, in composition of the masculine body it seems that Augustine adds six days." But the continuator of Tournely says (*ibid.* qu. 1) in this one must adhere more to the Gloss and the theologians who nearly all (as he says) think males are animated on the 40th day and on the 80th day for women; and the Poenitentiary follows this opinion when it treats on the irregularity and punishments, as Sylvius hands down from Navarre (2.2. q. 65 art. 7 p. 419, near the end).[5]

395.—*Quaeritur IV:* To what penalties should those procuring abortion be subjected? Pope Sixtus V, in the year 1588, published a bull which begins *Effrænatam*. In it, the Pope subjected those who procure the abortion of the fetus, whether it is animated or not, and *knowingly* offering a poison of sterility to women in any manner, to the same penalties which are due to murderers in civil and canonical law, such as deprivation of every clerical privilege, dignity, or ecclesiastical benefice, still, disqualification for their

---

[5] Translator's note: This opinion has been superseded by subsequent determinations of the Holy See responding to advances in science not available to the ancients. It would warrant no further commentary if it were not for the fact that some people today attempt to justify procuring abortions based on this discussion in the scholastics and older moralists. Thus we add for the reader the editorial remark from the Gaude edition of St. Alphonsus, letter *n* on this place: "This opinion of the ancients on the time in which the rational soul is animated is commonly rejected today, and it is more probable that the rational soul is infused into the body in the very moment of conception, or at least shortly thereafter. Obviously, the rational soul is the plasmative form of the organic body, or that which forms the human organism. Moreover, the fact is that the opposite opinion contends that the body before the formation of the organs is not suitable to the reception of a rational soul is asserted gratuitously. These sayings on the fetus, whether masculine or feminine, posited by the ancients on that vast disparity of time between the animation of a male and female rest upon no solid foundation, and therefore seem to demand rejection."

posterity to obtain them; moreover, he especially imposed irregularity and excommunication incurred *ipso facto* (following the effect) dispensation and absolution of which he reserved to the Roman Pontiff. Just the same, Gregory XIV, in his bull *Sedes Apostolica*, published in 1591, withdrew the irregularity and excommunication for the abortion of an unanimated fetus; but both the irregularity and the excommunication (reserved to the Pope) remain for the abortion of an animated fetus. Still, in regard to the excommunication, he conceded the faculty both to Bishops and those specially assigned to these cases to absolve them (The mendicant orders possess this faculty to absolve; see book 7, n. 99). Moreover, when Pope Sixtus inflicted the excommunication for those *knowingly* procuring an abortion, he excused those who did so from ignorance, even crass ignorance, as the doctors commonly teach with Sanchez (*de matr.* l. 9 d. 32) and others, as we will discuss in book 7 n. 47. But would affected ignorance excuse? See *ibid.* n. 48. And it seems the same thing must be said on the irregularity there imposed, according to the probable opinion which is adduced in the same place, book 7 n. 351.

Quaeritur V: Would pregnant women that procure an abortion for themselves incur excommunication?[6]

The first opinion is the most common and affirms it with Viva (*in prop. 34 Innoc. XI*, n. 18), Bonacina (*de rest.* d. 2 q. ult. sect. 1 p. 7 n. 6) who says this is received in use, and Sporer (*de matr.* c. 4 n. 718) with Filliuci, and Dicastillus, who holds it as certain. The reasons for this opinion, however, will be related below in the exposition of the second opinion.

The second opinion is very probable, and when we look at the intrinsic reasoning, it appears more probable and says no with Avila (*de Censur.* p. 2 c. 5 d. 3 dub. 12), Lezana (t. 3 v. *Abortus*, n.

---

[6] Translator's note: The discussion here turns on the canon law as it was in St. Alphonsus' time. The entire question is superseded today by Canon 1398 of the 1983 Code of Canon Law, which inflicts excommunication *latae sententiae* for anyone successfully procuring an abortion.

11) the Salamancans (*de rest*. c. 2 punct. 4 § 3, n. 70) with Naldus, Alphonse de Leone; and Cardinal de Lugo holds the same thing (*resp. Mor*. dub. 4 n. 4, although he says he must favor the common use if he explained the bull otherwise), and he does not call it improbable, nay more Roncaglia assiduously upholds it (*de 5 praec*. c. 2 q. 6). The whole resolution of this doubt depends on the words of the bull *Effraenatam* in the preceding question, which was published by Sixtus V, in which the aforesaid excommunication was inflicted against those procuring an abortion. The authors of the contrary opinion say that in the fulmination of the aforesaid excommunication, pregnant women were expressly embraced, because in § 1 of the bull it is said: "And even pregnant women themselves who would knowingly do the aforesaid." Likewise, in § 5, the Pope, while speaking about contraceptive potions,[7] says: "And women themselves, who knowingly, and of their own will take the same drink." But a response can be made to each paragraph that clearly the Pope speaks (as is carefully observed in the bull) only on temporal punishments constituted against homicide; for, when later the Pope meant to treat on the degree of spiritual penalties, especially to inflict the aforesaid excommunication, in § 7 he so adds: "Moreover, that we might ward off by means the gravity of this immense crime, not only with temporal punishments but even with spiritual ones, and that we might counsel each and everyone of whatever degree, state, etc., men or women who either as the principal agents, or as partners commit such a foul crime, would knowingly provide work, counsel, favor, potion or other medicine, etc." So, by speaking here on spiritual penalties, the Pope does not name pregnant woman, but only those men or women "who give such things as work, counsel, etc." Defenders of the first opinion insist, and say that at least in this § 7, pregnant women are embraced since there it is said: "Men or women who as the principal agents, or as partners commit such a

---

[7] *Venenatis potionibus sterilitatis.*

TREATISE IV: THE FIFTH & SIXTH PRECEPTS CH. I   449

foul crime," etc. But again we respond that here under the words *principal agents* pregnant women cannot also be understood, rather principal cooperators who the furnish the work, or counsel or medicines to the distinction of partners who agree mediately to the abortion. And really, in no way can pregnant women be understood here, for otherwise the Pope would not have said "men or women, who," etc. For how can men take medication to procure and abortion for women? Moreover, the reasoning whereby De Lugo, and the Salamancans (*ibid.* n. 71) with others as above, opine with the appearance of truth that the Pope is presumed to have exempted pregnant women from this excommunication is because perhaps that he had compassion on the weakness of women who, while driven on by a great fear of harm that is going to come about take these medicines provided that they abhor such a deed and demonstrably would be able to pay scant attention to an excommunication; thus the Pope, to avoid a new snare for the soul and other dangers, especially of sacrilegious confessions, refused to include them. At least Roncaglia says that when a doubt is present as to whether this excommunication has been imposed on pregnant women, they are much more probably excused, according to what we will say in book 7 *On Censures*, n. 67.

396.—*Quaeritur VI:* Would those procuring an abortion incur irregularity if they were in doubt as to whether the fetus were animated or not?

The first opinion affirms it, which several authors hold (Salamancans *de censur.* c. 7 punct. 3 num. 45 and *de rest.* c. 2 punct. 4 § 2 n. 59; Viva, *in prop. 34 damn. ab Innoc. XI*, n. 18; with Sanchez, Molina, *etc.* cited by Elbel, *de matr.* n. 479). The reasoning is on the one hand, because in every doubtful act of homicide irregularity is incurred, according to what is said in c. *Ad audientiam, de homic.* and c. *Significasti*, as well as c. *Petitio eodem tit.*; and on the other because in doubt the fetus is presumed to be male. Hence, they say, that procuring an abortion past 40 days must be held as irregular; so also Filliuci and others cited by Tamburinius say it must be judged in the external forum, and it is also carried on in the same way in the Sacred Poenitentiary.

Nevertheless, *the second opinion* is truer and denies this, and there are not authors lacking who hold this opinion (Tamburinius, *Dec.* l. 1 c. 3 § 6, v. *Irregularitas*, and *de censur.* l. 10 c. 5 n. 18, with Praepos. and Giballin, likewise Moya, tr. 5 q. 6 with Pell., Marchant, Leander and Verde, Elbel *loc. cit.* with Sporer, Diana, Bardi and others, and the learned author of a recent book with the title *Instruzzione per li novelli Conf.* part. 2, c. 18 n. 464 and 465). The conventional reason is that irregularity is not incurred unless it were expressed in law, as is said in c. *Is qui, de sent. exc.* in 6 (See what is going to be said in book 7, n. 345). Moreover, in this case, irregularity is not found expressed anywhere; although in the aforesaid texts irregularity was imposed on some, in regard to whom there was a doubt as to whether they were present or not for the sake of homicide, still a homicide was certainly committed. But in our case, when there is a doubt on the animation of the fetus, there is also a doubt on the accomplishment of a homicide; and this case is nowhere expressed in law, so procuring an abortion is not held as irregular. Still, we must address a different question: What if there were a doubt whether someone was an accomplice either by his own counsel or work in the certain death of a fetus that was animated for certain? See what is going to be said in book 7, n. 371. Moreover, there can be no presumption (as the Salamancans assert without any foundation) that the fetus might have been masculine; rather it can be presumed to be feminine because from the more frequent event, as I hear, the number of female is greater than that of male; at least on this there is equal doubt on both sides. Tamburinius does not improbably add (*l.c. in Dec.*) that possession in this case favors the earlier state, for a fetus is unanimated earlier than it is animated. Thus it is very probable from the aforesaid in question 3 above, that one must not be considered irregular, at least in the internal forum, who procured an abortion within 80 days of the conception of the fetus. But here we speak on irregularity, we must also speak on excommunication, according to what will be said in book 7 n. 67 on other punishments, as Elbel rightly says.

397.—*Quaeritur VII:* Who then, has the power to relax the punishments we have just reviewed for abortion? In regard to excommunication for abortion of an animated fetus, we already said from the bull of Gregory XIV, that only Bishops and others specially assigned by them to these cases, can absolve them. But there is a doubt as to whether confessors, who have the general faculty from their ordinary to absolve all cases reserved to them, could do it. The Salamancans (*de rest.* c. 2 punct. 4 § 3 n. 68), Diana (part. 7 tr. 5 r. 15 and 19), Roncaglia (*de 5 praec.* c. 2 q. 5 r. 1) and others deny it, saying that a specific deputation is required for this case of abortion. And they argue their case from the words of the aforesaid bull of Pope Gregory, related by Bonacina (tom. 3 d. 2 q. 2 p. 10 n. 15) where it is said: "Any priest, both secular or a regular of any Order, to hear the confessions of the faithful of Christ and specially assigned to these cases by the ordinary of the place have the full and free faculty to absolve only in the forum of conscience." Yet, Bonacina (*l.c.* n. 16) and Viva (*Opusc. de censur.* q. 7 d. 1 n. 7) very probably affirm the same could absolve, and Elbel adheres to them (*de matr.* n. 471), while Sporer does not think it is improbable (*de matr.* c. 4 n. 720). The reason is because those words, "specially assigned to these cases," do not refer to the case of abortion but to the confessor; so that whatever confessor certainly could not absolve in this case (as some cited by Diana falsely think), but one can do it rightly whose bishop specially assigns him to absolve the faithful from those cases, whether by specifically expressing the case of abortion, or by generally conceding the faculty to absolve from cases reserved to the ordinary. And Bonacina and Viva rightly say the use received use has interpreted the aforesaid concession in this way, since favor is interpreted broadly and I myself firmly witness that it is universally practiced in this way in missions for which, missionary priests have been pressed to absolve from this case of abortion because Bishops generally impart the faculty to them for all cases, even reserved ones.

Equally, Elbel (*d.n.* 471) by far says with probability that all the greater prelates of regulars can also absolve from this excommunication as if enjoying episcopal jurisdiction; but only their subjects, for whom they could also assign others. The Salamancans (tr. 6 c. 13 punct. 3 n. 52) add with Peyrin and Pell., Sporer (p. 4 c. 4 n. 721) and Elbel (*ibid.*), who assert in this that the common teaching of the doctors agrees, that the faculty to absolve from this excommunication is applicable to all Mendicant confessors in the internal forum because the Pope, even if he denied this faculty to confessors not specifically assigned by the Bishop, nevertheless is not considered to have denied privileged confessors, to whom the faculty is otherwise conceded in cases reserved to the Pope. Furthermore, after proposition 12 condemned by Pope Alexander VII, it should be certain that if a Bishop somewhere reserved to himself the case of abortion or voluntary homicide, no regular could absolve from it without a license of the Bishop (as the same Elbel, *eod. l.* and Cabassutius, T.J. l. 1 c. 11 n. 5 agree; see what will be said in book 7 n. 99).

Now, with what pertains to irregularity, speaking *per se* only the Pope can dispense against it, not Bishops even if the abortion were secret; because in the faculty conceded to them by the Council of Trent, in its 24th session, cap. *Liceat 6*, it expressly made the exception of voluntary homicide. But in regard to other penalties inflicted in the Bull of Sixtus V, namely the depravation of benefices, and incapacity to hold one, a condemnatory sentence is required to deprive him, or at least a declaratory sentence of the crime, since it would be a privation of an acquired right, as we said in book 1 n. 148 and as Elbel says in n. 478. In regard to the incapacity, we said it is incurred before every sentence, according to the aforesaid in book 1, and as we will speak about more profusely in book 6 n. 705 (whatever Sporer and Elbel might say); because incapacity does not deprive one of an acquired right, but from acquiring it. Now, could Bishops dispense against this incapacity? Elbel (*de leg.* n. 642 and *de matr.* n. 674), as well as Sporer (p. 4 c. 4 n. 722) concede, and Roncaglia (*de 5 praec.* c. 2 q. 6) does not unduly suppose it (against Anacletus). The reason is, because in all punishments imposed by law generally, and not specially reserved to the Pope, Bishops can dispense as St. Bonaventure, Scotus, de Elbel and others teach in common by speaking generically. And it is gathered from c. *Nuper* 29, *de sent. excomm.* where there is a discussion on excommunication. There it is said: "Still, because the maker of the canon did not specifically retain absolution for himself, by that very fact it seems he conceded the faculty of relaxing it to others." And the Gloss adds: "And this is the argument that Bishops can dispense where a dispensation has not been specifically inhibited and seems to have been conceded, because it is not forbidden." See what was said in book 1, n. 191, and also what will be said in book 6 n. 980.

398.—Lastly, it is fitting to add somethings here that are very necessary to know about *homicdium casuale*.[8] *Homicidum casuale* can contain two things, either by laboring on a licit thing, or an illicit thing. This is why St. Thomas gives these rules (II IIæ. q. 64 art. 8), saying: "According to laws, if someone were to labor on a licit thing, showing due diligence, and from this a homicide might follow, he does not incur guilt for homicide." And this, even if the homicide were foreseen in the cause (as the Salamancans note, following the common opinion, in *de V praec.* c. 1 punct. 6 § 1 n. 133). The Angelic Doctor continues: "But if he should labor in an

---

[8] Translator's note: Manslaughter.

illicit matter, he does not escape guilt for homicide." Therefore, there are two rules which are commonly assigned in this matter: I. When someone works on a licit thing, and a homicide follows from it *per accidens* he is excused even if he foresaw it, provided that he did not intend it, and he applied sufficient diligence to stop it; II. But it is otherwise if someone labors on an illicit thing and he would foresee a homicide; because then, although he does not intend it, and might apply diligence lest it would follow, he is not excused. But we must notice that to impute homicide for this, it does not suffice that the work was illicit in itself, but it is further required that it would be illicit precisely in respect to the homicide.

Hence, the question is what sort of work must be properly said to be illicit in respect to homicide? After omitting the diverse opinions on this uncertainty, we must rightly make a distinction with the Salamancans (*loc. cit.*).

And it must be said: I. That if the work of itself is frequently so dangerous, that death occurs from it as a common occurrence, then homicide is always imputed to him that places it, no matter how much diligence he might apply to guard against loss. This is why they are murderers who kick a pregnant woman, or terrify her, from which an abortion comes about; parents suffocating an infant in bed; those slaughtering a man by throwing stones from a sling for the sake of a game. See the Salamancans (with others, *loc. cit.* n. 136). Hence it was ratified in c. *fin. de hom.* in 6, he becomes irregular who hands someone over to be beaten, although he might prevent him from being killed, if the one entrusted with it should kill him.

It must be said: II. That if an illicit work were dangerous, but rarely, so that death rarely happened; then it suffices to excuse if diligence were applied to avoid it, at least in the forum of conscience. Hence a cleric is excused from homicide who might kill a man in some case, laboring in the hunt of wild beasts otherwise forbidden to him, if he applied due diligence. Thus

Roncaglia (*de cens.* c. 3 qu. 3 n. 147), with Palaus, Bonacina, Henriquez, Medina, etc.

It must be said: III. That if a work were not dangerous in itself, although it is illicit, homicide is never imputed to the one exercising it, if in that case death were to come about from it; *e.g.*, if a cleric would ring a bell during a time of interdict, and then the bell falls and strikes a wayfarer. Likewise, if following an act of fornication, the woman would die in childbirth. Add, if an adulterer, in an act of blameless self-defense were to kill the husband of the adulteress. So Lessius, l. 2 c. 9 d. 15 n. 13, Salamancans *ibid.* n. 138, with Suarez, Palaus, Covarruvias, etc. But this is certain in the order of restitution.

But in the order of irregularity, there is a great controversy between the doctors as to whether the adulterer avoids irregularity, who kills the husband when the latter makes an act of aggression, on account of the blameless defense of his life?

In common the doctors teach that if the adulterer could flee and not fleeing he kills the husband, he is not excused from irregularity. So the Salamancans (*de censur.* c. 8 punct. 4 n. 51 and 52 and Sporer, *de V. praec.* c. 2 n. 181) who asserted this is certain among all. The reason (as the Salamancans rightly say), is that it is not shameful for him to flee in that case; and if perhaps the flight would inflict some ignominy on him, he is held to suffer it since he mixed himself up in such difficulties by his own fault.

But what if he could not flee without danger to his life? There are three opinions.

The first opinion absolutely affirms it, although he still incurs irregularity. So Navarre, *Man* c. 27 n. 238, and St. Antoninus, Molina, Gugga, cited by Laymann, l. 3 *de just.* tr. 3 p. 3 c. 10 n. 2. And they prove it from c. *Dilectus, de homic.* where it is said that one laboring in an illicit act becomes irregular if death follows thence.

The second opinion is the opposite and absolutely denies that he incurs it; and Sylvester, Bonacina (d. 7, q. 4), Lessius, l. 2 c. 9 n.

106), with Bañez, Medina, etc., likewise Avila, del Soto, Tab, Leander, Diana, and Henriquez, cited by the Salamancans (*l.c.* n. 49). The reason is because the homicide is not a result of the adultery except *per accidens*; but *per se* it only arises from the unjust invasion of the husband, whose force the adulterer can literally repel with force to save his life. Moreover, they say the aforesaid text in *c. Dilectus* is understood when an illicit thing, upon which one works, is proximately and *per se* has the danger of homicide, but not when it is dangerous *per accidens* and remotely, as it would be in this case of adultery, because it would be rather more the occasion than the cause of the homicide, since homicide rarely comes about from it.

The third opinion, which other authors hold, distinguishes and says that if the adulterer foresaw the assault of the husband, he would continue on rashly and kill him, then he would become irregular; otherwise if he acted secretly and with due caution lest he would be discovered by the husband (Suarez d. 46 sect. 1 n. 12; Laymann, *l. c.*; Sporer, as above, n. 182; with Filliuci, Roncaglia, *de censur.* c. 3 q. 4; and the Salamancans *ibid.* n. 50 with Palaus, Coninck, Villalobos, Cornejo, etc.). And I attach myself to this opinion, if the danger of assault were foreseen to be proximate and very easy, as Roncaglia so rightly expresses it; because in that case the adultery carries the proximate danger of homicide; otherwise if the danger were remote and the adulterer can continue carefully, according to what we will say below. And so all the aforesaid opinions seem to be sufficiently reconciled. What if the man, after he learns of the adultery, were to kill his wife, will the adulterer be irregular? Navarre and others affirm it, but the more common teaching denies it, cited by Sporer, num. 82. But Sporer himself and Laymann (*l. c.*) distinguish in the same mode, as in the preceding question; I consent to them in the same mode if the slaying of the wife were foreseen to be proximate and a sure thing; otherwise if it is remote and difficult.

DUBIUM V
On Dueling and War

ARTICLE I
What is a duel, and is it lawful?

399. What is a duel and is it ever lawful to provoke one?
400. When would it be lawful to accept a duel? And would it be lawful to begin one against a false accuser?
401. What are the penalties imposed for dueling?

399.—"*Resp.* A duel is a contest of two people (or even of a "great many) which is made by an agreement, one declaring it "and the other accepting, taken up in such a way that it is not "to defend life but to expose it to danger. Because, even if it is "commonly a mortal sin, still it is licit for a just cause, which "always be applied. See the Council of Trent (Sess. 25 c. 19 *de* "*reformatione*), Sanchez, (*2. mor.* c. 39); likewise, on the "punishment for duelers, see below n. 401.

Wherefore, the following are resolved:

"1. A duel is not licit to investigate the truth or justice, or to "cleansing of the object of the crime, or to terminate a lawsuit, "because it is fallacious, nay more a superstitious medium to "that end, since even one that is innocent of homicide could "both do it and suffer (Trullenchus, l. 5 c. 2 d. 13 n. 12)" (And *c.* "*1 and 2 de purg.* with the Salamancans *de V praec.* c. 1 punct. 7 "§ 2 n. 181).

"2. Nor on account of enmity or to vindicate an injury, nor "for the reason of showing of manhood or enjoyment."

Here we ask the question: "Would it be lawful to take up a feigned duel to avoid infamy? Tamburinius (l. 7 c. 2 n. 17) upholds this with Escobar and Bossuet. But it must altogether be denied with Busembaum and the Salamancans (*ibid.* n. 163), Elbel (n. 135), Croix (l. 3 p. 1 n. 840), Holzmann (n. 604), with the common opinion. The reason is both to avoid scandal to others, and because Clement VIII, in his constitution *Illius vices* of 1592, forbade this by preventing "non-fatal duels". And therefore, it is not lawful for generals to permit duels for soldiers, even against the enemy to show manhood (Sanchez, *Dec.* l. 2 c. 39 num. 12; Salamancans *loc. cit.* with Navarre, Bonacina, Palaus, Cajetan).

"3. Likewise, it is not lawful to avoid ignominy because "among the good and prudent it does not destroy honor; nay "more, it would not diminish honor for others, if they were to "say to the one challenging them he does not think it is worthy "to proceed in a manner which is against divine and human "laws. Meanwhile, he will go freely on his way day by day and "will always be prepared, as he is now, to defend himself "against any assailant. Trullenchus, *l.c.* n. 4."

So Sanchez supposes, (*l. c.* n. 163, with del Soto, Navarre, Azor, Cajetan and others). But we must attend to proposition 2 condemned by Alexander VII, which said: "A knight challenged to a duel can accept it lest he appear a coward to others."

400.—"4. It is lawful to accept a duel, either to offer to "preserve an enemy's estimation of an army and weaken them, "or to end a war with lower casualties. See Sanchez, *l.c.*

"5. It is also lawful to accept if someone was going to kill "you anyway but conceded weapons so that you might test "fortune. This is only a defense, provided that you could not "avoid it in any other way." (Besides, Fr. Cuniliati thinks this is "probable (tr. 4 c. 9 § 5 n. 3) because if a nobleman were "challenged to a duel, he can licitly respond: *I, as a Christian,* "*cannot accept the duel; still I am prepared to defend myself* "*against unjust aggressors.*)

TREATISE IV: THE FIFTH & SIXTH PRECEPTS CH. I   459

"Likewise, if a judge were to will two men condemned to "death to meet in a duel, because then the other man is "constituted the minister of justice over the other. Trullenchus, "*l.c.*

"6. Lastly, if a nobleman at the royal court, or a soldier in a "camp, being challenged were to limit himself to making a mere "defense with the hope of prevailing, and would be deprived "otherwise on account of suspicion of being a coward from "dignity, office or favor of the prince, Laymann does not dare to "condemn him (lib. 3 t. 3 p. 3 c. 3) and Hurtius (2.2. d. 170, sect. "8 § 73), Lessius (c. 9 d. 8), Filliuci (cap. 8 q. 6), and Navarre (c. "13), all excuse the same."

Quaeritur I: Would it be lawful for a nobleman or a soldier to accept a duel or more still, offer it, if otherwise he would lose his honor, or would certainly be deprived of an office by which he sustains his household? Holzmann (*de 5 praec.* c. 3 n. 608) upholds it, with Pichler, and Anacletus. Likewise, Sporer (*eodem tit.* c. 2 n. 204) and Elbel (n. 118 and 128) with others. The reason is, as the aforesaid authors say, in this case, not only is honor defended but even the goods necessary for life, the loss of which is certainly supposed and cannot otherwise be renewed. Lessius (l. 2 c. 9 n. 49), Sanchez (*dec.* l. 2 c. 39 n. 7), Palaus (tr. 6 d. 6 p. 7 n. 9) also adhere to this opinion, as well as Concina and Valentia, provided (they say), he can licitly accept the duel as a necessary defense of goods of the greatest importance. Roncaglia (*de 5 praec.* c. 4 q. 2 r. 3) and Croix (l. 3 p. 1 n. 836) suppose this to be probable provided the other man invades those goods by act and must be fought in act, but not if he is not responsible for those goods.

Nevertheless, today both of the aforesaid opinions are no longer probable, from the first and fourth of five propositions recently condemned by our most Holy Father Benedict XIV in his constitution *Detestabilem*, published on 10 November 1752. The propositions which were annunciated and condemned are the following.

I. A military man who, unless he might offer or accept a duel, would be held as a coward, timid, abject and unsuited to military duties and thus would be deprived of his job, upon which he sustains himself and his own, or deprived of a promotion, and otherwise would perpetually lack hope of due honor, escapes all fault and penalty whether he offers or accepts a duel.

II. Those who accept a duel to safeguard their honor or escape human contempt, or challenging one to a duel for that purpose can be excused when they know for certain the fight is not going to be safe inasmuch as it is not going to be stopped by others.

III. A general, or army official that accepts a duel out of grave fear of loss of reputation or office does not incur the ecclesiastical penalties imposed by the Church against duelers.

IV. It is licit in the natural state of man to accept and offer a duel to preserve fortunes with honor when the loss of those cannot be averted by another remedy.

V. The license asserted for the natural state can also be applied to the state of a badly organized city, namely one in which justice is openly thwarted by the neglect or malice of the magistrate.

Quaeritur II: Is it licit for an innocent man to summon a duel against a false accuser when another remedy is not supplied to avoid an unjust sentence of death? Several authors uphold it, for the reason that it is lawful for anyone to defend his life against an unjust aggressor, precisely as the false accuser is reckoned here (de Lugo, *d.* 10. n. 184, Sanchez in *Dec.* l. 2 c. 39 n. 7; Bañez, Cajetan, Azor, Navarre, Trullenchus, cited by the Salamancans *de V. praec.* punct. 7 § 2 n. 167). But it must be held with the Salamancans, (*ibid.* n. 169) as well as Suarez, Aragon, Hozes, etc. (cited by the Salamancans) that it is illicit. The reason is, because the defense in this case would be excessive, as is proven from St. Thomas (II IIæ q. 64 art. 7) provided that death does not then proceed from the omission of the duel, but from the unjust sentence of the judge. Moreover, the contrary seems to have been condemned by Alexander VII in his condemned proposition 18, which said: "It is lawful to kill a false accuser, a false witness and even a judge, from whom an unjust sentence threatens for certain, if the innocent man can avoid harm by no other way."

401.—*Quaeritur III:* What are the penalties imposed for a duel? There are three from the Council of Trent (Sess. 25, cap. 19 *de Reformatione*): 1) Excommunication is incurred *ipso facto* and reserved to the Pope, which are also incurred by the second of each dueler, and those counseling it (namely those who efficaciously counsel), but it is otherwise if they did not persuade him, as Elbel says (*de hom.* num. 122). Likewise, those showing favor, and the owner of a place that provides it for the duel, as well as the spectators; but not those who are found there who were merely passing by on a journey, but those who purposely watch, and approve of it with their presence and cheer on the duelers, precisely as Gregory XIII and Clement VIII explain the Tridentine decree (see Elbel, *d.* n. 122); 2) The next penalty is proscription of all goods with perpetual infamy, but this penalty does not seem to be received in Naples. 3) Deprivation of ecclesiastical burial if the duelers die during the conflict itself. Elbel (n. 142), Tamburinus, Diana, etc. make the exception if they die elsewhere, or if they show a sign of penance before death. But in the aforesaid bull, *Detestabilem*, even they are deprived of ecclesiastical burial, although (as it is said there) "they died fortified with the Sacraments." Moreover, these punishments are only incurred for a duel taken strictly, namely, in a suitable place, time and in arms; but not due to an unplanned conflict, even if the fighters carry it out in some suitable place from the same violent quarrel. So Elbel (*De Duello*, num. 132) very probably thinks, with Diana (p. 3, tr. 6 resol. 1, v. *Dico* 11), Bonaspei (tom. 3, tr. 4 disp. 8 n. 145), and the common teaching. Tamburinius (*Dec.* l. 6 c. 1 § 3 n. 11), Diana (p. 5 tr. 13 r. 39) and Elbel (n. 137) with probability say the same thing if someone were to say: "I will fight with you the first time you meet me," for in that case, even after the fight took place, they do not incur the penalties because then they lack the designation of a specific place and time.

ARTICLE II
Whether war is lawful, and for how long?

402. When is war lawful?
403. What should a prince do to licitly carry out a war?
404. When could a war be fought with only a probable opinion?
405. To what are princes held?
406. Is it lawful to call in heretics and non-Christians as soldiers?
407. To what are generals held?
408. Could soldiers fight in a war when there is a doubt about it's justice?

402.—"Resp. A defensive war, namely one in which unjust "force is repelled, is licit even by private authority. On the other "hand, an offensive war, wherein force is initiated, requires "three conditions to be lawful: 1) That it is waged by the "authority of the prince or magistrate that knows no superior, "such as the Pope, emperor, kings and certain republics such as "those of the Venetians and Genoese, etc.; 2) That there is a just "and grave cause present, *e.g.* the necessity of the common "good, and to preserve the peace, recovery of unjust losses, "quelling a rebellion, defense of the innocent, etc. (see "Laymann, and Molina, t. 1 d. 114, Diana, p. 6 t. 4 r.); 3) That it "would be done with a right intention, *i.e.* not from hatred, but "from the love of the common good, although if this last were "lacking, there would be no obligation of restitution. So the "common opinion holds with St. Thomas, II IIæ q. 40, art. 1; "Laymann, l. 2 t. 3 c. 12." (We add in addition that a just cause for waging a war would be if the preaching of the Gospel were impeded, as the Salamancans say in tr. 21, c. 3 p. 2 n. 10).

Wherefore, the following are resolved:
"1. If anyone wages a just war, the other cannot licitly "defend himself because in regard to the same thing two cannot "have contrary rights. Still, it can happen that neither side sins "on account of invincible ignorance. Filliuci, n. 185.

403.—"2. A king is held to take care with all diligence that "he is certain about the justice of a war before he begins it, as "well as the grave cause. For which purpose the following are "profitable: a) He should see to it that he not only has "experienced counselors but also good ones; b) He should be "attentive as to whether they are impeded by his household, or "their letters intercepted, or his instructions to them; c) He "should not merely see to it that the justice of the war is "examined by his counselors and freely proclaimed, but also by "diverse theologians according to evangelical laws; d) If, after "everything has been heard, he were also to examine the matter "in the presence of God, let him decide to do what he would "wish to do at the point of death. Lastly, although a probable "opinion on the justice of the war would suffice, nevertheless, if "justice would remain equally doubtful and the other were in "possession, it would not be lawful to wage war since *melior sit* "*conditio possidentis* (Filliuci, tr. 29 c. 9 q. 4; Trullenchus l. 5 c. 2 "d. 3, where he teaches with Diana p. 4 tr. 4 r. 72), it is also "lawful for a prince to concede the right of *repressalia*, with "certain conditions preserved, which are cited by Palaus in tr. 1 "c. 6 disp. 5 p. 4 and in the following article)."

404.—*Quaeritur:* Could a prince wage war against another possessing his kingdom in good faith with only a probable opinion?

The first opinion upholds it, with Sanchez (*Dec.* l. 1 c. 9 n. 36) and Azor, Filliuci, Trullenchus, Escobar, etc., (cited by the Salamancans, tr. 21 c. 8 punct. 3 § 1 n. 20) and Sporer follows this (*de V. praec.* c. 2 n. 100). Their reasoning is that the prince should not be of a lower condition than a private person; for if the faculty to move a lawsuit is conceded to private people over a thing possessed by another when he has for himself only probable opinion that it is his, then why would the faculty to wage war against another not be conceded to the prince, at least to claim part of a kingdom possessed by another when there is no higher judge who would avail to decide the suit between them according to law?

The second opinion holds that, as the prince not in possession could wage war, he ought to exert his power at least by a more probable opinion. So think Suarez and Victoria; at least to obtain part of the kingdom, as Tournely, Bañez, Prado and Ledesma (cited by the Salamancans, *l.c.* n. 25) say. The reason is, because in that case his right is not more in possession, and just as for him, if he were a private person, the matter must be adjudicated by a judge according to the opinion that we will address in book 5, n. 210, *Quaeritur I,* so the prince, when he cannot go to a competent judge, can rightly claim the matter for himself in war. Croix call this opinion probable in lib. 3 p. 1 n. 869.

But the *third opinion*, to my mind more probable by far, teaches that a prince cannot wage war against another holding possession in good faith unless he had certitude of his right; the foremost reason is that the possessor (since possession attributes to him a certain right of retaining a thing, according to what was said in book 1, n. 35 and 36) cannot ever be despoiled of a thing he already possesses unless it were certain that he would retain it unjustly (Palaus t. 1 tr. 1 d. 2 punct. 7 n. 5; Elbel *de Bello Conf.* 6 n.

149, who holds our opinion as certain; Holzmann *de V. praec.* n. 602; the Salamancans *l.c.* n. 24 and 26, with Vasquez, Montesin, Villalobos and Salas). Laymann (l. 1 tr. 1 c. 5 § 3 n. 24) and Tamburinius (*Dec.* l. 1 c. 3 § 4 n. 50) hold the same thing, saying this is canonical law that must be observed even by kings, no man can plunder another that has possession in good faith—unless he had certitude of his right. And these authors reckon the contrary opinion improbable from the intrinsic principles. Moreover, although the second opinion seems probable enough to me speculatively and even intrinsically speaking, nevertheless, I agree with what Roncaglia says (to whom the Salamancans adhere, *dict.* n. 24), namely that war commonly advances such outrages and injuries to religion, the innocent, the honor of women, etc., that it seems it could scarcely ever be just in practice if it could be waged upon only probable reasons and not certain ones.

405.—"3. The evident justice of the war ought to be "proposed to the opposed party which, if it would offer "appropriate satisfaction, the war should not begin. Nay more, "as is more probable, if it begins, it should soon be ended if not "by the rigor of justice, then at least for the most part from "charity. See Molina as cited above, d. 103, Trullenchus, l. 5 c. 2 "d. 3."

"4. A prince can demand restitution for satisfaction of what "was stolen as well as expenses. Likewise something in "punishment for any injuries inflicted (Duval). Hence, he can "deprive the conquered of goods, even the innocent, command "tributes from them, raise citadels and whatever else is "necessary for security. Coninck, Diana, p. 6. 4 r. 22."

"5. Princes are held to pay wages to soldiers, otherwise they "are held to make compensation for injuries, both to the "soldiers themselves and others who receive loss from them. "Coninck, Palaus, Diana, p. 6. t. 4 r. 29."

"6. Catholic princes are also held at times to abstain from a war that is otherwise just *per se*, if from it scandal would arise, as well as the spiritual ruin of many and the detriment to the Church. See Palaus; Diana p. 6 t. 4 r. 7."

406.—"7. Even if, speaking *per se*, it would be lawful in a just war to summon infidels for assistance, *per accidens* frequently or all the time it would not be lawful by reason of scandal, or danger against the faith, *e.g.* lest subjects be perverted or sacred places profaned, etc. Regius, t. 2 l. 21 n. 10; Filliuci, n. 81."

"8. Similarly, it is lawful for another prince, even of another faith to assist in a just war unless there were danger of scandal, increase of heresy and loss of the true faith. See Coninck, tr. *de char.* d. *de bello*."

Quaeritur: Would it be lawful for Catholic kings in a just war to call upon heretics or non-Christians for aid against another Catholic prince?

The first opinion universally affirms it with Farinacio, Themudus, Salcedus, Aponte, etc. (cited by the Salamancans, *de praec. Dec.* tr. 21, cap. 8, punct. 3 § 2 num. 32).

The second opinion holds this is absolutely illicit from Exodus 34:12, where it says: "Beware lest you join in friendship with the inhabitants of that land which are to you in ruin." So Ramirez, Pizarrus, and many others whom Diana collected (p. 10, tr. 2, *Addit.*, Res. 2).

The third opinion says *per se* it is licit to summon heretics or non-Christians, but more often than not, *per accidens* it is illicit on account of the imminent damage to religion. So St. Antoninus, Sylvester, Suarez, Coninck, Prado, Tapia, Palaus, and Bonacina (cited by the Salamancans, *ibid.* n. 34) hold with Busembaum. Speculatively, this third opinion is indeed probable, but it appears that the second must altogether be held in practice, with Sporer (n. 107) and the Salamancans (*ibid.* n. 35), along with Molina,

Coninck, Diana, Prado, Lorca, and Villalobos. The reason is, because it is morally impossible that, after society has been contaminated with enemies of faith, the aforesaid damage to religion would not come about.

407.—"9. Generals, lieutenants, captains, and other officials "sin and are held to restitution: a) If they have fewer soldiers "than they show in the payment of wages; b) When it is their "duty to see to provisions and give spoiled food or drink to "soldiers, whereby plague arises; c) If in transit through regions "they receive money from various civilians lest they would "spend the night or tarry there; d) If they were to give a great "many contracts for different houses to one soldier. Molina, "Becan, Diana, p. 6 t. 4 r. 27 and 28; e) If, while taking away "wages from soldiers they permitted them to wrench necessities "from the innocent.

"10. A soldier who in war, both just and unjust, is prepared "[only] to earn a wage, he is in a bad state and is not fit for "absolution unless he would change his frame of mind; and "indeed, if he will fight in an unjust war, then he is held to "restitution of losses, unless inculpable ignorance were to "excuse him; for then the restitution would suffice of those "goods which he holds *in specie,* or of those, whereby he "became wealthier. See below."

"11. If a subject of a prince who wages war were called to "that war, or, was employed for it before it started, he is not "held to inquire on the justice of the war so long as no strong "suspicion to the contrary should appear that would positively "render it doubtful; because he can presume in favor of his "prince, whom he should obey in doubt, and his authority for "the most part suffices to form even positively a probable "judgment about the justice of the cause, so that he will not "carry out the work with doubtful faith. See Cardinal de Lugo, "*d.* 18 *de just.* s. 1 n. 21. But if he were not a subject, he is held

"first to inquire and then at least from a probable judgment that
"the war is just. Molina, d. 113, n. 171; Laymann, l. 2 t 3. c. 12, n.
"8; Azor, Mald., Regius, against certain authors cited by Diana,
"t. 2 tract. 5 *misc.* r. 96 and t. 3 r. 7, Card. de Lugo, *l.c.*, Escobar,
"e. 7 c. 8."

408.—*Quaeritur:* could soldiers fight in a war with a doubt about the justice of the war? We must distinguish with Busembaum if they are subjects of the king waging the war; then, unless they were certain about the injustice of the war, they can, or rather they are held, to obey the prince commanding it. So the authors commonly teach (Sanchez, *Dec.* l. 6 c. 3 n. 15; Sporer *de V. praec.* c. 2 num. 102 and the Salamancans, *de eod. V.* praec. c. 8 punct. 3 § 1 n. 29, with Suarez, Molina, Palaus, Bañez, Salas, and Villalobos). And it is expressly held in can. *Quid culpatur,* caus. 23, q. 1, where St. Augustine so teaches: "A just man, if perhaps he is under a king, even if he were a sacrilegious man, can be in the army and may rightly fight in a war at the prince's command because it is what is commanded of him, or it is certain that it is not against a precept of God, irrespective of whether it is or is not certain." The reason is, because subjects are held to obey where there is no certain sin; and moreover, they ought to presume the war is just as often as the contrary is not certain. But it must be said otherwise in regard to those who are not subjects, who are unable to fight unless they first become certain on the justice of the war. The reason is, because when it is a question of the loss of a third party, he cannot inflict it unless he is certain on the injustice of the possessor. So the common opinion runs (Cajetan, 2.2. qu. 169 art. 2 ad 4; Sanchez, Sporer *ll.cc.*; and the Salamancans, *ibid.* n. 30, with Ledesma, Molina, and Villalobos against a few authors cited by Palaus).

Furthermore, in regard to foreign soldiers that are hired for a wage, the same must be said as in regard to subjects. Nevertheless, understand if they are found to have been hired before the war was incited. Otherwise, if they are hired after the war has been started, even these ought to be made certain on the justice of the war. So Sporer, and the Salamancans with the cited authors.

12. A soldier understanding the war that he is fighting to be unjust cannot be absolved unless he were to will, as soon as he could, to see to his dismissal and in the meantime abstain from hostile actions, *e.g.*, slaughter, booty, etc. See Laymann, l. 2 t. 3 c. 12. But could such a man kill an enemy soldier invading him? See Escobar, e. 7 c. 8.

ARTICLE III
What is lawful in a just war?

409.—"*Resp.* Even if in regard to enemies in a just war it "were lawful to do all those things which are necessary to the "end of the war; *e.g.* to kill, despoil, etc., still they cannot "directly despoil the innocent of life (by which are understood "boys who cannot bear arms, women, old men, religious, "clerics, pilgrims, merchants, and country folk); nevertheless "they can from their external goods if they are part of an enemy "state, and otherwise the end of the war cannot be obtained "(Molina, Becan p. 2 c. 10 11 and 12; Laymann, Filliuci n. 191, "etc.). The reason is, because they are part of a state they can be "punished with its crime in those goods which in the dominion "of the state." (Nevertheless, Sporer, *de 5 praec.* n. 122, says that after the war has transpired, restitution must be made to ecclesiastics of everything taken, unless it was taken for use of the just war.)

410.—"1. *Per accidens*, sometimes it is lawful to burn even "Churches to extract enemies from them, to pillage them and "kill if, for example, a Church were used as a camp to fight "back. Sylvius, v. *Bellum*, n. 11, Sa, Bonacina, p. ult. § 3."

"2. Against the enemy it is lawful to use snares and "stratagems provided there is no fraud, albeit even these are not "mortal sins, such as when spies feign themselves to be friends. "But no discretion is granted to those things which must be "avoided, namely to put poison into well waters, bullets, etc. as "these are against the laws of war and are not permitted. "Molina, d. 3."

"3. Faith given to the enemy must be preserved unless "either coerced to surrender or to yield would be a grave loss to "the state or religion, or if the enemy will not preserve it; "thereupon the conditions and circumstances clearly have "changed. Duval, Palaus, Diana (*l.c.* r. 10). See Laymann, l. 3 t. 3 "c. 12."

"4. Those taken in war, even if they were justly taken, can "flee unless scandal or a special promise would hinder it, and "they can take away the goods of the enemy with them. "Laymann, l. 2 tr. 3 c. 12 n. 16. Is it lawful to kill besiegers? See "above, dub. 4 case 5."

"5. Sometimes, a city can be given over to be sacked (but "rarely and only for the most severe reasons); still, soldiers "cannot take spoils or inflict harm on enemies by their own "private authority because they are only executors and "ministers (See Sa, verb. *Bellum*, Laymann, tr. 3 c. 12, Filliuci n. "198, Diana, p. 6 t. 4). Moreover, were a city to be sacked "unjustly, rank and file soldiers are only held to the damage "which they inflict, as several authors teach is a probable "opinion. (Diana *l.c.* r. 31, following Sylvius, Navarre, etc. "likewise p. 3 t. 5 r. 86) See below, tr. 5 c. 2 d. 3."

"6. Soldiers sin with the burden of restitution if they steal "from country folk or others in whose homes they are billeted, "or from the homes of the places they pass through, or wrench "from them their possessions against their will, or even receive "presents (unless it were certain that it was done altogether "freely, seeing that those donations are usually not freely "offered but compelled); besides these, they can furnish these "from the constitution of the prince; nevertheless, only if they "were in extreme, or at least grave necessity. Molina, Coninck, "Palaus, Becan, etc. Diana p. 6 t. 4 r. 21."

Soldiers are held also to make restitution for all the damages that are inflicted by enemies when they themselves do not impede them. Thus Elbel, n. 154, because they are held from justice to impede damage to the state. Likewise, Soldiers sin if they desert while there is yet no despair of victory, or if they leave their camp without a just cause; it is otherwise if they leave due to grave necessity because their pay has gone into arrears. Elbel, n. 180, with Palaus, Laymann, Sporer, etc.

"7. *Repressalia* is licit under these conditions: a) It is "manifestly certain that citizens of another state caused injury; "b) When their superiors were asked they refused justice; c) It "were certain they culpably refused it; d) The supreme prince, "for a known cause, conceded it; e) That they do not inflict "more damage than just satisfaction requires; f) That it is not "conceded against Ecclesiastical persons.

411.—"One might ask, to whom do goods snatched away "from the enemy pertain?
"*Resp.* 1: They yield immovable goods to the prince or the "state while moveable goods become the property of those "taking them, unless custom would hold that a part should be "conceded to the prince and the community. 2) By Cesarean "Law, unless a contrary custom were in force, goods taken in a "just war which were possessed unjustly become the property

of those taking them, after they convey them as their spoils. Valentia, t. 3 d. 4 q. 3; Molina, d. 18 and Hurt. t. 2 d. 169, sect. 12 § 119, where he requires they possess them for at least one night. See also Sylvius, Bonacina, *loc. cit.*, on sins that are usually committed in war. Trullenchus, l. 2 d. 10 *et seq.*, Diana, p. 6 t. 4 r. 23, where he teaches against Durandus that this opinion is safe in practice."

TREATISE IV: THE FIFTH & SIXTH PRECEPTS CH. I

BOOK IV: ON THE PRECEPTS OF THE DECALOGUE

CHAPTER II
ON THE SIXTH AND NINTH COMMANDMENT

THOU SHALT NOT COMMIT ADULTERY AND THOU SHALT NOT COVET THY NEIGHBOR'S WIFE, etc.

412.—"These two precepts are joined because the same sins "are forbidden by them, either explicitly or implicitly, namely "sins of sexual impurity and lust.

"Moreover, lust is a disordered appetite, or delectation of "use, or even a venereal sensation which occurs with the "arousal of the passions serving generation in regard to the "venereal parts of the body. Inasmuch as the appetites, or other "delectations, even if they are also sensitive or of sensitive "appetites but are not venereal or of the venereal appetites, nor "ordered to them, they do not regard lust.

"Hence, the acts, or sins of lust are separated into: a) "Imperfect, in which the final *terminus* of the venereal appetites "is not discovered, namely the diminishment of semen, as are "acts of internal desires and morose delectation, which take "their species from their objects; and b) perfect and "consummated, which have the relevant terminus already "spoken of. These again are twofold. For some are natural, "which are not opposed to nature nor differ in species in the "reckoning of lust, (even if they were to differ in species by an "added deformity), *e.g.* adultery, incest, etc., while others are "unnatural, or contrary to nature, in which the conditions "established by nature (*e.g.* the identity of the species, the *vas* "*debitum*, etc.), are not preserved. And these also differ in the "reckoning of lust in their species, which vary according to the "modes in which they are committed, opposed to nature."

DUBIUM I
Whether kisses, hugs, touches, obscene words and similar things are sins outside of marriage, and how great?

413. What is sexual enjoyment, what is sensitive enjoyment?
414. Why is every venereal act [outside of marriage] bad?
415. Whether paucity of matter is granted in a venereal matter?
416. Whether it is granted in sensitive enjoyment?
417. Whether kisses would be licit at some point?
418. When are kisses excused from mortal sin?
419. On touch and the shameful gazing at one's own body, or at the mating of animals.
420. On touch and the shameful gazing at another's body; and on the touch of the genitals of animals.
421. Is it always a shameful mortal sin to gaze on the opposite sex? Or a beautiful youth? And whether these acts of looking cover the species of the object?
422. Is it lawful to gaze upon non-private parts of the opposite sex?
423. Whether it is a mortal sin to look at the chest, legs, etc. of a woman?
424. Whether it is a mortal sin to look at shameful pictures?
425. Whether it is lawful for a woman to adorn herself and put on makeup? What if she covers her breasts or uses men's garments? Review book 3, n. 52 and 54.
426. When do those mentioning foul words sin?
427. Whether those who spectate at foul comedic plays always sin gravely? Do those who cooperate with them by paying money or applause also sin gravely?
428. Do those who make the stages and dress sin?
429. Would it be lawful to dance?
430. Would a woman sin by permitted herself to be touched? Is a woman held to cry out in order to avoid unchaste touches?

431. *Would a touch be lawful, etc. among the married and the betrothed?*

413.—"*Resp.* To discern the matter, in the first place the "intention and sexual enjoyment must be distinguished from "intention, and sensitive enjoyment as well as other sensitive "appetites, which consists in a certain proportion and "conformity to the thing touched with the organ of touch. "Then it must be known that intention and sexual sensation is a "mortal sin and excludes one from the kingdom of God, "according to the Apostle in Galatians 5."

Now we reluctantly undertake to treat this matter, indeed the name of which is enough to infect the minds of men. I ask the chaste reader to forgive me if he will find discussed and clarified here a great many of the questions and circumstances omitted by Fr. Busembaum. Would that I were able to explain myself more briefly or obscurely! Yet, since this matter is the more frequent and abundant in confessions, and on account of which a greater number of souls fall into hell, I do not hesitate to assert that everyone who has been damned was damned on account of this one vice of sexual impurity (or at least not without it). Hence it has been necessary for me, in order to instruct those who desire to learn moral science, that I express myself clearly (although in the most chaste manner that can be done) and discuss a great many particulars. Nevertheless, I ask the students who are preparing themselves for the office of hearing confessions not to read this treatise on the sixth commandment, and in the same way the other on the conjugal debt until they will be near to receive confessions. And should they read, let them altogether cast out all curiosity, especially on account of this end, and also at that time often elevate the mind to God and commend themselves to the Immaculate Virgin so that while they are zealous to acquire the souls of others for God, they do not themselves suffer detriment.

414.—Although, under this precept "Thou shalt not commit adultery", only adultery is expressed (since the Greek word *mœchia* properly means this); just the same every sexual act outside of marriage is forbidden by the same precept. See the Salamancans, *de VI praec.* c. 1, punct. 1 n. 3, who profusely prove it from St. Augustine and St. Ambrose. For, even if fornication is less bad than adultery, nevertheless, since carnal relations, by the law of nature, are ordered only to matrimony, through which not only are children begotten but also educated, thus in this precept God forbade all sex outside of matrimony, and together every sexual act which is ordered to the process of procreation. Besides, that fornication was already expressly forbidden by God elsewhere can be found in Leviticus 19:29, Deuteronomy 23:17; and 1 Corinthians 6:9.

"1. Kisses, embracing, gazing, touch and similar things, if "they happen outside of matrimony and from intention for a "lustful act, or on account of sexual enjoyment, even if that is "not completed (which is insemination) are still always mortal "sins because in that mind, outside of matrimony, they are "unchaste and by their nature such enjoyment tends to "completion. Filliuci, t. 30, c. 9 n. 294; Lessius, lib. 4, c. 3 d. 8; "Sanchez, l. 9 d. 46."

415.—One might ask whether paucity of matter is granted to lust in general? We must preface that the Doctors make the distinction between sexual, or carnal enjoyment, namely with arousing of the genitals, from sensitive, or natural delight. Hence, two doubts arise:

Dubium I: Whether paucity of matter is granted in a sexual matter? Sanchez (*de Matrim.* l. 9 d. 46 n. 9) without danger of pollution or consent in a carnal act, thinks paucity of matter can be granted exactly as it would be to touch the hand or foot of a woman, to press an arm, to pinch or twist the fingers. And

Navarre, del Soto, Salas and many others cited by the Salamancans (*de VI praecept.*, c. 3 punct. 4 n. 79 ad 80) think the same thing. Tamburinius seems to have also held the same thing, *Dec. de impud.* c. 8 § 1 n. 8 and 9. But Tamburinius advances along another road; for he distinguishes, with Palaus (who calls this opinion the most common) and says paucity of matter is not given in a sexual matter, in which every small enjoyment is gravely evil; but still it is granted in the matter of lust, which is more broadly accessible to the sense of touch. Hence, he says a light touch from a joke, or without sexual enjoyment, does not exceed a venial sin. Nevertheless, these not withstanding, it altogether must be held with Viva (*in Trut. super prop. 40 damn. ab Alex. VII*), and the Salamancans (*ibid.* n. 81), as well as Moya and Corella, that every carnal or lustful delectation taken with knowledge and deliberation is a mortal sin, especially after the aforesaid proposition 40 that was condemned, which said: "It is a probable opinion which states that a kiss is only venial when performed for the sake of the carnal and sensible delight which arises from the kiss, if danger of further consent and pollution is excluded." For if in kisses light matter is not granted, nor must it be granted in other touches with carnal enjoyment. The reason is, because every carnal enjoyment, or arousal of the spirits serving generation, is a certain inchoate pollution, or a movement to pollution. Therefore, rightly, the Continuator of Tournely, de. 6 *dec.* praec. art. 8, concl. 2, and the Salamancans, *ibid.*, punct. 3 § 5 n. 65, with Cajetan, Bonacina, Tamburinus, Lopez, condemn the acts related, namely to pinch the hand of a woman, to intertwine fingers, etc., as a mortal sin due to the carnal enjoyment which then takes place, or at least on account of the proximate danger of it. And Croix equally rejects the opinion of Affiaga (l. 3 p. 1 n. 911), who says that one does not gravely sin who consents of his own will in such light carnal movements arising on their own.

416.—Dubium II: Whether paucity of matter is granted in sensible or natural enjoyment, namely, if anyone is delighted from contact of the hand of a woman exactly as they are from contact of a delicate thing, say a rose, silk garments, and similar things?

The first opinion affirms it, with St. Antoninus, Sylvius, Salas, Navarre, Filliuci, Hurtad, Moya, and a great many others with the Salamancans, *ibid.* § 3 n. 36, and Busembaum adheres to it below in n. 4, as well as the Cont. of Tournely, *de 6 praec.* art. 7 sect. 2 concl. 1, with Comitolus, Vincent Baronius, Sylvius and others.

Nevertheless, the *second opinion* denies it with Cajetan, Diana, and others, cited by the Salamancans, (*ibid.* n. 38 ad 40). The reasoning is that touches, following what are enjoyable according to the sense of touch of a girl, or an adolescent, are *per se* ordered to pollution. And I say this must altogether be held as the Salamancans rightly say (*l.c.* n. 40) with Filliuci, Trullenchus, Diana, etc. as well as Roncaglia, *de 6 praec.* c. 1, q. 2, that the first opinion is not practically probable, since due to the corruption of nature, it is morally impossible to have that natural enjoyment so that carnal and sexual enjoyment would not be perceived, especially by persons suited to intimate relation, and especially if these acts take place with some passion and time, as Elbel says (*de 6 praec.* n. 186). Hence, Sporer (*de matrim.* c. 3 n. 687) rightly says with Sanchez (l. 9 d. 46) and the common opinion, as well as Croix (l. 3 p. 1 n. 804), that by way of a general rule, the first opinion is not practically probable, because *per se* it is a mortal sin to expose oneself to the danger of consent in sexual enjoyment. Nevertheless, Croix makes some exception, in the case when such a proximate danger is absent. But I would only admit it (with Fr. Holzmann, *de 6 praec.* c. 2 n. 706) in some rare case, in which through long experience someone would be morally certain that no danger of consent threatened him; but when would this case be? Now, it must be noted (as the Continuator of Tournely rightly distinguished in *de 6 praec.* art. 7

sect. 1 concl. 3, *Verum*), that it is one thing to act so as to gain delectation, and another with delectation, which rises from the qualities connected to the body in which paucity of the matter can be granted if the delectation were merely sensible or natural; provided (it must be added) one does not permit it, but detests delectation in touch, otherwise he would not act with delectation but for delectation, which cannot be separated from the danger of following into sexual delectation.

"2. Such acts are of the same nature with perfected or "consummated acts, and therefore it must be explained in "confession whether they took place with the same sex or a "different one, with a free woman, or a married woman, a "relation, or a sacred person, etc. Lessius, d. 15, Sanchez, l. 1 c.2.

"3. Kisses, embracing, squeezing hands, and similar things "are not obscene if they are only done for duty,[9] or for the sake "of an increase of upright morals, or benevolence, even if sexual "enjoyment would arise (provided he did not consent to it) they "are not sins. Lessius, Filliuci, *l.c.* n. 171." (So jointly St. Antoninus p. 2 tit. 5 c. 1 § 10, and the Continuator of Tournely, *de 6 praec.* art. 7 sect. 1 concl. 1 etc., with Sylvius).

417.—Nevertheless, Croix properly notes (l. 3 part. 1 n. 900) that kisses, even those that are done from the custom of the country, if they happen for a space of time, or with vehemence, are ordinarily mortal sins. He says the same thing with Sporer on kisses in the mouth, or if anyone would put his tongue in the mouth of another. On the other hand, he adverts with Sanchez (*etc.* n. 902) that to kiss boys (it must be understood about very young boys), even with sensible delectation, is not ordinarily anything but venial because that delectation is not ordinarily anything but natural.

---

[9] As St. Thomas says in II IIæ. qu. 154 art. 4.

418.—"4. But if these very things are done from some "excusable vanity, a joke, curiosity, levity, petulance, nay more "even sensuality whether sensual and natural by disposition, "they do not exceed a venial sin" (Provided not with sexual delectation nor its cause, and if he is provided with more than an intention, after it has been repulsed, and then by abstaining from it). "See Filliuci, Lessius, Sanchez (*loc. cit.*), Diana, p. 4 t. 3 "r. 136. Nevertheless, the contrary is safer. See Turllenchus, l. 6 "c. 1 d. 12, num. 8." (Also see what was said in 416).

419.—"5. The same must be said about touch and gazing on "unwholesome parts of their own body, or watching the sexual "intercourse of animals, not with a sexual mind, but only from "curiosity or levity, still scandal avoided and the danger of "venereal consent."

To touch one's own revered parts from levity or curiosity is not a mortal sin *per se*, as the authors say (Salamancans *de 6 praec.* c. 3 punct. 3 § 5 n. 68) with Sanchez, and Bonacina, and the Continuator of Tourney, *loc. cit.* sect. 2 concl. 1 v. *Quaeres.* with Sylvius, and the common opinion); provided foul delectation were absent or danger of it, and it happened in passing, and not repeated time and again, as Tourney adverts, (*l.c.*) because otherwise the danger would already be present. Hence, one is not excused from mortal sin who, with the arousal of his spirits, and without a just cause, touched his own shameful parts. Hence, Tourney rightly says (*ibid.*) looking at one's own genitalia is a mortal sin if it is done zealously and morosely, without necessity (as it must be understood); it is otherwise if briefly, as Sylvius and Sanchez say. But would a spouse, touching themselves with great delight, sin? See what will be said on Matrimony, book 6 n. 936. Moreover, to gaze morosely at the mating of animals is dangerous, as the Salamancans note (n. 13 and Croix n. 903). But those causing horses, bulls and similar animals to mate so as to beget their young are excused; provided a lustful spirit were absent, as Cont. Tourn. says *v. Quod si*, as well as Tamburinus, l. 7 c. 8 § 2 n. 5, Elbel, n. 211, and Holzmann, n. 711).

"Nay more, if such a touch or gaze of one's own body were to happen with some natural end, and not a wicked one, it will not even be venial, *e.g.* if one extinguishes itching by friction of the skin it is not sexual; still provided that the danger of pollution or consent to it were absent, if perhaps it would come about unforeseen apart from any intention. Lessius, n. 63, Filliuci, n. 214, Sanchez, l. 9 d. 31.

420.—"Naked touches and gazing at the private parts of another's body, especially of the opposite sex, or from curiosity of human sex (for it is another thing from necessity even excluding sexual passion) seem not to be able to be excused from mortal sin on account of the grave indecency, and proximate danger of the sexual act: nevertheless, unless the sight took place from a place so remote as to be in passing, that these were absent. Sanchez, n. 25 and 29, Filliuci n. 281, Laymann, etc." (With Tamburinius and the Salamancans, *loc. cit.* punct. 1 n. 13).

We must note: 1) In regard to unchaste touches, which only necessity excuses; doctors touching or looking at the genitals of a person, even of the opposite sex, from necessity, do not sin, be it that they suffer involuntary pollution *per accidens*. Tamburinius, 6. dec. de impudic. c. 3 n. 49, from the common teaching, and the Salamancans, *ibid.* n. 12, and punct. 3 § 5., n. 68, from St. Thomas, II IIæ qu. 154, a. 4 and Sporer *de matrim.* n. 674. See what is going to be said from n. 481. This is true speculatively, still, would that in practice, doctors did not continually sin in these matters! For a doctor is not excused from mortal sin who without such a necessity touches the genitals of another, even a person of the same sex, unless perhaps it happened as a joke or from petulance, or curiosity (Tamburinus *dec.* c. 8 §2 n. 4; Croix n. 906, with Busembaum here, n. 7). But the Salamancans correctly say (*ibid.* §4 n. 50) that this must not be admitted practically, rather only speculatively, provided that touch happened lightly, and not *ex proposito*, and not for some notable space of time. What if someone were to touch the private parts of another from outside of their clothes? Croix (n. 904) with Sanchez, also does not excuse such a man from mortal sin, unless he were to act from some petulance, or with light delectation but not carnal. And the Salamancans rightly also condemn it as a mortal sin if he would so touch the genitals of a different sex, even if it were done through lattice, because it is very dangerous. Croix (n. 902), however, excuses with probability from mortal sin maidservants touching the genitals of boys while they vest them, unless it were for a space of time or they did this with carnal delectation.

We must note: 2) To touch the genitals of brute animals is not ordinarily anything but venial, as Croix (l. 3 part. 1 n. 903) and Sanchez (*de matr.* l. 9 d. 46 n. 15, etc.) say. It must more probably be said otherwise, if such a touch happened even to pollution, as the authorities say (Croix, *l.c.*, Holzmann, n. 711; Elbel, *de 6 praec.* n. 211, Cont. Tourn. *l.c. v. Nostro* at the end, and Sporer *de matr.* c. 3 n. 697, with Bonacina, Salas, and Tamburinus, against Diana and Sanchez, who thought this is not mortal). The reason is, because although this might only happen for the sake of levity, still, it is an action forcefully exciting venereal delight.

We must note: 3) With Busembaum (here in n. 7) and the Salamancans, *ibid.* punct. 1 n. 13, in regard to looking, it is not mortal of itself, short of the danger of sexual consent, to look at the genitals of the person of the same sex, unless the one looking would be very inclined to sodomy, as the Salamancans note (*loc. cit.* with Sanchez, and Filliuci) or unless, I would add, an adolescent male would appear beautiful naked.

421.—*Quaeritur I:* Would it be a mortal sin of itself to look at the private parts of a person of the opposite sex, or watch human sex with voluntary delectation at the sight? Cajetan and Navarre (cited by Sanchez, *de matrim.* l. 9 d. 45 n. 21) deny it, because, as they say, the delectation from sight is not such a thing as touch, that it would lead one to venereal delight; for someone can stop and only have natural delectation. But with Sanchez, n. 22 and other authors it must be said altogether that it is a mortal sin unless the vision happened in a far off place and for a very short time (St. Antoninus, Gerson, Lessius, Filliuci, etc. and the Salamancans, *de 6 praec.* c. 3 punct. 1 n. 7, 9. and 12, as well as n. 13, and Roncaglia, c. 1 q. 1). The reason is, because such a foul sight, far from doubt, excites to lust. Still, the Salamancans (*l.c.* n. 12 near the end) excuse from mortal sin if there is no danger of arousal by reason of prepubescent age, or even of old age, or of a frigid temperament. For this purpose, I think it must not be admitted, at least when from the foul sight the danger of lust arises. Likewise, the Salamancans say (*ibid.* n. 13) a man looking at the genitalia of young boys does not sin mortally unless he were forcefully prone to sodomy. But I would excuse with difficulty someone deliberately looking at a beautiful adolescent youth while naked.

Moreover, the Salamancans note (*ibid.*) with Sanchez, and Filliuci, that sinful stares, just as touches, cover the same species of the object; and therefore they say it must be explained in confession the quality of the person who was foully looked at. But Croix more truly contradicts this doctrine (l. 6 p. 2 n. 1030), where he says that one who without any longing looks venereally at a person, he is not held to say what sort of person it was, for how would a woman, by shamefully looking at a naked priest, commit a sacrilege, which consists in the violation of a sacred person, when there no violation existed? And how would someone, looking foully on a relative, commit incest?

422. *Quaeritur II*: Whether it is some sin to look at the non-private parts of a beautiful person of the opposite sex? St. Antoninus, Lessius, Toledo, Cajetan, Filliuci, Dicastillus, etc., with

the Salamancans (*ibid.* n. 2) say this is licit *per se*, precisely as it is licit to look on any beautiful things, created by God to be seen; consequently they hold there is no sin *per se*, curiosity removed, to look at a beautiful woman. And the Continuator of Tourely (*de 6 praec.* art. 7 sect. 2) sensed the same thing, by speaking about a secular man. But in practice I think this is rarely excused from venial sin, unless it happened from due manners or another just cause. Nevertheless, they duly say it is otherwise if the gaze were daily, because then he cannot be excused from venial sin nor even from mortal sin, if there were the proximate danger of shameful concupiscence or morose delectation, which will be present without a doubt, when there is a *commotio spirituum* in looking (the Salamancans, *ibid.* n. 3; with Lessius, Cajetan, St. Antoninus, Filliuci, etc. and Holzmann, n. 712 and Elbel, n. 188). Nay more, Roncaglia quite rightly says (*de 6 praec.* c. 1 reg. in praxi 1) staring at a beautiful woman for a long time, especially if it is influenced by a disordered love for her, is not without danger of grave sin. And he says the same thing about lengthy vain conversation with a girl one inordinately desires, to which opinion the Salamancans very much adhere (*ibid.* n. 22 and tr. 26 c. 7 punct. 2 n. 34, following St. Thomas) at least on account of the proximate danger of falling.

423.—To look at the less private parts of a woman (although by no means foul), namely the breast, arms, legs, without the danger of falling, and provided the look were not for a long time, as above, of itself is not a mortal sin (Navarre *in Sum.* c. 23 n. 19; Sanchez *de matr.* l. 9 d. 46 n. 25; Cajetan, v. *Ornatus*, and the Salamancans (*ibid.* c. 3 punct. 1 n. 13) with Armilla., and others). It was said *of itself*, for, as Holzmann rightly notes in the aforesaid (n. 712) that there is easily a mortal sin in a look, especially inclined to sexual enjoyment.

424.—To look at obscene pictures only from curiosity is not mortal, as Tamburinius says (*Dec.* c. 8 § 5 n. 1) if there is no foul delectation and danger of it. But in practice, a man looking morosely at unchaste paintings of women I think could only be excused from mortal sin with difficulty, because it will be hard to free himself from foul delectation or from probable danger of it as Elbel says, *n.* 195; unless he were to look for a short time and at a great distance, as Roncaglia notes (c. 1 q. 1).

425.—*Quaeritur III:* Is it lawful for a woman to adorn herself? It is answered in the affirmative if she adorns herself for the decency of her state or according to the custom of her country (Salamancans *de VI praec.* c. 3 punct. 1 n. 16). And the same thing if she should act so as to please her husband or that she might find a bridegroom, as St. Thomas teaches (II IIæ q. 169, art. 2). Moreover, a woman that dresses herself without a right end will certainly sin and indeed gravely if she were to do it to provoke men to lust after her, but venially if she only did it from levity or vanity (Cajetan, Lessius, Sylvius, etc., with the Salamancans, *l.c.* n. 15, from St. Thomas *eod. loc.*). And the same must be said about a woman disguising herself with cosmetics (Salamancans *ibid.* n. 16, with St. Thomas, *l.c.* art. 2 ad. 1 and 3, who equally excuses women that put makeup on their face to cover ugliness). See other things that were said on scandal in book 3, n. 55 where we said that a woman, according to the custom of a place that puts on makeup, or uncovering part of her breasts does not sin mortally, speaking *per se*, if perhaps thence others would be scandalized in general. There is a doubt if she knew someone would suffer scandal in particular. See what was said in the same book 3, n. 54. Moreover, a women using men's clothes does not commit a mortal sin of itself; but it will not rarely be mortal. See *ibid.* n. 52, vers. 2 *If women.*

TREATISE IV: THE FIFTH AND SIXTH PRECEPTS, CH. II 487

"7. The sight, and thereupon (though more rarely due to an "adjoined danger) touch from petulance, or curiosity of the "private parts of another's body, even of the same sex, short of "affectation and danger of sexual consent, can be excused from "mortal sin, say: when some people swim together or bath at "the same time, as the authors teach (Laymann, l. 3 sect. 4, from "Sanchez, l. 5 *mor.* c. 6 n. 12, 13 and n. 27, 28; Trullenchus, d. 12 "n. 15." (See the aforesaid in num. 420).

"8. Foul words, reading of obscene things, watching foul "plays, perverted songs, deeds, letters and amorous gifts, if they "are only done from curiosity, or vain consolation are not "mortal sins; nevertheless, it is otherwise if they are done with "a perverted mind, or a sexual end or with the danger of "spiritual ruin, or of other things. (Sanchez, d. 46, q. 3; Filliuci, t. "30 c. 10 q. 3."

426.—*Quaeritur I:* Is it a mortal sin to mention foul words? No matter the diversity of the doctors on this point, it must be said:

I. Of itself it is not evil to mention foul words or to hear them (for the same is said about the one mentioning what he heard); but this depends upon the good or evil end whereby the words are mentioned. So Sanchez, *de matr.* l. 9 d. 46, n. 34.

II. That to speak foul words on account of vain consolation or as a joke is not a mortal sin of itself (Busembaum in this place; St. Antoninus p. 2 tit. 5 c. 1 § 8; and Sanchez, n. 35 with Navarre, etc.). Tamburinius says (c. 8 § 4 n. 2), unless those listening are so weak in spirit that they would suffer scandal, as Sanchez says (n. 36) with Navarre, etc., or unless the words were very lustful, as the Salamancans add in tr. 26, c. 3 punct. 1 n. 19. Hence, they note (num. 20) with Dicastillus, foul jokes which are bandied about by harvesters, those gathering grapes, and muleteers, are not mortal because they are spoken and listened to in a sporting manner. St. Antoninus says the same thing: "Where such foul words are said from a certain levity on account of solace, although they are not mortal of themselves, nevertheless, it can be a mortal sin by reason of scandal, say when those listening are weak in spirit for whom the words would become very lustful. The same must be said about those making or singing ditties full of lustful things." Busembaum, Sanchez (n. 44), Tamburinius (§ 5, n. 1) and Sporer (*de matr.* n. 695) also say that it is of itself only venial to read foul books from curiosity without foul delectation, or the proximate danger of it (but confessors are hard pressed to carefully forbid this, as often as they may, to youth who, from readings of this sort always draw great ruin upon their soul). The same must also be said about those hearing the aforesaid words on account of a vain solace, as Sanchez says (n. 38) with Cajetan. Moreover, St. Antoninus (*l.c.*) rightly adverts that the one hearing foul words with *deliberate delectation* in their foulness, "do not seem able to be excused from mortal sin," just as one who takes morose delectation in a foul thought, *unless perchance* this was between spouses.

III. It must be said with Sanchez in the same place (n. 39) it is without doubt a mortal sin to speak foul words on account of delectation taken from the thought of these foul things, or with danger of such a delectation, as Tamburinius rightly adds (*l.c.* or with danger of grave scandal which is frequently present, when such words are advanced in the presence of youth or girls, as Elbel rightly adverts (n. 194). Hence, the Salamancans hold (*l.c.* n. 19) one is not excused from grave sin who names shameful things, or the manner of having sex, especially in the presence of adolescents and young women of upright life. Moreover, to name shameful things of the same sex in the presence of others of the same sex, I think, speaking commonly, is not grave.

Furthermore, they mortally sin who, on account of boasting, relate their foul sins: and then they will not only sin on account of the scandal to their listeners, but very easily they cause the sin of complacency for their own sins, as the Salamancans rightly say, with Dicastillus (*ibid.* n. 21). And therefore, they should explain in confession the species of the sin about which they boasted they had committed. Moreover, to speak honestly with someone else's children is not a sin, of itself it is not even venial but by reason of the danger, especially in daily conversation, it can be grave, as we said in n. 422 at the end, with the Salamancans, *loc. cit.* n. 22, Roncaglia c. 1 reg. 2 *in praxi.*

427.—*Quaeritur II:* Is it a mortal sin to attend foul plays? We answer: That if the play were not notably foul, one would not commit a mortal sin in hearing it unless he had proven very weak. So thinks Sanchez, *de matr.* l. 9 d. 46 n. 42. But if notably foul things are represented in the play, or in a foul manner, it is indeed a mortal sin to watch it on account of the delectation arising from those very foul things; but it is venial if only on account of curiosity or vain solace, excluding the danger of consent in foul delectation. (Sanchez, d. n. 41, and Tamburinius § 5 n. 1 with Diana, Rodriquez, Lorca, etc., whatever the case about cooperation (on which we will soon argue) in which someone furnishes agreement to such a representation with his money.

Moreover, would everyone sin that notably attends foul plays of this sort and support it with money or applause if the play would have been put on without them? Turrianus, Bald., and Baldel. cited by Croix , l. 2 n. 239 deny this. And I once adhered to this opinion, but now I regard it must be affirmed better with the same Croix and Holzmann (*de charit.* c. 4 n. 242). The reason is that they, even if materially, still positively cooperate with a gravely sinful action; such cooperation is not licit even if it were done for a grave cause of necessity, or utility. And Holzmann rightly says the same thing about those who are held to stop these by their office, or can otherwise suitably impede them. I do not condemn simple spectators, provided that the danger of foul delight is avoided as above, without which the play would take place anyway; for these cannot be the cause of this foul production because they did not positively influence it; nor the occasion, because (as is supposed) even without them the play would take place. The exception would be clergy or religious who cannot be present there without grave scandal to the laity. So, St. Benedict XIV rightly teaches *de Synodo* l. 11, c. 10. Except likewise laity without whom the play could not take place. But in no manner would I excuse a youth from mortal sin who, without necessity, wills for the sake of curiosity to be present at plays of this sort, unless someone were extremely fearful and moreover, experienced it many times, and he never mortally sinned by watching it; provided he does not furnish to other adolescents the occasion of assisting at plays of this sort.

428.—Moreover, it is certain those putting on or composing these plays, when they are notably foul, can in no way be excused from grave sin on account of the scandal to others, even if it was unintended (Sanchez *l.c.* n. 42, with St. Antoninus, Angel, etc.). Nor can any great profit excuse them, as Tamburinius rightly notes (*ibid.*) Further, note here that which the Angelic Doctor teaches (II IIæ q. 168 art. 3 ad 3), namely: "To all those matters which are useful for human conduct, some licit duties may be classified. Therefore, even the duty of actors, which is ordered to show consolation to men, is not illicit *secundum se*: nor are they in a state of sin, provided they moderately use entertainment, *i.e.* by not using some illicit words or deeds [*i.e.* foul things or those which incline to the harm of one's neighbor, as he explains in the body of the article] for entertainment and not by employing during business and undue times ... Wherefore they that moderately assist them do not sin ...; if some, however ... give sustenance to those actors who use illicit humor, they sin just as someone maintaining another in sin." St. Antoninus teaches the same thing in p 2 tit. 23 § 14, where in explaining the words of St. Thomas, "illicit words or deeds," says: "If foul plays are put on with disgusting words or acts, then it is illicit and a mortal sin." See other things said on scandal in book 3, n. 56.

429.—"9. Dances, unless they are done with a bad end, or "with danger of inciting others or oneself to lust, or with other "bad circumstances, are not evil according to what they are, nor "acts of lust, but of joy. But when the holy fathers exceedingly "rebuke them, they speak about foul dances and the abuse of "dancing. See Cajetan, *v. Chorea*, Filliuci n. 223."

Dances, as St. Antoninus teaches in p. 2 tit. 6 c. 6 are licit *per se*, provided they are done by secular persons with upright persons and in an upright manner, namely not with immoral gestures. The Salamancans say the same thing (*de 6 praecep.* c. 3 punct. 1 n. 17 and 18), with Azor, Cajetan, Filliuci, Bonacina, etc. Moreover, to lightly touch the hand of a woman in dances, will either be without fault or the lightest venial sin, as Cajetan notes (*ibid.* Sum. *v. Chorea*), and Sporer consents to this with probability (*de matr.* c. 3 n. 694). Still it was forbidden for clergy to assist in illicit dances by the Council of Trent in its 24th session *de Reformatione*, c. 12, or at least to lead them. See the Salamancans, *ibid.*

"10. Showing foul plays, likewise making books or pictures "inciting men to lust, sin mortally because they cause the ruin "of one's neighbor, since it is morally certain to incite many to "sin. (Filliuci n. 211). Similarly, Hurtius teaches that magistrates "who permit foul plays to be shown sin mortally, and Baldellus "concedes if the authorities that are over them approve and "foster them (tom. 1, lib. 3 disp. 18 n. 12 et 13). Nevertheless, he "adds that they can sometimes be excused if they did not "punish an evil to avoid a greater evil and merely tolerate it. See "Diana, p. 5 t. 15 r. 82.

"11. A single person, permitting themselves to be touched "by another with a touch that is commonly regarded as chaste, "such as holding a hand, contracting a hand, a hug and a kiss "according to the custom of the country do not sin, unless it "were certain it came about from a depraved affection; for it is not lawful to cooperate with the latter. Still, Filliuci teaches that it can even be admitted lest the one causing the touch were defamed." (Or lest he would gain suspicion of infamy or others be scandalized. So think the Continuator of Tournely, *de 6 praec.* art. 7 sect. 1 concl. 1 R ad 2, with Sylvius and Salamancans *loc. cit.* punct. 3 § 5 n. 62 with Sa, Azor, Cajetan, Bonacina. Still, the other is held to resist if the touch came about secretly and it were certain to become malicious. Salamancans *ibid.* Tamburinius § 4 n. 25, Croix lib. 2 n. 249).

"Moreover, the one admitting unchaste touches (such as of the breasts or of private parts) or furtive kisses whether morose or indecent would sin because evil passion is presumed. See Filliuci, tr. 30 n. 169, and above in book 2, c. 2 dub. 2."

430.—Furthermore, is a woman, when force has been applied, also held to cry out if she must to avoid the unchaste touches of a man?

The Salamancans (*ibid.* n. 63) affirm it with Cajetan from the common opinion; and they prove it from Deuteronomy 22:24 where a girl was condemned to death because she did not shout when she was in the city. But Navarre (*Summ.* cap. 16 n. 1), del Soto (*de justitia et jure*, l. 5 q. 1 art. 5) and Bonacina (*de VI praec.* q. un. n. 10) with Reginald, very probably argue she is not held to shout when in danger of notable harm, or infamy, or excessive shame; because then, if she can resist otherwise, as much as she can she is not held to repel the force with such an inconvenience except if a proximate danger of consent were present. The text of Deuteronomy related above causes no difficulty, for that precept was a judicial precept pertaining to an external judgment in which a girl was condemned that had been violated and had not cried out "when she was in the city," because she is presumed (according to the commentary of Cornelius à Lapide) to have consented to fornication and therefore did not shout out. And Menochius and Gordon think the same, with Philo (cited by Calmet), on the cited text. Besides, nobody doubts that all the judicial precepts of the old law altogether ceased by the more perfect judicial precepts of the law of the Gospel, as the learned Frassen proves (t. 6 *de legibus* d. 3 art. 2 q. 4 concl. 1 in fine). Still, it must not be denied that if a woman were in proximate danger of consenting to sex because of what passed previously, or on account of a known frailty, she is indeed held to cry out to free herself from that intercourse. Then, is a woman oppressed held to suffer death by repelling the invader of her chastity by force rather than permit sex? There is a twofold opinion, as we said in n. 386. But the negative, which del Soto, Navarre, Toledo and others hold is rather more speculative than it is probable in practice.

431.—"One might ask, are touches and gazes lawful between "spouses or the betrothed, and to what extent?"

"*Resp.* 1. It is lawful for spouses if they are ordered to "copulation, for then they licitly arouse themselves for this "purpose. If they are done for another end, *e.g.* for the sake of "pleasure, they are venial sins because matrimony makes these "touches respectable and a defect of a due end is not mortal "unless they take place with danger of pollution, which, with "touches of this sort it is illicit, and in that case they will be "mortal sins, at least regularly. Sanchez, l. 9 d. 46 n. 7, Filliuci, n. "357 and others (See book 6 n. 932 – 936)."

"*Resp.* 2. Unchaste touches are not licit to betrothed couples; "but chaste touches are lawful in non-private parts if they only "intend sensitive delight from them; otherwise if it is sexual "delight; Sanchez, *l.c.* n. 50, etc. Bonacina, p. 9 num. 6, etc." (But see what is going to be said in book 6, n. 854).

DUBIUM II
What are the species of natural lust?

432. Is fornication forbidden by natural law?
433. Does a woman sin not by not resisting sex on account of fear of death if she does not consent?
434. Could prostitutes be permitted?
435. In regard to concubinage it is asked: I. Whether a man can be absolved who cannot cast out a concubine without infamy?
436. II. Can a man be absolved that promises he will throw out his concubine?
437. III. Could a concubine be absolved that does not leave on account of necessity?
438. IV. Whether one who is in the proximate occasion, for the sake of exercising his craft can be absolved? What if he, after having applied remedies, always falls back in the same manner?
439. V. Whether a servant sinning with her master can be absolved?
440. VI. Whether a wife sinning with a husband can be absolved?
441. VII. Must the occasion also be removed with grave loss?
442. What are the penalties for concubinage, especially for clergy?
443. Whether "stuprum" (illicit sexual intercourse with a virgin) is a special sin?
444. To what is an abductor held?
445. What about adultery?
446. Whether heterosexual sodomy between spouses is adultery?
447. Is sex between the betrothed adultery?
448. In regard to incest it is asked: I. Whether all incest is of the same species?
449. II. Whether incest differs with in-laws?
450. III. Is it incest with spiritual kin?
451. IV. Whether it were a special sin for a confessor to have sex with a penitent? What about of a pastor with his subject?
452. V. Do near of kin commit incest having sex after a dispensation [but before the marriage]?
453. Would touches alone constitute incest?
454. How is sacrilege committed by masturbation?

455. *In regard to personal sacrilege, it is asked: I. Does a priest who is also a religious commit two sacrileges at the same time if he sins against chastity?*
456. *II. Is it a sacrilege to have sex with another consecrated person?*
457. *III. Does one commit a sacrilege having a vow of chastity if he induces another to masturbation? What if he takes morose delectation from the sin of the other?*
458. *In regard to "local" sacrilege, it is asked: I. Is secret or marital sex in a Church a sacrilege?*
459. *II. Are unchaste touches that take place in Church a sacrilege?*
460. *What is included by the term sacred places?*
461. *III. Are lustful words and gazes that take place in Church sacrileges?*
462. *IV. Are sexual thoughts in Church a sacrilege?*
463. *In regard to "real" sacrilege, when is it committed?*

432.—"*Resp.* The natural species of perfect lust are said to be "those in which sexual intercourse takes place in that mode, in "which nature instituted, *e.g.* when the opposite sex, the same "species, the vas, and natural mode, etc. are preserved.

Wherefore, it is resolved that such things as what follow which therefore must be expressed in confession:

"1. Fornication is a sexual union of a freeman with a free "woman (this is, one that is free from a vow, marriage, or "religion) by mutual consent. To this it is reduced: *a)* "Concubinage which is continued fornication. Wherefore, a "keeper of a concubine (just as even a harlot) should not "ordinarily be absolved unless he has first dismissed his "concubine or a woman suspected of it whose retention would "give scandal, even if he did not sin with her (Sanchez, lib. 1 "*mor.* cap. 8, Navarre, cap. 3, Filliuci tr. 30 c. 2 n. 56); *b)* Sex "with a woman betrothed to another, which is fornication "within a graver species, and must be made clear in confession; "at least in regard to the betrothed woman, as the authorities "teach (Rodriquez tr. 3 c. 109; Sanchez, *de matr.* t. 1. l. 1, dub. 2, "num. 6; Fagundez, t. 1 l. 4 c. 3; Filliuci, l. 2 tr. 30, c. 2 num. 52; "against Covarruvias, Vivaldi, Ledesma, Azor, whose opinion "even in respect to the spouse is probable and Diana regards it "as safe in practice p. 1 tr. 7 resp. 5)."

Here we must attend to proposition 25 condemned by Alexander VII, which said: "One that has sex with a single woman satisfies the precept of confession by saying 'I committed a grave sin against chastity with a single woman', while not explaining that he had sex with her."

Next, it must be noted that there is hardly any doubt that fornication is forbidden by natural law, since nature orders sex only to matrimony, wherein they not only can beget children, but also educate them well. —Consequently, fornication is always intrinsically evil, although some times *per* accidens the children of fornication may be well educated. The reason is not only because, in this matter due to the great danger of erroneous judgment, he could easily vacillate for the sake of excessive delectation, but also because nature considers such things which do not commonly come about *per accidens* and because it is, of itself, against the law of nature to be subject to the flesh, as happens in fornication on account of the delectation of the act. Moreover, in matrimony, be it that the same delectation occurs, still God disposes all things by his special providence that such a disorder is absent. See Roncaglia, *de VI praec.* c. 1 q. 2.

433.—*Quaeritur I:* Would a woman sin gravely by not resisting sex with another on account of fear of death if she does not consent? Some altogether affirm it, because such immobility would be a certain voluntary cooperation, since she could impede the sex by agitating herself in some manner. So think de Lugo, *de justitia et jure*, disp. 10 n. 197, Roncaglia, *ibid.* q. 3 with Filliuci,

Azor, whom I think must be followed at least in practice. Others deny it. See what was said in n. 368.

434.—*Quaeritur II:* Could prostitutes be permitted?

The first opinion affirms it as probable and the Salamancans hold it (*de 6 praecept.* c. 2 punct. 4 n. 84) with St. Thomas, Covarruvias, Trullenchus, Ledesma, etc., and St. Augustine clearly adheres to it (*de ord.* c. 4). The reason is, because after harlots have been removed worse evils may come about, namely sodomy, bestiality, masturbation, apart from the violation of upright women; therefore, St. Augustine (*loc. cit.*) says: "Remove harlots from human affairs, and you will agitate all manner of lust."

But the *second opinion* is more probable in practice which denies it; and Roncaglia holds this (*de 6 praec.* c. 2 q. 6), Navarre (*man.* c. 17, n. 195) with Cornel., Gutt., and others (cited by Salamancans *ibid.* n. 83). The reason is, because through prostitutes these graver evils do not come about to the extent that in lustful men lust plants deeper roots through easy and frequent sex with prostitutes; and so, when the frequency of this vice increases all the more, they do not cease committing pollution and heinous sins, at least with the harlots themselves, and therefore they do not abstain from soliciting upright women. On the other hand, when prostitution is permitted other innumerable evils are added, namely more girls enter prostitution, more youths pay little attention to their parents, they scatter goods, neglect their studies, arouse quarrels and spurn upright marriage. Moreover, Fr. Sarnelli both adverts and proves in his opisculum: *de abusu meretricii*, that although in large cities harlots can be permitted, still, in no way may they be permitted in other places.

435.—Concubinage, moreover, is properly the sexual intercourse of a single man with a single woman (and improperly with a married woman or man); provided they come together in the manner of husband and wife, or live as one in a house, or in another place, as is certain from the style of the Roman Curia, and from the Council of Trent (sess. 24 c. 8 *de Ref. matrimonio*). Note here, before all things, proposition 41 proscribed by Alexander VII, which says: "A man keeping a concubine is under no obligation to cast her out if she is useful to the pleasure of the former, in the vernacular called *regalo*; provided that, if she were gone, the keeper of the concubine would grow sick of life and banquets or social functions would bore him, and another female servant would be found with very great difficulty." Likewise, note three other propositions that were condemned by Pope Innocent XI, namely: "61. A man can sometimes be absolved who lives in the proximate occasion of sin which he can omit but does not wish to, and in fact intentionally seeks it out and lives in it. 62. The near occasion of sin does not need to be avoided when there is some useful or upright cause to not flee. 63. It is licit to directly seek an occasion of sin for a spiritual good whether our own temporal good or that of our neighbor."

Quaeritur I: Could a man keeping a concubine sometimes be absolved if he could not cast her out of the home without scandal or infamy? Speaking about common cases, he must not be absolved as the Salamancans say (tr. 26 c. 2 punct. 2 § 1 n. 27), with Busembaum. The reason is, because in daily concubinage it is morally impossible for the business not to be made known to others. Still, the Salamancans do not deny that in some very rare case he could be absolved, namely if he could not otherwise avoid grave loss of reputation or fortunes, according to what will be said in *de poenit.* n. 455. But in that case I say that it is altogether expedient that absolution should at least be delayed until the continence of the penitent is proven from experience. Unless it were the case that the penitent (supposing he were otherwise sufficiently disposed) could no longer return to confess sins; or if the necessity to communicate threatened, to avoid positive infamy.

436.—*Quaeritur II:* Outside of the aforesaid very rare case of infamy or scandal, could a man with a concubine be absolved before he dismisses her if he promises in earnest that he is going to dismiss her? Some concede for the first or second time, as Diana, Sancius, Megala and Fr. Antonio of the Holy Spirit (cited by the Salamancans, *ibid.* n. 28). Others altogether deny it even for the first time, when the occasion is proximate. So Navarre, Palaus, Azor, Toledo, Filliuci, etc., with Diana revoking himself (cited by the Salamancans, *ibid.* n. 31). Then others still, such as the Salamancans (*loc. cit.* n. 32) with Trullenchus, Sylvius, Rodriquez, Lopez, so distinguish: If the man is publicly known to have a concubine, he can hardly be absolved even if he were to give signs of great sorrow unless, he should dismiss the concubine or, unless after (when the concubine abides outside the house) he does not go to her for a notable period of time. The reason is not only because it would create a great scandal to see a man that still retains a concubine in his house or frequents her home to go to the Eucharist; but even more, because a public sinner should not be absolved unless he also does public penance and makes satisfaction for scandal. See what is going to be said in book 6, num. 512. But if the concubine is secret, he cannot also be absolved except in some rare case, say if a nobleman were to grieve with many tears either after hearing a fearful sermon or if he should be terrified and confess after the death of a friend, or if he escaped a great danger of death (Cardinal de Lugo, *de poen.* d. 10 sect. 10 n. 151, and the Salamancans *ibid.* n. 34, with Palaus, Laymann, Dicastillus, Trullenchus, etc.). Nevertheless, I think this can only be admitted when it is morally impossible that he could dismiss the concubine in so short a time before absolution, or when the necessity to communicate would urge due to avoiding great infamy, according to what was said in n. 435. For otherwise, absolution must always be delayed because, from experience it is most certain that after absolution has been obtained, the occasion is removed with difficulty and so the man will easily return to his vomit. See what is going to be said in book 6, n. 456.

437.—*Quaeritur III:* Whether a concubine who is given sustenance by the man keeping her, could be absolved before she departs from his house? The Salamancans rightly deny it (tr. 26, c. 2 punct. 2 § 2 n. 43). Still in n. 44 they make the exception: 1) if grave harm would come about due to her departure, or scandal to others; 2) if the woman cannot feed herself by the labor of her hands, or take up service in another house, or beg without dishonor, or from another grave disobliging condition. To beg for one's bread, however, when they are not suited to it, always seems to advance a grave disobliging condition, as Hurtius says (cited by the Salamancans, *loc. cit.*). But in these cases absolution must always be deferred as a rule.

438.—*Quaeritur IV:* Could someone be absolved who is in the proximate occasion of sin for the sake of carrying out a licit trade? The authors respond with probability that he can indeed be absolved if he would be morally powerless to desert his duty and would sin, not from the force of the occasion but from his own weakness and thence show signs of true penance with the intention of being wary of the occasion as much as he can (Suarez, t. 4 in 3 p. d. 32 sect. 2; Cajetan *v. Periculum*, and the Salamancans *ibid.* n. 46, with Cand.). Furthermore, commonly they can be excused from deserting the occasion when, by reason of their duty, they sin by being with women, as the authors say (Navarre, c. 3 n. 5 as well as Graff., Jann., Hurtius, Lopez, etc., with the Salamancans *loc. cit.* num. 47 and Militant., *in prop. 61 Innoc. XI*). The same is said about surgeons who, giving remedies to women are in the occasion of sin (Salamancans *ibid.*, with Sanchez, Navarre, Hurtius). The same about a pastor who, after hearing the confessions of women, commits voluntary pollution; they can be absolved for not deserting their duty; still it must be said otherwise about a simple confessor who is held to avoid hearing confessions unless he might be subjected to infamy from this (Salamancans *ibid.* n. 48, with Palaus, Navarre, Hurtius, etc.). A woman can also be absolved who lives as a host to lodgers and sins in the occasion of giving lodging, and therefore falls with different men, and even falls with someone in particular, provided she proposes thence to avoid interaction with anyone alone (Salamancans *ibid.* n. 49, with Navarre, and Trullenchus). Nevertheless, if after these remedies have been applied the one sinning still falls back into the same mode, and there appears no probable hope of amendment, then they must not be absolved in any way unless they forsake the occasion or show particular signs of sorrow, according to what is going to be said in *de poenit.* book 6, n. 457.

439.—*Quaeritur V:* Could female servants sinning with their masters be absolved if they had also sinned with them before? If they have sinned only once or twice and after the admonition of their confessor see to it to remove the occasion, then the Salamancans rightly say they can be absolved (tr. 26, c. 2 punct. 2 § 2 n. 50). It is otherwise if they do nothing to remove the occasion. For this reason, I would never absolve them if the sin were frequent, unless it were in a case of grave necessity, with the intention mentioned above in *quaeritur III*, and these women were sufficiently disposed, according to what will be said in book 6, n. 459. And even in that case I would look to experience.

440.—*Quaeritur VI:* Could a wife be absolved if she is in the proximate occasion of sin with her husband because she knows it is against nature to be subjected to an improper sexual act? We answer in the negative with the Salamancans (*ibid.* n. 52), with Sanchez. For then she is held to separate; but this must be understood, unless she was morally powerless to do this, as was said in *quaeritur IV* above.

441.—*Quaeritur VII:* Is someone held to remove the proximate occasion of sin with a concubine, even with grave temporal loss to himself, say if the lover were a debtor to the concubine in a financial matter of the greatest import? Tancred, Sanctius, and Antonius of the Holy Spirit (cited by the Salamancans *ibid.* n. 57) deny it. But the contrary must altogether be held with the Salamancans (*loc cit.* n. 58) because the spiritual harm must be guarded against more than the temporal. But this reasoning, if it would avail here, ought to avail even for the cases related above in questions III and IV, where the same Salamancans sometimes excuse with probability those who did not forsake the occasion to avoid grave harm. For this reason, I think the first opinion is probable if the lover could not pay without grave detriment to his reputation or state, so that he would be reduced to grave necessity (see what is going to be said in book 6, n. 455). But in all these cases it is altogether expedient that absolution be delayed even to amendment; see the same book, n. 456.

Here, we must add more things that are useful to know for this matter.

442.—I. The Council of Trent, sess. 14 c. 8, laid down the penalty of excommunication for concubinage imposed after the third warning, and moreover, the penalty of exile outside the town or diocese, to be asked of the secular arm; II. In this crime, since it is of a mixed forum, proceedings can be brought by a secular and ecclesiastical judge; III. A cleric guilty of concubinage (from the Council of Trent, sess. 25 c. 14) after the first warning is deprived of a third of the fruits of his benefice; after the second is deprived of his pensions and the administration of his benefice, and after the third, is altogether despoiled of the benefice. Then he is excommunicated and then can also be handed over to a secular court by the Bishop. See the Salamancans, c. 2 n. 60. Furthermore, the cleric (as has been said) is probably not deprived of a third of the fruits if he has only sinned once after

TREATISE IV: THE FIFTH AND SIXTH PRECEPTS, CH. II

the warning (Salamancans *ibid.* punct. 3 n. 64). It must be noted: 1) By the term "fruits" the daily distributions are not embraced, as the Sacred Congregation decided (cited by the Salamancans, *ibid.* n. 66); 2) monetary penalties for this crime must be applied to pious causes by the Bishop (Salamancans *eodem loc.* n. 67); 3) That the cleric is not deprived of the fruits of the benefice until after the sentence (Salamancans *ibid.* num. 68).

Would clergy guilty of public concubinage also be suspended by the law itself? Barbosa, St. Antoninus, Navarre, Sylvius, etc. (cited by the Salamancans, *loc. cit.* n. 70) answer in the affirmative, saying they incur such a suspension both from their office and from their benefice from *c. Sacerdotes,* dist. 50 and it was so declared by the Sacred Congregation of the Council. But, del Soto (in 4. disp. 5, q. 5 a. 6) Filliuci (tr. 27 cap. 7 n. 124) and Trullenchus, Suarez and Fagundez (cited by the Salamancans, *ibid.* and adhere to this opinion) probably deny it. The reason is that there is no certainty on such a suspension; rather, the opposite is proven from the Council of Trent, *loc. cit.* where it is said that if a cleric guilty of concubinage does not heed the second warning then he is suspended from the administration of his benefice by the Bishop. Therefore, the Council supposes no previous suspension imposed by the law itself. Furthermore, they respond to the declaration of the Sacred Congregation that it is not authentic, and even if it were authentic, it has no other authority than the probable opinion of doctors, according to what was said in book 1, n. 106.

443.—"2. *Stuprum,* this is the deflowering of a virgin, against "her will, since if she consented it would only be simple "fornication and the circumstance would not need to be "clarified in confession as Lessius and Sanchez prove (l. 7 *dis.* "12) against Navarre, Azor and others."

And the Salamancans (*de VI praec.* c. 4 punct. 1 n. 4) agree with Busembaum, as well as Roncaglia (c. 3 q. 2) with Barbosa,

Bonacina, etc. Moreover, Bonacina and the Salamancans (n. 13) with Lessius, Filliuci and Diana, say that fornication with a consenting virgin can be a special sin for another reason, namely the infamy or the sorrow of the parents, or of quarrels, hatred, etc. See what is going to be said on betrothals, book 6 n. 487.

444.—"3. Abduction, namely when some person (whether "male or female, married or unmarried) is abducted for the sake "of lust, carried out by force whether against the abducted or "those under whose power the one abducted is under." (Namely "parents, or tutors or a man; but not if they are brothers and "the woman is of her own right). "If the woman still leaves by "her own will with her lover, unknown to her parents, then it "will not properly be abduction, but flight, which does not add a "distinct malice to the species of fornication. (de Lugo d. 16 n. "137; Filliuci, n. 10. See Bonacina. Diana says the same thing, p. "1, tom. 7, r. 37, from Lessius, lib. 2 cap. 19 d. 1, Sanchez, *de* "*matr*. l. 7 d. 4 num. 5, etc.).."

From the Council of Trent, in its 24th session, ch. 6, an abductor is held to marry the woman or provide her with a dowry unless the woman is a prostitute or of ill repute. Nevertheless, when an abduction is present with violence against the will of a woman [*i.e.* rape], the matrimony is always null, even if betrothal were carried out with the abducted women. Importune pleas also constitute abduction. What about deceit? See the Salamancans, *ibid.* punct. 3 num. 28. See other things in book 6, *on Matrimony*, n. 1107 and 1108.

445.—"4. Adultery, namely when one or the other having "sex were married to someone else, even if the spouses of the "parties were content. For then, albeit an injury is not done to "them, still it is inflicted on their state, the sacrament and this "precept. But if the adulterous woman were married, it is held "as more grave than if she were a man, on account of the "graver disadvantages, namely the loss of inheritance, "uncertainty of the children, etc. But if both are married, it is "still more grave because there are two injuries against both "spouses that must be expressed in confession. Filliuci, t. 26, c. 4 "n. 85 and 89."

Note here proposition 50 condemned by Pope Innocent XI, which said: "Sex with a married woman, with the consent of her husband, is not adultery; thus it suffices to say in confession that it was fornication."

446.—A man who commits sodomy with his wife more probably also commits adultery because it is against a good *datae fidei*, as Sanchez says (*de matrimonio*, lib. 9 d. 18 n. 4) as well as Roncaglia (c. 4 q. 3) with Azor, the Salamancans (*de VI praec.* cap. 5 punct. 2 n. 15) with the common opinion against a few authors. And it ought to be explained [in confession] that he committed sodomy with his own wife, as the Salamancans teach in the same place, n. 17.

447.—Is sex with a betrothed woman adultery due to her future promise? Sanchez (*de matr.* lib. 1 d. 2 n. 2), the Salamancans (d. cap. 5 n. 11) and Roncaglia (*ibid.* q. 5) more probably deny it. Furthermore, Roncaglia and the Salamancans (*de matr.* cap. 1 punct. 1 n. 11) suppose that if one of the engaged were to fornicate with another person, they ought to make known the circumstance of the betrothals in confession as if changing the species, by reason of the injury inflicted on the other. But it is probable enough with Trullenchus, Pontian, Diana, Covarruvias, de Lugo, Sanchez, and Laymann that it is only an aggravating circumstance, since the betrothed acquires no rights over the body of the other through the *sponsalia*. See book 6, *on Matrimony*, n. 847.

448.—"5. Incest is sexual intercourse with kin or in-laws, "even to the fourth degree which is a graver sin the more near "the degree which hence, must be expressed in confession, at "least more securely, as Navare (c. 6), and Cardinal de Lugo "(disp. 16 n. 312) hold, just as incest is much graver with kin "than with in-laws in the same degree, *e.g.* with a mother than "with a mother-in-law; with one's own sister than with the "sister of his wife; and again more grave with an in-law than "with a spiritual or legal relation. It should be added, if it was in "the first degree, whether with a mother, or a daughter or "sister; *cf.* Cardinal de Lugo, *loc. cit.*, and Escobar, *de actibus "humanis*, e. 2 c. 6, where from Hurtad d. 9 *de poenit.* diss. 4 he "says it is probable that incest in the same degree and a line of "the same species (still the graver it is the nearer the degree is "to the post), and it is enough to say I had sex with kin in a "direct line."

"*Fornication with a daughter of confession* [spiritual "daughter] is recalled to this species since properly it is not a "spiritual kinship, nevertheless, such a circumstance must be "expressed in confession as the authors prove (Sanchez, l. 7 *de "matrimonio*, d. 55; Coninck, d. 32, Fagundez, and others "probably against Sa, *v. Confessio*, and Diana. See Cardinal de "Lugo, n. 355."

For greater clarity:

Quaeritur I: Is every act of incest in regard to a species of the same degree? See what is going to be said *On the Sacrament of Penance* in book 6, n. 470, where this is sufficiently affirmed with probability (except only in the first degree of consanguinity in a direct line) with Cajetan, del Soto, de Lugo, Bonacina, etc., with St. Thomas.

449.—*Quaeritur II:* Does incest with kin differ in species from incest with an in-law? Each opinion seems probable.

The *first* denies it, with Croix (l. 6 p. 2 n. 1073), Cajetan, de Lugo, Diana, from St. Thomas, because in each case one equally sins against the reverence due to spouses.

The *second opinion* with Vasquez, Dicastillus and others affirms it. Their reasoning, because it seems totally different from the reverence due on account of the marriage of blood, than on account of the union of affinity. See what is going to be said in book 6, n. 469.

450.—*Quaeritur III:* Is incest among spiritual kin different in species than among kin and in-laws? It absolutely must be affirmed with the Salamancans (tr. 26 c. 5 punct. 5 n. 39), and St. Thomas who teaches in II IIæ that through sex among spiritual kin *sacrilege is committed according to the mode of incest.* Then must the degree of relation be expressed? The Salamancans affirm (*ibid.* n. 40) although Croix more probably denies it (n. 1078). Equally, incest among legal relations, namely by reason of adoption, is of a different species from the others enunciated, and should be explained [in confession]. See the Salamancans, *ibid.* n. 41.

451.—*Quaeritur IV:* Should a confessor that has [carnal] involvement with a spiritual daughter in the occasion of confession, be held to explain this fact when making his confession?

The *first opinion* answers in the affirmative, because a father contracts with a spiritual daughter a certain extraordinary familiarity and the obligation of leading her to salvation, and therefore it seems a particular disgrace to drag her to perdition. The Salamancans, *ibid.* n. 43 with del Soto, Sanchez, Fagundez, etc.

The *second opinion* more probably denies it with Filliuci (tract. 30 n. 105), Sporer (*de matr.* cap. 3 n. 620), Elbel (*de 6 praec.* n. 141), Holzman (*eod. tit.* n. 669); likewise Vasquez, Bonacina, Pontian, Dicastillus Diana, Trullenchus, Leander, etc., cited by the Salamancans (*ibid.* n. 42). The continuator of Tourneley thinks the same thing (*de 6 Dec. praec.* art. 4 v. *Quaer.* 1. ex c. ult. *de Cogn. Spir.* in 6) where he says: "Spiritual kinship by no means arises from the giving of other sacraments [apart from baptism and confirmation]." The reason is, because it is not incest while among them no relation is discovered; nor is it a sacrilege (understand, in regard to this circumstance) while no injury is inflicted on the sacrament. But Elbel rightly adverts (*l.c.* with Henno), that a parish priest sinning with such a penitent, also sins against justice, since he is held from justice to feed his sheep (according to the Council of Trent), not only in word but also example.

452.—*Quaeritur V:* If it happens that those near in kinship, after they have obtained a dispensation to contract matrimony, if they committed fornication before the marriage, would they commit incest? Major and Callego (cited by Croix, lib. 6 part. 2 n. 1077) affirm it with probability, because an impediment of near relation is not thought to be taken away through a dispensation, except only that they can be joined to contract matrimony, but not to fornicate. But Sanchez (*de matr.* l. 7 d. 67 n. 9, with Cajetan, Arm. and Vega) no less probably contradict this, and de Lugo thinks the same (*de just.* d. 3 n. 13). The reason is, the dispensation does not indeed concede fornication, but abolishes the prohibition of matrimony; where, however, matrimony is not forbidden, there is no incest; therefore, when the prohibition ceases, just as accessories, a specific prohibition of fornication.

453.—Note here, that every touch among kin, at least of the first and second degree, is incest according to the received opinion. See the next Dubium, n. 469.

454.—"6. Sacrilege is the violation of a sacred thing through "a sexual act. Sacred things which are violated in this way are "place and person. So, the following constitute a sacrilege: 1)

"Every outward act of lust (such as pollution and probably also unchaste touches, see De Lugo, n. 464) in a sacred place, this is a Church or a cemetery, unless it would take place between spouses of necessity, *e.g.* to avoid incontinence; 2) Every lustful act both inward and outward in a person or with a person consecrated by a vow of chastity, in regard to which it is still probable that one need not express in confession whether it was a solemn or simple vow, just as it is not necessary to express whether one is consecrated by a twofold title, namely if one is both a priest and a religious, because morally the malice is one by number. (Sanchez, *de matrimonio*, l. 7 d. 27 n. 27; Henriquez, and other cited by Diana whom he follows in p. 1 t. 7 r. 3. See Cardinal de Lugo, in the aforesaid, *de poen*. d. 16 s. 4, Bonacina, q. 4 p. 17, Escobar E. 8)."

For a clearer understanding, I will explain questions in regard to sacrilege on this point separately, first in regard to *person*, then *place*, and then *thing*.

455.—I. In regard to *person*, we raise the following questions. *Quaeritur I:* Do priests who are also religious, commit two sacrileges when they sin against chastity?

The *first opinion* affirms it, because such as a religious, ought to preserve chastity by reason of his vow, but as a priest, by reason of the precept of the Church. So think Lessius (l. 4 c. 3 dub. 12 n. 87), Coninck, Ledesma, etc.

But other authors more truly deny this (Sanchez, *de matr.* lib. 7 disp. 27 n. 31 and 38, Palaus, Azor, Trullenchus, etc. with the Salamancans *de VI praec.* c. 6 punct. 2 n. 7). The reason is, because although such a priest remains bound by a vow of chastity via a twofold precept, nevertheless, he would sin against the same precept and from the same motive, while a priest, not yet from a constitution of the Church, as the authors of the first opinion suppose, but only by reason of the vow connected to sacred orders, obliged to chastity according to the more probable opinion. See *de Ordine*, book 6 n. 808. Besides, even if the obligation of chastity in the priest were immediately only from a precept of the Church, he still, by wounding chastity, also would sin against religion according to the common opinion of the doctors cited above, because the Church from the motive of religion alone, on account of the reverence for the sacrament of Order, imposes celibacy on her ministers. For the Church can rightly effect this, that the matter of some one of its precepts were a matter of some virtue, as Croix proves (lib. 3 p. 1 n. 57) with Suarez, and Cardenas. See more about this in book 6, n. 470.

456.—*Quaeritur II:* Would a sacred person, having relations with another consecrated person commit a double sacrilege? Whatever Sa might say, it must altogether be affirmed with Lessius (lib. 4 c. 4 n. 84), Elbel (*de 6. praec.* n. 248) the Salamancans (*ibid.* n. 5) with Filliuci, Bonacina and the common opinion, because then he would doubly offend religion, namely by his own sin and by the other's sin, in which he cooperated.

457.—*Quaeritur III:* If someone had a vow of chastity, would he commit a sacrilege if he were to lead another to carnal sin by his own counsel? De Lugo, Leander, Perez, and the Salamancans (*ibid.* punct. 3 num. 10) affirm it with probability. Their reasoning is that he would not lead others to wound chastity unless he himself were positively affected with lust, and therefore he also offends chastity. But Sanchez denies this with enough probability (*dec.* t. 2 lib. 5 cap. 6 num. 11) as well as Dicastillus (cited by the Salamancans, *loc. cit.* n. 9) because one pronouncing a vow of chastity regards only his own chastity, not another. Just the same, the first opinion certainly seems more probable to me if from a positive disposition to lust were to induce another to sin; otherwise if for another depraved reason. Moreover, it must altogether be held with the Salamancans (*ibid.* num. 13 and 14) against a few authors, that a religious indeed commits a sacrilege who takes morose delectation from the carnal sin of another, or who pollutes another with his own hands, even without his own delectation.

458.—II. In regard to *place*, we ask the following questions:

Quaeritur I: Whether marital sex taking place in a church, if it is secret or without any other fault, is a sacrilege? We must preface that according to *c. un. de consec. Eccl.* in 6 and *c. Ecclesiis* 20 *de consec.* dist. 1, the voluntary effusion of blood or seed in a Church is forbidden, whereby (provided the effusion were certainly a mortal sin and a sacrilege) the Church remains polluted until it shall be blessed again. But there is a doubt as to what sort of effusion suffices for this? There are three opinions, all of which are probable enough, as the Salamancans rightly say (*de matr.* c. 15 punct. 5 n. 61 in fine).

The *first opinion* holds, scandal avoided, marital sex is never a sacrilege just as the shedding of blood done in self defense is not; because the aforesaid law, since it is penal, must be understood strictly, namely on the illicit effusion alone. Thus the Gloss (*in d.c. Ecclesiis*, 20, *v. Semine*, saying this is according to Pope Hyginus in *c. 19 antecedenti*, where he says: "If a Church has been violated by homicide or adultery, let it be cleansed." Also Pontius (*de matr.* lib. 10 cap. 10 n. 13), Sa (*v. Ecclesia* n. 14) likewise Alensis, Rosell, and Henriquez, and del Soto and Dicastillus think it is probable (cited by the Salamancans, *l.c.*)

The *second opinion* makes a distinction and says that a sacrilege is certainly committed and the Church polluted through the public effusion of blood or seed, but not through the secret effusion, namely an effusion that is not known to anyone, or only two or three. Thus the Gloss (*l.c.* c. *un. de consecr.* in 6 *v. Si polluit*) which notes: "If the pollution were secret the Church need not be restored; for the theologians say that a Church is restored so that when men see a Church is washed they think such a great labor is carried out to wash away sins." Likewise Pontius (*l.c.* n. 9, calling it common), Toledo (l. 15 c. 8), Sa (*v. Ecclesia*, n. 19), Navarre (c. 27 n. 230), Azor, t. 1 l. 10 c. 26 q. 3, and Vasquez, Coninck, Rodriquez, etc. cited by the Salamancans (*d*. c. 15 n. 63 and 64). The reasoning is (as they say) that such an effusion is not a sacrilege by divine law, but only by ecclesiastical law, in which only a public effusion seems to be forbidden, as long as the reverence due to a sacred place in the opinion of men is removed by it (Salamancans *ibid*. n. 65). Nevertheless, they note that when the effusion is made public, it suffices if it is manifested in words or if the husband and wife are thought to lie in the same bed.

The *third opinion* more probably says that even through secret marital sex a sacrilege is committed and a Church polluted unless it were done from a moral necessity. The reason is, because the cited text speaks in general terms about any effusion and so is more correctly understood that by secret and licit sex a grave injury is inflicted on the Church; and it is more probably polluted. Nevertheless, if the crime were secret, there is no obligation to refrain from the divine office. (Sanchez, *de matr*. l. 9 d. 15 n. 12, Bonacina *de matr*. q. 4 p. ult. n. 6, Holzman, *de 6 pr*. n. 667, Croix, l. 6 p. 2 n. 1071, Salamancans *ibid*. n. 65 and 66, with Suarez, Lessius, Sylvius). Moreover, the cited doctors opine that then the spouses are in moral necessity when they are in danger of incontinence, or, if at some time they must remain in the Church for a long time, namely for 10 days, as some think; others for 20, while others still a month. And in the case where spouses judge that they will remain in the Church for a month, they can copulate even from the beginning. So think Sanchez, *loc. cit.*, the Salamancans, *ibid.* n. 67 and 68, with others.

459.—*Quaeritur II*: Would only unchaste touches in the Church be a sacrilege? Many authors deny this provided there was no danger of pollution. (Sanchez, *de matr*. l. 9 d. 15 n. 21, with Cajetan, Navarre and Bonacina, Fagundez, Zanardus, Diana, Candidus, Leander, and others cited by Moya, tr. 3, disp. 3, qu. 4

cap. 3 n. 19). The reason is, because a Church is not violated by such touches to the extent that the divine offices would be impeded, and therefore the accounting of a sacrilege. But other authors more probably contradict this (Elbel *de sacril.* n. 576, Holzmann, *de 6 praec.* n. 721, likewise Sylvester, Corduba, Lopez and Manuel, cited by Sanchez *l.c.* n. 15). The reasoning is, because shameful touches have the same malice as sex itself and therefore are a sacrilege, not on account of the violation of the Church, which is only constituted by pollution, but on account of grave irreverence which is inflicted upon a sacred place. Consequently, pollution is not a sacrilege because the Church is polluted, but rather the Church is polluted because pollution is a sacrilege.

460.—The words *sacred place*, however, embrace every place blessed by a bishop, assigned for divine offices or to bury the dead from the roof to the very pavement. But this does not embrace the cell, cloister, sacristy, dormitory, above the roof over the Church, the door outside the threshold of the Church, or the atrium. (Salamancans *loc. cit.* n. 69 and 70, and *de VI praec.* c. 6 punct. 4 § 2 n. 27 *et seqq.* with Sanchez, Dicastillus, Basilius). But private oratories do not come under this heading, unless they were erected by the authority of the Bishop as usually happens in hospitals, because then they are true Churches and there everyone can hear Mass as the Salamancans say (*de privil.* tr. 18, cap. 3 punct. 3 § 1 n. 87) with Palaus, Suarez, Fagundez, etc. But it is otherwise if they are merely private oratories, although there Mass can be said from a concession of the Pope or the Bishop, according to what we will say *On the Holy Eucharist*, book 6 n. 357 and 359.

461.—*Quaeritur III:* Are lustful words or stares in Church considered to be sacrileges? There are also three opinions on this question.

The *first opinion* says that every external act that takes place in Church, even if it is lightly indecent, is a sacrilege. (Sylvius, Corduba, cited by the Salamancans *de VI praec.* c. 6 punct. 4 § 1 n. 20).

The *Second opinion* condemns as sacrilegious only gravely indecent external acts (Sanchez, *de matr.* l. 9 d. 15 n. 20, the Salamancans *ibid.* n. 21, with Suarez, Molina, Decastillus, and others).

The *third opinion* denies that such acts, whether lightly or gravely indecent, are sacrilegious (Toledo, Coninck, Vasquez, Basilius, Diana, Valentia, etc., cited by the Salamancans, *l.c.* n. 19, Holzmann *de 6 praec.* n. 721, calling it common and the Salamancans elsewhere follow it as certain, namely *de matr.* c. 15 punct. 5 n. 68, although here they contradict themselves). The reasoning is, because indecent conversation or stares, or even a lustful kiss (always with the danger of pollution avoided), although they are mortal sins as well as morally disgraceful, still they do not contain of themselves a grave physical deformity against the reverence due to the sacred place. Nevertheless, this not withstanding, I think the second opinion is absolutely more probable.

462.—*Quaeritur IV:* Are indecent thoughts which take place in a Church sacrilegious? The Salamancans rightly make a distinction: they affirm it if the desire to sin outwardly in the Church is deliberate, even if it takes place outside of the Church (*de VI praec.* c. 6 punct. 4 § 1 n. 24, with del Soto, Navarre, Azor, Suarez, etc.). It must be said otherwise, if the desires are to sin outside the Church, contrary to Medina. But if there was consent to sin within the Church, though secretly, it is a sacrilege according to the opinion we advanced just recently in n. 458.

463.—III. In regard to *sacred things*, it is also a sacrilege to abuse sacred things to sin disgracefully, therefore, one indeed commits a sacrilege who, having vested for Mass, would pollute himself, etc., as Diana, and Tancred, cited by the Salamancans *ibid.* punct. 5 n. 37.

There is an uncertainty as to whether the priest, carrying the sacrament of the Eucharist, by sinning outwardly or inwardly against chastity, would commit another sacrilege? In common Tamburinius (*de Sacram. poen.* l. 2 c. 7 n. 12), Sanchez (c. 6 n. 36) and others affirm it. The reasoning is, because holy things must be treated in a holy manner. Also see book 6, n. 35, near the end. So the Salamancans (cit. n. 37) equally say with Cardinal de Lugo and Tamburinius, etc., that one cannot be excused from sacrilege who will have polluted himself immediately after communion, namely half an hour after.

However, one does not commit a sacrilege that carries relics or an *agnus dei*, and not if he were to give them to a lover under the pretext of a donation. It is otherwise if he would give them as the price for the sin, for then it would be a sacrilege and simony. (Salamancans *loc. cit.* n. 38 and 39, with Azor and Filliuci).

Would it be a sacrilege to commit a carnal sin on feast days? Some affirm this, but it is more probably denied with the Salamancans (*de* 3 praec. c. 1 p. 11 § 1 n. 218) because the end of that precept does not fall under this precept. See what was said in book 4, n. 46, and 273.

DUBIUM III
What are the species of lust carried out against nature?

464. *What of unnatural sexual intercourse?*
465. *What about masturbation (mollities)?*
466. *What is sodomia imperfecta and sodomia perfecta?*

467. *Whether pollution that takes place by touching a boy or a woman is a different species?*
468. *Whether in confessing sodomy it must be explained if one was the agent or the patient?*
469. *Whether heterosexual sodomy adds the species of incest?*
470. *What are the penalties for those guilty of sodomy?*
471. *What is required to incur these? Would a cleric who is patient in an act of sodomy incur these penalties?*
472. *Are the penalties incurred before the sentence?*
473. *Does a cleric committing acts of bestiality incur these penalties?*
474. *What is the sin of bestiality?*
475. *On sin with a demon. What if the demon represented itself as a married or consecrated woman?*

464.—"Response: When we speak of those things against "nature, we mean those wherein the effusion of seed takes place "in manners repugnant to the institution of nature, so that "according to such modes the species are changed, hence it is "resolved, such a species are the following:

"1. Disordered sexual intercourse, this is unnatural whether "it is a manner of having sex that is not due, namely when the "same identity of the species, the opposite sex and due organ of "nature are preserved, but it is merely done in a disordered "mode; *e.g.* a man submits [lies underneath] or comes from "behind after the fashion of animals, or from the side, or while "standing or sitting, or by another unusual reckoning; which is "against mortal nature when thence there is a danger of "impeding generation or of spilling the seed; otherwise, if this "danger is guarded against, or if it is not, to the extent that the "womb of the woman sufficiently takes the seed and retains it, "then it is rather more done apart from nature than against it, "and is a weighty venial sin, or none at all if grave cause is "present; *e.g.* the woman is pregnant or because of the "disposition of the body of either spouse it cannot be suffered to

TREATISE IV: THE FIFTH AND SIXTH PRECEPTS, CH. II 517

"be done otherwise. Filliuci, tract. 30, cap. 8, q. 8 n. 137" (See "what will be said *on Matrimony*, book 6 n. 917).

465.—"2. Masturbation, or pollution, is when, without "human commerce or sex one voluntarily procures the flow of "semen whether it is shed outwardly, as in males, or inwardly "as in women. And this sin, apart from its own malice, often "has another adjoined to it, *e.g.* fornication, adultery, incest, "etc., namely when someone imagines and at the same time "desires to have sex with another person that is free, or married, "etc., which hence, if it happens, must be clarified in "confession. See more on masturbation in the next dubium."

466.—"3. *Sodomia imperfecta* is also carnal relations with the "proper sex, namely of a man with a woman, but outside of the "natural *vas*. It can also have at the same time other malices, "*e.g.* adultery, if it is done with a married woman; incest if with "kin. Bonacina, q. 4 *de matrimonio*, p. 11 n. 1; Filliuci *l.c.* n. 158."

"4. *Sodomia perfecta* is the sexual relations of two people of "the same sex, that as a man with a man or a woman with a "woman, and it can also have other malices joined to it, *e.g.* "incest; in which case, the degree of relation does not "necessarily have to be explained, as Escobar teaches (*de act.* "*hum.* e. 2 c. 6) but it is enough to say, I had sex with a blood "relation, or kin; because the flesh is not mixed nor is affinity "contracted, nor does the line change the species. But it must "also be explained whether he was the agent or patient, as de "Lugo says (d. 16 n. 425) against Diana, tom. 2 t. 4 *de sactr.* r. 159 "and p. 6 t. 6 r. 36."

There is a great question, in what act does sodomy consist of? Some hold it consists in sexual coitus in a *vas indebitum*. Others, coitus among those of the same sex. Each opinion is probable and in each opinion a special deformity is discerned, which holds sodomy against nature and requires both to be preserved for generation, *i.e.* a *vas debitum* and the opposite sex.

The *first opinion* is that sodomy is defined in the sexual act directed to a *vas indebitum*, as Trullenchus, Reginald, Henriquez, Covarruvias, Lez., Leander, Llamas and commonly the jurists cited by the Salamancans (*de VI praec.* cap. 7 punct. 5 § 1 num. 81). Hence, they say one commits true sodomy who has sex in a *vas praeposterum* even with a person of the opposite sex.

The *second opinion* is more probable and is the common teaching of theologians, which holds that sodomy consists in carnal relations *ad indebitum sexum*.[10] (St. Thomas, II IIæ, q. 154 art. 11 in the body of the article; Lessius, l. 4 c. 3 dubium 13 n. 89; Holzmann *de 6 praec.* n. 676; Elbel, n. 263 and the Salamancans *ibid.* n. 82 with Sa, Azor, Bonacina, Cajetan and many others). The reason is, because true and proper sodomy is committed in sexual relations with a person with whom generation can in no way take place.

Hence it is inferred I: Coitus of a woman with a woman is true sodomy, as the authors say (St. Thomas, *loc. cit.*; Roncaglia, *de 6 praec.* c. ult. q. 1, Holzmann *loc. cit.*; Sporer *de matrimonio* c. 3 n. 626; the Salamancans *ibid.* n. 80 with Cajetan, etc.). Although, Elbel (*l.c.*) with Felix Potianus (*de 6 praec. n. 2171*) think that sex of this sort, even with entry to a *vas praeposterum*, does not seem anything but *sodomia impropria*, since perfect copulation cannot take place between women.

It is inferred II: Every sexual act is true sodomy which either entails the union of bodies taking place with a person of the same sex, or in a *vas preposterum*, or in another part; for then, speaking plainly, the disposition to an undue sex is always present, as the authors hold (Tamburinius, *in meth. Conf.* c. 7 n. 64; Roncaglia, *l.c.*; the Continuator of Tounrely, *de 6 dec. praec.* art. 6 sect. 2; Croix lib. 3 p. 1 n. 910 and l. 6 p. 2 n. 1082; the Salamancans *loc.*

---

[10] Translator's note: *Indebitum* means undue, or not where an act should be ordered. So, as *vas indebitum* means an undue vessel, *i.e.* outside the vagina where sexual acts are ordered by nature, so also *indebitum sexum* means an undue sex, or not the opposite sex to which sexual acts tend by nature.

cit. n. 81). Hence, Roncaglia, Tamburinius (n. 70) and the Salamancans (*ibid.* n. 87 near the end against Graff), say that it must not necessarily be explained in confession if the pollution happened inside or outside the *vas*, for it suffices to confess "I sinned with a boy," that the confessor would judge sodomy was present with pollution. But if pollution was not present, it should be explained.

It is inferred III: With the Salamancans (*ibid.* n. 82) and Cajetan, Sa, Bonacina, Tamburinius and the more common opinion, sex of a man in a *vas praeposterum* of a woman is only *sodomia imperfecta* distinct in species from *sodomia perfecta*, as the Continuator of Tourney says (*loc. cit.*) and Tamburinius (*num.* 74), who notes in n. 64 with Filliuci (and Holzman, n. 720 and Sporer n. 336 with the common opinion rightly agree), as he asserts that if a man were to have sex between the legs, arms or other parts of a woman, would be a certain *copula inchoata*, at least in disposition. This is why, according to this doctrine, a man lying with a virgin outside the *vas* commits two sins, certainly against the same chastity but of a different species, one of fornication in disposition, the other against nature in effect. Moreover, the aforesaid authors (Sporer, Holzmann and Tamburinius n. 77 with Angelus) say that a confessor, understanding that a woman was known outside the natural *vas* or a *vas praeposterum*, ought not to inquire in what place, or how. Moreover, pollution in the mouth is of a different species, as Sporer affirms (n. 637) with some cited by Diana and this sin they call *irrumatio*. But other authors say more probably that if a man is polluted in the mouth of a woman, it will be *copula inchoata*, as above, but if in the mouth of a male, it will be sodomy (Holzmann, *loc. cit.* and Filliuci tr. 30 n. 155 with Cajetan, Graff., etc.). What sort of sin is it to have sex with a dead woman? It must be said with Holzmann, num. 720, Salamancans num. 74, Sporer n. 639 with Tamburinius etc. in common, it is not fornication, because it takes place with a cadaver, nor bestiality, as some would have it, but it is pollution and affective fornication.

467.—There is a doubt: 1) Would pollution that takes place when touching a boy or a woman that is asleep, or incapacitated by a trick, or shameful acts with beasts, but without coitus, be of a different species from simple pollution?

The *first opinion* affirms it, and says such pollution with a boy is sodomy, with a woman is *inchoate copulation* (Sporer, n. 635, and Dicastillus and Diana cited by Salamancans *de 6 praec.* c. 7 punct. 2 n. 9).

But the *second opinion* holds that it is simple pollution (Cajetan 2. 2. q. 154 art. 11; Azor, l. 3 p. 3 c. 23, qu. 1; Bonacina *de matr.* q. 4 p. 10 n. 15; Salamancans n. 10 with Trullenchus, Marchant, Sayr, Filliuci, Bassaeus, etc.). The reason is because when sex is absent, they speak about something that is of itself material, that pollution takes place with one's own touches or another's. Then it suffices to confess, "I had pollution from someone else's touches." For when coitus is not present, there is no affect toward the sex, but to pollution: then it is intended, even if it happens materially, if it came about by the touches of a man or woman. Still it must be said otherwise if it takes place from the touches of one's wife or one having a vow of chastity.

468.—There is a doubt: 2) Whether it must be explained in the sin of sodomy whether, if someone were the agent, or patient? The Salamancans deny it (*eodem tr.* c. 7 punct. 5 § 1 n. 87 with Diana, etc.) because, they say, those having sex in this way are commonly both polluted. But it must be explained more truly according to what other authors say. Because pollution is easier in the agent than in the patient (Holzmann n. 678, the Continuator of Tournely, *l.c.* n. 2, Mazotta t. 1 p. 13 and Tamburinius, Leander, de Lugo, etc., cited by the Salamancans, *ibid.* n. 86).

469.—There is a doubt: 3) Does sodomy between blood relations or in-laws add the species of incest? There are three opinions.

The *first* generally denies it with some authors cited by Diana, who seems to follow them; because they say, incest is only committed when the act of coitus takes place in a *vas debitum* with a mixing of relations. But this does not seem sufficiently probable.

The *second opinion*, which other authors hold, says sodomitical coitus between blood relations within the first and second degree is certainly incest, since that is forbidden by natural law, but not coitus between relations in the third and fourth degree which is merely forbidden by positive law between a male and female in matrimony, which is why they say that sodomitical coitus, which is not ordered to matrimony, is not forbidden between such relations by positive law, precisely by reason of proximity (Bonacina, *de matr.* p. 4 punct. 11 n. 10 and 11; likewise, Azor, Cand., etc. cited by the Salamancans tr. 26 c. 7 punct. 5 § 2 n. 90).

The *third opinion,* which I think is more probable, teaches that all coitus, whether natural or unnatural among blood relations even to the fourth degree, whether they are blood relations or in-laws, whether legal or spiritual, introduces the malice of incest (de Lugo *de poen.* d. 16 n. 345 to 351; Cont. Tourney, *l.c.* art. 4 quaer. 2; Roncaglia, last chapter, q. 2; Croix, l. 6 p. 2 n. 1082, with Sylvius, and Graff., likewise Leander, Dicastillus, etc. with the Salamancans *ibid.* n. 92). The reason is, because from the law of the Church reverence is now due in all things, as well as piety which is defiled by natural coitus, so much more by unnatural coitus. So also the Salamancans say (*loc. cit.* n. 94) that he commits incest who commits pollution with the touches of someone he is related to in the fourth degree. And the same must be said about other unchaste touches, wherein one must express the species of an accomplice whether he is a blood relation, related, etc. (with the Cont. Tournely, *l.c.* art. 7 sect. 1 v. *Hic* near the end, and Viva, as well as the Salamancans who assert it is the common opinion). But we must note that it is certain that one must explain in confession if the sodomy took place with violence or with a person bound by a vow of chastity. Moreover, if with a married woman; because the trust of matrimony demands that the spouse would not divide her flesh in sex with others. Sanchez, Trullenchus, with the Salamancans, *ibid.* from nu. 98.

470.—In regard to the penalties for this crime, it must be known that sodomy carries with it the death penalty in civil law as well as burning, but by canon law, from the bull of St. Pius V (which the Salamancans cite, tr. 26 c. 7 punct. 6 § 1 n. 107) both clergy and religious laity, the words of the bull say those "committing these dreadful sins are deprived from every clerical privilege, office, or benefice by the authority of the present canon." And furthermore, the saintly Pontiff commands that they be handed over to the civil power.

471.—Here, many questions are raised in regard to those things which—for the sake of brevity—we say it is probably required to incur the aforesaid penalties: 1) That the sodomy were carried out with pollution within the *vas*, as Roncaglia holds (against Laguna in *de VI praec.* c. ult. q. 5; Bonacina, *de matr.* q. 4 p. 11 n. 2; Holzmann c. 3 n. 719; likewise Suarez, Navarre, Filliuci, Azor, Barbosa, with the Salamancans *ibid.* § 2 n. 109 and the common opinion); for the penal law always demands that the crime be perfect and consummated; 2) That the sodomy be a male with a male; for sodomitical coitus of a male with a female is not true sodomy, as Bonacina (*loc. cit.* n. 5) and with Azor, Hurtius, Dicastillus and the more common opinion holds with the Salamancans (*ibid.* n. 111) against Lessius and Garcia. Hence, the Salamancans note with probability (*ibid.* n. 112 with Bonacina, etc.) that sodomy with a woman is not embraced under the reservation of sodomy. But it is otherwise if it were a reserved sin against nature. Then, would pollution be embraced under a reserved sin against nature? It seems that of itself it is included, but the Salamancans (*loc. cit.* n. 115, with Hurtad.) deny it, because bishops (as they say) commonly do not intend to include pollution in a reservation of this sort; 3) What pertains to the penalties for clergy, that an act of sodomy were frequented, or continued by use, as Navarre says. For this imports the word *exercentes*, as expressed above in the Bull. So Bonacina (num. 2) and the Salamancans (*ibid.* n. 121) with Barbosa, Suarez, Hurtad, Henriquez and the common opinion, against Lopez, Farinac., etc. Hence he is excused who sinned in this way once or twice.

But there is a greater doubt: 1) Whether clergy that are patients in sodomy incur the penalties? Hurtad, Graff, etc. (cited by the Salamancans *ibid.* n. 116) deny it because they say the word *exercentes* properly means being active, not passive, and this seems probable enough. But the Salamancans duly hold the contrary is probable (n. 117) with Diana, Bonacina, Barbosa, etc., because the patients are also true sodomites. In equal mode, even women are not excused from the penalties for adultery, even though they are merely patients.

472.—There is a doubt: 2) Whether the aforesaid penalties are incurred before the sentence?

The *first opinion* affirms it, because the Pope says, "We deprive [them] by the authority of the present canon." So think Azor, Dicastillus, Far., Garcia, etc., cited by the Salamancans, tr. 26, c. 7 punct. 6 § 3 n. 124.

Nevertheless, the *second opinion* is truer and more common and it denies this. The reason is, because (as the Salamancans prove, tr. 11 c. 2 punct. 3 § 2 ex. n. 59), no penalty depriving someone from an acquired right is incurred before the sentence, although it is expressed in law that the penalty is incurred *ipso facto*. (Navarre, c. 27 n. 249; Suarez, *de cens.* t. 5 d. 31, sect. 4 n. 22;

Bonacina, *de matr.* q. 4 p. 11 n. 3; Lessius, l. 2 c. 29 n. 63 and the Salamancans, *ibid.* n. 125, with Barbosa, Filliuci, Trullenchus, Diana, Hurtad, etc.). Nay more, even if there it was said "Not awaiting the sentence of a judge," then at least a declaratory sentence of the crime would be required. The reason is, because the law would be excessively hard in that *per se* someone who is held to undergo punishment would be condemned earlier than the sentence. See what was said in book 1, n. 148.

473.—There is a doubt: 3) Whether a cleric committing bestiality would incur the penalties for sodomitical acts? Quaranta, Ledesma, Rodriquez, etc. (cited by the Salamancans tr. 26 n. 128) uphold this, because (as they say), the penal law ought also to be extended from case to case, when the same reasoning occurs and the crime is of a graver malice as it is in this case. But the opposite must be held with Fr. Concina (c. 5), the Salamancans (*ibid.* n. 129) with Barbosa, Bonacina, Diana, etc., because the reasoning of the first opinion proceeds in the penal law, which depends not only on the reasoning of the law, but also the will of the legislator; and therefore, in that the argument does not avail in like manner.

474.—"5. Bestiality, which is the most serious of all, is also a "sexual action in which the identity of the species is not "preserved; *e.g.* if a man has coitus with a beast whether of the "same sex or not." (Bestiality is a graver sin than sodomy because there, just as the *vas debitum* is not preserved, nor the sex so neither is the *genus debitum*. Salamancans, *ibid.* punct. 7 n. 139).

"It is also not necessary to explain what kind of animal it "was or what species it was because the difference is merely "material and in the kind of being; but not formal and in the "kind of moral. Escobar, e. 2 cap. 6, Filliuci t. 2 tr. 30, c. 7 n. 131."

TREATISE IV: THE FIFTH AND SIXTH PRECEPTS, CH. II

(This is the common opinion with the Salamancans, *ibid.* num. 140, and Elbel n. 260, with Henno, etc.).

But there is a doubt as to whether one needs to explain whether the beast was male or female? Croix (l. 3 p. 2), Elbel (n. 261), Holzmann (n. 681) affirm this, because (as they say), morally, the difference is a deformity of sexual intercourse with a male beast and with a female. But in common (the same Elbel affirms) and more probably other authors deny it (Cont. Tournely, *de 6 Dec. praec.*, art. 6 sect. 2 n. 3; Filliuci tr. 30 c. 8 n. 161; Tamburinius *Dec. praec.* l. 7 c. 8 § 5 n. 1; Felix Potianus *de 6 praec.* n. 2182; Azor, l. 3 c. 22 q. 3; Renzi *de 6 pr.* c. 8 q. 16 with Fragg., and *de Januar.*). The reason is, because the whole essential deformity of this deed consists in entering into a different species; wherefore the circumstance of sex is altogether accidental and involves no difference in the kind of moral. Moreover, unchaste touches with a beast, although they are not properly sins of bestiality, nevertheless, have some particular foulness, as Elbel says (*l.c.*) and are at least venial.

475.—"A sin with a demon, either a succubus or incubus, is "recalled to bestiality; to which sin is added in addition a malice "against religion. In addition to that, sodomy, adultery or incest "if he were to have coitus with the demon by the affect of a "man, or woman, in a fashion that is sodomitical, adulterous or "incestuous. See Bonacina, *de matr.* q. 4 p. 12 n. 3; Filliuci, num. "162."

Fr. Busembaum rightly says that sexual relations with demons are reduced to the sin of bestiality, as Tamburinius (*l.c.*), Elbel, n. 262, with Bonacina, Filliuci, and the Salamancans (*loc. cit.* n. 141, with Cajetan, Azor, and Trullenchus. Besides the crime of bestiality he adds the crime of superstition. Moreover, would someone that has sex with a demon appearing in the form of a married woman, a nun, or a blood relation always affectively sin with the sin of adultery, sacrilege or incest? It seems in general that Busembaum affirms this with others (as above), but it is very probable that it must be denied if the man having such relations takes delight in the woman represented by the demon not because she were married, or a nun, but because she was beautiful, according to de Lugo, Palaus, Vasquez, and a great many others, who teach with probability that morose delectation does not involve the species of the object, from which someone takes delight, unless the circumstances of person would enter into delectation. See book 2, n. 15.

DUBIUM IV
Is it a sin to procure pollution?

476. *Is pollution forbidden by natural law?*
477. *Is the voluntary effusion of seminal fluid a mortal sin?*
478. *Is it lawful to expel corrupt semen?*
479. *Are we held to impede pollution that has already begun?*
480. *Is it lawful on account of an upright end to desire or take delight in it?*
481. *What if it were foreseen that pollution will follow from an upright act? What if it were foreseen from an illicit act?*
482. *Pollution is certainly a mortal sin when it arises from a foul cause gravely influencing toward it.*
483. *What if the action were posited on account of a just cause? Namely: I. To heal, or to hear confessions, to give an address according to morals, etc.; II. To satisfy an itch; III. To ride a horse; IV. To recline in some position; V. To eat moderately, etc. What if a surgeon or a pastor were to consent several times in pollution? And what about a simple confessor? What if someone nearly always fell back into this sin?*
484. *Is pollution a mortal sin when it arose from a cause lightly influencing it? What if the cause were in the same genus of lust? And what if the fall were frequent? What if the cause were in another genus? Can venial sin at least be posited for it?*

485. *On pollution following a dream. Does mutual pollution have a different malice?*

476.—"*Resp.* By the authority of Scripture, which excludes "the effeminate from the kingdom of heaven (1. Corinthians 6), "everyone teaches that there is no licit cause to intend or "directly procure masturbation, not even for the sake of health "or avoid certain death. Sanchez (l. 9 d. 17) grants the reason "that nature denies to man in every event the administration of "semen outside of matrimony precisely because the sense of "delight in it is so vehement that men, blinded by passion "would easily persuade themselves that they have a just cause "to arouse the seed wherefore, many and very grave vices "against the common good and to impede generation would "emerge."

Notice here: 1) Before anything else, number 49 of the propositions condemned by Pope Innocent XI, which said: "Masturbation is not forbidden by natural law; this is why if God did not forbid it, it is often good and sometimes obligatory under mortal sin." This was rightly condemned since if fornication is evil because it is against the education of children, pollution is worse which is against the generation of children. Notice: 2) That pollution of eunuchs and children (even if they do not have completed seed) is no different from the pollution of adults. Notice: 3) That all pollutions of themselves are of the same species in whatever way they are done if it is without sex, as the authors say (Azor, p. 3 l. 3 c. 21; Bonacina, *de matr.* q. 4 p. 10 n. 15; Anacletus, *de 6 praec.* n. 49; see what was said in n. 467). It is said *of itself,* because by reason of the circumstances it can be joined to another malice distinct in species, namely if a priest commits pollution, a sacrilege is added; if a married man, adultery; if with the desire to sin with another person, a malice is added according to the quality of the person desired; likewise another malice is added if someone pollutes himself by delectation from imagining sex with some male person or a married woman, or from habit, according to what was said in book 2, n. 15. Likewise, if one is polluted by someone else's touches.

477.—"1. Distillation, which is the flow of a humor as a "medium among urine and semen (with which it bears the "similitude of color and viscosity) without that immoderate "delectation, is not true pollution, and if it happens without all "commotion of venereal sense then one should not be any more "troubled over it than sweat, as Cajetan says. But if it were to "happen with the sense of the flesh and arousal of the spirits "serving generation, then, one must not cooperate or provide "the occasion, or it is a sin; and at that venial or mortal to the "same mode on which we spoke in regard to pollution. Sanchez, "l. 9 d. 45 n. 32, Laymann, l. 3 t. 4 n. 18."

Quaeritur: Is voluntary distillation a mortal sin? We must make the distinction; if it comes to pass with a notable arousal of the spirits, then there is no doubt that it is a mortal sin; because such a notable commotion is inchoate pollution. And the same must be said if the distillation were in a great quantity, because such a notable distillation cannot be without a notable rebellion of the flesh. This is why just as one gravely sins who procures a notable arousal, so also who procures a great distillation (Sanchez, *de matrimonio*, l. 9 d. 17 n. 17 and d. 45 n. 41; Sporer *eod. tit.* n. 659; Elbel *de 6 praec.* n. 259; Holzmann *eod. tit.* n. 692; Tamburinius *dec.* l. 7 c. 3 § 5 n. 53 and others in common). Hence, we are held under grave obligation not only to directly avoid a distillation of this sort, but also indirectly by avoiding all proximate causes influencing it, in equal manner we will speak about pollution below in n. 484. But if distillation were in a modest quantity and without delectation and arousal, then without sin we could permit it, as Cajetan and Marg. say (cited by Sanchez, l. 9 d. 45 n. 2; the Salamancans *de 6 praec.* c. 7 punct. 2 n.

35, with St. Thomas, Sayr, Bonacina and others in common; because on such a flow one need not take more care than on the emission of any sort of excrement, from which is customarily discharged by nature. Cajetan says: "In regard to that, unless it takes place with a rebellion of the flesh, it seems one should not be any more troubled over it than sweat." (*Opusc.* 22, q. 1 § *Animadverte*). The Continuator of Tourney speaks likewise (*de 6 praec.* art. 6 sect. 1 v. *Hic obiter*, with Henriquez of St. Ignatius. Nay more, Holzmann, Tamburinius, Sporer, and Elbel (*ll.cc.*) say it is also permitted with a mild commotion of the flesh. But Sanchez rightly adverts (and Bonacina consents to him in *de matr.* q. 4 p. 8 n. 17) that directly and with full attention to procure any distillation, even light, can in no way be excused from mortal sin; because really, each distillation always, or for the most part, advance with it some arousal and the effusion of some small amount of semen.

478.—"If the semen, in the judgment of doctors, became "putrid, it is lawful for him to expel it with medication, even if "some loss of true seed might unintentionally follow. Sanchez, "*de matr.* l. 9 d. 17 n. 16; Filliuci, tr. 30 c. 8 n. 150; Trullenchus, l. "6 c. 1 d. 8 §1."

The Salamancans do not admit this opinion (*ibid.* n. 27) nor Roncaglia (*eod. tit.* c. 7 q. 3) both because (as they say) it is impossible to expel corrupted semen and not true semen at the same time; and because they do not lack other remedies to heal someone from corrupted semen so that it would not be necessary to eject it. But the more common opinion embraces the position of our Fr. Busembaum. The reason is, because these medications tend, *per se*, to only directly expel corrupted semen; moreover, the effusion of some true seed follows *per accidens*, and besides the intention, which cannot be illicit, since all concede it is licit to expel other harmful humors with remedies, although *per accidens* pollution might follow just as it is licit to take poison to expel a plague, even if an unanimated fetus must be indirectly expelled (*Cf.* above, n. 394, *Quaeritur I*; Sanchez, l. 9 d. 17 n. 15 and d. 45, n. 9; Sporer *de matrim.* n. 643; Tamburinius l. 7 c. 7 § 2 n. 8; Anacletus *de 6 praec.* n. 47; Bonacina *de matr.* q. 4 p. 10 n. 12; Diana p. 2 tr. 19 r. 55; Croix l. 3 p. 1 n. 926, with Laymann). I believe this second opinion is probable enough provided that: 1) The seed were corrupted for certain, but not if it were in doubt; 2) the expulsion of the corrupted seed could be done without a sense of lust, as Anacletus adverts; 3), but not if there are other remedies to heal the corrupted seed; nevertheless it is never licit to expel corrupted seed by touch, even if the danger of consent were absent; for so it must be altogether held with the authors (Sporer n. 643; Croix *l.c.* n. 926, with Laymann, Filliuci and the common teaching against Bonacina *l.c.* and Tamburinius d. § 2 n. 8) The reason is, although the remedy is permitted for that very reason it only tends of itself to expel the corrupted seed, still by no means may one permit it by rubbing because this tends of itself to provoke the sensual spirits; and it is never licit to expel true seed. Hence, the very wise and pious Sanchez, although he earlier held the contrary in his treatise *De Matrimonio*, still, in *Dec.* l. 5 c. 6 n. 12) he did not hesitate to retract himself.

But, is it permitted to take medication to taint the semen and later eject it released in blood, or another humor? Sporer (d. n. 643) with Diana denies it, because (as he says) it is opposed to the institution of the semen. But other authors concede it with probability (Sanchez, l. 9 d. 17 n. 15; Bonacina, p. 10 n. 12; Anacl. n. 47; Roncaglia q. 3, etc.). The reason is, because nature does not oblige one to preserve the semen with danger to life, for if (as Sanchez says) it is lawful to remove the testicles to save one's life, although without them a man is rendered altogether powerless to beget [children], why will it not be lawful to taint semen?

479.—"3. A man is not held (provided there is no danger of "consent in the will, nor that he would voluntarily continue) to "impede pollution happening by itself, or already begun, e.g. to "repress it in a dream. But he can permit nature to discharge "itself for the sake of health since this is not to procure but to "suffer the flow which, otherwise being corrupted, would harm "his health. Wherefore, Sanchez admits the same thing, even if "earlier it arose from fault, provided he was sorry for it and he "removes further consent. Furthermore, he adds that it is "expedient for the man to fortify himself with the cross and, "without another touch, while his hands are at rest, asks God to "not permit his fall into delectation. Sanchez, d. 17, num. 17; "Trullenchus, l. 6 c. 1 d. 10."

When pollution begins in a dream and the discharge happens while half-awake, then if a man experiences some delectation, it is not fully deliberate and he does not sin except venially, as the authors note (St. Antoninus, p. 2 tit. 6 c. 5 in fin.; Navarre c. 16 n. 8 v. *Non est*; the Salamancans *de 6 praec.* c. 7 punct. 4 n. 74 and Concina, n. 48, and it is clear from the aforesaid in book 2, num. 3 and 5). Yet, when an discharge began in a dream but later were consummated while fully awake, in that case (provided there is no consent to delectation or proximate danger of consent from past experience), a man is not held to restrain it; both because it is very difficult to avert the exit of seed that has already fallen from his arousal, as the authors commonly say with the Salamancans, *l.c.* near the end; Navarre, Azor, Trullenchus, etc. and because a person is not held with danger of death from retaining corrupt seed, to impede that effusion, as the authors teach (Sanchez, *de matr.* l. 9 d. 17 n. 16; Concina, *l.c.*; Sporer *de matr.* n. 657; Holzmann *de 6 praec.* n. 688; Tamburinius l. 7 c. 7 § 2 n. 17 and others in common); for then he does not will that pollution, but merely suffers it. Still, Gerson correctly warns (*Alph* 38. l. 3 prop. 9) that in that case "for the execution of virtue and the avoidance of danger, it seems expedient that a man

532   BOOK IV: ON THE PRECEPTS OF THE DECALOGUE

should try to stop it, as much as he feels it and as suitably as it can be done." At least (it must be said with Sanchez) then it is expedient to fortify one's self with the sign of the Cross and to turn the mind away from that foul delectation, and by invoking the most holy names of Jesus and Mary, to fervently pray to them lest they would permit any fall.

480.—"4. It is licit on account of an upright end, *e.g.* to "diminish temptation, for health, tranquility of mind, to desire "from the simple affect a voluntary and natural release of "nature; provided that desire were not the efficacious cause of "pollution." (and the Salamancans think this is probable, *ibid.* n. 75 with St. Antoninus, Trullenchus, Fagundez, Diana, etc.). "Similarly, it is also lawful to rejoice in that it was done by a "natural means and without sin because the object of that desire "and rejoicing is not evil;" (And so St. Antoninus, p. 2 tit. 6 c. 5 *in fin*, only that you must understand that pollution has not arisen from some foul dream or one's own touch, as we said in book 2 n. 20. But it is always lawful to take delectation not from the cause but from the effect that followed, namely from the discharge; see *ibid.*) "although simple desires of this sort are "useless and do not lack danger as certain men rightly observe. "Lessius, d. 14 num. 15; Laymann, n. 17.

481.—"5. If anyone is going to do some necessary, or licit "and upright thing and foresees that from there pollution is "naturally going to follow (and it avails much more in regard to "distillation) which he nevertheless in no way wants or intends, "then, provided the danger of consent in delectation is removed, "he is not held to abstain from such an action because the "effects are not imputed to one exercising his right *per accidens* "and following apart from the intention. Hence, not "withstanding the danger of pollution, it is permitted to hear "the confessions of women, to be zealous in cases of conscience,

"to touch one's self from necessity, and to carefully and with
"necessity to address, kiss, and embrace women according to
"the custom of the country, unless it were otherwise uncivil.
"Yet, if there were a danger of consenting to delectation (which
"thence is gathered, if one more often falls into mortal sin from
"a similar occasion) from that cause, he must refrain from it as
"often as it is licit; and hence, the confessor in such a case is
"held to relinquish his office. (Filliuci, Sanchez l. 9 d. 45;
"Navarre, c. 16; Laymann, n. 16). Moreover, Layman advises one
"that experiences such misery in upright and advantageous
"actions, that he is more easily freed by having scant regard
"than by making much of it, because it is increased by
"imagination and fear."

482.—"6. If pollution were foreseen to follow from an illicit,
"idle or less necessary thing, and this were a proximate cause
"ordered to sex by its own nature, as are all lustful acts,
"touches, gazes, reading, hearing, foul speech, then it is a
"mortal sin to not stay away from. This is because in that case
"the one consenting is reckoned to morally consent to the
"effect. But if the matter were only a remote cause, *per accidens*
"only coinciding with pollution, *e.g.* eating or hot drinks, horse
"riding, vain conversation, games, even the mortal sin of
"drunkenness (provided one does not intend pollution and the
"danger of consent to sex is absent, then the pollution which
"follows is not a mortal sin; because in such a matter the one
"consenting, is not reckoned to have willed the effect. Filliuci,
"tr. 30 c. 8 q. 6 n. 152; Sanchez, *l.c.*; Lessius, l. 4 c. 3 d. 14. See
"Diana, p. 5 tr. 13 r. 4. Certain authors add this rule, that
"pollution is only a mortal sin as much as it is itself willed; just
"as if the cause were desired; that, if the cause were a mortal
"sin, even perhaps mortal itself, if it were venial, then venial,
"but if the cause were not a sin, nor were it perchance (always
"excluding the danger of consent); then it is venial; *e.g.* that

"which follows from curious reading, or a look that is not a "mortal sin *per se*. Trullenchus, l. 6 c. 1 d. 9 from Lopez, "Henriquez, Vasquez, Bonacina *de matr.* p. 10. See Diana, p. 1 t. "2 misc. r 56."

Here it will be worthwhile to explain and discuss all these things more clearly and distinctly. If the cause of pollution is gravely influencing in the vary matter, and a man does not refrain from the cause or that action placing it, it is clear that pollution is regarded as a sin even if it were not intended, provided it was foreseen in at least a confused state of mind. Moreover, all the causes of this sort are, without a doubt, those which, per se, are grave sins in the genus of lust, namely touches and unchaste stares at one's own or someone else's body with foul and deliberate delectation; watching human sex, as well as morose thoughts about sexual matters. Therefore, all acts of pollution proceeding from these causes are certainly mortal sins (St. Thomas II IIæ, q. 154, a. 5 and others in common). And then that foul act, which is the cause of the pollution, has a special malice against nature as Sanchez says (*de matr.* l. 9 d. 45, n. 21) and it is certain with all. Sporer rightly says the same thing about actions arising from pollution (*de matrimonio*, n. 647), which, although, if they are *per se* venial, and objectively, nevertheless they end up being mortal sins by reason of the proximate danger of consent to the foul delectation from it. So it must be said that one is not excused from the malice of pollution who is polluted from lengthy discussion with a young woman that he takes inordinate delight in, at least on account of the danger of consent, as the authors rightly say (Petroc. *de 6 praec.* c. 4 and the Salamancans, *de 6 praec.* c. 7 punct. 2 n. 34, with St. Thomas in *Opusc.* 65, c. *de Fluxu libid.* where he expressly teaches that).

483.—Nevertheless, an exception is made is the aforesaid actions are posited from a necessary or useful cause, or suitable to soul or body, for then the pollutions proceeding from those things, though foreseen, are not sins, provided that consent and danger of it are absent, as the authors commonly hold (Sylvius, 2.2. q. 154, a. 11 ad 2; Tournely, *l.c.* art. 6 sect. 1 concl. 2 with Henriquez a St. Ignatius; the Salamancans *ibid.* punct. 2 § 2 n. 45 and 46; Croix l. 3 p. 1 n. 925; Roncaglia *de 6 praec.* . 7 qu. 9 and others from St. Thomas, *l.c.*). The reason is, because then a man rather suffers than causes it, provided the pollution does not proceed from his malice but from the weakness of nature, as St. Gregory says in *can. Testamentum*, distinction 6, and according to what St. Thomas says: "When the twofold effect of one cause is equally immediate, one good and the other bad, and the good is equivalent to the bad, nothing forbids the good to be intended and the evil permitted." Hence, even from foreseen involuntary pollution, it is lawful:

I. For parish priests and even other confessors, to hear the confessions of women and to read treatises on foul things; surgeons to look and touch the parts of sick women and to be zealous for medical matters; it is also lawful for others otherwise to kiss or embrace women according to the custom of the country, to take service in bath houses, and similar things. So St. Thomas, p. 3 q. 80 a. 7; Sanchez, *dict.* d. 45, n. 4-8; Bonacina *de matr.* q. 4 p. 10 n. 6; Sporer *l.c.* n. 650; Anacletus *de 6 praec.* n. 53; P. Holzmann *eod. tit.* n. 690; the Salamancans *l.c.* n. 45 near the end, and likewise Petrocor. tom. 2 *de Temp.* p. 215; with Navarre, Cajetan and St. Antoninus, p. 2 tit. 6 c. 4, near the end, where he says: "But where pollution is altogether involuntary, and against intention it is not a sin, just as when someone hears a foul confession or speaks to a woman from an upright cause, and thereafter pollution follows." And Navarre teaches the same thing (c. 16 n. 7).

II. It is licit for someone who suffers from great itching in his private places to expel it by touch, even if pollution might follow (Busembaum, above, n. 419; Bonacina *l.c.* n. 8; Laymann, l. 3 sect.

4 n. 13; Sanchez, Filliuci tr. 30 n. 150; Sporer n. 650; Croix n. 926 with Marchant, the Salamancans *ibid.* n. 49; with Trullenchus and Diana, along with Cajetan, Navarre, Villalobos, Ledesma, Zanard., Basseus cited by Moya). Maybe someone will say it can happen that the itch proceeds from the very ardor of lust, whereby the removal of the itch that is done by friction ought to be accomplished better by sexual delectation. But we respond that it is more rational to judge that such an itch, when it is very aggravating, arises from the quality of blood than the ardor of lust. At least in doubt, *libertas possidet* for a man to free himself from aggravations of this sort through what is of itself a licit touch, since anyone can licitly drive away an itch of the body by touch; and if pollution happens, without danger of consent, *per accidens* and involuntarily, then it happens inculpably; moreover, for this man to be held to refrain from that touch it would need to be proved for certain that the touch proceeded from lust. Moreover, Croix wisely advises those who love itching to refrain (understand as often as it is morally possible) from touches of this sort. And Roncaglia (*loc. cit.*) forbids it absolutely if the itch were not very aggravating; still, he permits it in a case where one suffers some arousal if the man does not have the strength to tolerate it.

III. So it is also lawful, even if the pollution were foreseen, to ride a horse for the sake or utility (Bonacina, n. 7; Sanchez n. 7 with Navarre, Armilla, Vasquez, Lopez, etc., the Salamancans tr. 26 c. 7 punct. 3 § 2 n. 53 with Lessius, Azor, and Dicastillus). It is also licit for the sake of recreation as many authors assert (Sporer, n. 650, Anacletus, n. 53, likewise Laymann, Palaus, Sanchez, etc., cited by Croix n. 925 and Henno as well as Holzmann, n. 690 with Pichler, and the common opinion).

IV. It is lawful to recline in some place to rest more agreeably. (Salamancans, *ibid.* n. 55; Sporer n. 650; Sanchez, Palaus, Laymann, etc. cited by Croix n. 925; Holzmann, n. 690; with others in common).

V. Hot food or drink taken moderately, as well as upright dances (Sporer n. 650; Salamancans *l.c.* with St. Antoninus, Toledo, Lessius, Holzmann, *d.* n. 690; with Pichler etc).

What if a physician that consents to pollution as often as he heals a woman; is he held to lay aside his office?

It is probable that he is not held provided that he proposes due means to fortify himself against it, as the authors say (Navarre, *Summ.* c. 3 in fine from the Salamancans, *ibid.* n. 47 with Hurt., Antonio of the Holy Spirit, etc. See what was said in book 2, n. 63). The same is said about a parish priest who falls into the same misery when hearing confessions [of women]; but it is otherwise for a simple confessor who, without grave detriment to his reputation, or faculties, can desert the exercise of hearing confessions, as the Salamancans teach (*l.c.* n. 48) with Palaus and other authors whom we have cited. But what if persons of this sort will always or nearly always fall and give off no reasonable hope of amendment? Then we say they are held to lay aside their office no matter what the loss, according to what was said in n. 438 above, and what will be said more profusely in book 6, n. 457.

484.—Now we take up a great question, namely whether pollution that was foreseen, which follows involuntarily from causes lightly influencing it is a mortal sin? There are many different opinions present.

I. The *first opinion* affirms that all pollutions which were foreseen and not impeded are mortal sins, even if the causes were otherwise licit. (Valentia, Medina, Manuel, etc., cited by Sanchez, l. 9 d. 45 n. 10).

II. The *second opinion* which Armilla holds, says that any cause, even venially illicit, makes pollution a mortal sin.

III. The *third* opinion, which del Soto, Angelus, Gerson, Lopez (and others cited by Sanchez, n. 12) follow, holds that every cause, which is in itself a mortal sin, also constitutes pollution which follows from it a mortal sin. And it seems St. Thomas favors this opinion (III, q. 80 a. 7) where he says: "Whenever (nocturnal pollution) is from a sin, say, when it comes about from superfluous food or drink, then this can be a venial or mortal sin."

IV. The *fourth opinion* is common and more probable, which teaches that pollution is not a mortal sin unless it comes about from a cause that is itself mortal in the genus of lust. (Lessius, l. 4 c. 3 dubit. 14 n. 102; Sylvius, 2. 2. quaest. 154, art. 11 ad 2; Sporer *de matrimonio* c. 3 n. 647; Croix, l. 3 part. 1 n. 922; Sanchez *de matrimonio* c. 3 n. 16; with Sylvester, Abulensis, Sa, Angelus, Turrianus, Henriquez, etc. Likewise Roncaglia, c. 7 p. 9 r. 2; Elbel *de 6 praec.* n. 257; Anacletus *eod. tit.* n. 54; Holzmann n. 690; Bonacina q. 4 p. 10 n. 5; Salamancans tr. 26 c. 7 punct. 3 § 2 n. 52 and 54 with St. Antoninus, Suarez, etc). The reason why the cause should be mortal *per se* is that when pollution were not willed in itself, but only in the cause, it will be evil to the degree which the cause itself was evil. Moreover, the reason why it should be mortal in the same genus of lust is that when the cause lightly coincides with pollution, it is not a grave obligation to avoid that cause due to pollution which happens apart from the intention.

Hence it is inferred: 1) Pollution which arises from lengthy discussion with a girl, or a brief look, or curious reading of a venially foul book, is no more than a venial sin; because, as it was said, since these causes lightly influence, the subsequent pollution is more from a natural cause than it proceeds from the former. (Sanchez, *dict.* d. 45, n. 18; Slam. *ibid.* n. 50 with others, as above). Fr. Cunilati thinks the same thing (tract. 2 c. 2 n. 15) saying: "One sins mortally that places foul actions which of themselves excite and arouse one to pollution. It is otherwise if the cause were remote, such as to ride, sleep, eat hot food, or speak with women, even if it were posited without a virtuous end; then he will only sin venially." The same in regard to pollution arising involuntarily from foul reading done from curiosity, without a wicked intention, or danger of taking delectation from these obscene things, as Lessius (l. 3 c. 3 n. 102) with Sa, Bonacina, quaest. 4 p. 10 n. 9, with Vasquez, Tamburinius, § 2 n. 8; Sporer n. 648, with Sanchez. But in practice, I would never concede it, and so much the less if due to foul reading taken up only for the sake of curiosity, pollution would frequently occur. The Salamancans (n. 48, with whom Roncaglia agrees in qu. 7 n. 11) rightly say a man is not excused from mortal sin that experiences frequent pollution from such causes that are in the same genus of lust, which more forcefully influence him to pollution, and that he places voluntarily and without necessity, even if they do not pertain to mortal sins *per se*, such as curious reading or an indecent look at obscene pictures, or the sex of animals, touches of his own or another person's private parts from levity, and similar things; the reason is, because in respect to this person, on account of his wicked disposition, such a cause does not lightly influence. But they say otherwise if pollution rarely came about from causes of this sort. And it is also otherwise if the causes were altogether light, such as the sight of the non-private parts of a woman's body, reading something only mildly shameful, short conversation with a woman, or if it was mildly obscene; the reason is that it is almost morally impossible for a man to commonly avoid all these causes (Sanchez, num. 18 and the Salamancans, *ibid.* num. 50).

It is inferred: 2) Pollution is not a mortal sin when it happens apart from the intention from illicit causes but is still mortal in another genus than lust, say from drunkenness, or from very immoderate consumption of meat, or that on a forbidden day. So with Busembaum, Sanchez, n. 20; Navarre, c. 16 n. 8; Suarez, 3. part. tom. 3 qu. 80 art. 7; Bonacina p. 10 num. 6 Lessius l. 4 c. 3 n. 99; the Salamancans *l.c.* n. 54 with Vasquez, Dicastillus, etc.; Sporer n. 649 with Laymann, and others cited above in n. 484. Therefore, St. Gregory in can. *Testamentum*, dist. 6, speaking about pollution arising from superfluous food or drink, he said only some guilt is contracted. In the words of the Pope: "When beyond the mode of appetite in taking nourishment one falls, ... the mind thereafter has some guilt." Now, the Gloss, explaining that word *some* [*aliquem*], says "*i.e.* venial sin." So much more will pollution not be a mortal sin when it arises from venial sins in another genus, such as from riding, eating of hot foot, being in a certain place, and other similar actions. But here the controversy is over whether it is at least a venial sin to place these lightly illicit causes in another matter without a rational motive when he foresees from them that he is going to suffer pollution? Several authors deny it because (as they say) then the pollution arises rather from the weakness of nature than from that cause, which is nothing other than *per accidens* and remotely concurrent with the pollution (Holzmann, *de sexto praecepto*, cap. 1 num. 690; Croix lib. 2 part. 1 num. 924; with Arriaga, and Rodriguez). But other authors more probably uphold it. The reason is, because to permit pollution without a reasonable cause always seems to be indecent and disordered (Sanchez, n. 21; Lessius, c. 3 n. 99; Roncaglia q. 7; Sporer d. n. 649; Bonacina p. 10 n. 6; the Salamancans tr. 26 cap. 7 punct. 3 § 2 num. 52, with St. Gregory, St. Antoninus, Navarre, Suarez, and Dicastillus). But some reasonable cause of necessity, utility or convenience excuses from this venial sin, as the authors cited in n. 483 teach with Laymann (l. 3 sect. 4 n. 12). And this, even if that cause were venially illicit in the same matter of lust, as the Salamancans commonly teach (*ibid.* n. 51 and § 3 n. 63; Roncaglia, q. 7, r. 3; Sporer n. 650; Holzmann n. 690, as we recently said).

485.—"7. Pollution that occurred in a dream is a mortal sin: "a) If beforehand it were procured directly or formally, and the "cause were not retracted; b) When one takes pleasure after the "dream and approves of it due to the sexual delectation; "otherwise it is not a sin. Filliuci, q. 5 n. 148; Trullenchus, *loc.* "*cit.* n. 9." (See book 2 n. 20 for more on this).

"Someone will ask, whether mutual pollution, procured "between male or female, is only masturbation or sodomy?

"We respond: If it happened from the disposition alone to "venereal lust without coitus, it is only masturbation; but if it "were done from an affect to the person of an undue sex "(especially if some union and sexual intercourse were present) "it is sodomy in regard to the malice. Filliuci, t. 30 c. 8. See "above in book 2, cap. 1 d. 2 art. 2 about sin in general and the "cited authors." (See more about this in the preceding n. 467).

END OF VOLUME II

www.ingramcontent.com/pod-product-compliance
Lightning Source LLC
Chambersburg PA
CBHW010824070526
44583CB00022B/2919